Survival Communications in Connecticut

John E. Parnell, KK4HWK

ISBN 978-1-62512-019-9

Cover design by:
Lynda Colón
FREELANCE GRAPHIC DESIGN &
MARKETING COMMUNICATIONS
www.hirelynda.webs.com

Titles available in this series:

Survival Communications in Alabama
Survival Communications in Alaska
Survival Communications in Arizona
Survival Communications in Arkansas
Survival Communications in California
Survival Communications in Colorado
Survival Communications in Connecticut
Survival Communications in Delaware
Survival Communications in Florida
Survival Communications in Georgia
Survival Communications in Hawaii
Survival Communications in Idaho
Survival Communications in Illinois
Survival Communications in Indiana
Survival Communications in Iowa
Survival Communications in Kansas
Survival Communications in Kentucky
Survival Communications in Louisiana
Survival Communications in Maine
Survival Communications in Maryland
Survival Communications in Massachusetts
Survival Communications in Michigan
Survival Communications in Minnesota
Survival Communications in Mississippi
Survival Communications in Missouri

Survival Communications in Montana
Survival Communications in Nebraska
Survival Communications in Nevada
Survival Communications in New Hampshire
Survival Communications in New Jersey
Survival Communications in New Mexico
Survival Communications in New York
Survival Communications in North Carolina
Survival Communications in North Dakota
Survival Communications in Ohio
Survival Communications in Oklahoma
Survival Communications in Oregon
Survival Communications in Pennsylvania
Survival Communications in Rhode Island
Survival Communications in South Carolina
Survival Communications in South Dakota
Survival Communications in Tennessee
Survival Communications in Texas
Survival Communications in Utah
Survival Communications in Vermont
Survival Communications in Virginia
Survival Communications in Washington
Survival Communications in West Virginia
Survival Communications in Wisconsin
Survival Communications in Wyoming

The above titles are available from your favorite online or brick-and-mortar bookstore or directly from the publisher at Tutor Turtle Press LLC, 1027 S. Pendleton St. – Suite B-10, Easley, SC 29642.

TABLE OF CONTENTS

Appendix A – Connecticut Ham Radio Clubs

ARRL Affiliated Amateur and Ham Radio Clubs – By City

Appendix B – Connecticut Ham Licensees by City

Survival Communications in Connecticut

Perhaps you have prepared for WTSHTF or TEOTWAWKI with respect to food, water, self-defense and shelter. But what about communication?

Whenever there is a disaster (hurricane, earthquake, economic collapse, nuclear war, EMF, solar eruption, etc.), the normal means of communication that we're all reliant upon (cell phone, land line phone, the Internet, etc.) will probably be, at best, sporadic and at worst, non-existent.

As this author sees it, short of smoke signals and mirrors, there are three options for communication in "trying times": (1) GMRS or FRS radios; (2) CB radios; and (3) ham or amateur radio. Let's consider each of these options to come up with the most acceptable one.

GMRS (General Mobile Radio Service) / FRS (Family Radio Service)

GMRS (General Mobile Radio Service) / FRS (Family Radio Service) radios work optimally over short distances where there is minimal interference. Originally designed to be used as pagers, particularly inside a building or other such confined area, these radios are low-cost and convenient to carry. Unfortunately their small size and light weight comes with a trade-off – short range and short battery life. These radios are supposed to be able to communicate for up to 25-30 miles. Right. That's on level terrain, without buildings or trees getting in the way. While battery life technology is constantly improving, you will need spare batteries to keep communicating or someway of recharging the ones in the radio. In this author's opinion, GMRS/FRS radios are not first choice when concerned with medium or long range communication.

CB (Citizens Band)

CB (Citizens Band) radios operate in a frequency range originally reserved for ham or amateur radio operation. Because of the overwhelming number of people wishing quick, low-cost, regulation-free communication, the FCC (Federal Communication Commission) split off a portion of the frequency spectrum and allowed anyone to purchase a CB radio and start communicating. No test. No license. Just personal/business communication. Today, CB radios are readily available in such outlets as eBay and Craigslist. This author has seen them at yard/garage/tag sales and at flea markets.

CB radios come in a variety of "flavors." Fixed units, sometimes referred to as base units are intended for home use. For the most part, they derive their power from the utility company. In the event of loss of electricity, most base units can also be connected to a 12-volt battery, like that in your car/truck. If you choose to obtain a fixed unit, make sure you know how to connect the unit to the battery – ahead of time. Trying to figure this out when you're under extra stress is not a good situation.

A second type of CB radio is designed to be mobile, that is, installed in your car/truck. It gets its power from the vehicle's battery. You can either attach an antenna permanently to the vehicle or have a removable, magnetic type antenna.

The third type of CB radio is designed for handheld use. They are small and light. Most weigh less than a pound and operate on batteries. Yes, using batteries in a CB poses the same limitations as those by the GMRS/FRS radios, but have the added advantage that most handheld units come with a cigarette lighter adapter. Comes in handy when you are on the move and wish to be able to communicate both from a vehicle and also when you have to abandon it.

While they have a greater range than GMRS/FRS radios, CB radios are, legally, limited to operate on 40 channels, with a power rating of four (4) watts or less. Yes, it is possible to alter CB radios to get around these limitations, but not legally,

Ham/Amateur Radio

Ham/Amateur radio is very appealing. With a ham radio, you are not limited to less than 50 miles, but can communicate with anyone in the world (who also has access to a ham radio, of course).

Standardized Amateur Radio Prepper Communications Plan

In the event of a nationwide catastrophic disaster, the nationwide network of Amateur Radio licensed preppers will need a set of standardized meeting frequencies to share information and coordinate activities between various prepper groups. This Standardized Amateur Radio Communications Plan establishes a set of frequencies on the 80 meter, 40 meter, 20 meter, and 2 meter Amateur Radio bands for use during these types of catastrophic disasters.

Routine nets will not be held on all of these frequencies, but preppers are encouraged to use them when coordinating with other preppers on a routine basis. Routine nets may be conducted by The American Preparedness Radio Net (TAPRN) on these or other frequencies as they see fit. However, TAPRN will promote the use of these standardized frequencies by all Amateur Radio licensed preppers during times of catastrophic disaster. The promotion of this Standardized Amateur Radio Communications Plan is encouraged by all means within the prepper community, including via Amateur Radio, Twitter, Facebook, and various blogs.

Standardized Frequencies and Modes
80 Meters – 3.818 MHz LSB (TAPRN Net: Sundays at 9 PM ET)
40 Meters – 7.242 MHz LSB
40 Meters Morse Code / Digital – 7.073 MHz USB (TAPRN: Sundays at 7:30 PM ET on CONTESTIA 4/250)
20 Meters – 14.242 MHz USB
2 Meters – 146.420 MHz FM

Nets and Network Etiquette

In times of nationwide catastrophic disaster, the ability of any one prepper to initiate and sustain themselves as a net control may be limited by the availability of power and other resource shortages. However, all licensed preppers are encouraged to maintain a listening watch on these frequencies as often as possible during a catastrophic disaster. Preppers may routinely announce themselves in the following manner:

• This is [Your Callsign Phonetically] in [Your State], maintaining a listening watch on [Standard Frequency] for any preppers on frequency seeking information or looking to provide information. Please call [Your Callsign Phonetically]. Preppers exchanging information that may require follow up should agree upon a designated time to return to the frequency and provide further information. If other stations are utilizing the frequency at the designated time you return, maintain watch and proceed with your communications when those stations are finished. If your communications are urgent and the stations on frequency are not passing information of a critical nature, interrupt with the word "Break" and request use of the frequency.

For More Information

Catastrophe Network: http://www.catastrophenetwork.org or @CatastropheNet on Twitter The American Preparedness Radio Network: http://www.taprn.com or @TAPRN on Twitter

© 2011 Catastrophe Network, Please Distribute Freely

In order to use a ham radio, legally, one must be licensed to do so by the FCC (other countries have analogous governmental bodies to regulate ham radio). To obtain a license is quite easy – take a test and pay your license fee. There are currently three classes of license – Technician, General, and Amateur Extra. With each of these licenses come specific abilities.

Technician class is the beginning level. The exam consists of 35 multiple choice questions randomly drawn from a pool of 395 questions. The question pool is readily available online for free downloading (http://www.ncvec.org/downloads/Revised%20Element%202.Pdf) or in such publications at *Ham Radio License Manual Revised 2nd Edition* (ISBN 978-0-87259-097-7). The current Technician pool of questions is to be used from July 1, 2010 to June 30, 2014. Be sure the question pool you are studying from is current. You will need to score at least 26 correct to pass. (Do not worry, Morse Code is no longer on the test, although many ham operators use it anyway.) You do not need to take a formal class in order to qualify to take the exam. You can learn the material on your own. Most people spend 10-15 hours studying and then successfully take the exam. The cost of taking the exam is under $20. The exam is given in MANY locations throughout the US. Usually the exam is given by area ham clubs. You do not have to belong to the club to take the exam. Check Appendix A for a listing of clubs in Connecticut.

Topics for the Technician License in Amateur Radio

The Technician license exam covers such topics as basic regulations, operating practices, and electronic theory, with a focus on VHF and UHF applications. Below is the syllabus for the Technician Class.

Subelement T1 – FCC Rules, descriptions and definitions for the amateur radio service, operator and station license responsibilities

[6 Exam Questions – 6 Groups]

T1A – Amateur Radio services; purpose of the amateur service, amateur-satellite service, operator/primary station license grant, where FCC rules are codified, basis and purpose of FCC rules, meanings of basic terms used in FCC rules

T1B – Authorized frequencies; frequency allocations, ITU regions, emission type, restricted sub-bands, spectrum sharing, transmissions near band edges

T1C – Operator classes and station call signs; operator classes, sequential, special event, and vanity call sign systems, international communications, reciprocal operation, station license licensee, places where the amateur service is regulated by the FCC, name and address on ULS, license term, renewal, grace period

T1D – Authorized and prohibited transmissions

T1E – Control operator and control types; control operator required, eligibility, designation of control operator, privileges and duties, control point, local, automatic and remote control, location of control operator

T1F – Station identification and operation standards; special operations for repeaters and auxiliary stations, third party communications, club stations, station security, FCC inspection

---

Subelement T2 – Operating Procedures

[3 Exam Questions – 3 Groups]

T2A – Station operation; choosing an operating frequency, calling another station, test transmissions, use of minimum power, frequency use, band plans

T2B – VHF/UHF operating practices; SSB phone, FM repeater, simplex, frequency offsets, splits and shifts, CTCSS, DTMF, tone squelch, carrier squelch, phonetics

T2C – Public service; emergency and non-emergency operations, message traffic handling

---

Subelement T3 – Radio wave characteristics, radio and electromagnetic properties, propagation modes

[3 Exam Questions – 3 Groups]

T3A – Radio wave characteristics; how a radio signal travels; distinctions of HF, VHF and UHF; fading, multipath; wavelength vs. penetration; antenna orientation

T3B – Radio and electromagnetic wave properties; the electromagnetic spectrum, wavelength vs. frequency, velocity of electromagnetic waves

T3C – Propagation modes; line of sight, sporadic E, meteor, aurora scatter, tropospheric ducting, F layer skip, radio horizon

Subelement T4 - Amateur radio practices and station setup

[2 Exam Questions – 2 Groups]

T4A – Station setup; microphone, speaker, headphones, filters, power source, connecting a computer, RF grounding

T4B – Operating controls; tuning, use of filters, squelch, AGC, repeater offset, memory channels

Subelement T5 – Electrical principles, math for electronics, electronic principles, Ohm's Law

[4 Exam Questions – 4 Groups]

T5A – Electrical principles; current and voltage, conductors and insulators, alternating and direct current

T5B – Math for electronics; decibels, electronic units and the metric system

T5C – Electronic principles; capacitance, inductance, current flow in circuits, alternating current, definition of RF, power calculations

T5D – Ohm's Law

Subelement T6 – Electrical components, semiconductors, circuit diagrams, component functions

[4 Exam Groups – 4 Questions]

T6A – Electrical components; fixed and variable resistors, capacitors, and inductors; fuses, switches, batteries

T6B – Semiconductors; basic principles of diodes and transistors

T6C – Circuit diagrams; schematic symbols

T6D – Component functions

Subelement T7 – Station equipment, common transmitter and receiver problems, antenna measurements and troubleshooting, basic repair and testing

[4 Exam Questions – 4 Groups]

T7A – Station radios; receivers, transmitters, transceivers

T7B – Common transmitter and receiver problems; symptoms of overload and overdrive, distortion, interference, over and under modulation, RF feedback, off frequency signals; fading and noise; problems with digital communications interfaces

T7C – Antenna measurements and troubleshooting; measuring SWR, dummy loads, feedline failure modes

T7D – Basic repair and testing; soldering, use of a voltmeter, ammeter, and ohmmeter

Subelement T8 – Modulation modes, amateur satellite operation, operating activities, non-voice communications

[4 Exam Questions – 4 Groups]

T8A – Modulation modes; bandwidth of various signals

T8B – Amateur satellite operation; Doppler shift, basic orbits, operating protocols

T8C – Operating activities; radio direction finding, radio control, contests, special event stations, basic linking over Internet

T8D – Non-voice communications; image data, digital modes, CW, packet, PSK31

Subelement T9 – Antennas, feedlines

[2 Exam Groups – 2 Questions]

T9A – Antennas; vertical and horizontal, concept of gain, common portable and mobile antennas, relationships between antenna length and frequency

T9B – Feedlines; types, losses vs. frequency, SWR concepts, matching, weather protection, connectors

Subelement T0 – AC power circuits, antenna installation, RF hazards

[3 Exam Questions – 3 Groups]

T0A – AC power circuits; hazardous voltages, fuses and circuit breakers, grounding, lightning protection, battery safety, electrical code compliance

T0B – Antenna installation; tower safety, overhead power lines

T0C – RF hazards; radiation exposure, proximity to antennas, recognized safe power levels, exposure to others

Once your name and call sign are available in the FCC database, you have the privilege of operating on all VHF (2 m) and UHF (70 cm) frequencies above 30 megahertz (MHz) and HF frequencies 80, 40, and 15 meter, and on the 10 meter band using Morse code (CW), voice, and digital mode. For a Technician license in Connecticut, your call sign will consist of a two-letter prefix beginning with K or W, the number one (1), and a three-letter suffix. The single digit number in the call sign is determined according to which area of the US you obtain your first license. Even though you may move to another state, you keep this number in your call sign. This is also true should you upgrade to a higher license and get a new call sign. The numeral portion of your call sign stays the same.

Call Sign Numbers

Below is a chart showing the various numbers and the state(s) in which you would obtain the number.

Call Sign Number	State(s)
0	CO, IA, KS, MN, MO, NE, ND, SD
1	CT, ME, MA, NH, RI, VT
2	NJ, NY
3	DE, DC, MD, PA
4	AL, FL, GA, KY, NC, SC, TN, VA
5	AR, LA, MS, NM, OK, TX
6	CA
7	AZ, ID, MT, NV, OR, WA, UT, WY
8	MI, OH, WV
9	IL, IN, WI

Residents of Alaska may have any of the following call sign prefixes assigned to them: AL0-7, KL0-7, NL0-7, or WL0-7. Likewise, residents of Hawaii may have the prefix AH6-7, KH6-7, NH6-7, or WH6-7 assigned.

Once you obtain your Technician license, do not stop there. Go and get your General license.

General is the second of three ham license classes. Like the Technician license, to get a General license, you merely have to take a 35-question multiple choice exam and pay your license fee. Passing is still at least 26 correct answers and the fee is the same (less than $20). Again the question pool is available for free online (http://www.ncvec.org/page.php?id=358). It is also available in such print publications as *The ARRL General Class License Manual 7th Edition* (ISBN 978-0-87259-811-9). The current General pool of questions is to be used from July 1, 2011 to June 30, 2015. Be sure the question pool you are using is current. Being a bit more comprehensive than the Technician license, the General license usually requires 15-20 hours of study to learn the material. Check Appendix A for a listing of clubs in Connecticut where you might take your exam. Once your name and NEW call sign is listed in the FCC database, you're good to go. For a General license in Connecticut, your call sign will consist of a one-letter prefix beginning with K, N or W, the number one (1), and a three-letter suffix.

Topics for the General License in Amateur Radio

The General license exam covers regulations, operating practices and electronic theory. Below is the syllabus for the General Class.

Subelement G1 – Commission's Rules
(5 Exam Questions – 5 Groups)
G1A – General Class control operator frequency privileges; primary and secondary allocations
G1B – Antenna structure limitations; good engineering and good amateur practice, beacon operation; restricted operation; retransmitting radio signals
G1C – Transmitter power regulations; data emission standards
G1D – Volunteer Examiners and Volunteer Examiner Coordinators; temporary identification
G1E – Control categories; repeater regulations; harmful interference; third party rules; ITU regions

Subelement G2 – Operating procedures
(5 Exam Questions – 5 Groups)
G2A – Phone operating procedures; USB/LSB utilization conventions; procedural signals; breaking into a OSO in progress; VOX operation
G2B – Operating courtesy; band plans, emergencies, including drills and emergency communications
G2C – CW operating procedures and procedural signals; Q signals and common abbreviations; full break in

G2D – Amateur Auxiliary; minimizing interference; HF operations

G2E – Digital operating; procedures, procedural signals and common abbreviations

Subelement G3 – Radio wave propagation

(3 Exam Questions – 3 Groups)

G3A – Sunspots and solar radiation; ionospheric disturbances; propagation forecasting and indices

G3B – Maximum Usable Frequency; Lowest Usable Frequency; propagation

G3C – Ionospheric layers; critical angle and frequency; HF scatter; Near Vertical Incidence Sky waves

Subelement G4 – Amateur radio practices

(5 Exam Questions – 5 Groups)

G4A – Station Operation and setup

G4B – Test and monitoring equipment; two-tone test

G4C – Interference with consumer electronics; grounding; DSP

G4D – Speech processors; S meters; sideband operation near band edges

G4E – HF mobile radio installations; emergency and battery powered operation

Subelement G5 – Electrical principles

(3 Exam Questions – 3 Groups)

G5A – Reactance; inductance; capacitance; impedance; impedance matching

G5B – The Decibel; current and voltage dividers; electrical power calculations; sine wave root-mean-square (RMS) values; PEP calculations

G5C – Resistors; capacitors and inductors in series and parallel; transformers

Subelement G6 – Circuit components

(3 Exam Questions – 3 Groups)

G6A – Resistors; capacitors; inductors

G6B – Rectifiers; solid state diodes and transistors; vacuum tubes; batteries

G6C – Analog and digital integrated circuits (ICs); microprocessors; memory; I/O devices; microwave ICs (MMICs); display devices

Subelement G7 – Practical circuits

(3 Exam Questions – 3 Groups)

G7A – Power supplies; schematic symbols

G7B – Digital circuits; amplifiers and oscillators

G7C – Receivers and transmitters; filters, oscillators

Subelement G8 – Signals and emissions

(2 Exam Questions – 2 Groups)

G8A – Carriers and modulation; AM; FM; single and double sideband; modulation envelope; overmodulation

G8B – Frequency mixing; multiplication; HF data communications; bandwidths of various modes; deviation

Subelement G9 – Antennas and feed lines

(4 Exam Questions – 4 Groups)

G9A – Antenna feed lines; characteristic impedance and attenuation; SWR calculation, measurement and effects; matching networks

G9B – Basic antennas

G9C – Directional antennas

G9D – Specialized antennas

Subelement G0 – Electrical and RF safety

(2 Exam Questions – 2 Groups)

G0A – RF safety principles, rules and guidelines; routine station elevation

G0B – Safety in the ham shack; electrical shock and treatment, safety grounding, fusing, interlocks, wiring, antenna and tower safety

With a General license, you can use all VHF and UHF frequencies and most of the HF frequencies. You would have access to the 160, 30, 17, 12, and 10 meter bands and access to major parts of the 80, 40, 20, and 15 meter bands. Of course, this is in addition to all bands available to Technician license holders.

Amateur Extra is the third of three ham license classes. Like the Technician and General classes, you merely have to pass a test and pay your fee to get your Amateur Extra license. This class of license is more comprehensive than the lower license classes. The exam is longer – 50 questions – and the minimum passing score is higher – 37. However, once you get your Amateur Extra license, all ham frequencies, VHF, UHF and HF are available for your enjoyment. The Extra exam covers regulations, specialized operating practices, advanced electronics theory, and radio equipment design.

Like for the other license classes, the question pool for the Amateur Extra license is available online for downloading (http://www.ncvec.org/downloads/REVISED%202012-2016%20Extra%20Class%20Pool.doc). It is also available in print form in such publications as *The ARRL Extra Class License Manual Revised 9th Edition* (ISBN 978-0-87259-887-4).

Topics for the Extra License in Amateur Radio

Below is the syllabus for the Amateur Extra Class for July 1, 2012 to June 30, 2016.

Subelement E1 – Commission's Rules

[6 Exam Questions – 6 Groups]

E1A – Operating Standards: frequency privileges; emission standards; automatic message forwarding; frequency sharing; stations aboard ships or aircraft

E1B – Station restrictions and special operations: restrictions on station location; general operating restrictions, spurious emissions, control operator reimbursement; antenna structure restrictions; RACES operations

E1C – Station control: definitions and restrictions pertaining to local, automatic and remote control operation; control operator responsibilities for remote and automatically controlled stations

E1D – Amateur Satellite service: definitions and purpose; license requirements for space stations; available frequencies and bands; telecommand and telemetry operations; restrictions, and special provisions; notification requirements

E1E – Volunteer examiner program: definitions, qualifications, preparation and administration of exams; accreditation; question pools; documentation requirements

E1F – Miscellaneous rules: external RF power amplifiers; national quiet zone; business communications; compensated communications; spread spectrum; auxiliary stations; reciprocal operating privileges; IARP and CEPT licenses; third party communications with foreign countries; special temporary authority

Subelement E2 – Operating procedures

[5 Exam Questions – 5 Groups]

E2A – Amateur radio in space: amateur satellites; orbital mechanics; frequencies and modes; satellite hardware; satellite operations

E2B – Television practices: fast scan television standards and techniques; slow scan television standards and techniques

E2C – Operating methods: contest and DX operating; spread-spectrum transmissions; selecting an operating frequency

E2D – Operating methods: VHF and UHF digital modes; APRS

E2E – Operating methods: operating HF digital modes; error correction

Subelement E3 – Radio wave propagation

[3 Exam Questions – 3 Groups]

E3A – Propagation and technique, Earth-Moon-Earth communications; meteor scatter

E3B – Propagation and technique, trans-equatorial; long path; gray-line; multi-path propagation

E3C – Propagation and technique, Aurora propagation; selective fading; radio-path horizon; take-off angle over flat or sloping terrain; effects of ground on propagation; less common propagation modes

Subelement E4 – Amateur practices

[5 Exam Questions – 5 Groups]

E4A – Test equipment: analog and digital instruments; spectrum and network analyzers, antenna analyzers; oscilloscopes; testing transistors; RF measurements

E4B – Measurement technique and limitations: instrument accuracy and performance limitations; probes; techniques to minimize errors; measurement of "Q"; instrument calibration

E4C – Receiver performance characteristics, phase noise, capture effect, noise floor, image rejection, MDS, signal-to-noise-ratio; selectivity

E4D – Receiver performance characteristics, blocking dynamic range, intermodulation and cross-modulation interference; 3rd order intercept; desensitization; preselection

E4E – Noise suppression: system noise; electrical appliance noise; line noise; locating noise sources; DSP noise reduction; noise blankers

Subelement E5 – Electrical principles

[4 Exam Questions – 4 Groups]

E5A – Resonance and Q: characteristics of resonant circuits: series and parallel resonance; Q; half-power bandwidth; phase relationships in reactive circuits

E5B – Time constants and phase relationships: RLC time constants: definition; time constants in RL and RC circuits; phase angle between voltage and current; phase angles of series and parallel circuits

E5C – Impedance plots and coordinate systems: plotting impedances in polar coordinates; rectangular coordinates

E5D – AC and RF energy in real circuits: skin effect; electrostatic and electromagnetic fields; reactive power; power factor; coordinate systems

Subelement E6 – Circuit components

[6 Exam Questions – 6 Groups]

E6A – Semiconductor materials and devices: semiconductor materials germanium, silicon, P-type, N-type; transistor types: NPN, PNP, junction, field-effect transistors: enhancement mode; depletion mode; MOS; CMOS; N-channel; P-channel

E6B – Semiconductor diodes

E6C – Integrated circuits: TTL digital integrated circuits; CMOS digital integrated circuits; gates

E6D – Optical devices and toroids: cathode-ray tube devices; charge-coupled devices (CCDs); liquid crystal displays (LCDs); toroids: permeability, core material, selecting, winding

E6E – Piezoelectric crystals and MMICs: quartz crystals; crystal oscillators and filters; monolithic amplifiers

E6F – Optical components and power systems: photoconductive principles and effects, photovoltaic systems, optical couplers, optical sensors, and optoisolators

Subelement E7 – Practical circuits

[8 Exam Questions – 8 Groups]

E7A – Digital circuits: digital circuit principles and logic circuits: classes of logic elements; positive and negative logic; frequency dividers; truth tables

E7B – Amplifiers: Class of operation; vacuum tube and solid-state circuits; distortion and intermodulation; spurious and parasitic suppression; microwave amplifiers

E7C – Filters and matching networks: filters and impedance matching networks: types of networks; types of filters; filter applications; filter characteristics; impedance matching; DSP filtering

E7D – Power supplies and voltage regulators

E7E – Modulation and demodulation: reactance, phase and balanced modulators; detectors; mixer stages; DSP modulation and demodulation; software defined radio systems

E7F – Frequency markers and counters: frequency divider circuits; frequency marker generators; frequency counters

E7G – Active filters and op-amps: active audio filters; characteristics; basic circuit design; operational amplifiers

E7H – Oscillators and signal sources: types of oscillators; synthesizers and phase-locked loops; direct digital synthesizers

Subelement E8 – Signals and emissions

[4 Exam Questions – 4 Groups]

E8A – AC waveforms: sine, square, sawtooth and irregular waveforms; AC measurements; average and PEP of RF signals; pulse and digital signal waveforms

E8B – Modulation and demodulation: modulation methods; modulation index and deviation ratio; pulse modulation; frequency and time division multiplexing

E8C – Digital signals: digital communications modes; CW; information rate vs. bandwidth; spread-spectrum communications; modulation methods

E8D – Waves, measurements, and RF grounding: peak-to-peak values, polarization; RF grounding

Subelement E9 – Antennas and transmission lines

[8 Exam Questions – 8 Groups]

E9A – Isotropic and gain antennas: definition; used as a standard for comparison; radiation pattern; basic antenna parameters: radiation resistance and reactance, gain, beamwidth, efficiency

E9B – Antenna patterns: E and H plane patterns; gain as a function of pattern; antenna design; Yagi antennas

E9C – Wire and phased vertical antennas: beverage antennas; terminated and resonant rhombic antennas; elevation above real ground; ground effects as related to polarization; take-off angles

E9D – Directional antennas: gain; satellite antennas; antenna beamwidth; losses; SWR bandwidth; antenna efficiency; shortened and mobile antennas; grounding

E9E – Matching: matching antennas to feed lines; power dividers

E9F – Transmission lines: characteristics of open and shorted feed lines: 1/8 wavelength; 1/4 wavelength; 1/2 wavelength; feed lines: coax versus open-wire; velocity factor; electrical length; transformation characteristics of line terminated in impedance not equal to characteristic impedance

E9G – The Smith chart

E9H – Effective radiated power; system gains and losses; radio direction finding antennas

Subelement E0 – Safety

[1 exam question – 1 group]

E0A – Safety: amateur radio safety practices; RF radiation hazards; hazardous materials

Once your new call sign is listed in the FCC database, you are good to go. For an Amateur Extra license in Connecticut, your call sign will consist of a prefix of K, N or W, the number one (1), and a two-letter suffix, or a two-letter prefix beginning with A, N, K or W, the number one (1), and a one-letter suffix, or a two-letter prefix beginning with A, the number one (1), and a two-letter suffix.

Ham radio equipment can be expensive or you can do it "on the cheap." The cost will run from a couple hundred dollars to well in the thousands, depending on what you have available. eBay, and Craigslist are good places to start looking. Most ham clubs do some sort of hamfest annually wherein club members or others are willing to part with older equipment. See Appendix A for a list of clubs in Connecticut.

Another excellent source of equipment, as well as advice on setting the equipment up and how to use it properly, is current ham operators. In Appendix B, the author has listed all the FCC licensed ham operators in Connecticut, listed by city, and then sorted by street and house number on the street. Who knows, maybe someone who lives close to you is a ham operator. Be a good neighbor, stop by and have a chat with him/her.

Like CB radios, ham radios come in three formats – base, mobile, and handheld. They can use the electric company for power, or operate off a car battery. In the opinion of this author, in spite of the slightly higher cost of the equipment and having to take a test to legally use the equipment, ham radio is the way to go when concerned about communication during times of crisis.

Canadian Call Sign Prefixes

Because of our proximity to Canada, many times ham contact is made with our northern neighbors. Below is a chart showing the origin of Canadian call sign prefixes.

Call Sign Prefix	Provence or Territory
CY0	Sable Island
CY9	St. Paul Island
VA1, VE1	New Brunswick, Nova Scotia
VA2, VE2	Quebec
VA3, VE3	Ontario
VA4, VE4	Manitoba
VA5, VE5	Saskatchewan
VA6, VE6	Alberta
VA7, VE7	British Columbia
VE8	North West Territories
VE9	New Brunswick
VO1	Newfoundland
VO2	Labrador
VY0	Nunavut
VY1	Yukon
VY2	Prince Edward Island

Common Radio Bands in the United States

Certain radio bands are more popular with ham radio enthusiasts than others. Below is a chart showing these bands and when they are most popular.

	Band (meter)	Frequency (MHz)	Use
HF	160	1.8 – 2.0	Night
	80	3.5 – 4.0	Night and Local Day
	40	7.0 – 7.3	Night and Local Day
	30	10.1 – 10.15	CW and Digital
	20	14.0 – 14.350	World Wide Day and Night
	17	18.068 – 18.168	World Wide Day and Night
	15	21.0 – 21.450	Primarily Daytime
	12	24.890 – 24.990	Primarily Daytime
	10	28.0 – 29.70	Daytime during Sunspot highs
VHF	6	50 – 54	Local to World Wide
	2	144 – 148	Local to Medium Distance
UHF	70 cm	430 – 440	Local

Common Amateur Radio Bands in Canada

160 Meter Band - Maximum bandwidth 6 kHz
1.800 - 1.820 MHz - CW
1.820 - 1.830 MHz - Digital Modes
1 830 - 1.840 MHz - DX Window
1.840 - 2.000 MHz - SSB and other wide band modes

80 Meter Band - Maximum bandwidth 6 kHz
3.500 - 3.580 MHz - CW
3.580 - 3.620 MHz - Digital Modes
3.620 - 3.635 MHz - Packet/Digital Secondary
3.635 - 3.725 MHz - CW
3.725 - 3.790 MHz - SSB and other side band modes*
3.790 - 3.800 MHz - SSB DX Window
3.800 - 4.000 MHz - SSB and other wide band modes

40 Meter Band - Maximum bandwidth 6 kHz
7.000 - 7.035 MHz - CW
7.035 - 7.050 MHz - Digital Modes
7.040 - 7.050 MHz - International packet
7.050 - 7.100 MHz - SSB
7.100 - 7.120 MHz - Packet within Region 2
7.120 - 7.150 MHz - CW
7.150 - 7.300 MHz - SSB and other wide band modes

30 Meter Band - Maximum bandwidth 1 kHz

10.100 - 10.130 MHz - CW only
10.130 - 10.140 MHz - Digital Modes
10.140 - 10.150 MHz - Packet

20 Meter Band - Maximum bandwidth 6 kHz

14.000 - 14.070 MHz - CW only
14.070 - 14.095 MHz - Digital Mode
14.095 - 14.099 MHz - Packet
14.100 MHz - Beacons
14.101 - 14.112 MHz - CW, SSB, packet shared
14.112 - 14.350 MHz - SSB
14.225 - 14.235 MHz - SSTV

17 Meter Band - Maximum bandwidth 6 kHz

18.068 - 18.100 MHz - CW
18.100 - 18.105 MHz - Digital Modes
18.105 - 18.110 MHz - Packet
18.110 - 18.168 MHz - SSB and other wide band modes

15 Meter Band - maximum bandwidth 6 kHz

21.000 - 21.070 MHz - CW
21.070 - 21.090 MHz - Digital Modes
21.090 - 21.125 MHz - Packet
21.100 - 21.150 MHz - CW and SSB
21.150 - 21.335 MHz - SSB and other wide band modes
21.335 - 21.345 MHz - SSTV
21.345 - 21.450 MHz - SSB and other wide band modes

12 Meter Band - Maximum bandwidth 6 kHz

24.890 - 24.930 MHz - CW
24.920 - 24.925 MHz - Digital Modes
24.925 - 24.930 MHz - Packet
24.930 - 24.990 MHz - SSB and other wide band modes

10 Meter Band - Maximum band width 20 kHz

28.000 - 28.200 MHz - CW
28.070 - 28.120 MHz - Digital Modes
28.120 - 28.190 MHz - Packet
28.190 - 28.200 MHz - Beacons
28.200 - 29.300 MHz - SSB and other wide band modes
29.300 - 29.510 MHz - Satellite
29.510 - 29.700 MHz - SSB, FM and repeaters

160 Meters (1.8-2.0 MHz)

1.800 - 2.000 CW
1.800 - 1.810 Digital Modes
1.810 CW QRP
1.843-2.000 SSB, SSTV and other wideband modes
1.910 SSB QRP
1.995 - 2.000 Experimental
1.999 - 2.000 Beacons

80 Meters (3.5-4.0 MHz)

3.590 RTTY/Data DX
3.570-3.600 RTTY/Data
3.790-3.800 DX window
3.845 SSTV
3.885 AM calling frequency

40 Meters (7.0-7.3 MHz)

7.040 RTTY/Data DX
7.080-7.125 RTTY/Data
7.171 SSTV
7.290 AM calling frequency

30 Meters (10.1-10.15 MHz)

10.130-10.140 RTTY
10.140-10.150 Packet

20 Meters (14.0-14.35 MHz)

14.070-14.095 RTTY
14.095-14.0995 Packet
14.100 NCDXF Beacons
14.1005-14.112 Packet
14.230 SSTV
14.286 AM calling frequency

17 Meters (18.068-18.168 MHz)

18.100-18.105 RTTY
18.105-18.110 Packet

15 Meters (21.0-21.45 MHz)

21.070-21.110 RTTY/Data
21.340 SSTV

12 Meters (24.89-24.99 MHz)

24.920-24.925 RTTY
24.925-24.930 Packet

10 Meters (28-29.7 MHz)

28.000-28.070 CW
28.070-28.150 RTTY
28.150-28.190 CW
28.200-28.300 Beacons
28.300-29.300 Phone
28.680 SSTV
29.000-29.200 AM
29.300-29.510 Satellite Downlinks
29.520-29.590 Repeater Inputs
29.600 FM Simplex
29.610-29.700 Repeater Outputs

6 Meters (50-54 MHz)

50.0-50.1 CW, beacons
50.060-50.080 beacon subband
50.1-50.3 SSB, CW
50.10-50.125 DX window
50.125 SSB calling
50.3-50.6 All modes
50.6-50.8 Nonvoice communications
50.62 Digital (packet) calling
50.8-51.0 Radio remote control (20-kHz channels)
51.0-51.1 Pacific DX window
51.12-51.48 Repeater inputs (19 channels)
51.12-51.18 Digital repeater inputs
51.5-51.6 Simplex (six channels)
51.62-51.98 Repeater outputs (19 channels)
51.62-51.68 Digital repeater outputs
52.0-52.48 Repeater inputs (except as noted; 23 channels)
52.02, 52.04 FM simplex
52.2 TEST PAIR (input)
52.5-52.98 Repeater output (except as noted; 23 channels)
52.525 Primary FM simplex
52.54 Secondary FM simplex
52.7 TEST PAIR (output)
53.0-53.48 Repeater inputs (except as noted; 19 channels)
53.0 Remote base FM simplex
53.02 Simplex
53.1, 53.2, 53.3, 53.4 Radio remote control
53.5-53.98 Repeater outputs (except as noted; 19 channels)
53.5, 53.6, 53.7, 53.8 Radio remote control
53.52, 53.9 Simplex

2 Meters (144-148 MHz)

144.00-144.05 EME (CW)
144.05-144.10 General CW and weak signals
144.10-144.20 EME and weak-signal SSB
144.200 National calling frequency
144.200-144.275 General SSB operation
144.275-144.300 Propagation beacons
144.30-144.50 New OSCAR subband
144.50-144.60 Linear translator inputs
144.60-144.90 FM repeater inputs
144.90-145.10 Weak signal and FM simplex (145.01,03,05,07,09 are widely used for packet)
145.10-145.20 Linear translator outputs
145.20-145.50 FM repeater outputs
145.50-145.80 Miscellaneous and experimental modes
145.80-146.00 OSCAR subband
146.01-146.37 Repeater inputs
146.40-146.58 Simplex
146.52 National Simplex Calling Frequency
146.61-146.97 Repeater outputs
147.00-147.39 Repeater outputs
147.42-147.57 Simplex
147.60-147.99 Repeater inputs

1.25 Meters (222-225 MHz)

222.0-222.150 Weak-signal modes
222.0-222.025 EME
222.05-222.06 Propagation beacons
222.1 SSB & CW calling frequency
222.10-222.15 Weak-signal CW & SSB
222.15-222.25 Local coordinator's option; weak signal, ACSB, repeater inputs, control
222.25-223.38 FM repeater inputs only
223.40-223.52 FM simplex
223.52-223.64 Digital, packet
223.64-223.70 Links, control
223.71-223.85 Local coordinator's option; FM simplex, packet, repeater outputs
223.85-224.98 Repeater outputs only

70 Centimeters (420-450 MHz)

420.00-426.00 ATV repeater or simplex with 421.25 MHz video carrier control links and experimental
426.00-432.00 ATV simplex with 427.250-MHz video carrier frequency
432.00-432.07 EME (Earth-Moon-Earth)
432.07-432.10 Weak-signal CW
432.10 70-cm calling frequency
432.10-432.30 Mixed-mode and weak-signal work
432.30-432.40 Propagation beacons

432.40-433.00 Mixed-mode and weak-signal work
433.00-435.00 Auxiliary/repeater links
435.00-438.00 Satellite only (internationally)
438.00-444.00 ATV repeater input with 439.250-MHz video carrier frequency and repeater links
442.00-445.00 Repeater inputs and outputs (local option)
445.00-447.00 Shared by auxiliary and control links, repeaters and simplex (local option)
446.00 National simplex frequency
447.00-450.00 Repeater inputs and outputs (local option)

33 Centimeters (902-928 MHz)

902.0-903.0 Narrow-bandwidth, weak-signal communications
902.0-902.8 SSTV, FAX, ACSSB, experimental
902.1 Weak-signal calling frequency
902.8-903.0 Reserved for EME, CW expansion
903.1 Alternate calling frequency
903.0-906.0 Digital communications
906-909 FM repeater inputs
909-915 ATV
915-918 Digital communications
918-921 FM repeater outputs
921-927 ATV
927-928 FM simplex and links

23 Centimeters (1240-1300 MHz)

1240-1246 ATV #1
1246-1248 Narrow-bandwidth FM point-to-point links and digital, duplex with 1258-1260.
1248-1258 Digital Communications
1252-1258 ATV #2
1258-1260 Narrow-bandwidth FM point-to-point links digital, duplexed with 1246-1252
1260-1270 Satellite uplinks, reference WARC '79
1260-1270 Wide-bandwidth experimental, simplex ATV
1270-1276 Repeater inputs, FM and linear, paired with 1282-1288, 239 pairs every 25 kHz, e.g. 1270.025, .050, etc.
1271-1283 Non-coordinated test pair
1276-1282 ATV #3
1282-1288 Repeater outputs, paired with 1270-1276
1288-1294 Wide-bandwidth experimental, simplex ATV
1294-1295 Narrow-bandwidth FM simplex services, 25-kHz channels
1294.5 National FM simplex calling frequency
1295-1297 Narrow bandwidth weak-signal communications (no FM)
1295.0-1295.8 SSTV, FAX, ACSSB, experimental
1295.8-1296.0 Reserved for EME, CW expansion
1296.00-1296.05 EME-exclusive
1296.07-1296.08 CW beacons

1296.1 CW, SSB calling frequency
1296.4-1296.6 Crossband linear translator input
1296.6-1296.8 Crossband linear translator output
1296.8-1297.0 Experimental beacons (exclusive)
1297-1300 Digital Communications

2300-2310 and 2390-2450 MHz

2300.0-2303.0 High-rate data
2303.0-2303.5 Packet
2303.5-2303.8 TTY packet
2303.9-2303.9 Packet, TTY, CW, EME
2303.9-2304.1 CW, EME
2304.1 Calling frequency
2304.1-2304.2 CW, EME, SSB
2304.2-2304.3 SSB, SSTV, FAX, Packet AM, Amtor
2304.30-2304.32 Propagation beacon network
2304.32-2304.40 General propagation beacons
2304.4-2304.5 SSB, SSTV, ACSSB, FAX, Packet AM, Amtor experimental
2304.5-2304.7 Crossband linear translator input
2304.7-2304.9 Crossband linear translator output
2304.9-2305.0 Experimental beacons
2305.0-2305.2 FM simplex (25 kHz spacing)
2305.20 FM simplex calling frequency
2305.2-2306.0 FM simplex (25 kHz spacing)
2306.0-2309.0 FM Repeaters (25 kHz) input
2309.0-2310.0 Control and auxiliary links
2390.0-2396.0 Fast-scan TV
2396.0-2399.0 High-rate data
2399.0-2399.5 Packet
2399.5-2400.0 Control and auxiliary links
2400.0-2403.0 Satellite
2403.0-2408.0 Satellite high-rate data
2408.0-2410.0 Satellite
2410.0-2413.0 FM repeaters (25 kHz) output
2413.0-2418.0 High-rate data
2418.0-2430.0 Fast-scan TV
2430.0-2433.0 Satellite
2433.0-2438.0 Satellite high-rate data
2438.0-2450.0 WB FM, FSTV, FMTV, SS experimental

3300-3500 MHz

3456.3-3456.4 Propagation beacons

5650-5925 MHz

5760.3-5760.4 Propagation beacons

10.00-10.50 GHz
10.368 Narrow band calling frequency 10.3683-10.3684 Propagation beacons
10.3640 Calling frequency

Now that you have your license (you do, don't you?), and your equipment, you are ready to go live. Below is a suggested start.

1) Assuming you have the HT set up to the appropriate frequency, and offset, press the mic button on the HT and say, "KK4HWX listening." Replace the KK4HWX with your own call sign, the one assigned to you by the FCC (it's the law). If no one responds to your call, you may wish to try again. Hopefully someone will respond to your call.

2) Once you get a response, it will be in the form of something like, "KK4HWX this is ??1??? in Eastport returning. My name is Florence. Back to you. ??1???" then a tone. Let us examine the response more closely. She first acknowledged your call sign (KK4HWX), then identified hers (??1???). From the 1 in her call sign, you know that she first got her license in Region 1, meaning she got it while a resident of CT, ME, MA, NH, RI, or VT. She then told you where she's transmitting from (Eastport). The term "returning" means that she is returning your call. Her name is Florence. The phrase, "Back to you" indicates that she is turning over the conversation to you. She then repeats her call sign. The tone indicates to you that it is okay to proceed with your response. BTW if she had used the term "Over" instead of "Back to you," it would mean the same thing, just fewer words.

3) At this point, press the mic button and continue with the conversation. You should restate your call sign often during the conversation (perhaps every 10 minutes or less and whenever you begin transmitting). Don't forget to say, "Over" or "Back to you" whenever you are giving Florence control of the conversation again.

4) When you are ready to stop the conversation, you should say goodbye or use the phrase "73", meaning "best wishes." Your conversation would end something like, "??1??? 73, this is KK4HWX clear and monitoring." The "clear and monitoring" indicates that you are going to continue to monitor the frequency. If you are not going to continue monitoring, you may wish to end the conversation with Florence with, "clear and QRT" instead. The QRT means that you are stopping transmissions.

Call Sign Phonics

Because of different accents of various people, sometimes it is difficult to understand call sign letters when spoken. For this reason, most ham operators verbalize their call sign using phonics. Below is a table listing the accepted phonics for letters and numbers.

A = ALFA	D = DELTA
B = BRAVO	E = ECHO
C = CHARLIE	F = FOXTROT

G = GOLF	V = VICTOR
H = HOTEL	W = WHISKEY
I = INDIA	X = X-RAY
J = JULIETT	Y = YANKEE
K = KILO	Z = ZULU (ZED)
L = LIMA	1 = ONE
M = MIKE	2 = TWO
N = NOVEMBER	3 = THREE (TREE)
O = OSCAR	4 = FOUR
P = PAPA (PA-PA')	5 = FIVE (FIFE)
Q = QUEBEC (KAY-BEK')	6 = SIX
R = ROMEO	7 = SEVEN
S = SIERRA	8 = EIGHT
T = TANGO	9 = NINE (NINER)
U = UNIFORM	0 = ZERO

The words in parentheses are the pronunciation or the alternate pronunciations for the words or numbers, but you will hear both used. With the letter Z, (ZED) is by far the most commonly used. With the number 9, NINER is the most common and easiest to understand ON THE AIR.

If you wish to use Morse code (CW) instead of voice communication, the "conversation" would follow the same steps, with a few modifications. To type out each word would require a lot of typing and translating. If you are like this author, more means more, i.e., more typing means more typos are likely. To help with this situation, CW enthusiasts have developed a language all their own – they use abbreviations for common phrases. Below is a chart showing some of these abbreviations.

Abbreviation	Use
AR	Over
de	From or "this is"
ES	And
GM	Good Morning
K	Go
KN	Go only
NM	Name
QTH	Location
RPT	Report
R	Roger
SK	Clear
tnx	Thanks
UR	Your, you are
73	Best Wishes

Morse Code and Amateur Radio

If you wish to use CW, but are concerned about accuracy, you might consider purchasing a Morse code translator. This is an electronic device that you place in front of your speakers. It takes the CW sounds and translates them into English and displays the transmission on an LCD display. For the reverse, you can pick up a CW keyboard. With the keyboard, you type in your message and it converts the text to Morse code. The translator does not need to be attached to your ham equipment, whereas the keyboard would.

For your convenience, below is a table showing the Morse code signals and their meaning.

Character	Code
A	• —
B	— • • •
C	— • — •
D	— • •
E	•
F	• • — •
G	— — •
H	• • • •
I	• •
J	• — — —
K	— • —
L	• — • •
M	— —
N	— •
O	— — —
P	• — — •
Q	— — • —
R	• — •
S	• • •
T	—
U	• • —
V	• • • —
W	• — —
X	— • • —
Y	— • — —
Z	— — • •
0	— — — — —
1	• — — — —
2	• • — — —
3	• • • — —
4	• • • • —
5	• • • • •
6	— • • • •
7	— — • • •

8	— — — · ·
9	— — — — ·
Ampersand [&], Wait	· — · · ·
Apostrophe [']	· — — — — ·
At sign [@]	· — — · — ·
Colon [:]	— — — · · ·
Comma [,]	— — · · — —
Dollar sign [$]	· · · — · · —
Double dash [=]	— · · · —
Exclamation mark [!]	— · — · — —
Hyphen, Minus [-]	— · · · · —
Parenthesis closed [)]	— · — — · —
Parenthesis open [(]	— · — — ·
Period [.]	· — · — · —
Plus [+]	· — · — ·
Question mark [?]	· · — — · ·
Quotation mark ["]	· — · · — ·
Semicolon [;]	— · — · — ·
Slash [/], Fraction bar	— · · — ·
Underscore [_]	· · — — · —

An advantage of using Morse Code is that when broadcasting CW, you are using reduced power, thereby saving your battery. Your battery is used only while actually transmitting or receiving.

International Call Sign Prefixes

As was stated earlier, all ham radio call signs begin with letters (or numbers) taken from blocks assigned to each country of the world by the *ITU - International Telecommunications Union,* a body controlled by the United Nations. The following chart indicates which call sign series are allocated to which countries.

Call Sign Series	Allocated to
AAA-ALZ	**United States of America**
AMA-AOZ	Spain
APA-ASZ	Pakistan (Islamic Republic of)
ATA-AWZ	India (Republic of)
AXA-AXZ	Australia
AYA-AZZ	Argentine Republic
A2A-A2Z	Botswana (Republic of)
A3A-A3Z	Tonga (Kingdom of)
A4A-A4Z	Oman (Sultanate of)
A5A-A5Z	Bhutan (Kingdom of)
A6A-A6Z	United Arab Emirates
A7A-A7Z	Qatar (State of)

A8A-A8Z	Liberia (Republic of)
A9A-A9Z	Bahrain (State of)
BAA-BZZ	China (People's Republic of)
CAA-CEZ	Chile
CFA-CKZ	Canada
CLA-CMZ	Cuba
CNA-CNZ	Morocco (Kingdom of)
COA-COZ	Cuba
CPA-CPZ	Bolivia (Republic of)
CQA-CUZ	Portugal
CVA-CXZ	Uruguay (Eastern Republic of)
CYA-CZZ	Canada
C2A-C2Z	Nauru (Republic of)
C3A-C3Z	Andorra (Principality of)
C4A-C4Z	Cyprus (Republic of)
C5A-C5Z	Gambia (Republic of the)
C6A-C6Z	Bahamas (Commonwealth of the)
C7A-C7Z	World Meteorological Organization
C8A-C9Z	Mozambique (Republic of)
DAA-DRZ	Germany (Federal Republic of)
DSA-DTZ	Korea (Republic of)
DUA-DZZ	Philippines (Republic of the)
D2A-D3Z	Angola (Republic of)
D4A-D4Z	Cape Verde (Republic of)
D5A-D5Z	Liberia (Republic of)
D6A-D6Z	Comoros (Islamic Federal Republic of the)
D7A-D9Z	Korea (Republic of)
EAA-EHZ	Spain
EIA-EJZ	Ireland
EKA-EKZ	Armenia (Republic of)
ELA-ELZ	Liberia (Republic of)
EMA-EOZ	Ukraine
EPA-EQZ	Iran (Islamic Republic of)
ERA-ERZ	Moldova (Republic of)
ESA-ESZ	Estonia (Republic of)
ETA-ETZ	Ethiopia (Federal Democratic Republic of)
EUA-EWZ	Belarus (Republic of)
EXA-EXZ	Kyrgyz Republic
EYA-EYZ	Tajikistan (Republic of)
EZA-EZZ	Turkmenistan
E2A-E2Z	Thailand
E3A-E3Z	Eritrea
E4A-E4Z	Palestinian Authority
E5A-E5Z	New Zealand - Cook Islands (WRC-07)
E7A-E7Z	Bosnia and Herzegovina (Republic of) (WRC-07)

FAA-FZZ	France
GAA-GZZ	United Kingdom of Great Britain and Northern Ireland
HAA-HAZ	Hungary (Republic of)
HBA-HBZ	Switzerland (Confederation of)
HCA-HDZ	Ecuador
HEA-HEZ	Switzerland (Confederation of)
HFA-HFZ	Poland (Republic of)
HGA-HGZ	Hungary (Republic of)
HHA-HHZ	Haiti (Republic of)
HIA-HIZ	Dominican Republic
HJA-HKZ	Colombia (Republic of)
HLA-HLZ	Korea (Republic of)
HMA-HMZ	Democratic People's Republic of Korea
HNA-HNZ	Iraq (Republic of)
HOA-HPZ	Panama (Republic of)
HQA-HRZ	Honduras (Republic of)
HSA-HSZ	Thailand
HTA-HTZ	Nicaragua
HUA-HUZ	El Salvador (Republic of)
HVA-HVZ	Vatican City State
HWA-HYZ	France
HZA-HZZ	Saudi Arabia (Kingdom of)
H2A-H2Z	Cyprus (Republic of)
H3A-H3Z	Panama (Republic of)
H4A-H4Z	Solomon Islands
H6A-H7Z	Nicaragua
H8A-H9Z	Panama (Republic of)
IAA-IZZ	Italy
JAA-JSZ	Japan
JTA-JVZ	Mongolia
JWA-JXZ	Norway
JYA-JYZ	Jordan (Hashemite Kingdom of)
JZA-JZZ	Indonesia (Republic of)
J2A-J2Z	Djibouti (Republic of)
J3A-J3Z	Grenada
J4A-J4Z	Greece
J5A-J5Z	Guinea-Bissau (Republic of)
J6A-J6Z	Saint Lucia
J7A-J7Z	Dominica (Commonwealth of)
J8A-J8Z	Saint Vincent and the Grenadines
KAA-KZZ	**United States of America**
LAA-LNZ	Norway
LOA-LWZ	Argentine Republic
LXA-LXZ	Luxembourg
LYA-LYZ	Lithuania (Republic of)

LZA-LZZ	Bulgaria (Republic of)
L2A-L9Z	Argentine Republic
MAA-MZZ	United Kingdom of Great Britain and Northern Ireland
NAA-NZZ	**United States of America**
OAA-OCZ	Peru
ODA-ODZ	Lebanon
OEA-OEZ	Austria
OFA-OJZ	Finland
OKA-OLZ	Czech Republic
OMA-OMZ	Slovak Republic
ONA-OTZ	Belgium
OUA-OZZ	Denmark
PAA-PIZ	Netherlands (Kingdom of the)
PJA-PJZ	Netherlands (Kingdom of the) - Netherlands Antilles
PKA-POZ	Indonesia (Republic of)
PPA-PYZ	Brazil (Federative Republic of)
PZA-PZZ	Suriname (Republic of)
P2A-P2Z	Papua New Guinea
P3A-P3Z	Cyprus (Republic of)
P4A-P4Z	Netherlands (Kingdom of the) - Aruba
P5A-P9Z	Democratic People's Republic of Korea
RAA-RZZ	Russian Federation
SAA-SMZ	Sweden
SNA-SRZ	Poland (Republic of)
SSA-SSM	Egypt (Arab Republic of)
SSN-STZ	Sudan (Republic of the)
SUA-SUZ	Egypt (Arab Republic of)
SVA-SZZ	Greece
S2A-S3Z	Bangladesh (People's Republic of)
S5A-S5Z	Slovenia (Republic of)
S6A-S6Z	Singapore (Republic of)
S7A-S7Z	Seychelles (Republic of)
S8A-S8Z	South Africa (Republic of)
S9A-S9Z	Sao Tome and Principe (Democratic Republic of)
TAA-TCZ	Turkey
TDA-TDZ	Guatemala (Republic of)
TEA-TEZ	Costa Rica
TFA-TFZ	Iceland
TGA-TGZ	Guatemala (Republic of)
THA-THZ	France
TIA-TIZ	Costa Rica
TJA-TJZ	Cameroon (Republic of)
TKA-TKZ	France
TLA-TLZ	Central African Republic
TMA-TMZ	France

TNA-TNZ	Congo (Republic of the)
TOA-TQZ	France
TRA-TRZ	Gabonese Republic
TSA-TSZ	Tunisia
TTA-TTZ	Chad (Republic of)
TUA-TUZ	Côte d'Ivoire (Republic of)
TVA-TXZ	France
TYA-TYZ	Benin (Republic of)
TZA-TZZ	Mali (Republic of)
T2A-T2Z	Tuvalu
T3A-T3Z	Kiribati (Republic of)
T4A-T4Z	Cuba
T5A-T5Z	Somali Democratic Republic
T6A-T6Z	Afghanistan (Islamic State of)
T7A-T7Z	San Marino (Republic of)
T8A-T8Z	Palau (Republic of)
UAA-UIZ	Russian Federation
UJA-UMZ	Uzbekistan (Republic of)
UNA-UQZ	Kazakhstan (Republic of)
URA-UZZ	Ukraine
VAA-VGZ	Canada
VHA-VNZ	Australia
VOA-VOZ	Canada
VPA-VQZ	United Kingdom of Great Britain and Northern Ireland
VRA-VRZ	China (People's Republic of) - Hong Kong
VSA-VSZ	United Kingdom of Great Britain and Northern Ireland
VTA-VWZ	India (Republic of)
VXA-VYZ	Canada
VZA-VZZ	Australia
V2A-V2Z	Antigua and Barbuda
V3A-V3Z	Belize
V4A-V4Z	Saint Kitts and Nevis
V5A-V5Z	Namibia (Republic of)
V6A-V6Z	Micronesia (Federated States of)
V7A-V7Z	Marshall Islands (Republic of the)
V8A-V8Z	Brunei Darussalam
WAA-WZZ	**United States of America**
XAA-XIZ	Mexico
XJA-XOZ	Canada
XPA-XPZ	Denmark
XQA-XRZ	Chile
XSA-XSZ	China (People's Republic of)
XTA-XTZ	Burkina Faso
XUA-XUZ	Cambodia (Kingdom of)
XVA-XVZ	Viet Nam (Socialist Republic of)

XWA-XWZ	Lao People's Democratic Republic
XXA-XXZ	China (People's Republic of) - Macao (WRC-07)
XYA-XZZ	Myanmar (Union of)
YAA-YAZ	Afghanistan (Islamic State of)
YBA-YHZ	Indonesia (Republic of)
YIA-YIZ	Iraq (Republic of)
YJA-YJZ	Vanuatu (Republic of)
YKA-YKZ	Syrian Arab Republic
YLA-YLZ	Latvia (Republic of)
YMA-YMZ	Turkey
YNA-YNZ	Nicaragua
YOA-YRZ	Romania
YSA-YSZ	El Salvador (Republic of)
YTA-YUZ	Serbia (Republic of) (WRC-07)
YVA-YYZ	Venezuela (Republic of)
Y2A-Y9Z	Germany (Federal Republic of)
ZAA-ZAZ	Albania (Republic of)
ZBA-ZJZ	United Kingdom of Great Britain and Northern Ireland
ZKA-ZMZ	New Zealand
ZNA-ZOZ	United Kingdom of Great Britain and Northern Ireland
ZPA-ZPZ	Paraguay (Republic of)
ZQA-ZQZ	United Kingdom of Great Britain and Northern Ireland
ZRA-ZUZ	South Africa (Republic of)
ZVA-ZZZ	Brazil (Federative Republic of)
Z2A-Z2Z	Zimbabwe (Republic of)
Z3A-Z3Z	The Former Yugoslav Republic of Macedonia
2AA-2ZZ	United Kingdom of Great Britain and Northern Ireland
3AA-3AZ	Monaco (Principality of)
3BA-3BZ	Mauritius (Republic of)
3CA-3CZ	Equatorial Guinea (Republic of)
3DA-3DM	Swaziland (Kingdom of)
3DN-3DZ	Fiji (Republic of)
3EA-3FZ	Panama (Republic of)
3GA-3GZ	Chile
3HA-3UZ	China (People's Republic of)
3VA-3VZ	Tunisia
3WA-3WZ	Viet Nam (Socialist Republic of)
3XA-3XZ	Guinea (Republic of)
3YA-3YZ	Norway
3ZA-3ZZ	Poland (Republic of)
4AA-4CZ	Mexico
4DA-4IZ	Philippines (Republic of the)
4JA-4KZ	Azerbaijani Republic
4LA-4LZ	Georgia (Republic of)
4MA-4MZ	Venezuela (Republic of)

4OA-4OZ	Montenegro (Republic of) (WRC-07)
4PA-4SZ	Sri Lanka (Democratic Socialist Republic of)
4TA-4TZ	Peru
4UA-4UZ	United Nations
4VA-4VZ	Haiti (Republic of)
4WA-4WZ	Democratic Republic of Timor-Leste (WRC-03)
4XA-4XZ	Israel (State of)
4YA-4YZ	International Civil Aviation Organization
4ZA-4ZZ	Israel (State of)
5AA-5AZ	Libya (Socialist People's Libyan Arab Jamahiriya)
5BA-5BZ	Cyprus (Republic of)
5CA-5GZ	Morocco (Kingdom of)
5HA-5IZ	Tanzania (United Republic of)
5JA-5KZ	Colombia (Republic of)
5LA-5MZ	Liberia (Republic of)
5NA-5OZ	Nigeria (Federal Republic of)
5PA-5QZ	Denmark
5RA-5SZ	Madagascar (Republic of)
5TA-5TZ	Mauritania (Islamic Republic of)
5UA-5UZ	Niger (Republic of the)
5VA-5VZ	Togolese Republic
5WA-5WZ	Samoa (Independent State of)
5XA-5XZ	Uganda (Republic of)
5YA-5ZZ	Kenya (Republic of)
6AA-6BZ	Egypt (Arab Republic of)
6CA-6CZ	Syrian Arab Republic
6DA-6JZ	Mexico
6KA-6NZ	Korea (Republic of)
6OA-6OZ	Somali Democratic Republic
6PA-6SZ	Pakistan (Islamic Republic of)
6TA-6UZ	Sudan (Republic of the)
6VA-6WZ	Senegal (Republic of)
6XA-6XZ	Madagascar (Republic of)
6YA-6YZ	Jamaica
6ZA-6ZZ	Liberia (Republic of)
7AA-7IZ	Indonesia (Republic of)
7JA-7NZ	Japan
7OA-7OZ	Yemen (Republic of)
7PA-7PZ	Lesotho (Kingdom of)
7QA-7QZ	Malawi
7RA-7RZ	Algeria (People's Democratic Republic of)
7SA-7SZ	Sweden
7TA-7YZ	Algeria (People's Democratic Republic of)
7ZA-7ZZ	Saudi Arabia (Kingdom of)
8AA-8IZ	Indonesia (Republic of)

8JA-8NZ	Japan
8OA-8OZ	Botswana (Republic of)
8PA-8PZ	Barbados
8QA-8QZ	Maldives (Republic of)
8RA-8RZ	Guyana
8SA-8SZ	Sweden
8TA-8YZ	India (Republic of)
8ZA-8ZZ	Saudi Arabia (Kingdom of)
9AA-9AZ	Croatia (Republic of)
9BA-9DZ	Iran (Islamic Republic of)
9EA-9FZ	Ethiopia (Federal Democratic Republic of)
9GA-9GZ	Ghana
9HA-9HZ	Malta
9IA-9JZ	Zambia (Republic of)
9KA-9KZ	Kuwait (State of)
9LA-9LZ	Sierra Leone
9MA-9MZ	Malaysia
9NA-9NZ	Nepal
9OA-9TZ	Democratic Republic of the Congo
9UA-9UZ	Burundi (Republic of)
9VA-9VZ	Singapore (Republic of)
9WA-9WZ	Malaysia
9XA-9XZ	Rwandese Republic
9YA-9ZZ	Trinidad and Tobago

Third-Party Communications and Amateur Radio

If all of this information about ham radios is somewhat intimidating, do not despair. "You" can still use ham radios for communications without being a licensed operator. Yes, you do have to have a ham license in order to legally transmit by ham equipment (or be under the direct supervision of someone else who is licensed), but there is an alternative – third-party communication.

Third-party communications occur when a licensed operator sends either written or verbal messages on behalf of unlicensed persons or organizations. There are two "controls" on third-party communication.

First, the communication must be noncommercial and of a personal nature. Asking a ham operator to contact another ham operator located in an area just hit by tornados and, because of being without power, phones do not work in Grandma Sally's city so you can check up on her, is okay. Asking a ham to send a message out that you have an old Chevy for sale would not be okay.

Second, the message must be going to a permitted area. Transmitting from a US location to another US location is okay, but transmitting from the US to another country may not. Because third-party communications bypass a country's normal telephone and postal systems, many foreign governments forbid such communications. In order to transmit from one country to another, the other country must have signed a third-party agreement with the US. What follows is a list of those countries that do have third-party a communications agreement with the US.

V2	Antigua / Barbuda
LU	Argentina
VK	Australia
V3	Belize
CP	Bolivia
T9	Bosnia-Herzegovina
PY	Brazil
VE	Canada
CE	Chile
HK	Colombia
D6	Comoros (Federal Islamic Republic of)
TI	Costa Rica
CO	Cuba
HI	Dominican Republic
J7	Dominica
HC	Ecuador
YS	El Salvador
C5	Gambia, The
9G	Ghana
J3	Grenada
TG	Guatemala
8R	Guyana
HH	Haiti
HR	Honduras
4X	Israel
6Y	Jamaica
JY	Jordan
EL	Liberia
V7	Marshall Islands
XE	Mexico
V6	Micronesia, Federated States of
YN	Nicaragua
HP	Panama
ZP	Paraguay
OA	Peru
DU	Philippines
VR6	Pitcairn Island
V4	St. Christopher / Nevis
J6	St. Lucia
J8	St. Vincent and the Grenadines

9L	Sierra Leone
ZS	South Africa
3DA	Swaziland
9Y	Trinidad / Tobago
TA	Turkey
GB	United Kingdom
CX	Uruguay
YV	Venezuela
4U1ITUITU	Geneva
4U1VICVIC	Vienna

Remember, before TSHTF, keep your pantry well stocked, your powder dry, and your batteries fully charged. 73

APPENDIX A

American Radio Relay League

Affiliated Amateur Radio Clubs in

Connecticut

ARRL Affiliated Club	**Bethel Educational Amateur Radio Society**
City	Bethel, CT
Call Sign	KA1KD
Section	CT
Links	people.mags.net/boem/bears.htm

ARRL Affiliated Club	**Bloomfield Amateur Radio Club**
City	Bloomfield, CT
Call Sign	W1CWA
Section	CT

ARRL Affiliated Club	**Southcentral Connecticut Amateur Radio Association**
City	Branford, CT
Call Sign	W1GB
Section	CT
Links	www.scara.us

ARRL Affiliated Club	**Chippens Repeater/ Bristol Radio Club**
City	Bristol, CT
Call Sign	W1DHT
Section	CT

ARRL Affiliated Club	**Candlewood Amateur Radio Association**
City	Danbury, CT
Call Sign	W1QI
Section	CT
Links	www.danbury.org/cara/

ARRL Affiliated Club	**Connecticut AM Society**
City	Danielson, CT
Call Sign	KW1AM
Section	CT

ARRL Affiliated Club	**Trinity College Alumni Radio Club**
City	Dayville, CT
Call Sign	W1JUD
Links	w1jud.blogspot.com

ARRL Affiliated Club	**Eastern Connecticut Amateur Radio Association**
City	Dayville, CT
Call Sign	K1MUJ
Section	CT
Links	www.qsl.net/k1muj

ARRL Affiliated Club	**CT Amateur Radio League of Youth (CARLY)**
City	East Hampton, CT
Call Sign	K3KID
Section	CT

ARRL Affiliated Club	**Greater Fairfield Amateur Radio Association**
City	Fairfield, CT
Call Sign	WB1CQO
Section	CT

ARRL Affiliated Club	**Middlesex Amateur Radio Society**
City	Glastonbury, CT
Call Sign	W1EDH
Section	CT
Links	www.w1edh.org

ARRL Affiliated Club	**Tri-City Amateur Radio Club - CT**
City	Groton, CT
Call Sign	W1QV
Section	CT
Links	www.tricityarc.com

ARRL Affiliated Club	**Manchester Radio Club**
City	Manchester, CT
Call Sign	W1KKS
Section	CT

ARRL Affiliated Club	**Bears OF Manchester Inc.**
City	Manchester, CT
Call Sign	W1BRS
Section	CT
Links	www.w1brs.com

ARRL Affiliated Club	**Pioneer Valley Radio Association**
City	Manchester, CT
Call Sign	W1HDN
Section	CT
Links	www.pvra.net

ARRL Affiliated Club	**Meriden Amateur Radio Club**
City	Meriden, CT
Call Sign	W1NRG
Section	CT
Links	www.meridenarc.org

ARRL Affiliated Club	**Milford Amateur Repeater Association**
City	Milford, CT
Call Sign	KB1CBD
Section	CT
Links	www.qsl.net/kb1cbd/

ARRL Affiliated Club	**Yale University Amateur Radio Club**
City	New Haven, CT
Call Sign	W1YU
Section	CT
Links	www.yale.edu/w1yu

ARRL Affiliated Club	**Northville Amateur Radio Association**
City	New Preston Marble Dale, CT
Call Sign	NA1RA
Section	CT
Links	www.na1ra.com

ARRL Affiliated Club	**NARL (Newington Amateur Radio League)**
City	Newington, CT
Call Sign	W1OKY
Section	CT
Links	www.NARL.net

ARRL Affiliated Club	**Greater Norwalk Amateur Radio Club**
City	Norwalk, CT
Call Sign	W1NLK
Section	CT
Links	www.gnarc.org

ARRL Affiliated Club	**Radio Amateur Society of Norwich (Rason)**
City	Norwich, CT
Call Sign	N1NW
Section	CT
Links	www.rason.org

ARRL Affiliated Club	**Orange Amateur Radio Association**
City	Orange, CT
Section	CT
Links	orangeradio.org

ARRL Affiliated Club	**Insurance City Repeater Club**
City	Plainville, CT
Call Sign	K1CRC
Section	CT
Links	www.icrcweb.org

ARRL Affiliated Club	**Valley Amateur Radio Assn.**
City	Seymour, CT
Call Sign	W1VAR
Section	CT

ARRL Affiliated Club	**Southern Berkshire Amateur Radio Club**
City	Sharon, CT
Call Sign	W1BAA
Section	CT
Links	www.w1baa.org

ARRL Affiliated Club	**The Stratford Amateur Radio Club, Inc.**
City	Shelton, CT
Call Sign	W1ORS
Section	CT
Links	www.qsl.net/w1ors/

ARRL Special Service Club	**Southington Amateur Radio Association**
City	Southington, CT
Call Sign	W1ECV
Section	CT
Links	www.chetbacon.com/sara.htm

ARRL Affiliated Club	**Natchaug Amateur Radio Club**
City	Stafford Springs, CT
Call Sign	NA1RC
Section	CT
Links	www.na1rc.org

ARRL Affiliated Club	**Stamford Amateur Radio Association Inc**
City	Stamford, CT
Call Sign	W1EE
Section	CT
Links	www.ctsara.org

ARRL Affiliated Club	**Connecticut Amateur Radio Association**
City	Stamford, CT
Call Sign	KB1OAS
Section	CT

ARRL Affiliated Club	**CQ Radio Club**
City	Torrington, CT
Section	CT
Links	www.CQRadioClub.com

ARRL Affiliated Club	**Shore Point Amateur Radio Club - SPARC**
City	Wallingford, CT
Call Sign	K1SOX
Section	CT

ARRL Affiliated Club	**Waterbury Amateur Radio Club**
City	Waterbury, CT
Call Sign	W1LAS
Section	CT
Links	www.qsl.net/w1las/

ARRL Affiliated Club	**Greater Bridgeport Amateur Radio Club, Inc.**
City	Waterbury, CT
Call Sign	WA1RJI
Section	CT
Links	www.gbarc.net/

ARRL Affiliated Club	**Southeastern CT Radio Amateur**
City	Waterford, CT
Call Sign	W1NLC
Section	CT
Links	www.QSL.net/W1NLC, www.scrams.webs.com/

ARRL Affiliated Club	**Huckleberry Mountain Contest Club**
City	West Suffield, CT
Call Sign	W1SSB
Section	CT

ARRL Affiliated Club	**Shoreline ARC Inc**
City	Westbrook, CT
Call Sign	W1BCG
Section	CT
Links	www.shorelinearc.org

ARRL Affiliated Club	**Connecticut DX Association**
City	Windsor, CT
Section	CT

ARRL Affiliated Club	**Wireless Operators of Winsted**
City	Winsted, CT
Call Sign	WB1DJU
Section	CT

APPENDIX B

Amateur Radio License Holders

in

Connecticut
(by City)

FCC Amateur Radio Licenses in Abington

Call Sign: N1PTC
Jeannette A Knight
585 Mashamoquet Rd
Abington CT 06230

Call Sign: N1PTE
Warren H Knight Sr
585 Mashamoquet Rd
Abington CT 06230

FCC Amateur Radio Licenses in Amston

Call Sign: KB1DNH
Thomas R Corris
59a 59a Burrows Hill Rd
Amston CT 06231

Call Sign: KC5LUT
David R Case
45 Ames Road
Amston CT 06231

Call Sign: K5IZM
David R Case
45 Ames Road
Amston CT 06231

Call Sign: KB1FBR
Thomas R Corris
59a Burrows Hill Rd
Amston CT 06231

Call Sign: K1ELT
Alexander J Joseph Jr
36 Crouch Rd
Amston CT 06231

Call Sign: KA1QLW
John D Avallone
197 Hillcrest Dr
Amston CT 06231

Call Sign: KA1QLX
J David Avallone Jr
197 Hillcrest Dr
Amston CT 06231

Call Sign: W1NUE
Stanley J Misorski
56 Hoadly Rd
Amston CT 06231

Call Sign: W1HTZ
John F Richmond
276 Hope Valley Rd
Amston CT 06231

Call Sign: N1NRQ
Richard V Daddi
469 Hope Valley Rd
Amston CT 06231

Call Sign: W9JJ
Bart J Jahnke
275 Jones
Amston CT 06231

Call Sign: K1FNT
Thomas J Doucette
299 Old Colchester Rd
Amston CT 06231

Call Sign: KB1FCH
David A Schroeder
305 Old Colchester Rd
Amston CT 06231

Call Sign: N1GOX
Ted L Adams Sr
20 Turner Rd
Amston CT 06231

Call Sign: N1GOY
Lisa D Adams
20 Turner Rd
Amston CT 06231

Call Sign: KA3DRL
Russell C Seeger
36 Uncas Drive
Amston CT 06231

Call Sign: WA1PFE
Robert J Beyus
633 W Main St
Amston CT 06231

Call Sign: KA1LBZ
Barbara V Muzzulin
Amston CT 06231

Call Sign: WA1USD
Guerin V Muzzulin
Amston CT 06231

FCC Amateur Radio Licenses in Andover

Call Sign: KE1K
Steven T Nakos
300 Boston Hill Rd
Andover CT 06232

Call Sign: N1EGB
Grace A Nakos
300 Boston Hill Rd
Andover CT 06232

Call Sign: KA1DTV
Joan M Merritt
41 Burnap Brook Rd
Andover CT 06232

Call Sign: W1FCV
John F Roache Iii
50 Gilead Rd
Andover CT 06232

Call Sign: KA1OXC
Christopher E Caovette
41 Kingsley Dr Apt B1

Andover CT 06232

Call Sign: KB1EMJ
Bert A Bowen Iii
173 Lake Rd
Andover CT 06232

Call Sign: KB1PKW
Carol L Bowen
173 Lake Rd
Andover CT 06232

Call Sign: AB1NG
Bert A Bowen Iii
173 Lake Rd
Andover CT 06232

Call Sign: KB1EMJ
Carol L Bowen
173 Lake Rd
Andover CT 06232

Call Sign: N1EAI
Joseph A Poland Iii
300 Lake Rd
Andover CT 06232

Call Sign: N1TST
Milton A Glew
78 Merritt Valley Rd
Andover CT 062321323

Call Sign: K1JTX
Lawrence Billiel
25 Riverside Dr Apt 25
Andover CT 06232

Call Sign: W1MQQ
Richard B Kent
674 Rt 6
Andover CT 06232

Call Sign: KA1KZC
Joseph R King
86 School Road

Andover CT 06232

Call Sign: KB1RMV
Todd J Hunter
37 Shoddy Mill Rd
Andover CT 06232

Call Sign: N1BSE
Nancy R Breadheft
55 Wales Rd
Andover CT 06232

Call Sign: N1BSF
Martin W Breadheft
55 Wales Rd
Andover CT 06232

FCC Amateur Radio Licenses in Ansnoia

Call Sign: N1NHC
Anthony K Soriano
46 Elm
Ansnoia CT 06401

Call Sign: KB1TLB
Kevin S Pasacreta
14 Arbor Terr
Ansonia CT 06401

Call Sign: KA1LSD
David J Lombard
29 Bartholomew Ave
Ansonia CT 06401

Call Sign: N1XGT
John A Siebert
21 Beechwood Dr
Ansonia CT 06401

Call Sign: KB1AUL
Joseph A Palombo
28 Beechwood Dr
Ansonia CT 06401

Call Sign: KB1VCR
Michael J Lake
29 Beechwood Dr
Ansonia CT 06401

Call Sign: KA1LGA
John Honas
17 Belleview Ter
Ansonia CT 06401

Call Sign: KB1EHV
Connecticut Radio Society
32 Benz St
Ansonia CT 06401

Call Sign: W1CTN
David M Arruzza
32 Benz St
Ansonia CT 06401

Call Sign: KB1GXN
Greater North American
Transmitting Society
32 Benz Street
Ansonia CT 06401

Call Sign: NA1QP
Greater North American
Transmitting Society
32 Benz Street
Ansonia CT 06401

Call Sign: KB1CPD
Jonathan R Awalt
19 Beverly Dr
Ansonia CT 06401

Call Sign: KB1UKS
Ann M Fisher
4 Birchwood Dr
Ansonia CT 06401

Call Sign: N1ACE
Ann M Fisher
4 Birchwood Dr

Ansonia CT 06401　　　　　　　Ansonia CT 06401　　　　　　　Ansonia CT 06401

Call Sign: K1CRD　　　　　　Call Sign: KB1DPR　　　　　　Call Sign: KR1CW
Anthony C Sawicki　　　　　　Ct Southwest Radio Society　　Voa Radio Club
6 Birchwood Dr　　　　　　　2 Ford St　　　　　　　　　　21 Glen Dr
Ansonia CT 06401　　　　　　Ansonia CT 064012730　　　　Ansonia CT 06401

Call Sign: WA1HCH　　　　　Call Sign: WA1UHY　　　　　Call Sign: KB1VFE
Ralph W Tingley Jr　　　　　　Jacqueline E Howard　　　　　Joseph J Navin Ii
5 Bruns Rd　　　　　　　　　2 Ford St　　　　　　　　　　38 Glen Dr
Ansonia CT 06401　　　　　　Ansonia CT 06401　　　　　　Ansonia CT 06401

Call Sign: WA1HSR　　　　　Call Sign: WK1M　　　　　　Call Sign: K1JJN
Ralph E Tingley　　　　　　　George A Howard Jr　　　　　Joseph J Navin Ii
5 Bruns Rd　　　　　　　　　2 Ford St　　　　　　　　　　38 Glen Dr
Ansonia CT 06401　　　　　　Ansonia CT 06401　　　　　　Ansonia CT 06401

Call Sign: N1ZIX　　　　　　Call Sign: W1TXL　　　　　　Call Sign: K2RS
Eric M Rivera　　　　　　　　Ct Southwest Radio Society　　John K Russell
34 Church St　　　　　　　　2 Ford St　　　　　　　　　　21 Glen Drive
Ansonia CT 06401　　　　　　Ansonia CT 064012730　　　　Ansonia CT 06401

Call Sign: KB1FKJ　　　　　　Call Sign: KB1WJS　　　　　Call Sign: KB1UWU
Andres A Rosado　　　　　　Angelique M Fitzmorris　　　　Ryan Hunt
80 Clifton Ave　　　　　　　23 Francis St　　　　　　　　7 Hale Dr
Ansonia CT 06401　　　　　　Ansonia CT 06401　　　　　　Ansonia CT 06401

Call Sign: KB1PZA　　　　　Call Sign: N1NQT　　　　　　Call Sign: K9RMH
Pasquale S Librandi　　　　　Michael A Pawlyk　　　　　　Ryan Hunt
11 Clover St　　　　　　　　37 Franklin St　　　　　　　7 Hale Dr
Ansonia CT 06401　　　　　　Ansonia CT 06401　　　　　　Ansonia CT 06401

Call Sign: KA1LZT　　　　　　Call Sign: KB1NLP　　　　　Call Sign: W1NZG
Harry Lysak Sr　　　　　　　Michael E Marganski　　　　　Andrew W Knapp
39 Clover Street　　　　　　14 Franklin Street　　　　　　8 Hickory Ln
Ansonia CT 06401　　　　　　Ansonia CT 06401　　　　　　Ansonia CT 06401

Call Sign: KB1SIW　　　　　Call Sign: WB1IAN　　　　　　Call Sign: W1LBZ
Anthony J Wyrembek　　　　Michael E Marganski　　　　　Daniel R De Marco
19 Colony St　　　　　　　　14 Franklin Street　　　　　　33 Highland Ave
Ansonia CT 06401　　　　　　Ansonia CT 06401　　　　　　Ansonia CT 06401

Call Sign: N1QXA　　　　　　Call Sign: KB1TTS　　　　　Call Sign: KA1UGU
Frank Perry　　　　　　　　Voa Radio Club　　　　　　　Roger J Begnoche
72 Dwight St　　　　　　　　21 Glen Dr　　　　　　　　　176 Hill St

Ansonia CT 06401

Call Sign: N1PFE
Andrew D Motes
18 Hillside Lane
Ansonia CT 06401

Call Sign: K1QR
Ronald W Chopski
10 Hoinski Way
Ansonia CT 06401

Call Sign: KA1QN
Ronald W Chopski
10 Hoinski Wy
Ansonia CT 06401

Call Sign: N1FRG
Richard R Lewis
130 Howard Ave
Ansonia CT 06401

Call Sign: N1NXY
Kevin Cochran
143 Jackson St
Ansonia CT 06401

Call Sign: KB1SJG
John Merkowitz
157 Jackson St
Ansonia CT 06401

Call Sign: KA1HVG
Edward E Wilkinson
15 Lester St
Ansonia CT 06401

Call Sign: N1WOY
Joseph W Glogowski
10 Michael St
Ansonia CT 06401

Call Sign: WK1X
Nathaniel G Wadsworth
5 Morningside Dr

Ansonia CT 06401

Call Sign: N1EGL
William A Blewett
29 N Coe Ln
Ansonia CT 06401

Call Sign: KB1PZB
Lisa M Shamansky
165 North State St
Ansonia CT 06401

Call Sign: AB1OQ
Kenneth W Bryant
255 North State St
Ansonia CT 06401

Call Sign: KB1RJK
Timothy F Gilroy
2 Prospect St
Ansonia CT 06401

Call Sign: KA1IBS
Edwin M Seufert
209 Prospect St
Ansonia CT 06401

Call Sign: KA1IBT
Peter M Seufert
209 Prospect St
Ansonia CT 06401

Call Sign: KB1QZX
Rebecca L Vives
10 Rev Taylor Dr
Ansonia CT 06401

Call Sign: N1SQB
Manfred E Vives
10 Reverend Taylor Drive
Ansonia CT 06401

Call Sign: N1SWO
Leticia Vives
10 Reverend Taylor Drive

Ansonia CT 06401

Call Sign: KB1FKI
Freddy Martin
106 S Cliff St
Ansonia CT 06401

Call Sign: WA1EHK
May E Blakley
118 Silver Hill Road
Ansonia CT 06401

Call Sign: N1FHG
Richard J Harkins Jr
80 Star St
Ansonia CT 06401

Call Sign: K1RKT
Thomas M Marchulitis
185 Sunset Dr
Ansonia CT 064011323

Call Sign: KB1MKX
John T Mellor Jr
107 Westfield Ave
Ansonia CT 06401

Call Sign: AB1IJ
John T Mellor Jr
107 Westfield Ave
Ansonia CT 06401

Call Sign: WB1GNK
James T Sherwood
120 Westfield Ave
Ansonia CT 06401

Call Sign: KB1WUY
Danilo Cantil
164 Westfield Ave
Ansonia CT 06401

Call Sign: KA1JVF
Raymond T Dudginski
8 Winter St

Ansonia CT 06401

Call Sign: KA1LZV
Michael J Nowak
Ansonia CT 06401

**FCC Amateur Radio
Licenses in Ashford**

Call Sign: NT1N
David C Patton
324 Ashford Center Rd
Ashford CT 06278

Call Sign: N1VDB
Rose M Dupre
387 Ashford Center Rd
Ashford CT 06278

Call Sign: N1VKX
Richard A Dupre
387 Ashford Center Rd
Ashford CT 06278

Call Sign: KB1PYR
Christopher L Curylo
149 Ashford Center Rd Apt
B6
Ashford CT 06278

Call Sign: K1VGF
Kevin T A Mc Carthy
436 Bebbington Rd
Ashford CT 062781615

Call Sign: KA1JZN
Kevin S Mc Carthy
436 Bebbington Rd
Ashford CT 06278

Call Sign: N1PXQ
Frederick J Smith Jr
80 Bicknell Rd Apt 15
Ashford CT 06278

Call Sign: KA1TBZ
Pamela Sirois
6 Broad Oak Dr
Ashford CT 06278

Call Sign: KA1YRS
Wojciech K Kowalczewski
18 Broad Oak Dr
Ashford CT 06278

Call Sign: KD1SH
William A Scott Jr
11 Campert Dr
Ashford CT 06278

Call Sign: W1TR
Terry G Glagowski
25 Hnath Road
Ashford CT 062782322

Call Sign: WB1CCL
Linda D Glagowski
25 Hnath Road
Ashford CT 06278

Call Sign: KB1KUL
Martin A Kiss Jr
93 Howard Rd
Ashford CT 06278

Call Sign: KA1KEJ
William J Mihancki Jr
3-Jul Kent Ct
Ashford CT 06278

Call Sign: N1NEF
Ramon M Caraballo
9-1 Kent Ct
Ashford CT 06278

Call Sign: KE1MD
Ramon M Caraballo
1-Sep Kent Ct
Ashford CT 06278

Call Sign: KB1DGY
Bernard M Dubb
83 Lakeside Dr
Ashford CT 062780066

Call Sign: KB1IYF
James J Martin
117 Mansfield Rd
Ashford CT 06278

Call Sign: WA1GVZ
Ulrich W Eschholz
49 Portland Dr
Ashford CT 06278

Call Sign: N4IKX
Maurice T Smith
219 Pumkin Hill Rd
Ashford CT 06278

Call Sign: KB1BSF
Natchaug Amateur Radio
Club
168 Pumpkin Hill Rd
Ashford CT 062781709

Call Sign: K1NIX
Donald A Soucie Jr
168 Pumpkin Hill Rd
Ashford CT 06278

Call Sign: N1SPK
Bruce A Wilbur
139 Squaw Hollow Rd
Ashford CT 06278

Call Sign: W1FDU
Oliver W Norton
49 Tremko Lane Apt 211
Ashford CT 06278

Call Sign: KB1VRQ
Stephanie A Seaburg
58 Varga Rd
Ashford CT 06278

Call Sign: K1AFP
Find C C Pedersen Jr
411 Zaicek Road
Ashford CT 06278

Call Sign: KC1LL
David B Garron
Ashford CT 06278

Call Sign: N1RCH
James E Clarke Jr
Ashford CT 06278

Call Sign: W1VSI
Robert C Britton
Ashford CT 062780240

Call Sign: KB1GAT
Carol B Patton
Ashford CT 06278

Call Sign: NN1N
David C Patton
Ashford CT 06278

**FCC Amateur Radio
Licenses in Avon**

Call Sign: N1NBI
Jan Rosow
10 Acorn Glen
Avon CT 06001

Call Sign: W1EFJ
Norman Z Rosow
10 Acorn Glen
Avon CT 06001

Call Sign: K1JQT
Philip K Schenck Jr
19 Applewood Lane
Avon CT 06001

Call Sign: KE6WRQ

Stephen J Tranovich
40 Avonridge
Avon CT 06001

Call Sign: KB1BWE
Monica N Brown
75 Avonwood Rd.
Avon CT 06001

Call Sign: KE1DP
George D Brown
75 Avonwood Rd.
Avon CT 06001

Call Sign: KB1HKW
Robert S Bell Jr
24 Brownstone Dr
Avon CT 06001

Call Sign: W1AAD
Robert S Bell Jr
24 Brownstone Dr
Avon CT 06001

Call Sign: W1KE
Robert S Bell Jr
24 Brownstone Dr
Avon CT 06001

Call Sign: KB1CAP
John M Baleshiski
43 Burnham Rd
Avon CT 060012258

Call Sign: KB1OXH
D Kay T Compton
11 Canal Court
Avon CT 06001

Call Sign: K1GBC
Peter A Sauerwein
23 Candlewood Ln
Avon CT 06001

Call Sign: KI4QMN

Marie D Gauvin
7 Catalpa Court
Avon CT 06001

Call Sign: N4RCR
David S Burns
61 Chevas Road
Avon CT 06001

Call Sign: N1PWF
Leonard D Pearce
38 Cold Spring Road
Avon CT 06001

Call Sign: KA1HHS
Andrew S Beres
332 Country Club Rd
Avon CT 06001

Call Sign: KA1KBY
Helen Ann W Gerli
500 Country Club Rd
Avon CT 060012406

Call Sign: WA1NEV
James F Mc Givern Jr
56 Craigemore Cir
Avon CT 06001

Call Sign: W1DLW
Patrick E Clark
13 Day Rd
Avon CT 06001

Call Sign: W1VG
Peter P Chenausky
151 Deercliff Rd
Avon CT 06001

Call Sign: W1JHD
George D Royster Jr
189 Deercliff Rd
Avon CT 06001

Call Sign: KA1HHT

Howard S Pfirman
600 Deercliff Rd
Avon CT 06001

Call Sign: N1GOK
Thomas L Voorhees
29 E Woodhaven Dr
Avon CT 06001

Call Sign: N1OWL
Joel Deutsch
13 Finch Run
Avon CT 06001

Call Sign: KB1EJX
James J Longworth
80 Forge Dr
Avon CT 06001

Call Sign: N1ILC
Russell K Puryear
25 Grant Dr
Avon CT 06001

Call Sign: KM1T
Louis O Roy Jr
23 Greenwich Lane
Avon CT 06001

Call Sign: KA1NST
Robert D Loeffler
36 Hawley Hill Rd
Avon CT 06001

Call Sign: WA1YYO
Albert J Quartiero
25 Helena Rd
Avon CT 06001

Call Sign: KA1RNW
Robert M Doherty
11 Hillcrest Dr
Avon CT 06001

Call Sign: W1HJO

John S Przybyszewski
46 Juniper Dr
Avon CT 060013438

Call Sign: KB1CBO
Secret Lake Contest Club
27 Lakeview Blvd
Avon CT 06001

Call Sign: KB4LY
Ronald M Horrell
15 Lawrence Ave
Avon CT 06001

Call Sign: KB1DCO
Marjorie E Bourgoin
95 Lawrence Ave
Avon CT 060013623

Call Sign: KB1ETN
David D Bourgoin
95 Lawrence Ave
Avon CT 06001

Call Sign: KB1ETO
Adam B Bourgoin
95 Lawrence Ave
Avon CT 06001

Call Sign: WA1CKT
George C Arvanetaki
553 Lovely St
Avon CT 06001

Call Sign: WA1VGN
Joseph Tourville
257 Lovely St.
Avon CT 06001

Call Sign: W8KWB
Glen L Anderson
16 Madison Lane
Avon CT 06001

Call Sign: KB1LPL

Talcott Mountain Science
Center
Montevideo Rd
Avon CT 06001

Call Sign: W1TMS
Talcott Mountain Science
Center
Montevideo Rd
Avon CT 06001

Call Sign: N1XVT
Gary M Balich
71 Moravia Rd
Avon CT 06001

Call Sign: N1KCH
David J Mazur
670 New Road
Avon CT 06001

Call Sign: KD1LA
Joseph H Mc Isaac Iii
52 Northington Dr
Avon CT 06001

Call Sign: N1TMA
Richard C Tenan
44 Old Town Rd
Avon CT 06001

Call Sign: N1TMC
Bridget A Clancy Tenan
44 Old Town Rd
Avon CT 06001

Call Sign: KA1TDG
John M Pardy
15 Old Wood Rd
Avon CT 06001

Call Sign: N1EID
Joy C Bacci
4 Overlook Ct
Avon CT 060014526

Call Sign: KA1EUH
Dean C Graham
41 Oxbow Dr
Avon CT 06001

Call Sign: WA1TRK
Gerald R Graham
41 Oxbow Dr
Avon CT 06001

Call Sign: NC1B
Shawn M Mc Cormick
6 Oxford Ct
Avon CT 06001

Call Sign: KB1VNU
Dennis V Mancini
42 Parkview Dr
Avon CT 06001

Call Sign: W1IUZ
Arthur Masthay
54 Parkview Dr
Avon CT 06001

Call Sign: N1NTG
Jerry S Zarwanski
33 Pine Hill Road
Avon CT 06001

Call Sign: WB1FMZ
Bon R Smith
4 Pioneer Dr
Avon CT 060012201

Call Sign: W1OHM
William H Ohm
8 Putnam Lane
Avon CT 06001

Call Sign: KB1CGD
Peter M Sanford
2 Reverknolls
Avon CT 06001

Call Sign: KB1SVZ
Karen L Isakson
17 Richard St
Avon CT 06001

Call Sign: W1KLI
Karen L Isakson
17 Richard St
Avon CT 06001

Call Sign: KB1CRW
Christina E Fitch
45 Sarah Dr
Avon CT 06001

Call Sign: W2IPI
Charles S Fitch Pe
45 Sarah Dr
Avon CT 06001

Call Sign: KB1VIB
James R Phillips
13 Sedgewood Rd
Avon CT 06001

Call Sign: KB1SVK
Eric B Spencer
28 Sheffield Lane
Avon CT 06001

Call Sign: KB1EIT
Alison K Spencer
28 Sheffield Ln
Avon CT 06001

Call Sign: KB1EOB
Mark R Hamel
86 Somerset Dr
Avon CT 06001

Call Sign: N1EKK
Robert A Marshall
27 Stony Corners Rd
Avon CT 060012623

Call Sign: N1OLH
Frank A Stratton
11 Sycamore Ln
Avon CT 06001

Call Sign: KD1LU
Robert J Pratt
49 Sylvan St
Avon CT 06001

Call Sign: W1FYH
Robert E Ennis
5 Templeton Ct
Avon CT 060013950

Call Sign: KA1HO
Philip J Bieluch
60 Toll Gate Lane
Avon CT 06001

Call Sign: W1PJB
Philip J Bieluch
60 Toll Gate Lane
Avon CT 06001

Call Sign: KB1KEZ
Tim J Ellsworth
563 W Avon Rd
Avon CT 06001

Call Sign: K4LOW
Henry B C Low
333 Waterville Rd
Avon CT 06001

Call Sign: N1ASO
John J Kohler
71 Wheeler Rd
Avon CT 06001

Call Sign: KB1SID
Jaymin Mehta
95 Wild Wood Dr
Avon CT 06001

Call Sign: KB1OKE
Robert P Eckhoff
1 Wills Walk
Avon CT 06001

Call Sign: N1LCB
Robert T Hepburn
58 Winding Ln
Avon CT 06001

Call Sign: N1ZRZ
James Hepburn
58 Winding Ln
Avon CT 06001

Call Sign: N1VOL
Thomas A Kline
12 Windrush Ln.
Avon CT 06001

Call Sign: W1HRF
Herbert A Vance Jr
167 Woodford Hills Dr
Avon CT 060013925

Call Sign: N1YYF
Miles Q Thomason
Avon CT 06001

Call Sign: W1AFF
Alvin Liftig
Avon CT 06001

Call Sign: W1MEA
Mark E Anderson
Avon CT 06001

FCC Amateur Radio Licenses in Ballouville

Call Sign: W1MKM
Michael K Mavor
Box 196 Chestnut Hill Rd
Ballouville CT 06233

FCC Amateur Radio Licenses in Baltic

Call Sign: W1WML
George D Dennis
185 High St
Baltic CT 06330

Call Sign: W1OOW
Vincent E Chrzanowski
128 Pautipaug Hill Rd
Baltic CT 06330

Call Sign: KA1FNP
John P Kane
221 Pautipaug Hill Rd
Baltic CT 06330

Call Sign: KB1HYG
Gary W Divan
67 Plain Hill Rd
Baltic CT 06330

Call Sign: N1NW
Radio Amateur Society Of
Norwich
102 Plain Hill Rd
Baltic CT 06330

Call Sign: WT1SND
Gary W Divan
102 Plain Hill Rd
Baltic CT 06330

Call Sign: KB1FUO
Christopher S Poss
26 Potash Hill Road
Baltic CT 06330

Call Sign: AA1SP
Elliott J Robert
104 Riverside Dr
Baltic CT 06330

Call Sign: K7UGO
Donald A Bastien
23 Rose Street
Baltic CT 06330

Call Sign: KB1RPH
Rebecca M Cipriani
55 Salt Rock Rd
Baltic CT 06330

Call Sign: KB1RPQ
Erik L Reyer
55 Salt Rock Rd
Baltic CT 06330

Call Sign: AB1KJ
Erik L Reyer
55 Salt Rock Rd
Baltic CT 06330

Call Sign: KB1DZB
Mary C Turner
187 Willimantic Rd
Baltic CT 06330

Call Sign: N1REI
Scott H Turner
187 Willimantic Rd
Baltic CT 06330

Call Sign: KB1OGG
George D Dennis
Baltic CT 06330

FCC Amateur Radio Licenses in Bantam

Call Sign: KA1BZB
Tracey P Eykelhoff
59 Case Ave
Bantam CT 06750

Call Sign: WA1YWG
John G Eykelhoff
59 Case Rd

Bantam CT 06750

Call Sign: N1WYF
Elmer L Perry Jr
159 Old Forge Hollow
Bantam CT 06750

Call Sign: K1BUN
Bantam Radio Club
Bantam CT 067500787

Call Sign: KA1IZN
Michael D Roth
Bantam CT 06750

Call Sign: N1UXB
Kathleen F Roth
Bantam CT 067500787

FCC Amateur Radio Licenses in Barhamstead

Call Sign: N1YOZ
Jack P Bouckaert
134 Goosegreen Rd
Barhamsted CT 06063

Call Sign: KB1PIW
George W Washington
43 Briarwood Rd
Barkhamsted CT
060631102

Call Sign: KB1API
Raymond L Arnold
223 E Hartland Rd
Barkhamsted CT 06063

Call Sign: KE1IH
John F Corini
498 E Hartland Rd
Barkhamsted CT 06063

Call Sign: N1ZLE
Patrick J Lefebvre

173 W West Hill Road
Barkhamsted CT 06063

Call Sign: KB1OLE
Leo R Fournier Jr
201 West Hill Rd
Barkhamsted CT 06063

Call Sign: K2GAV
Theodore H Szypulski
73 West West Hill Rd
Barkhamsted CT 06063

FCC Amateur Radio Licenses in Beacon Falls

Call Sign: K1CRU
Frank J Krasnicki
94 Andrasko Rd
Beacon Falls CT 06403

Call Sign: K1FRC
Steven E Sawyer
333 Bethany Rd #1
Beacon Falls CT 06403

Call Sign: KA1VIR
Earl J Moran
374 Burton Rd
Beacon Falls CT 06403

Call Sign: WB1ARZ
Richard Botelho Sr
527 Burton Rd
Beacon Falls CT 06403

Call Sign: KA7PFB
Jennifer D Nimons
57 Cambridge Court
Beacon Falls CT 06403

Call Sign: N1MIB
Stanley Durinski
201 Cook Ln
Beacon Falls CT 06403

Call Sign: N1SKH
Herbert L Tripp
202 Cook Ln
Beacon Falls CT 06403

Call Sign: N1VOU
William F Mc Casland
4 Coventry Ln
Beacon Falls CT 06403

Call Sign: N1AKF
William F Mc Casland Iii
4 Coventry Ln
Beacon Falls CT 06403

Call Sign: N1CMJ
Gordon L Stewart
20 Ellen Dr
Beacon Falls CT 06403

Call Sign: WB1HGW
Chester Mrozinski
29 Fairfield Pl
Beacon Falls CT 06403

Call Sign: AJ2C
Edward P Chromczak
19 Fieldstone Ln
Beacon Falls CT 064031481

Call Sign: WB1GVQ
Thomas S Mulinski
13 Haley Ridge Road
Beacon Falls CT 06403

Call Sign: KA1UTS
Cheryl A Flyte
98g Highland Ave
Beacon Falls CT 06403

Call Sign: WA1WMX
Michael G Lawrence
42 Kaleas Way
Beacon Falls CT 06403

Call Sign: N1YGL
Patrick G Dionne
474 Lopus Rd
Beacon Falls CT 06403

Call Sign: N1BF
Patrick G Dionne
474 Lopus Rd
Beacon Falls CT 06403

Call Sign: N1LPR
Donald P Mays
3 Pamanata Meadow
Beacon Falls CT 06403

Call Sign: KA1DVD
Joseph Mis
2 Pamanta Meadows
Beacon Falls CT 06403

Call Sign: N1LXT
James D Lanci
161 Pines Bridge Rd
Beacon Falls CT 06403

Call Sign: KA1OJG
Jonathan E Lee
67 Railroad Ave
Beacon Falls CT 06403

Call Sign: N6VFJ
Richard J Gard
121 Rice Lane Ext
Beacon Falls CT 06403

Call Sign: K1EPX
Ronald E Doolittle Jr
433 Skokorat Rd
Beacon Falls CT 06403

Call Sign: WU1E
Robert C Morin
458 Skokorat Rd
Beacon Falls CT 06403

Call Sign: KB1FTD
Charles C Woodin
516 Skokorat Rd
Beacon Falls CT 06403

Call Sign: NG1S
Ralph J Thomas
848 South Main St
Beacon Falls CT 06403

Call Sign: W6QY
Ralph J Thomas
848 South Main St
Beacon Falls CT 06403

Call Sign: W1RJT
Ralph J Thomas
848 South Main St
Beacon Falls CT 06403

Call Sign: KB1ROP
William E Chellis
29 Stoddard Pl
Beacon Falls CT 06403

Call Sign: N1QMT
Edward T Zebrowski
8 White Birch Ln
Beacon Falls CT 06403

**FCC Amateur Radio
Licenses in Berlin**

Call Sign: KA1CCY
Frederick M Meeker
97 Apple Tree Xing
Berlin CT 06037

Call Sign: KB1EIA
Garrett R Weinberg
409 Beckley Road
Berlin CT 06037

Call Sign: KB1EIB

Lori J Weinberg
409 Beckley Road
Berlin CT 06037

Call Sign: KB1POO
Michael A Lentini
Memorial Station
221 Christian Lane
Berlin CT 06037

Call Sign: W1VLA
Michael A Lentini
Memorial Station
221 Christian Lane
Berlin CT 06037

Call Sign: KB1VXW
Eric R Becker
41 Cliffview Dr
Berlin CT 06037

Call Sign: W1ERB
Eric R Becker
41 Cliffview Dr
Berlin CT 06037

Call Sign: KB1KRQ
Kevin J D Aquila
165 Deerfield Dr
Berlin CT 06037

Call Sign: KB1ORU
Peter J Vernesoni
261 Deerfield Dr
Berlin CT 06037

Call Sign: K9BLA
Peter J Vernesoni
261 Deerfield Dr
Berlin CT 06037

Call Sign: KA1UGC
Mary B Basch
1443 Farmington Ave
Berlin CT 06037

Call Sign: W1RN
George H Woodward
33 Fernstead Ln
Berlin CT 06037

Call Sign: KB1SSS
Craig L Freeman
555 Four Rod Road
Berlin CT 06037

Call Sign: KB1VXX
David B Jones
204 Grandview Ave
Berlin CT 06037

Call Sign: K1DBJ
David B Jones
204 Grandview Ave
Berlin CT 06037

Call Sign: AA1IY
Herb B Watson
181 Hudson St
Berlin CT 06037

Call Sign: WA1LOB
Sebastian J Sorrentino
165 Hummingbird Dr
Berlin CT 06037

Call Sign: KB1TCQ
Walter Korfel
1623 Kensington Rd
Berlin CT 06037

Call Sign: KB1UYC
Philip J Mader
27 Kenton St
Berlin CT 06037

Call Sign: KB1XP
Michael S Samulenas
338 Lamentation Dr
Berlin CT 06037

Call Sign: N1PRQ
Carlo J Lapollo
112 Ledge Dr
Berlin CT 06037

Call Sign: N1PAF
Thomas F Cosgrove
333 Lower Ln
Berlin CT 06037

Call Sign: N1VIL
Joan M Borriello
706 Lower Ln
Berlin CT 06037

Call Sign: N1VIM
Ralph L Borriello
706 Lower Ln
Berlin CT 06037

Call Sign: KB1WUX
Kimberly A Mcneill
453 New Britain Rd 1
Berlin CT 06037

Call Sign: KE1EP
Bruno Ciccio
1085 Orchard Rd
Berlin CT 06037

Call Sign: AB1CJ
Bruno Ciccio
1085 Orchard Rd
Berlin CT 06037

Call Sign: KB1OLX
Robert Hall
38 Overhill Dr
Berlin CT 06037

Call Sign: N1FXJ
Edward T Schufer Ii
189 Patterson Way
Berlin CT 06037

Call Sign: N1JZD
John J Pajor
9 School St
Berlin CT 060373162

Call Sign: KB1WEZ
Thomas A Chapman
39 Sea Green Dr
Berlin CT 06037

Call Sign: K1MNX
Paul N Wotkiewich
33 Smoky Hill Rd
Berlin CT 06037

Call Sign: KA1UHK
Lawrence R Richotte
101 Spruce Brook Rd
Berlin CT 06037

Call Sign: KB1FQS
Edward W Kimmerle
140 Spruce Brook Road
Berlin CT 06037

Call Sign: K1TD
Gerald L Hall
116 Stonebridge Way
Berlin CT 060372519

Call Sign: KC5KYE
Gary A Jansma
9 Streamside Lane
Berlin CT 06037

Call Sign: W1HHD
J L Eugene Chartrand
38 Valley Dr
Berlin CT 06037

Call Sign: KM4VB
Michael P Szoke
167 Watch Hill
Berlin CT 06037

Call Sign: KE1MF
Michael P Szoke
167 Watch Hill
Berlin CT 06037

Call Sign: KB1KWX
Michael C Faiaz
1326 Wilbur Cross Hwy
Berlin CT 06032

Call Sign: KA1YFU
John A Facca
Berlin CT 06037

FCC Amateur Radio Licenses in Bethany

Call Sign: KB1DFU
Clifford C Rosson
15 Atwater Rd
Bethany CT 06524

Call Sign: KA1BJV
Joseph D Craddock Jr
205 Bear Hill Rd
Bethany CT 065243251

Call Sign: KA1GCA
Mark Kirschbaum
469 Bethmour Rd
Bethany CT 06524

Call Sign: KB1VUP
Janice M Wivagg
53 Bethridge Rd
Bethany CT 06524

Call Sign: KB1VUQ
Daniel P Wivagg
53 Bethridge Rd
Bethany CT 06524

Call Sign: W1GNA
Mary L Relyea

25 Brookwood Rd
Bethany CT 065243148

Call Sign: W1GNB
Douglas I Relyea
25 Brookwood Rd
Bethany CT 06524

Call Sign: K2SS
David F Donnelly
40 Brookwood Rd
Bethany CT 06524

Call Sign: KB1DSF
Thomas G Hunt Sr
807 Carrington Rd
Bethany CT 06524

Call Sign: W1DSF
Thomas G Hunt Sr
807 Carrington Rd
Bethany CT 065243141

Call Sign: N1HDW
John R Masotta
413 Downs Rd
Bethany CT 06525

Call Sign: KB1ZC
Johnson Parker
58 Falls Rd
Bethany CT 06525

Call Sign: NC1AE
Nicholas M Di Giorgi
254 Falls Rd
Bethany CT 06524

Call Sign: KB1EWZ
Edward C Digiorgi
254 Falls Rd
Bethany CT 06524

Call Sign: K1ZP
Nicholas M Digiorgi

254 Falls Rd
Bethany CT 06524

Call Sign: KB1HVF
Jacques P Dumas
98 Farm View Rd
Bethany CT 06524

Call Sign: W1GB
Southcentral Connecticut
Amateur Radio Association
24 Gaylord Mountain Road
Bethany CT 06524

Call Sign: KB1IUD
Victor D Calhoun
55 Hatfield Hill Rd
Bethany CT 06524

Call Sign: KB1IUE
Andrew M Calhoun
55 Hatfield Hill Rd
Bethany CT 06524

Call Sign: KB1VSN
Astronomical Society Of
New Haven
111 Hilldale Rd
Bethany CT 06524

Call Sign: KB1DKJ
Christian A Hungerford
136 Hilldale Rd
Bethany CT 06524

Call Sign: N1ZJR
Herbert G Howard
160 Hoadley Rd
Bethany CT 06524

Call Sign: N1OOB
Kenneth D Wenning
135 Humiston Dr
Bethany CT 06524

Call Sign: N1KSW
Avi Zelnick
664 Litchfield Tpke
Bethany CT 06524

Call Sign: AB1QL
Felix Tang
811 Litchfield Turnpike
Bethany CT 06524

Call Sign: WB2YXC
Joseph J Cuccia
59 Meyers Rd
Bethany CT 06524

Call Sign: KA1UYW
Scott D Burbank
201 Miller Rd
Bethany CT 06525

Call Sign: WA1SFL
Willis E Copeland
53 Munson Rd
Bethany CT 06525

Call Sign: KB1IUF
Brendan J Rieger
25 Old Fairwood Rd
Bethany CT 06524

Call Sign: KA1UYZ
Amy M Lizotte
46 Rolling Green Rd
Bethany CT 06525

**FCC Amateur Radio
Licenses in Bethel**

Call Sign: N1UMU
Bridget K Schaefer
63 A Taylor Ave
Bethel CT 06801

Call Sign: KB1SOU
Lillian W Riley

8 Adams Dr
Bethel CT 06801

Call Sign: N1WTI
Matthew T Farrell
25 Adams Dr
Bethel CT 06801

Call Sign: N1MDR
Jennifer M Leonard
18 Andrews St
Bethel CT 06801

Call Sign: N1ZYK
Patricia A Kunz
6 Ann Terrace
Bethel CT 06801

Call Sign: N1HGT
Matthew L Bardani
19 Appletree Rd
Bethel CT 06801

Call Sign: N1PCU
Joseph F J Coniglio
29 Appletree Rd
Bethel CT 06801

Call Sign: KB3HYB
Bonnie Feldstein
10 Aunt Pattys Ln East
Bethel CT 06801

Call Sign: KB3JFX
Joshua I Feldstein
10 Aunt Patty's Ln East
Bethel CT 06801

Call Sign: KB1DVO
John W Robinson
11 Aunt Pattys Ln W
Bethel CT 06801

Call Sign: K1JR
John W Robinson

11 Aunt Pattys Ln W
Bethel CT 06801

Call Sign: KA1RYQ
Heath D Durlester
4a Beach St
Bethel CT 06801

Call Sign: N1WXG
Alison L Goodman
5 Bethpage Dr
Bethel CT 06801

Call Sign: KB1CPP
Justin B Travis
32 Bethpage Dr
Bethel CT 06801

Call Sign: N1ZAB
Jason D Travis
32 Bethpage Dr
Bethel CT 06801

Call Sign: KA1RGR
Brian C Olmstead
34 Bethpage Dr
Bethel CT 06801

Call Sign: N1OAL
Donald J Lee
22 Birch Dr
Bethel CT 06801

Call Sign: N1UNB
David F Keating
3 Blue Spruce Ct
Bethel CT 06801

Call Sign: KA1TGF
Joseph N Colombo
6 Blue Spruce Ct
Bethel CT 06801

Call Sign: KB1SJ
Lawrence A Ryan Jr

4 Bonnett Dr
Bethel CT 06801

9 Buckboard Ridge Rd
Bethel CT 06801

20 Castle Hill Dr
Bethel CT 06801

Call Sign: N1PDC
Evelyn F Ryan
4 Bonnett Dr
Bethel CT 06801

Call Sign: KB1SQU
Laurie E Kommritz
9 Buckboard Ridge Rd
Bethel CT 06801

Call Sign: N1WTH
Jacqueline A De Pace
5 Cawley Ave
Bethel CT 06801

Call Sign: N1VIS
Thomas J Pace Iii
3 Bonnette Dr Ext
Bethel CT 06801

Call Sign: KB1SQX
William R Kommritz
9 Buckboard Ridge Rd
Bethel CT 06801

Call Sign: KI1N
Robert M Banasik
5 Cedar Dr
Bethel CT 06801

Call Sign: N1WTE
Jared S Gottlieb
4 Briar Cliff Manor
Bethel CT 06801

Call Sign: KA1UPN
Eric A Terry
4 Budd Dr
Bethel CT 06801

Call Sign: N1BYR
Carol M Banasik
5 Cedar Dr
Bethel CT 06801

Call Sign: KA1RGN
Christopher M Fairchild
6 Brookview Ct
Bethel CT 06801

Call Sign: N1WZC
James M Reynolds
18 Budd Dr
Bethel CT 06801

Call Sign: KA1WQI
Douglas P Fischer
6 Cedar Dr
Bethel CT 06801

Call Sign: KA1VEQ
Thomas M Keenan Jr
8 Brookview Ct
Bethel CT 06801

Call Sign: KA1VEN
Lisa M Mc Closkey
19 Budd Dr
Bethel CT 06801

Call Sign: KA1KPT
William J Fesh Iii
13 Cherry Ln
Bethel CT 06801

Call Sign: KA1UOL
Nicole R Kolba
9 Brookwood Dr
Bethel CT 06801

Call Sign: N1HMN
Lisa M Burak
22 Budd Dr
Bethel CT 06801

Call Sign: N1UMS
Andrew H Ackermann
18 Cherry Ln
Bethel CT 06801

Call Sign: KA1UPF
Michael F Larson
12 Brookwood Dr
Bethel CT 06801

Call Sign: KB1SOO
Dzintra Liepkalns
1 Carriage Dr
Bethel CT 06801

Call Sign: KA1TCT
Winsor J Lee
29 Cherry Ln
Bethel CT 06801

Call Sign: KB1RVZ
Adam B Cornwell
2 Buckboard Ridge
Bethel CT 06801

Call Sign: KA1UOS
Chad A Sibbitt
10 Castle Hill Dr
Bethel CT 06801

Call Sign: KA1WJH
James B Seeley
135 Chestnut Ridge Rd
Bethel CT 06801

Call Sign: N1KWV
Herbert K Kommritz

Call Sign: KA1VBD
Emily A Wragg

Call Sign: KA1VJW
Rachel E Fiddes

204 Chestnut Ridge Rd
Bethel CT 06801

Call Sign: N1LGT
Brett M Lefferts
69 Chestnut St
Bethel CT 06801

Call Sign: N1MDQ
Seth A Lefferts
69 Chestnut St
Bethel CT 06801

Call Sign: N1HUJ
Mark E Richard
79 Chestnut St
Bethel CT 06801

Call Sign: KA1UPU
David M Morris
95h Chestnut St
Bethel CT 06801

Call Sign: KA1STJ
Andrew J Gay
99e Chestnut St
Bethel CT 06801

Call Sign: KB1QPB
Adam Iaizzi
80 Chestnut St Unit E
Bethel CT 06801

Call Sign: KA1VEO
Jason R Wajert
28 Chimney Dr
Bethel CT 06801

Call Sign: N1GHX
Joshua W Van Natter
14 Chipmunk Ter
Bethel CT 06801

Call Sign: N1DNA
Louis J Macol

16 Chipmunk Ter
Bethel CT 06801

Call Sign: N1WZD
Alexis N Sachin
24 Chipmunk Ter
Bethel CT 06801

Call Sign: N1HGQ
Richard H Barton Jr
14 Cindy Ln
Bethel CT 06801

Call Sign: KA1RHA
Holly A Hunter
4 Clearview Ave
Bethel CT 06801

Call Sign: KA1YNS
Brendan P Dempsey
130 Codfish Hill
Bethel CT 06801

Call Sign: KA1RHI
Sean P Mc Inerney
484 Codfish Hill
Bethel CT 06801

Call Sign: N1IRJ
Gary N Svenson
28 Codfish Hill Ext
Bethel CT 06801

Call Sign: N1EBI
Edmond C Ryan
34 Codfish Hill Rd Ext
Bethel CT 06801

Call Sign: KA1YNW
Gregory P Crisci
35 Codfish Hill Rd Ext
Bethel CT 06801

Call Sign: N1UNA
Sarah A Menegay

36 Codfish Hill Rd Ext
Bethel CT 06801

Call Sign: KA1WQP
Richard C Morgan
14 Colonial Dr
Bethel CT 06801

Call Sign: N1PCS
Adam V Young
15 Colonial Dr
Bethel CT 06801

Call Sign: KA1RGH
Joshua J Rourke
6 Country Way
Bethel CT 06801

Call Sign: KA1YCR
Maria Eulal Chiriboga
9 Country Way
Bethel CT 06801

Call Sign: KB1CPJ
Joseph A Henits
12 Country Way
Bethel CT 06801

Call Sign: N1YZZ
John F Henits
12 Country Way
Bethel CT 06801

Call Sign: N1ZYQ
John Henits
12 Country Way
Bethel CT 06801

Call Sign: N1IBQ
Ronald J Willson
15 Country Way
Bethel CT 06801

Call Sign: KB1PSK
Arthur A Chickneas

26 Country Way
Bethel CT 06801

88 Dodgingtown Rd
Bethel CT 0680

18 Elizabeth St
Bethel CT 06801

Call Sign: KA1UOM
Erick A Roos
6 Crest View Rd
Bethel CT 06801

Call Sign: KB1NWF
Todd M Smith
92 Dodgingtown Rd
Bethel CT 06801

Call Sign: N1HGL
Carrie L Redin
16 Evergreen Dr
Bethel CT 06801

Call Sign: N1PDA
David J Kearns
19 Deepwood Dr
Bethel CT 06801

Call Sign: K1TMS
Todd M Smith
92 Dodgingtown Rd
Bethel CT 06801

Call Sign: KA1YHE
Steven N Fancher
17 Evergreen Dr
Bethel CT 06801

Call Sign: KA1STF
Michelle B Manning
3 Deer Run
Bethel CT 06801

Call Sign: KA1TGJ
Christopher A Gall
11 Drummers Ln
Bethel CT 06801

Call Sign: KA1UEZ
Andrew R Pisani
14 Far Horizons Dr
Bethel CT 06801

Call Sign: KA1SGJ
Ian K Quigley
3 Dittmar Rd
Bethel CT 06801

Call Sign: KA1STE
Alex K Martin
37 Drummers Ln
Bethel CT 06801

Call Sign: KA1VJM
Charles W Parks Iii
27 Far Horizons Dr
Bethel CT 06801

Call Sign: N1WTB
Erin M Driscoll
15 Dittmar Rd
Bethel CT 06801

Call Sign: KA1TGK
Francois M Perres
28c Durant Ave
Bethel CT 06801

Call Sign: KA1EZL
Ferdinand C Miller Jr
1 Farmview Dr
Bethel CT 06801

Call Sign: N1NBW
Amy M Bruno
14 Dittmar Road
Bethel CT 06801

Call Sign: KA1WQG
James A Elliott
20 Elgin Ave
Bethel CT 06801

Call Sign: KA1STI
Andrew R George
29 Fleetwood Ave
Bethel CT 06801

Call Sign: N1YZY
Brian J Cyr
12 Dodgingtown
Bethel CT 06801

Call Sign: N1LGU
William E Noyce
18 Elizabeth St
Bethel CT 06801

Call Sign: KA1UNX
Robert G George
29 Fleetwood Ave
Bethel CT 06801

Call Sign: WU1L
John W Mc Donald
23 Dodgingtown Rd
Bethel CT 06801

Call Sign: N1NCF
Elaine M Noyce
18 Elizabeth St
Bethel CT 06801

Call Sign: KA1NZH
Dana M Westerberg
38 Fleetwood Ave
Bethel CT 06801

Call Sign: KA1WQB
Anthony Conte

Call Sign: N1OAN
Elizabeth C Noyce

Call Sign: N1WTF
Thomas L Gioielli

22 Fox Den
Bethel CT 06801

6 Grandview Ave
Bethel CT 06801

112 Grassy Plain St
Bethel CT 06801

Call Sign: KA1RGQ
Joseph P Pezik
12 Fox Den Rd
Bethel CT 06801

Call Sign: N1TIW
William T Thoren
6 Grandview Ave
Bethel CT 06801

Call Sign: N1HGR
Brockton G Mc Grath
152a Grassy Plain St
Bethel CT 06801

Call Sign: KA1VBG
Paul E Rapp Iii
5 Gale Ct
Bethel CT 06801

Call Sign: N1WXH
Jessica P Kies
13 Granite Dr
Bethel CT 06801

Call Sign: KA1RGY
Anthony J Carta
97 Grassy Plain St 23
Bethel CT 06801

Call Sign: N1NBX
Erik C Berube
10 Golden Hill
Bethel CT 06801

Call Sign: KB1CPI
Alan W Byxbee
32 Granite Dr
Bethel CT 06801

Call Sign: N1FNL
Katherine R Hoyt
97 Grassy Plain St Apt 25
Bethel CT 06801

Call Sign: N1WXO
Sokpoleak So
20 Golden Hill
Bethel CT 06801

Call Sign: KA1WQU
Matthew D Whelton
144a Grassy Plain Rd
Bethel CT 06801

Call Sign: N1HMM
Eugene J Linnhoff Iii Iii
97 Grassy Plain St Apt 31
Bethel CT 06801

Call Sign: WA1VFC
Charles J Cristofalo Jr
11 Governors Ln
Bethel CT 068012707

Call Sign: N1NIP
Kimberly A Burnside
15 Grassy Plain St
Bethel CT 06801

Call Sign: KB1DVS
Kristen M Barra
12 Green Pasture Rd
Bethel CT 06801

Call Sign: KA1YNR
James A Dever
13 Governors Ln
Bethel CT 06801

Call Sign: N1WYX
Amanda G Burnside
15 Grassy Plain St
Bethel CT 06801

Call Sign: N1HGP
Richard A Richardson
44 Green Wood Ave
Bethel CT 06801

Call Sign: N1EPG
Robert G Quayle
19 Governors Ln
Bethel CT 06801

Call Sign: KA1UPV
Christopher S Christov Jr
74 Grassy Plain St
Bethel CT 06801

Call Sign: KA1VBJ
Michael S Brown
46 Green Wood Ave
Bethel CT 06801

Call Sign: KA1STD
Matthew J Wallace
25 Governors Ln
Bethel CT 06801

Call Sign: N1WYI
Charles W Sterling
94 Grassy Plain St
Bethel CT 06801

Call Sign: KA1TGG
Saki A Karakostas
14 Greenwood Ave
Bethel CT 06801

Call Sign: KB1AXZ
Mark W Thoren

Call Sign: KA1WQF
George R Ehrhard Jr

Call Sign: N1GWB
David M Nelson

39 Greenwood Ave
Bethel CT 06801

8 Highland Ave
Bethel CT 06801

106 Hoyts Hill Rd
Bethel CT 06801

Call Sign: N1JSV
Sara A Wasylean
72 Greenwood Ave
Bethel CT 06801

Call Sign: KA1UPQ
Joshua D Reilly
32 Highland Ave
Bethel CT 06801

Call Sign: N1IYF
Edward A Bruey
10 Hudson St
Bethel CT 06801

Call Sign: KA1VEM
Michelle L Blair
49 Hawleyville Rd
Bethel CT 06801

Call Sign: N1SLD
Ansel J Halliburton
44 Highland Ave
Bethel CT 06801

Call Sign: KA1VJL
Jason A Selleck
8 Huntington Ct
Bethel CT 06801

Call Sign: KA1RHB
Kristina M Hanson
22 Hearthstone Dr
Bethel CT 06801

Call Sign: KA1VJO
Puneet K Gupta
2 Hilldale Ln
Bethel CT 06801

Call Sign: KA1RGI
Douglas D Griffin Ii
21 Huntington Ct
Bethel CT 06801

Call Sign: WB1ESU
James H Lambertson Jr
31 Hearthstone Dr
Bethel CT 06801

Call Sign: KA1SGA
Judith L Palardy
103 Houts Hill
Bethel CT 06801

Call Sign: KA1SGG
Terrance L Kalka Ii
3 Ichabod Ln
Bethel CT 06801

Call Sign: KA1SGE
Thomas M Ricci
37 Hearthstone Dr
Bethel CT 06801

Call Sign: N1SLF
Chris T Raabe
80 Hoyt Hill Rd
Bethel CT 06801

Call Sign: N1JTW
Heather S Ferson
12 Ichabod Ln
Bethel CT 06801

Call Sign: N1YZW
Paula A Muhlfeld
2 Henry St
Bethel CT 06801

Call Sign: N1UMW
William A Simon
6 Hoyt Rd
Bethel CT 06801

Call Sign: KB1TJB
Paula Antolini
19 Jacobs Lane
Bethel CT 06801

Call Sign: N1WXL
Eric J Portante
5 High View Ter
Bethel CT 06801

Call Sign: KD1DD
Kenneth B Weith
8a Hoyt Rd
Bethel CT 06801

Call Sign: N1PCV
Janice E Ferris
9 Juniper Rd
Bethel CT 06801

Call Sign: N1IYM
Christian M Aitchison
11 High View Ter
Bethel CT 06801

Call Sign: N1TGM
Nancy L Weith
8a Hoyt Rd
Bethel CT 06801

Call Sign: N1POM
Daniel L Hatt
20 Juniper Rd
Bethel CT 06801

Call Sign: N1HOO
Seth J Grahame Smith

Call Sign: N1WXM
P Michael Ryan

Call Sign: KA1TGH
Jorge L Wolff

30 Juniper Rd
Bethel CT 06801

8b Kayview Ave
Bethel CT 068011527

15 Kingswood Dr
Bethel CT 06801

Call Sign: N1OAK
Dov G Gold Medina
47 Juniper Rd
Bethel CT 06801

Call Sign: KA1KD
Bears
8b Kayview Dr
Bethel CT 06801

Call Sign: KA1UOW
Javier P Araya
52 Kingswood Dr
Bethel CT 06801

Call Sign: N1WSX
Matthew J Gies
48 Juniper Rd
Bethel CT 06801

Call Sign: N1HOP
Christine J Markosky
6 Kellogg St
Bethel CT 06801

Call Sign: N1YZX
Wallace P Kunin
56 Kinkswood Dr
Bethel CT 06801

Call Sign: KA1RGV
Steven J Moore
49 Juniper Rd
Bethel CT 06801

Call Sign: N1IBP
Edward J Markosky Jr
6 Kellogg St
Bethel CT 06801

Call Sign: N1HUK
Daniel P Almeida
33 Knollwood Dr
Bethel CT 06801

Call Sign: KA1YNT
William N Holland
64 Juniper Rd
Bethel CT 06801

Call Sign: N1WXJ
Markosky E Karol
6 Kellogg St
Bethel CT 06801

Call Sign: N1LHJ
Clarence A Rees
51 Knollwood Dr
Bethel CT 06801

Call Sign: W1CUB
Ronald P Lindsay
11 Karen Dr
Bethel CT 06801

Call Sign: N1UMT
Brendan T Spain
17 Kellogg St
Bethel CT 06801

Call Sign: N1RQJ
Arthur W Rees
51 Knollwood Dr
Bethel CT 06801

Call Sign: N1UMR
Gregory D Brown
41 Katrina Cir
Bethel CT 06801

Call Sign: N1WXK
Amy C Polkowski
18 Kellogg St
Bethel CT 06801

Call Sign: N1UMY
James P Rees
51 Knollwood Dr
Bethel CT 06801

Call Sign: KA1VEK
Christopher R Urban
36 Kayview Ave
Bethel CT 06801

Call Sign: KA1RGW
David J D Amura
20 Kellogg St
Bethel CT 06801

Call Sign: KB1DVP
Vanele Da Costa
71 Knollwood Dr
Bethel CT 06801

Call Sign: KA1WQN
Erica L Kronewitter
41 Kayview Ave
Bethel CT 06801

Call Sign: N1ZAA
Aditya A Habbu
71 Kingswood
Bethel CT 06801

Call Sign: N1WXE
Kinsey E Finden
9 Kristy Dr
Bethel CT 06801

Call Sign: KD1YV
James F Ritterbusch

Call Sign: KB1DVR
Matthew R Alongi

Call Sign: KA1UOU
Andrew P Nero

12 Kristy Dr
Bethel CT 06801

2 Linda Ln
Bethel CT 06801

18 Lindberg St
Bethel CT 06801

Call Sign: N1JTA
Meghan M Bennett
18 Kristy Dr
Bethel CT 06801

Call Sign: KA1YHH
Alfred V Battista Jr
5 Linda Ln
Bethel CT 06801

Call Sign: KA1YOA
Kelly A Zimmermann
5 Long Hill Rd
Bethel CT 06801

Call Sign: KA1SGI
Kimberli A Pickhardt
22 Kristy Dr
Bethel CT 06801

Call Sign: KB1CPK
Stephen A Hermes
6 Linda Ln
Bethel CT 06801

Call Sign: N1GSO
Jason S Turenchalk
11 Long Hill Rd
Bethel CT 06801

Call Sign: N1IYG
Thomas M Grosse Jr
28 Kristy Dr
Bethel CT 06801

Call Sign: K1UOL
Robert D Stevenson Jr
11 Linda Ln
Bethel CT 06801

Call Sign: KA1YNX
Jennifer Perec
13 Long Hill Rd
Bethel CT 06801

Call Sign: N1ZYL
Shay B Beninson
9 Lime Kiln Ct
Bethel CT 06801

Call Sign: N1HGK
Melina N Arcano
11 Linda Ln
Bethel CT 06801

Call Sign: KA1VJX
Jason A Rehm
5 Main St Apt 14
Bethel CT 06801

Call Sign: N1ZYM
Edward T Davison
9 Lime Kiln Ct
Bethel CT 06801

Call Sign: N1WSZ
Dana E Cullen
25 Linda Ln
Bethel CT 06801

Call Sign: N1PCW
Heather L A Schaad
11 Mansfield St
Bethel CT 06801

Call Sign: N1ZYN
Susan A Davison
9 Lime Kiln Ct
Bethel CT 06801

Call Sign: KA1STG
Benjamin J Guerrette
27 Linda Ln
Bethel CT 06801

Call Sign: KA1SFZ
Christopher M Esposito
41 Maple Ave
Bethel CT 06801

Call Sign: N1PCZ
Brian M Whaley
5 Limekiln Ct
Bethel CT 06801

Call Sign: N1APL
Eugene G Ellertson
70 Linda Ln
Bethel CT 068011632

Call Sign: KA1QFH
Thomas J Andrews
20 Maple Ave Ext
Bethel CT 06801

Call Sign: N1LGR
Daniel A Gerlich
7 Limekiln Ct
Bethel CT 06801

Call Sign: N1HHK
Robert W Santore
71 Linda Ln
Bethel CT 06801

Call Sign: N1ZYR
Robert Germinaro Sr
22 Maple Ave Ext
Bethel CT 06801

Call Sign: KA1STH
Eric A Gould

Call Sign: KA1UOP
Jennifer A Reynolds

Call Sign: WB1GSZ
Arthur S Blackman

36 Maple Ave Ext
Bethel CT 06801

6 Midway Dr
Bethel CT 06801

125 Milwaukee Ave
Bethel CT 06801

Call Sign: KA1UOQ
Donna M Cherniske
1a Maple Ln
Bethel CT 06801

Call Sign: WA1CEU
Robert C Frazer
8 Midway Dr
Bethel CT 06801

Call Sign: N1EPJ
Robert D Light
7 Mountain Orchard Rd
Bethel CT 06801

Call Sign: KA1TCM
Heather E White
12 Maple Row
Bethel CT 06801

Call Sign: KA1RGM
Jannette L Sykora
13 Midway Dr
Bethel CT 06801

Call Sign: KA1SGB
Adam V Reynolds
40 Nashville Rd
Bethel CT 06801

Call Sign: KA1RGT
Wendy M Weiss
16 Maple Row
Bethel CT 06801

Call Sign: KA1RGX
Douglas G Dangaard
66 Midway Dr
Bethel CT 06801

Call Sign: K1YOY
Morgan J Williams Sr
89 Nashville Rd
Bethel CT 06801

Call Sign: KA1UPC
Jessica R Renda
19 Maple Row
Bethel CT 06801

Call Sign: KA1TCO
Stacy A Sullivan
68 Midway Dr
Bethel CT 06801

Call Sign: N1XCQ
Dirk V Meyer
89 Nashville Rd
Bethel CT 06801

Call Sign: KA1UPI
George R Costa Jr
20 Maple Row
Bethel CT 06801

Call Sign: N1HML
Sopheap Sun
78 Midway Dr
Bethel CT 06801

Call Sign: N1UMZ
Erin A Guild
90 Nashville Rd
Bethel CT 06801

Call Sign: N1GSZ
Jennifer M Maxa
1 Meadow Ln
Bethel CT 06801

Call Sign: KB1SI
Pasquale A Sarracco Jr
34 Milwaukee Ave
Bethel CT 06801

Call Sign: N1UMX
Kristen M Regan
96 Nashville Rd
Bethel CT 06801

Call Sign: N1JSZ
Laura S Farcas
8 Meadow Ln
Bethel CT 06801

Call Sign: N1LHG
Pat L Sarracco
34 Milwaukee Ave
Bethel CT 06801

Call Sign: N1JUA
James L Bouse
140 Nashville Rd
Bethel CT 06801

Call Sign: KA1WQC
Aurora G Daley
17 Meckauer Cir
Bethel CT 06801

Call Sign: KB1JBY
John J Read
73 Milwaukee Ave
Bethel CT 06801

Call Sign: KA1WQS
John J Poklemba Iii
8 Nashville Rd Ext
Bethel CT 06801

Call Sign: KA1SFW
James M Beard Jr

Call Sign: N1YZV
Pierce A Banza

Call Sign: N1JUC
Devon M Mc Guinness

23 Nashville Rd Ext
Bethel CT 06801

Call Sign: KA1RHF
Matthew C Johnson
24 Nashville Rd Ext
Bethel CT 06801

Call Sign: KC1NQ
Lawrence A Ryan Iii
60 Nashville Rd Ext
Bethel CT 06801

Call Sign: N1PDB
Melanie J Stout
60 Nashville Rd Ext
Bethel CT 06801

Call Sign: KA1UPW
Robert H Brunner Jr
62 Nashville Rd Ext
Bethel CT 06801

Call Sign: KA1WQR
Thomas A Oswald Jr
3 Nature View Trail
Bethel CT 06801

Call Sign: WA1UFI
Warren K Atkins
13 Oak Ridge Rd
Bethel CT 06801

Call Sign: N1IXZ
Robert D Pasqualone
15 Oak Ridge Rd
Bethel CT 06801

Call Sign: N1SLA
Amy M Amin
23 Oak Ridge Rd
Bethel CT 06801

Call Sign: KA1OLH
Edward M Gilsenan

38 Oak Ridge Rd
Bethel CT 06801

Call Sign: KB1DVQ
Brian N Tilford
5 Old Field Dr
Bethel CT 06801

Call Sign: KB1VIS
William P Keller
26 Old Hawleyville Rd
Bethel CT 06801

Call Sign: N1PTV
Fred Pollard Jr
53 Old Hawleyville Rd
Bethel CT 06801

Call Sign: KA1SQO
Madison T Rutherford
74 Old Hawleyville Rd
Bethel CT 06801

Call Sign: N1URB
Lawrence Pennington
75 Old Hawleyville Rd
Bethel CT 06801

Call Sign: KA1RGJ
Donald H Jack
119 Old Hawleyville Rd
Bethel CT 06801

Call Sign: KA1VJG
Bradley A Shepherd
128 Old Hawleyville Rd
Bethel CT 06801

Call Sign: KA1WPZ
Joseph A Arigo
4 Old Lantern Dr
Bethel CT 06801

Call Sign: KB1PKS
William Jacobs

9 Old Lantern Dr
Bethel CT 06801

Call Sign: N1UMV
Sebastian S Hindman
10 Old Town Ln
Bethel CT 06801

Call Sign: N1WXN
Michelle Skelly
3 Oven Rock Rd
Bethel CT 06801

Call Sign: KA1WQV
Nicole Y Williams
9 Payne Rd
Bethel CT 06801

Call Sign: KA1WQW
Michele E Yursik
16 Payne Rd
Bethel CT 06801

Call Sign: KA1UPD
Jason M Schade
32 Payne Rd
Bethel CT 06801

Call Sign: KA1YNP
Kelly B White
63 Payne Rd
Bethel CT 06801

Call Sign: KA1UPK
Eric C Boccuzzi
83 Payne Rd
Bethel CT 06801

Call Sign: KA1RGS
Nathan C Swafford
12 Pell Mell Dr
Bethel CT 06801

Call Sign: KA1VEP
Heather Conley

13 Pell Mell Dr
Bethel CT 06801

22 Plumtrees Rd
Bethel CT 06801

4 Prospect St
Bethel CT 06801 ·

Call Sign: KB1VAM
Michael R Natal
17 Pell Mell Dr
Bethel CT 06801

Call Sign: KA1NPG
Quoc A Bui
36 Plumtrees Rd
Bethel CT 06801

Call Sign: N1HUH
Paul R Bagley
8 Prospect St
Bethel CT 06801

Call Sign: KB1WBG
Joseph Natal
17 Pell Mell Dr
Bethel CT 06801

Call Sign: KA1VBK
Kevin J Perreault
38 Plumtrees Rd
Bethel CT 06801

Call Sign: KA1UOX
Kenneth J Reyes
20 Putnam Park Rd
Bethel CT 06801

Call Sign: NA1AL
Michael R Natal
17 Pell Mell Dr
Bethel CT 06801

Call Sign: KA1TCU
Karen E Boyd
40 Plumtrees Rd
Bethel CT 06801

Call Sign: KA1YNZ
Anne C Hochsprung
79 Putnam Park Rd
Bethel CT 06801

Call Sign: KA1RHC
Kelly C M Heres
31 Pell Mell Dr
Bethel CT 06801

Call Sign: KA1VJI
Tiffany S Boyd
40 Plumtrees Rd
Bethel CT 06801

Call Sign: KA1VEL
Jason R Mortara
145 Putnam Park Rd
Bethel CT 06801

Call Sign: N1GSJ
Matthew G Smith
32 Pell Mell Dr
Bethel CT 06801

Call Sign: KA1RZK
Leigh A Rondano
75 Plumtrees Rd
Bethel CT 06801

Call Sign: WA1YNF
John P Lopiano
53b Putnam Park Rd
Bethel CT 06801

Call Sign: N1FNJ
Jeffrey C Tufts
40 Pell Mell Dr
Bethel CT 06801

Call Sign: N1FNK
Patrick J Rondano
75 Plumtrees Rd
Bethel CT 06801

Call Sign: KA1RHE
Craig J C Calvert Jr
6b Putnam Park Rd
Bethel CT 06801

Call Sign: N1WTA
Keith G Boshell
21 Pleasant St
Bethel CT 06801

Call Sign: KA1NPY
Anthony M Pecoraro
107 Plumtrees Rd
Bethel CT 06801

Call Sign: N1HUL
Geoff D Bandura
37 Quaker Ridge
Bethel CT 06801

Call Sign: KA1UPS
Jennifer N Rogers
23 Pleasant St
Bethel CT 06801

Call Sign: N1MFG
Daniel P Settanni
149 Plumtrees Rd
Bethel CT 06801

Call Sign: N1XMA
Anthony F Sacco
10 Quaker Ridge Rd
Bethel CT 06801

Call Sign: KA1WQH
Jacklyn P Goodwin

Call Sign: KA1YNY
Samantha A Sniffin

Call Sign: KA1RGU
Carey L Brown

33 Quaker Ridge Rd
Bethel CT 06801

47 Redwood Dr
Bethel CT 06801

26 Ridgedale Rd
Bethel CT 06801

Call Sign: N1IGQ
Charles W Brown Jr
33 Quaker Ridge Rd
Bethel CT 06801

Call Sign: N1IGR
Jeffrey A Chaudhari
47 Redwood Dr
Bethel CT 06801

Call Sign: N1IGP
Kyle C Walsh
27 Ridgedale Rd
Bethel CT 06801

Call Sign: KA1NEW
Richard J Reynolds Jr
35 Quaker Ridge Rd
Bethel CT 06801

Call Sign: KA1WQM
Theodore L Kelsey
22 Reservoir St
Bethel CT 06801

Call Sign: N1GSL
William J Foster
55 Ridgedale Rd
Bethel CT 06801

Call Sign: KA1IAB
James M Connolly
43 Quaker Ridge Rd
Bethel CT 06801

Call Sign: W1ENL
Albert T German
62 Reservoir St
Bethel CT 06801

Call Sign: N1HHL
Paul B Tripi
3 Roberts Dr
Bethel CT 06801

Call Sign: KA1JDD
Barry J Connolly
43 Quaker Ridge Rd
Bethel CT 06801

Call Sign: N1WXF
Diana L Gaita
6 Ridge Rd
Bethel CT 06801

Call Sign: KA1UOR
Stacey L Gordon
15 Roberts Dr
Bethel CT 06801

Call Sign: KB1RBB
Jeremy J Cohn
6 Raven Crest Dr
Bethel CT 06801

Call Sign: KB1ODD
Michael Judice
28 Ridge Rd
Bethel CT 06801

Call Sign: N1JCW
Joshua A Rigney
13 Rockwell Rd
Bethel CT 06801

Call Sign: KA1TCN
Colleen H Webb
31 Redwood Dr
Bethel CT 06801

Call Sign: KB1OES
Joseph M Peterson Jr
26 Ridge Road
Bethel CT 06801

Call Sign: KB1SOW
Diane E Miska
21 Rockwell Rd
Bethel CT 06801

Call Sign: KA1VMN
William M Webb
31 Redwood Dr
Bethel CT 06801

Call Sign: KA1RGG
Walter A Sudik Iv
2 Ridgedale Rd
Bethel CT 06801

Call Sign: KB1SPA
James J Mangi
21 Rockwell Rd
Bethel CT 06801

Call Sign: KB1SOV
Patrick Sheridan
45 Redwood Dr
Bethel CT 06801

Call Sign: KA1TCW
James J Howarth
6 Ridgedale Rd
Bethel CT 06801

Call Sign: KA1WQO
Lauren A Minor
81 Rockwell Rd
Bethel CT 06801

Call Sign: KA1STM
Jimshade A Chaudhari

Call Sign: KA1VBI
Leah A Kocse

Call Sign: N1PCX
Jeffrey R Daigle

126 Rockwell Rd
Bethel CT 06801

Call Sign: N1WTG
Barbara J Caro
20 S St Unit 1
Bethel CT 06801

Call Sign: KA1STN
Christian A Atwood
2 Saxon Rd
Bethel CT 06801

Call Sign: KA1RHG
Jason W Gill
15 Sharon Ct
Bethel CT 06801

Call Sign: N1PXS
Michael J Brown
11 Shelley Rd
Bethel CT 06801

Call Sign: KA1UPJ
James J Luchsinger Jr
27 Shelley Rd
Bethel CT 06801

Call Sign: KA1UPP
Aaron W Arbesman
31 Sky Edge Dr
Bethel CT 06801

Call Sign: KA1WQT
Timothy R Smith
3 Sky Edge Ln
Bethel CT 06801

Call Sign: KA1UPA
Jeremy J Kasack
83 South St
Bethel CT 06801

Call Sign: KA1YNQ
Richard W Burghoff

89 South St
Bethel CT 06801

Call Sign: N1NBY
Matthew M Burghoff
89 South St
Bethel CT 06801

Call Sign: KA1TGI
Jeffrey H Rehm
99 South St
Bethel CT 06801

Call Sign: KA1SGH
David S Friedman
34 Spring Hill Ln
Bethel CT 06801

Call Sign: KA1UOV
Brooke R O Dwyer
37 Spring Hill Ln
Bethel CT 06801

Call Sign: KA1UOY
Michael C Byrnes
23 Springhill Ln
Bethel CT 06801

Call Sign: WB4OGU
James H Nelson
2b Starr Ln
Bethel CT 06801

Call Sign: KB1CPM
Carol L Ogdon
73 Stony Hill Rd
Bethel CT 06801

Call Sign: N1WXI
Erin B Holliday
14 Sunny Acres Rd
Bethel CT 06801

Call Sign: KB1CPL
Heidi Leigh Klussmann

5 Taylor Ave
Bethel CT 06801

Call Sign: N1JHL
Gerard T Johansen Jr
52 Taylor Ave
Bethel CT 06801

Call Sign: N1MFH
Honorah C O Neill
54 Taylor Ave
Bethel CT 06801

Call Sign: N1PJG
William L Schaefer Iii
63a Taylor Ave
Bethel CT 06801

Call Sign: KA1SGC
Meliah A Mc Namara
65c Taylor Ave
Bethel CT 06801

Call Sign: KA1WQD
Carrie A Delaney
37 Taylor Rd
Bethel CT 06801

Call Sign: KA1WQE
Robin L Delaney
37 Taylor Rd
Bethel CT 06801

Call Sign: N1EPM
Jonathan F Waggoner
51 Taylor Rd
Bethel CT 06801

Call Sign: KA1VJQ
Jason Grunstra
6 Terry Dr
Bethel CT 06801

Call Sign: N1WXP
Gary K Tepper

3 Topstone Dr
Bethel CT 06801

43 Vail Rd
Bethel CT 06801

166 Walnut Hill Rd
Bethel CT 06801

Call Sign: KA1SWQ
Matthew K Keating
7 Topstone Dr
Bethel CT 06801

Call Sign: N1MFI
Margo A Kopec
11 Van Campen Ln
Bethel CT 06801

Call Sign: KA1UQN
Deborah A Kapteina
1 Webb Rd
Bethel CT 06801

Call Sign: N1WSY
Jason M Greene
38 Topstone Dr
Bethel CT 06801

Call Sign: KA1SFY
Aaron M Kelly
15 Van Campen Ln
Bethel CT 06801

Call Sign: KA1RGF
William J Higgins Jr
3 Webb Rd
Bethel CT 06801

Call Sign: KA1VJF
Andrew S Holbrook
45 Turkey Plain Rd
Bethel CT 06801

Call Sign: KA1SGD
Wayne R Hammond
3 Vining Rd
Bethel CT 06801

Call Sign: N1ZAC
Anne V Korin
47 Whipoorwill Rd
Bethel CT 06801

Call Sign: KB1SOM
Laura L Vasile
27 Vail Rd
Bethel CT 06801

Call Sign: N1RQM
Donald S Hammond
3 Vining Rd
Bethel CT 06801

Call Sign: N1WYZ
Benjamin T Korin
47 Whippoorwill
Bethel CT 06801

Call Sign: N1HON
Thomas S Montana
35 Vail Rd
Bethel CT 06801

Call Sign: KA1WQK
Jason J Horvath
8 Wagon Rd
Bethel CT 06801

Call Sign: N1WTD
Brandy L Frazao
3 Whippoorwill Rd
Bethel CT 06801

Call Sign: KB1SOX
Roger W Strong
35 Vail Rd
Bethel CT 06801

Call Sign: KA1VBA
Aditya S Karande
88 Walnut Hill Rd
Bethel CT 06801

Call Sign: N1FQI
Richard M Huff
23 Whippoorwill Rd
Bethel CT 06801

Call Sign: KB1NYY
Roger W Strong
35 Vail Rd
Bethel CT 06801

Call Sign: N1NCA
Benjamin M Strano
166 Walnut Hill Rd
Bethel CT 06801

Call Sign: N1GHV
Deborah M Huff
23 Whippoorwill Rd
Bethel CT 06801

Call Sign: N1OAM
Shefali V Mehta
37 Vail Rd
Bethel CT 06801

Call Sign: N1SLG
Orazio J Strano
166 Walnut Hill Rd
Bethel CT 06801

Call Sign: N1GHY
Cynthia J Huff
23 Whippoorwill Rd
Bethel CT 06801

Call Sign: KA1VJH
Jennifer L Pimentel

Call Sign: N1SLJ
Mary Lou Strano

Call Sign: KA1VBL
Yancy L Irwin

8 Whitlock Ave
Bethel CT 06801

Call Sign: N1IAI
Lora D Irwin
8 Whitlock Ave
Bethel CT 06801

Call Sign: N1WYY
Megan A Irwin
8 Whitlock Ave
Bethel CT 06801

Call Sign: KB1SOR
Sandra W Cole
7 Whitney Rd
Bethel CT 06801

Call Sign: N1NED
Richard O Wallace
6 Windaway Road
Bethel CT 06801

Call Sign: N1WZA
Paul A La Terra Jr
21 Wine Sap Run
Bethel CT 06801

Call Sign: KA1RYP
Jonathan S Shapiro
20 Winthrop Rd
Bethel CT 06801

Call Sign: KA1RHD
Michael W Carlson
21 Winthrop Rd
Bethel CT 06801

Call Sign: N1DPR
David B Carlson
21 Winthrop Rd
Bethel CT 06801

Call Sign: N1SLC
Michael J Renzulli

12 Wolfpits Rd
Bethel CT 06801

Call Sign: KB1HQE
Kenneth Frey
15 Wooster St
Bethel CT 06801

Call Sign: N1JSX
Steven P Valenti
48 Wooster St
Bethel CT 06801

Call Sign: N1XWQ
Patrick M Perrefort
50 Wooster St
Bethel CT 06801

Call Sign: KA1SFX
Jesse A Thompson
53 Wooster St
Bethel CT 06801

Call Sign: KA1UPO
Carlye A Thompson
53 Wooster St
Bethel CT 06801

Call Sign: KA1WQQ
Andrew Y Oguma
59 Wooster St
Bethel CT 06801

Call Sign: KA1PDI
William H Ochs Iv
68 Wooster St
Bethel CT 06801

Call Sign: KA1TCV
Joseph A Douskey
73 Wooster St
Bethel CT 06801

Call Sign: KA1RGZ
Jennifer L Cyr

77 Wooster St
Bethel CT 06801

Call Sign: N1WTC
Jessica H Costanzo
79 Wooster St
Bethel CT 06801

Call Sign: KA1STL
Michael G Dobsevage
Bethel CT 06801

Call Sign: KA1UON
Dana K Shaw
Bethel CT 06801

Call Sign: KD1RY
Rocco R Grosso
Bethel CT 06801

Call Sign: N1MFJ
Bernard L Grauer
Bethel CT 06801

Call Sign: KB1HYW
Thomas H Barnola
Bethel CT 06801

**FCC Amateur Radio
Licenses in Bethlehem**

Call Sign: KB1KZC
Peter F Paradis
48 Deerwood Dr
Bethlehem CT 06751

Call Sign: K9MAN
Kent D Mac Farlane
75 Green Hill Road
Bethlehem CT 06751

Call Sign: KB1EVR
Robert G Hamilton
69 Guilds Hollow
Bethlehem CT 06751

Call Sign: W1GBP
Robert G Hamilton
69 Guilds Hollow Rd
Bethlehem CT 06751

Call Sign: W1FHP
Robert J O Neil
Hard Hill Rd N
Bethlehem CT 06751

Call Sign: KA1UUI
Robert C Miller
167 Lakes Rd
Bethlehem CT 06751

Call Sign: KB1PTX
Anthony M Gruber
30 Lakeview Dr
Bethlehem CT 06751

Call Sign: N1TFU
Jennifer L Stauff
611 Main Street South
Bethlehem CT 06751

Call Sign: KB1QXN
Thomas G Wilson
53 Munger Lane
Bethlehem CT 06751

Call Sign: K1TGW
Thomas G Wilson
53 Munger Lane
Bethlehem CT 06751

Call Sign: N1LXX
James M Lee
366 Munger Ln
Bethlehem CT 06751

Call Sign: KB1VCJ
Seamus C Mclaughlin
128 Nonnewaug Rd
Bethlehem CT 06751

Call Sign: K1VTM
Ronald W Nevers Sr
109 Todd Hill Rd
Bethlehem CT 06751

Call Sign: KB1MMZ
Daniel B Decker
92 Townline Rd
Bethlehem CT 06751

Call Sign: N1ECA
John G O Keefe Jr
500 Wood Creek Rd
Bethlehem CT 067511017

Call Sign: KA1EVN
Gerald L Assard
484 Woodcreek Road
Bethlehem CT 06751

Call Sign: KB2WTO
Peter A Silverstein
Bethlehem CT 06751

Call Sign: N1TOL
Linda A Stauff
Bethlehem CT 067510190

Call Sign: W2HCV
Roger M Bogin
Bethlehem CT 06751

Call Sign: WA1THV
Arthur W Stauff
Bethlehem CT 067510190

Call Sign: KB1KJT
David A Rahmlow
Bethlehem CT 06751

Call Sign: KB1KME
Kenneth A Stauff
Bethlehem CT 06751

FCC Amateur Radio Licenses in Black Rock

Call Sign: KB1CJY
Michael F Cunningham
340 Sailors Ln
Black Rock CT 06605

FCC Amateur Radio Licenses in Bloomfield

Call Sign: KB1MHN
Johnny Gonzalez
123 Barry Circle Apt 123
Bloomfield CT 06002

Call Sign: W1UVU
Herbert C Fishman
41 Bath Crescent Ln
Bloomfield CT 06002

Call Sign: WB1FNK
Karl F Witter
7 Bear Ridge Dr
Bloomfield CT 06002

Call Sign: WA1GDX
Bruce M Lomasky
1 Benton Drive
Bloomfield CT 06002

Call Sign: N1JWG
Adrian B Batey
4 Bestor Ln Apt 9
Bloomfield CT 06002

Call Sign: KC1EX
Brad A Thomas
1 Birch Rd
Bloomfield CT 06002

Call Sign: WA1VVB
Mark E Simcik
657 Bloomfield Ave
Bloomfield CT 060023043

Call Sign: KB1HSW
Kerstin M Simcik
657 Bloomfield Ave
Bloomfield CT 060023043

Call Sign: KB1HTA
Linnea F Simcik
657 Bloomfield Ave
Bloomfield CT 060023043

Call Sign: KB1HTB
Loris J Simcik
657 Bloomfield Ave
Bloomfield CT 060023043

Call Sign: KB1HTF
Brita E Simcik
657 Bloomfield Ave
Bloomfield CT 060023043

Call Sign: KA1BYQ
Dennis A Hubbs
16 Brooke St
Bloomfield CT 06002

Call Sign: NB1N
Aaron B Hubbs
16 Brooke St
Bloomfield CT 06002

Call Sign: N1PBV
Steven A Hubbs
16 Brooke Street
Bloomfield CT 060022711

Call Sign: N1MTH
Ben E Schaffer
5 Burnwood Dr
Bloomfield CT 06002

Call Sign: N1TKJ
Carlos O Cintron
55 Burnwood Dr
Bloomfield CT 06002

Call Sign: N1OKA
Harlan J Shakun
23 Chateau Margaux
Bloomfield CT 06002

Call Sign: N1PBG
Eric H Shakun
23 Chateau Margaux
Bloomfield CT 060022153

Call Sign: W1CNI
Daniel M Arnold
7 Cliffmount Dr
Bloomfield CT 060022225

Call Sign: KB9IKI
Jeremy Sachs
2 Curran Cir.
Bloomfield CT 06002

Call Sign: KB1LUS
Judith A Miller
29 Douglas St
Bloomfield CT 06002

Call Sign: KB1FWC
Connecticut Amateur Radio
League Of Youth Carly
29 Douglas Street
Bloomfield CT 06002

Call Sign: KA1VME
Jerome Bertuglia
11 Duncaster Rd
Bloomfield CT 06002

Call Sign: KA1NEE
Jeanette A Lowe
48 Duncaster Rd
Bloomfield CT 06002

Call Sign: KA1NEF
Richard I Lowe
48 Duncaster Rd

Bloomfield CT 06002

Call Sign: KA1NEI
Celia L Lowe
48 Duncaster Rd
Bloomfield CT 06002

Call Sign: W1AI
William A Teso
252 Duncaster Rd
Bloomfield CT 06002

Call Sign: K1EBS
Edgar B Spencer Iii
255 Duncaster Rd
Bloomfield CT 06002

Call Sign: N3YAR
Joshua I Rozovsky
272 Duncaster Road
Bloomfield CT 060021105

Call Sign: AC1N
Joshua I Rozovsky
272 Duncaster Road
Bloomfield CT 060021105

Call Sign: KB1KIV
James D Humphrey
101 East Harold Street
Bloomfield CT 06002

Call Sign: KA1AMJ
Robert L Nay
7 Fern Dr
Bloomfield CT 08002

Call Sign: KB1BE
Paul R Shafer
7 Fern Dr
Bloomfield CT 06002

Call Sign: W1VNO
Gordon P Barnard
60 Filley St

Bloomfield CT 06002

Call Sign: W1NIK
Julian Mandell
1 Font Hill Park
Bloomfield CT 06002

Call Sign: KB1FCQ
Ronald F Barbour
95 Glenwood Ave
Bloomfield CT 06002

Call Sign: N1CAM
I Martin Fierberg
35 High Hill Rd
Bloomfield CT 06002

Call Sign: N1NQQ
Marshall H Weaver
20 J Wedgewood Dr
Bloomfield CT 06002

Call Sign: KB1CQ
Leon Goolsby
24 Jackson Rd
Bloomfield CT 06002

Call Sign: KB1KCB
Clifford J Aldrich Jr
21 Ledyard Ave
Bloomfield CT 06002

Call Sign: WB1EEU
Charles F Ridolfo
41 Linwood Dr
Bloomfield CT 060021716

Call Sign: KB1FQZ
Kenneth M Jones
59 Linwood Drive
Bloomfield CT 06002

Call Sign: KB1SWR
Cedric R Green
20 Louis Dr

Bloomfield CT 06002

Call Sign: KA1DJ
Erwin P Cohen
8 Maple Edge Drive
Bloomfield CT 060021616

Call Sign: K1QPN
Donald E Moore
171 Mountain Ave
Bloomfield CT 06002

Call Sign: W1CWA
Bloomfield Amateur Radio
Club
171 Mountain Ave
Bloomfield CT 06002

Call Sign: W1SL
Sherwood C Lewis
30 Old Village Rd
Bloomfield CT 06002

Call Sign: KA1LOR
Leonard R Woods
3 Partridge Ln
Bloomfield CT 06002

Call Sign: N1WHK
Johanna N Rivera
5 Pasture Ln
Bloomfield CT 06002

Call Sign: KA1ZDL
Denise C Durant
50 Prospect St
Bloomfield CT 06002

Call Sign: WB7RSE
Elizabeth H Swanson
331 Seabury Dr
Bloomfield CT 06002

Call Sign: N1BMC
Richard S Bagnall Md

400 Seabury Dr Apt 2123
Bloomfield CT 06002

Call Sign: AA1T
Caleb G Warner
319 Seabury Drive
Bloomfield CT 06002

Call Sign: KB1EYZ
Robert B Stanwood
21 Stuart Dr
Bloomfield CT 060021524

Call Sign: N1HVC
Paul L Corrette
8 Sunset Ln
Bloomfield CT 06002

Call Sign: KB1GGF
David J Lahey
190 Tunxis Ave
Bloomfield CT 06002

Call Sign: N1OCU
Christos Kraverotis
315 Tunxis Ave
Bloomfield CT 06002

Call Sign: KB1RJJ
Luke K Ionno
41 Woodland Ave
Bloomfield CT 06002

Call Sign: W1RWK
Joseph B Matczak
22 Woops Rd
Bloomfield CT 06002

Call Sign: N1RED
Scott A Mac William
10 Wyndemere Rd
Bloomfield CT 06002

Call Sign: WA1ZQJ
Robert B Katz

Bloomfield CT 06002

Call Sign: KB1BBP
Dustin T Taksar
105 Birch Mtn Rd
Bolton CT 06043

Call Sign: N1VIE
Derek S Green
148 Brandy St
Bolton CT 06043

Call Sign: KB1QNO
Austin B Vernesoni
10 Brookside Lane
Bolton CT 06043

Call Sign: KE1C
Patrick T Tracy
33 Carter St
Bolton CT 06043

Call Sign: K1NYK
David R Malley
26 Fiano Rd
Bolton CT 06043

Call Sign: W1IG
Bolton Amateur Radio Net
26 Fiano Rd
Bolton CT 06043

Call Sign: KB1UHF
Christopher M Trudeau
624 Hop River Rd
Bolton CT 06043

Call Sign: K1CMT
Christopher M Trudeau
624 Hop River Rd
Bolton CT 06043

Call Sign: KB1LPG
Joseph K Gore
88 Loomis Rd
Bolton CT 06043

Call Sign: KB1TGI
Pauline M Silva
35 Mount Sumner Dr
Bolton CT 06043

Call Sign: AB1CR
Charles A Rexroad Jr
35 Mt Sumner Dr
Bolton CT 06043

Call Sign: KB1PJJ
Digital Amateur Radio Club
35 Mt Sumner Dr
Bolton CT 06043

Call Sign: K1LBU
Malcolm L Hilton
37 Plymouth Ln
Bolton CT 06043

Call Sign: KA1DFK
Donald E Cassells
15 Riga Ln
Bolton CT 06043

Call Sign: KB1CXA
Francis Stadmeyer
24 Rocco Rd
Bolton CT 06043

Call Sign: KA1HVS
Dorothy B Reiss
41 School Rd
Bolton CT 06043

Call Sign: KB1PTB
Anthony J Girasoli
13 Stonehedge Ln
Bolton CT 06043

Call Sign: W1TTL
Anthony J Girasoli
13 Stonehedge Ln
Bolton CT 06043

Call Sign: KB1SQE
Levi R Schneider
6 Sunset Lane
Bolton CT 06043

Call Sign: WA1ZNT
Eugene E Hattin
36 Tunxis Trl
Bolton CT 06043

Call Sign: K1SBO
Calvin F Trumbull
28 Volpi Rd
Bolton CT 06043

Call Sign: KB1NRP
Stephen P Coffey
70 Volpi Rd
Bolton CT 06043

Call Sign: N1YAB
Richard J Malota
10 Watrous Rd
Bolton CT 06043

Call Sign: K1HOP
Russell A Reiss
Bolton CT 06043

Call Sign: N1ZFB
David H Hodgman Jr
Botsford CT 06404

Call Sign: KB1PII

Jeremiah D Stover
154 Bishop Rd
Bozrah CT 06334

Call Sign: KB1PIJ
Craig H Stover
154 Bishop Rd
Bozrah CT 063341507

Call Sign: KB1PIK
Nathanael J Stover
154 Bishop Rd
Bozrah CT 06334

Call Sign: KB1PIL
Zechariah B Stover
154 Bishop Rd
Bozrah CT 06334

Call Sign: KB1WOK
Julia K Stover
154 Bishop Rd
Bozrah CT 06334

Call Sign: N1OTT
George W Gager
45 Bozrah St
Bozrah CT 06334

Call Sign: K1ZF
Eugene M Henson
229 Bozrah St
Bozrah CT 06334

Call Sign: KB1FSH
Bozrah Beer Chowder &
Propagation Society
229 Bozrah St
Bozrah CT 06334

Call Sign: AI1D
Bozrah Beer Chowder &
Propagation Society
229 Bozrah St
Bozrah CT 06334

Call Sign: WB3IOS
Jean A Wolfgang
30 Cottage Rd
Bozrah CT 063341410

Call Sign: WR1B
Larry D Wolfgang
30 Cottage Rd
Bozrah CT 06334

Call Sign: WA1BSA
Connecticut Amateur Radio
Scouters
30 Cottage Rd
Bozrah CT 063341410

Call Sign: KB1JQI
Connecticut Amateur Radio
Scouters
Larry Wolfgang - 30
Cottage Rd
Bozrah CT 063341410

Call Sign: KB1VMS
Herbert C Zickwolf Jr
117 Lake Rd
Bozrah CT 06334

Call Sign: WA1WQG
Bruce R Danielson
62 Lebanon Rd
Bozrah CT 06334

Call Sign: W1WQG
Bruce R Danielson
62 Lebanon Rd
Bozrah CT 06334

Call Sign: KA1NOD
Barry E Weinsteiger
127 Scotthill Rd
Bozrah CT 06334

Call Sign: KA1NOF

Elaine C Weinsteiger
127 Scotthill Rd
Bozrah CT 06334

Call Sign: K1DQD
Walter P Postovoit
39 South Rd
Bozrah CT 06334

Call Sign: KB1QFU
Leigh A Williams
2 Stockhouse Rd Apt 4
Bozrah CT 06334

Call Sign: KB1QGQ
Leigh A Williams
2 Stockhouse Rd Apt 4
Bozrah CT 06334

FCC Amateur Radio Licenses in Branford

Call Sign: N1QFG
Patrick F Cassell Sr
21 Aceto St
Branford CT 06405

Call Sign: N1MUS
Sandra J Mac Lean
57 Alps Rd
Branford CT 06405

Call Sign: KB1SJJ
Joseph A Kolodej
231 Austin Ryer Lane
Branford CT 06405

Call Sign: N1GGA
George W Mc Gann
200 Austin Ryer Ln
Branford CT 06405

Call Sign: N1SWP
Paul A Lehr
10 Avon Rd

Branford CT 06405

Call Sign: KA1WXF
Kevin D Seales
31 Baypath Way
Branford CT 06405

Call Sign: N1XKQ
Holmes A Lattime
3 Beach Pl
Branford CT 06405

Call Sign: KA1ADS
Alan P Daniels
34 Bradley Ave
Branford CT 06405

Call Sign: KB1DFT
Samuel J Stewart Iv
75 Bradley St 4c
Branford CT 06405

Call Sign: K1MLW
John E Hall
131 Brushy Plain Rd
Branford CT 06405

Call Sign: KB1TWI
Stanley R Laska
137 Brushy Plain Rd
Branford CT 06405

Call Sign: K1HTI
Stanley R Laska
137 Brushy Plain Rd
Branford CT 06405

Call Sign: KA1ZTT
Christopher A Guzzi
175 Brushy Plain Road 2
Branford CT 06405

Call Sign: N1UGK
Jesse B Bertier
45 Cedar Knolls Drive

Branford CT 06405

Call Sign: K1PEP
John H Roch
113 Cedar St Apt A
Branford CT 06405

Call Sign: K1YRW
Richard C Crispi
116 Cedas Knolls Drive
Branford CT 06405

Call Sign: KA1FZS
Robert C Prahovic
169 Chestnut St
Branford CT 06405

Call Sign: N1UTL
Celeste Krahl
348 Clark Ave
Branford CT 064054706

Call Sign: KC1AV
Douglas N Turnbull
18 Cove Ter
Branford CT 06405

Call Sign: N1MRK
William M Perrelli
3 Crescent Bluff Ave.
Branford CT 06405

Call Sign: WA1YTU
Daniel R Gellatly
125 E Main St
Branford CT 06405

Call Sign: WA1ZWB
David W Smith
395 E Main St
Branford CT 064052944

Call Sign: N1ZZT
Christopher C Platt
211 East Main St E53

Branford CT 06405

Call Sign: N1MFF
Donald J Siclari Jr
765 East Main Street
Branford CT 06405

Call Sign: N1TXM
Alan M Karenko
14 Evergreen Pl
Branford CT 064054508

Call Sign: N1OX
Alan M Karenko
14 Evergreen Place
Branford CT 06405

Call Sign: WB2JVZ
Jeffrey S Kahn
312 Field Pt Rd
Branford CT 06405

Call Sign: KB1NXS
Thomas D Powers
38 Griffing Pond Rd
Branford CT 06405

Call Sign: W1TDP
Thomas D Powers
38 Griffing Pond Rd
Branford CT 06405

Call Sign: N1KZF
Daniel R Snyder
47 Griffing Pond Rd
Branford CT 06405

Call Sign: KB1RDQ
Peter J Darco
218 Harbor St
Branford CT 06405

Call Sign: W1SF
Harry H Johnson
231 Harbor St Box 48

Branford CT 06405

Call Sign: K1DZA
Stanson G Nimiroski
Harbour Village Unit 5a
Branford CT 06405

Call Sign: N1KZI
Dale E Johnson
35 Harrison Ave
Branford CT 06405

Call Sign: N1TGG
Alfred L Angelo
65 Harrison Ave
Branford CT 06405

Call Sign: KA1QJ
James H Revkin
12 Highland Ave.
Branford CT 06405

Call Sign: KB1FSC
William J Ludwig
39 Hotchkiss Grove Rd
Branford CT 06405

Call Sign: W1IH
Jonathan D Katz
41 Island View Ave
Branford CT 06405

Call Sign: KB1PDK
George J O'brien
45 Jefferson Rd Unit 1-14
Branford CT 06405

Call Sign: KA1LHE
Paul J Zakur
10 Lakeview Terr
Branford CT 06405

Call Sign: W1AP
Akihiro Hashimoto
47 Laurel Street

Branford CT 06405

Call Sign: W1MRI
Mirai Hashimoto
47 Laurel Street
Branford CT 06405

Call Sign: W1CHI
Chizu Hashimoto
47 Laurel Street
Branford CT 06405

Call Sign: KB1GTM
Dov Toren
177 Leetes Island Rd
Branford CT 06405

Call Sign: KB1FZE
Michael J Modzelewski
16 Lincoln Avenue
Branford CT 064053015

Call Sign: K1BGZ
Alan B Gilchrist
13 Lomartra Ln
Branford CT 06405

Call Sign: N1CJ
CHRISTOPHER J
Mcmillian
622 Longfellow Dr
Branford CT 06405

Call Sign: N1HUI
Thomas M Raiola
169 Maple St
Branford CT 06405

Call Sign: KB1IIS
Sharon Raiola
169 Maple St
Branford CT 06405

Call Sign: N1YVV
David M Ocame

10 Marion Road
Branford CT 06405

Call Sign: KB1INW
Patricia A Santoro
10 Marion Road
Branford CT 06405

Call Sign: WS1ETI
David M Ocame
10 Marion Road
Branford CT 06405

Call Sign: W1CLM
Charles L Mason
48 Midwood Rd
Branford CT 064054852

Call Sign: W5UIM
Masahito Fujiwara
130 Montoya 12288
Branford CT 06405

Call Sign: KB1QYT
Hiroyuki Toba
130 Montoya Dr
Branford CT 06405

Call Sign: W5OTE
Yuji Shimizu
130 Montoya Dr
Branford CT 06405

Call Sign: WA5OP
Hiroyuki Toba
130 Montoya Dr
Branford CT 06405

Call Sign: AA3TD
Shuji Ito
130 Montoya Drive
Branford CT 06405

Call Sign: KB1RNM
Chizu Hashimoto

130 Montoya Drive
Branford CT 06405

Call Sign: N1GVX
Michael T Smaga Sr
22 Old Smugglers Rd
Branford CT 06405

Call Sign: KA1FLU
Norman R Esborn
33 Old Smugglers Rd
Branford CT 06405

Call Sign: N1EEP
Robert N Dreyer
202 Opening Hill Rd
Branford CT 06405

Call Sign: AA3RV
Akihiro Hashimoto
46 Park Pl Apt 3
Branford CT 06405

Call Sign: K1AH
Akihiro Hashimoto
46 Park Pl Apt 3
Branford CT 06405

Call Sign: KB1QYU
Yuji Shimizu
A Hashimoto 46 Park Pl
Apt 3
Branford CT 06405

Call Sign: KB1QGX
Mirai Hashimoto
46 Park Place Apt 3
Branford CT 06405

Call Sign: KB1REW
Masahito Fujiwara
C/O A Hashimota 46 Park
Place Apt 3
Branford CT 06405

Call Sign: AA3QM
Takashi Morioka
46 Park Place Apt#3
Branford CT 06405

Call Sign: KB1HWJ
Kurt R Volk
167 Pawson Rd
Branford CT 06405

Call Sign: K1KRV
Kurt R Volk
167 Pawson Rd
Branford CT 06405

Call Sign: KA3MNU
Shauket A Gadiwalla
59 Peddlers Dr
Branford CT 06405

Call Sign: N1EHV
Ralph S Bonanno
19 Peddlers Dr.
Branford CT 06405

Call Sign: W1OKG
James W M Monde
241 Pine Orchard Rd
Branford CT 06405

Call Sign: N1ODM
Alan R Safford
5c Pineview Dr
Branford CT 06405

Call Sign: N1ZNB
Adolph J Brink
105 Plymouth Colony
Branford CT 06405

Call Sign: K1VHF
Morton H Krantz
28 Quarry Dock Rd
Branford CT 06405

Call Sign: WA1LBC
Leonard I Spear
33 Quarry Dock Rd
Branford CT 06405

Call Sign: N1HLS
Dorrance R Johnson
9 Riverside Dr
Branford CT 06405

Call Sign: N1GLF
Richard J Walker
35 Riverside Dr
Branford CT 06405

Call Sign: KA1MLR
June W Scharf
52 Riverside Dr
Branford CT 06405

Call Sign: WB1FGQ
Kenneth R Donovan
260 Shore Dr
Branford CT 06405

Call Sign: K1MBH
Victor J Machutas
154 Short Beach Rd
Branford CT 06405

Call Sign: KA1RPS
Scott M Beisiegel
49 Summer Island Rd
Branford CT 06405

Call Sign: KB1VI
Ernest L Johnson Jr
15 Swift St
Branford CT 06405

Call Sign: N1WEU
Paul D Sansone
36 Taylor Pl
Branford CT 06405

Call Sign: N1WHT
Christopher S Meffert
64 Thimble Island Rd
Branford CT 06405

Call Sign: W1OCH
George N Dunbar Jr
11 Tweed Rd Pine Orchard
Branford CT 06405

Call Sign: KB1JNV
Mark R Howard-Flanders
5 Valley St
Branford CT 06405

Call Sign: KA1JGI
John T Roach
135 Village Ln
Branford CT 06405

Call Sign: KB1QBG
Raymond E Sylvester
72 Waverly Park Road
Branford CT 06405

Call Sign: WU1I
Raymond E Sylvester
72 Waverly Park Road
Branford CT 06405

Call Sign: N1ITV
Gregory G Weltin
32 Waverly Rd
Branford CT 06405

Call Sign: NA1M
Mathias Hettinger Sr
18 Wilford Ave
Branford CT 064053823

Call Sign: AA6E
Martin S Ewing
28 Wood Road
Branford CT 06405

Call Sign: KA1TZD
Thomas W Grantland Jr
34 Woodvale Rd
Branford CT 06405

Call Sign: N1DZR
Jay F Ewer
Branford CT 06405

Call Sign: N1SLI
Pedro J Melendez
Branford CT 06405

Call Sign: KB1TTN
Robert K Barba
Branford CT 06405

Call Sign: W1QYC
Robert A Valley
32 Meadow Wood Rd
Branfort CT 06504

**FCC Amateur Radio
Licenses in Bridgeport**

Call Sign: N1GXG
Robert L Warren
27 Abner Ct
Bridgeport CT 06606

Call Sign: KB1ZB
Remco D Weidema
60 Accadia Ave
Bridgeport CT 06604

Call Sign: KB1BYS
Armando L Rodriguez
36 Allen St Blvd 12
Bridgeport CT 06610

Call Sign: KB1IQH
Richard C Pfeifer Jr
130 Anton St
Bridgeport CT 06606

Call Sign: KA1ULF
Omar Montalvo Jr
494 Atlantic St
Bridgeport CT 06604

Call Sign: KA1ULH
Ricardo Montalvo
494 Atlantic St
Bridgeport CT 06604

Call Sign: KB1CFT
Pablo Rivera
140 Austin St Apt 1
Bridge Port CT 06604

Call Sign: WN1CRX
Philip A Segneri Jr
260 B Edgemoor Road
Bridgeport CT 066062104

Call Sign: N1WYM
Miguel A Bonilla
196 Barcley
Bridgeport CT 06608

Call Sign: WB1CVH
Joseph J Feher
8 Beachview Ave
Bridgeport CT 06605

Call Sign: KE1LH
Enrique G Medina
108 Bearsaire Ave
Bridgeport CT 06608

Call Sign: W1WHT
Albino W Ciotti
356 Beechmont Ave
Bridgeport CT 06606

Call Sign: KB1TGZ
Sandra M Russell
207 Beechwood Ave
Bridgeport CT 06604

Call Sign: KB1THA
Joshimar C Russell
207 Beechwood Ave
Bridgeport CT 06604

Call Sign: KB1BZY
Brenda Castro
108 Berkshire Ave
Bridgeport CT 06608

Call Sign: N1FPN
Juan Fiol
159 Black Rock Ave
Bridgeport CT 06604

Call Sign: N1EOC
Paul Mendes
41 Blackman Pl
Bridgeport CT 06604

Call Sign: AB1MU
Joel A Lambert
Box 5953
Bridgeport CT 06610

Call Sign: KB1AYK
Vincent J Kravec
721 Brewster St
Bridgeport CT 066052936

Call Sign: AA1BS
Charles E Butler
390 Broad St
Bridgeport CT 06604

Call Sign: KA1JVR
Joseph E Scala Jr
327 Broad Street
Bridgeport CT 06604

Call Sign: N1OLQ
Edward M Allen
287 Brooks St
Bridgeport CT 06608

Call Sign: KA1PPF
Jorge A Valle
563 Brooks St
Bridgeport CT 06608

Call Sign: N1NGR
Howard Kinsinger
1093 Capitol Ave
Bridgeport CT 06606

Call Sign: N1SUH
Miguel Rodriguez
28 Carrie St
Bridgeport CT 06607

Call Sign: KB1EQ
Roy Rogers
151 Cedar St Apt 15
Bridgeport CT 06608

Call Sign: N1VWO
Luis Lugo
235 Chamberlain St
Bridgeport CT 066064847

Call Sign: N1DUI
Patrick J Loturco
4 Chatham Ter
Bridgeport CT 066062321

Call Sign: WA1HNM
Donald A O Brien
40 Cityview Ave
Bridgeport CT 06606

Call Sign: WA1IIK
Allen S Carnicke
29 Clarkson St
Bridgeport CT 06605

Call Sign: KB1BYT
Fernando Monginho
114 Cleveland Ave
Bridgeport CT 06606

Call Sign: KB1PQK
Don Hei Ming Wong
955 Connecticut Ave
Bridgeport CT 06606

Call Sign: WA1ZPT
Edward C Mattison
162 Cottage St
Bridgeport CT 06605

Call Sign: KB1INP
James R Elliott
666 Courtland Ave. 3rd
Floor
Bridgeport CT 06605

Call Sign: WB1GVW
William P Haynes
60 Daniel Dr
Bridgeport CT 06606

Call Sign: WA1EDX
Joseph T Pelham
322 Dayton Rd
Bridgeport CT 06606

Call Sign: N1XLH
Peter T Joseph
136 Dogwood Dr
Bridgeport CT 06606

Call Sign: WW1X
Harry Seymour Jr
124 E Eaton St
Bridgeport CT 06604

Call Sign: N1OLN
Ben Edl
3110 E Main
Bridgeport CT 06610

Call Sign: N1ZWS
Maria M Villanueva
2136 E Main St
Bridgeport CT 06610

Call Sign: W1MJL
Mary Janice Ligouri
352 East Pasadena Place
Bridgeport CT 06610

Call Sign: KA1RBZ
Kenneth R Ayhens
330 Fairview Ave
Bridgeport CT 06606

Call Sign: KA1RFP
Antonio Pagan
127 Garfield Ave
Bridgeport CT 06606

Call Sign: N1YGT
Jose Ramon R Rodriguez
146 Eastwood Rd
Bridgeport CT 06606

Call Sign: N1HIZ
Vincent A Johnson Sr
281 Fiske Ave
Bridgeport CT 06606

Call Sign: KA1DVB
John A De Cesare
87 Geduldig St
Bridgeport CT 06606

Call Sign: KB1BHZ
Gonzalo G Otero
28 Edwards St
Bridgeport CT 06608

Call Sign: N1KJP
Elaine M Johnson
281 Fiske Ave
Bridgeport CT 06606

Call Sign: W1JVQ
Albert J Kaufman
84 Glendale Ave
Bridgeport CT 06606

Call Sign: KE1HD
Emilio A Medina
48 Elmwood Ave
Bridgeport CT 06605

Call Sign: KB1SJI
Edward J Wheatcraft
53 Flower Street
Bridgeport CT 06605

Call Sign: KB1BES
John T Killian
463 Goldenrod Ave
Bridgeport CT 06606

Call Sign: KB1CPQ
Angel L Garcia
61 Elmwood Ave 3rd Floor
Bridgeport CT 06605

Call Sign: N1XFI
Edwin Escalera
117 Frank St
Bridgeport CT 06604

Call Sign: KB1CGU
Abisail Andino
145 Granfield Ave
Bridgeport CT 06610

Call Sign: N1EAA
Teodosio M Ortega Sr
40 Evans St
Bridgeport CT 06606

Call Sign: N1XLL
Orlando Escalera
117 Frank St
Bridgeport CT 06604

Call Sign: KA1QMW
Robert E Hennessey
361 Gurdon St
Bridgeport CT 06606

Call Sign: KA1TZQ
Lazaro J Alberto
500 Ezra St
Bridgeport CT 06606

Call Sign: N1PCJ
Dinh C Traw
70 Fremont St
Bridgeport CT 06605

Call Sign: N1CAQ
Patrick W Domkowski
505 Gurdon St
Bridgeport CT 06606

Call Sign: KB1FDK
Anthony D Davis
509 Ezra St
Bridgeport CT 06606

Call Sign: N3PQD
John M Zenner
836 Frenchtown Rd
Bridgeport CT 06606

Call Sign: W1ZQX
Tim G English
44 Haddon Street
Bridgeport CT 06605

Call Sign: N1QOS
Dinh C Tran
1035 Fairfield Ave Apt B3
Bridgeport CT 06604

Call Sign: KB1SKE
Edward T Lomax
331 Funston Avenue
Bridgeport CT 06606

Call Sign: KA1KGO
Laszlo Deutsch
111 Hale Ter
Bridgeport CT 06610

Call Sign: N1ZMJ
Hector Retamar
724 Hancock Ave
Bridgeport CT 066051908

Call Sign: N1PLI
Thanh Nguyen
1152 Hanlak Ave
Bridgeport CT 06605

Call Sign: KB1BNS
Ismael Ponce
341 Harriet
Bridgeport CT 06608

Call Sign: KB1BUE
Carmen M Ponce
341 Harriet St
Bridgeport CT 06608

Call Sign: KB1BIA
Ramon J Martinez
15 Harvey St
Bridgeport CT 06610

Call Sign: KB1HWV
Antonio J Marcano
603 Hawley Ave
Bridgeport CT 06606

Call Sign: AA1QE
Miguel Perez
170 Hickory St
Bridgeport CT 06610

Call Sign: KA1UUS
Robert H Schaefer Ii
146 Hillside Ave
Bridgeport CT 06604

Call Sign: KB1BZM
Freddy M Martinez
120 Holland Hill Cir
Bridgeport CT 066101043

Call Sign: W1WML
George F Dennis
81 Houston Ave
Bridgeport CT 06606

Call Sign: WB1CYU
Mark A Schickler
72 Intervale Rd
Bridgeport CT 06610

Call Sign: KY1A
Joseph Diaz Jr
327 Iranistan Ave
Bridgeport CT 06604

Call Sign: N1ORN
Jesse B Henman Jr
1169 Iranistan Ave
Bridgeport CT 06605

Call Sign: KA1PFA
David E Weed
1176 Iranistan Ave
Bridgeport CT 06605

Call Sign: KD1BM
Rita A Weed
1176 Iranistan Ave
Bridgeport CT 066051121

Call Sign: N1DUF
B Elliott Weed
1176 Iranistan Ave
Bridgeport CT 06605

Call Sign: W1RMZ
Darren P Zapotocky Jr
214 Iranistan Avenue
Bridgeport CT 06604

Call Sign: W1WAV
Darren P Zapotocky Jr
214 Iranistan Avenue
Bridgeport CT 06604

Call Sign: KA1VXR
John S Diaz
321 Irianistan Ave
Bridgeport CT 06604

Call Sign: KB1BUT
Angel M Morales
65 James St   Apt 30
Bridgeport CT 06604

Call Sign: KA1SJQ
Felipe Rodriguez
196 Jones Ave
Bridgeport CT 06604

Call Sign: KB1IJP
John P Mcdermott
128 Judson Pl
Bridgeport CT 06610

Call Sign: KA1YTB
Joseph L Rosenthal
124 Keeler Ave
Bridgeport CT 06606

Call Sign: KB1BXM
Jennifer C Sanchez
115 King Burry Rd
Bridgeport CT 06610

Call Sign: N2VMG
Salvador Davila
1360 Kossth St
Bridgeport CT 06608

Call Sign: WP4FZJ
Jorge A Ramos
854 Kossuth St
Bridgeport CT 06608

Call Sign: N1ENP
Joseph J Larcheveque Jr
500 Lake Avenue
Bridgeport CT 066053517

Call Sign: KB1AAI
Wesner J Ovide Jr
438 Lakeside Dr
Bridgeport CT 06606

Call Sign: KA1VZH
Luis A Martinez
1604 Laurel Ave
Bridgeport CT 06604

Call Sign: KB1BSZ
David Arroyo
897 Lindley St
Bridgeport CT 06606

Call Sign: KB1PJA
Stella Yeotsas
1161 Madison Ave
Bridgeport CT 06606

Call Sign: KA1SUM
Annette L Cooney
1267 Madison Ave
Bridgeport CT 06606

Call Sign: N1CJC
Elbert F Blackburn
2954 Madison Ave
Bridgeport CT 06606

Call Sign: KB1OIC
St Vincents Medical Center
Amateur Radio Club
2800 Main St
Bridgeport CT 066060482

Call Sign: W1SVM
St Vincents Medical Center
Amateur Radio Club
2800 Main St
Bridgeport CT 066060482

Call Sign: KE1JC
Robert H Kamens

3319 Main St
Bridgeport CT 06606

Call Sign: KA1UCT
Anthony Castellini
96 Manila Pl
Bridgeport CT 06610

Call Sign: N1LBX
Charles I Hunziker
508 N Summerfield Ave
Bridgeport CT 06610

Call Sign: KB1THD
Laurie A Brown
67 Nash Lane
Bridgeport CT 06605

Call Sign: KA1AAQ
Janis L Cole
13 Nash Ln Apt 5
Bridgeport CT 06605

Call Sign: KA1IOW
Stanley F Perry
123 Nautilus Rd
Bridgeport CT 06606

Call Sign: KB1BJN
Alexander C Otero
632 Noble Ave
Bridgeport CT 06608

Call Sign: N1CBM
Joseph Franco Jr
1318 Noble Ave
Bridgeport CT 06608

Call Sign: N1DUP
Geny Franco
1318 Noble Ave
Bridgeport CT 06608

Call Sign: N1UGO
Joseph L Franco

1318 Noble Ave
Bridgeport CT 06608

Call Sign: N1UGP
Neil R Franco
1318 Noble Ave
Bridgeport CT 06608

Call Sign: KA1TSL
Carlos F Lopez
1320 Noble Ave
Bridgeport CT 06608

Call Sign: N1HAY
Adriano Garcia
1320 Noble Ave
Bridgeport CT 06608

Call Sign: WA1UCQ
Joel A Lambert
1407 Norman St
Bridgeport CT 06604

Call Sign: KB1TGT
Joel Lambert
1273 North Ave
Bridgeport CT 06604

Call Sign: WA1UCQ
Joel A Lambert
1273 North Ave
Bridgeport CT 06604

Call Sign: KA1SWS
Enrique Vazquez Jr
2109 North Ave
Bridgeport CT 06604

Call Sign: KC2AEW
Rafael Serrano
292 Ogden St
Bridgeport CT 06608

Call Sign: KA1WIR
Bernardo Rodriguez

391 Ogden St
Bridgeport CT 06608

Call Sign: N1DUH
Jose I Bujosa
604 Ogden St
Bridgeport CT 06608

Call Sign: W1FWD
George W Murray Jr
1979 Old Town Rd
Bridgeport CT 066061321

Call Sign: N1FYH
Richard J Lombard
2825 Old Town Rd
Bridgeport CT 066061242

Call Sign: KA1BQX
Charles P Prokop Sr
2830 Old Town Rd
Bridgeport CT 066061243

Call Sign: N1YIG
Benito M Mejias
146 Olive St
Bridgeport CT 06605

Call Sign: KC1ZY
Lloyd Holmes Jr
57 Orange St
Bridgeport CT 06607

Call Sign: KA1VXS
Fernando J Medina
183 Orland St
Bridgeport CT 06605

Call Sign: N1ZAU
Kelly Pierre
59 Pacific St
Bridgeport CT 06604

Call Sign: W1RGP
Ulious L Raiford Sr

730 Palasade Ave Apt B2
Bridgeport CT 06604

Call Sign: N1DUO
Jose Solano
275 Palisade Ave
Bridgeport CT 06610

Call Sign: KB1BUU
Diana Morales
26 Palmer St
Bridgeport CT 06606

Call Sign: WA1UKN
Saul L Nowitz
2057 Park Ave
Bridgeport CT 066041911

Call Sign: N1XQZ
David Yasner
3030 Park Ave
Bridgeport CT 06604

Call Sign: KB1HHP
Alfred J Mallozzi
3300 Park Ave
Bridgeport CT 06604

Call Sign: W2RNM
Thomas P O Connell
3900 Park Ave
Bridgeport CT 06604

Call Sign: N1JNE
Mary J Scoran
3030 Park Ave 2
Bridgeport CT 06604

Call Sign: KE1XK
Robert H Kamens
4180 Park Ave Apt 20
Bridgeport CT 066041039

Call Sign: KB1TGR
Israel J Soto

1447 Park Avenue
Bridgeport CT 06604

Call Sign: KB1BNR
Jorge L Maldonado
29 Park St
Bridgeport CT 06608

Call Sign: KA1YUP
Evan C Betts
256 Pennsylvania Ave
Bridgeport CT 06610

Call Sign: WA1JXL
Herbert E Backus
170 Prince St
Bridgeport CT 06610

Call Sign: WB1CYZ
Arthur J Wendell
377 Queen St
Bridgeport CT 06606

Call Sign: KA1QGY
Herbert H Steinhardt
199 Ranch Dr
Bridgeport CT 06606

Call Sign: W1BIQ
Freddy Martin
299 Remington Street
Bridgeport CT 06610

Call Sign: KA1UUA
Cassandra Y Weidema
Houston
1156 Reservoir Ave
Bridgeport CT 06606

Call Sign: W1IKB
John V Yacovelli Sr
95 Richfield Rd
Bridgeport CT 066061040

Call Sign: N1APB

Carlos Vazquez
85 Rose St
Bridgeport CT 066101724

Call Sign: KB1IRB
Philip L Smith
230 Rosewood Place
Bridgeport CT 06610

Call Sign: KA1QIQ
Manuel L Batlle
51 S Pequonnock St
Bridgeport CT 06604

Call Sign: KB1VAT
Ashley Burton
315 Seaview Ave Unit
58706
Bridgeport CT 06607

Call Sign: AC8IA
Wilhelm Alm
315 Seaview Ave # 56144
Bridgeport CT 066072433

Call Sign: AC1WA
Wilhelm Alm
315 Seaview Ave # 56144
Bridgeport CT 066072433

Call Sign: KB1TWY
Christoph Krumbholz
315 Seaview Ave #31434
Bridgeport CT 06607

Call Sign: AB1QQ
Takehiro Tsubata
315 Seaview Ave 109454
Bridgeport CT 066072433

Call Sign: KB1UEJ
Francis Asuquo
315 Seaview Ave 36389
Bridgeport CT 06607

Call Sign: NA1JA
Francis Asuquo
315 Seaview Ave 36389
Bridgeport CT 06607

Call Sign: KB1VZP
Masanao Wakahara
315 Seaview Ave 79733
Bridgeport CT 06607

Call Sign: AB1QD
Masanao Wakahara
315 Seaview Ave 79733
Bridgeport CT 06607

Call Sign: KB1WFG
Erik De Man
315 Seaview Ave 83642
Bridgeport CT 06607

Call Sign: AB1PP
Hisashi Yoshida
315 Seaview Ave 88080
Bridgeport CT 06607

Call Sign: AB1PT
Masaru Tanaka
315 Seaview Ave 88117
Bridgeport CT 06607

Call Sign: KU1D
Masaru Tanaka
315 Seaview Ave 88117
Bridgeport CT 06607

Call Sign: AB1LM
Robert Froehling
315 Seaview Ave.
Bridgeport CT 066072433

Call Sign: N7BCP
Lorenzo M Da Ponte
315 Seaview Ave. # 47758
Bridgeport CT 066072433

Call Sign: WA1ZQW
Ioannis D Raditsas
27 Sedfewick
Bridgeport CT 06606

Call Sign: N1HGW
Michael J Slutzky
55 Shell St Apt 318
Bridgeport CT 06605

Call Sign: KA1RFQ
Antonio Castillo
157 Shelton St
Bridgeport CT 06608

Call Sign: KA1RFR
Nicolas Medina
157 Shelton St
Bridgeport CT 06608

Call Sign: KA1YJE
Luis E Orriola
446 Shelton St
Bridgeport CT 06608

Call Sign: N1FNS
Juan A Gonzalez
67 Sherwood Ave
Bridgeport CT 06605

Call Sign: N1OXQ
Phuc M Ly
147 Sherwood Ave
Bridgeport CT 06605

Call Sign: KA1STQ
Francene S Sanchione
29 Sidney St
Bridgeport CT 06606

Call Sign: K1MML
Lawrence D Mammone
71 Sidney St
Bridgeport CT 06606

Call Sign: KA1RQQ
Wayne M Pettway
53 Sixth St
Bridgeport CT 06607

Call Sign: KA1WKA
Bryan D Hamilton
175 Sixth St
Bridgeport CT 06607

Call Sign: KB1BSY
Marva C Hamilton
175 Sixth St
Bridgeport CT 06607

Call Sign: KB1BUS
Olga Lopez Quinones
361 Stratford Ave
Bridgeport CT 06608

Call Sign: N1QOG
Keith A Morris
10 Sturtevant Pl
Bridgeport CT 06610

Call Sign: N1UDI
Ronnie Parker
221 Sunshine Cir
Bridgeport CT 06606

Call Sign: KD1HV
Rodney J Harris Sr
65 Texas Ave
Bridgeport CT 06610

Call Sign: KB1BYU
Ariel Rodriguez
66 Tom Thumb St
Bridgeport CT 06606

Call Sign: N1PWG
John G Turek
665 W Taft Ave
Bridgeport CT 06604

Call Sign: WA1UKU
Phylipp Dilloway
105 Walnut St
Bridgeport CT 066045350

Call Sign: KB1DZU
Angel J Melendee
629 Washington Ave 4th Fl
Apt 526
Bridgeport CT 06604

Call Sign: N1LQW
Donald A Mac Lean
25 Westfield Ave
Bridgeport CT 06606

Call Sign: W1ALZ
Thomas C Nicholson Jr
178 Wilson St
Bridgeport CT 06605

Call Sign: KB1WFT
Larry D Robinson
566 Wood Ave
Bridgeport CT 06604

Call Sign: K1BKL
Frank A Sanchione
Bridgeport CT 06606

Call Sign: KA1TUW
Ralf Hross
Bridgeport CT 06601

Call Sign: KB1CBA
Luz E Avila
Bridgeport CT 066100267

Call Sign: KB1CUH
Ruben D Rivera
Bridgeport CT 06610

Call Sign: KB1DRP
Ulysses Serpa
Bridgeport CT 066010393

Call Sign: N1HJZ
Stanley Dlugolenski
Bridgeport CT 06601

Call Sign: N1NVH
James A Christensen
Bridgeport CT 06610

Call Sign: N1WKF
Henry I Sanchez
Bridgeport CT 06606

Call Sign: KB1NTZ
Edward J Vizi
Bridgeport CT 06606

FCC Amateur Radio Licenses in Bridgewater

Call Sign: KA2WQZ
Scott L Smith
136 Beach Hill Road East
Bridgewater CT 06752

Call Sign: W1BEM
David C Cooper
Blueberry Hill 193
Bridgewater CT 06752

Call Sign: N1FXV
Douglas J Delisle
189 Blueberry Hill Rd
Bridgewater CT 06752

Call Sign: KA1VZD
Christopher D Davison
25 Canfield Dr
Bridgewater CT 06752

Call Sign: KB1HYI
George K Lalak
188 Clapboard Rd
Bridgewater CT 06752

Call Sign: KA1RFM
Kit D Sagendorf
Hat Shop Hill
Bridgewater CT 06752

Call Sign: K1CVF
Martin C Sagendorf
Hat Shop Hill Rd
Bridgewater CT 06752

Call Sign: K1UQJ
Douglas S Smyth
72 Henry Sanford Rd
Bridgewater CT 06752

Call Sign: KB1MWT
Jerry O Stern
30 Lakewood Dr
Bridgewater CT 06752

Call Sign: N1PQU
Peter B Mancino
210 Skyline Ridge
Bridgewater CT 06752

Call Sign: K1LXE
Ronald H Beerbaum
5 Sunrise Lane
Bridgewater CT 067520473

Call Sign: AB1BW
George K Lalak
Bridgewater CT 06752

Call Sign: KB1BYC
Isidro Nieves
361 Stratford Ave
Bridgport CT 06608

FCC Amateur Radio Licenses in Bristol

Call Sign: N1ZKX
Michael C Cousins
64 Allentown Rd

Bristol CT 06010

Call Sign: WA1SJO
Gerald T Chicoine
141 Allentown Rd
Bristol CT 06010

Call Sign: N1WZP
Jose Manuel Rubert
39 Armand Rd.
Bristol CT 06010

Call Sign: N1GJT
Gerald P Mel
67 Ashley Rd
Bristol CT 06010

Call Sign: KA1EI
Maurice R Lajoie
398 Baldwin Dr
Bristol CT 06010

Call Sign: N1GUF
David P Champagne
382 Baldwin Dr.
Bristol CT 06010

Call Sign: KB1EAC
Geoffrey E Parker
76 Bellevue Ave Apt 4
Bristol CT 06010

Call Sign: KA1WGE
Cathleen S Cianci
148 Ben St
Bristol CT 06010

Call Sign: N1AMB
F John Cianci Jr
148 Ben St
Bristol CT 06010

Call Sign: KA1ONN
Wayne M Halsdorf
148 Beth Ave

Bristol CT 06010

Call Sign: KE1FM
Tracy N Gordienko
156 Beths Ave
Bristol CT 06010

Call Sign: N1COS
Leonard J Lapollo
191 Birch St
Bristol CT 06010

Call Sign: KA1QXG
Bette J Gebrian
715 Birch St
Bristol CT 06010

Call Sign: K1DII
William C Stapleford
191 Bird Road
Bristol CT 06010

Call Sign: WA4BID
Ronald H Smith
252 Blakeslee St 3
Bristol CT 06010

Call Sign: WB1DAV
Joseph H St Amant
43 Boardman Rd
Bristol CT 06010

Call Sign: KB1NMK
Kimberly Ploszaj
71 Boardman Street
Bristol CT 06010

Call Sign: W1SO
William P Carpenter
Box 453
Bristol CT 06010

Call Sign: W1OD
Michael B Kaczynski
70 Braeburn Rd

Bristol CT 06010

Call Sign: KA1OTF
Edward W Gurtowsky
64 Brentwood Rd
Bristol CT 06010

Call Sign: WA1LJD
August J Lukacovic
6 Broadview St.
Bristol CT 06010

Call Sign: N1QHM
Michael C Probert
90 Brook St
Bristol CT 06010

Call Sign: K1EZZ
John G Greenlaw
150 Brookside Dr
Bristol CT 06010

Call Sign: N1BWY
Mary J Lee
410 Burlington Ave
Bristol CT 06010

Call Sign: WA1ZVH
Melvin E Sherman
634 Burlington Ave
Bristol CT 06010

Call Sign: K1FNP
Clayton A Wheeler Jr
184 Burton St
Bristol CT 060104808

Call Sign: WB1EOB
Steve A Avritch
268 Burton St
Bristol CT 060104873

Call Sign: KB1WPE
Worldwide Amateur Radio
Club

C/O Theodore H Szypulski
President ESPN Plaza
Bristol CT 06010

Call Sign: WE1SPN
Worldwide Amateur Radio
Club
C/O Theodore H Szypulski
President ESPN Plaza
Bristol CT 06010

Call Sign: KB1BJJ
Robert K Morgan
200 Carriage Rd
Bristol CT 06010

Call Sign: N1MUY
Kevin M Mellon
64 Chapel St
Bristol CT 06010

Call Sign: N1NAQ
Jeffrey E Du Pont
59 Charles St
Bristol CT 06010

Call Sign: N1LCE
Edward A Sobuta Jr
565 Clark Ave Unit 48
Bristol CT 06010

Call Sign: N1OQD
Chris F Garcia
565 Clark Ave. #57
Bristol CT 06010

Call Sign: WA1TCN
Wayne J Zadrick
39 Cold Springs Rd
Bristol CT 06010

Call Sign: KB1LE
Richard J Moris
46 Collins Rd
Bristol CT 060103843

Call Sign: N1PVL
Barbara C Moris
46 Collins Rd
Bristol CT 06010

Call Sign: KB1CQL
Ronald M Melanson
43 Colony St
Bristol CT 06010

Call Sign: WK1U
George E Roman
29 Colony Street
Bristol CT 06010

Call Sign: AA1JM
David J Twiggs
65 Consolation St
Bristol CT 06010

Call Sign: K1DCR
Joseph J D Angelo
88 Council Ring Dr
Bristol CT 06010

Call Sign: KA1ZOL
Francis G Marek
111 Council Ring Dr
Bristol CT 06010

Call Sign: KA1UCJ
Karen D Parenti
9 Deering Ln
Bristol CT 06010

Call Sign: WA1ECZ
James B Orr Sr
128 Divinity St
Bristol CT 06010

Call Sign: N3TLX
Roger A Nevers
280 Divinity St - Unit 5
Bristol CT 06010

Call Sign: WA1YHM
Henry A Swenton
353 East Rd
Bristol CT 06010

Call Sign: KA1UCH
Dolores B Ricker
80 Edrow Rd
Bristol CT 06010

Call Sign: WA1OOP
Charles E Ricker
80 Edrow Rd
Bristol CT 06010

Call Sign: N1NBH
Thomas E Kulowski
44 Empire Way
Bristol CT 06010

Call Sign: KB1PGL
Francis N Dragon
33 Fall Mt Rd
Bristol CT 06010

Call Sign: N1JGT
Lawrence E Tallman
415 Farmington Ave
Bristol CT 06010

Call Sign: N1LD
Lawrence E Tallman
415 Farmington Ave
Bristol CT 06010

Call Sign: KA1SIV
Richard A Balboni
111 Fleetwood Rd
Bristol CT 06010

Call Sign: N1PYZ
John D Kriniske
116 Fleetwood Rd
Bristol CT 06010

Call Sign: WB1A
Gerald R Mackie
129 Fox Den Rc
Bristol CT 06010

Call Sign: N1HFN
Joan M Mackie
129 Fox Den Rd
Bristol CT 06010

Call Sign: KB1ADE
Daniel S Jester
14 Foxwood Rd
Bristol CT 06010

Call Sign: KB1ADW
Sharon L Roys
14 Foxwood Rd
Bristol CT 06010

Call Sign: K1RPQ
Frederick J Davis
24 French St
Bristol CT 06010

Call Sign: W1SBU
Stanley J Swenton
10 Garden Ter
Bristol CT 06010

Call Sign: WB1ACK
John J Brophy
27 Garfield Rd
Bristol CT 06010

Call Sign: N1RYF
Bunna O Phin
113 Georetown Rd
Bristol CT 06010

Call Sign: KB1MLU
Robert A Mccarthy
45 Grove St
Bristol CT 06010

Call Sign: KB1HHO
David A Smarkus
223 Hart St
Bristol CT 06010

Call Sign: WV1D
David P Banker
39 Harvest Ln
Bristol CT 06010

Call Sign: KB1BJT
Anna P Mc Knight
40 Hawthorne St
Bristol CT 060107064

Call Sign: N1DNB
Paula M Place
40 Hawthorne St
Bristol CT 060107064

Call Sign: WB1EYI
Stephen C Place
40 Hawthorne St
Bristol CT 060107064

Call Sign: N1IKM
Roy E Johnson Jr
71 Hill St
Bristol CT 06011

Call Sign: W1DHT
Chippens Repeater / Bristol
Radio Club Inc
65 Hill Street
Bristol CT 06010

Call Sign: W1GY
William H Flaherty Jr
65 Hill Street
Bristol CT 06010

Call Sign: KA1IXI
Cheryl L Sowers
44 Hull St

Bristol CT 06010

Call Sign: NA1L
Wyland D Clift
44 Hull St
Bristol CT 06010

Call Sign: WB1EDP
Maurice V Leger
26 Hurley Commons
Bristol CT 06010

Call Sign: W1SHW
Edward W Cushing
48 Ingraham Pl
Bristol CT 06010

Call Sign: N1SSL
Camille L Lord
68 Ingraham St 3
Bristol CT 06010

Call Sign: KB1LXA
Anthony G Korytko
25 Ipswitch Rd
Bristol CT 06010

Call Sign: W1YDO
Edward W Bunnell
98 Jacqueline Dr
Bristol CT 06010

Call Sign: N1SQH
Sivert R Jacobson
21 Jefferson Ave
Bristol CT 06010

Call Sign: KA1PGH
Jay A Stephenson Jr
7 Jennings Ter
Bristol CT 06010

Call Sign: KB1KDG
James J Brown
104 Jewel St

Bristol CT 06010

Call Sign: KB1VFM
Carol L Jackson
103 Judson Ave
Bristol CT 06010

Call Sign: WN1ROB
Michael F Hudak
151 Judson Ave
Bristol CT 06010

Call Sign: KB1OLD
Lisa M Lonicki
483 King St
Bristol CT 060105242

Call Sign: N3ZXF
Deborah A Fusaro
586 King St
Bristol CT 06010

Call Sign: W3IZ
Norman Fusaro
586 King St
Bristol CT 06010

Call Sign: KB1NVG
Brute Force Kilowatts
586 King St
Bristol CT 06010

Call Sign: N1ZQ
Magnum Force
586 King St
Bristol CT 06010

Call Sign: KB1PHU
Brute Force Kilowatts
586 King St
Bristol CT 06010

Call Sign: W1SRT
Strange Radio Team Usa
586 King St

Bristol CT 06010

Call Sign: NT3S
Strange Radio Team Usa
586 King St
Bristol CT 06010

Call Sign: KB1PAM
Matteo Copetti
C/O Norman Fusaro 586
King St
Bristol CT 06010

Call Sign: K1NNB
William W Thompson
10 Knibbs Circle
Bristol CT 06010

Call Sign: KB1EVL
Wendell R Cody
69 Knoll St
Bristol CT 06010

Call Sign: KB1UFO
Wendell R Cody
69 Knoll St
Bristol CT 06010

Call Sign: KB1VFJ
Craig A Pocock
16 Lake Ave
Bristol CT 06010

Call Sign: WB1DBA
Weldon L Adams
14 Lakeside Dr
Bristol CT 06010

Call Sign: WA3HAI
James R Kerins
114 Lakeside Dr 78
Bristol CT 06010

Call Sign: N1JRX
Chester F Brzozowski

24 Lancaster Rd
Bristol CT 06010

Call Sign: K1TEW
Anthony Calbi
50 Lancaster Rd
Bristol CT 06010

Call Sign: WB1BYU
Harrison Alderson
77 Lawndale Ave
Bristol CT 06010

Call Sign: NJ1Q
Joseph P Carcia Iii
66 Leon Rd
Bristol CT 06010

Call Sign: WA1BUA
Roland L Crapo I
228 Longview Ave
Bristol CT 060107166

Call Sign: WA1YID
Frank Peronace Jr
29 Madison Dr
Bristol CT 06010

Call Sign: WA1ZQG
Claudia G Peronace
29 Madison Dr
Bristol CT 06010

Call Sign: KB1HRX
Susan Brzozowy
121 Magnolia Ave
Bristol CT 06010

Call Sign: N1EOS
William N Bresnahan
70 Magnolia Ave.
Bristol CT 06010

Call Sign: N1SQE
Jean Marie A Dionne

26 Mark St
Bristol CT 06010

Call Sign: WA1WNK
Anthony J Schiavone
91 Martin Rd
Bristol CT 06010

Call Sign: KA1OXD
James R Ritchie
27 Matilda Dr
Bristol CT 06010

Call Sign: KA1BXR
Carl W Shields Sr
177 Matthews St
Bristol CT 06010

Call Sign: KB1VFN
Harland S Graime
520 Matthews St
Bristol CT 06010

Call Sign: N1QGY
Jayson C Tautic
820 Matthews St #16
Bristol CT 06010

Call Sign: KC1UP
Joseph P Mel
28 Maywood Ln
Bristol CT 06010

Call Sign: N1HFP
Mary E Mel
28 Maywood Ln
Bristol CT 06010

Call Sign: WA1LMV
Richard H Swenton
106 Melinda Ln
Bristol CT 060107199

Call Sign: KC1NL
Raymond L Greene

18 Merriman St
Bristol CT 06010

Call Sign: K1QYD
Richard J Zack
89 Metro St
Bristol CT 060107826

Call Sign: N1SIB
Dory Avritch
60 Michigan Ave
Bristol CT 06010

Call Sign: WB1EOA
Richard T Avritch
60 Michigan Ave
Bristol CT 06010

Call Sign: KA1AZX
Lawrence L Palin Sr
215 Middle St
Bristol CT 06010

Call Sign: K1HXJ
Peter S Tranchida
41 Miller Rd - Apt 2
Bristol CT 060105954

Call Sign: WA1SHC
David M Zabel
114 Mines Rd
Bristol CT 06010

Call Sign: N1ZLF
Justin M Pearson
142 Minnesota Ln
Bristol CT 06010

Call Sign: N1PSP
Patricia L Mielniczuk
52 Missal Ave
Bristol CT 06010

Call Sign: KB1BSH
Michael C Jefferson

71 Morningside Dr West
Bristol CT 06010

Call Sign: WA1PKS
Victor J Nejfelt
86 Mossa Dr
Bristol CT 06010

Call Sign: W1FAN
Victor J Nejfelt
86 Mossa Dr
Bristol CT 06010

Call Sign: N1UVA
Robert A Hess
178 Mountain View Ave
Bristol CT 06010

Call Sign: W1IMP
Theodore H Maceieski
284 N Main St
Bristol CT 060104921

Call Sign: N1XNR
James J Wargo
1 Neuman Pl
Bristol CT 06010

Call Sign: KB1QCO
John W Kane Ii
36 Noel Ln
Bristol CT 06010

Call Sign: KA1UCK
Timothy R Peterson
124 North St
Bristol CT 06010

Call Sign: KB1RBD
Stephen W Perkins
21 Northmont Rd Ext
Bristol CT 06010

Call Sign: W1PRK
Stephen W Perkins

21 Northmont Rd Ext
Bristol CT 06010

Call Sign: KA1OUZ
Godelieve Koninckx
60 Northwestern Dr
Bristol CT 06010

Call Sign: N1WDE
Mark Van Hout
60 Northwestern Dr
Bristol CT 06010

Call Sign: W1CKA
Paul A Neveu Jr
60 Northwestern Dr
Bristol CT 06010

Call Sign: K1QJ
Ireneusz S Biernat
66 O Sullivan Dr
Bristol CT 06010

Call Sign: N2OK
Ralph T Voigt
83 Oakhill Rd
Bristol CT 06010

Call Sign: W1MES
William F Potter Jr
352 Peck Ln
Bristol CT 06010

Call Sign: W1SQ
Michael A Churchill
1955 Perkins St
Bristol CT 06010

Call Sign: KB1LV
Bent Jensen
2116 Perkins St
Bristol CT 06010

Call Sign: AA1GY
Ted L Theriault

30 Pierce St
Bristol CT 06010

Call Sign: KA1QWS
Daniel B Knope
40 Pinebrook Ter Apt 2
Bristol CT 06010

Call Sign: WA1YND
Allen J Beattie Jr
66 Pinnacle Rd
Bristol CT 06010

Call Sign: KD1DB
Dennis W Sadowsky
94 Poitras Rd
Bristol CT 06010

Call Sign: K1OLT
Russell P Wedge
40 Putnam St
Bristol CT 06010

Call Sign: KB1VFK
Elizabeth M Gionfriddo
39 Rathdun Rd
Bristol CT 06010

Call Sign: KB1RDM
Lionel G Sousa
295 Redstone Hill Rd Apt
29
Bristol CT 06010

Call Sign: N1IYL
Joseph D Terrien Jr
736 Redstone Hill Road
Bristol CT 06010

Call Sign: WA1SSU
Mark P Benvenuto
43 Richmond Pl
Bristol CT 06010

Call Sign: W4MCK

Real E Downing
276 Riverside Ave
Bristol CT 06010

Daniel O Wall
94 Rowe Pl
Bristol CT 06010

Brent R Landeen
300 Sonstrom Rd
Bristol CT 06010

Call Sign: KB1VFL
Edward G Litherland
20 Robertson St
Bristol CT 06010

Call Sign: W1ZFG
Daniel O Wall
94 Rowe Pl
Bristol CT 06010

Call Sign: KS1P
Gilles R Charbonneau
112 South St Ext
Bristol CT 060106419

Call Sign: KA1RQU
Lauren M Roy
14 Robin St
Bristol CT 06010

Call Sign: N1LEV
James E Palmer
68 Saw Mill Road
Bristol CT 060102427

Call Sign: K1OLS
George R Wedge
502 South St. Apt. 3c
Bristol CT 06010

Call Sign: KB1OLB
Kimberly R Stuart
33 Rockwell Ave
Bristol CT 06010

Call Sign: KB1KNV
William F Reyor Iii
150 Seneca Rd
Bristol CT 06010

Call Sign: WA1ZLV
Daniel L Dallaire
124 Stafford Ave
Bristol CT 060104612

Call Sign: N1RPO
Sharon A Sweet
126 Rockwell Ave
Bristol CT 060105942

Call Sign: N1NYK
Mark J Paparello Sr
49 Sherman St
Bristol CT 060104951

Call Sign: K1LDO
David M Rimmer
1466 Stafford Ave
Bristol CT 060102542

Call Sign: KB1SUJ
Steven Massey
18 Rogers Rd
Bristol CT 06010

Call Sign: N1NIN
Jeffrey A Walden
35 Sherwood Rd
Bristol CT 06010

Call Sign: KB1ARZ
Timothy J Benson
42 Stafford Ave Apt B4
Bristol CT 06010

Call Sign: KB1OKZ
Monica Reynolds
20 Root Ave
Bristol CT 06010

Call Sign: W1PNB
Howard F Wright Jr
55 Sigourney St
Bristol CT 060106883

Call Sign: N1MFD
Jason K Zakrzewski
163 Stafford Ave.
Bristol CT 06010

Call Sign: WB1GKS
Stephen T Starre
84 Rosemont Ave
Bristol CT 06010

Call Sign: K1IUY
John Demerski
150 Sixth St
Bristol CT 060105363

Call Sign: KB1OLC
Cynthia L Morin
163 Stearns St
Bristol CT 06010

Call Sign: WO1X
Thomas M Samulenas
71 Round Hill Rd.
Bristol CT 06010

Call Sign: N1ODI
K Elizabeth E Cook
125 Skyridge Rd
Bristol CT 060107254

Call Sign: WA1BRD
Harold L Roy
80 Stonecrest Dr
Bristol CT 060105319

Call Sign: WA1PAT

Call Sign: N1YST

Call Sign: W1YI

Victor J Nejfelt
32 Summer Glen
Bristol CT 06010

Call Sign: K1LFH
Norman A Cucuel
9 Susan Ln
Bristol CT 06010

Call Sign: N1JXX
David R Norton
25 Terryville Ave
Bristol CT 06010

Call Sign: KB1DVF
Zachary N Fisk
257 Terryville Ave
Bristol CT 06010

Call Sign: KA1MJV
Donna P Frank
46 Timber Ln
Bristol CT 06010

Call Sign: N1QAC
Wesley A Going
85 Twining St
Bristol CT 06010

Call Sign: KB1RHV
John H Scott
42 Tyler Way
Bristol CT 06010

Call Sign: KA1MVO
Tammy A Wotton
154 Union St
Bristol CT 06010

Call Sign: KA1SPN
Ramon A Wotton Jr
154 Union St
Bristol CT 06010

Call Sign: KI1U

Michael P Corey
149 Union St Apt 5
Bristol CT 06010

Call Sign: W5MPC
Michael P Corey
149 Union Stapt 5
Bristol CT 06010

Call Sign: KB1RHU
Scott A Robidoux
173 Vera Rd
Bristol CT 06010

Call Sign: N1TMB
Sean P Clancy
59-4 W Washington St
Bristol CT 06010

Call Sign: N1SQJ
Richard W Valentine
226 Westwood Rd
Bristol CT 060108928

Call Sign: W1RWV
Richard W Valentine
226 Westwood Rd
Bristol CT 060108928

Call Sign: WA1UAE
Thomas J Young
625 Willis St
Bristol CT 06010

Call Sign: KB1VJL
Christine U Moulis
665 Willis St
Bristol CT 06010

Call Sign: N1SQD
Walter D Polochanin
104 Winding Brook Rd
Bristol CT 06010

Call Sign: WA1ATW

Allen L Simmons
575 Witches Rock Rd
Bristol CT 06010

Call Sign: KB1LCR
Mark E Creamer
17 Woodbine St
Bristol CT 06010

Call Sign: N1XSK
Deborah L Foss
4 Woodridge Rd
Bristol CT 060107631

Call Sign: W1ZTQ
Daniel E David
4 Woodridge Rd
Bristol CT 06010

Call Sign: K1FPJ
Richard F Jackman
Bristol CT 060111224

Call Sign: KA1OYR
Steven S Decker
Bristol CT 06010

Call Sign: KB1BOT
Bird Rd Connecticut Dx
Assn
Bristol CT 060111093

Call Sign: KD1KR
James L Bower
Bristol CT 06011

Call Sign: N1OTA
Carl G Mason
Bristol CT 06011

Call Sign: N1XVO
Carol A Johnson
Bristol CT 060111775

Call Sign: WA1SZU

Clifford J Cayer
Bristol CT 060113211

Call Sign: K1IFF
Clifford J Cayer
Bristol CT 060113211

**FCC Amateur Radio
Licenses in Broad Brook**

Call Sign: KB1KUR
Richard U Sherman
12 Allen Dr
Broad Brook CT 06016

Call Sign: KB1WRB
Barbara I Sherman
12 Allen Dr
Broad Brook CT 06016

Call Sign: KB1HSH
Michael A Donlon
19 Deerfield Dr
Broad Brook CT 06016

Call Sign: KB1MET
Kelly J Easton
30 Deerfield Dr.
Broad Brook CT 06016

Call Sign: KA1MAR
Kelly J Slate
30 Deerfield Dr.
Broad Brook CT 06016

Call Sign: N1IZS
Remo S Bonali
120 Depot St
Broad Brook CT 06016

Call Sign: KA1SRW
Michael C Garcia
4 Eastwood Dr
Broad Brook CT 06016

Call Sign: WB1FDR
Elaine P Perron
5 Elaine Dr
Broad Brook CT 06016

Call Sign: K1AGI
Halle D Clisby
58 Highland Ave
Broad Brook CT 06016

Call Sign: WA1YEF
Floyd E Colvin
10 Joseph Ct
Broad Brook CT 06016

Call Sign: W1EPG
E Paul Galica
14 Margaret Drive
Broad Brook CT 060169622

Call Sign: K1GHU
John W Read
11 Melrose Rd
Broad Brook CT 06016

Call Sign: N1QVQ
William P Thim Jr
50 Miller Rd
Broad Brook CT 06016

Call Sign: KB1NFV
Andrew J Shustock
61 Miller Rd
Broad Brook CT 06016

Call Sign: KB1UNF
Christine A Schwartz
52 Norton Rd
Broad Brook CT 06016

Call Sign: KB1UNO
Mark A Musante
52 Norton Rd
Broad Brook CT 06016

Call Sign: KB1UNP
David M Schwartz Jr
52 Norton Rd
Broad Brook CT 06016

Call Sign: KB1GGG
David M Schwartz
52 Norton Road
Broad Brook CT 06016

Call Sign: K1AEM
Leslie George
52 Old Ellington Rd
Broad Brook CT 06016

Call Sign: WB1AET
Nelson L Koehler Jr
11 Pine Dr
Broad Brook CT 06016

Call Sign: KB1DMZ
Harold G Skinner
34 Skinner Rd
Broad Brook CT 06016

Call Sign: AA1YV
Harold G Skinner
34 Skinner Rd
Broad Brook CT 06016

Call Sign: WA1TLB
Roger C Rowe
4a Spring Ct
Broad Brook CT 06016

Call Sign: N1ST
Scott A Thomas
17 Stiles Rd
Broad Brook CT 06016

Call Sign: W1VLT
Vicki L Thomas
17 Stiles Rd
Broad Brook CT 06016

Call Sign: KB1GVP
Timothy S Belmonte
Broad Brook CT 06016

Call Sign: KB1IQX
Cub Scout Pack 89
Broad Brook CT 06016

**FCC Amateur Radio
Licenses in Brookfield**

Call Sign: N1LEI
Michael E Mayes
12 A West Whisconier Rd
Brookfield CT 068043735

Call Sign: KB1JAG
James F Mclaughlin
11 Ashwood Lane
Brookfield CT 06804

Call Sign: N1IXJ
Thomas G Osenkowsky
5 Beachwood Grove
Brookfield CT 06804

Call Sign: W1QI
Candlewood Amateur Radio
Assn
121 Candlewood Lake Rd
Brookfield CT 06804

Call Sign: W1QK
Daniel N Fegley
121 Candlewood Lake Rd
Brookfield CT 06804

Call Sign: KB1AXS
Michael E Cavallo
179 Candlewood Lake Rd
Brookfield CT 06804

Call Sign: KA1VHQ
Karin N Wuhrer
21 Drover Rd

Brookfield CT 06804

Call Sign: N1HKX
Andrew A Wuhrer
21 Drover Rd
Brookfield CT 06804

Call Sign: KA1URO
Edward F Fitch
31 Drover Rd
Brookfield CT 06804

Call Sign: KB1ELA
Lawrence G Stevens
19 Falmouth Ct
Brookfield CT 068042709

Call Sign: N1WOX
Robert C Conley
520 Federal Rd
Brookfield CT 06804

Call Sign: K1PHG
Peter H Gagne
9 Fieldstone Rd
Brookfield CT 068042305

Call Sign: N1HGS
John B Avallone
13 Forty Acre Moutain
Road
Brookfield CT 06804

Call Sign: N1XLZ
Myron J Wheichel Jr
13 Green Ridge Dr
Brookfield CT 06804

Call Sign: N2OOM
Bohdan M Dackow
9 Hgih Ridge Rd
Brookfield CT 06804

Call Sign: WB1GYQ
Thomas Muricchio

17 Huckleberry Hill Rd
Brookfield CT 06804

Call Sign: W1ESJ
Richard F Cronin
21 Indian Trl
Brookfield CT 06804

Call Sign: N1RNF
Kristina M Root
16 Ledgwood Dr
Brookfield CT 06804

Call Sign: N1ULD
Richard P Urkiel
85 Long Meadow Hill Rd
Brookfield CT 06804

Call Sign: KA1OLP
Linne M Waldo
175 Long Meadow Hill Rd
Brookfield CT 06804

Call Sign: NA1O
Robert C Waldo Jr
175 Long Meadow Hill Rd
Brookfield CT 06804

Call Sign: N1JXG
Francis R Brodeur
41 Longview Dr
Brookfield CT 06804

Call Sign: N1EPH
Susan A Hurley
23 Longview Drive
Brookfield CT 068041413

Call Sign: KA1VZE
Jay R Dzubak
4 Marldon Dr
Brookfield CT 06804

Call Sign: N1LQU

Mary Ann Mac Knight
Palmer
30 Meadow Brook Rd
Brookfield CT 06804

Call Sign: W1GMP
Joseph P Bupivi
42 Mist Hill Dr
Brookfield CT 06804

Call Sign: AB1QA
Christopher Roper
14 N Beech Tree Rd
Brookfield CT 06804

Call Sign: KD1WK
Bert W Sheppard
147 N Lakeshore Dr
Brookfield CT 06804

Call Sign: N1NRR
John J Birmingham
45 N Mountain Rd
Brookfield CT 06804

Call Sign: N1PFV
Bonnie L Birmingham
45 N Mountain Rd
Brookfield CT 06804

Call Sign: KB1PCL
Steven A Anderlot
29 N. Beech Tree Rd.
Brookfield CT 06804

Call Sign: KA1WAY
Kenneth R Eriksen
8 Nabby Rd
Brookfield CT 06804

Call Sign: KC2ALL
Maria B Morrisett
3 Oak Crest Drive
Brookfield CT 068042324

Call Sign: N2WRM
Warren R Morrisett
3 Oak Crest Drive
Brookfield CT 068042324

Call Sign: W1WRM
Warren R Morrisett
3 Oak Crest Drive
Brookfield CT 068042324

Call Sign: K1EDU
Raymond S James
66 Obtuse Rd S
Brookfield CT 06804

Call Sign: WA1OKX
William S Meltzer
75 Obtuse Rd S
Brookfield CT 06804

Call Sign: KB1VLQ
Michael J Smith
15 Obtuse Rd South
Brookfield CT 06804

Call Sign: WA1DGU
Richard W Gaylor
17 Old Middle Rd
Brookfield CT 06804

Call Sign: K1EPE
Alfred P Hantsch
53 Old Middle Rd
Brookfield CT 06804

Call Sign: W1ICF
Richard T Carroll
12 Ox Dr
Brookfield CT 068043631

Call Sign: KB1FZA
Andrey E Stoev
12 Pleasant Rise
Brookfield CT 06804

Call Sign: AE1Z
Andrey E Stoev
12 Pleasant Rise
Brookfield CT 06804

Call Sign: AE1S
Andrey E Stoev
12 Pleasant Rise
Brookfield CT 06804

Call Sign: KB1LTQ
Sean M Aikman
11 Shamrock Dr
Brookfield CT 06804

Call Sign: N1GUV
Bret J Nemeth
16 Skyline Dr
Brookfield CT 06804

Call Sign: KB1GDT
John N Nuzzi
94 So Lake Shore Dr
Brookfield CT 06804

Call Sign: W1AFX
William J Webb
12 Stage Rd
Brookfield CT 068043636

Call Sign: WA1WXG
Alice M Webb
12 Stage Rd
Brookfield CT 068043636

Call Sign: N1IWL
Douglas P Bradley
9 Tommys Ln
Brookfield CT 06804

Call Sign: N1OFZ
Dana S Rawding
80 Tower Road
Brookfield CT 06804

Call Sign: KB1VNP
Matthew Eirich
222 Whisconier Rd
Brookfield CT 06804

Call Sign: KB1ROL
Edward Briggs
12 Woodcreek Rd
Brookfield CT 06804

Call Sign: KA4EJQ
Allison L Lake
Brookfield CT 06804

Call Sign: N1KPY
Frederick A Pachaly
Brookfield CT 068040809

Call Sign: KB1EVG
Felicia R O Donohue-
Pachaly
Brookfield CT 068040809

**FCC Amateur Radio
Licenses in Brookfield
Center**

Call Sign: W1DZS
Tore N Anderson
49 High Ridge Rd
Brookfield Center CT
06805

Call Sign: KA1EUD
George N Crocker
29 Powder Horn Hill
Brookfield Center CT
06805

Call Sign: N1CII
William F Bethke
81 Whisconier Rd
Brookfield Center CT
06805

Call Sign: KC1WW
John R Marcin
5 Woodland Ter
Brookfield Center CT
06804

**FCC Amateur Radio
Licenses in Brooklyn**

Call Sign: KC1ZM
Robert D Young
69 Allen Hill Rd
Brooklyn CT 06234

Call Sign: W1AWS
David A Kowolenko
575 Allen Hill Rd
Brooklyn CT 06234

Call Sign: N1QLU
Matthew R Kivela
766 Allen Hill Rd
Brooklyn CT 06234

Call Sign: KB1PRX
Keith P Gregoire
441 Allen Hill Road
Brooklyn CT 06234

Call Sign: KT1NG
Tad A Church
12 B Fairway Dr
Brooklyn CT 06234

Call Sign: K1JPH
Keith L Knowlton
30 Canterbury Rd
Brooklyn CT 06234

Call Sign: W1BRF
Keith L Knowlton
30 Canterbury Rd
Brooklyn CT 06234

Call Sign: KB1SBA

Mark A Johola
164 Christian Hill Rd
Brooklyn CT 06234

Call Sign: KA1VNY
Antonio P Therrien Ii
314 Christian Hill Rd
Brooklyn CT 06234

Call Sign: KA1VVI
Joseph J Therrien
314 Christian Hill Rd
Brooklyn CT 06234

Call Sign: WA1YRZ
David J Kowolenko
37 Dawn Dr
Brooklyn CT 06234

Call Sign: K1CPU
David R Brumbaugh
202 Day St
Brooklyn CT 06234

Call Sign: KA1VYR
Hilary B Nelson
79 Fitzgerald Rd
Brooklyn CT 06234

Call Sign: KB1WRN
Amie M Polverari
122 Fortin Dr
Brooklyn CT 06234

Call Sign: KA1BKL
Thomas J Sullivan
272 Gorman Rd
Brooklyn CT 06234

Call Sign: KA1ILZ
Louise E Billings
272 Gorman Rd
Brooklyn CT 06234

Call Sign: KB1UWB

Luke W Green
15 Green Dr
Brooklyn CT 06234

Call Sign: KA1ZUR
Stephen M Chesnowitz
293 Hartford Rd
Brooklyn CT 06234

Call Sign: KA1ZUV
Jeanne M Chesnowitz
293 Hartford Rd
Brooklyn CT 06234

Call Sign: N1BBI
Gary M Peck
34 Hartford Road
Brooklyn CT 06234

Call Sign: KA1HSB
James H Lennon
70 Old Kimball Rd
Brooklyn CT 06234

Call Sign: WB1DXY
Joseph Stanley
Paradise Lake
Brooklyn CT 06234

Call Sign: KA1HID
Violet J Sandholm
Box 846 Route 6
Brooklyn CT 06234

Call Sign: KB1DRY
Brian N Caya
151 South Main St
Brooklyn CT 06234

Call Sign: KA1QED
Olison L Best
209 Tatnic Rd
Brooklyn CT 06234

Call Sign: WB1AQM

Robert E Best
209 Tatnic Rd
Brooklyn CT 06234

Call Sign: KB1SHR
Patricia R Luboda
252 Tatnic Rd
Brooklyn CT 06234

Call Sign: N1TAO
William F Welz Jr
93 Tripp Hollow Rd
Brooklyn CT 06234

Call Sign: W1CJ
Charles P Jaworski
362 Tripp Hollow Rd
Brooklyn CT 062342323

Call Sign: KB1TIW
Kenneth J Rutt
Brooklyn CT 06234

Call Sign: K1RAX
Kenneth J Rutt
Brooklyn CT 06234

FCC Amateur Radio Licenses in Burlington

Call Sign: KB1WSD
Jonathan J Glastris
42 Barberry Dr
Burlington CT 06013

Call Sign: WA1YJE
Gary W Richards
58 Barberry Dr
Burlington CT 06013

Call Sign: KA1KHN
Richard W Crowe
104 Belden Rd
Burlington CT 06013

Call Sign: KB1FV
Mark D Brasche
118 Belden Rd
Burlington CT 06013

Call Sign: WA1RHT
William S Robotham Jr
14 Blueberry Ln
Burlington CT 06013

Call Sign: K1FVQ
Raymond A Berggren
15 Brookside Dr
Burlington CT 06013

Call Sign: WB1CAR
Walter R Zaniewski
39 Burlwood Dr
Burlington CT 060132502

Call Sign: KA1PKJ
Bruce G Mullen
89 Canton Rd
Burlington CT 06013

Call Sign: WB1DAR
Ralph R Mele
15 Charles Pl
Burlington CT 06013

Call Sign: KA1MNX
Marc M Mele
15 Charles Place
Burlington CT 06013

Call Sign: K1NFE
Aniello L Depascale
19 Charles Place
Burlington CT 06013

Call Sign: KB1IZY
Jason E Rama
22 Cider Mill Rd
Burlington CT 06013

Call Sign: K1DOD
Jason E Rama
22 Cider Mill Rd
Burlington CT 06013

Call Sign: N1YZS
John Sway
46 Covey Rd
Burlington CT 06013

Call Sign: N1ASH
Russell T Butts
224 Covey Rd
Burlington CT 06013

Call Sign: WB1GIY
Roger S Durant
14 Cricket Ln
Burlington CT 06013

Call Sign: WA1WEU
Thomas A Carmody
18 Daniel Trace
Burlington CT 06013

Call Sign: K1TAC
Thomas A Carmody
18 Daniel Trace
Burlington CT 06013

Call Sign: NQ1K
John P Larson
34 Donna Dr
Burlington CT 06013

Call Sign: KB1IBM
Louis M Calvo Jr
27 Eastshore Blvd
Burlington CT 06013

Call Sign: WB1CAV
John M Zaniewski
30 George Washington
Tpke
Burlington CT 06013

Call Sign: KA1YQU
David P Czerwinski
161 George Washington
Tpke
Burlington CT 06013

Call Sign: KB1GOZ
David P Czerwinski
161 George Washington
Tpke
Burlington CT 06013

Call Sign: KA1CZ
David P Czerwinski
161 George Washington
Tpke
Burlington CT 06013

Call Sign: W1RFI
Edward F Hare Jr
304 George Washington
Tpke
Burlington CT 06013

Call Sign: KB1EIC
Benjamin P Budnik
13 Gilbert Lane
Burlington CT 06013

Call Sign: W1BEN
Benjamin P Budnik
13 Gilbert Lane
Burlington CT 06013

Call Sign: N1PRP
David C Poppel
35 Gilbert Lane
Burlington CT 060132114

Call Sign: KB1HY
Peter L Budnik
13 Gilbert Ln
Burlington CT 06013

Call Sign: W1BEN
Burlington Hills Contest
Club
13 Gilbert Ln
Burlington CT 06013

Call Sign: KA1URM
Arthur C Geisel
35 Heather Ln
Burlington CT 06013

Call Sign: W1RQF
Michael A Iacovazzi
47 Hunters Crossing
Burlington CT 06013

Call Sign: KA1BED
Willard B Green Iii
22 Jerome Ave
Burlington CT 06013

Call Sign: KA1QNT
Joseph F Furnari
Johnny Cake Mountain Rd
Burlington CT 06013

Call Sign: KG6FT
James E Bransfield
10 Laurel Crest
Burlington CT 06013

Call Sign: K1QYG
Ronald J Bumstead
76 Lyon Rd
Burlington CT 060131313

Call Sign: WB1EXU
John J Holleran
9 Merritt Woods
Burlington CT 06013

Call Sign: WA1ZIQ
Ernest G Glastris
72 Nassahegan Dr
Burlington CT 06013

Call Sign: WA1CVN
David G Grossmann
57 Nepaug Rd
Burlington CT 06013

Call Sign: W1CKC
Christian H Robison
2 Oak St
Burlington CT 06013

Call Sign: KB1MPH
David A Yudelson
8 Old Field Rd
Burlington CT 06013

Call Sign: WB1CLF
Robert W Kenefick
10 Orchard Rd
Burlington CT 06013

Call Sign: KA1SZU
Nancy L Goodwin
56 Pine Hill Rd
Burlington CT 06013

Call Sign: N1FNH
Harold C Goodwin
56 Pine Hill Rd
Burlington CT 06013

Call Sign: W1VD
Jay B Rusgrove
15 Polly Dan Rd
Burlington CT 06013

Call Sign: N1BTU
David C Lillibridge
Rt 4
Burlington CT 06013

Call Sign: WO0DIE
Thomas L Calo
29 Savarese Lane
Burlington CT 06013

Call Sign: W1RM
G Peter Chamalian
81 Savarese Ln
Burlington CT 06013

Call Sign: WB1ADL
Roberta J Chamalian
81 Savarese Ln
Burlington CT 06013

Call Sign: KA1SOD
Paul L Lyons
35 School St
Burlington CT 06013

Call Sign: WX1SKY
Michael J Boucher
277 Spielman Hwy
Burlington CT 06013

Call Sign: KB1RNA
Michael J Boucher
43 Stage Coach Rd
Burlington CT 06013

Call Sign: WA1ZJP
Edward Bendza Jr
23 Stagecoach Rd
Burlington CT 06013

Call Sign: N1CWT
Richard H St Laurent
82 Stagecoach Rd
Burlington CT 06013

Call Sign: N1DYW
Thomas R Carbone
3 Stanwich Lane
Burlington CT 060132011

Call Sign: NF1U
Frederick W Rosenbaum
11 Stone Rd
Burlington CT 06013

Call Sign: KB1AEF
Daniel D Positano
7 Stony Hill Rd
Burlington CT 06013

Call Sign: KA1VCA
Brian A Topolski
40 Taine Mountain Rd
Burlington CT 060131912

Call Sign: WA1BOZ
Carl J Russo
106 Taine Mountain Road
Burlington CT 06013

Call Sign: KB1RHP
Mark F Augustine
22 Vineyard Rd
Burlington CT 06013

Call Sign: W1BL
Alan J Blank
37 W Chippens Hill Rd
Burlington CT 06013

Call Sign: N1OLV
Carlos E Mason
185 W Chippens Hill Rd
Burlington CT 06013

Call Sign: KA1WWP
Tammy Beth Ubides
2 Yorkshire Way
Burlington CT 06013

FCC Amateur Radio Licenses in Byram

Call Sign: KA1GIY
Stanley E Olszewski
142 Mead Ave
Byram CT 06830

Call Sign: KA1POA
Kathy J Williams
C/O Mitchell Vhf
Canaan CT 06018

Call Sign: W1NED
John W Post
Rfd 1 North Elm St
Canaan CT 06018

Call Sign: KB1IND
William C Palmer
29 Old Turnpike Rd S
Canaan CT 06018

Call Sign: N1KVA
Robert S Gray
132 Quinn St Apt 9
Canaan CT 060182053

Call Sign: WB3FRZ
Francis J Golden
21 Railroad St Box 202
Canaan CT 06018

Call Sign: KA1BYU
C Gunnar Svala
Geer Village - 77 S Canaan
Rd - Apt 109
Canaan CT 06018

Call Sign: KD2ICK
Richard Lang
342 Salisbury Rd
Canaan CT 06018

Call Sign: WA1BAM
Richard J Phair
260 W Main St
Canaan CT 06018

Call Sign: N1MTF

Keith N Beebe
W Main St 227
Canaan CT 06018

Call Sign: KB1LQM
Joseph London
Canaan CT 060180853

Call Sign: KB1UMP
Joshua Hammel
151 Barstow Rd
Canterbury CT 06331

Call Sign: KB1TMQ
Curtis A Troup
305 Brooklyn Rd
Canterbury CT 06331

Call Sign: N1FBF
Robert D Murphy Ii
20 Campbell Dr
Canterbury CT 063311807

Call Sign: NQ1I
Nicholas J Carchidi
7 Hanover Rd
Canterbury CT 06331

Call Sign: KB1GLS
Phillip S Zapadka
102 Lisbon Rd
Canterbury CT 06331

Call Sign: KB1SHO
Jesse M Yeager
482 Lisbon Rd
Canterbury CT 06331

Call Sign: KA1ZNZ
Denis Morin
95 N Canterbury Rd
Canterbury CT 06331

Call Sign: N1PUD
Dean B Wysocki
220 Albany Tnpk
Canton CT 06019

Call Sign: KB1SSJ
Dean B Wysocki
220 Albany Tnpk
Canton CT 06019

Call Sign: K5GMX
William A Conner Jr
8 Andrew Dr
Canton CT 06019

Call Sign: KB1GAZ
Keith E Viering
35 Atwater Rd
Canton CT 06019

Call Sign: KB1GBA
Kevin A Viering
35 Atwater Rd
Canton CT 06019

Call Sign: WA2AHA
Timothy E Healy
11 Bidwell Farm Rd
Canton CT 060193600

Call Sign: WB1GHL
Mark I Jurras Iii
43 Cherry Brook Rd
Canton CT 06019

Call Sign: KB1DBI
Alan D Normand
75 E Hill Rd
Canton CT 060192215

Call Sign: N1SSK

Stephen P Chomak
81 E Hill Rd
Canton CT 06019

Call Sign: K1ERU
Michael Adajian
232 E Hill Rd
Canton CT 06019

Call Sign: KB1JDI
Dale Nies
41 East Hill Rd
Canton CT 060192418

Call Sign: N1TCQ
George H Parson
4 Frey Rd
Canton CT 06019

Call Sign: W1GHP
George H Parson
4 Frey Rd
Canton CT 06019

Call Sign: KA2MUH
David Bondanza
109 High Valley Dr
Canton CT 06019

Call Sign: KA1OBK
Stephen R Griswold
116 Lawton Rd
Canton CT 060190074

Call Sign: N1OVE
Robert J Donovan Jr
3 Noja Trail
Canton CT 06019

Call Sign: N1OVF
Lorraine F Donovan
3 Noja Trail
Canton CT 06019

Call Sign: KB1TIG

Michael N Sesto
26 Old Mill
Canton CT 06019

Call Sign: KB1SCU
Michael L Campbell
9 Pond Road
Canton CT 06019

Call Sign: W1CUT
Michael L Campbell
9 Pond Road
Canton CT 06019

Call Sign: N1NHV
Eugene A White
20 Sunrise Dr
Canton CT 06019

Call Sign: WB2SGI
Kenneth R Jones
8 Uplands Dr
Canton CT 06019

Call Sign: KA1WEB
Jessica E Littmann
2 Whitney Ln
Canton CT 06019

Call Sign: KB1VTH
Athan E Chekas
114 Wright Rd
Canton CT 06019

Call Sign: W1VNG
William W R Hughes Jr
Canton CT 06019

Call Sign: KB1KIW
Paul A Gregory
Canton CT 06019

**FCC Amateur Radio
Licenses in Centerbrook**

Call Sign: KB1PJW
Jon S Korper
9 Charles Street
Centerbrook CT 06409

Call Sign: K1DNR
Charles S Socci
124 Main Street
Centerbrook CT 06409

**FCC Amateur Radio
Licenses in Central Village**

Call Sign: KB1CRN
Glen L J Cote
25 East Main St
Central Village CT
063320126

Call Sign: NR1O
David E Hawley Sr
76 School St
Central Village CT 06332

**FCC Amateur Radio
Licenses in Chaplin**

Call Sign: WB1AVW
Joseph W Miller Jr
Rt 198 235
Chaplin CT 06245

Call Sign: KB1VMJ
Christopher S Komuves
122 Bedlam Rd
Chaplin CT 062352324

Call Sign: KB1VMH
James W Randall
27 Canada Lane
Chaplin CT 06235

Call Sign: KB1VCC
Robert E Demaio
132 Chappell St

Chaplin CT 06235

Call Sign: KB1VMK
Broc N Smith
203 Davis Rd
Chaplin CT 06235

Call Sign: KB0UGR
Edward A Murray
416 Hampton Rd.
Chaplin CT 062352646

Call Sign: KB1JAI
Edward A Murray
416 Hampton Rd.
Chaplin CT 062352646

Call Sign: N1ULI
David R Morris
23 Mountain Laurel Lane
Chaplin CT 06235

Call Sign: WB1CCN
Robert W Prochorchik
376 Phoenixville Rd.
Chaplin CT 06235

Call Sign: WB1GLS
Merrill R Lucia
Ridge Rd
Chaplin CT 06235

Call Sign: W1DMY
James H Gifford
37 Singleton Rd
Chaplin CT 062352229

Call Sign: N1HUE
Robert P Tamburri Jr
210 Singleton Rd
Chaplin CT 062352221

Call Sign: KB1VML
Jason P Chilly
90 South Bedlam Rd

Chaplin CT 06235

Call Sign: KB1VMG
Robert K Williamson Jr
210 Tower Hill Rd
Chaplin CT 06235

Call Sign: KB1VMI
Pietro Fiasconaro
68 Willimantic Rd
Chaplin CT 06235

FCC Amateur Radio Licenses in Cheshire

Call Sign: KA1WCN
Halleem Coury Jr
5 Amherst Dr
Cheshire CT 06410

Call Sign: KB1BZT
Seth G Dalton
15 Amherst Dr
Cheshire CT 06410

Call Sign: KA1NYF
Amy C Hart
1015 Amherst Pl
Cheshire CT 06410

Call Sign: K2HVA
Michael A Terminiello
19 Applewood Dr
Cheshire CT 06410

Call Sign: KB1TNQ
Daniel S Fusco
400 Beacon Hill Dr
Cheshire CT 06410

Call Sign: AB1LU
Daniel S Fusco
400 Beacon Hill Dr
Cheshire CT 06410

Call Sign: KB1TTQ
Frank M Fusco
400 Beacon Hill Dr
Cheshire CT 06410

Call Sign: KB1TTR
Mark L Fusco
400 Beacon Hill Dr
Cheshire CT 06410

Call Sign: KA1QYC
Alfred L Ehrenfels
687 Boulder Rd
Cheshire CT 06410

Call Sign: KB1SIP
Edward J Hines
30 Brentwood Dr
Cheshire CT 06410

Call Sign: W3ICE
James T Nawracay
75 Briar Ct
Cheshire CT 06410

Call Sign: N1OKO
Lynne S Baxter
13 Brigadoon Dr
Cheshire CT 06410

Call Sign: KB1TBQ
Matthew A Petroff
11 Brookfield Ct
Cheshire CT 06410

Call Sign: N1EPU
Kevin R Webster
1564 Byam Rd
Cheshire CT 06410

Call Sign: N6OBQ
Jay M Sabot
80 Charter Oak Dr
Cheshire CT 06410

Call Sign: WJ1B
Harold R Kramer
77 Cherry St
Cheshire CT 06410

Call Sign: KB1PXM
Kw Amateur Radio Club
77 Cherry Street
Cheshire CT 06410

Call Sign: N1EPU
Kw Amateur Radio Club
77 Cherry Street
Cheshire CT 06410

Call Sign: WA1ZSH
Joseph J Gilgallon Sr
1509 Cheshire St
Cheshire CT 06410

Call Sign: N1RDT
Philip Fostini
1248 Cheshire Street
Cheshire CT 06410

Call Sign: W1LAS
Waterbury Amateur Radio
Club
30 Cliff Edge Cir
Cheshire CT 06410

Call Sign: N1ABY
Craig S Kalley
30 Cliff Edge Circle
Cheshire CT 06410

Call Sign: W1NFG
George D Steele
150 Cook Hill Rd 3317
Cheshire CT 064103763

Call Sign: W1UKL
Martha J Steele
150 Cook Hill Rd 3317
Cheshire CT 06410

Call Sign: W1AKJ
George E Johnson
150 Cook Hill Rd 4223
Cheshire CT 06410

Call Sign: WA1ZLF
Robert E Moseley
150 Cook Hill Rd Apt 1307
Cheshire CT 06410

Call Sign: WX1P
Roy E M Reid
150 Cook Hill Rd Apt 2301
Cheshire CT 064103763

Call Sign: KB1IR
John J Hryb Iii
150 Cook Hill Rd Apt 4225
Cheshire CT 06410

Call Sign: W1FD
Frank S Darmofalski
150 Cook Hill Rd Apt 6210
Cheshire CT 064103777

Call Sign: W1ULF
Gertrude P Hines
100 Cranberry Ln
Cheshire CT 06410

Call Sign: KB1UTM
Donald J Shanly Jr
208 Cricket Court
Cheshire CT 06410

Call Sign: WA1DJS
Donald J Shanly Jr
208 Cricket Court
Cheshire CT 06410

Call Sign: WB1ASG
Richard H Tenney
46 Currier Way
Cheshire CT 06410

Call Sign: KB1FWZ
Erik M Pedersen
101 Curve Hill Rd
Cheshire CT 06410

Call Sign: KA1IHM
Charlan K Walston
180 Curve Hill Rd
Cheshire CT 06410

Call Sign: KA1WF
Edwin D Walston
180 Curve Hill Rd
Cheshire CT 06410

Call Sign: WB0OLY
Clark N Eid Jr
53 Dundee Dr
Cheshire CT 06410

Call Sign: KB1UWR
Barry C Spaulding
809 E Johnson Ave
Cheshire CT 06410

Call Sign: KA1UEC
Julie A Troyer
159 Eastgate Dr
Cheshire CT 06410

Call Sign: KA1UFA
Christopher M Troyer
159 Eastgate Dr
Cheshire CT 06410

Call Sign: W1HHP
Harry C Marotto Sr
840 Farmington Dr
Cheshire CT 064104216

Call Sign: N1IWJ
James Kalach
81 Flagler Ave
Cheshire CT 06410

Call Sign: N1WHX
Charles K Falsey
33 Glenbrook Dr
Cheshire CT 06410

Call Sign: KA1TMA
Jeffrey E Fowler
945 Marion Rd
Cheshire CT 06410

Call Sign: KA1OZM
Peggy D Hoffmann
145 Paul Ney Rd
Cheshire CT 06410

Call Sign: KC1PB
Arthur D Siegel
24 Goldenrod Ct
Cheshire CT 06410

Call Sign: KB1KFD
Richard P Borecki
1147 Marion Road
Cheshire CT 06410

Call Sign: WZ1P
Gotfred O Hoffmann
145 Paul Ney Rd
Cheshire CT 06410

Call Sign: KA1QQG
Richard S Hylinski
330 Greenwood Dr
Cheshire CT 06410

Call Sign: KA1KJV
Robert D Trussell
134 Mountain Rd
Cheshire CT 06410

Call Sign: KB1HWF
James M Hackett
319 Payne Dr
Cheshire CT 06410

Call Sign: K1NMO
David S Mac Donald
26 Hemlock Ridge Rd
Cheshire CT 06410

Call Sign: KB1LQ
Stanley J Slogeris
1697 Musso View Ave
Cheshire CT 06410

Call Sign: KB1RHQ
Eugene G Caputo
1203 Peck Lane
Cheshire CT 06410

Call Sign: AB1AE
David M Sack
60 Hidden Place
Cheshire CT 06410

Call Sign: WA1CBG
Joseph J Lamontagne
1320 Notch Rd
Cheshire CT 06410

Call Sign: WA1UFZ
Victor J Coppa
354 Radmere Rd
Cheshire CT 06410

Call Sign: K1DMS
David M Sack
60 Hidden Place
Cheshire CT 06410

Call Sign: N1RBC
Richard J De Vito
138 Oak Ave
Cheshire CT 06410

Call Sign: KA1ZFI
Jane R Capo
454 Riverside Dr
Cheshire CT 06410

Call Sign: KB1ZT
Laurence S Levine
5 Inverness Ct
Cheshire CT 06410

Call Sign: K1OVG
Edward C Duda
48 Old Towne Rd
Cheshire CT 06410

Call Sign: N1HQS
Andrew J Levada
640 S Brooksvale Rd
Cheshire CT 06410

Call Sign: K1TGX
Gerald S Molaver
50 Inverness Ct
Cheshire CT 06410

Call Sign: K1VDZ
Joseph C Lanoue
82 Old Towne Rd
Cheshire CT 06410

Call Sign: N1GDV
Robert B Weed
200 S Meriden Rd
Cheshire CT 06410

Call Sign: KA1YGD
Scott E Howland
530 Jarvis St
Cheshire CT 06410

Call Sign: WY3S
Charles B Cooper
233 Patton Dr
Cheshire CT 064104235

Call Sign: N1OKN
Elbert K Linsley
295 S Rolling Acres Rd
Cheshire CT 06410

Call Sign: WA1ZSI
Joseph J Gilgallon Jr
27 Saint Joseph St
Cheshire CT 06410

Call Sign: WA1LIT
Richard T Slusarz
499 Sharon Dr
Cheshire CT 06410

Call Sign: KA1PEM
John E Deko Jr
12 Sheila Ln
Cheshire CT 06410

Call Sign: K1FRD
Dean W Spencer
341 South Rolling Acres
Cheshire CT 06410

Call Sign: W1DQ
John J Elengo
50 Surrey Dr
Cheshire CT 064102813

Call Sign: K1AMI
Allan E Cooper
180 Timber Ln
Cheshire CT 06410

Call Sign: KA1SIO
Arthur D Lowden
205 Timber Ln
Cheshire CT 06410

Call Sign: KA1ZCF
Jessica A Brodnik
258 Timber Ln
Cheshire CT 06410

Call Sign: N1LEQ
John S Freismuth
55 Towpath Ln
Cheshire CT 06410

Call Sign: W1HAP
Ario P Hadinoto
56 Trout Brook Rd
Cheshire CT 064101250

Call Sign: KA1SL
Ronald D Hansen
1775 Tuttle Ave
Cheshire CT 06410

Call Sign: KA1DMS
Robert N D Amato Jr
55 Vanessa Court
Cheshire CT 06410

Call Sign: K1RJC
Richard J Castaldo
981 Ward Ln
Cheshire CT 06410

Call Sign: N1SRO
Richard J Frantz Jr
1672 Waterbury Rd
Cheshire CT 06410

Call Sign: KA1WCP
Gregory B Wasko
2159 Waterbury Rd Rear
Cheshire CT 06410

Call Sign: KB1FWH
John J O Luanaigh
300 Weatherside Road
Cheshire CT 064104330

Call Sign: N1BVW
John J O Luanaigh
300 Weatherside Road
Cheshire CT 064104330

Call Sign: WA2PNB
Kevin A Coogan
393 Westland Ave
Cheshire CT 06410

Call Sign: KB1SMM
Xiaopeng R Niu
10 Whispering Hollow Ct
Cheshire CT 06410

Call Sign: K1NIU
Xiaopeng R Niu
10 Whispering Hollow Ct
Cheshire CT 06410

Call Sign: W1IDB
John S Purtill Jr
353 Wiese Rd
Cheshire CT 06410

Call Sign: KB1VAU
Richard M Levy
478 Woodpond Road
Cheshire CT 06410

Call Sign: W1RML
Richard M Levy
478 Woodpond Road
Cheshire CT 06410

Call Sign: KB1FZY
Thomas F Veivia
Cheshire CT 06410

Call Sign: KB1SAQ
Jonathan E Hasson
Cheshire CT 06410

Call Sign: N1VGR
Christopher F Slater
1537 Byam Rd
Chesire CT 06410

Call Sign: KB1EYA
Michael S Nitkowski
1628 Plank Rd
Chesire CT 06410

Call Sign: N1JPN

Robert J Hourigan
805 Resivior Rd
Chesire CT 06410

Call Sign: WB2KAF
Gary B Stevens
20 Castle View Dr
Chester CT 06412

FCC Amateur Radio Licenses in Chester

Call Sign: KA1OSY
Vincent Nevins
28 Castleview Dr
Chester CT 06412

Call Sign: KB1JVT
Robert L Dona
7 Ferry Rd
Chester CT 06412

Call Sign: W1FDX
Jack E Gretta
41 Gilbert Hill Rd
Chester CT 06412

Call Sign: AB1BV
Peter W Harding
41 Gilbert Hill Road
Chester CT 06412

Call Sign: KB1QLJ
Charles F Greeney Jr
4 Grote Rd
Chester CT 06412

Call Sign: KA1WXE
Harvey E Redak
21 Laurel St
Chester CT 06412

Call Sign: KB1HDS
Charles W Tower
1 Liberty St

Chester CT 06412

Call Sign: N1TUA
William F Horan
9 Maple St Apt G
Chester CT 06412

Call Sign: WA1TOU
Albert G Pearson
272 Middlesex Ave
Chester CT 064121226

Call Sign: W1KZX
Richard R Carlson
3 S Wig Hill Rd Aaron
Manor
Chester CT 064121106

Call Sign: KA1JTJ
William J Zimmerman
34 Straits Rd
Chester CT 06412

Call Sign: KA1SMK
Robert S Rayner
117 W Main St
Chester CT 06412

Call Sign: W1IUN
Gordon B Hayes
317 W Main St Apt 9203
Chester CT 06412

Call Sign: KA1KQM
Carroll S Dewey
Chester CT 06412

FCC Amateur Radio Licenses in Clinton

Call Sign: N1ISO
George C Heck Iii
220 Airline Road
Clinton CT 06413

Call Sign: KA1FAH
Patricia A Quackenbush
35 Brickyard Road
Clinton CT 06413

Call Sign: K1JBS
Robert J O Connell
12 Bright Hill Dr
Clinton CT 06413

Call Sign: N1RFG
Martha B O Connell
12 Bright Hill Dr
Clinton CT 06413

Call Sign: N1REA
Barbara P Clark
8 Brookside Dr
Clinton CT 06413

Call Sign: WB0MSE
Ralph Clark
8 Brookside Dr
Clinton CT 06413

Call Sign: W1TKG
Carl L Bixby Jr
36 Brush Hill Rd
Clinton CT 06413

Call Sign: KA1PKO
Edmund H Davenport
32 Cedar Island Ave
Clinton CT 06413

Call Sign: KA1GKG
Nancy D Finch
22 Chittenden Hill
Clinton CT 064131228

Call Sign: WA1YCE
Peter B Finch
22 Chittenden Hill
Clinton CT 06413

Call Sign: KB1FSB
Maryrose F Shamp
13 Circle Drive
Clinton CT 064131213

Call Sign: WB4OYC
Harold E Hill
3 Coachlight Dr
Clinton CT 06413

Call Sign: KV1Q
William G Russell Iv
5 Colonial Dr
Clinton CT 06413

Call Sign: K1LBB
Robert C Butcher
133a Cow Hill Road
Clinton CT 06413

Call Sign: WA1SDX
Byron A Baisden
85 Cowhill Rd
Clinton CT 06413

Call Sign: N1ES
Erwin R Sparks
6 Deerfield Dr
Clinton CT 064131012

Call Sign: KB1GYH
Comer A Wilson
7 Deerfield Dr
Clinton CT 06413

Call Sign: W1WZZ
Comer A Wilson
7 Deerfield Dr
Clinton CT 06413

Call Sign: KB1BMD
Erik D Armando
13 Elmwood Way
Clinton CT 06413

Call Sign: KB1CG
David S Kendle
25 Fairy Dell Rd
Clinton CT 06413

Call Sign: KB1HDU
Robert C Butcher Jr
14 Fir Ridge Rd
Clinton CT 06413

Call Sign: KB1HDV
Susan K Butcher
14 Fir Ridge Rd
Clinton CT 06413

Call Sign: K1BCB
Robert C Butcher Jr
14 Fir Ridge Rd
Clinton CT 06413

Call Sign: K1SKB
Susan K Butcher
14 Fir Ridge Rd
Clinton CT 06413

Call Sign: WA2JGW
Gloria Fessina
36 Founders Rd
Clinton CT 06413

Call Sign: WR2J
Antonio Fessina
36 Founders Rd
Clinton CT 06413

Call Sign: KB1RBE
Trudie M Cardone
57 Founders Village
Clinton CT 06413

Call Sign: N1BVI
Trudie M Cardone
57 Founders Village
Clinton CT 06413

Call Sign: KA1NQS
George G Spratt
33 Grove Way
Clinton CT 06413

Call Sign: AA1UO
Mark A Capuano
1 Hemlock Hill Rd
Clinton CT 06413

Call Sign: W1OCN
William H Huggins
26 Heritage Cir
Clinton CT 06413

Call Sign: W1RLW
Morris E Austin
27 High St
Clinton CT 06413

Call Sign: W1BDN
Loren E Baker
60 High St
Clinton CT 06413

Call Sign: WA1DCK
Douglas M French
24 Indian Dr
Clinton CT 06413

Call Sign: W1RJA
North East Weak Signal
Group
52 Jefferson Cir
Clinton CT 06413

Call Sign: WZ1V
Ronald J Klimas
52 Jefferson Cir
Clinton CT 06413

Call Sign: W1SAM
Larry R Sorensen
94 Kelseytown Rd
Clinton CT 06413

Call Sign: K0IKR
Benedict W Bangerter
109 Kelseytown Rd
Clinton CT 06413

Call Sign: KA1NRA
Margaret S Krny
13 Kings Grant Rd
Clinton CT 06413

Call Sign: N1JVU
Philip Krupnikoff
30 Mallard Ln
Clinton CT 06413

Call Sign: KB1KKV
John J Sevanick
11 Neck Rd
Clinton CT 06413

Call Sign: KB1JSJ
Jeff A Yacobucci
19 Oak Ridge Dr
Clinton CT 06413

Call Sign: AA1AT
Gregory G Di Sisto
17 Old Post Rd 1
Clinton CT 06413

Call Sign: N1OFG
Thomas B Wissenbach
5 Oscela Trl
Clinton CT 06413

Call Sign: NV1M
James T Clinton
9 Pratt Rd
Clinton CT 06413

Call Sign: WA1FRG
John W Conover
18 Shore Grove Dr
Clinton CT 06413

Call Sign: WB1EBJ
Mark A Marsella
67 Shore Rd
Clinton CT 06413

Call Sign: N1PLS
Randy S Naimo
29 Stanton Rd
Clinton CT 06413

Call Sign: KD1L
Ronald W Parker
20 Uncas Rd
Clinton CT 06413

Call Sign: N1WZW
James A Falconer
11 Valley Rd
Clinton CT 06413

Call Sign: N1TTY
Richard D Kook
24 Valley Rd
Clinton CT 06413

Call Sign: N1TTZ
Eric M Kook
24 Valley Rd
Clinton CT 06413

Call Sign: N3AGA
Charles I Bruder
11 Waterside Ln
Clinton CT 06413

Call Sign: W1JTD
Harold A Bubb
83 West Main St
Clinton CT 06413

Call Sign: KA1NHQ
Christopher G Peterson
6 Whitewood Rd
Clinton CT 06413

Call Sign: KA1PQS
Jeremy D Hansen
1 Woodcock Ln
Clinton CT 06413

FCC Amateur Radio Licenses in Cobalt

Call Sign: KB1WA
Vernon E Curneal
12 Grist Mill Ln
Cobalt CT 06414

FCC Amateur Radio Licenses in Colchester

Call Sign: KB1FYE
Francis M Kurowski
5 Ackley Cemetery Rd
Colchester CT 06415

Call Sign: N1GLK
Wasiley Kisley
27 Alexander Dr
Colchester CT 06415

Call Sign: KG4VRB
Christian A Beisel
35 Alexander Rd
Colchester CT 06415

Call Sign: KB1NSZ
Dennis F Dolan
452 Amston Rd
Colchester CT 06415

Call Sign: W1PYZ
Dennis F Dolan
452 Amston Rd
Colchester CT 06415

Call Sign: W1RKW
Robert K Walter Iii
55 Ashley Lane

Colchester CT 06415

Call Sign: KB1UMN
Richard E Joaquin
20 Balaban Rd 610
Colchester CT 06415

Call Sign: KA1DM
David W Menge
65 Blackledge Drive
Colchester CT 064152543

Call Sign: N1JMM
James C Thisdale
39 Boretz Rd
Colchester CT 06415

Call Sign: WA1USF
Keith A Post
51 Buckley Hill Rd
Colchester CT 06415

Call Sign: KA1EBZ
John P Conshick
375 Cabin Rd
Colchester CT 06415

Call Sign: KA1YFA
Laura R Sonnichsen
46 Cemetery Rd
Colchester CT 06415

Call Sign: N1PSH
Peter J Blackman
52 Cherry Tree Ln
Colchester CT 06415

Call Sign: KA1EHO
Kenneth H Reinholdt
187 Chestnut Dr
Colchester CT 06415

Call Sign: KB1UAH
Marc R Warren
64 Clark Rd

Colchester CT 06415

Call Sign: KB1ULS
Karie L Parker
64 Clark Rd
Colchester CT 06415

Call Sign: KB1RR
Rudolf I Breisach
74 Colchester Commons
Colchester CT 06415

Call Sign: N1MUG
Henry C Setterstrom
96 Colchester Commons
Colchester CT 06415

Call Sign: N1IHX
David J Thomas
80 David Dr
Colchester CT 06415

Call Sign: KA1RMV
Edmond A Fontaine
164 Elm St
Colchester CT 06415

Call Sign: N1SPT
Jacqueline M Fontaine
164 Elm St
Colchester CT 06415

Call Sign: KB1NUM
Colchester EOC
315 Halls Hill Rd
Colchester CT 06415

Call Sign: KF6QIU
Robert W Newton
156 Halls Hill Rd 5
Colchester CT 06415

Call Sign: W1JKV
Kenniston W Lord Sr
12 Kennedy Dr

Colchester CT 06415

Call Sign: N1GUN
Peter A Lewis
86 Lake Hayward Road
Colchester CT 06415

Call Sign: AA1ZC
Robert S Williams
67 Linwood Ave
Colchester CT 06415

Call Sign: KB1OTK
Norman R Gustafson
120 Longwood Drive
Colchester CT 06415

Call Sign: K1EMD
Norman R Gustafson
120 Longwood Drive
Colchester CT 06415

Call Sign: N1RVX
Walter J Cox Jr
256 Middletown Rd
Colchester CT 06415

Call Sign: WA1CAP
Daniel M Wrobel
668 Middletown Rd.
Colchester CT 06415

Call Sign: KA1JZ
Mary J Graves
44 Midland Dr
Colchester CT 06415

Call Sign: NN1G
David J Benson
32 Mountain Rd
Colchester CT 06415

Call Sign: KA1TEF
Christian J Tyrrell
48 Nelkin Road

Colchester CT 06415

Call Sign: KA1LLX
Daniel S Black
42 O Connell Rd
Colchester CT 064150303

Call Sign: KB1NCE
Stephen E Loomis
5 Sandy Lane
Colchester CT 06415

Call Sign: W1ZKE
Donald W Standish
175 Standish Rd
Colchester CT 06415

Call Sign: WB1CKL
John F Grottole
100 Stollman Rd
Colchester CT 06415

Call Sign: N2ANX
Barry R Bruun
47 Ude Way
Colchester CT 064151784

Call Sign: WA1JMP
Ronald R Benatti
102 Van Cedarfield Rd
Colchester CT 06415

Call Sign: KB1CCP
Wethersfield Amateur
Radio Society
198 Waterhole Road
Colchester CT 06415

Call Sign: KE1DX
Angelo S Arcaria
198 Waterhole Road
Colchester CT 06415

Call Sign: KA2FFI
Richard S Hill

368 West Rd
Colchester CT 06415

Call Sign: N1WWY
David N Tiefenbrunn
315 Westchester Road
Colchester CT 06415

Call Sign: N1XQP
Adelaide M Tiefenbrunn
315 Westchester Road
Colchester CT 06415

Call Sign: N1XDP
Leo P Tupay
40 Windham Ave
Colchester CT 06415

Call Sign: AL7QS
Douglas J Mc Bournie
Colchester CT 064150451

Call Sign: N1MCF
Jo Ann Di Pietro
Colchester CT 06415

Call Sign: N1MCH
Sean Hoskins
Colchester CT 06415

Call Sign: N1ZHS
Charles R Dutch
Colchester CT 06415

Call Sign: WH6SW
Kevin M Mc Manus
Colchester CT 06415

Call Sign: AA1XN
Sean Hoskins
Colchester CT 06415

**FCC Amateur Radio
Licenses in Colebrook**

Call Sign: WV1E
Adam S Macek
107 Beech Hill Rd
Colebrook CT 060210211

Call Sign: KB1GAG
Alan J Chidester
32 Cobb City Rd
Colebrook CT 06021

Call Sign: KB1GAH
Joel C Chidester
32 Cobb City Rd
Colebrook CT 06021

Call Sign: KB1GAI
Seth C Chidester
32 Cobb City Rd
Colebrook CT 06021

Call Sign: N1EFY
Hillarie B Speziale
467 Colebrook Rd - P O
Box 10
Colebrook CT 06021

Call Sign: N1QVE
Harry E White
199 Sandy Brook Rd
Colebrook CT 06021

Call Sign: N1UNJ
Ann M White
199 Sandy Brook Rd
Colebrook CT 06021

Call Sign: W1ALF
Norman F Thompson
467 Smith Hill Rd
Colebrook CT 06021

**FCC Amateur Radio
Licenses in Collinsville**

Call Sign: N1PSW

Lawrence E Sullivan
20 Bunker Hill Rd
Collinsville CT 06019

Call Sign: N1RSH
Richard J Grayson
139 Bunker Hill Rd
Collinsville CT 06022

Call Sign: KB1QZS
Susan L Bentley
69 Dunne Ave
Collinsville CT 06019

Call Sign: W1VPF
Susan L Bentley
69 Dunne Ave
Collinsville CT 06019

Call Sign: KB1KJD
Donald R Walck
79 Dunne Ave
Collinsville CT 06019

Call Sign: WA1UQC
David J Faucher Sr
23 Freedom Dr
Collinsville CT 06022

Call Sign: KA1VDJ
John M Kulick
9 Gemstone Dr
Collinsville CT 06022

Call Sign: KA1CAS
Walter R Hampton Jr
46 Gildersleeve Avenue
Collinsville CT 06022

Call Sign: N1SPL
Anupam Narula
154 Robbin Dr
Collinsville CT 06022

Call Sign: K1EHU

James M Dexter
93 Torrington Ave
Collinsville CT 06022

Call Sign: W1IAR
James M Dexter
93 Torrington Ave
Collinsville CT 060193326

FCC Amateur Radio Licenses in Columbia

Call Sign: N1TJL
Kenneth N Nickerson
34 Cards Mill Rd
Columbia CT 06237

Call Sign: KA1MXI
Dennis M Hoddinott
47 Doubleday Rd
Columbia CT 06237

Call Sign: N1IDP
Brian G Ingalls
53 Erdoni Road
Columbia CT 06237

Call Sign: KB1EXP
Bruce E Brettschneider
2 Hickory Ct
Columbia CT 06237

Call Sign: N1XN
Andrew P Weise
28a Hunt Rd
Columbia CT 06237

Call Sign: KD1JB
Kurt R Johnson
30 Lake Rd
Columbia CT 06237

Call Sign: WB1EIO
Robert C Wason
42 Lake Rd

Columbia CT 062371316

Call Sign: N1JCZ
Gary J Tettelbach
103 Lake Rd
Columbia CT 06237

Call Sign: N1UJN
Waldon R Melo
28 Lake Rd Box 178
Columbia CT 06237

Call Sign: N1PSG
Warren R Hartzell
8 Lake Ridge Dr
Columbia CT 06237

Call Sign: NX1Q
Andrejs I Emars
4 Latham Hill Rd
Columbia CT 06237

Call Sign: KB1MMU
John J Edenburn
211 Pine St
Columbia CT 06237

Call Sign: K1ZDO
Bryant A Andrews
99 Route 87
Columbia CT 06237

Call Sign: KF1K
Charles R Logan
576 Rt 87
Columbia CT 062371414

Call Sign: KA1AQN
Edgar E Sellers
Rt 87
Columbia CT 06237

Call Sign: N1JMF
James F Cushing
279 Rte 66

Columbia CT 06237

Call Sign: KA1TBT
David R Chase
144 Rte 87
Columbia CT 06237

Call Sign: W1HNX
John C Pokorny
9 Thompson Hill Rd
Columbia CT 06237

Call Sign: N1GPC
Peter J Nosal
6 Wells Woods Rd
Columbia CT 062371525

Call Sign: K1BV
Theodore F Melinosky Jr
12 Wells Woods Rd
Columbia CT 062371525

Call Sign: KB1THV
Gary W Root
16 West St
Columbia CT 06237

Call Sign: KG1D
Lester R Kemble Jr
26 West St
Columbia CT 06237

Call Sign: W1HHR
John C Sullivan
62 Whitney Rd
Columbia CT 06237

Call Sign: WB1FTR
Frances K Sullivan
62 Whitney Rd
Columbia CT 06237

Call Sign: N1JBT
William B Halverson
45a Whitney Rd

Columbia CT 06237

FCC Amateur Radio Licenses in Cornwall

Call Sign: KA1YTE
Gordon S Cady
60 Furnace Brook Rd
Cornwall CT 06753

Call Sign: KA1HHN
Tony E Downer
Jewel St Box 162
Cornwall CT 06753

Call Sign: KB1TRN
David E Beasley
82 Valley Rd
Cornwall CT 06753

Call Sign: AA1BZ
David E Beasley
82 Valley Rd
Cornwall CT 06753

FCC Amateur Radio Licenses in Cornwall Bridge

Call Sign: N1YBO
Axel Gronborg
108 Pretchard Rd
Cornwall Bridge CT 06754

Call Sign: N1YBP
Birthe E Gronborg
108 Pretchard Rd
Cornwall Bridge CT 06754

Call Sign: KA1OEQ
Joshua A Reynolds
Rfd 1
Cornwall Bridge CT 06754

FCC Amateur Radio Licenses in Cos Cob

Call Sign: KB1HCH
Timothy J Wall
95 Bible St Apt 2
Cos Cob CT 068070251

Call Sign: N1ZKD
Bryan A Scales
7 Calbalbo Pl
Cos Cob CT 06807

Call Sign: KB1HZB
Christopher W Southern
453 E Putnam Ave 4b
Cos Cob CT 06807

Call Sign: KB1WCJ
Richard A Hofer
44 Frontier Rd
Cos Cob CT 06807

Call Sign: KA1JPF
John T Gallagher
65 Gregory Rd
Cos Cob CT 06807

Call Sign: KA3NQJ
Theodore L Dysart
41 Harold St Apt 4
Cos Cob CT 06807

Call Sign: N1LQV
Larry Liaw
7 Nassau Pl
Cos Cob CT 06807

Call Sign: K1JQX
Samuel R Santoro
3 North St
Cos Cob CT 06807

Call Sign: N1FZG
Hugh K Evans

78 River Rd
Cos Cob CT 06807

Call Sign: N1HAH
Carol A Rogers
70 River Road
Cos Cob CT 068072516

Call Sign: WA0VPG
Richard L Flaskegaard
98 Valley Rd #5
Cos Cob CT 06807

Call Sign: AB1PG
Marcin Toczyolowski
10 Valleywood Rd
Cos Cob CT 06807

FCC Amateur Radio Licenses in Coventry

Call Sign: K1JCL
Alan J Koepke
1976 Boston Tpke
Coventry CT 06238

Call Sign: N1YON
Corey R Freeto
2000 Boston Tpke
Coventry CT 06238

Call Sign: KB1RNC
Willard A Beane
68 Brenda Lane
Coventry CT 06238

Call Sign: KB1AIR
Stephen G Sandberg
57 Brewster St
Coventry CT 06238

Call Sign: KA1VRH
Michael D Hoyt
127 Broadway
Coventry CT 06238

Call Sign: AA1KD
Karl Heinz Merscher
684 Cedar Swamp Rd
Coventry CT 06238

Call Sign: K1ZD
Residence Radio Club
684 Cedar Swamp Rd
Coventry CT 06238

Call Sign: K1ZZ
David G Sumner
684 Cedar Swamp Rd
Coventry CT 06238

Call Sign: KA1ZD
Linda A Churma Sumner
684 Cedar Swamp Rd
Coventry CT 06238

Call Sign: N1UCI
Deryn A Sumner
684 Cedar Swamp Rd
Coventry CT 06238

Call Sign: N1YU
Marijan M Miletic
684 Cedar Swamp Rd
Coventry CT 06238

Call Sign: AD4UC
Colin J Thomas
684 Cedar Swamp Road
Coventry CT 062381062

Call Sign: KB1ODW
Stephen I Williams
205 Cooper Lane
Coventry CT 06237

Call Sign: N1JWT
John F Kobetitsch
149 Cornwall Dr
Coventry CT 06238

Call Sign: N1YOM
Michael T Vance
484 Geraldine Dr
Coventry CT 06238

Call Sign: KA1VVH
Lauren E Felix
436 Hemlock Point
Coventry CT 06238

Call Sign: KB1SHN
Dick J Bluto
181 Hemlock Point Dr
Coventry CT 06238

Call Sign: N1XGW
Dan S Goodin
411 Hemlock Pt
Coventry CT 06238

Call Sign: N1UCL
John E Brazeau
15 Hickory Dr
Coventry CT 06238

Call Sign: KB1ITX
Stephen W Pacholski
114 High St
Coventry CT 06238

Call Sign: KB1KTW
William J Burinskas
101 Highland Rd
Coventry CT 06238

Call Sign: N1XJP
David C Rappe
153 Lancaster Rd Box 280
Coventry CT 06238

Call Sign: KB1KTX
William A Snyder
64 Laurel Trail
Coventry CT 06238

Call Sign: N1FHE
Dudley A Brand
1630 Main St
Coventry CT 06238

Call Sign: KB1BSK
David E La More
163 Main St Apt 72
Coventry CT 062381620

Call Sign: KA1LYR
Kenneth P Donovan
299 Pine Lake Dr
Coventry CT 06238

Call Sign: KB1RRS
Barbara L Andrew
1921 Main St
Coventry CT 06238

Call Sign: N1OBX
Anthony Ochtera
1712 Main Street
Coventry CT 06238

Call Sign: N1YOL
Trista L Mc Getrick
230 Plains Rd
Coventry CT 06238

Call Sign: KB1RVU
Lisa A Beauchamp
1921 Main St
Coventry CT 06238

Call Sign: K1YYX
James K Rau
305 Merrow Rd
Coventry CT 06238

Call Sign: KG4FKS
Roger L Story Jr
Po Box 391
Coventry CT 06238

Call Sign: K1TQH
John C Burchard Jr
2883 Main St
Coventry CT 06238

Call Sign: N1TYP
Gary S Groskritz
139 N River Rd
Coventry CT 06238

Call Sign: N1TMV
David E La More
68 Prospect St
Coventry CT 062383129

Call Sign: KB1GAC
Grace E Burchard
2883 Main St
Coventry CT 06238

Call Sign: K1AOX
Henry W Kent Sr
91 N School Rd
Coventry CT 06238

Call Sign: KH6JUK
Timothy M Dwyer
766 Pucker St
Coventry CT 062383445

Call Sign: KB1GAD
Jayne Burchard
2883 Main St
Coventry CT 06238

Call Sign: KA1KTH
Carol A Kent
91 N School Rd
Coventry CT 06238

Call Sign: WD1U
Joseph A Faraci
190 Richmond Rd
Coventry CT 062381699

Call Sign: KB1GAE
John C Burchard Iii
2883 Main St
Coventry CT 06238

Call Sign: N1NXK
Clark R Kent
1640 North River Rd
Coventry CT 06238

Call Sign: KB1SHJ
Lori J Boucher
349 Ripley Hill Rd
Coventry CT 06238

Call Sign: KB1GAF
Katherine J Burchard
2883 Main St
Coventry CT 06238

Call Sign: KB1WQT
Jeffrey M Foran
65 Parker Bridge Rd
Coventry CT 06238

Call Sign: KB1SHQ
Trena Gale
349 Ripley Hill Rd
Coventry CT 06238

Call Sign: KA1WCK
Christopher T Solomon
3204 Main St
Coventry CT 06238

Call Sign: KA1KMJ
Ann L Polcari
153 Pine Lake Dr
Coventry CT 06238

Call Sign: KC1HK
Laurence Diamond
498 Root Rd
Coventry CT 06238

Call Sign: KB1FCM
Owen M Swift
89 S River Rd
Coventry CT 062381510

Call Sign: WA8EMT
Richard L Merrifield
45 Seneca Trail
Coventry CT 06238

Call Sign: W8CIA
Richard L Merrifield
45 Seneca Trail
Coventry CT 06238

Call Sign: KB1FBS
Edward Werner Cook
534 Silver St
Coventry CT 06238

Call Sign: W1UK
James P Parise
164 South River Rd
Coventry CT 06238

Call Sign: KA1RWY
Katherine D Allison
1552 South St
Coventry CT 06238

Call Sign: WB1GCM
Robert S Allison
1552 South St
Coventry CT 06238

Call Sign: N1FPM
Maurice J Du Bois
220 Springdale Ave
Coventry CT 06238

Call Sign: NR1L
Kevin S Hilinski
184 Stone Bride Road
Coventry CT 06238

Call Sign: KB1CWO
Lawrence J Margavich
20 Wall St
Coventry CT 062383143

Call Sign: KB1VPX
Richard P Collette
36 Windswept Way
Coventry CT 06238

Call Sign: KC1EW
Kenneth W Carvell
98 Woodland Rd
Coventry CT 062380019

Call Sign: WA1LD
Laurence Diamond
22 Zeya Drive
Coventry CT 06238

Call Sign: KA1RMQ
Kelly B Carvell
Coventry CT 06238

Call Sign: KA1TBR
Brian K Carvell
Coventry CT 06238

Call Sign: N1ERK
Richard L Merrifield
Coventry CT 06238

Call Sign: W0EMT
Richard L Merrifield
Coventry CT 06238

**FCC Amateur Radio
Licenses in Cromwell**

Call Sign: KB1NAJ
Sean J Angus
21 Alexander Dr
Cromwell CT 06416

Call Sign: KC1OK
Demetrio L Tindoy
6 Beechwood Cir
Cromwell CT 06416

Call Sign: KB1UUB
Jonathan R Beatty
9 Bellaire Manor
Cromwell CT 06416

Call Sign: W1WRL
Gregory D Ginnetti
15 Black Haw Dr
Cromwell CT 064161236

Call Sign: N1FHV
Gregory D Ginnetti
66 Black Haw Dr
Cromwell CT 064161236

Call Sign: N1OTV
Wayne B Ripley
4 Briadon Dr
Cromwell CT 06416

Call Sign: N1IUT
Noel S Smith
5 Carroll Pl
Cromwell CT 06416

Call Sign: KB1QQP
William J Miller
8 Centerwood Drive
Cromwell CT 06416

Call Sign: KA1WDS
Lori A Manwaring
18 Chelsea Dr
Cromwell CT 06416

Call Sign: WA1BRN
Emilio J Branciforte
8 Diane Dr
Cromwell CT 06416

Call Sign: N1EBU
Alex P Lentini
1 Doering Dr
Cromwell CT 06416

Call Sign: KA1KRO
George F Damroth
1 Edgewood Street
Cromwell CT 06416

Call Sign: KA1UAY
Stephanie L Carta
206 Evergreen Rd
Cromwell CT 06416

Call Sign: KB1KWD
Nicholas E Tomassone
119 Field Rd
Cromwell CT 06416

Call Sign: KA1PLF
Ervin W Peterson Jr
28 Goodrich Ave
Cromwell CT 06416

Call Sign: N1XGD
Emily E Pember
1 Greendale Ave
Cromwell CT 06416

Call Sign: K1LW
Carl V Brinck Jr
20 Hicksville Rd
Cromwell CT 06416

Call Sign: N1NWQ
Jason M Fox
4 Highridge Rd
Cromwell CT 06416

Call Sign: N1LOC
John Liseo
43 Hillside Road
Cromwell CT 06416

Call Sign: KA1UFG
Daniel B Armet
26 Iron Gate Ln
Cromwell CT 06416

Call Sign: KB1PUT
Eric M Parham
367 Main St
Cromwell CT 06416

Call Sign: N1UTF
Kristine M Haswell
373 Main St
Cromwell CT 06416

Call Sign: N1XKO
Christin E Bloor
462 Main St
Cromwell CT 06416

Call Sign: KB1NAI
Paul M Rice
563 Main St
Cromwell CT 06416

Call Sign: KS1V
George R Johnson
583 Main St
Cromwell CT 064161428

Call Sign: N1VEK
Francisco J Perrotta
613 Main St
Cromwell CT 06416

Call Sign: K1NQJ
James A Post
629 Main St
Cromwell CT 06416

Call Sign: KA1AAA
Raymond C Sabb Sr
586 Main Street
Cromwell CT 06416

Call Sign: K1PL
Paul Lux
5 North Rd
Cromwell CT 064162614

Call Sign: WB1EOS
Patricia G Lux
5 North Rd
Cromwell CT 064162614

Call Sign: KB1PJV
Town Of Cromwell Eoc
5 North Rd
Cromwell CT 06416

Call Sign: W1CWL
Town Of Cromwell Eoc
5 North Rd
Cromwell CT 06416

Call Sign: WB1DWZ
Maxime P Toussaint
5 Oak Rd
Cromwell CT 06416

Call Sign: WB2VZW
Christine A Meyers
3 Pine Ct
Cromwell CT 06416

Call Sign: KB2ZZI
Steven J Damon
25 Raymond Pl
Cromwell CT 06416

Call Sign: N1ZZS
Robert A Yordan
2 Riverdale Dr
Cromwell CT 06416

Call Sign: KB1FQP
Robert A Yordan Jr
2 Riverdale Drive
Cromwell CT 06416

Call Sign: WA1NKZ
Roger Dauphinais
3 Ronald Dr
Cromwell CT 06416

Call Sign: KB1KIO
Roy Charity
213 Rook Rd
Cromwell CT 06416

Call Sign: KB1KIP
Pamela Charity
213 Rook Rd
Cromwell CT 06416

Call Sign: KD1LS
Michael A Dickerson
2 Shanley Ct
Cromwell CT 06416

Call Sign: WA1K
John P Chapman
147 Shunpike Rd
Cromwell CT 06416

Call Sign: KD1PH
Mark K Vincent
34 Shunpike Rd Suite 249
Cromwell CT 06416

Call Sign: NX1V
Mark K Vincent
34 Shunpike Rd Suite 249
Cromwell CT 06416

Call Sign: KB1GEX
Michael J Chadukiewicz
161 Shunpike Road
Cromwell CT 06416

Call Sign: WB1EGY
Mitchell C Sawicki
5 St. John's Court
Cromwell CT 06416

Call Sign: K1CBV
Herbert G Clark
59 Timber Hill Rd
Cromwell CT 06416

Call Sign: N1PVY
Angelo T Fazio
8 Vincy Dr
Cromwell CT 06416

Call Sign: WA1VNO
James F Mullen
210 Winthrop Blvd
Cromwell CT 06416

Call Sign: N1RGI
Lawrence C Lentini
131 Woodland Dr
Cromwell CT 06416

Call Sign: KD1EN
Steven P Knapp
Cromwell CT 06416

Call Sign: W4TAI
Raymond C Sabb Sr
Cromwell CT 06416

Call Sign: W1TAI
Raymond C Sabb Sr
Cromwell CT 06416

Call Sign: N1TAI
Raymond C Sabb Sr
Cromwell CT 06416

FCC Amateur Radio Licenses in Danbury

Call Sign: KA1RVV
Thomas H Andersen
90 A Clapboard Ridge Rd
Danbury CT 068113643

Call Sign: N1KNO

William J Schlichtig
6 Advocate Pl
Danbury CT 06810

Call Sign: WB2DSO
Arthur D Miller
46 Aunt Hack Rd
Danbury CT 06811

Call Sign: WA1JGA
David M Coelho
52 Aunt Hack Road
Danbury CT 06811

Call Sign: KB1OLY
Jason L Jett
317 Avalon Lake Rd
Danbury CT 06810

Call Sign: KB1LIJ
Jennifer A Mackenzie
33 Ball Pond Rd
Danbury CT 06811

Call Sign: KB1MBM
Terry R Lynch
75 Ball Pond Rd
Danbury CT 06811

Call Sign: K1TRL
Terry R Lynch
75 Ball Pond Rd
Danbury CT 06811

Call Sign: KF6AJ
Steven M Simons
33 Ball Pond Road
Danbury CT 06811

Call Sign: W1SMS
Steven M Simons
33 Ball Pond Road
Danbury CT 06811

Call Sign: W1QJ

Louis A Parascondola
75 Ball Pond Road
Danbury CT 06811

Call Sign: AA1RE
Rocco Cardillo Jr
14 Barnum Ct
Danbury CT 06810

Call Sign: N2OQL
Donald E Daggett Jr
72 Bear Mountain Road
Danbury CT 06811

Call Sign: N1DJK
Duane P Kish
8 Belair Dr
Danbury CT 06811

Call Sign: WV1V
Victor A Schirmer
15 Belmont St
Danbury CT 068106424

Call Sign: N1VTK
Joe Marie L Garcia
1 Benson Dr
Danbury CT 06810

Call Sign: K2BGU
John A Vossler
147 Boulevard Dr
Danbury CT 06810

Call Sign: W1DQH
Richard A Mahler
11-1 Boulevard Dr
Danbury CT 06810

Call Sign: KA1TZN
Kevin J Holick
4 Brookside Padanaram Rd
Danbury CT 06811

Call Sign: N1NNH

George A Hoyt Jr
18 Buckskin Hghts Dr
Danbury CT 06811

Call Sign: KA1MIS
Mark R Burke
31 Bullet Hill Road
Danbury CT 068112906

Call Sign: N1NEE
Leonard A Casacalenda Jr
19 Candlelight Dr
Danbury CT 06810

Call Sign: KB1ILY
Harlan A Ford
159 Candlewood Park
Danbury CT 06811

Call Sign: W1QH
Harlan A Ford
159 Candlewood Park
Danbury CT 06811

Call Sign: KB1FKM
John F Mccarthy Jr
11 Cannonball Drive
Danbury CT 06810

Call Sign: KB2TWI
Ionel Vilceanu
12 Capitola Rd
Danbury CT 06811

Call Sign: KB1LQV
Oscar P Fuller Jr
32 Carriage House Dr
Danbury CT 06810

Call Sign: KO1F
Oscar P Fuller Jr
32 Carriage House Dr
Danbury CT 06810

Call Sign: KA1WGA

John A Fegley
111 Chambers Rd
Danbury CT 06811

Call Sign: KA1VEE
Sheron L Mottola
7b Cherry St
Danbury CT 06810

Call Sign: N1KUN
Brian P Sullivan
3 Chestnut Trail
Danbury CT 06811

Call Sign: N1ZUH
Michael K Skrocki
179 Clapboard Ridge Road
Danbury CT 06811

Call Sign: KA1KS
John P Ziegler
25 Clayton Rd
Danbury CT 06811

Call Sign: N1NKX
Chris A Ziegler
25 Clayton Rd
Danbury CT 06811

Call Sign: KB1FGP
Kurt Wetter
Co Ken Glezer Old
Neversink Rd
Danbury CT 06811

Call Sign: N1HSL
Linda E Votier
75 Coalpit Hill Rd 10
Danbury CT 06810

Call Sign: WB1CTW
Martin R Paul
6 Crestwood Dr
Danbury CT 06811

Call Sign: K1NP
Martin R Paul
6 Crestwood Dr
Danbury CT 06811

Call Sign: KE4DNR
Angela Blakely
27 Crows Nest Lane Unit
18r
Danbury CT 06810

Call Sign: KA1NEX
Richard J Meskill
27 Crows Nest Lane Unit
20d
Danbury CT 068102019

Call Sign: N2FEX
Rostyslaw O Slabicky
105 Deer Hill Ave
Danbury CT 06810

Call Sign: WC1AAX
Danbury Dept Of Civil
Preparedness
155 Deer Hill Ave
Danbury CT 06810

Call Sign: KB1EWI
Rodney T Quinn
130-11 Deer Hill Ave
Danbury CT 06810

Call Sign: KB1PXC
Danbury Civil Preparedness
155 Deer Hill Ave - Attn
Paul Estefan
Danbury CT 06810

Call Sign: KX1DXR
Danbury Civil Preparedness
155 Deer Hill Ave - Attn
Paul Estefan
Danbury CT 06810

Call Sign: W1DST
Walter B Mitchell
8 Dogwood Dr
Danbury CT 06811

Call Sign: N2KUG
Douglas E Spelman
8 Durham Road
Danbury CT 06811

Call Sign: W1FRJ
George W Waters
44 E Hayestown Rd 2
Danbury CT 06811

Call Sign: KC1HG
Benino Fragomeli
90 E Pembroke Rd
Danbury CT 06811

Call Sign: KB4ANR
Jaime Carvajal
85 East Dr
Danbury CT 06810

Call Sign: N1WZB
Vincent R Pisani
3105 Eaton Court
Danbury CT 06811

Call Sign: KB1NCU
Robert Gasiorowski
2904 Eaton Ct
Danbury CT 06811

Call Sign: W1ACR
John S Gruss
20 Edgewood St
Danbury CT 06810

Call Sign: N1IXI
Brian P Gruss
22 Edgewood St
Danbury CT 06810

Call Sign: KA1ODF
Robert F Mc Gran
2 Elmcrest Dr
Danbury CT 06811

Call Sign: WB1EDT
David A Abrantes
12 Fanton Rd
Danbury CT 06811

Call Sign: KA1VZF
Peter A Hylenski
13 Firelight Dr
Danbury CT 06810

Call Sign: N1RHJ
Kenneth E Nawyn
13 Fleetwood Dr
Danbury CT 06810

Call Sign: N1JXN
Seth S Boughton
54 Forty Acre Mt Rd
Danbury CT 06811

Call Sign: KB1HMI
Peter J Porrazzo
124 Forty Acre Mt Rd
Danbury CT 068113354

Call Sign: KB1SOQ
Albert A Russo
220 Franklin St Ext
Danbury CT 06811

Call Sign: N1JXI
Kenneth E Stilson
5 Golden Hill Ln
Danbury CT 06811

Call Sign: WA1CJM
Richard M Rand
17 Golden Hill Rd
Danbury CT 06811

Call Sign: KB1NFJ
Peter J Perrone
75 Great Plain Rd
Danbury CT 06811

Call Sign: N1SEZ
Paul R Levin
132 Great Plain Rd
Danbury CT 06811

Call Sign: N1TFO
Suzanne J Levin
132 Great Plain Rd
Danbury CT 06811

Call Sign: KD1PL
Paul R Levin I
132 Great Plain Rd
Danbury CT 06811

Call Sign: W9QZY
Suzanne J Levin
132 Great Plain Rd
Danbury CT 06811

Call Sign: N1SEZ
Paul R Levin
132 Great Plain Rd
Danbury CT 06811

Call Sign: N1SUZ
Suzanne J Levin
132 Great Plain Rd
Danbury CT 06811

Call Sign: WQ1I
Paul R Levin
132 Great Plain Rd
Danbury CT 06811

Call Sign: KB1WUT
Dana B Cassel
191 Great Plain Rd
Danbury CT 06811

Call Sign: KB1EYH
John J Casey
247 Great Plain Rd
Danbury CT 06811

Call Sign: KA1IJC
Charles F Bovaird Jr
4 Gregory St
Danbury CT 06811

Call Sign: N1NRP
Jay V Albano Sr
8 Harmony Street
Danbury CT 06810

Call Sign: N1OEN
Christian C Roberts
20 Harrison St
Danbury CT 06810

Call Sign: KB1TJL
Susan E Nyahay
16 Harvard Rd
Danbury CT 06810

Call Sign: N1DFM
John F Pitrelli
34 Hawley Road
Danbury CT 06811

Call Sign: KB1VIR
Alexandrea M Composto
6 Hawthorne Cove Rd
Danbury CT 06811

Call Sign: KB1VLO
Henry Abbott Tech
Amateur Radio Club
21 Hayestown Ave
Danbury CT 06811

Call Sign: K1HAT
Henry Abbott Tech
Amateur Radio Club
21 Hayestown Ave

Danbury CT 06811

Call Sign: KK1DF
Donald E Ferguson
2005 Heartwood Lane
Danbury CT 068112620

Call Sign: WA1LWF
Frederick H Max
5004 Heartwood Lane
Danbury CT 068112623

Call Sign: KA1JOM
William B Hoyer Jr
7 Hickory St
Danbury CT 06810

Call Sign: AA1GO
Michael G Jacobs
84 Highland Ave
Danbury CT 06810

Call Sign: KB1IJV
Michael J Erickson
11 Hillandale Rd
Danbury CT 06811

Call Sign: N1HGU
Edward H Burger Jr
37 Hollandale Road
Danbury CT 06811

Call Sign: N1RXP
Thomas A Nejame
4 Huntington Dr
Danbury CT 06811

Call Sign: KA1MPR
Richard D Vanasse
17 Indian Head Rd
Danbury CT 06811

Call Sign: NO0Q
Scott E Shipper
10 Ironwood Dr

Danbury CT 068112703

Danbury CT 06810

Danbury CT 06811

Call Sign: KB1KBI
Edward R Shipper
10 Ironwood Dr
Danbury CT 06811

Call Sign: N1HHE
Joseph F Callahan
1 Lexington Ave
Danbury CT 06810

Call Sign: KB1EWG
Jon J Secor
81a Merrimac St Apt 3
Danbury CT 06810

Call Sign: N1CBI
Anthony M Fraticelli
32 Jefferson Ave
Danbury CT 06810

Call Sign: KB1SSU
Vernon B Hadden Iii
14 Locust Ave Apt 1a
Danbury CT 06810

Call Sign: KB1CJX
Barry A Pirro
235 Middle River Rd
Danbury CT 06811

Call Sign: WA2IZQ
Mark A Hertzberg
19 Joes Hill Road
Danbury CT 06811

Call Sign: KB1ILX
Douglas A Bushong
38 Locust Ave Apt 2
Danbury CT 06810

Call Sign: N1IGU
Joanna D Tinios
55 Mill Plain Rd 15-1
Danbury CT 06811

Call Sign: KG4IQI
Mary A Sirchia
14 Josh Lane
Danbury CT 06811

Call Sign: KB1SQH
Daniel W Barile
51 Main St -24
Danbury CT 06810

Call Sign: NU2K
Engelbertus Oosterveer
55 Mill Plain Rd 30
Danbury CT 06810

Call Sign: KC2HUV
Michael F Scalia
41 Judith Drive
Danbury CT 06811

Call Sign: N1LAV
Norman A Wolfe
18 Mallory St 2
Danbury CT 06810

Call Sign: KB1BNB
Neil J Marceau
55 Mill Plain Rd Bldg 31
Danbury CT 06810

Call Sign: WB3DLG
Jeffrey A Cantor
37 King Street
Danbury CT 06811

Call Sign: KE1H
Joseph M Davidson
26 Maplewood Dr
Danbury CT 06811

Call Sign: N1PJO
Martin D Cohn
113 Mill Ridge Rd
Danbury CT 06811

Call Sign: KB1TT
Stephen J Potpan
147 Kohanza Street
Danbury CT 06811

Call Sign: N1NIT
Kate D Davidson
26 Maplewood Dr
Danbury CT 06811

Call Sign: N1NY
Robert D Dugan
43 Morris St
Danbury CT 06810

Call Sign: KB1WKZ
Russell F Chartier
92 Lake Ave
Danbury CT 06810

Call Sign: N1EKH
Jack M Lesser
6 Marion St
Danbury CT 06810

Call Sign: N1PJH
Melissa M Dugan
43 Morris St
Danbury CT 06810

Call Sign: N1ZSE
John J Riska
6 Lancey St

Call Sign: K1IRG
John J Mc Keever
11 Mendes Rd

Call Sign: W1UZ
Robert D Dugan
43 Morris St

Danbury CT 06810

Call Sign: KC9NNI
Matthew L Hadaway
2 Mountainview Terrace
Unit 5214
Danbury CT 06810

Call Sign: K1QJG
Edward Lasky
45 Myrtle
Danbury CT 06810

Call Sign: KB1ONB
Takao Yanase
C/O K Kihara 5 Nabby Rd
Unit A50
Danbury CT 06811

Call Sign: AB1GS
Yasuhiro Yamada
C/O K Kihara 5 Nabby Rd
Unit A50
Danbury CT 06811

Call Sign: KR2Y
Yasuhiro Yamada
C/O K Kihara 5 Nabby Rd
Unit A50
Danbury CT 06811

Call Sign: AB1HP
Takao Yanase
C/O K Kihara 5 Nabby Rd
Unit A50
Danbury CT 06811

Call Sign: KB1SOT
Natalie Dos Santos
19 Nancy Dr
Danbury CT 06811

Call Sign: N1SVK
Dana E Dewan
3a Oak Ln

Danbury CT 06811

Call Sign: W1KAY
Kenneth M Gleszer
26 Old Neversink Rd
Danbury CT 06811

Call Sign: KB1TWE
Martin J Folan
99 Old Neversink Rd
Danbury CT 06811

Call Sign: KB1DGQ
Henry W Szymanski Jr
3 Olive St
Danbury CT 06810

Call Sign: W1DFD
Henry W Szymanski Jr
3 Olive St
Danbury CT 06810

Call Sign: KA1NSP
Glenn A Mc Kague
35 Olympic Drive
Danbury CT 06810

Call Sign: N1XD
Glenn A Mckague
35 Olympic Drive
Danbury CT 06810

Call Sign: W1HBR
Hugh L Lupo
4 Overlook Dr
Danbury CT 06811

Call Sign: NI2B
Raoul Elton
60 Padanaram Rd 18
Danbury CT 06811

Call Sign: WS1I
Ann E Ross
60 Padanaram Rd Unit 18

Danbury CT 06811

Call Sign: KB1AGS
Radu Timosca
8 Parker St Apt 2
Danbury CT 06811

Call Sign: N1NEB
Louis F Andreko Sr
35 Patch St Apt C
Danbury CT 06810

Call Sign: KC0RHX
Joseph G Hartwell
6 Paul Street
Danbury CT 06810

Call Sign: N1GFE
Thomas A Goodwin
11 Prospect St
Danbury CT 06810

Call Sign: KC2SYT
Richard J Martucci
1303 Revere Rd
Danbury CT 06811

Call Sign: N1PCY
Jeremy A Schaefer
1902 Revere Road
Danbury CT 068112661

Call Sign: KA1PVV
Judith A Slater
4 Richter Dr
Danbury CT 06811

Call Sign: N1GS
George M Slater
4 Richter Dr
Danbury CT 068113453

Call Sign: N1NLA
Kristen A Slater
4 Richter Dr

Danbury CT 06811

Call Sign: KB1KIJ
Danbury Eoc Radio Club
4 Richter Dr
Danbury CT 068113453

Call Sign: KX1EOC
Danbury Eoc Radio Club
4 Richter Dr
Danbury CT 068113453

Call Sign: KB1WUR
Brian P Waldron
26 Ridge Rd
Danbury CT 06810

Call Sign: KB1WYT
Christine R Waldron
26 Ridge Rd
Danbury CT 06810

Call Sign: KB1WYU
Joseph S Waldron
26 Ridge Rd
Danbury CT 06810

Call Sign: KB1SXW
Michael D Orawsky Jr
5 Rodline Rd
Danbury CT 06811

Call Sign: N1OK
Michael D Orawsky Jr
5 Rodline Rd
Danbury CT 06811

Call Sign: KB1FYZ
Todd R Palmer
47 Rolf's Dr
Danbury CT 06810

Call Sign: KA2VAW
Michael Gallo
24 S King St

Danbury CT 06811

Call Sign: W1PJ
Shiro Sakai
50 Saw Mill Road (Unit 4325)
Danbury CT 06810

Call Sign: W6IMJ
Fumio Ikeda
50 Saw Mill Road Unit 4325
Danbury CT 06810

Call Sign: K1YG
Masaharu Yasumitsu
50 Saw Mill Road Unit 4325
Danbury CT 06810

Call Sign: KB1KED
John P Bucci
29 School House Dr.
Danbury CT 06811

Call Sign: N1WJF
Pasquale Cavalieri
157 Shelter Rk Rd 12
Danbury CT 06810

Call Sign: KB1GXC
Lawrence E Graham
151 Shelter Rock Rd 29
Danbury CT 06810

Call Sign: N1YXC
James P Andersen
200 Siboney Terrace
Danbury CT 06811

Call Sign: KA1LSL
Ralph J Johnson
11 Side Hill Ln
Danbury CT 06810

Call Sign: KB1STT
Roger A Mitchell
103 Sienna Dr
Danbury CT 06810

Call Sign: NG1R
Roger A Mitchell
103 Sienna Dr
Danbury CT 06810

Call Sign: KA1WSR
Brian Z Johnston
12 Sleepy Hollow Dr
Danbury CT 06810

Call Sign: KA1NLB
Tracy A Heron
24 South St
Danbury CT 06810

Call Sign: KB1BKC
Robert J Taylor
63 South St
Danbury CT 06810

Call Sign: KB1HYH
Eric L Johnson
14 South St 18
Danbury CT 06810

Call Sign: K1ELJ
Eric L Johnson
14 South St 18
Danbury CT 06810

Call Sign: KB1QM
Christopher E Vargo
10 South Street Unit 86
Danbury CT 06810

Call Sign: N1DVS
Kimberly L Manzi
4 Stable Dr
Danbury CT 068108223

Call Sign: N1USQ
Terry L Genaway
41 Stadley Rough Rd
Danbury CT 06811

Call Sign: N1CPA
Norman G Asmar
57 Stadley Rough Rd
Danbury CT 06811

Call Sign: W2MCJ
Thomas M Smith
31 Staple St - Hancock Hall
Room 122
Danbury CT 068106323

Call Sign: KB1MJF
Thomas Q Kimball
34 Stevens St Apt 2f
Danbury CT 06810

Call Sign: N1KZY
Roy W Hadden Jr
3 Stuart Dr
Danbury CT 068113622

Call Sign: N1BOG
William C Fleischer
21 Sunrise Rd
Danbury CT 06810

Call Sign: KB1SVC
Thayer C Syme
25 Sunrise Rd
Danbury CT 06810

Call Sign: W1FMM
Edmund C De Veaux
30 Tammany Trail
Danbury CT 06810

Call Sign: KA1WBA
Arvind N Bakhru
24 Tanglewood Dr
Danbury CT 06811

Call Sign: KB1LIK
Paul A Puccio
8 Timber Crest Dr
Danbury CT 06811

Call Sign: KA1GAF
Charles P Chelso
10 Tomlinson Ave
Danbury CT 06810

Call Sign: KB1US
Harold F Keenan Jr
85 Topstone Dr
Danbury CT 06810

Call Sign: KB1SOZ
Sally M Estefan
156 Triangle St
Danbury CT 06810

Call Sign: N1TEG
Michael G Hernandez Sr
126 Triangle St B18
Danbury CT 06810

Call Sign: KB1VVY
Ashley L Cwikla
14 Triangle Terrace Apt 3
Danbury CT 06810

Call Sign: N1NIS
Paul A Ziegler
30 Valerie Ln
Danbury CT 06811

Call Sign: KB9SSS
Dana L Hoggatt
10 Valley View Dr
Danbury CT 06810

Call Sign: N1GQR
Lee Steuber
40 Well Ave
Danbury CT 06810

Call Sign: WB1DSB
Donald Wicks
3 West Redding Rd
Danbury CT 06810

Call Sign: KB1BLY
Jeffrey D Hyer
66 Westville Ave
Danbury CT 06810

Call Sign: KA1PYL
Gerald E Keeler
115 Westville Ave
Danbury CT 06810

Call Sign: N1RLU
Robert W Gibb Jr
15 Whaley Street
Danbury CT 06810

Call Sign: KA1RBS
Francis J Bartholomew
164 White St
Danbury CT 06810

Call Sign: KA1VUW
Richard K Bennett
8 Wilson St Apt 2
Danbury CT 06810

Call Sign: KA1SMN
Sean R Votier
17 Woodbury Dr
Danbury CT 068103916

Call Sign: K1LTJ
Allan P Matthews
Danbury CT 06813

Call Sign: N1NBZ
Joseph C Simon Sr
Danbury CT 06813

Call Sign: NX8G

Gregory M Smith
Danbury CT 06813

Call Sign: W1MHT
Michael H Tjader Sr
Danbury CT 06813

Call Sign: KB1QAU
Andre J Boucher
Danbury CT 06813

Call Sign: WN1LEC
Rocco Cardillo Jr
Danbury CT 06813

Call Sign: KB1SOY
Paul D Estefan
Danbury CT 06813

Call Sign: KB1UQF
Patrick T Hackett
Danbury CT 06813

Call Sign: W1LSD
Patrick T Hackett
Danbury CT 06813

Call Sign: KQ2Y
Patrick T Hackett
Danbury CT 06813

**FCC Amateur Radio
Licenses in Danielson**

Call Sign: KB1GYQ
Bernard S Lovell
204 Bailey Hill
Danielson CT 06239

Call Sign: KB1ORW
Maureen E Frey
204 Bailey Hill Rd
Danielson CT 06239

Call Sign: WA1MNS

George F Bisson
304 Bailey Hill Rd
Danielson CT 062393424

Call Sign: KB1QVP
Mark L Edmonds
17 Brick House Rd
Danielson CT 06239

Call Sign: KB1QGZ
John-Mark S Edmonds
17 Brickhouse Rd
Danielson CT 06239

Call Sign: KB1HSS
Connecticut A. M. Society
37 Cady St
Danielson CT 06239

Call Sign: N1ROZ
Lawrence D Scott
42 Cranberry Bog
Danielson CT 06239

Call Sign: KW1AM
Connecticut A. M. Society
42 Cranberry Bog
Danielson CT 06239

Call Sign: K1NLX
Peter A Johnson
3029 David Ave
Danielson CT 06239

Call Sign: KB1VBY
Christy L Johnson
3029 David Ave
Danielson CT 06239

Call Sign: N7BEO
Christy L Johnson
3029 David Ave
Danielson CT 06239

Call Sign: KB1TMP

Charles P Weimer Iii
64 Edwardsen St
Danielson CT 06239

Call Sign: N1TYN
Gerald W Royce
30 Jolley Rd
Danielson CT 06239

Call Sign: KD1FK
Jeffrey C Lalumiere
33 Kent St
Danielson CT 06239

Call Sign: WD1F
Edgar R Lachance
29 L Homme St
Danielson CT 06239

Call Sign: K1ZFN
Syl Pauley Jr
68 L Homme St
Danielson CT 06239

Call Sign: K1BUZ
Dorothy J Hutchins
8 Maple Ct
Danielson CT 062391418

Call Sign: WA1YVX
Florence D La Belle
375 Maple St
Danielson CT 06239

Call Sign: NW1Q
Edward G Walsh
226 Maple Street
Danielson CT 06239

Call Sign: N1YFA
Hamilton L Gavitt
672 North Main St
Apt.C
Danielson CT 06239

Call Sign: KB1VCA
Brian R Gosper
64 Picabo St
Danielson CT 06239

Call Sign: KB1MOK
Robert A Ferriere
81 Picabo St
Danielson CT 06239

Call Sign: K1TTF
Robert A Ferriere
81 Picabo St
Danielson CT 06239

Call Sign: WB1AOC
Charles P Weimer Jr
3 Plainview Dr
Danielson CT 06239

Call Sign: N1XLM
Donald J Dumond
24 Plainview Dr
Daneielson CT 06239

Call Sign: K1AS
Alan R Sherman
44 Polly Ave
Danielson CT 06239

Call Sign: N1NUX
Sandra L Cote
1022 Providence Pike
Danielson CT 06239

Call Sign: KB1JDX
Vincenzo P Mazzarella
6 Ruth Street
Danielson CT 06239

Call Sign: KB1QFV
Eldon L Griffiths
685 S Frontage Rd
Danielson CT 06239

Call Sign: W1AV
Robert A Ruzzo
44 Schoonman Avenue
Danielson CT 06239

Call Sign: KB1QVD
Marvin L Harris
35 Steven St
Danielson CT 06239

Call Sign: N1RFV
Harold J Hendricks
6 Tunk City Rd
Danielson CT 06239

Call Sign: WH6MY
James R Miller
53 Waterman Street
Danielson CT 06239

Call Sign: KS1SSN
James R Miller
53 Waterman Street
Danielson CT 06239

Call Sign: WA2UOF
Bruce D Lundgren
488 Wauregan Road
Danielson CT 062394233

Call Sign: K2IOM
Gordon E Reese
111 Westcottd Rd Ron Calli
Health Ctr
Danielson CT 06239

**FCC Amateur Radio
Licenses in Darien**

Call Sign: KB1GFF
Michael J Tangney
18 B Swifts Ln
Darien CT 06820

Call Sign: N5DLE

Jack H Hartfelder
31 Blueberry Ln.
Darien CT 06820

Call Sign: KA2DQF
David T Bellingham
2697 Boston Post Road
Darien CT 06820

Call Sign: K1TJ
Thomas J Alessi
53 Brookside Drive
Darien CT 068205000

Call Sign: KB1VPB
David H Martin
275 Brookside Rd
Darien CT 06820

Call Sign: KA1ZTA
Fred W Sinon
30 Contentment Island
Darien CT 06820

Call Sign: N1RRB
Peter R Gray
43 Delafield Island Rd
Darien CT 06820

Call Sign: N1RRC
Peter R Gray Jr
43 Delafield Island Rd
Darien CT 06820

Call Sign: N1SRP
Sandra B Mac Pherson
13 Dickinson Rd
Darien CT 06820

Call Sign: KB1MFD
Gustav W Hedlund
91 Dorchester Rd
Darien CT 06820

Call Sign: W1GUS

Gustav W Hedlund
91 Dorchester Rd
Darien CT 06820

David L Hughes Jr
197 Hoyt St
Darien CT 06820

Christopher C Wallhagen
27 Maple St
Darien CT 06820

Call Sign: W1BV
Gustav W Hedlund
91 Dorchester Rd
Darien CT 06820

Call Sign: N1UJG
Edward J Rondano
28 Lake Dr
Darien CT 068203121

Call Sign: KA1UGX
Crans B Baldwin Iv
26 Middlesex Rd
Darien CT 06820

Call Sign: W1YWP
John S Durland Jr
27 Edgerton St
Darien CT 06820

Call Sign: KB1PFH
Richard K Brook
27 Lake Drive
Darien CT 06820

Call Sign: KB1VQZ
Branislav A Raskovic
61 Nearwater Ln
Darien CT 06820

Call Sign: W1SYZ
Herbert R Lester
34 Edgerton St
Darien CT 06820

Call Sign: K1RKB
Richard K Brook
27 Lake Drive
Darien CT 06820

Call Sign: KE1DT
Richard E Gunzel
170 Nearwater Ln
Darien CT 06820

Call Sign: WB6KRW
Brian Y Ike
18 Fox Hill Lane
Darien CT 06820

Call Sign: KB1DIY
Herman Shacter
50 Ledge Rd Apt 223
Darien CT 068204441

Call Sign: NB1D
Richard E Gunzel
170 Nearwater Ln
Darien CT 06820

Call Sign: N1ESC
Steven S May
21 Gardiner Street
Darien CT 06820

Call Sign: KC2CQA
Shawn P Seale
225 Leroy Avenue
Darien CT 06820

Call Sign: N1BMW
Michael K Lorelli
15 Norman Lane
Darien CT 06820

Call Sign: KA1TKT
Stuart Duffield
27 Georgian Ln
Darien CT 06820

Call Sign: N1JNX
Robert J Moore
21 Lighthouse Way
Darien CT 06820

Call Sign: KB1GUH
Martin K Reid
48 Noroton Avenue
Darien CT 06820

Call Sign: KA1IZ
Paul Romanos
21 Harriet Ln
Darien CT 06820

Call Sign: KB1GHD
Ben H Millard
115 Long Neck Point
Darien CT 068205815

Call Sign: KA1RIZ
A James Boris
35 Old Parish Rd
Darien CT 06820

Call Sign: K1DZH
Michael E Casciolo
45 Hollow Tree Ridge Rd
Darien CT 068205033

Call Sign: W1OFE
Peter Chowka
10 Mansfield Pl
Darien CT 06820

Call Sign: KB1VXS
Cindy L Smith
72 Peach Hill Rd
Darien CT 06820

Call Sign: WB4DYW

Call Sign: KA1UGY

Call Sign: KA1RAU

Adam G Gebauer
170 Pear Tree Point Rd
Darien CT 06820

Call Sign: KB1GQB
Christopher A Horan
2 Petticoat Lane
Darien CT 06820

Call Sign: W1CF
Christopher A Horan
2 Petticoat Lane
Darien CT 06820

Call Sign: W1CNU
Ralph E Nichols Sr
4 Pine St
Darien CT 06820

Call Sign: K1RQV
Charles L Du Vivier
76 Sedgwick Ave
Darien CT 06820

Call Sign: KB1GUG
Julie E Reid
15 Shady Acres Rd
Darien CT 06820

Call Sign: N1MMB
Carol E Kennedy
19 Stephanie Lane
Darien CT 06820

Call Sign: KA1VWN
Susan F Doorlay
11 Sunset Rd
Darien CT 06820

Call Sign: N1IOV
Jack P Doorlay
11 Sunset Rd
Darien CT 06820

Call Sign: KB1SPM

Ryan P Green
27 Sunset Road
Darien CT 06820

Call Sign: W1EAK
Ryan P Green
27 Sunset Road
Darien CT 06820

Call Sign: WA1QEP
Scott G Randall
27 Tulip Tree Lane
Darien CT 06820

Call Sign: KA1DU
Richard C Mc Curdy
1 Weed Ln Contentment Is
Darien CT 06820

Call Sign: KB1ABR
Daniel J Sharkey
130 West Ave
Darien CT 06820

Call Sign: N1DPC
Ronald E Konitshek
385 West Ave
Darien CT 06820

Call Sign: WA1SPK
Julius C Japon
385 West Ave
Darien CT 06820

Call Sign: ND1F
Ronald E Konitshek
385 West Ave
Darien CT 06820

Call Sign: N1LCZ
Alfred Mezquida
411 West Ave
Darien CT 06820

Call Sign: WA1FXO
Joseph W Miller
206 Ballouville Rd
Dayville CT 06241

Call Sign: KB1SBF
Kenneth A Rohan
293 Coomer Hill Rd
Dayville CT 06241

Call Sign: KB1DFB
Kim A Provencher
287 Lake Rd
Dayville CT 06241

Call Sign: N1WK
Kim A Provencher
287 Lake Rd
Dayville CT 06241

Call Sign: KB1KAB
Jason R Richardson
1002a North Main Street
Dayville CT 06241

Call Sign: K1MYF
William B Simmons
1436 North Rd
Dayville CT 062411404

Call Sign: W1CBJ
Albert L Chartier
1459 North Rd
Dayville CT 06241

Call Sign: KB1PYX
Jason M Stanislawski
1619 North Rd
Dayville CT 06241

Call Sign: KB1NRB
Allan E Richardson

P.O.Box 396
Dayville CT 06241

Call Sign: NR1X
Allan E Richardson
P.O.Box 396
Dayville CT 06241

Call Sign: W1NAP
Siesta Wireless Society
57 Pine Knolls Dr
Dayville CT 06241

Call Sign: W1JUD
Trinity College Alumni
Radio Club
57 Pine Knolls Dr
Dayville CT 062411857

Call Sign: WA1CT
Connecticut Wireless
Society
57 Pine Knolls Dr
Dayville CT 06241

Call Sign: W1MJC
Siesta Wireless Society
57 Pine Knolls Dr
Dayville CT 06241

Call Sign: KB1QWT
Sam Cassarino Memorial
Station
57 Pine Knolls Dr
Dayville CT 02641

Call Sign: N1NAP
Sam Cassarino Memorial
Station
57 Pine Knolls Dr
Dayville CT 02641

Call Sign: W1EDT
George H Vowles
102 Primrose Crossing

Dayville CT 06241

Call Sign: WB1EAW
Vilda E Mathurin
10 Primrose Village
Dayville CT 06241

Call Sign: N1VXM
Eve M Andrews
304 Putnam Pike
Dayville CT 06241

Call Sign: N1PYI
Andrea J Sadler
437 Putnam Pike
Dayville CT 06241

Call Sign: KB1QHB
Elina A Van Den Berg
136 Thompson Pike
Dayville CT 06241

Call Sign: K1KKK
Richard R Busher
1805 Upper Maple St
Dayville CT 06241

Call Sign: KA1ELO
Frederick L Peabody
473 Valley Rd
Dayville CT 06241

Call Sign: K1MUJ
Eastern Connecticut
Amateur Radio Assn
Dayville CT 06241

Call Sign: WB1EKU
Robert F Desrochers
Dayville CT 06241

Call Sign: KB1NTT
Jim Dalterio Memorial
Station
Dayville CT 06241

Call Sign: KZ1M
Jim Dalterio Memorial
Station
Dayville CT 06241

FCC Amateur Radio Licenses in Deep River

Call Sign: K1WWZ
Ludwig M Spokas
33 Acorn Rd
Deep River CT 06417

Call Sign: KB1QLK
Thomas A Law
22 Acorn Road
Deep River CT 06417

Call Sign: KB1OZJ
Eric C Stanley
69 B Main St
Deep River CT 06417

Call Sign: KA1MHE
Michael T Hagerth
50 Barn Rd
Deep River CT 06417

Call Sign: N1QHU
John T Baldwin
108 Cedar Lake Rd
Deep River CT 06417

Call Sign: K1UYZ
Gregory B Alexander
3 Colonial Dr
Deep River CT 06417

Call Sign: KB1MND
Peter L Greeley
14 Elm St
Deep River CT 06417

Call Sign: WA1HKW

William C Greeley
14 Elm Street
Deep River CT 06417

Call Sign: WB2DFK
William E Maguire
177 Falls Landing Road
Deep River CT 06417

Call Sign: N1RRI
John T Benton
8 Grove St
Deep River CT 06417

Call Sign: WA1JJF
John L Simcheski
11b High St
Deep River CT 06417

Call Sign: KA1LAN
Barrie V Potter
28 Prospect St
Deep River CT 06417

Call Sign: KB1OZE
Andrew P Faust
47 Rosemont Dr
Deep River CT 06417

Call Sign: KA1MHD
Sandra M Sorensen
36 Sylvan Ter
Deep River CT 06417

Call Sign: WA1YRY
Everett M Bradley
47 Tower Hill Rd
Deep River CT 06417

Call Sign: N1OFH
Dale Winchell
143 Union Street
Deep River CT 06417

Call Sign: N1HFJ

Donald C Paulson
183 W Elm St
Deep River CT 06417

Call Sign: KA1CCH
Lawrence M Moneypenny
46 Westbrook Rd
Deep River CT 06417

Call Sign: KB1WTD
Donald F Stadolnik Jr
142 Winthrop Rd
Deep River CT 06417

Call Sign: WA1RVR
Craig L Hanson
64 Witch Hazel Dr
Deep River CT 06417

Call Sign: WB1BQM
Ronald D Tower
Deep River CT 06417

FCC Amateur Radio Licenses in Derby

Call Sign: WB1FSO
Helen R Clifford
140 Bradley Tr
Derby CT 06418

Call Sign: N1KCF
Dawn A Kanicsar
209 Caroline St
Derby CT 06418

Call Sign: KB1RCT
Dale C Martin
16 Chatfield St
Derby CT 06418

Call Sign: N1UNV
Ferdinando Aiello
53 Commodore Commons
Derby CT 06418

Call Sign: KB1RCU
William J Korolyshun
1 Dale Dr
Derby CT 06418

Call Sign: KA9SCR
Timothy J Gomolak
315 David Humphreys Rd
Derby CT 06418

Call Sign: KD1BD
David J Kostrey
196 Derby Ave
Derby CT 06418

Call Sign: WB1FWG
Joseph R Owens Jr
278 Derby Ave
Derby CT 06418

Call Sign: KB1SJH
Joann M Raytar
196 Derby Ave 2nd Floor
Derby CT 06418

Call Sign: KA1IBU
Carol J Lembo
233 Derby Ave Unit 614
Derby CT 06418

Call Sign: WA1ZPM
Louis F Lembo
233 Derby Ave Unit 614
Derby CT 06418

Call Sign: WB1EXP
Charles H Mosman Jr
2 Hillcrest Ave
Derby CT 06418

Call Sign: KB1URZ
Marianne Samokar
22 New Haven Avenue 2nd
Floor

Derby CT 06418

Call Sign: KB1SWP
Tadeusz Janicki
25 Paugassett Rd
Derby CT 06418

Call Sign: KA1EWY
James S Emmett
1025 Roosevelt Dr
Derby CT 06418

Call Sign: N1CNJ
Leonard G Pearce
257 Sentinel Hill Rd
Derby CT 064182427

Call Sign: KB1RQS
Stanley J Sroka
262 Sentinel Hill Rd
Derby CT 06418

Call Sign: N1WKL
George J Pasuth
256 Shagbark Dr
Derby CT 06418

Call Sign: KB7XJ
Manuel S Perez
262 Shagbark Drive
Derby CT 06418

Call Sign: WW3K
Dominick Tuzzo
69 Smith St
Derby CT 06418

Call Sign: WB1GRJ
Bedri Hassan
47 Sunset Dr
Derby CT 06418

Call Sign: KB1KHN
Valley Amateur Radio
Association

Derby CT 06418

Call Sign: W1VAR
Valley Amateur Radio
Association
Derby CT 06418

FCC Amateur Radio Licenses in Devon

Call Sign: KA1UJF
Gus A Betso
75 Berwyn St
Devon CT 06460

Call Sign: N1LFH
Roger B Brelsford
6 Clayton St
Devon CT 06460

Call Sign: KB1BU
Fred A Traut
17 Granville Ave
Devon CT 06460

FCC Amateur Radio Licenses in Durham

Call Sign: NZ1G
Susan M Peak
28 Cedar Dr.
Durham CT 06422

Call Sign: N1PYR
Susan L Mc Candless
28 Clearidge Dr
Durham CT 06422

Call Sign: N1KSX
Scott T Wright
106 Creamery Road
Durham CT 06422

Call Sign: KB1OAR
Mark A Sergi Jr

181 David Rd
Durham CT 06422

Call Sign: KA1RIL
Daniel K Baeschlin
David Rd
Durham CT 06422

Call Sign: KD1PO
Harold J Ruhl Jr
95 Dunn Hill Rd
Durham CT 06422

Call Sign: KB1BFJ
Jerry A Stross
21 Edwards Rd
Durham CT 06422

Call Sign: N1AD
Alexander J Nytch
117 Guilford Rd
Durham CT 06422

Call Sign: W1UMN
John T De Nunzio
96 Haddam Quarter Rd
Durham CT 064221619

Call Sign: KA1FXR
Seeley C Kellogg
Higganuna Rd
Durham CT 06422

Call Sign: KB1WLI
Brian T Dumas
41 Little Ln
Durham CT 06422

Call Sign: W1SQK
Frederick A Stone
153 Madison Rd
Durham CT 064222910

Call Sign: NK1J
Christopher M Soulias

456 Maiden Lane
Durham CT 06422

Call Sign: KB1MMR
Daniel S Geary Jr
388 Maiden Ln
Durham CT 06422

Call Sign: K1BOI
Arlene E Dudley
460 Main St
Durham CT 06422

Call Sign: N1LQP
Jeffery A Van Arsdale
447 Main St.
Durham CT 06422

Call Sign: KA1RJT
William W Martin Sr
Oak Ter
Durham CT 06422

Call Sign: N1QYB
William S Witecki Jr
108 Oak Terrace
Durham CT 06422

Call Sign: KA1UXQ
Jan Exman
66 Old Blue Hills Rd
Durham CT 064223004

Call Sign: WB1DQT
William H Bacon
97r Old Blue Hills Rd
Durham CT 06422

Call Sign: KA1RIM
Ruth S Bacon
Old Blue Hills Rd
Durham CT 06422

Call Sign: KA1RJW
Andrew J Bacon

Old Blue Hills Rd
Durham CT 06422

Call Sign: KB1RPW
Wayne R Grohs
88 Old Pent Rd
Durham CT 06422

Call Sign: KA1RIP
Steven A Levy
190 Parmelee Hill Rd
Durham CT 06422

Call Sign: KB1QEC
Steven Leiler
297 R Higganum Rd
Durham CT 06422

Call Sign: KD4MFK
William B Du Brosky
15 Side Hill Dr
Durham CT 06422

Call Sign: N1SBA
Joseph G Roselli
377 Stage Coach Rd
Durham CT 06422

Call Sign: W1WAT
Joseph G Roselli
377 Stage Coach Rd
Durham CT 064223611

Call Sign: KA1SZP
Daniel M Murphy
162 Tri Mountain Rd
Durham CT 06422

Call Sign: W1DMM
Daniel M Murphy
162 Tri Mountain Rd
Durham CT 06422

Call Sign: N1GDI
Lucinda D Schulte

54 Wheeler Hill Dr
Durham CT 06422

Call Sign: WK1N
Robert R Schulte
54 Wheeler Hill Dr
Durham CT 06422

Call Sign: KB1MHF
Christopher W Mielke
Durham CT 06422

FCC Amateur Radio Licenses in East Berlin

Call Sign: N1TPX
Thomas D Mucha
31 Mattabassett St Apt 1
East Berlin CT 06023

Call Sign: N1JQY
Oscar J Dietrich
1068 Mill St
East Berlin CT 06023

FCC Amateur Radio Licenses in East Glastonbury

Call Sign: KA1SXU
Jeffery D Russell
Box 174
East Glastonbury CT 06025

Call Sign: KA1NUE
Peter A Klock
East Glastonbury CT 06025

Call Sign: K1XU
Jeffery D Russell
East Glastonbury CT
060250174

Call Sign: AB1LK
Jeffery D Russell

East Glastonbury CT
060250174

Call Sign: K1XU
Jeffery D Russell
East Glastonbury CT
060250174

**FCC Amateur Radio
Licenses in East Granby**

Call Sign: KA1CEF
Joseph J Jasienski
11 Cedar Ridge Rd
East Granby CT 06026

Call Sign: KB1HXH
Joseph J Jasienski
11 Cedar Ridge Rd
East Granby CT 060269707

Call Sign: KB1WSF
Dennis Morgan
21 Concord Dr
East Granby CT 06026

Call Sign: WA1VE
Dennis Morgan
21 Concord Dr
East Granby CT 06026

Call Sign: KA1COV
David G Stannard
6 Cricket Ln
East Granby CT 06026

Call Sign: WA1RGE
Charles G Stannard
6 Cricket Ln
East Granby CT 06026

Call Sign: KA1JGO
Jupp O Norhausen
154 Kimberly Rd
East Granby CT 06026

Call Sign: W1KGQ
Kenneth W Johnson
47 N Main Street Apt 5d
East Granby CT 06026

Call Sign: W1CCX
Plez Z Reid Jr
76 Newgate Rd
East Granby CT 06026

Call Sign: KB1WUO
Becky R Schoenfeld
111 Peak Mountain Dr
East Granby CT 06026

Call Sign: WB1AEX
Robert F Connelly
10 Pinewood Rd
East Granby CT 06026

Call Sign: W1AEX
Robert F Connelly
10 Pinewood Rd
East Granby CT 06026

Call Sign: K1PYU
Leonard S Cowles
56 S Main St
East Granby CT 06026

Call Sign: KA1BYY
James R Birmingham
Saddle Dr
East Granby CT 06026

Call Sign: KB1OOU
Robert D Michaud
10 Sanford Ridge
East Granby CT 06026

Call Sign: KB1PWA
William G Worcester
103 South Main St
East Granby CT 06026

Call Sign: KB1IXV
Charles E Hoadley
10 Southwood Ln
East Granby CT 06026

Call Sign: WA1VJQ
Andrew R Rossetti
9 Stark Dr
East Granby CT 06026

Call Sign: KB1QZR
Paul L Soucy
47 Talcott Range Dr
East Granby CT 06026

Call Sign: N1HUB
Russell P Rourke Jr
154 Turkey Hills Rd
East Granby CT 06026

Call Sign: K1GBV
Joseph F Colletti Jr
4 Woodledge
East Granby CT 06026

Call Sign: W1KAA
Joseph F Colletti Jr
4 Woodledge
East Granby CT 06026

Call Sign: K1GQV
David A Barton
60 Wynding Hills Rd
East Granby CT 06026

Call Sign: W1CBL
Andrew R Rossetti
East Granby CT 060260124

**FCC Amateur Radio
Licenses in East Haddam**

Call Sign: N1RSW
Gregory E Salisbury

29 Alger Rd
East Haddam CT 06423

Call Sign: KB1HU
Richard P Strang
63 Alger Rd
East Haddam CT 06423

Call Sign: KA1WGM
Scott J Godin
10 Babcock Rd
East Haddam CT 06423

Call Sign: KA1IDZ
Harry D Mc Cutcheon Jr
128 Clark Hill Rd
East Haddam CT 06423

Call Sign: KB1SEC
James F Stewart
10 Evergreen Ln
East Haddam CT 06423

Call Sign: WB1DUF
Zygmunt K Ciucias
66 Haywardville Rd
East Haddam CT 06423

Call Sign: WA1SUO
W Cameron Beard
81 Honey Hill Rd
East Haddam CT 06423

Call Sign: KB1HYZ
Carol P O Hare
7 Juda Lane
East Haddam CT 06423

Call Sign: W1LRR
Carol P O Hare
7 Juda Lane
East Haddam CT 06423

Call Sign: N1RNQ
Philip E Miller

11 Long Pasture Ln
East Haddam CT 06423

Call Sign: K1IKE
Joseph Szczech Jr
155 Newberry Rd
East Haddam CT
064230360

Call Sign: N1QHS
Dale L Szczech
155 Newberry Rd
East Haddam CT
064230360

Call Sign: KZ1R
Clarence G Jeffers
279 Norwich Salem Rd
East Haddam CT 06423

Call Sign: KB1UXF
John A Hartzell
74 Palmer Martin Rd
East Haddam CT 06423

Call Sign: N1LEY
Timothy P Kunsa
87 Petticoat Ln
East Haddam CT 06423

Call Sign: K1GC
George F Clark
37 Ridgewood Rd
East Haddam CT 06423

Call Sign: KA1NTF
Cassandra Z Ciullo
138 Sheepskin Hollow Rd
East Haddam CT 06423

Call Sign: N1ID
John P Ciullo
138 Sheepskin Hollow Rd
East Haddam CT 06423

Call Sign: KA4MQN
Elizabeth L Cox
23 Three Bridges Rd
East Haddam CT 06423

Call Sign: KB1UCW
Brian K Mcdougall
46 Warner Rd
East Haddam CT 06423

Call Sign: N1QLG
Phillip J Moore
East Haddam CT 06423

Call Sign: N1QLI
Walter J Wassil
East Haddam CT 06423

Call Sign: WB1FGX
Matthew E Lux
East Haddam CT 06423

FCC Amateur Radio Licenses in East Hampton

Call Sign: N1VID
Bruce A Weitzman
2 Bevin Court
East Hampton CT 06424

Call Sign: N1NEU
Rockford G Gibbons
6 Cedar Ridge Rd
East Hampton CT 06424

Call Sign: AK1N
Joel A Wilks
27 Champion Hill Rd
East Hampton CT 06424

Call Sign: KB1BQM
Champion Hill Dxers
27 Champion Hill Rd
East Hampton CT 06424

Call Sign: N1KVK
Lynne B Wilks
27 Champion Hill Rd
East Hampton CT 06424

Call Sign: K1LEF
Leland E Farkas
12 Glenwood Dr
East Hampton CT 06424

Call Sign: KA1OQW
Kevin E Gosselin
188 Lake Dr
East Hampton CT 06424

Call Sign: N4MUE
Paul S Paloski Jr
53 Champion Hill Road
East Hampton CT 06424

Call Sign: KB1JRZ
Victoria L Farkas
12 Glenwood Dr
East Hampton CT 06424

Call Sign: KA1OQX
Andrea B Gosselin
188 Lake Dr
East Hampton CT 06424

Call Sign: K1MET
Lance Q Johnson
204 Chestnut Hill Road
East Hampton CT 06424

Call Sign: KB1LUW
Haley R Farkas
12 Glenwood Dr
East Hampton CT 06424

Call Sign: N1SVZ
Gary E Nichols
191 Lake Dr
East Hampton CT 06424

Call Sign: WA1WJL
William V De Pietro Iii
26 Colbhester Ave
East Hampton CT 06424

Call Sign: KB1MMD
Monica S Farkas
12 Glenwood Dr
East Hampton CT 06424

Call Sign: WB1DBQ
Walter E Nichols Sr
191 Lake Dr
East Hampton CT 06424

Call Sign: KB1MME
James A Mckinney
44 Crestwood Dr
East Hampton CT 06424

Call Sign: KB1MOJ
Philip A Farkas
12 Glenwood Dr
East Hampton CT 06424

Call Sign: WB1DQY
Dennis J Lavigne Jr
195 Lake Dr
East Hampton CT 06424

Call Sign: KB1NAC
Matthew J Mckinney
44 Crestwood Dr
East Hampton CT 06424

Call Sign: KB1NAB
Caroline E Farkas
12 Glenwood Dr
East Hampton CT 06424

Call Sign: KA1SNO
John J Smedick
1 Middletown Ave
East Hampton CT 06424

Call Sign: N1HIH
Aldo M Zovich
164 Daly Rd
East Hampton CT 06424

Call Sign: AB1AN
Thomas R Corris
47 Haddam Neck Rd
East Hampton CT 06424

Call Sign: N5HBO
Wayne E Tanguay
21 Oak Knoll Rd
East Hampton CT 06424

Call Sign: KB1SPY
Adam J Smith
16 Forest St
East Hampton CT 06424

Call Sign: KB1BXJ
Jarret J Coleman
58 Haddam Neck Rd
East Hampton CT 06424

Call Sign: KB1FNX
Jerry F Houff
9 Old Chestnut Hill Rd
East Hampton CT 06424

Call Sign: N1PYS
Leland E Farkas
12 Glenwood Dr
East Hampton CT 06424

Call Sign: N1WMN
Drew M Coleman
58 Haddam Neck Rd
East Hampton CT 06424

Call Sign: N1LGB
John P Tierney
26 Old Middletown Ave
East Hampton CT 06424

Call Sign: N1XIV
Wendy H Tierney
26 Old Middletown Ave
East Hampton CT 06424

Call Sign: KB1MMA
Ian F Tierney
26 Old Middletown Ave
East Hampton CT 06424

Call Sign: KB1MMB
Mckeighry W Tierney
26 Old Middletown Ave
East Hampton CT 06424

Call Sign: KB1MMC
Austin P Tierney
26 Old Middletown Ave
East Hampton CT 06424

Call Sign: KB1NAD
Robert R Kochuk
41 Old Middletown Ave
East Hampton CT 06424

Call Sign: N1KPH
Carl J Hansen
12 Pine Trail
East Hampton CT 06424

Call Sign: W1LT
Lawrence L Titus
74 Pocotopaug Dr
East Hampton CT 06424

Call Sign: KB1NUO
Jeremy C Broad
36 Ridgeview Dr
East Hampton CT 06424

Call Sign: K1EFK
Robert A States Sr
35 Staeth Rd
East Hampton CT
064240238

Call Sign: W1EGX
George A Scott
9 Viola Dr
East Hampton CT
064241683

Call Sign: KB1FAP
David J Macdonald
127 W High St
East Hampton CT
064242115

Call Sign: K1DEX
David J Macdonald
127 W High St
East Hampton CT
064242115

Call Sign: KB1VTV
Robert L Ashton Jr
42 White Birch Rd
East Hampton CT 06424

Call Sign: W1RLA
Robert L Ashton Jr
42 White Birch Rd
East Hampton CT 06424

Call Sign: K1QCR
Walter J Rutkoski
33 Wildwood Ln
East Hampton CT 06424

Call Sign: KC1ZO
Joel B Wilks
60 Wopawog Rd
East Hampton CT 06424

Call Sign: KB1MZD
Ronald L Shepherd
East Hampton CT 06424

**FCC Amateur Radio
Licenses in East Hartford**

Call Sign: N1IRX
Barry J Forbes
66 Amy Drive
East Hartford CT 06108

Call Sign: KB1KUM
Guy S Bishop
5 Anchor Rd
East Hartford CT 06118

Call Sign: KB1DME
Marc J D'aloisio
78 Anita Dr
East Hartford CT 06118

Call Sign: KB1GRN
Dwight Knowlton
13 Arawak Dr
East Hartford CT 06118

Call Sign: WA1QPK
Richard M Souza
72 Arbutus Street
East Hartford CT 06108

Call Sign: KB1MLD
Kristen E Dube
61 Barbara Dr
East Hartford CT 06118

Call Sign: K1GEN
Kristen E Dube
61 Barbara Dr
East Hartford CT 06118

Call Sign: KB1KJA
John M Proctor
37 Birchwood Road
East Hartford CT 06118

Call Sign: KB1KJB
H J Pete Warner
37 Birchwood Road
East Hartford CT 06118

Call Sign: K1JMP
John M Proctor
37 Birchwood Road
East Hartford CT 06118

Call Sign: K1HJW
H J Pete Warner
37 Birchwood Road
East Hartford CT 06118

Call Sign: KB1NAG
Michael J Trudeau
88 Brentmoor Rd
East Hartford CT 06118

Call Sign: N1EYL
Marvin C Mc Gowan
385 Brewer St
East Hartford CT 06118

Call Sign: WA1IGQ
Judy H Burnham
18 Brook St
East Hartford CT 06108

Call Sign: KB1QBO
Gary J Vollinger
36 Brookfield Dr
East Hartford CT 06118

Call Sign: WB1CJO
Richard J Betz
36 Brown St
East Hartford CT 06118

Call Sign: N1VKD
Bernard H Meyers
68 Buena Vista Dr
East Hartford CT 06118

Call Sign: KB1TVS
John P Ryan
172 Burke St
East Hartford CT 06118

Call Sign: KB1MMG
Craig L Hancock
100 Burnbrook Rd
East Hartford CT
061182008

Call Sign: N1IWI
James C Soderquist
405 Burnside Ave
East Hartford CT 06108

Call Sign: N1TJO
Thomas J Hoffman
1333 Burnside Ave
East Hartford CT 06108

Call Sign: KA1GYB
Craig S Miller
99 Burnside Ave Apt 6
East Hartford CT 06108

Call Sign: KB1QNT
Joseph J Weber
793 Burnside Avfe
East Hartford CT 06108

Call Sign: N1OTU
Francis S Sullivan Jr
92 Cambridge Dr
East Hartford CT 06118

Call Sign: WB1FVF
Gordon R Mac Farlane
15 Cherry Tree Dr
East Hartford CT 06118

Call Sign: KB1VPY
Susan J Tukey
51 Cheyenne Rd
East Hartford CT 06118

Call Sign: KB1EYR
Raymond V Chevalier
82 Cheyenne Rd

East Hartford CT 06118

Call Sign: W1TLV
James L Warmolts
16 Christine Dr
East Hartford CT
061082931

Call Sign: KB1WSC
Marybeth N Warmolts
16 Christine Dr
East Hartford CT 06108

Call Sign: KB1RPG
Larry W Hardin
46 Christine Dr
East Hartford CT 06108

Call Sign: KK1S
Roland J Michaud
81 Christine Dr
East Hartford CT 06108

Call Sign: K1GZH
Francis G Charest
93 Christine Dr
East Hartford CT 06108

Call Sign: WA1LGQ
Lawrence M Bearse
132 Christine Dr
East Hartford CT 06108

Call Sign: KB1RUP
Anthony T Bearse
132 Christine Dr
East Hartford CT 06108

Call Sign: KB1LBE
Albert G Bolduc
23 Clayton Rd
East Hartford CT 06118

Call Sign: KB1IXU
Gladys N Kielb

32 Clement Rd
East Hartford CT 06118

Call Sign: W1TEE
Eugene M Kowalewski
23 Clune Ct
East Hartford CT 06108

Call Sign: N1MUZ
Garrett C Fitzpatrick Iii
195 Colby Dr
East Hartford CT 06108

Call Sign: KB1ETP
Genaro Gonzalez Jr
37 Comstock Pl
East Hartford CT 06108

Call Sign: K1SJ
Stanley W Jasut
21 Concord St
East Hartford CT 06108

Call Sign: KB1MLE
Leola J Davenport
101 Conn Blvd - 9-M
East Hartford CT 06108

Call Sign: KB1JYX
George E Carbonell Jr
16 Crescent Ct
East Hartford CT
061182710

Call Sign: N1RMF
George E Carbonell Jr
16 Crescent Ct
East Hartford CT
061182710

Call Sign: KB1TFS
Catherine A Carbonell
16 Crescent Ct
East Hartford CT 06118

Call Sign: K1MUT
L Philip Cormier
21 Davis Rd
East Hartford CT 06118

Call Sign: KA1NYS
Eloise Cormier
21 Davis Rd
East Hartford CT 06118

Call Sign: W1PTS
Paul W Comer
75 Davis Rd
East Hartford CT 06118

Call Sign: KB1TFU
Marie Fredrickson
26 Elms Village Dr
East Hartford CT 06118

Call Sign: KB1TFT
Theresa A Meares
57 Elms Village Dr
East Hartford CT 06118

Call Sign: WB1EEK
Marshall P Souza
35 Elms Village Dr A-3
East Hartford CT 06118

Call Sign: KB1WRE
Frank K Roberts Jr
24 Ensign St
East Hartford CT 06118

Call Sign: WA1COA
James F O Keefe
125 Farmstead Rd
East Hartford CT 06118

Call Sign: KB1QNX
Janit P Romayko
340 Forbes St
East Hartford CT 06118

Call Sign: N1PSI
Francis P Le Prohon Jr
1260 Forbes Street
East Hartford CT 06118

Call Sign: WB1GDH
Richard M O Keefe
61 Glenn Rd
East Hartford CT 06118

Call Sign: N4EFF
James E Hobbick
272 Goodwin St
East Hartford CT 06108

Call Sign: W1UFV
Wallace Blake
75 Great Hill Rd
East Hartford CT 06108

Call Sign: WA1QLQ
Jenner A Restrepo
11 Green Manor Dr
East Hartford CT
061183519

Call Sign: KA1OYU
Stephen H Jensen
148 Green Manor Dr
East Hartford CT 06118

Call Sign: N1UKE
Ruben S Blanco
17 Hartz Ln
East Hartford CT 06118

Call Sign: KA1TMO
Eric J Whyte
39 Hartz Ln
East Hartford CT
061181718

Call Sign: KB1VRE
Richard L Gatewood
37 Harvard Dr

East Hartford CT 06108

Call Sign: KB1MLO
Bruce F Gaudette Jr
22 Higbie Dr
East Hartford CT 06108

Call Sign: KB1FDM
Daniel A Wilson
23 Higbie Dr
East Hartford CT 06108

Call Sign: N1BGE
Gisele M Lamoureux
54 High Ct Apt 1
East Hartford CT 06118

Call Sign: KB1TBO
Albert L Abrams
31 High St 3208
East Hartford CT 06118

Call Sign: KB1TOK
Albert L Abrams
31 High St 3208
East Hartford CT 06118

Call Sign: KA1IFB
Steffie F Nelson
99 Highview St
East Hartford CT 06108

Call Sign: W1RW
John Huntoon
574 Hills St
East Hartford CT 06118

Call Sign: W1BJY
Aurelio S Silveira
4 Hilton Dr
East Hartford CT 06118

Call Sign: W1DX
Byron H Goodman
75 Holland Ln

East Hartford CT
061181725

Call Sign: N1GSQ
John B Olsen
81 Holland Ln
East Hartford CT 06118

Call Sign: N1HRC
Peter J Lombardo
80 Hollister Dr
East Hartford CT 06118

Call Sign: KB1GXF
Andrew R Greaney
12 Judy Drive
East Hartford CT 06118

Call Sign: KT1G
Tristam I Greaney
12 Judy Drive
East Hartford CT 06118

Call Sign: KB1UST
Connecticut D-Star Group
25 Kimberly Lane
East Hartford CT 06108

Call Sign: KB1USU
Connecticut D-Star Group
25 Kimberly Lane
East Hartford CT 06108

Call Sign: KB1USZ
Connecticut D-Star Group
25 Kimberly Lane
East Hartford CT
061081914

Call Sign: W1CDG
Connecticut D-Star Group
25 Kimberly Lane
East Hartford CT 06108

Call Sign: KD1STR

Connecticut D-Star Group
25 Kimberly Lane
East Hartford CT
061081914

Call Sign: K1CDG
Connecticut D-Star Group
25 Kimberly Lane
East Hartford CT 06108

Call Sign: KA1SPW
Lucille G Miele
25 Kimberly Ln
East Hartford CT 06108

Call Sign: N1GAU
Francis J Miele
25 Kimberly Ln
East Hartford CT 06108

Call Sign: W1FJM
Francis J Miele
25 Kimberly Ln
East Hartford CT 06108

Call Sign: KB1SWQ
Connecticut D-Star Group
25 Kimberly Ln
East Hartford CT 06108

Call Sign: N1GAU
Connecticut D-Star Group
25 Kimberly Ln
East Hartford CT 06108

Call Sign: KB1UHR
Connecticut D-Star Group
25 Kimberly Ln
East Hartford CT 06108

Call Sign: KB1UHS
Connecticut D-Star Group
25 Kimberly Ln
East Hartford CT 06108

Call Sign: KB1IIM
Eugene D Palin
51 Kimberly Ln
East Hartford CT 06108

Call Sign: KB1MLJ
Paul Belanger
316 King St
East Hartford CT 06108

Call Sign: KB1RRX
Thomas H Benoit
51 Larrabee St
East Hartford CT 06108

Call Sign: KB1TVM
Patrick D Gay
39 Lexington Rd
East Hartford CT 06118

Call Sign: N1JYF
Paul J Leger
92 Linwood Dr
East Hartford CT 06118

Call Sign: WB1EKK
Margaret T Berner
151 Long Hill St
East Hartford CT 06108

Call Sign: WA1ZSK
Nicholas A Tambone
143 Madison St
East Hartford CT 06118

Call Sign: KB1TFX
John R Ranney
1663 Main St
East Hartford CT 06108

Call Sign: KB1TFV
Anand Hingorani
227 Main St Apt 3
East Hartford CT 06118

Call Sign: KB1KUS
Freeman M Sargent
1403 Main St Apt 4f
East Hartford CT 06108

Call Sign: W1GNR
Robert L Anger
67 Manor Cir
East Hartford CT 06118

Call Sign: KB1GJK
Edward N Landry Jr
100 Maple Street
East Hartford CT 06118

Call Sign: KB1GJL
Patrick J Brick Jr.
83 Margery Dr
East Hartford CT 06118

Call Sign: KB1RM
Lawrence A La Penta
380 May Rd
East Hartford CT 06118

Call Sign: WA1FJG
Graydon R Dyer Sr
112 Milbrook Dr
East Hartford CT 06118

Call Sign: KB1TFW
Laurie J Beley
22 Milwood Rd
East Hartford CT 06118

Call Sign: K1LJB
Laurie J Beley
22 Milwood Rd
East Hartford CT 06118

Call Sign: WB1AIJ
Robert W Tomlin
114 Milwood Rd
East Hartford CT 06118

Call Sign: KA1DWI
Fernand E Nadeau
67 Mohawk Dr
East Hartford CT 06108

Call Sign: KB1HUX
Michael J Haviland
145 Mohawk Drive
East Hartford CT 06108

Call Sign: N1MGE
Julio A Moreno
23 Nelson St
East Hartford CT 06108

Call Sign: AI4OA
Julio A Moreno
23 Nelson St
East Hartford CT 06108

Call Sign: KB1MLF
David L Pelletier
22 Noch Lane
East Hartford CT 06118

Call Sign: KB1CIG
Scott E Doucette
52 Northfield Dr
East Hartford CT
061182053

Call Sign: AA1VD
Scott E Doucette
52 Northfield Dr
East Hartford CT
061182053

Call Sign: N1SFB
Robert D Welk
103 O Connell Dr
East Hartford CT 06118

Call Sign: WB1DBT
Eugene F Rojas
239 O Connell Dr

East Hartford CT 06118

Call Sign: N1SSI
William G Mederos
158 Oak St
East Hartford CT 06118

Call Sign: N1JW
Alexander J Meleg Jr
224 Oak St
East Hartford CT 06118

Call Sign: KA1TCL
Lucille M Vignone
615 Oak St
East Hartford CT 06118

Call Sign: N1GHB
Michael D Giannetti
633 Oak St
East Hartford CT 06118

Call Sign: WA1JPP
Peter R Glass
15 Oakwood St
East Hartford CT 06108

Call Sign: KB1RFR
Craig Mclea
205 Oconnell Drive
East Hartford CT 06118

Call Sign: N1HSA
Vincent J La Bella Sr
114 Oxford Dr
East Hartford CT 06118

Call Sign: KB1KIT
John F Winkley
105 Oxford Drive
East Hartford CT 06118

Call Sign: KB1MLK
Elizabeth J Cardoso
152 Oxford Drive

East Hartford CT 06118

Call Sign: N1LEW
Henry T Seegers
40 Parkview Dr
East Hartford CT 06108

Call Sign: K1OER
Robert B Merrigan
15 Piper Ln
East Hartford CT
061182065

Call Sign: N1XKP
James E Campbell
15c Racebrook Dr
East Hartford CT 06108

Call Sign: N1IDO
Ki Kwang Sung
30d Racebrook Dr
East Hartford CT 06108

Call Sign: KB1TVF
Michael R Brinius
60 Rentschler St
East Hartford CT 06118

Call Sign: KB1TVG
Victoria G Brinius
60 Rentschler St
East Hartford CT 06118

Call Sign: KB1MLC
Daniel M Dube
31 School St
East Hartford CT 06108

Call Sign: KB1UEL
East Hartford Cert
31 School St
East Hartford CT 06108

Call Sign: K1YLE
Daniel M Dube

31 School St
East Hartford CT 06108

Call Sign: W1EHC
East Hartford Cert
31 School St
East Hartford CT 06108

Call Sign: KB1BGZ
Monika S Swietek
93 Scott St
East Hartford CT 06118

Call Sign: N1UTE
Mark F Swietek
93 Scott St
East Hartford CT 06118

Call Sign: KD1II
Michael T Regan
25 Shannon Road
East Hartford CT 06118

Call Sign: KB1HWK
Carl M Balanoff
35 Shawnee Rd
East Hartford CT 06118

Call Sign: N1LEP
George J Tatzmann
16 Sherman Ave
East Hartford CT 06108

Call Sign: N1KIY
Lee W Kirk
21 Silver Ln A1
East Hartford CT 06118

Call Sign: N1JGH
Dale J Hogan
80 Simmons Rd Apt B4
East Hartford CT 06118

Call Sign: WB1CCK
Joseph C Amirault

41 Skyline Dr
East Hartford CT 06118

Call Sign: KB1VSH
Keith B Victor
44 Suffolk Drive
East Hartford CT 06118

Call Sign: NX1T
Alexander Alper
124 Summerset Drive
East Hartford CT 06118

Call Sign: N1WAM
Scott T Stanchfield
13 Sunnydale Rd
East Hartford CT 06118

Call Sign: KA1VYZ
Robert J Sheahan Jr
90 Sunnyreach Dr
East Hartford CT
061183150

Call Sign: WB1AIZ
James G Lanzo
68 Sunrise Lane
East Hartford CT 06118

Call Sign: WA1DAW
Martin J O Meara Jr
60 Sunset Ridge
East Hartford CT 06118

Call Sign: AA1JO
James C Bills Jr
11 Taylor St
East Hartford CT 06118

Call Sign: N1NAO
Frederick R Ladue
98 Terrace Ave
East Hartford CT 06108

Call Sign: N1TGW

Robert F Amodio
31 Timber Trail
East Hartford CT 06118

Call Sign: KA1EFE
Vaughn O Wilson
1153 Tolland St
East Hartford CT 06108

Call Sign: KB1UNE
Raul Ayala
33 Tower Rd
East Hartford CT 06108

Call Sign: N1XHJ
Catherine M Gnat
181 Walnut St
East Hartford CT 06108

Call Sign: KB1MMF
Edwardo Ruiz
31 Warren Dr
East Hartford CT 06118

Call Sign: KB1RUF
James J O'keefe Jr
118 Washington Ave
East Hartford CT 06118

Call Sign: KB1SLF
Jason P Dever
24 Whitney St
East Hartford CT 06118

Call Sign: WN1T
Jason P Dever
24 Whitney St
East Hartford CT 06118

Call Sign: KD4JNE
Linda T Darcy
110 Wickham Dr
East Hartford CT 06118

Call Sign: WB1FTC

John M Benker Jr
46 Woodbridge Ave
East Hartford CT 06108

Call Sign: KB1MLM
Bridget E O Donnell
16 Woodlawn Cir
East Hartford CT 06108

Call Sign: KE1LE
Edward T Seaward Jr
202 Woodlawn Cir
East Hartford CT 06108

Call Sign: KB1MLI
Debra L Beauliew
14 Woodlawn Circle
East Hartford CT
061082857

Call Sign: WA1FVJ
Edward T Seaward Jr
202 Woodlawn Circle
East Hartford CT 06108

Call Sign: KB1PZS
Robert M Delgreco
East Hartford CT 06138

**FCC Amateur Radio
Licenses in East Hartland**

Call Sign: N1PFJ
Francis A Jansen
43 Granville Rd
East Hartland CT 06027

Call Sign: W1EN
Leon Stoltze
536 Granville Rd
East Hartland CT
060271117

Call Sign: N1LJW
Max R Schmitter

32 Kensington Acres Rd
East Hartland CT 06027

187 Angela Dr
East Haven CT 06512

279 Cosey Beach Ave
East Haven CT 06512

Call Sign: W1ZGP
Robert E Leaver
58 Mountain Rd
East Hartland CT 06027

Call Sign: N1OXT
Ralph Valanzuolo
112 Bennett Rd
East Haven CT 06513

Call Sign: KB1DSJ
Charles F Simjian
26 Eddon Dr
East Haven CT 065121056

Call Sign: WA1IAO
John J Shelley
186 Mountain Rd
East Hartland CT
060271517

Call Sign: KA1SPB
Paul R Deschamps
142 Borrmann Rd
East Haven CT 06512

Call Sign: W1RMG
William E Cummings
5 Edgehill Dr
East Haven CT 06512

Call Sign: W1TJL
Thomas J Le Clerc
111 Pell Road
East Hartland CT 06027

Call Sign: KA1QGG
Anthony F Pannone
33 Bradely Ave
East Haven CT 06512

Call Sign: N1TAZ
Stephen B Robillard
8 Elm Court
East Haven CT 06512

Call Sign: K1YON
Theodore A Jansen
East Hartland CT 06027

Call Sign: N1ESO
John C Santanello
16 Bradley Ave
East Haven CT 06512

Call Sign: K1UCW
Karl S Paecht
23 Englewood Dr
East Haven CT 06513

Call Sign: KA0TZX
Bruce A Wright Jr
East Hartland CT 06027

Call Sign: N1DJJ
Joseph R Hopkinson
18 Burr St.
East Haven CT 06512

Call Sign: KA1EFD
Anthony J Laudano
20 Fisco Dr
East Haven CT 06512

Call Sign: KB1DTC
Philip E Mikan
East Hartland CT 06027

Call Sign: N1GPB
James D Williams
219 Coe Ave
East Haven CT 06512

Call Sign: KA1UWB
William H Prout
12 Fisco Drive
East Haven CT 06513

Call Sign: N1QVP
Frederick G Wright
East Hartland CT 06027

Call Sign: N1RDH
Richard D Pohle
130-14 Coe Ave
East Haven CT 06512

Call Sign: N1ROW
Gennaro Muoio
143 Foxon Rd
East Haven CT 06512

**FCC Amateur Radio
Licenses in East Haven**

Call Sign: N1ODN
Marshall L Hood
197 And A Half Coe Ave
East Haven CT 06512

Call Sign: N1GDR
Craig M Lang
279 Cosey Beach Ave
East Haven CT 06512

Call Sign: KQ4NE
James F Kellas
70 French Ave
East Haven CT 06512

Call Sign: N1KLB
James Pompano

Call Sign: W1MHZ
Craig M Lang

Call Sign: W1PYF
George J Hugo

140 French Avenue
East Haven CT 06512

15 Joyce Rd
East Haven CT 06512

1301 N High St
East Haven CT 06512

Call Sign: KH2GS
Mitsuhiro Ito
90 Gerrish Ave. #104
East Haven CT 06512

Call Sign: AA1NQ
Meyer J Moquet
514 Main St 12
East Haven CT 065122749

Call Sign: KA1OFN
Thomas F Griffith Mr
28 Nicesca Dr
East Haven CT 06513

Call Sign: N1KLC
Daniel L Steeves
40 Hellstrom Rd
East Haven CT 06512

Call Sign: N1SWR
Maria C Moquet
514 Main St Apt 12
East Haven CT 065122749

Call Sign: WA1VRZ
Andrew N Janer
5 Nicholas Dr
East Haven CT 06512

Call Sign: KA1TYJ
Lorraine Scalia
113 Highland Ave
East Haven CT 06513

Call Sign: WP3QV
Steven Lecodet-Cabasquini
500 Main St Apt 327
East Haven CT 06512

Call Sign: N1XCB
Ralph A Colavolpe
11 Oregon Ave
East Haven CT 065124120

Call Sign: KA1OSA
Michael R Esposito
46 Hobson St
East Haven CT 06512

Call Sign: KB1SYD
Kevin P Morann
166 Meadow St
East Haven CT 06512

Call Sign: KB1PIP
John B Torello
58 Oregon Ave
East Haven CT 06512

Call Sign: N1IES
Dan T Laudano
67 Holmes St
East Haven CT 06512

Call Sign: N1RCI
Robert B Schmaling Jr
171 Mill Street
East Haven CT 06512

Call Sign: W1NYY
John B Torello
58 Oregon Ave
East Haven CT 06512

Call Sign: WC1Q
Lawrence A Fusco
64 Hughes St
East Haven CT 065122615

Call Sign: KB1HEW
William H Kershaw Jr
1057 N High St
East Haven CT 065121021

Call Sign: KA1EZX
Raymond A Nuzzo
65 Osmond St
East Haven CT 06512

Call Sign: KT1T
Paul M Gauvin
18 Hurlburt Dr
East Haven CT 06512

Call Sign: AA1OZ
Joseph V Anyzeski
1295 N High St
East Haven CT 06512

Call Sign: KB1MYI
Eric W Traester
43 Ozone Rd
East Haven CT 06512

Call Sign: K1RGO
Salvatore J De Francesco
17 Jeffrey Rd
East Haven CT 06513

Call Sign: KA1LSX
Vincent J Anyzeski Sr
1301 N High St
East Haven CT 06512

Call Sign: W1YZR
Andrew A Cangiano
139 S End Rd
East Haven CT 06512

Call Sign: KB1ECV
Albert P Kacerguis Jr

Call Sign: KB1MT
Vincent J Anyzeski

Call Sign: K1XJ
Kevin M Buchanan

82 Saltonstall Parkway
East Haven CT 06512

Call Sign: N1AKN
Joseph J Dwyer
277 Short Beach Rd.
East Haven CT 06512

Call Sign: WA1TUT
Douglas E Losty
33r Stevens St
East Haven CT 06512

Call Sign: WB1FUS
Casimir P Jasudowich
543 Strong St
East Haven CT 06512

Call Sign: N1TVL
James R Gomme
11 Sunset Rd
East Haven CT 06512

Call Sign: KB1TTW
David P Slater
26 Weber St
East Haven CT 06512

Call Sign: N1TAK
Albert V Cahoon
61 Wheaton Rd
East Haven CT 06512

Call Sign: WA1PER
Frank Pandolfi
28 Wilson St
East Haven CT 06512

Call Sign: KA1OVT
Frank A Baldassare
62 Windsor St
East Haven CT 06512

Call Sign: KA1HUU
Jorgen P Christensen

East Haven CT 06512

FCC Amateur Radio Licenses in East Killingly

Call Sign: KB1FOX
The Barnstormers Contest
Group
East Killingly CT 06243

Call Sign: NZ1U
The Barnstormers Contest
Group
East Killingly CT 06243

Call Sign: KB1H
Richard R Pechie
East Killingly CT 06243

Call Sign: N1NAP
Santo J Cassarino
East Killingly CT
062430043

FCC Amateur Radio Licenses in East Lyme

Call Sign: N1AMD
George L White
392 Boston Post Rd
East Lyme CT 063331403

Call Sign: KB1IME
Christopher B Johnson
480 Boston Post Rd
East Lyme CT 06333

Call Sign: W1ANK
Ronald A Soccoli
543 Boston Post Rd
East Lyme CT 06333

Call Sign: KB1WBY
James J Fleishell
172 Boston Post Rd Apt B

East Lyme CT 06333

Call Sign: N4JTN
Hadley W Duprey Jr
543 Boston Post Rd.
East Lyme CT 06333

Call Sign: K1OIY
Clarence R Noel
15 Brookfield Dr
East Lyme CT 063331305

Call Sign: KB1TL
David E Kelly
12 Cavasin Dr
East Lyme CT 06333

Call Sign: K1FOB
Richard J Nielsen
62 Charter Oak Dr
East Lyme CT 06333

Call Sign: KA1FNS
John A Deane Jr
59 Dean Rd
East Lyme CT 06333

Call Sign: KB5BVF
Robert F White
109 Dean Rd
East Lyme CT 063331510

Call Sign: KB5BVG
Linda K White
109 Dean Rd
East Lyme CT 063331510

Call Sign: KB1RPN
Ronald J Luich
13 Enid Ln
East Lyme CT 06333

Call Sign: KB1KCA
James E Curley
11 Ferro Drive

East Lyme CT 063331515

Call Sign: N1PUP
Susannah L Rochester-
Bolen
3 Greentree Dr
East Lyme CT 06333

Call Sign: N1GEH
Richard W Goode
38 Heritage Rd
East Lyme CT 06333

Call Sign: KA1PQB
Earl D Johnson
73 Holmes Rd
East Lyme CT 06333

Call Sign: N1TMS
Francis J De Fazio
23 Marion Dr
East Lyme CT 06333

Call Sign: N1CLV
Wayne R Gronlund
11 Monticello Dr
East Lyme CT 063331228

Call Sign: AI0Z
Michael J Avery
16 Monticello Dr
East Lyme CT 06333

Call Sign: N1XK
Michael J Avery
16 Monticello Dr
East Lyme CT 06333

Call Sign: KC2WQO
Rosellen A Daddario
72 Plants Dam Rd
East Lyme CT 063331427

Call Sign: N2GZ
Gregory M Zenger

72 Plants Dam Road
East Lyme CT 063331427

Call Sign: KB1MAC
Beth K Fitzpatrick
7 River Rd
East Lyme CT 06333

Call Sign: KB1MMT
Ronald J Fitzpatrick
7 River Rd
East Lyme CT 06333

Call Sign: K1CV
William M Haigh
85 Scott Rd
East Lyme CT 06333

Call Sign: N1YL
Diane E Haigh
85 Scott Rd
East Lyme CT 063331124

Call Sign: WA1VOC
Robin N Haigh
85 Scott Rd
East Lyme CT 06333

Call Sign: WA2SKK
William J Lambert
17 Spring Rock Rd
East Lyme CT 06333

Call Sign: KA3ETD
Michael F Palladino
36 Spring Rock Rd
East Lyme CT 06333

Call Sign: WA1WEQ
Stephen C Lattanzi
7 Tanglewood Dr.
East Lyme CT 06333

Call Sign: W1DCR
Stephen C Lattanzi

7 Tanglewood Dr.
East Lyme CT 06333

Call Sign: KB1FXR
Joshua M Madore
211 Upper Patt Rd
East Lyme CT 06333

Call Sign: KA1YJH
David M O Connor
44 Upper Pattagansett Rd
East Lyme CT 06333

Call Sign: KB1VMU
Robert D Williamson
137 Upper Pattagansett Rd
East Lyme CT 06333

Call Sign: K1LE
Jeffrey A Madore
211 Upper Pattagansett Rd
East Lyme CT 06333

Call Sign: W1GTT
William H Covey
14 Village Dr
East Lyme CT 06333

Call Sign: W2XU
Stephen J Libby
48 Webster Rd
East Lyme CT 06333

Call Sign: KA1GKT
Brian A Dargel
8 Williw Lane
East Lyme CT 06333

Call Sign: KA1BB
Robert H Dargel
8 Willow Ln
East Lyme CT 063331526

Call Sign: N1AMR
Michael R Dargel

8 Willow Ln
East Lyme CT 063331526

Call Sign: KB1GVX
Timothy J Wilbur
4 Woodrow Drive
East Lyme CT 06333

**FCC Amateur Radio
Licenses in East Norwalk**

Call Sign: KA1QXX
Robert H Heise
11 Bond St
East Norwalk CT 06855

Call Sign: W1AXB
William A Whitbeck
16 Fourth St
East Norwalk CT 06855

Call Sign: KA1EFT
Frank T Fasanella
88 Old Saugatuck Rd
East Norwalk CT 06855

Call Sign: KA1ZTO
Sergio Serrano
49 Olmstead Pl
East Norwalk CT 06855

Call Sign: N1RRH
Jason P Borner
1 Sycamore St
East Norwalk CT 06855

Call Sign: K1YYC
Theodore A White
14 Tonetta Cir
East Norwalk CT 06855

Call Sign: K1UFM
Theodore A White
14 Tonetta Cir
East Norwalk CT 06855

Call Sign: KA1ZVP
Raymond Marrero
44 Van Zant St
East Norwalk CT 06855

Call Sign: N1LUZ
George Albano
18 Winfield St
East Norwalk CT 06855

Call Sign: KA1WTW
William P Biase
East Norwalk CT 06855

**FCC Amateur Radio
Licenses in East Windsor**

Call Sign: KB1NOZ
James M Kloter
64 Abbe Rd
East Windsor CT 06088

Call Sign: N1SAT
Richard J Pangburn
156 C North Rd
East Windsor CT 06088

Call Sign: W1RQD
Edward J Grazik
17 Cricket Rd Box 106
East Windsor CT 06088

Call Sign: KA1JGG
Andrew J Tripp
4 Gardner St
East Windsor CT 06088

Call Sign: K3WJM
William J Mccusker
12 Pleasant Street
East Windsor CT 06088

Call Sign: WT1V
Sydney C Faria

---

30 Prospect Hill Drive
East Windsor CT 06088

Call Sign: N1LCV
Lawrence D Quinn
13c Riverview Dr
East Windsor CT 06088

Call Sign: WB1DNL
Jonathan F Towle
134 S Main St
East Windsor CT 06088

Call Sign: KB1HCD
Mark B Farmer
249 S Water St
East Windsor CT 06088

Call Sign: KC9NNV
Blake J Wischer
228 S Water Street Apt K8
East Windsor CT 06088

Call Sign: KD5GIW
Ronald A Hocutt Mr.
199 Scantic Road
East Windsor CT 06088

Call Sign: ND1T
Brian H Bickford
35 Stoughton Rd
East Windsor CT 06088

Call Sign: KB1QQB
Raymond A Parker
91 Tromley Rd
East Windsor CT 06088

Call Sign: N1VTJ
Kenneth L Card
160 Tromley Rd
East Windsor CT 06088

Call Sign: N1VTM
Keith L Card

160 Tromley Rd
East Windsor CT 06088

Call Sign: KB1NPU
Raymond G Parker
91 Trowley Rd
East Windsor CT 06088

Call Sign: WB1ETR
Michael J Krull Sr
136 Wells Rd
East Windsor CT
060889716

Call Sign: K1GHX
Michael J Krull Sr
136 Wells Rd
East Windsor CT
060889716

Call Sign: K1MIB
Michael J Krull
136 Wells Rd
East Windsor CT
060889716

Call Sign: WA1LWB
Frederic W Stucklen
148 Winkler Rd
East Windsor CT 06088

Call Sign: N1VKE
Louis B Rychling
41 Winton Rd
East Windsor CT 06088

Call Sign: KB1QQE
Irene V Rychling
41 Winton Road
East Windsor CT 06088

Call Sign: KB1GWO
Paul E Gruhn
16 Woolam Rd
East Windsor CT 06088

Call Sign: K1DXB
A Ward Machesney
East Windsor CT 06088

Call Sign: KB1SMB
Robert J Petrelli
East Windsor CT 06088

FCC Amateur Radio Licenses in East Windsor Hill

Call Sign: W1MYB
George Bancroft
1985 Rt 5
East Windsor Hill CT 06028

FCC Amateur Radio Licenses in Eastford

Call Sign: N1HZP
John R Owens
117 Ashford Rd
Eastford CT 06242

Call Sign: KB1JQA
Philip N Mazzarella Jr
265 Chaplin Rd
Eastford CT 06242

Call Sign: KB1LYF
Jana R Mazzarella
265 Chaplin Rd
Eastford CT 06242

Call Sign: KB1NTA
Quiet Corner Amateur
Radio Club
265 Chaplin Rd
Eastford CT 06242

Call Sign: W1QFF
Eugene H French
County Rd

Eastford CT 06242

Call Sign: N1MVW
Lucien R Guilbault
193 Old Colony Rd
Eastford CT 06242

Call Sign: N1SKE
Susan N Kerr
9 Old Rt 44
Eastford CT 06242

FCC Amateur Radio Licenses in Easton

Call Sign: WA1NEI
John N Fedick
51 Bartling Dr
Easton CT 06612

Call Sign: K1BNQ
Fairfield County Contesters
Ars
330 Center Rd
Easton CT 06612

Call Sign: K1PX
James E Monahan Iii
330 Center Rd
Easton CT 06612

Call Sign: W1QS
Eastern Top Band Arc
330 Center Rd
Easton CT 06612

Call Sign: W1LU
Eastern Top Band Arc
330 Center Rd
Easton CT 06612

Call Sign: KB1SVJ
Arthur W Dugas Jr
115 Church Rd
Easton CT 066121411

Call Sign: KD1AWD
Arthur W Dugas Jr
115 Church Rd
Easton CT 066121411

Call Sign: K1NGL
August D Rosati
11 Crestwood Dr
Easton CT 06612

Call Sign: W0RGC
John D Sarsgard
31 Golf View Drive
Easton CT 06612

Call Sign: K1RXR
John D Sarsgard
31 Golf View Drive
Easton CT 06612

Call Sign: N1EE
Conrad B Senior
56 High Ridge Rd
Easton CT 06612

Call Sign: KB1FEW
Russell P Senior
56 High Ridge Rd
Easton CT 066122022

Call Sign: W1RPS
Russell P Senior
56 High Ridge Rd
Easton CT 06612

Call Sign: KB7MFM
Theresa A D'ausilio
124 Mile Common Rd
Easton CT 066121506

Call Sign: W1RT
John L D'ausilio
124 Mile Common Rd
Easton CT 066121506

Call Sign: K1TB
Tree Bangers Field Day
Society
124 Mile Common Rd
Easton CT 06612

Call Sign: W1XF
James A Frier Jr
150 Mile Common Road
Easton CT 06612

Call Sign: N1FOA
Michael Cordelli
18 Mill Road
Easton CT 06612

Call Sign: KB1THM
Brandon Harvey
150 North Park Ave
Easton CT 06612

Call Sign: KC1KT
Robert M Carroll
7 Old Redding Rd
Easton CT 06612

Call Sign: WA1NCK
Randolph L Stone
77 Rock House Rd
Easton CT 06612

Call Sign: WD5EIJ
Eric J Cieplik
21 Rosewood Dr
Easton CT 066122116

Call Sign: K1MOG
Joseph L Silhavy
45 Silver Hill Rd
Easton CT 06612

Call Sign: KB1WFX
Arthur R Greiser
314 Westport Rd

Easton CT 06612

Call Sign: WR1G
John P Salva Jr
80 Woodend Dr
Easton CT 06612

Call Sign: K1RT
Edward B Kalin
Easton CT 06612

FCC Amateur Radio Licenses in Ellington

Call Sign: N1EQL
David J Bessette
26 Abbott Rd
Ellington CT 06029

Call Sign: N1TTB
Robert G Hoffman
1 Abbott Rd Unit #3
Ellington CT 06029

Call Sign: KB1QKA
Gary Tautkus Sr
1 Angel Trace Rd
Ellington CT 06029

Call Sign: WR1Z
James B Smith Sr
5 Anthony Way
Ellington CT 06029

Call Sign: N1JNW
Douglas T Metheny
27 Ardsley Lane
Ellington CT 06029

Call Sign: W1DTM
Douglas T Metheny
27 Ardsley Lane
Ellington CT 06029

Call Sign: N1XMZ

Frank G Henderson Ii
307 Autumn Chase
Ellington CT 06029

Sara S Tavares
25 Crane Rd
Ellington CT 06029

Allen P Tracy
1 Gem Dr
Ellington CT 06029

Call Sign: K1DDX
Reed A Seitz
88 Burbank Rd
Ellington CT 06029

Call Sign: N1OQA
John K Richert
159 Crystal Lake Rd
Ellington CT 06029

Call Sign: N1UFE
John A Douglass
7 Glenwood Rd
Ellington CT 06029

Call Sign: K1IDJ
Reed A Seitz
88 Burbank Rd
Ellington CT 06029

Call Sign: W1DRO
Charles J Dobrowolski
14 Deborah Dr
Ellington CT 06029

Call Sign: KB1RMO
John R Streiber
4 Hatheway Rd
Ellington CT 06029

Call Sign: K1DDX
Reed A Seitz
88 Burbank Rd
Ellington CT 06029

Call Sign: K2KKH
Jonathan H Allen
33 Dogwood Ln
Ellington CT 06029

Call Sign: KB1TIH
Kenlyn J Streiber
4 Hatheway Rd
Ellington CT 06029

Call Sign: W1WON
Reed A Seitz
88 Burbank Rd
Ellington CT 06029

Call Sign: KB1LOF
Carolyn J Allen
33 Dogwood Ln
Ellington CT 060292205

Call Sign: WA1FKX
Robert B Lockhart Jr
32 Hayes Ave
Ellington CT 06029

Call Sign: N9NJF
Salvitore J Decina Jr
100 Burbank Rd
Ellington CT 06029

Call Sign: N1CJA
Carolyn J Allen
33 Dogwood Ln
Ellington CT 060292205

Call Sign: KA1GIC
Lawrence Chestnut Iii
8 Heather Rd
Ellington CT 06029

Call Sign: KB1UHX
Scott T Hiestand
127 Burbank Rd
Ellington CT 06029

Call Sign: N1VSN
Joseph B Botti
32 Florence Ave
Ellington CT 06029

Call Sign: KD6RRN
Gregg M Gallant
47 Hillside Dr
Ellington CT 06029

Call Sign: KB1TIN
Melissa Ocasio-Willbrant
22 Charter Rd
Ellington CT 06029

Call Sign: K1AYR
James R Hazen Sr
25 Gail Dr
Ellington CT 06029

Call Sign: KD6RRO
Suzette C Gallant
47 Hillside Dr
Ellington CT 06029

Call Sign: K1MQU
Gerald J Tavares
25 Crane Rd
Ellington CT 06029

Call Sign: N1NAT
Carl H Slicer
14 Gail Drive
Ellington CT 06029

Call Sign: KE6CVQ
Basil X Gallant
47 Hillside Dr
Ellington CT 06029

Call Sign: WA1INH

Call Sign: KB1AMM

Call Sign: K1GMG

Gregg M Gallant
47 Hillside Dr
Ellington CT 06029

Call Sign: KB1NAH
William J Gallant
47 Hillside Dr
Ellington CT 06029

Call Sign: N1FOO
James B Kelley
110 Jobs Hill Rd Apt 70
Ellington CT 06029

Call Sign: KB1TIU
Paricia E Davis
11 Lee Lane
Ellington CT 06029

Call Sign: AD1A
Daniel W Schoell
21 Ludwig Rd
Ellington CT 06029

Call Sign: AA1KN
Robert M Gorcynski
1 Maple St 26
Ellington CT 06029

Call Sign: K1RVB
Clyde S Harting
23 Maplewood Dr
Ellington CT 06029

Call Sign: NC7R
Charles R Nelson
34 Maplewood Dr
Ellington CT 060292313

Call Sign: N7ZXI
Susan M Nelson
34 Maplewood Dr.
Ellington CT 060292313

Call Sign: N1YYA

Lisa A Wadhams
222 Mountain Rd
Ellington CT 06029

Call Sign: N1GUT
Robert L Townsend
226 Mountain Road
Ellington CT 06029

Call Sign: KA2ZFP
Lynn T Walker
2 Mountainview Circle
Ellington CT 06029

Call Sign: N1IDU
Geoffrey A Wadhams
222 Mtn Rd
Ellington CT 060293704

Call Sign: KB1VIP
William R Smith Jr
89 Muddy Brook Road
Ellington CT 06029

Call Sign: KG4DZW
Daniel Mc Menamin
8 Overlook Pass
Ellington CT 06029

Call Sign: K4ZXW
Daniel Mc Menamin
8 Overlook Pass
Ellington CT 06029

Call Sign: WA1ZKW
Ronald J Daley
6 Pinewood Ln
Ellington CT 06029

Call Sign: W1GTU
Jeffrey J Murray
63 Pinnacle Rd
Ellington CT 060293515

Call Sign: KB1GSY

Richard A Henderson
239 Pinney St
Ellington CT 06029

Call Sign: W1HEN
Richard A Henderson
239 Pinney St
Ellington CT 06029

Call Sign: N1URW
Harold Chase
60 Pinney St 87
Ellington CT 06029

Call Sign: N1VGU
Henry Chapman
60 Pinney St Apt 145
Ellington CT 06029

Call Sign: KB1TIL
Robert J Parlante
26 Pinney St Apt 38
Ellington CT 06029

Call Sign: KB1SEA
Regina M Hurley
26 Pinney Street #64
Ellington CT 06029

Call Sign: K1AHB
Kevin A Holian Borgnis
10 Quarry Street
Ellington CT 06029

Call Sign: KB1VQR
Susan M Trisler
20 Sandy Beach Rd
Ellington CT 06029

Call Sign: KB1VQS
William Trisler
20 Sandy Beach Rd
Ellington CT 06029

Call Sign: KB1SME

John M Wrynn
73 Sandy Beach Rd
Ellington CT 06029

Call Sign: KA1PCQ
Dale T Cunningham
3 South Rd
Ellington CT 06029

Call Sign: NK1D
Dale T Cunningham
3 South Road
Ellington CT 06029

Call Sign: N1ND
Daniel B Henderson
9 Strawberry Rd - Apt 14
Ellington CT 06029

Call Sign: KB1CIH
Brian D Bari
9 Strawberry Rd 27
Ellington CT 06029

Call Sign: K1NO
Century Club Contest
Group
9 Strawberry Rd Apt 14
Ellington CT 06029

Call Sign: KB1ELO
Sante Lillo
9 Strawberry Rd Apt 14
Ellington CT 06029

Call Sign: KB1VQW
Weining Wu
4 Teaberry Ridge
Ellington CT 06029

Call Sign: KB1QJS
Brandon J Bartell
35 Wapping Wood Rd
Ellington CT 06029

Call Sign: KA1BSC
John T Whitten
55 Webster Rd
Ellington CT 060292727

Call Sign: W1JTW
John T Whitten
55 Webster Rd
Ellington CT 060292727

Call Sign: KB1SMC
Harry J Wambolt
108 Webster Rd
Ellington CT 06029

Call Sign: KB1SMD
Kristen M Picard-Wambolt
108 Webster Rd
Ellington CT 06029

Call Sign: KB1ITU
Randal F Mcintire
153 Webster Rd
Ellington CT 06029

Call Sign: W1FXS
Francis Stadmeyer
155 Windermere Ave #1108
Ellington CT 06029

Call Sign: KB1WAP
Francis Stadmeyer
155 Windermere Ave 1108
Ellington CT 06029

Call Sign: NO1Z
Christopher Martin
155 Windermere Ave Unit
1207
Ellington CT 06029

Call Sign: WA1ODD
Gordon D Underwood
Ellington CT 06029

Call Sign: KB1EPH
John J Mccormick Sr
Ellington CT 06029

FCC Amateur Radio Licenses in Elmwood

Call Sign: K1CFE
James R Vann
22 Grove St
Elmwood CT 061101841

Call Sign: N1WKZ
Maurice P Samuelian
26 Lewis Ln
Elmwood CT 06110

Call Sign: W1GYR
Charles S Griffen
1225 New Britain Ave
Elmwood CT 061102405

Call Sign: N1MZ
Zvonimir Makovec
Elmwood CT 061330941

Call Sign: W1BCD
Michael Pupin Memorial
Radio Club
Elmwood CT 061330941

Call Sign: KB1NDO
Sky Contest Club
Elmwood CT 061330941

Call Sign: WW6SKY
Sky Contest Club
Elmwood CT 061330941

FCC Amateur Radio Licenses in Enfield

Call Sign: KA1CEA
Eugene E Allard
194 Abbe Rd

Enfield CT 06082

Enfield CT 06082

Enfield CT 06082

Call Sign: W1ESR
Robert R Bell
33 Alban Rd
Enfield CT 06082

Call Sign: KX1P
David C Miller
42 Bigelow Ave
Enfield CT 06082

Call Sign: W1ZVF
Joseph D Gagne
41 Broadleaf Ln
Enfield CT 06082

Call Sign: KB1FRA
Paul J Steneri
26 Allen Street
Enfield CT 06082

Call Sign: WA1FTI
Scott B Welton
6 Birchwood Rd
Enfield CT 06082

Call Sign: KB1SLU
Dawn L Brock-Belford
44 Brook Rd
Enfield CT 06082

Call Sign: N1RUU
Rodney H Bungard Jr
10 Ann St
Enfield CT 06082

Call Sign: N1FWF
Richard J Chrzan
58 Booth Rd
Enfield CT 06082

Call Sign: KB1SLV
Richard E Belford Jr
44 Brook Rd
Enfield CT 06082

Call Sign: KA1LIW
Frederick J Stroiney
14 Armstrong Rd
Enfield CT 060822709

Call Sign: KA1CRI
Carmine J Morrone
15 Booth St
Enfield CT 06082

Call Sign: N1YGD
Allan P Davis
14 Campania Rd
Enfield CT 06082

Call Sign: KA1ZUN
Gary T Desrosiers
414 Ashmead Commons
Enfield CT 06082

Call Sign: WA1VQK
Anthony C Kondracki
64 Brewster Rd
Enfield CT 06082

Call Sign: N1XSD
Andrew J Chabot
32 Carriage Dr
Enfield CT 06082

Call Sign: N1MFN
Gary T Desrosiers
414 Ashmead Commons
Enfield CT 06082

Call Sign: W1TDE
William J Czipulis
37 Bridge Ln
Enfield CT 06082

Call Sign: NA1H
Robert B Kirby
25 Central St Apt 6b
Enfield CT 06083

Call Sign: K1WTA
Leonard H Pauze Jr
15 Avon St
Enfield CT 060824550

Call Sign: WA1PVM
Stephen J Skarzynski
5 Bright St
Enfield CT 06082

Call Sign: KB1FDU
Neal A Haggerty
90 Church Street
Enfield CT 06082

Call Sign: KB1UUQ
Brandon Cislak
2 Betty Rd
Enfield CT 06082

Call Sign: N1WCB
Gene L Giuliano Jr
17 Broadleaf Ln
Enfield CT 06082

Call Sign: KB1EGL
Shirley C Cooper
4 Circle Dr
Enfield CT 06082

Call Sign: K1NFL
Brandon Cislak
2 Betty Rd

Call Sign: N1WHZ
Jason W Gauthier
17 Broadleaf Ln

Call Sign: W1NWE
Thomas T Leiper
11 Circle Dr

Enfield CT 06082

Enfield CT 06082

Enfield CT 06082

Call Sign: N1LZI
John F Malley
19 Claremont Ave
Enfield CT 06082

Call Sign: KA1RT
W Michael Lachniet
28 Deepwood Rd
Enfield CT 060826121

Call Sign: KB1SLT
Gerald P Barnett
26 Ellis Rd
Enfield CT 06082

Call Sign: K1PC
Paul Cappa
16 Colonial Dr
Enfield CT 06082

Call Sign: KB1HLC
Donald J Lee Jr
23 Diamond Dr
Enfield CT 06082

Call Sign: KB1VV
Robert A Pancavage
56 Elm St Unit 11
Enfield CT 060823655

Call Sign: KA1ONX
William J Snyder Sr
35 Colonial Dr
Enfield CT 06082

Call Sign: N1EWY
Alexander Filatov Ii
6 Dicardee Dr
Enfield CT 06082

Call Sign: N1GOO
Annette M Pancavage
56 Elm St Unit 11
Enfield CT 060823655

Call Sign: WA1GFZ
Francis A Carcia Jr
181 Columbia Rd
Enfield CT 06082

Call Sign: KB1AEV
Dana L Underhill
42 Douglas Dr
Enfield CT 06082

Call Sign: W1SQ
Robert M Laflamme
335 Elm Street
Enfield CT 06082

Call Sign: N1IRB
Scott R Norris
1 Coolidge Drive
Enfield CT 060825309

Call Sign: K1LNB
Paul R Pearson
30 Edgewood Dr
Enfield CT 06082

Call Sign: K1MVR
David L Olson
1371 Enfield St
Enfield CT 06082

Call Sign: N1KIP
Randall S Duchesneau
75 Cornell Dr
Enfield CT 06082

Call Sign: N1XVZ
Matthew Malinoski
36 Edgewood Dr
Enfield CT 060825916

Call Sign: N1GVV
Adam D Olson
1371 Enfield St
Enfield CT 06082

Call Sign: N1YWU
Daniel M Mc Carthy
66 Cottage Rd
Enfield CT 06082

Call Sign: WB1HAM
William P Malinoski
36 Edgewood Dr
Enfield CT 06082

Call Sign: KB1TWL
Richard D Fusco
7 Fairfield Rd
Enfield CT 06082

Call Sign: KA1HPI
Allen G Alward
37 Dale Rd
Enfield CT 06082

Call Sign: KA1BBW
Lillian L Dow
4 Eds Dr
Enfield CT 06082

Call Sign: WB1CKI
Gordon D Young
12 Fairlane Rd
Enfield CT 06082

Call Sign: N1QCJ
Dale H Ulrich
24 David St

Call Sign: KB1VRI
Nicholas P Levasseur
8 Elizabeth St

Call Sign: KA1JES
William J Spokes
4 Gamello Ave

Enfield CT 060821806

Call Sign: KB1SLZ
Howard L Lunt Jr
4 Glen Arden Ln
Enfield CT 06082

Call Sign: WA1IYJ
Arthur C Birch
15 Glendale Rd
Enfield CT 06082

Call Sign: KB1SLW
Emily A Clifford
8 Gordon Lane
Enfield CT 06082

Call Sign: WA1EMI
Russell H Mc Clintock
56 Granny Ter
Enfield CT 060823006

Call Sign: KA1TBA
Paul J Faille
6 Grove Rd
Enfield CT 06082

Call Sign: N1EHZ
Richard A Prior
1 Hampton Rd
Enfield CT 06082

Call Sign: KB1EDX
William I Basser
347 Hazard Ave
Enfield CT 06082

Call Sign: KB1UJV
Carl E Gabbert Jr
368 Hazard Ave
Enfield CT 06082

Call Sign: N1QKP
Knut E Finnevolden
2 Hillyer Dr

Enfield CT 06082

Call Sign: KB1OFZ
Joshua J Finnie
7 Hillyer Dr
Enfield CT 06082

Call Sign: KB1KTE
Richard T Stebbins
2 Hoover Ln
Enfield CT 06082

Call Sign: KB1PXV
Ross B Perreault
18 Howard St
Enfield CT 06082

Call Sign: KA1DDV
Frank C Cooper
23 Impala Dr
Enfield CT 06082

Call Sign: K1FWK
George L Egerton
27 Indian Run
Enfield CT 06082

Call Sign: N1GEG
Franklin A Deming
118 Jackson Rd
Enfield CT 06082

Call Sign: N1FNU
Howard F Jansma
162 Jackson Rd
Enfield CT 06082

Call Sign: KB1IPY
David B Smith
2 Joan Dr
Enfield CT 060823010

Call Sign: N1DBS
David B Smith
2 Joan Dr

Enfield CT 060823010

Call Sign: KB1LTU
Patricia K Smith
2 Joan Dr
Enfield CT 06082

Call Sign: N1LCC
Kieth M Bergendahl
33 Kimberly Dr
Enfield CT 06082

Call Sign: N1XZF
Steven L De Capua
47 Laurel Pk
Enfield CT 06082

Call Sign: KB1JH
Vincent J Motto
8 Louise Dr
Enfield CT 060825923

Call Sign: N1MN
Vincent J Motto
8 Louise Dr
Enfield CT 060825923

Call Sign: K1AH
Vincent J Motto
8 Louise Dr
Enfield CT 060825923

Call Sign: KD1TB
Gerard A Cote
5 Lox Ln
Enfield CT 06082

Call Sign: KB1DGG
Joseph L Nadeau Jr
16 Magnolia Dr
Enfield CT 060822016

Call Sign: KY1W
Richard A Hickson
40 Mathewson Ave

Enfield CT 06082   Enfield CT 06082   Enfield CT 06082

Call Sign: KB1LWD
Robert J West
1 Michael Dr
Enfield CT 06082

Call Sign: KB1DMB
Douglas J Metivier
30 Montano Rd
Enfield CT 060822449

Call Sign: AB1JA
Wilfried Klein
115 Oldefield Farms
Enfield CT 06082

Call Sign: N1TPV
William L Trumper
41 Middlesex Dr
Enfield CT 06082

Call Sign: N1XPL
Karen M Marinaccio
243 Moody Rd
Enfield CT 06082

Call Sign: KB1EWR
Charles L Johnson Iii
19 Orbit Dr
Enfield CT 06082

Call Sign: NM1K
Russell T Hack Jr
21 Montano
Enfield CT 06082

Call Sign: N1CLR
Roland E Buzzell
275 Moody Rd
Enfield CT 06082

Call Sign: K7XDY
Charles L Johnson Iii
19 Orbit Dr
Enfield CT 06082

Call Sign: KB1IRV
Connecticut Signalmen
21 Montano
Enfield CT 06082

Call Sign: KB1LFD
Frank Sedlik
1 Moon St
Enfield CT 06082

Call Sign: KB1TVC
Francis J Boyer
23 Oxford Dr
Enfield CT 06082

Call Sign: KA1VEC
Connecticut Signalmen
21 Montano
Enfield CT 06082

Call Sign: K2KXJ
Martin E Boyle
195 N Maple St
Enfield CT 06082

Call Sign: KB1TVD
Zachary R Boyer
23 Oxford Dr
Enfield CT 06082

Call Sign: KA1VEC
Russell T Hack Sr
21 Montano Rd
Enfield CT 06082

Call Sign: N1YQR
Melissa A Flaherty
375 N Maple St
Enfield CT 060830814

Call Sign: KB1JVK
Kevin J Smith
47 Park Ave
Enfield CT 06082

Call Sign: KA1VED
Edith K Hack
21 Montano Rd
Enfield CT 06082

Call Sign: KB1WHA
Robert A Rocconella
79 North St
Enfield CT 06082

Call Sign: W0ASS
Kevin J Smith
47 Park Ave
Enfield CT 06082

Call Sign: KB1UIG
Enfield Ct Cert
21 Montano Rd
Enfield CT 06082

Call Sign: N1SPJ
Dennis L Rembiesa
4 Northfield Rd
Enfield CT 06082

Call Sign: K1EVN
Kevin J Smith
47 Park Ave
Enfield CT 06082

Call Sign: K1ENF
Enfield Ct Cert
21 Montano Rd

Call Sign: N1SPM
Suzanne C Rembiesa
4 Northfield Rd

Call Sign: KB1DCD
Kevin J Reilly
37 Plainfield

Enfield CT 060825813

Call Sign: WA1SFM
Philip D Corini
11 Plainfield St
Enfield CT 06082

Call Sign: N1VRI
Christopher B Reilly
37 Plainfield St
Enfield CT 060825813

Call Sign: KE1DK
Theodore J Polinski
4 Play Rd
Enfield CT 06082

Call Sign: KB1MDT
Philip H Williams Iii
38 Pleasant St
Enfield CT 06082

Call Sign: AB1R
Francis H Morrison
16 Poplar St
Enfield CT 06082

Call Sign: KB1MCI
Leverett R Clark
24 Powder Ridge Rd
Enfield CT 06082

Call Sign: KA1PRM
Albert J Merkt
33 Powder Ridge Rd
Enfield CT 06082

Call Sign: KB1IQV
Clifford D Champlin Jr
78 Prospect St
Enfield CT 06082

Call Sign: KB1ISV
Michael J Merrill
78 Prospect St

Enfield CT 06082

Call Sign: N1XHN
Mark A Marinaccio
22a Prospect St
Enfield CT 06082

Call Sign: KB1GTD
E Paul Galica
15 Robbin Rd
Enfield CT 06082

Call Sign: KD6CCB
Stephanie M Bustos
24 Robbin Rd
Enfield CT 060822117

Call Sign: KI6DYG
Santiago Bustos Iii
24 Robbin Rd
Enfield CT 060822117

Call Sign: N1FB
Paul K Pagel
4 Roberts Rd
Enfield CT 06082

Call Sign: N1CRR
Frederick Goodman
4 Rocket Run
Enfield CT 060825050

Call Sign: N1CRS
Sandra O Goodman
4 Rocket Run
Enfield CT 060825050

Call Sign: AK1WI
Larry Hurst
19 Rockland Dr
Enfield CT 06082

Call Sign: KB1LNT
Karen B Bartlett
77 Roosevelt Blvd

Enfield CT 06082

Call Sign: K1MPD
Michael P Dailey
79 Roosevelt Blvd
Enfield CT 06082

Call Sign: KB1CZT
Todd B Punderson
1 Roseland Ave
Enfield CT 060823709

Call Sign: N1ALZ
Ludwig Kreho
27 Rye Field Dr
Enfield CT 06082

Call Sign: AA1WB
Ludwig Kreho
27 Rye Field Dr
Enfield CT 06082

Call Sign: K1WH
Ludwig Kreho
27 Rye Field Dr
Enfield CT 06082

Call Sign: KA1YUD
Mario Saccoccio
19 Saint James Ave
Enfield CT 06082

Call Sign: WB1I
Fred I Caswell Jr
13 Salerno Drive
Enfield CT 06082

Call Sign: W1VWP
Gordon R Zuchegna
9 Sandpiper Rd
Enfield CT 060825718

Call Sign: KB1IXA
Daniel L Zuchegna
9 Sandpiper Rd

Enfield CT 06082

Call Sign: WA1FYB
Peter S Eslinger
4 Shady Oak Dr
Enfield CT 06082

Call Sign: N1YHA
Keith T Henneberry
1 Silver Ln
Enfield CT 06082

Call Sign: KA1YBB
James T Walpole
22 Silver Ln
Enfield CT 06082

Call Sign: WB1AEU
Glenn L Layne
1 Sky St
Enfield CT 06082

Call Sign: WA1KQC
John H Waller
20 Somers Rd
Enfield CT 06082

Call Sign: N1EEC
Henry F Tetrault
110 South Road Apt 23
Enfield CT 060824445

Call Sign: K1DBP
Frank J Colletti
35 Southwood Rd
Enfield CT 06082

Call Sign: KE1DQ
Peter N Russell
9 Spring Garden Rd
Enfield CT 060823037

Call Sign: KB1BJK
Edward M Dugan
22 St James Ave

Enfield CT 06082

Call Sign: KB1LEW
Ralph C Gedney
11 Summer St 2nd Fl
Enfield CT 06082

Call Sign: KB1DVE
Lynn J Anfinson
1 Tolland Dr
Enfield CT 06082

Call Sign: KB1FQQ
Eugene G Warmouth Jr
2 Trevor Drive
Enfield CT 06082

Call Sign: KA1JKI
Garth J Hallett
2 Vernon Rd
Enfield CT 06082

Call Sign: N1QVR
Jennifer B Vesci
5 Wallop School Rd.
Enfield CT 06082

Call Sign: KA1OGT
William J Mazza
15 Washington Ave
Enfield CT 06082

Call Sign: KA1ERU
Irving M Pease
549 Washington Rd
Enfield CT 06082

Call Sign: K1CEX
Robert A Manning
12 West Forrest Dr
Enfield CT 06082

Call Sign: N1YPE
Paul R Meunier
17 Weymouth Rd

Enfield CT 06082

Call Sign: N1IKE
Harry G Hartzell
92 Willard Dr
Enfield CT 06082

Call Sign: KD1ZD
Robert E Thoelen Iii
27 Willard Drive
Enfield CT 06082

Call Sign: KA1ONY
John M Holland
16 Windham Rd
Enfield CT 06082

Call Sign: KB1LVY
Russ A Belanger
6 Windmill Rd
Enfield CT 06082

Call Sign: N1RWG
Andrew J Zander
59a Windsor St
Enfield CT 06082

Call Sign: N1XST
Jonathan J Zander
59a Windsor St
Enfield CT 06082

Call Sign: KB1QGN
Wilfried Klein
707 Woodgate Circle
Enfield CT 06082

Call Sign: KB1EEY
Michael P Dailey
1210 Woodgate Circle
Enfield CT 06082

Call Sign: KB1FGM
Michael P Dailey
1210 Woodgate Circle

Enfield CT 06082

Call Sign: KB1FMK
Michael P Dailey
1210 Woodgate Circle
Enfield CT 06082

Call Sign: KB1NJV
Robert M Laflamme
4 Woodlawn Ave
Enfield CT 060822436

Call Sign: AA1RK
John A Badura
Enfield CT 060830605

Call Sign: N1NOC
Patricia A Knapp
Enfield CT 06083

Call Sign: KB1HDD
Maria T Johnson
Enfield CT 060830623

Call Sign: KB1LEX
John P Shea
Enfield CT 06083

**FCC Amateur Radio
Licenses in Essex**

Call Sign: K1OBJ
Ogden Bigelow Jr
30 Bokum Road
Essex CT 06426

Call Sign: N1KZM
Ram Dulari Collier
15 Brookside Ln
Essex CT 06426

Call Sign: KB1OZB
Bette J Buckridge
8 Collins Lane
Essex CT 06427

Call Sign: KB1OZC
William E Buckridge
8 Collins Lane
Essex CT 06426

Call Sign: KA1WN
Stewart L De Vausney
118 Essex Meadows
Essex CT 064261522

Call Sign: W1ECG
Howland B Jones Jr
217 Essex Meadows
Essex CT 06427

Call Sign: N1PYU
Robert G Luburg
251 Essex Meadows
Essex CT 06426

Call Sign: K1RFY
Turner Marsh
266 Essex Meadows
Essex CT 064261525

Call Sign: W2BGL
Henry R Wilsey
267 Essex Meadows
Essex CT 06426

Call Sign: N1ZQD
David W Sykes Sr
593 Essex Meadows
Essex CT 06426

Call Sign: KB1PEN
Clarke
F G E
Essex CT 064260099

Call Sign: K1FGE
Clarke
F G E
Essex CT 064260099

Call Sign: K9GTH
Scott L Harris
22 Fordham Road
Essex CT 06426

Call Sign: N1KZK
Earl J Fowler
18 Gates Rd
Essex CT 06426

Call Sign: WA3TRN
Joseph R Reifer
31 Prospect St
Essex CT 064261031

Call Sign: KB1NN
William P Herlihy Sr
45 River Rd
Essex CT 06426

Call Sign: N1WHD
Timothy W Howell
151 River Rd
Essex CT 06426

Call Sign: WB1FMW
Dale S Dickinson
85 River Rd Unit L5
Essex CT 06426

Call Sign: N1ATG
Michael M Perl
71 South Main Street
Essex CT 06426

Call Sign: N1CUA
Jonathan L Perl Mr.
71 South Main Street
Essex CT 06426

Call Sign: KS4US
Edward C Mc Caffrey
20 South Winds Drive
Essex CT 06426

Call Sign: K1VZA
Roger J Kern
6 Turnstone Road
Essex CT 06426

Call Sign: KA1TAQ
Geoffrey M Kerrigan
3 Waterside Lane
Essex CT 06426

Call Sign: KB1QLL
Stewart H Schenck
39 West Ave
Essex CT 06426

Call Sign: KA1NGR
Kathleen J Harris
Essex CT 06426

**FCC Amateur Radio
Licenses in Fairfield**

Call Sign: KM1B
Thomas H Lang
245 1j Warde Ter
Fairfield CT 06425

Call Sign: N1HAQ
Jack T Wargo
70 Alton Pl
Fairfield CT 06825

Call Sign: N1WLP
David A St Germain
130 Baros St
Fairfield CT 06430

Call Sign: N1VHT
Roger L Anderson
171 Baros St
Fairfield CT 06824

Call Sign: WB1FDU
Bruce E Moore

303 Beach Rd
Fairfield CT 06430

Call Sign: N1ZU
Bruce E Moore
303 Beach Rd
Fairfield CT 06824

Call Sign: KA1HTH
Sylvia M Zigun
12 Beechwood Ln
Fairfield CT 06825

Call Sign: K2GTY
John V Von Sneidern Jr
125 Bennett St
Fairfield CT 06825

Call Sign: KC1OF
Terence Roach
238 Bennett St
Fairfield CT 06432

Call Sign: AA1VP
Terence Roach
238 Bennett St
Fairfield CT 06432

Call Sign: NA1SV
Stephen E Verbil
43 Berkeley Rd
Fairfield CT 068254417

Call Sign: WB2IUL
John M Bruderman Jr
50 Berkeley Rd
Fairfield CT 064324418

Call Sign: N1LNR
Paul M Haydu
108 Bibbins Ave
Fairfield CT 06430

Call Sign: KA1UGS
William M Carter

808 Black Rock Tpke
Fairfield CT 06430

Call Sign: N1TVN
John J Masi Jr
1838 Black Rock Tpke Apt
301
Fairfield CT 06825

Call Sign: WQ3J
Jason Foster Bey
564 Black Rock Turnpike
Fairfield CT 06825

Call Sign: KB1UJY
Emma F Ellis
38 Blake Drive
Fairfield CT 06824

Call Sign: KB1OEC
T Devitt Allen
100 Bradley Street
Fairfield CT 06824

Call Sign: N1FIR
Peter Kiako
101 Brookfield Ave
Fairfield CT 06432

Call Sign: KB1LTP
Christopher M Coyle
74 Brookside Dr
Fairfield CT 068242416

Call Sign: KC2AJM
Richard M Paul
133 Bungalow Ave
Fairfield CT 06430

Call Sign: WA1YCG
Abraham I Gordon
960 Burr St
Fairfield CT 06430

Call Sign: W1BSM

Brian S May
1176 Burr St
Fairfield CT 06430

Call Sign: KA1IIL
Andrew R Medvegy Jr
2001 Burr St
Fairfield CT 06430

Call Sign: W1DHI
Michael J Brienza
714 Burr Street
Fairfield CT 068247156

Call Sign: KB1FXC
Brian S May
1176 Burr Street
Fairfield CT 06430

Call Sign: N1HAF
Dimitris Kotzailias
744 Burroughs Rd
Fairfield CT 06430

Call Sign: N1KSC
Stella Kotzailias
744 Burroughs Rd
Fairfield CT 06430

Call Sign: KA1LWM
William E Dunn
10 Centerbrook Rd
Fairfield CT 06430

Call Sign: KA1GWE
Anna Godrie
105 Churchill St
Fairfield CT 06430

Call Sign: N1XCO
Frank E Baron
84 Cobblers Hill Rd
Fairfield CT 06824

Call Sign: N3AQJ

Gary H Weddle
71 Colonial Dr
Fairfield CT 064306817

Call Sign: W1GHW
Gary H Weddle
71 Colonial Dr
Fairfield CT 064306817

Call Sign: KA1MYP
Robert M Geoghegan
2161 Congress St
Fairfield CT 064307116

Call Sign: K1MYM
Edward L Cheffetz
38 Crest Terrace
Fairfield CT 06825

Call Sign: N1AK
Alexander G Kuhn
107 Cynthia Drive
Fairfield CT 06824

Call Sign: KB1EMY
Duncan M March
100 Dalewood Ave
Fairfield CT 06824

Call Sign: KA1FSR
Christopher W De Witt
289 Davis Road
Fairfield CT 06825

Call Sign: KA1YQI
Joseph V Loiacono
78 Deer Run
Fairfield CT 06430

Call Sign: KB1WIC
Peter R Cimino
618 Duck Farm Rd
Fairfield CT 06824

Call Sign: W1NS

Norman S Dick
250 Eastfield Dr
Fairfield CT 06432

Call Sign: KB1QAB
Joshua D Dick
250 Eastfield Drive
Fairfield CT 06825

Call Sign: KB1BNO
Nancy Docherty
100 Eunice Ave
Fairfield CT 06430

Call Sign: KE1BU
Laszlo Radocz
261 Fairchild Av
Fairfield CT 06432

Call Sign: WA1PYU
Jozsef G Debreceni
261 Fairchild Av
Fairfield CT 06432

Call Sign: KA1L
James T Louloudes
228 Fairfield Beach Rd
Fairfield CT 06430

Call Sign: KA1OLI
Robert T Reed
254 Fairfield Woods Rd
Fairfield CT 06430

Call Sign: KA1CZQ
Joseph T Faria
117 Fairland Dr
Fairfield CT 064323222

Call Sign: W1SQL
Joseph T Faria
117 Fairland Dr
Fairfield CT 068253222

Call Sign: NJ1C

Gyula Palmai
69 Flax Rd
Fairfield CT 068246365

Call Sign: W1NU
Victor D Politi
69 Flax Rd
Fairfield CT 068246365

Call Sign: KA1OKU
Emile C Schaffner
114 Flora Blvd
Fairfield CT 06430

Call Sign: KB1UZR
Kenneth A Von Holtz
70 Fox St
Fairfield CT 06824

Call Sign: KA1IBZ
Frank J Thompson
1090 Galloping Hill Rd
Fairfield CT 068247130

Call Sign: KB1UZQ
Donald F Peterson
1061 Galloping Hill Road
Fairfield CT 06824

Call Sign: W2FYJ
Carl B Adolphson Jr
65 Gate Ridge Rd
Fairfield CT 06430

Call Sign: KA1OJH
Staffan O Grigholm
83 Geneva Ter
Fairfield CT 06430

Call Sign: KB1EED
Kirk S Mc Donald
141 Gorham Rd
Fairfield CT 06430

Call Sign: WB6HPT

Don Lebell
190 Governors Lane
Fairfield CT 06824

Call Sign: WB1FYY
Marion B Yourwith
54 Greenlawn Drive
Fairfield CT 06825

Call Sign: N2ACG
John H Mahar
71 High Point Ln
Fairfield CT 064302063

Call Sign: WC1ACK
Fairfield Civil Preparedness
461 High St
Fairfield CT 06430

Call Sign: W1LRW
Andrew Gura Jr
126 Highlawn Rd
Fairfield CT 06430

Call Sign: N1ZIL
Matthew J Galya
2305 Hillside Rd
Fairfield CT 064302019

Call Sign: N1ZIK
Raymond E Galya
2361 Hillside Rd
Fairfield CT 06430

Call Sign: W1EZA
Eugene I Herman
358 Katona Dr
Fairfield CT 06430

Call Sign: KB1MZL
Jeffrey N Cronin
750 Knapps Highway
Fairfield CT 06824

Call Sign: W1XW

Anthony L Szilagyi
107 Knollwood Dr
Fairfield CT 06430

Call Sign: KB1UJX
Connie D Lasky
290 Knollwood Dr
Fairfield CT 06824

Call Sign: KB1VXR
Rebecca L Zwally
290 Knollwood Dr
Fairfield CT 06824

Call Sign: N1BYX
Werner Graser
23 Lakeview Ct
Fairfield CT 06430

Call Sign: KB1SJB
Linda C Crowley
112 Lalley Boulevard
Fairfield CT 06824

Call Sign: WB1CYW
Everett H Herbert
15 Limerick Rd
Fairfield CT 06430

Call Sign: W1HIX
Thomas A Giordano
155 Lisbon Dr
Fairfield CT 068252641

Call Sign: KB1PGS
Gazal Gulati
492 Lockwood Rd
Fairfield CT 06825

Call Sign: KB1PGT
Mona Gulati
492 Lockwood Rd
Fairfield CT 06825

Call Sign: KB1PGU

Jay Gulati
492 Lockwood Rd
Fairfield CT 06825

Call Sign: KB1PGV
Sagar Gulati
492 Lockwood Rd
Fairfield CT 06825

Call Sign: W1HT
Ralph E Green
129 Lucille St
Fairfield CT 06825

Call Sign: N1LQS
Douglas S Lee
13 Meadowbrook Rd
Fairfield CT 06430

Call Sign: KB1QPV
Phillip J Rodriguez
33 Melville Ave
Fairfield CT 06825

Call Sign: KA1ICB
Norbert C Lux
49 Melville Ave
Fairfield CT 06432

Call Sign: KA1SDR
John Gawron Jr
234 Melville Dr
Fairfield CT 06430

Call Sign: KA1GGP
Harold E Rhame Jr
501 Mine Hill Rd
Fairfield CT 06430

Call Sign: WA1OMJ
Caron J Keenan
139 Miro St
Fairfield CT 06430

Call Sign: WA1UZC

Jason F Mallette
192 Miro St
Fairfield CT 064323616

Call Sign: KA1EFS
Ronald H Knight
38 Morehouse Dr
Fairfield CT 06432

Call Sign: W1LLV
Carl A Mitchell
78 Nepas Rd
Fairfield CT 06825

Call Sign: KB1LRW
Kenneth G Lehman
346 Nepas Rd
Fairfield CT 06825

Call Sign: W1MEH
Kenneth G Lehmann
346 Nepas Rd
Fairfield CT 06825

Call Sign: W1RLD
William E Bannay Jr
60 New St
Fairfield CT 06432

Call Sign: KB1UKB
Myra S Rustin
29 Newton Street
Fairfield CT 068246925

Call Sign: KB1QMR
John P Markey
108 Nichols St
Fairfield CT 06824

Call Sign: KB1IAJ
David O Jackson
533 North Benson Rd
Fairfield CT 06430

Call Sign: WA1ZOX

Lois Bird
2307 North Benson Rd
Fairfield CT 06824

Call Sign: N1XQS
Vincent A Sanfilippo
1400 North Benson Road
Fairfield CT 06824

Call Sign: W1GWA
Dennis J Bird
2307 North Benson Road
Fairfield CT 068243135

Call Sign: N1PCI
Will E Banks Iii
180 Old Academy Rd
Fairfield CT 06430

Call Sign: N1HPE
Victor M Gracer
198 Old Blackrock Tpke
Fairfield CT 06430

Call Sign: W1FIV
Robert Berliner
290 Old Spring Rd
Fairfield CT 06824

Call Sign: KB1HMH
William C Taylor
72 Old Stratfield Rd
Fairfield CT 06432

Call Sign: KB1TGY
CONOR T Lahiff
166 Old Stratfield Road
Fairfield CT 06825

Call Sign: KD1OP
Alexander G Kuhn
74 Oldfield Dr
Fairfield CT 06430

Call Sign: N1GPE

Gasper F Kuhn
74 Oldfield Dr
Fairfield CT 06430

Call Sign: K1INQ
John L Kmetzo
53 Oldfield Rd
Fairfield CT 06430

Call Sign: WA2PRM
Mark A Potter
87 Oldfield Road
Fairfield CT 06824

Call Sign: KB1UKC
DOUGLAS J Defauw
110 Orchard Hill Drive
Fairfield CT 06824

Call Sign: N8ANQ
Eric Geil
149 Orchard Hill Drive
Fairfield CT 068247318

Call Sign: KA1GX
Frank G Moycik
149 Oyster Rd
Fairfield CT 06430

Call Sign: W1TTJ
Arthur B Duel Iii
136 Palmer Bridge
Fairfield CT 064307830

Call Sign: K4SF
John B Englund
123 Papurah Rd
Fairfield CT 06825

Call Sign: WA1NLJ
John R Hafele
3467 Park Ave
Fairfield CT 06432

Call Sign: KB1RJN

Vincent A Pennatto Jr
3609 Park Ave
Fairfield CT 06825

Call Sign: WA1BDO
George E Classy
118 Partridge Ln
Fairfield CT 06430

Call Sign: N1KOE
Larry A Strickland
259 Pemburn Dr
Fairfield CT 06430

Call Sign: KB1QPY
James M Eastwood
41 Pepperbush Lane
Fairfield CT 06824

Call Sign: KB1UBA
Benjamin H Feintzeig
36 Pequot Rd
Fairfield CT 06825

Call Sign: WU1K
John M Colonnese
35 Perry St
Fairfield CT 064303814

Call Sign: WA1RUS
Brian C Beuershausen
Po Box 320294
Fairfield CT 06825

Call Sign: WB1BSN
Fred J Baechtold Jr
21 Pompano Pl
Fairfield CT 06430

Call Sign: KB1NLU
North Stratfield School
Amateur Radio Association
190 Putting Green Rd
Fairfield CT 06825

Call Sign: WA1NSS
North Stratfield School
Amateur Radio Association
190 Putting Green Rd
Fairfield CT 06825

Call Sign: K1RBF
William S Britt
33 Reef Ct
Fairfield CT 06430

Call Sign: KA1PGZ
John B Lindsay
130 Rockland Rd
Fairfield CT 06432

Call Sign: WB1CQO
Greater Fairfield Amateur
Radio Assn
1 Rod Highway
Fairfield CT 068246365

Call Sign: KB1TGV
Mark T Kennedy
409 Rolling Hills Drive
Fairfield CT 06824

Call Sign: KB1TGU
Haydn E Kennedy
409 Rollington Hills Drive
Fairfield CT 06824

Call Sign: KA1CVV
Edmund C Bassick
75 Romanock Pl
Fairfield CT 06432

Call Sign: KA1NRU
William B Moran
344 Romanock Rd
Fairfield CT 06432

Call Sign: K1HWL
Paul Carroll
20 Ronald Dr

Fairfield CT 06430   Fairfield CT 06824   Fairfield CT 06824

Call Sign: W1THC
Phillip J D Ostilio
116 Ronald Dr
Fairfield CT 06432

Call Sign: K1IJW
Anthony V Adams
60 Short Hill Ln
Fairfield CT 06432

Call Sign: WB1GRV
Roy M Bobowick
152 Stratfield Rd
Fairfield CT 06432

Call Sign: KA1OKZ
Frank R Suich
96 Roseville St
Fairfield CT 06430

Call Sign: W1RPD
Robert P Daly
587 Shrub Oak Lane
Fairfield CT 068247813

Call Sign: KB1NPI
Brian C Beurshausen
1820 Stratfield Rd
Fairfield CT 06825

Call Sign: N1CDM
Raymond L Weber
450 Round Hill Rd
Fairfield CT 06824

Call Sign: N6HKD
Walter R Baranger Iii
480 Silver Spring Rd
Fairfield CT 068241947

Call Sign: N8ASQ
Vincent E Barmann
46 Sunfield Ln
Fairfield CT 06824

Call Sign: W1GDZ
Joseph P Ull
366 Ruane St
Fairfield CT 068245840

Call Sign: KB1NBX
Sungkey L Paik
125 Sky Top Terrace
Fairfield CT 06825

Call Sign: KB1UZS
Eileen B Lynam
245 Sunnyridge Ave 16
Fairfield CT 06824

Call Sign: KB1QFQ
Jeffrey E Tang
164 S 20st Dr
Fairfield CT 06824

Call Sign: KA1AC
S Stuart Gibbons
280 Spring Hill Rd
Fairfield CT 064301940

Call Sign: KA1ZQF
Anthony J Szost
442 Szost Dr
Fairfield CT 06430

Call Sign: KB1UBJ
Ari A Jones
203 Samp Morear Drive
Fairfield CT 06824

Call Sign: K1NYT
Robert H Horen
236 Stevenson Rd
Fairfield CT 06432

Call Sign: KC1BK
Earl M De Witt
164 Tanglewood Ln
Fairfield CT 06430

Call Sign: N1CRM
John K Anderson
52 Sasco Hill Terrace
Fairfield CT 06430

Call Sign: N1QLJ
Louis J Havanich
487 Stillson Rd
Fairfield CT 06824

Call Sign: KF1J
Robert A Nevins
108 Tide Mill Ter
Fairfield CT 068245653

Call Sign: KA1MJK
Erik J Sporre
65 Sedan Terrace
Fairfield CT 06825

Call Sign: N1TKT
Robert J Zadrovicz
559 Stillson Rd
Fairfield CT 06430

Call Sign: KB1UKT
Andrew K Fox
460 Toll House Lane
Fairfield CT 06825

Call Sign: W1EUR
Richard D Evans
128 Shady Hill Rd

Call Sign: WB2UJA
James V Lettera
220 Stonewall Ln

Call Sign: KD6UVC
Al Nasir Sultan
403 Unquowa Road

Fairfield CT 06824

Call Sign: KB1UJW
Edward E Smith
51 Villa Avenue
Fairfield CT 06825

Call Sign: KB5VVX
Michael D Fox
343 Villa Ave
Fairfield CT 06432

Call Sign: KA1USX
Cathy F Coburn
558 Villa Ave
Fairfield CT 06432

Call Sign: N1DRB
Paul J Coburn
558 Villa Ave
Fairfield CT 06432

Call Sign: N1VNV
William B Allinger
84 Warde Terr
Fairfield CT 06825

Call Sign: N1CFE
Cyril J Clancy
310 Wilson St
Fairfield CT 06432

Call Sign: W1HFL
Salvatore B Passos
206 Windermere Street
Fairfield CT 06825

Call Sign: WA1YFO
Jay L Ringelheim
135 Woody Ln
Fairfield CT 06432

Call Sign: N2UXA
Michael R Fabrico
74 York Road

Fairfield CT 06825

Call Sign: KB1BOZ
Mitchell Memorial Radio
Assn
Fairfield CT 06432

Call Sign: KB1BWA
Pacific Radio Association
Fairfield CT 06432

Call Sign: KB1BZR
Low Frequency Research
Society
Fairfield CT 06432

Call Sign: KB1CDP
North American Dx Group
Fairfield CT 06432

Call Sign: N1SBB
Thomas F Davis
Fairfield CT 064326590

Call Sign: WL7WO
Gary Carl Mitchell
Fairfield CT 06825

Call Sign: WO1T
Christian H Hansen
Fairfield CT 06430

Call Sign: KB1JZA
Maureen S Davis
Fairfield CT 06825

Call Sign: KB1JZB
Elaine T Davis
Fairfield CT 06825

Call Sign: N1ETD
Elaine T Davis
Fairfield CT 06825

Call Sign: W1MSD

Maureen S Davis
Fairfield CT 06825

Call Sign: W1TFD
Thomas F Davis
Fairfield CT 068256590

Call Sign: KB1RQY
City Of Bridgeport
Emergency Operations Club
Fairfield CT 06825

Call Sign: KB1TNM
Department Of Chemistry
Fairfield University
Fairfield University
Amateur Radio Club
Fairfield CT 06824

Call Sign: N3AQJ
Department Of Chemistry
Fairfield University
Fairfield University
Amateur Radio Club
Fairfield CT 06824

Call Sign: KH8AC
Gary Carl Mitchell
Fairfield CT 06825

FCC Amateur Radio Licenses in Falls Village

Call Sign: N1RXN
David A Archer
164 Canaan Mt Rd
Falls Village CT 06031

Call Sign: KA1LRH
Arthur B Cross
52 Kellogg Rd
Falls Village CT 06031

Call Sign: N1PJN
Jonathan E Vakassian

109 Rte 7
Falls Village CT 06031

FCC Amateur Radio Licenses in Farmington

Call Sign: N1NWL
Donald P Chmielewski Sr
12 Arwood Rd
Farmington CT 06032

Call Sign: N1OEM
Donald P Chmielewski Jr
12 Arwood Rd
Farmington CT 06032

Call Sign: KA1SK
Elizabeth A Walton
24 Berkshire Dr
Farmington CT 06032

Call Sign: N1FPL
Robert T Winter
149 Birdseye Rd
Farmington CT 06032

Call Sign: N1PSK
Christina M Perugini
3 Blue Ridge Dr
Farmington CT 06032

Call Sign: W1WEA
Edward L De Freitas
3 Blue Ridge Dr
Farmington CT 060322001

Call Sign: W1FAJ
Edward F Nowak
36 Bonnie Dr
Farmington CT 06032

Call Sign: N1NIR
Anthony E Voytovich
47 Carriage Dr
Farmington CT 06032

Call Sign: KB1RRR
Stephen M Paradis
22 Case St
Farmington CT 06032

Call Sign: KB1TLM
Amy A Leary
304 Colt Hgwy -36
Farmington CT 06032

Call Sign: W1SVR
Douglas W Grimshaw
369 Colt Hwy
Farmington CT 06032

Call Sign: K1EUS
David H Roy
39 Crosswood Rd
Farmington CT 06032

Call Sign: KA1HUG
Sandra A Roy
39 Crosswood Rd
Farmington CT 06032

Call Sign: KB1EID
Michael D Roy
39 Crosswood Road
Farmington CT 06032

Call Sign: N1TFZ
Larry R Graves
4 Cutler
Farmington CT 06032

Call Sign: KA1HXN
Laurie G Nolan
3 Cutler Ln
Farmington CT 06032

Call Sign: N1CHU
William M Nolan
3 Cutler Ln
Farmington CT 06032

Call Sign: KA1SJP
Dan Eisenberg
7 Cutler Ln
Farmington CT 06032

Call Sign: W1TDU
Frank C Ferola
15 Elizabeth Rd
Farmington CT 06032

Call Sign: W3GTI
Donald D Reefe
2 Essex Ct
Farmington CT 06032

Call Sign: KB1DFR
Brian M Bentio
1 Evergreen Trail
Farmington CT 06032

Call Sign: W1NI
Wtic Amateur Radio
Association
10 Executive Dr
Farmington CT 06032

Call Sign: KB1GKT
Geoffrey F Butland
8 Fable Lane
Farmington CT 06032

Call Sign: N1KV
Geoffrey F Butland
8 Fable Lane
Farmington CT 06032

Call Sign: KB1BQQ
American Red Cross
Farmington Chapter
209 Farmington Ave
Farmington CT 060321911

Call Sign: KB1TXP
Philip G Hanson

774 Farmington Ave
Farmington CT 06032

Call Sign: N1NKO
Philip G Hanson
774 Farmington Ave
Farmington CT 06032

Call Sign: N1SHU
Robb J Conlon
1677 Farmington Ave
Farmington CT 06085

Call Sign: N1SHW
Corey A Conlon
1677 Farmington Ave
Farmington CT 08085

Call Sign: N1SZR
Shawn M Conlon
1677 Farmington Ave
Farmington CT 06085

Call Sign: N1TCT
Diana L Conlon
1677 Farmington Ave
Farmington CT 06085

Call Sign: WA1ARC
American Red Cross Ct
Regional Chapter
209 Farmington Ave 3rd Fl
Farmington CT 060321911

Call Sign: WB1FEH
Elliott H Mini
67 Farmington Chase Crscnt
Farmington CT 06032

Call Sign: KB1KUP
Larry L Kirin
21 Field Rock Rd
Farmington CT 060322152

Call Sign: W1VTU

John P Reno
37 Forest Hills Dr
Farmington CT 06032

Call Sign: N1HEA
Mark A Ladisky
25 Fox Run Rd
Farmington CT 06085

Call Sign: WC1AAB
Bristol Emergency
Management
25 Fox Run Rd
Farmington CT 06085

Call Sign: WB1J
Richard B Ladisky
25 Fox Run Road
Farmington CT 06085

Call Sign: W1KGD
Alex J Bednarek
34 Gail Rd
Farmington CT 06032

Call Sign: N1TUO
Aleta M Gleason
185 Garden St
Farmington CT 06032

Call Sign: W4ZUJ
Donald D Reefe
1 Gleneagles Drive
Farmington CT 06032

Call Sign: KB1WR
David W Findley
3 Glenmore Dr
Farmington CT 06032

Call Sign: KB1MYJ
Frank W Scalia
11 Greenbriar Dr Unit D
Farmington CT 06032

Call Sign: KA1SJN
Trung X Le
6 Half Acre Dr
Farmington CT 06032

Call Sign: KA1GZY
Jacqueline M Hogerty
83 Harold Rd
Farmington CT 06032

Call Sign: AA1VG
Ronald H Smith
83 Harold Rd
Farmington CT 06032

Call Sign: K1THP
David A Karpiej
100 Harold Rd
Farmington CT 06032

Call Sign: KA1DTU
Elizabeth H Karpiej
100 Harold Rd
Farmington CT 06032

Call Sign: N1CEM
Deane G Williams
6 Harvest Ln
Farmington CT 06032

Call Sign: N1CRQ
Ronald A Wysocki
9 Harvest Ln
Farmington CT 06032

Call Sign: N1URR
Karol M Hernas
17 Hotchkiss Rd
Farmington CT 06032

Call Sign: KA1SXT
Kenneth H Mathewgon
31 Jeffrey Dr
Farmington CT 06032

Call Sign: KB1HTE
Steven C Cote
78 Knollwood Rd
Farmington CT 06032

Call Sign: AB1BQ
Steven C Cote
78 Knollwood Rd
Farmington CT 06032

Call Sign: KJ4IJJ
David E Dressler
16 Lake Garda Dr.
Farmington CT 06085

Call Sign: WB8TWP
Patricia M Buttero
5 Lakeview Drive
Farmington CT 06032

Call Sign: W1HID
Philip B Clegg
221 Main St A4
Farmington CT 06032

Call Sign: KB1EPI
Charles E Rogers 3rd
287 Main St Apt A1
Farmington CT 06032

Call Sign: W1RMU
John T Kneeland
10 Maple Ridge Dr
Farmington CT 06032

Call Sign: N1HVR
Dorothy G Perkins
465 Middle Rd Apt 56
Farmington CT 06032

Call Sign: N1WLA
Gregory C Scholz
115 Mountain Rd
Farmington CT 06032

Call Sign: KA1RSC
Antonio Lagana
929 New Britain Ave
Farmington CT 06032

Call Sign: KB1KLU
Courtney Arthur
14 Northeast Rd
Farmington CT 060321719

Call Sign: KB1WTE
James P Moran Jr
30 Paper Chase Dr
Farmington CT 06032

Call Sign: KA1DZK
Alan B Schienda
25 Peggy Ln
Farmington CT 06032

Call Sign: KB1DNJ
Matthew J Walston
14 Pheasant Hill
Farmington CT 06032

Call Sign: W1VOS
Marjorie C Snow
870 Plainville Ave
Farmington CT 06032

Call Sign: W1VOV
Arnold E Snow
870 Plainville Ave
Farmington CT 06032

Call Sign: KA1SXY
Robert E Waugh
8 Poplar Hill Dr
Farmington CT 06032

Call Sign: KA1SYA
Elizabeth K Waugh
8 Poplar Hill Dr
Farmington CT 06032

Call Sign: WA2HOX
Marti J Rothe
57 Portage Crossing
Farmington CT 06032

Call Sign: N1ZLX
Michael J Drew
2 Portage Xing
Farmington CT 06032

Call Sign: W1MAU
Frank J Lipski
146 Red Oak Hill Rd
Farmington CT 06032

Call Sign: K1TLY
James P Thompson
55 Reservoir Rd
Farmington CT 060322400

Call Sign: W1COJ
Owen J Mc Cabe
Village Gate 88 Scott
Swamp Rd
Farmington CT 060322986

Call Sign: N4BUI
Sidney Doroff
88 Scott Swamp Rd 208
Farmington CT 06032

Call Sign: W1SWM
Harry W Peterson
88 Scott Swamp Road Apt
215
Farmington CT 06032

Call Sign: KB1NPE
Edmund A Lescoe Jr
10 Stream Court
Farmington CT 060322143

Call Sign: W1EAL
Edmund A Lescoe Jr
10 Stream Court

Farmington CT 060322143

Call Sign: N1WIC
John B Delaney
Suncrest Ln
Farmington CT 06032

Call Sign: KB1KTD
Richard W Monahan
6 Sunningdale
Farmington CT 06032

Call Sign: KB1OOV
Alfred J Santos
8 Tanglewood Rd
Farmington CT 06032

Call Sign: W1DDP
Irving A Stannard
88 Tunxis Village
Farmington CT 06032

Call Sign: KA1ZOI
Edward J O Reilly
71 W Meath Ln
Farmington CT 06085

Call Sign: KB1HRW
David L Tabol
26 Walnut Farms Drive
Farmington CT 06032

Call Sign: KB1RBF
Eugen G Wichmann
157 Waterville Rd
Farmington CT 06032

Call Sign: KB1UYF
Jeremiah J Piescik
20 Wells Dr
Farmington CT 06032

Call Sign: KA1FEY
Constance A Castro
20 West Gate Rd

Farmington CT 06032

Call Sign: WA1YQB
Frank A Castro Jr
20 West Gate Rd
Farmington CT 06032

Call Sign: N1DNE
Arthur G Simonian
72 Westview Terr
Farmington CT 06085

Call Sign: WD8OZF
Phillip P Smith
5 Willow Lane
Farmington CT 06032

Call Sign: KC2AQM
David Santiago
Farmington CT 06034

Call Sign: N1TLL
Gary E Lavelle
Farmington CT 06034

FCC Amateur Radio Licenses in Forestville

Call Sign: N1QDH
Jong Soo Kim
371 Birch St
Forestville CT 06010

Call Sign: W1VLQ
Roger W Raymond
31 Brace Ave
Forestville CT 060104844

Call Sign: WA1DYH
Richard M Borders
482 Broad St 16
Forestville CT 06010

Call Sign: N1RIB
Andy Janson

50 Curtiss Ave
Forestville CT 06010

Call Sign: WL7B
Bruce E Brightman
28 Daley St
Forestville CT 06010

Call Sign: K1TUQ
Edwin S Kloss
184 Diane Ln
Forestville CT 06010

Call Sign: KA1PLE
Mary C Dion
76 Georgetown Rd
Forestville CT 06010

Call Sign: WA1LAP
Michael P Dion
76 Georgetown Rd
Forestville CT 06010

Call Sign: KA1YYM
Lorenzo P Martell
67 Hepworth St
Forestville CT 06010

Call Sign: N1XDO
David J Drezek
107 Lincoln Ave
Forestville CT 06010

Call Sign: KA1VJB
Steven B Pike
27 Pleasant Ave
Forestville CT 06010

Call Sign: N1SQC
John C Fitzgerald
728 Redstone Hill Rd
Forestville CT 06010

Call Sign: KA1FKB
Denis A Thiede

72 Robertson St
Forestville CT 06010

Call Sign: W1ZFG
Oscar Wall
94 Rowe Pl
Forestville CT 06010

Call Sign: KB1IGA
Jean-Luc N Bilodeau
60 Surrey Dr
Forestville CT 06010

Call Sign: KB1AGE
David W Messner
14 Village St
Forestville CT 06010

FCC Amateur Radio Licenses in Foxon

Call Sign: KB1HEV
James V Ranelli
6 Sylvan Hills Rd
Foxon CT 06512

Call Sign: AJ1D
James V Ranelli
6 Sylvan Hills Rd
Foxon CT 06512

FCC Amateur Radio Licenses in Franklin

Call Sign: WB1FWQ
Robert B Munro
55 Ayer Rd
Franklin CT 062541201

Call Sign: KN1DPS
Dennis N Goderre
205 Baltic Rd
Franklin CT 06254

Call Sign: K1WJ

Ernest W Jennings
17 Lydia Ln
Franklin CT 06254

Call Sign: KB1EEO
Glen A Manning
26 Meeting House Hill Rd
Franklin CT 06254

FCC Amateur Radio Licenses in Gales Ferry

Call Sign: KB1GDN
Matthew K Runkle
36 Bittersweet Dr
Gales Ferry CT 06335

Call Sign: K1RJA
John D Blachuta
18 Bobwhite Trail
Gales Ferry CT 06335

Call Sign: N8CDI
Michael G Minich
21 Bobwhite Trail
Gales Ferry CT 06335

Call Sign: K1FUG
Kenneth P Bailey Sr
14 Devonshire Dr
Gales Ferry CT 06335

Call Sign: N1DTK
Lee A Cornett
2 Forest Ln
Gales Ferry CT 06335

Call Sign: KB1CRB
Peter E Beers
6 Garden Court
Gales Ferry CT 06335

Call Sign: N1YXA
Deane F Terry
49 Harvard Terrace

Gales Ferry CT 06335

Call Sign: KA1BTF
Liston R Harley
6 Hemlock Cir
Gales Ferry CT 06335

Call Sign: K1EQ
Liston R Harley
6 Hemlock Cir
Gales Ferry CT 06335

Call Sign: W1DIT
Cletus M Dunn
3 Hermitage Dr
Gales Ferry CT 06335

Call Sign: KE6PUU
Matthew L Rutschky
14 Inchcliffe Dr
Gales Ferry CT 06335

Call Sign: KB1GYI
Salvinu C Vella
30 Ledgewood Dr
Gales Ferry CT 06335

Call Sign: K1LBE
James Culley
6 Library Ln
Gales Ferry CT 06335

Call Sign: N1MHW
George F Kindel
35 Lincoln Dr
Gales Ferry CT 06335

Call Sign: W8QDX
George R Fagan
6 Little John Ct
Gales Ferry CT 06335

Call Sign: WA1IKN
David F Carberry
845 Long Cove Rd

Gales Ferry CT 063351913

Gales Ferry CT 063351516

Gales Ferry CT 06335

Call Sign: KA1LNS
Paul H Banker Jr
979 Long Cove Rd
Gales Ferry CT 06335

Call Sign: KB1GDJ
Lee P O Connell
18 Norman Drive
Gales Ferry CT 06335

Call Sign: KF6QKL
Doris Spencer
43 Pinelock Dr.
Gales Ferry CT 06335

Call Sign: K1SRF
Nelson W Treadway Jr
1098 Long Cove Rd
Gales Ferry CT 06335

Call Sign: KA1ZQR
Richard M Burke
33 North Glenwoods Road
Gales Ferry CT 06335

Call Sign: WA8SME
Mark S Spencer
43 Pinelock Dr.
Gales Ferry CT 06335

Call Sign: KA1RPC
James J Sheridan
1 Meadow Dr
Gales Ferry CT 06335

Call Sign: N1RW
Robert L Williams Jr
19 Oakwood Dr
Gales Ferry CT 063351630

Call Sign: KB1UQD
Joannis C Roussakies
42 Richard Rd
Gales Ferry CT 06335

Call Sign: N1YFD
Barry B Baker
7 Merry Ln
Gales Ferry CT 06335

Call Sign: NJ1W
Robert S Williams
19 Oakwood Dr
Gales Ferry CT 06335

Call Sign: AB1ND
Steven J Smith
132 Stoddards Wharf Rd
Gales Ferry CT 06335

Call Sign: N7GZA
Donald R Palko
94 Military Hwy
Gales Ferry CT 06335

Call Sign: N1LAF
Paul A Felgate
11 Oakwood Drive
Gales Ferry CT 06335

Call Sign: KB1ICA
William A Lacy
260 Stoddards Wharf Rd
Gales Ferry CT 063351130

Call Sign: KC7LFA
Geraldine Pfeuffer
8 Mt. Vernon Drive
Gales Ferry CT 06335

Call Sign: WA2RYV
Thomas E Scott
4 Overlook Rd
Gales Ferry CT 06335

Call Sign: KB1DTB
Brian M Jolicoeur
8 Tanglewood Dr
Gales Ferry CT 063351323

Call Sign: KW1K
Joseph J Pfeuffer
8 Mt. Vernon Drive
Gales Ferry CT 06335

Call Sign: WY1W
Howard L Bacon Iii
36 Overlook Rd
Gales Ferry CT 06335

Call Sign: KA1HOB
Alan S Lundie
23 Terry Rd
Gales Ferry CT 06335

Call Sign: KB1GDM
Ryan P O Connell
18 Norman Dr
Gales Ferry CT 06335

Call Sign: N3ABN
William B Higgins
59 Partridge Hollow Rd
Gales Ferry CT 06335

Call Sign: KB1GJT
Noel N Coe
26 Terry Rd
Gales Ferry CT 06335

Call Sign: KA1QI
Michael J Mc Lane
20 Norman Dr

Call Sign: W3IFD
William B Higgins
59 Partridge Hollow Rd

Call Sign: KA1IRG
Jack K Allen
21 Van Tassell Dr

Gales Ferry CT 06335

Call Sign: KB1CMI
William Bauer Ii
5 Vinegar Hill Rd
Gales Ferry CT 06335

Call Sign: KA1QPV
Sylvia M Wooten
102 Vinegar Hill Rd
Gales Ferry CT 06335

Call Sign: W1LW
Walter L Wooten
102 Vinegar Hill Rd
Gales Ferry CT 06335

Call Sign: N1FAM
Harrison H Solt Iii
110 Vinegar Hill Rd
Gales Ferry CT 063351713

Call Sign: WB1EOH
Michael J Jacey
236 Whalehead Rd
Gales Ferry CT 06335

Call Sign: N4BLU
John D Wright
9 Whippoorwill Dr
Gales Ferry CT 06335

Call Sign: K1MRL
Thomas M Lees
35 Woodridge Cir
Gales Ferry CT 06335

**FCC Amateur Radio
Licenses in Gaylordsville**

Call Sign: WB1GGT
Joseph R Snow
9 Beverly Dr
Gaylordsville CT 06755

Call Sign: KB1UUY
David J Zullo
656 Kent Rd
Gaylordsville CT 06755

Call Sign: W1HX
Robert G Fuller
549 Kent Road
Gaylordsville CT
067551504

**FCC Amateur Radio
Licenses in Georgetown**

Call Sign: N1NSL
Ronald Lusky
Box 464
Georgetown CT 06829

Call Sign: KA1LBE
Andrew W Morris
Georgetown CT 06829

Call Sign: N1MG
Mark R Gilbert
Georgetown CT 068290117

Call Sign: N1UTA
Boris Moreyn
Georgetown CT 068290933

**FCC Amateur Radio
Licenses in Glastonbury**

Call Sign: KD1QK
Thomas M Walsh
158 Barrington Way
Glastonbury CT 06033

Call Sign: AB1GY
Thomas M Walsh
158 Barrington Way
Glastonbury CT 06033

Call Sign: AG1R

Thomas M Walsh
158 Barrington Way
Glastonbury CT 06033

Call Sign: N1UXA
Thomas J Boscarino
62 Bayberry Rd
Glastonbury CT 06033

Call Sign: N1WZN
Julie M Boscarino
62 Bayberry Rd
Glastonbury CT 06033

Call Sign: N1XG
Bruce S Marcus
866 Birch Mountain Rd.
Glastonbury CT 06033

Call Sign: WA1NXG
Bruce S Marcus
866 Birch Mtn Dr
Glastonbury CT 06033

Call Sign: W1PHG
Lucretia B Seidel
55 Bunker Hill Rd
Glastonbury CT 06033

Call Sign: KB1MXP
Charles R Winston Jr
109 Cambridge Dr
Glastonbury CT 06033

Call Sign: KB1QJQ
Frederick A Jacobs Iii
148 Candelight Dr
Glastonbury CT 06033

Call Sign: KB1QJI
Austin M Jacobs
148 Candlelight Dr
Glastonbury CT 06033

Call Sign: KB1QJJ

Alexander F Jacobs
148 Candlelight Dr
Glastonbury CT 06033

Call Sign: KB1QJO
Holly June Jacobs
148 Candlelight Dr
Glastonbury CT 06033

Call Sign: N1LUS
Peter S Wilson
210 Cavan Ln
Glastonbury CT 06033

Call Sign: WB1GIE
James P Todd
145 Cedar Ridge Dr
Glastonbury CT 060331815

Call Sign: KA1TKW
Helen M Weigel
458 Cedar Ridge Dr
Glastonbury CT 06033

Call Sign: N1GLY
William K Weigel
458 Cedar Ridge Dr
Glastonbury CT 06033

Call Sign: WA1NMI
Ira R Lefkowitz
143 Cedar Ridge Drive
Glastonbury CT 06033

Call Sign: AD1J
Neil F Kelly
645 Chestnut Hill Rd
Glastonbury CT 06033

Call Sign: KB1PQI
Anthony D Rita Jr
98 Chimney Sweep Hill Rd
Glastonbury CT 06033

Call Sign: W1ADR

Anthony D Rita Jr
98 Chimney Sweep Hill Rd
Glastonbury CT 06033

Call Sign: N1LMQ
James T Mc Vey
223 Cider Mill Rd
Glastonbury CT 06033

Call Sign: K1NCD
James B Burke
25 Crossroads Ln
Glastonbury CT 06033

Call Sign: KA1NLA
Jonathan H Brey
6 Deerfield Dr
Glastonbury CT 06033

Call Sign: KA1NYV
Andrew P Brey
6 Deerfield Dr
Glastonbury CT 06033

Call Sign: KB9UQZ
Jeremy C Ball
149 Deerfield Drive
Glastonbury CT 06033

Call Sign: NS1T
Mark E Bonadies
1331 Diamond Lake Rd
Glastonbury CT 060334052

Call Sign: KB1IXO
Jerome M Zott
233 E Opal Dr
Glastonbury CT 060331455

Call Sign: KB1VWM
Joseph A Zott
233 East Opal Dr
Glastonbury CT 06033

Call Sign: N3ASJ

Stanley P Focht
44 Gayfeather Lane
Glastonbury CT 06033

Call Sign: WA1MXA
George A Upton
288 Georgetown Dr
Glastonbury CT 060332306

Call Sign: KB1SFB
Steven L Sleeper
68 Granite Rd
Glastonbury CT 06033

Call Sign: N1CTS
Arthur A Ostrowitz
63 Greentree Dr
Glastonbury CT 06033

Call Sign: KA1MCV
Beatriz R Milne
699 Griswold St
Glastonbury CT 06033

Call Sign: WB2LED
Richard E Beach
121 Hale Rd
Glastonbury CT 06033

Call Sign: KB1EDW
Sharon A Bennett
2345 Hebron Ave
Glastonbury CT 06033

Call Sign: KA1DSQ
J James Bodnar
1177 Hebron Avenue - Apt.
312
Glastonbury CT 060335008

Call Sign: KB1WQW
Brent S Lorraine
35 Heritage Dr
Glastonbury CT 06033

Call Sign: N1QZJ
David J Closson
20 Holmes Rd
Glastonbury CT 06033

Call Sign: N1ZNC
Christopher D Eiswerth
155 Homestead Dr
Glastonbury CT 06073

Call Sign: N1JBS
William E Simpson Jr
214 House Street
Glastonbury CT 06033

Call Sign: KB1PTA
Raymond F Carpenter
21 Indian Hill Trail
Glastonbury CT 06033

Call Sign: WR1D
Ralph J Frank Jr
104 Johnny Cake Ln
Glastonbury CT 06033

Call Sign: KU7G
Robert J Schetgen
21 Juniper Ln
Glastonbury CT 06033

Call Sign: W1FVH
Robert J Bires
60 Ladyslipper Ln
Glastonbury CT 06033

Call Sign: KA1ST
Francis J Ritchie
35 Linden St
Glastonbury CT 06033

Call Sign: KA1KQW
William P Caruso
1238 Main St
Glastonbury CT 06033

Call Sign: N1VEO
Sarah E Chaffee
1732 Main St
Glastonbury CT 06033

Call Sign: KB1BUA
The Glastonbury
Communications Pioneers
2155 Main St
Glastonbury CT 06033

Call Sign: KE1CW
Kenneth A Ferner
2113 Main Street
Glastonbury CT 06033

Call Sign: KB1VWP
Mark L Richard
1712 Manchester Rd
Glastonbury CT 06033

Call Sign: WB1DWO
Robert A Pulito
32 Maple St
Glastonbury CT 060332951

Call Sign: KB1GUM
John W Walton
113 Marilyn Drive
Glastonbury CT 060334130

Call Sign: W1JWW
John W Walton
113 Marilyn Drive
Glastonbury CT 060334130

Call Sign: KB1OLU
Albert T Mollegen Jr
49 Millstone Rd
Glastonbury CT 06033

Call Sign: N1OIX
Alvah A Russell Jr
237 Mountain Rd
Glastonbury CT 06033

Call Sign: N1SBJ
Mark A Hermann
378 Neipsic Road
Glastonbury CT 06033

Call Sign: KM1W
George S Stingel
649 Oakwood Dr
Glastonbury CT 06033

Call Sign: KA1JKQ
Karen L Williams
35 Old Musket Rd
Glastonbury CT 06033

Call Sign: KB1DFZ
Edward J Daly Jr
123 Olde Stage Road
Glastonbury CT 06033

Call Sign: N1JBN
John E Harper
76 Overlook Rd
Glastonbury CT 06033

Call Sign: W1FYM
Edward M Harper
76 Overlook Rd
Glastonbury CT 06033

Call Sign: W1TCJ
Fred D Manganelli Jr
234 Overlook Rd
Glastonbury CT 060333616

Call Sign: KA1SUU
Susan H Klock
505 Overlook Rd
Glastonbury CT 06033

Call Sign: N1YJZ
Barry L Stoner
12 Pane Dr
Glastonbury CT 06033

Call Sign: W1KOJ
Frederick R Joslin Sr
11 Pearl St
Glastonbury CT 06033

Call Sign: N1TIU
Samuel F Mc Kay
96 Pheasant Crossing
Glastonbury CT 06033

Call Sign: W1ORI
Henry H Hunt
6 Pine Tree Ln
Glastonbury CT 060333620

Call Sign: WB1HDB
Philip S Sanborn
41 Pinnacle Rd
Glastonbury CT 06033

Call Sign: KB1WQU
Mary Jane B Greissle
132 Prospect St
Glastonbury CT 06033

Call Sign: K1TIS
Jeffrey D Kearney
17 Prospect St. Apt. 2s
Glastonbury CT 06033

Call Sign: KF4VSD
Anthony M Zimmerman
76 Ridgecrest Road
Glastonbury CT 06033

Call Sign: KB1ZG
Douglas H Pagett
68 Rockhaven Drive
Glastonbury CT 060333014

Call Sign: WB1BXQ
Charles R Harris
82 Shady Hill Ln
Glastonbury CT 06033

Call Sign: KB1CN
Bradley O Hurley
146 Shagbark Rd
Glastonbury CT 06033

Call Sign: N1DTS
Michael S Smith
150 Shallowbrook Ln
Glastonbury CT 06033

Call Sign: W1GWZ
Richard E L Heureux
45 Shelley Ln
Glastonbury CT 06033

Call Sign: N1XFE
Nancy L Manter
103 Sherman Rd
Glastonbury CT 060332954

Call Sign: KA1UJN
Marc F Petruzzi
56 Shipman Rd
Glastonbury CT 06033

Call Sign: KB1VRB
Bree M Berner
240 Spring St Ext
Glastonbury CT 06033

Call Sign: KB1DAV
Mario J Bruno
458 Stanley Drive
Glastonbury CT 060332624

Call Sign: KB1LMT
Debra M Johnson
135 Stevens Ln
Glastonbury CT 06033

Call Sign: AB1EW
Debra M Johnson
135 Stevens Ln
Glastonbury CT 06033

Call Sign: K1DMJ
Debra M Johnson
135 Stevens Ln
Glastonbury CT 06033

Call Sign: KB1FFV
Richard J Sisca
12 Stoney Brook Drive A4
Glastonbury CT 06033

Call Sign: KB2NSR
Maryconcepta I Panetta
252 Strickland St
Glastonbury CT 060332529

Call Sign: WO2D
John C Panetta
252 Strickland Street
Glastonbury CT 060332529

Call Sign: KB1GFD
Michael J Mc Mahon
227 Sunset Dr
Glastonbury CT 060334144

Call Sign: KB1IPX
Jeffrey K Bagley
47 Tara Dr
Glastonbury CT 060332423

Call Sign: W1WEF
Jack S Schuster
408 Thompson St
Glastonbury CT 06033

Call Sign: KB1RDV
Sean P Clark
259 Three Mile Rd
Glastonbury CT 06033

Call Sign: KA1CEO
Sean P Clark
259 Three Mile Rd
Glastonbury CT 06033

Call Sign: W1MDE
Michael D Ersevim
260 Trinity Ave
Glastonbury CT 06033

Call Sign: WA2CHJ
Scott H Reagan
251 Trinity Avenue
Glastonbury CT 060331339

Call Sign: K1WKB
Bruce A Bodnar
34 Twelve Acre Ln
Glastonbury CT 06033

Call Sign: KB1NXB
Brent A Murcia
355 Weir St
Glastonbury CT 06033

Call Sign: KB1NXC
Penny L Murcia
355 Weir St
Glastonbury CT 06033

Call Sign: KB1QIQ
Aurelio Bombagi
128 Wells Street
Glastonbury CT 06033

Call Sign: KA1SXD
Alan G Hecht
24 Wesleyan Rd
Glastonbury CT 06033

Call Sign: N1QCF
Wil L Brown
13 Williams Glen
Glastonbury CT 06033

Call Sign: W1AMZ
Anthony M Zimmerman
222 Williams St. East   Unit
312

Glastonbury CT 06033

Call Sign: KB1RMW
Taylor S Gilman
173 Woodfield Crossing
Glastonbury CT 06033

Call Sign: KB1RMX
Albert E Gilman
173 Woodfield Crossing
Glastonbury CT 06033

Call Sign: WA1YCK
Anthony S Lincoln
26 Woodhaven Rd
Glastonbury CT 06033

Call Sign: KB1FGR
Anthony S Lincoln
26 Woodhaven Rd
Glastonbury CT 06033

Call Sign: N1GTR
Gerald S Young
Glastonbury CT 06033

Call Sign: N1RFM
Michael K Roberts
Glastonbury CT 06033

Call Sign: KB1URD
Scott F Higgins
Glastonbury CT 06033

FCC Amateur Radio Licenses in Goshen

Call Sign: WA1EQC
L Michael Gourd
43 Ashley Dr
Goshen CT 06756

Call Sign: N1SRJ
Joseph A Alicata
38 Bentley Circle

Goshen CT 06756

Call Sign: KA1JVN
Henrietta C Horvay
43 Breguet Rd
Goshen CT 067561420

Call Sign: KU1Q
Walter M Horvay
43 Breguet Rd
Goshen CT 06756

Call Sign: WB2MED
Guy I Smiley
18 Chatham Court
Goshen CT 06756

Call Sign: WA1GS
Guy I Smiley
18 Chatham Court
Goshen CT 06756

Call Sign: WA1VUY
Lawrence M Sirignano
518 East Hyerdale Dr.
Goshen CT 06756

Call Sign: KB1KPE
William J Papp
217 North St.
Goshen CT 06756

Call Sign: KB1QQD
Devin Lowe
55 Paxton Ct
Goshen CT 06756

Call Sign: N1ZCV
Frank Jankowics
10 Squire Court
Goshen CT 06756

Call Sign: W1LCR
Frank Jankowics
10 Squire Court

Goshen CT 06756

Call Sign: WB1DNR
Craig A Gagnier
140 Weldon Court
Goshen CT 06756

Call Sign: KB1QQC
Thomas E Gregoire
Goshen CT 06756

**FCC Amateur Radio
Licenses in Granby**

Call Sign: N1ABN
Richard J Lydon
7 Boxwood Ct
Granby CT 06035

Call Sign: N1UYL
James P Donaldson
97 Bushy Hill Rd
Granby CT 06035

Call Sign: K1CCT
James P Donaldson
97 Bushy Hill Rd
Granby CT 06035

Call Sign: KA1NZZ
John I Swenson
26 Buttles Rd
Granby CT 06035

Call Sign: KB1EO
Peter E Favolise Jr
74 Canton Rd
Granby CT 060352501

Call Sign: N1HEB
Mary Ann Favolise
74 Canton Rd
Granby CT 060352501

Call Sign: WA1PLJ

Donald F Kehn
14 Chatsworth Rd
Granby CT 06035

Call Sign: W1IHH
David M Hildreth
118 Day St
Granby CT 06035

Call Sign: KB1LMK
Sunrise Freedom Amateur
Radio Association
34 E Granby Rd
Granby CT 06035

Call Sign: W1SFA
Sunrise Freedom Amateur
Radio Association
34 E Granby Rd
Granby CT 06035

Call Sign: W1CBL
Christopher J Rossetti
31 East St
Granby CT 06035

Call Sign: K1PZS
Harvey A Broverman
20 Griffin Rd
Granby CT 06035

Call Sign: N1VWL
David A Yoreo
3 Halwood Dr
Granby CT 06035

Call Sign: KA1CPQ
Bruce A Laudenat
49 Harmony Hill Rd
Granby CT 06035

Call Sign: KG4BBP
Mark W Lockwood
15 Heather Ln
Granby CT 06060

Call Sign: W1FTE
Charles L Colton
12 Kelly Ln
Granby CT 06035

Call Sign: KB1DZV
Nicholas B Eddy
53 Lakeside Dr
Granby CT 06035

Call Sign: W1LAW
Nicholas B Eddy
53 Lakeside Drive
Granby CT 06035

Call Sign: KB1NKS
Jeffrey A Gorton
54 Lakeside Drive
Granby CT 06035

Call Sign: KB1NQP
Christine W Gorton
54 Lakeside Drive
Granby CT 06035

Call Sign: KB1EVO
Matthew J Dooley
10 Maple Hill Dr
Granby CT 06035

Call Sign: KB1FFL
Matthew J Dooley
10 Maple Hill Dr
Granby CT 06035

Call Sign: W1MJD
Matthew J Dooley
10 Maple Hill Dr
Granby CT 06035

Call Sign: KB1ELK
Robert W Wagner
52 Meadowbrook Rd
Granby CT 06035

Call Sign: WA1KKD
Alfred J Brewer
199 N Granby Rd
Granby CT 06035

Call Sign: KB1BPP
Austin Organs Wireless
Society
213 N Granby Rd
Granby CT 06035

Call Sign: W1CKV
Frederick G Heffner
213 N Granby Rd
Granby CT 06035

Call Sign: KB1BWO
Of Qcwa Nutmeg Chapter
149
213 North Granby Rd
Granby CT 06035

Call Sign: W1EFW
Of Qcwa Nutmeg Chapter
149
213 North Granby Rd
Granby CT 060351302

Call Sign: KB1BFH
Doreen E M Veazie
124 North Granby Rd.
Granby CT 06035

Call Sign: N1FUV
John A Thompson
29 Notch Rd
Granby CT 06035

Call Sign: KB1TMU
John A Thompson
29 Notch Rd
Granby CT 06035

Call Sign: N1UOO

Leland E Mack
127 Notch Rd
Granby CT 06035

Call Sign: N1GAM
Linda E Sade
24 Peterson Road
Granby CT 06035

Call Sign: N1MOM
John Carvalho
31 Quarry Rd
Granby CT 06035

Call Sign: KB1FFU
Jennifer L Christensen
364 Salmon Brook Rd
Granby CT 06035

Call Sign: KB1EYT
Kathleen M Christensen
364 Salmon Brook St
Granby CT 06035

Call Sign: KB1EYY
Irving H Christensen Jr
364 Salmon Brook St
Granby CT 06035

Call Sign: W1SV
George A Rossetti Sr
51 Salmonbrook St
Granby CT 06035

Call Sign: KA1CTV
Elliot C Rundquist
50 Shelley Dr
Granby CT 06035

Call Sign: N1KWW
Fred H Hogaboom
183 W. Granby Rd.
Granby CT 06035

Call Sign: K1DH

Donald E Huntington
55 Windmill Springs
Granby CT 06035

Call Sign: KA1FHX
Roger C Phillips
9 Winter Village Road
Granby CT 06035

Call Sign: N1EOH
Douglas P Modeen
26 Woodcliff Dr
Granby CT 06035

Call Sign: K1BOS
Walter C Mission
15 Woodland Dr
Granby CT 06035

Call Sign: N1MAT
Dennis W Lombard
20 Zimmer Rd
Granby CT 06035

Call Sign: KB1IIL
Dennis W Lombard
20 Zimmer Rd
Granby CT 06035

Call Sign: W1PG
Gary E Norman
Granby CT 06035

Call Sign: KB1OLW
Jason M Osborne
Granby CT 06035

**FCC Amateur Radio
Licenses in Green Farms**

Call Sign: KA1NYE
Susan M Roberts
Greens Farms CT 06436

Call Sign: N1INF

Bryan D Sivak
75 Maple Ave S
Greens Farms CT 06436

Call Sign: WH6ANY
James M Alexander
Mitchell Repeater Group
Greens Farms CT 06436

Call Sign: KB1AUG
Martha M Buzel
Greens Farms CT
064360645

**FCC Amateur Radio
Licenses in Greenwich**

Call Sign: K1VJH
William A Quigley
23 Annjim Dr
Greenwich CT 06830

Call Sign: KB1QXO
Michael C Lewis
22 Armstrong Ct Apt 11
Greenwich CT 06830

Call Sign: N1JEP
David V Roscetti
Barn Hill Rd
Greenwich CT 06831

Call Sign: NY1X
Engel P Hevenor
29 Birchwood Dr
Greenwich CT 06831

Call Sign: AD2TA
Takanori Adachi
82 Brookside Drive
Greenwich CT 06831

Call Sign: N1AZF
Thomas J Greco
49 Burdsall Dr

Greenwich CT 06831

Call Sign: N1BFE
Katherine A Greco
49 Burdsall Dr
Greenwich CT 06831

Call Sign: KB1SGY
Frederick W Scholz
45 Byram Shore Rd
Greenwich CT 06830

Call Sign: KB1AJT
Jessica A Catalano
134 Byram Shore Rd
Greenwich CT 06830

Call Sign: N1LYK
Richard G Cimino
39 Chapel St
Greenwich CT 06831

Call Sign: KB1KTU
Stephan M Laska
21 Chestnut St
Greenwich CT 06830

Call Sign: N1NLE
William K Josephson
130 Clapboard Ridge Rd
Greenwich CT 06830

Call Sign: N1OEY
Keith B Josephson
130 Clapboard Ridge Rd
Greenwich CT 06830

Call Sign: K2LBJ
Salvatore G Schimenti
214 Clapboard Ridge Rd
Greenwich CT 06831

Call Sign: WT1F
David C Stauffer
64 Cliffdale Rd

Greenwich CT 06831

Call Sign: N1ZKG
Lilit Karayan
177 Davis Ave
Greenwich CT 06830

Call Sign: KB1UKD
Robert C Stanton
410 Davis Ave
Greenwich CT 06830

Call Sign: KB1UKG
Jesse F Stanton
410 Davis Ave
Greenwich CT 06830

Call Sign: WA1LXL
Robert Wolf
14 E Lyon Farm
Greenwich CT 06831

Call Sign: N2GAT
Tina L Woetzel
15 E Putnam Ave 300
Greenwich CT 06830

Call Sign: KB1RLH
Arjun Talwar
75 Fairfield Rd
Greenwich CT 06830

Call Sign: AA1CI
Frank J Cusare
140 Field Pt Rd Unit 1
Greenwich CT 06830

Call Sign: KB2UCC
Dean Gerardi
45 Fletcher Ave.
Greenwich CT 068314910

Call Sign: KB1AJU
Priya A Verma
3 Gaston Farms Rd

Greenwich CT 06831

Call Sign: KB1VQY
Dominique Murrle
251 Glenville Road
Greenwich CT 06831

Call Sign: KB1OQD
Robert E Nebel
60 Glenville St
Greenwich CT 06831

Call Sign: KB4GFD
Robert E Nebel
60 Glenville St
Greenwich CT 06831

Call Sign: N2YNJ
Andrew Guthrie
60 Gold Street
Greenwich CT 06830

Call Sign: N1VHU
Janine M Oxer
24 Greenway Dr
Greenwich CT 06831

Call Sign: K1AOA
Donald A Hartmann
27 Grey Rock Dr
Greenwich CT 06830

Call Sign: N1UNF
Nicole E Mink
18 Hickory Dr
Greenwich CT 06831

Call Sign: W1VJU
Arthur E French
39 Hickory Dr
Greenwich CT 06831

Call Sign: N1PQD
Andrew J Spyreas
7 Highland Farm Rd

Greenwich CT 06831

Call Sign: KB1LHO
Robert J Salvatore
3 Hollow Wood Ln
Greenwich CT 06831

Call Sign: KB1MUE
Austin S Collins
2 Homestead Lane #112
Greenwich CT 06831

Call Sign: WA1MUB
Bruce S Nicholas
40 Howard Rd
Greenwich CT 06830

Call Sign: WA1MUC
Phyllis W Nicholas
40 Howard Rd
Greenwich CT 06831

Call Sign: KB1UNQ
Ed Heflin
50 Indian Field Rd
Greenwich CT 06830

Call Sign: N1IQH
Winthrop A Brignoli
65 Indian Field Rd
Greenwich CT 06830

Call Sign: KA1SLG
Andrew J Laska
925 King St
Greenwich CT 06831

Call Sign: KB1AKA
Bradford J Parker
1065 King St
Greenwich CT 06831

Call Sign: N1OHU
Edward R Parker
1065 King St

Greenwich CT 06831

Call Sign: N1UND
Deborah M Parker
1065 King St
Greenwich CT 06831

Call Sign: W1CWS
Christopher W Southern
9 Lafayette Ct Apt 1b
Greenwich CT 06830

Call Sign: KB1HS
Harold E Armbruster
50 Lafayette Pl Apt 2i
Greenwich CT 06830

Call Sign: N1XGZ
Robert A Cervoni
145 Mason St
Greenwich CT 06830

Call Sign: N1IXH
George R Finn
43 Moshier St
Greenwich CT 06830

Call Sign: KA1TZK
Robert Gluck
12 Norias Rd
Greenwich CT 06830

Call Sign: KA1JUV
George Wells
918 North St
Greenwich CT 06831

Call Sign: N1VDD
David Harvey
980 North St
Greenwich CT 06831

Call Sign: N1XND
Adam M Aurelia
72 Oak Ridge St

Greenwich CT 06830

Call Sign: AB1HI
Jonathan S Shapiro
128 Old Church Rd
Greenwich CT 068304821

Call Sign: KN1U
Robert E Enslein
166 Parsonage Rd
Greenwich CT 068303943

Call Sign: AB1FJ
Luigi Belvederi
1 Perry Ridge Rd
Greenwich CT 06830

Call Sign: KA1RN
Spencer J Schedler
10 Ponderosa Dr
Greenwich CT 06830

Call Sign: KB1AJV
Amy L Belmonte
69 Prospect St
Greenwich CT 06830

Call Sign: KA1MJD
Elizabeth A Crawford
32a Putnam Green
Greenwich CT 06830

Call Sign: N1LNA
Paul F Curtis
8 Rex St
Greenwich CT 06831

Call Sign: N1TKS
Anthony J Salvate
25 Richland Rd
Greenwich CT 06830

Call Sign: W1IEO
Ardenus F Mc Bride Sr
36 Richland Rd

Greenwich CT 06830

Call Sign: KB1NFS
Clark Burgard
256 Riversville Rd
Greenwich CT 06831

Call Sign: N1ZKF
John E Schmeltzer Iv
239 Round Hill Rd
Greenwich CT 06831

Call Sign: WQ1P
John A Friel
591 Round Hill Rd
Greenwich CT 068312717

Call Sign: KA1WSJ
Frank V Snyder
640 Round Hill Rd
Greenwich CT 06831

Call Sign: KA1WSK
Jessie P Snyder
640 Round Hill Rd
Greenwich CT 06831

Call Sign: KE5EJX
Norman E Jorgensen
47 Round Hill Road
Greenwich CT 06831

Call Sign: KB1VKB
Yusuke Ochiai
21 Sachem Rd
Greenwich CT 06830

Call Sign: KA1IGM
Runo L Larson
72 Sherwood Pl
Greenwich CT 06830

Call Sign: WA2UVC
Thomas J Cirillo
155 Stanwich Rd

Greenwich CT 06830

Call Sign: AA0EZ
Alexander E Patterson Iii
289 Stanwich Rd
Greenwich CT 06830

Call Sign: N0LLO
Carol A Patterson
289 Stanwich Rd
Greenwich CT 06830

Call Sign: N1ESQ
Alexander E Patterson Jr
291 Stanwich Rd
Greenwich CT 06830

Call Sign: N1ZKE
Robert T Thompson Iii
328 Stanwich Rd
Greenwich CT 06830

Call Sign: KP2BR
Richard W Geary
559 Steamboat Rd
Greenwich CT 06830

Call Sign: AA1EH
Lawrence R Jacobs
67 Sumner Rd
Greenwich CT 06830

Call Sign: KA1MFC
Michael V Buddy
104 Taconic Rd
Greenwich CT 06831

Call Sign: K1IYK
Richard E Bishop Jr
212 Taconic Rd
Greenwich CT 06831

Call Sign: WA2CMK
Werner A Roder
11 Thistle Ln

Greenwich CT 06831

Call Sign: KB9SAW
Wesley C Chang
6 Upland Road
Greenwich CT 068314425

Call Sign: N1YGV
Allen S Gramlich
3 Upland St
Greenwich CT 06831

Call Sign: KB1ISO
Dennis F Hanlon
127 W Putnam Ave
Greenwich CT 06830

Call Sign: KU0Q
Takashi Matsuzawa
96 Weaver Street
Greenwich CT 06830

Call Sign: KA3LPA
Stephen J Salzer
23 West Brother Drive
Greenwich CT 06830

Call Sign: W2COF
Stephen J Salzer
23 West Brother Drive
Greenwich CT 06830

FCC Amateur Radio Licenses in Griswold

Call Sign: N1UKV
Kenneth N Fargo
35 Bow Ln
Griswold CT 06351

Call Sign: KA1KDB
Bruce F Bousquet Jr
85 Colonel Brown Road
Griswold CT 06351

Call Sign: N1MLG
Elizabeth Griffin
1672 Glasgo Rd
Griswold CT 06351

Call Sign: N1MIE
George E Griffin
1672 Glasgo Road
Griswold CT 06351

Call Sign: KB1HNQ
Emmet T Griffin
1672 Glasgo Road
Griswold CT 06351

Call Sign: KB1OUX
Elizabeth Griffin
1672 Glasoo Rd
Griswold CT 06351

Call Sign: KE6IVY
Guy R Cashman
257 Lester Rd
Griswold CT 06351

Call Sign: N1QQL
Scott W Powell
79 Monroe Ave
Griswold CT 06351

Call Sign: KB1EXW
Dustin N Laro
79 Pachaug River Dr
Griswold CT 06351

Call Sign: KB1EZT
Mark J Hamel Jr
79 Pachaug River Dr
Griswold CT 06351

Call Sign: KB1FRE
Scott E Jodoin
4 Pond Lane
Griswold CT 06351

Call Sign: W1FAA
William J Stachnik
9 Sheldon Circle
Griswold CT 06351

Call Sign: N1SVF
John J Dick Jr
559 Stonehill Rd
Griswold CT 06351

FCC Amateur Radio Licenses in Groton

Call Sign: KA1UKQ
Jenoe Gordon
5 Benham Rd
Groton CT 06340

Call Sign: KA1YXZ
Michel C Cooper
203 Benham Rd
Groton CT 06340

Call Sign: KB1KHA
Michel C Cooper
203 Benham Rd
Groton CT 063405005

Call Sign: KB1GJU
Francis J Wehner Jr
220 Benham Rd
Groton CT 063405006

Call Sign: W1FJW
Francis J Wehner Jr
220 Benham Rd
Groton CT 063405006

Call Sign: KA1YEB
Darren L Henson
266 Benham Rd
Groton CT 06340

Call Sign: NU1D
Hart P Martin

266 Benham Rd
Groton CT 06340

Call Sign: N1REH
Joseph J Carter
233 Benham Rd Apt 18
Groton CT 06340

Call Sign: KA1PFK
Charles H Hewitt Sr
76 Benham Rd Apt 2
Groton CT 06340

Call Sign: KC1LV
Albert J Lindsey
107 Benham Rd Apt 2
Groton CT 06340

Call Sign: WB2RYQ
James F Grisoli
107 Benham Rd Apt 24
Groton CT 06340

Call Sign: KB1PWO
Roger D Reeves Jr
14 Birch St
Groton CT 06340

Call Sign: KB1EJP
Mark E Bronson
95 Brandegee Ave
Groton CT 06340

Call Sign: KB1IRQ
Phillip S T Wu
25 Broad Street Ext Apt B3-1
Groton CT 06340

Call Sign: KB1DYY
Paul G Ludwig
170 Brook St
Groton CT 06340

Call Sign: KB1PKH

Lindsey A Roberts
34 Brookshaven Rd
Groton CT 06340

Call Sign: N1GZA
William H Winterholer
62 Brookshaven Rd
Groton CT 06340

Call Sign: KA1STR
Allen J Robinson
173 Buckeye Rd
Groton CT 06340

Call Sign: KA1ZMQ
David G Cochran
301 Buddington Rd 50
Groton CT 06340

Call Sign: KC8VSN
Sreeram Koneru
74 Buddington Rd Apt 6]
Groton CT 06341

Call Sign: N1VZI
Paul F Murphy
60 Burgess Pl
Groton CT 06340

Call Sign: KB1OZZ
Harold C Haugland Sr.
164 Candlewood Rd
Groton CT 06340

Call Sign: KA1HRT
Thomas E Fish
191 Candlewood Rd
Groton CT 06340

Call Sign: N1OBU
Douglas M Pervine
161 Charter Oak Dr
Groton CT 06340

Call Sign: KA1ZNX

Jeffrey T Nelson
23 Chase Oaks Court #20
Groton CT 06340

Call Sign: K5DTR
Jamie R Koula
114 Cherry Circle
Groton CT 06340

Call Sign: KA1ZYV
Derek M Steinhoff
Navsubscol Box 700 Code 475
Groton CT 06349

Call Sign: N1UYR
Shaun R Lickliter
Box 700 Code N13
Groton CT 06349

Call Sign: N1ENM
Wallace W Mac Peek
127 Colony Rd
Groton CT 06340

Call Sign: KA1ZPX
William R Wagner Ii
40 Country Club Road
Groton CT 06345862

Call Sign: N1LHN
David P Wagner
40 Country Club Road
Groton CT 063405862

Call Sign: WY1F
David S Lang
72 Courtland Dr
Groton CT 06340

Call Sign: N1ISN
Peter W Eccleston
156 D Street
Groton CT 06340

Call Sign: KA1RQC
Matt A Shepker
90 Deerwood Dr
Groton CT 06340

Call Sign: KA1SJV
Ricky L Shepker
90 Deerwood Dr
Groton CT 06340

Call Sign: K2OXW
William E Carle
425 Drozdyk Dr Apt 213
Groton CT 06340

Call Sign: W1NZP
Philip G James
425 Drozdyk Drive Apt 141
Groton CT 06340

Call Sign: W1JIO
Robert W Turner
25 Eastwood Rd
Groton CT 06340

Call Sign: KE1DA
Robert A Zagorac
4b Elderkin Avenue
Groton CT 063404912

Call Sign: KB1BVL
Grasso Tech Arc
169 Fort Hill Rd
Groton CT 06340

Call Sign: N1RJG
Leo Di Mella
62 Fort Hill Rd Lot 15
Groton CT 06340

Call Sign: KB1FPC
Daniel S Bowers
175 Gales Ferry Rd
Groton CT 06340

Call Sign: KB1QFT
John I Suarez
166 Grove Ave
Groton CT 06340

Call Sign: KA1HOA
Martin Schames
16 Haley Crescent
Groton CT 06340

Call Sign: KF4IMO
Matthew L Piper
16 Hawthorn Road
Groton CT 06340

Call Sign: KA4WJM
Marcia P Bruner
15 Heron Ln
Groton CT 06340

Call Sign: KA1RPB
Richard C Moravsik
8 Island Ave
Groton CT 06340

Call Sign: N1UWQ
Todd Kigas
20 Knoxville Ct
Groton CT 06340

Call Sign: KB1GDO
Todd Kigas
20 Knoxville Ct
Groton CT 06340

Call Sign: W1TDK
Todd Kigas
20 Knoxville Ct
Groton CT 06340

Call Sign: KB1RAY
Mark M Horka
83 Leafwood Lane Apt 222
Groton CT 06340

Call Sign: KA1SLI
Fred S Wardwell Jr
600 Meridian St Ext Apt
324
Groton CT 06340

Call Sign: N1TVH
Jerry E Molonson
15 Miami Ct
Groton CT 06340

Call Sign: WA1YRB
Richard H Pelletier
28 Miami Ct
Groton CT 063404708

Call Sign: KB1AEG
James C Husaby
255 Michelle Ln 108
Groton CT 06340

Call Sign: N1TSZ
Leonard L Kimes
55 Mirra Dr
Groton CT 06340

Call Sign: N1PLU
George C Card
150 Mitchell St
Groton CT 06340

Call Sign: KB1JIJ
Thomas R Dean
5 Mohegan Rd
Groton CT 06340

Call Sign: KB1JTA
Jonathan M Dean
5 Mohegan Rd
Groton CT 06340

Call Sign: KA1YKB
Niccolas L Franz
163 Monument St
Groton CT 06340

Call Sign: WA1CTB
Erwin Eckhoff
1290 N Rd Rte 117
Groton CT 06341

Call Sign: KA1YIR
Vincent L Carter
Mars Box 200 Nav Subbase
Nlon
Groton CT 06349

Call Sign: KA1ZDV
Richard P Acuti
Arc Bldg 119 Navsubase
Groton CT 06349

Call Sign: KU1U
Warren C Stoker
4 Neptune Dr
Groton CT 06340

Call Sign: N1PKS
David M Stockwell
266 Neptune Dr
Groton CT 063405441

Call Sign: KA1J
Gary D Smith Dc
295 Neptune Dr
Groton CT 063405416

Call Sign: W1BML
Earl W Smith
295 Neptune Dr
Groton CT 06340

Call Sign: N1ITC
Larry L Cleman
246 Ohio Ave
Groton CT 06340

Call Sign: W5XQM
Kent A Shafer
111 Orion Ave

Groton CT 06340

Call Sign: KA1ZLB
Richard W Santor Jr
118 Orion Ave
Groton CT 06340

Call Sign: KB1KMV
Howard W Martin
34 Pegasus Dr
Groton CT 06340

Call Sign: N1HWM
Howard W Martin
34 Pegasus Dr
Groton CT 06340

Call Sign: KG4ULU
Kimberly D Lynn
106 Pelican Drive
Groton CT 06340

Call Sign: N1PLR
Kenneth H Miller
147 Peters Dr
Groton CT 06340

Call Sign: WB1GUC
James F Ferrie
99 Pine Island Rd
Groton CT 063406024

Call Sign: KD1AA
Edward D Kravat
1145 Poqounnoch Rd
Groton CT 06340

Call Sign: N1RVW
George L Durfee
1042 Poquonnock Rd
Groton CT 063404222

Call Sign: K1HOX
Donald C Neilan
1145 Poquonnock Rd

Groton CT 06340

Call Sign: N1TSY
Elsie M Dart
1042 Poquonnock Rd 4
Groton CT 06340

Call Sign: KA1BOK
Calvin E Green Sr
787 Poquonnock Rd Apt Q
Groton CT 06340

Call Sign: KB1VNS
Bernard T O'neill Iii
143 Proteus Ave
Groton CT 06340

Call Sign: WB1ADY
Harold G Page
58 R Warner St
Groton CT 06340

Call Sign: KA1SHZ
Louise A Page
58 Rear Warner Street
Groton CT 06340

Call Sign: N1VIA
Michael T Adams
Box 92 Rm 722
Groton CT 063495092

Call Sign: WA1RHW
Erling E F Andersen
78 Ronald Rd
Groton CT 06340

Call Sign: W1CUH
Arthur M Card Jr
1352 Rt 117
Groton CT 06340

Call Sign: KA1RWJ
David D Ferrara
255 Rt 12 Ste 1-678

Groton CT 06340

Call Sign: KB1VFZ
William D Havens
51 School St
Groton CT 06340

Call Sign: KA1ONP
Beryl W Dominy
189 Seneca Dr
Groton CT 06340

Call Sign: W1AAM
William C Spicer Jr
930 Shennecosset Rd
Groton CT 06340

Call Sign: N1TVG
Steven S Carle
215 Shennecossett Pky
Groton CT 063405829

Call Sign: N7HSX
John A Fisher
Comintice Pat 1082
Shennecossett Rd
Groton CT 063406096

Call Sign: KB1CWX
Matthew J Torchia
73 Sound Breeze Ave
Groton CT 06340

Call Sign: W1QV
Robert Y Chapman
28 South Rd
Groton CT 06340

Call Sign: KB1RPI
Kamal W Matta
82 Spyglass Circle
Groton CT 06340

Call Sign: KB1BLL
Andrea G Johnson Kennett

58 Starr Hill Rd
Groton CT 06340

Call Sign: N1GYI
Robert W Twiddy
Sub Ron 10 State Pier Rd
Groton CT 06320

Call Sign: N1BQH
John R Murphy
30 Stonecrest Rd
Groton CT 06340

Call Sign: W1LVS
John R Murphy
30 Stonecrest Rd
Groton CT 06340

Call Sign: KB1KMU
Joseph A Parant
20 Sutton Pl
Groton CT 06340

Call Sign: N1QHQ
Henry D Jorsz
420 Thames Street
Groton CT 06340

Call Sign: WA1WKT
Dennis A Bacchiocchi
15 Triton Pl
Groton CT 06340

Call Sign: N1SXU
Thomas M Barnhart
205 Virgo Dr
Groton CT 06340

Call Sign: WU1P
Elizabeth R Wagner
122 Warner Street
Groton CT 06340

Call Sign: KB1QDB
Robert A Tarabek

27 Woodland Dr East
Groton CT 06340

Call Sign: K1KQV
Robert A Tarabek
27 Woodland Dr East
Groton CT 06340

Call Sign: KA1VHR
Michael W Taylor
Groton CT 06340

Call Sign: KA1ZKL
Dustin A Demorest
Groton CT 06340

Call Sign: N1FUN
Thomas W Kintz
Groton CT 06340

Call Sign: N1ITF
William R Wagner
Groton CT 063407184

Call Sign: N1UYQ
Julie M Jones
Groton CT 06340

Call Sign: N1VHZ
Donald E Jones Jr
Groton CT 06340

Call Sign: KB1KTH
Tri-City Amateur Radio
Club
Groton CT 06340

Call Sign: W1QV
Tri-City Amateur Radio
Club
Groton CT 06340

FCC Amateur Radio Licenses in Groton Long Point

Call Sign: N1YPR
Douglas R Beucler
10 Ridge Rd
Groton Long Point CT
06340

Call Sign: K1RSI
Robert G Scrivener
365 West Shore Ave
Groton Long Point CT
06340

**FCC Amateur Radio
Licenses in Guilford**

Call Sign: KB1NDX
Ted F Vander Wiede
725 Boston Post Rd
Guilford CT 06437

Call Sign: N1DIO
James G Clarke
1960 Boston Post Rd
Guilford CT 06437

Call Sign: N1QLH
Philip H Sands
20 Bunker Hill Rd
Guilford CT 06437

Call Sign: KA1Z
William G Mc Mahon
20 Canary Ct
Guilford CT 064371428

Call Sign: N1NOL
Stewart R Thomas
20 Cardinal Drive
Guilford CT 06437

Call Sign: N1VKL
Raymond Bower
83 Catullo Drive
Guilford CT 06437

Call Sign: WA1HKV
Frederick E Stoehr
99 County Rd
Guilford CT 06437

Call Sign: KB1VHA
Robert C Schimmel
31 Dover Ct
Guilford CT 06437

Call Sign: AB1FW
Oscar F Hills
2519 Durham Rd
Guilford CT 06437

Call Sign: WV1C
Oscar F Hills
2519 Durham Rd
Guilford CT 06437

Call Sign: WB2CLV
Kenneth W Gilstein
2657 Durham Rd
Guilford CT 06437

Call Sign: KA1UWA
Jonathan C Prout
185 Elm St
Guilford CT 06437

Call Sign: N1OXN
Richard W Prout
185 Elm St
Guilford CT 06437

Call Sign: N1YLK
Mary T Gunther
47 Fair St
Guilford CT 06437

Call Sign: N1YLM
Robert E Drew
47 Fair St
Guilford CT 06437

Call Sign: KB1DNG
Kurt A Paskiewicz
111 Fire Tower Rd
Guilford CT 06437

Call Sign: N1MVM
Sidney F Gale
250 Flag Marsh Rd
Guilford CT 06437

Call Sign: W1LAM
Leon A Morgan
43 Forest Brook Rd
Guilford CT 064372245

Call Sign: WA1WUF
David J Moffat
111 Glenwood Dr
Guilford CT 06437

Call Sign: AA1VE
David J Moffat
111 Glenwood Dr
Guilford CT 06437

Call Sign: N1SCN
Jeremy J Fulkerson
474 Granite
Guilford CT 06437

Call Sign: KB1RCH
Marianne I Valley
300 Granite Rd
Guilford CT 06437

Call Sign: KB1RCI
Robert Valley Jr
300 Granite Rd
Guilford CT 06437

Call Sign: N1FTK
Robert E Handschumacher
97 Great Harbor
Guilford CT 06437

Call Sign: N1FTL
Joan G Handschumacher
97 Great Harbor
Guilford CT 064373036

Call Sign: KM1R
Michael J Castellano
631 Great Hill Rd
Guilford CT 06437

Call Sign: NI1U
Guilford Radio Society
631 Great Hill Rd
Guilford CT 06437

Call Sign: KA1PNX
Howard C Davidson
49 Hawthorn Rd
Guilford CT 06437

Call Sign: WA1VAC
Cornell M Lattanzi
150 High Meadow Rd
Guilford CT 06437

Call Sign: KB1GZK
Michael K Loukides
30 Hungry Hill Circle
Guilford CT 06437

Call Sign: W1JQ
Michael K Loukides
30 Hungry Hill Circle
Guilford CT 06437

Call Sign: KB1LGK
Craig P Carter
24 Indian Cove Rd
Guilford CT 06437

Call Sign: KA1PI
Richard G Loomis
71 Indian Rd
Guilford CT 06437

Call Sign: KA1WXK
Stephen Bencivengo Jr
242 Jefferson Dr
Guilford CT 06437

Call Sign: KB1CEX
Aaron M Silidker
323 Jefferson Dr
Guilford CT 06437

Call Sign: KB1IPD
Stephen M Packard Jr
67 Kendel Court
Guilford CT 06437

Call Sign: N1ORP
Richard A Mentelos
5 Lantern Hill Ln
Guilford CT 06437

Call Sign: KB1NDW
Frithjof Volker
63 Ledgeview Lane
Guilford CT 06437

Call Sign: W1NGQ
William S Mc Neil
169 Little Meadow Rd
Guilford CT 06437

Call Sign: KB1GCP
Jacob D Hunt
2047 Little Meadow Road
Guilford CT 06437

Call Sign: N1CCO
Edward J Dill Jr
84 Long Hill Farm
Guilford CT 06437

Call Sign: KA1PRY
Joseph F Lipinski Jr
2320 Long Hill Rd
Guilford CT 06437

Call Sign: K2RNY
Paul W Schrader
38 Maplecrest Dr
Guilford CT 06437

Call Sign: KB1LGY
Mark A Gilbertie
55 Maupas Rd N
Guilford CT 06437

Call Sign: KA1NRB
Meredith M Thompson
19 Michael Dr
Guilford CT 06437

Call Sign: KA1WLK
Dean J Russo
59 Middle Rd
Guilford CT 06437

Call Sign: K1YYQ
Donald E Cloud
56 Mohawk Trail
Guilford CT 06437

Call Sign: KB1SEL
Scott R Mitchell
778 Mulberry Pt Rd
Guilford CT 06437

Call Sign: W1IWM
John F Daly Jr
524 N Madison Rd
Guilford CT 06437

Call Sign: N1KZV
Robert D Grant
373 New Whitfield St Apt
A
Guilford CT 06437

Call Sign: KA1TLF
Howard A Lawrence
288 Northwood Dr

Guilford CT 06437

Guilford CT 06437

Guilford CT 06437

Call Sign: KA1RQB
Joseph D Cantey
132 Nortontown Rd
Guilford CT 064372224

Call Sign: KB1SBL
Thomas P Martin
213 Sam Hill Rd
Guilford CT 064372525

Call Sign: KB1NUE
Ct & Western Ma Mensa
Communications
Committee
1121 W Lake Ave
Guilford CT 06437

Call Sign: N1IZF
James B Mc Candless
520 Nut Plains Rd
Guilford CT 06437

Call Sign: W1EEE
William H Sexton
35 Seaside Ave
Guilford CT 06437

Call Sign: K1HIQ
Ct & Western Ma Mensa
Communications
Committee
1121 W Lake Ave
Guilford CT 06437

Call Sign: KB1LSL
Richard Stegina
50 Red Coat Ln
Guilford CT 06437

Call Sign: N1KGO
Kathleen B Magness
23 Snow Bird Ct
Guilford CT 06437

Call Sign: N1BWG
Richard A Joslyn Jr
47 Walden Hill Rd
Guilford CT 06437

Call Sign: KB1LYK
Carolyn D Jagielski
110 Round Hill Road
Guilford CT 06437

Call Sign: K1CXT
Pieter V Keogh
194 State Street
Guilford CT 06437

Call Sign: KA1WXJ
Frederick E Yale
137 Water St
Guilford CT 06437

Call Sign: KB1NZS
Robert O Rawson
55 Ruggles Rd
Guilford CT 06437

Call Sign: W1EVH
Daniel C Clark
27 Sunset Cir
Guilford CT 06437

Call Sign: WB8RJV
Lauren E Gaunt
60 Wauwinet Ct
Guilford CT 06437

Call Sign: N1KEC
Robert O Rawson
55 Ruggles Rd
Guilford CT 06437

Call Sign: W1CKG
Robert L Walker Jr
58 Three Corners Rd
Guilford CT 06437

Call Sign: KB1UEH
Colin C Souney
70 Wauwinet Trail
Guilford CT 06437

Call Sign: KB1UKI
Carl C Cooper
111 Russo Drive
Guilford CT 06437

Call Sign: N1LBB
Kirk E Sullivan
61 Three Corners Road
Guilford CT 06437

Call Sign: N1KHB
Joseph P Wonoski
1121 West Lake Ave
Guilford CT 06437

Call Sign: KA1DHE
Norman H Yeo
61 Saddle Hill Dr
Guilford CT 06437

Call Sign: KA1UVZ
Preston M Kampmeyer
450 Vineyard Point Rd
Guilford CT 06437

Call Sign: N1MHI
Robert E Russo
580 West St
Guilford CT 06437

Call Sign: KA1UVN
Joseph S Raiola
66 Saddle Hill Drive

Call Sign: KB1EBF
Helene Wonoski
1121 W Lake Ave

Call Sign: N1OFK
Joseph J Hurley
650 West St
Guilford CT 06437

Call Sign: N1JJT
Edward W Perkins
1398 West St
Guilford CT 06437

Call Sign: KA1ACB
Donald J Gillette
149 White Birch Dr
Guilford CT 06437

Call Sign: K1SEO
Irving Glassman
446 Whitfield St Unit M
Guilford CT 06437

Call Sign: KA1RJR
Stacy M Magness
Guilford CT 06437

Call Sign: NI1U
Clark S Magness
Guilford CT 06437

Call Sign: KB1LMI
Michael Mc LAUGHLIN
Guilford CT 06437

FCC Amateur Radio Licenses in Haddam

Call Sign: KB1JUB
John J Breton
30 Camp Bethel Rd
Haddam CT 06438

Call Sign: KB1SHT
John F Tary
144 Cedar Lake Rd
Haddam CT 06438

Call Sign: KB1SIC
John F Tary
144 Cedar Lake Rd
Haddam CT 06438

Call Sign: KA1MZF
William F Snigg
230 Hayden Hill Rd
Haddam CT 06438

Call Sign: KB1IXY
Ervin L Lowery
77 Oak Ridge Dr
Haddam CT 06438

Call Sign: KB1MTC
James S Carlson
52 Old Ponsett Road
Haddam CT 06438

Call Sign: N1LOB
Allen D Alonzo
246 Plains Rd
Haddam CT 06438

Call Sign: KA1GNP
Gregory J Campagnano
259 Plains Rd
Haddam CT 06438

Call Sign: K1WWI
Randal L Hale Jr
380 Plains Rd
Haddam CT 06438

Call Sign: W1IN
Randal L Hale Jr
380 Plains Rd
Haddam CT 06438

Call Sign: KB1TTU
Steven J Wytas
428 Plains Road
Haddam CT 06438

Call Sign: KB1BCR
Jon H Lyons
39 Rutty Lane
Haddam CT 06438

Call Sign: KB1UZL
Katherine E Gill
661 Saybrook Rd
Haddam CT 06438

Call Sign: N1UQR
Matthew T Wolak
1158 Saybrook Rd
Haddam CT 06438

Call Sign: N1JXM
Leona M Trudel
211 Turkey Hill Rd
Haddam CT 06438

Call Sign: KB1NKQ
Barclay M Thomas
Haddam CT 064380255

Call Sign: WU1B
Barclay M Thomas
Haddam CT 064380255

Call Sign: KB1TTP
Gary D'amico
Haddam CT 06438

FCC Amateur Radio Licenses in Haddam Neck

Call Sign: KA1OLD
Michael J Tacinelli
4 Hurd Park Rd
Haddam Neck CT 06424

FCC Amateur Radio Licenses in Hadlyme

Call Sign: KB1UMO

Richard P Prowell
150 Ferry Rd
Hadlyme CT 06439

Call Sign: WA1UJT
Edwin H Tanguay
10 Town St
Hadlyme CT 06439

Call Sign: N1IBE
Wade E Martell
Hadlyme CT 06439

Call Sign: N1KZH
Graham N Raynolds
Hadlyme CT 06439

Call Sign: N1QLE
Julia H Smith
Hadlyme CT 06439

FCC Amateur Radio Licenses in Hamden

Call Sign: KG6JGV
Glenn R Johnson
704 Aspen Glen Dr
Hamden CT 065183799

Call Sign: KB1KPN
Joshua A Mennone
94 Beacon St
Hamden CT 06514

Call Sign: N1XLK
Cheryl L Smith
99 Beacon St
Hamden CT 06514

Call Sign: KA1QFQ
George S Blondeck
156 Belden Rd
Hamden CT 06514

Call Sign: KB1IXB

John H Condon Jr
90 Benham St
Hamden CT 06514

Call Sign: KB1KQE
John H Condon Iii
90 Benham St
Hamden CT 06514

Call Sign: KB1IQU
James Distefano
629 Benham St
Hamden CT 06514

Call Sign: KB1ITB
Michael Distefano
629 Benham St
Hamden CT 06514

Call Sign: N1DTE
Arlene J Alegi
747 Benham St
Hamden CT 06514

Call Sign: N1DTF
John A Taruska
747 Benham St
Hamden CT 06514

Call Sign: KB1HPZ
Peter M Sloan
25 Benton St
Hamden CT 06517

Call Sign: N1GRK
Armand J Gherlone Jr
46 Bliss Ave
Hamden CT 065172505

Call Sign: W1NEW
Armand J Gherlone Jr
46 Bliss Ave
Hamden CT 065172505

Call Sign: KB1HRH

Robert Oliveira
25 Brinsmade Rd
Hamden CT 06514

Call Sign: N1FJS
Herbert Kolodny
74 Brook Hill Rd
Hamden CT 06514

Call Sign: N1ZNE
Frank N Czerwinski
144 Brooksvale Avenue
Hamden CT 06518

Call Sign: N1ZSH
Kathleen A Ramunni
144 Brooksvale Avenue
Hamden CT 06518

Call Sign: KA1WTA
David A Webb Jr
124 Bryden Ter
Hamden CT 06517

Call Sign: KB1WJW
Gregory T Rondinone
10 Busher Lane
Hamden CT 06518

Call Sign: KA1KMB
Arthur A Mc Clure
40 Busher Ln
Hamden CT 065181100

Call Sign: KA1ZFG
Jesse E Schachter
77 Cardo Rd
Hamden CT 06517

Call Sign: KA1ZFH
Dean A Schachter
77 Cardo Rd
Hamden CT 06517

Call Sign: N1TAY

Derek A Schachter
77 Cardo Rd
Hamden CT 06517

Zdenek Markovic Sr
51 Colony St
Hamden CT 06518

Mary D Agostino
19 Douglas Drive
Hamden CT 06518

Call Sign: KB1TBP
Frank P Platt
84 Carelton St
Hamden CT 06517

Call Sign: KB1DKK
Monica L Fitzpatrick
1 Deer Pond Trl
Hamden CT 065181031

Call Sign: KA1SVK
Peter H Freiler
38 Duane Rd
Hamden CT 06514

Call Sign: W1AMM
Abraham Bettigole
51 Charlton Hill
Hamden CT 06518

Call Sign: KN1V
Jim H Bershtein
1186 Dixwell Ave
Hamden CT 065144732

Call Sign: W1AIR
Peter H Freiler
38 Duane Rd
Hamden CT 06514

Call Sign: WA1QOF
Roger F Hawley
79 Charlton Hill Rd
Hamden CT 06518

Call Sign: K2LFP
Paul D Landman
2015 Dixwell Ave
Hamden CT 06514

Call Sign: N1KVT
Christopher G Senger
946 Dunbar Hill Rd
Hamden CT 06514

Call Sign: WA1U
Geoffrey J Fox
15 Chatterton Woods
Hamden CT 06518

Call Sign: N1SLB
Susan M Ritterbusch
1732 Dixwell Ave Apt 2e
Hamden CT 06514

Call Sign: KB2KDK
Jose S Landin
1120 Dunbar Hill Rd
Hamden CT 06514

Call Sign: K1GF
Geoffrey J Fox
15 Chatterton Woods
Hamden CT 06518

Call Sign: KA1PYN
Louis Phillips
25 Dorrance St
Hamden CT 06518

Call Sign: KB2KSR
Claire Cucurullo
1120 Dunbar Hill Rd
Hamden CT 06514

Call Sign: WA1D
Darrow F Loucks
103 Chester Street
Hamden CT 065143429

Call Sign: N1ELZ
S Charlotte Phillips
25 Dorrance St
Hamden CT 06518

Call Sign: K1JSL
Jose S Landin
1120 Dunbar Hill Rd
Hamden CT 06514

Call Sign: N1RBK
Donald A Scialla
745 Choate Ave
Hamden CT 06518

Call Sign: N1HJN
Karl G Wildman
151 Dorrance St
Hamden CT 06518

Call Sign: W1HUG
Robert A Seemann
89 Earl Ave
Hamden CT 06514

Call Sign: N1KCD
James C Hopkinson
94 Church St
Hamden CT 06514

Call Sign: WB1DMK
William L D Agostino
19 Douglas Dr
Hamden CT 06518

Call Sign: WA1HKT
James R Anderson
128 East Gate Lane
Hamden CT 065142233

Call Sign: WV1O

Call Sign: KB1FRD

Call Sign: KB1UPE

Christopher M Battista
122 Eastgate Lane
Hamden CT 06514

Call Sign: WA1AHG
Joseph L Farrell
151 Fans Rock Rd
Hamden CT 065182016

Call Sign: K1JCF
Joseph L Farrell
151 Fans Rock Rd
Hamden CT 065182016

Call Sign: KA1BHJ
Joseph R Raccio
20 Fourth St
Hamden CT 06514

Call Sign: KA1OWW
Francis D Cavallaro Jr
60 Gate Way
Hamden CT 06518

Call Sign: KB1DFV
Thomas A Talmadge
315 Gaylord Mt Rd
Hamden CT 06518

Call Sign: N1PQR
James Sakelarakis
515 Gilbert Ave
Hamden CT 06514

Call Sign: WA1ZVY
Anthony J Martin
571 Gilbert Ave
Hamden CT 06514

Call Sign: KB1NYA
Lewis L Sutherland
45 Glen Ham Rd
Hamden CT 06518

Call Sign: KB1LXB

Donald F Mccarthy
11 Goebel Rd
Hamden CT 06514

Call Sign: KB1PXQ
Willie M Mills
47 Grafton Rd
Hamden CT 06517

Call Sign: N1CUP
Vilmars Fimbers
25 Hamden Hills Drive Unit
41
Hamden CT 065185353

Call Sign: N1XQR
Joseph L Kantrow
130 Hearn Ln
Hamden CT 06514

Call Sign: KB1FKK
Craig D Schultz
31 Hideaway Ln.
Hamden CT 06518

Call Sign: N9NVM
Robert W Ellis
265 Highland Ave
Hamden CT 06518

Call Sign: KB1EMX
Nick Amento
273 Highland Ave
Hamden CT 06518

Call Sign: KB1DSH
Eric P Carney
30 Highview Ter Apt D3
Hamden CT 06514

Call Sign: N1LUK
Robert J Scott
154 Hill Street
Hamden CT 06514

Call Sign: KB1UZO
Ralph J Candela Iii
240 Hill Street
Hamden CT 06514

Call Sign: KB1FYK
Donald G Cofrancesco
104 Hillfield Road
Hamden CT 06518

Call Sign: KA1MDF
Nicholas T Brignola Jr
327 Howard Dr
Hamden CT 065141517

Call Sign: K1IRI
Charles E Brewer
240 Ives St
Hamden CT 06518

Call Sign: N1DOG
Philip B Applewhite
330 Ives St
Hamden CT 06518

Call Sign: N1FIF
Douglas R Applewhite
330 Ives St
Hamden CT 06518

Call Sign: N4MIG
Mark N Templeton
39 Jackson Road
Hamden CT 06517

Call Sign: WA1TUU
Thomas A Barker
63 Jaenicke Ln
Hamden CT 06517

Call Sign: N1ROE
George W Turner
71 Lake St
Hamden CT 06517

Call Sign: WA1MAC
Paul D Clark
120 Laura Rd
Hamden CT 065141007

Call Sign: WA1ZHU
Paula A Clark
120 Laura Rd
Hamden CT 065141007

Call Sign: K1FUE
Roy T Fredricksen
24 Leatherman Trl
Hamden CT 06518

Call Sign: WA1EUK
Kenneth J Reuben
200 Leeder Hill Dr Apt 336
Hamden CT 06517

Call Sign: W2UKJ
James M Garry
200 Leeder Hill Dr Apt 603
Hamden CT 06517

Call Sign: KB1SIY
Michael J Brennan
92 Leonard Rd
Hamden CT 06514

Call Sign: KA1GSW
Henry Doll Jr
44 Longmeadow Ave
Hamden CT 06514

Call Sign: KB2AOH
Kenneth A Kirchoff
10 Maplecrest Lane
Hamden CT 06514

Call Sign: N1OIK
Weitzer Wong
365 Mather St 164
Hamden CT 06514

Call Sign: KA1KHZ
Douglas J Toth
59 Michael Rd
Hamden CT 06514

Call Sign: N1FHH
Caroline S Toth
59 Michael Rd
Hamden CT 06514

Call Sign: KB1HFU
Edmund F Turner
175 Mill Pond Rd Unit 332
Hamden CT 06514

Call Sign: KB1INX
Craig S Roser
120 Mill Rock Rd
Hamden CT 06517

Call Sign: N1JVM
Arnold Perez
725b Mix Ave
Hamden CT 06514

Call Sign: WB1CLT
Steve B Deuss
905 Mix Ave Apt 1h
Hamden CT 06514

Call Sign: WA1YJK
Jerrold H Koret
900 Mix Ave Unit 102
Hamden CT 065145141

Call Sign: W1RPE
Grady L Garner
28 Myra Rd
Hamden CT 06517

Call Sign: K1FGM
Frank A Jomini
121 Norman Rd
Hamden CT 06514

Call Sign: WA1DOU
Sid M Miller
135 Old Hartford Turnpike
Hamden CT 06517

Call Sign: N1DJI
Philip A De Vit
1960 Paradise Ave
Hamden CT 06518

Call Sign: N1NQD
Barry A Kuehl
42 Paramount Ave
Hamden CT 06517

Call Sign: W2HDU
Richard Chocolate
82 Perry Rd
Hamden CT 06514

Call Sign: KB1KPM
Arthur H Simoneau
391 Pine Rock Ave
Hamden CT 06514

Call Sign: N1JIW
Brian A Pulisciano
687 Pine Rock Ave
Hamden CT 06514

Call Sign: NW1K
Bradford W Little
22 Pine St
Hamden CT 06514

Call Sign: N1UFY
Dennis M Smith
53 Piper Rd
Hamden CT 065143335

Call Sign: W1PTZ
Dennis M Smith
53 Piper Rd
Hamden CT 065143335

Call Sign: N1ZRQ
Lawrence F Walls
72 Piper Rd
Hamden CT 06514

Call Sign: K1LK
Louis I Kuslan
90 Robinwood Rd
Hamden CT 06517

Call Sign: K1POS
Erwin C Wetmore
1287 Sherman Ave
Hamden CT 06514

Call Sign: KB1AYG
Arthur W Mallory
146 Piper Rd
Hamden CT 06514

Call Sign: N1WZX
John M Sanford
115 Rogers Rd
Hamden CT 06517

Call Sign: KC2SYY
George C Braen
2950 State St Unit 3
Hamden CT 06518

Call Sign: N1DFB
Edwin J Stewart
85 Putnam Ave
Hamden CT 06517

Call Sign: KA1CFA
Allan B Schwartz
18 Russo Dr
Hamden CT 06518

Call Sign: KB1RDP
Paul Hemingway Jr
86 Still Hill Rd
Hamden CT 06518

Call Sign: KB1SQT
Henry J Eschmann Iii
140 Putnam Ave
Hamden CT 06517

Call Sign: KA1UWC
Robert D Kelsey
95 School St
Hamden CT 065183158

Call Sign: KA1ATW
Christian G Kohler Jr
316 Still Hill Rd
Hamden CT 06518

Call Sign: KB1STI
Henry J Eschmann Iv
140 Putnam Ave
Hamden CT 06517

Call Sign: KE1SEY
Robert D Kelsey
95 School St
Hamden CT 065183158

Call Sign: W1UDW
Warren R Gilmore
539 Still Hill Rd
Hamden CT 06518

Call Sign: WA7TZE
Henry J Eschmann Iii
140 Putnam Ave
Hamden CT 06517

Call Sign: W1UKX
Americo A Aranci
128 School St
Hamden CT 065183127

Call Sign: N1TXN
Frank D Grelle
25 Sunny Side Ave
Hamden CT 06518

Call Sign: AB1M
Mahdiy K Abdulrahim
364 Putnam Ave 10
Hamden CT 06517

Call Sign: KB1TBN
Janice L Ammons
16 Seminole St
Hamden CT 06518

Call Sign: KA6FIC
Michael C Saleski
13 Sunwoods Cir
Hamden CT 06518

Call Sign: N3NFP
Scott A Matheson
60 Ralston Ave
Hamden CT 06517

Call Sign: N1OFJ
David W Malicki
1650 Shepard Avenue
Hamden CT 06518

Call Sign: N1YQO
Doris K Preston
33 Taft St
Hamden CT 06514

Call Sign: KC0YOH
Peter J Downhour
60 Ralston Ave
Hamden CT 06517

Call Sign: KC7YJT
Robert L Doering
90 Shepards Knoll Dr
Hamden CT 06514

Call Sign: KB1UUX
Ronald H Gershman
34 Towne House Rd
Hamden CT 06514

Call Sign: KC1AE
Joel P Tilley
89 Towne House Rd
Hamden CT 06514

Call Sign: KB1FC
Edward F De Mott
90 West Shepard Ave
Hamden CT 06514

Call Sign: N1ORO
Thomas J Wagner
48 Windsor Rd
Hamden CT 06517

Call Sign: KB1OGE
Andrew L Masto
245 Treadwell Street
Hamden CT 06517

Call Sign: N1VAJ
Richard E Papa
285 West Shepard Ave
Hamden CT 065141010

Call Sign: KA1HBP
Anthony J Niesz
31 Winnett St
Hamden CT 06517

Call Sign: K1ALM
Andrew L Masto
245 Treadwell Street
Hamden CT 06517

Call Sign: KB6KXY
Richard G Nista
63 Whiting St
Hamden CT 06514

Call Sign: N1NQE
Helga F Niesz
31 Winnett St
Hamden CT 06517

Call Sign: W1LVX
Frank J Di Elsi
90 Troiano Rd
Hamden CT 06518

Call Sign: KB1MHV
Frank J Ardizzone
1548 Whitney Ave
Hamden CT 06517

Call Sign: N1ESZ
Anthony J Niesz
31 Winnett St
Hamden CT 06517

Call Sign: WA1HRC
Weli Ham Radio Club
104 Twin Brook Rd
Hamden CT 065143725

Call Sign: K1MHV
Frank J Ardizzone
1548 Whitney Ave
Hamden CT 06517

Call Sign: KA1CEZ
John T Buciak
51 Winnett St
Hamden CT 06517

Call Sign: WA1MIK
Robert W Meister
104 Twin Brook Rd
Hamden CT 065143725

Call Sign: NT1W
Sylvester P Civitello
2669 Whitney Ave
Hamden CT 06518

Call Sign: KB1SWN
John G Collins
199 Woodin St
Hamden CT 06514

Call Sign: N1PQQ
Greg S Cartier
119 Warner St
Hamden CT 06514

Call Sign: W1NUL
Philip S Lewis
3145 Whitney Ave
Hamden CT 06518

Call Sign: AD2G
George J Gerard
25 Woodlawn St
Hamden CT 06517

Call Sign: N1XLI
Jo Ann M Cartier
119 Warner St
Hamden CT 06514

Call Sign: N1PJS
Joseph A Scully Iii
1748 Whitney Avenue
Hamden CT 06517

Call Sign: NN1X
Alan R Plotnick
77 Woodlawn St
Hamden CT 06517

Call Sign: KB1MXQ
Nicholas Cartier
119 Warner St
Hamden CT 06514

Call Sign: KB1MCN
Michael P Vasil
16 Wilmont Dr
Hamden CT 06514

Call Sign: N1RWE
Allen H Silberstein
169 Worth Ave
Hamden CT 06518

Call Sign: N1XLR
Marla J Silberstein
169 Worth Ave
Hamden CT 06518

Call Sign: N1JVV
Raymond R Latini
Hamden CT 06517

Call Sign: KB1FYL
Robert W Carruthers
Hamden CT 06517

FCC Amateur Radio Licenses in Hampton

Call Sign: KB1FZC
William M Pipitone
66 Calvin Burnahm Rd
Hampton CT 06247

Call Sign: W1TJ
Timothy Jajliardo
135 Kemp Rd
Hampton CT 06247

Call Sign: KB1OOT
Walter J Ball Jr
25 Littlefield Rd
Hampton CT 06247

Call Sign: W1NOO
Malcolm D Burdick
156 Station Rd
Hampton CT 06247

Call Sign: N1LUX
Russell A Fors Jr
149 W Old Rt 6
Hampton CT 06247

Call Sign: N1ILB
Stuart Case
71 W Old Rte 6
Hampton CT 06247

Call Sign: KA1NCO
Lenore B Case
71 West Old Rte 6
Hampton CT 06247

Call Sign: W1JEY
Roderick K Nichols Jr
185 Windy Hill Rd
Hampton CT 06247

Call Sign: WA1YOU
Roger R Caridad
195 Windy Hill Road
Hampton CT 06247

Call Sign: N1HUY
Gary A Warzocha
Hampton CT 06247

FCC Amateur Radio Licenses in Hartford

Call Sign: KA1TKA
Ernesto Santiago
97 A Van Block Ave
Hartford CT 06106

Call Sign: KP4RMM
Ramiro Marin
188 Adelaide St
Hartford CT 06114

Call Sign: KB1FOE
Charles Esquilin
64 Ashley St
Hartford CT 06105

Call Sign: NU0U
Hugh Barker
143 Avery Heights
Hartford CT 061064264

Call Sign: KC4ANJ
Lawrence E Kwapich

13 Babcock St
Hartford CT 06103

Call Sign: KB1CKY
Anibal Agron
57 Barker Street
Hartford CT 061340613

Call Sign: KA1WMW
Lionel Thompson Sr
294 Bellevue St
Hartford CT 06120

Call Sign: KB1INQ
Jose Trejo
30 Bliss St
Hartford CT 06114

Call Sign: KB1UFX
Evelyn Fuentes
121 Bond St
Hartford CT 06114

Call Sign: KP4JM
Jorge L Fuentes
121 Bond St
Hartford CT 06114

Call Sign: K1EHB
Henry R Rannou
75 Bonner St
Hartford CT 06106

Call Sign: KB1FNW
Luis J Sanchez
214 Bonner St
Hartford CT 06106

Call Sign: KB1BSQ
Connecticut Office Of
Emergency Management
360 Broad St
Hartford CT 06105

Call Sign: KD1OT

Leon Goolsby Ii
94 Campfield Ave. 3rd Fl.
Hartford CT 06114

Call Sign: KB1FXT
Richard R Charron
225 Capen St 1e
Hartford CT 06112

Call Sign: KB1HBZ
Hiram A Alvarado
80 Catherine St
Hartford CT 06106

Call Sign: KB1MLN
Joseph S Manke
50 Chapman St
Hartford CT 06114

Call Sign: WA1JSM
Joseph S Manke
50 Chapman St
Hartford CT 06114

Call Sign: KB1MLN
Joseph S Manke
50 Chapman St
Hartford CT 06114

Call Sign: KA1YEM
Manuel Perez
150 Clark St
Hartford CT 06120

Call Sign: KB1ALO
Luis De Jesus
59 Coleman Dr A1
Hartford CT 06106

Call Sign: K1MVQ
Gregory C Secord
23 Columbia Street
Hartford CT 061061313

Call Sign: KB1KUK

Paul A Hoff
125 Cromwell St
Hartford CT 06114

Call Sign: KA9PXX
Derick J Norskog
62 Curtiss St
Hartford CT 06106

Call Sign: KB1FNV
Phillip L Mccalla
56 E Euclid St
Hartford CT 06112

Call Sign: WA2KJN
Richard D Pomp
65 Elizabeth St
Hartford CT 06105

Call Sign: KA1OPM
Henry J Lach
346 Fairfield Ave
Hartford CT 06114

Call Sign: KA1WWR
Leo J Mathew
662 Farmington Ave Apt
210
Hartford CT 06105

Call Sign: KB1RDL
Alexander Alper
665 Farmington Ave Apt 4
Hartford CT 06105

Call Sign: N1SUM
Erik W Bowen
381 Farmington Ave Apt
401-D
Hartford CT 06105

Call Sign: W1SDJ
John S Erisoty
16 Forster St
Hartford CT 06106

Call Sign: KA1MCZ
Joseph D Restrepo
30 Franklin Ave
Hartford CT 06114

Call Sign: WB1BXS
Roger W Taksar
93 Franklin Ave
Hartford CT 06114

Call Sign: AA1OX
Andrew Dumas
407 Franklin Ave
Hartford CT 06114

Call Sign: KA1TFR
Cruz L Rivas
5 Frederick St
Hartford CT 06105

Call Sign: N1YIE
Jose A Rivera
53 Gidding St
Hartford CT 06110

Call Sign: KA1JUM
Howard E Oakley
109 Gilman St
Hartford CT 06114

Call Sign: KA1ZRX
Alice L Wisniewski
180 Gilman St
Hartford CT 06114

Call Sign: KA1WJU
Stephen C Mc Guire
34 Goshen St
Hartford CT 06106

Call Sign: N1XJQ
Stephen Douglass
63 Greenfield St
Hartford CT 06112

Hartford CT 061102220

Hartford CT 06114

Call Sign: KB1BUH
Ss Cyril And Methodius
School Amateur Radio Clb
35 Groton St
Hartford CT 06106

Call Sign: N1LWA
Salvatore M Mennella
14 Hubbard Rd
Hartford CT 06114

Call Sign: N1ZND
James R Cox Chapman
229 Kenyon
Hartford CT 06105

Call Sign: KB1BHA
Ursula M Gromek
38 Groton St
Hartford CT 06106

Call Sign: N1UIS
Richard E Tefft
425 Hudson St
Hartford CT 06106

Call Sign: KB4KJ
James W Spellman
221 Laurel St Apt 101
Hartford CT 06105

Call Sign: N1WHL
Violet R Gromek
38 Groton St
Hartford CT 06106

Call Sign: KA1WXP
Domingo H Cotto
23 Humphrey St
Hartford CT 06106

Call Sign: KA1YCA
Fay M Gill
50 Litchfield St
Hartford CT 06112

Call Sign: WA1JZS
Albert O Pfeiffer
11 Haddam St
Hartford CT 06106

Call Sign: KB1NQR
Frankie Perez
32 Huntington St - 3f
Hartford CT 06105

Call Sign: N1MTD
Andrew S P Lindh
32 Lorraine St
Hartford CT 06105

Call Sign: K1SUS
Robert J Dillon Jr
32 Hanmer St
Hartford CT 06114

Call Sign: N1NAG
Penny E Harts
52 Kenneth St
Hartford CT 06114

Call Sign: KB1BGX
Kristen L Carrion
24 Madison St
Hartford CT 06106

Call Sign: KA1WGW
Wendy G Krol
90 Heath St
Hartford CT 06106

Call Sign: KB1MNM
Tristan D Gunn
52 Kenneth St
Hartford CT 06114

Call Sign: KA1VMD
Amanda L Schumaker
66 Main St Apt H
Hartford CT 06106

Call Sign: KA1UQJ
George A De Jesus
100 Henry St
Hartford CT 06114

Call Sign: N1TDG
Tristan D Gunn
52 Kenneth St
Hartford CT 06114

Call Sign: KB1PVS
Peter Hsieh
450 Main Street
Hartford CT 06103

Call Sign: KA1YEI
Guillermo Martinez
213 Hillside Avenue
Hartford CT 06106

Call Sign: KB1PVT
Tyrique J Harts
52 Kenneth St
Hartford CT 06114

Call Sign: KA1RTS
Ramon Quinones
218 Mather St
Hartford CT 06112

Call Sign: KB1CYN
Tammy L Krauss
148 Hollywood Ave

Call Sign: N1TJH
Tyrique J Harts
52 Kenneth St

Call Sign: KA1RTY
Maria Rivera
218 Mather St

Hartford CT 06112

Call Sign: KA1RSO
Ruperta Rodriguez
220 Mather St
Hartford CT 06112

Call Sign: KP4OE
Nemesio Zambrana
220 Mather St
Hartford CT 06112

Call Sign: W1LB
Arturo I Rodriguez
220 Mather St
Hartford CT 06112

Call Sign: N1ZHX
Aneta Draka
69 Mountford St Apt 6a
Hartford CT 06114

Call Sign: KA1AEY
Joseph Ferlazzo
475 New Britain Ave
Hartford CT 06106

Call Sign: W1NJM
George Hart
705 New Britain Ave
Brainard Building Rm 78
Hartford CT 06106

Call Sign: KB3KEI
Thomas C Murphy
85 New Park Ave.
Hartford CT 06106

Call Sign: WB1AOY
Luann C Skwara
199 Newbury St
Hartford CT 06114

Call Sign: KB1ULU
William M Large

242 Newbury St
Hartford CT 06114

Call Sign: KA1TFP
Anthony Velez
2 O Neil Rd Chater Oak
Hartford CT 06106

Call Sign: KW1J
Peter P Tolisano Jr
141 Otis St
Hartford CT 06114

Call Sign: KB1CKX
Eugenio Bonilla
199 Otis St
Hartford CT 061141429

Call Sign: KB1PRO
Hamilton Arroyo
21 Owen St Apt 202
Hartford CT 06105

Call Sign: KA1RNB
Robert D Palochko
2 Park Pl 8c
Hartford CT 06106

Call Sign: N1YPD
Felix A Zayas
1618 Park Street
Hartford CT 06106

Call Sign: N1OVD
Stephen P Peterson
18 Pawtucket St
Hartford CT 06114

Call Sign: KB1FQT
Clyde C White
83 Pliny Street
Hartford CT 06120

Call Sign: N1RSN
Carlene B Peterson

33 Preston St
Hartford CT 06114

Call Sign: KB1GTB
University Of Connecticut
School Of Law Amateur
Radio Club
633 Prospect Ave - Apt C-1
Hartford CT 061054207

Call Sign: KA1YEH
Jose A Colon
446 Prospet Ave
Harford CT 06105

Call Sign: KA1YEE
Gladis Martinez
446 Prospet Ave
Hartford CT 06105

Call Sign: KB1KWY
Angel Diaz
249 Putnam
Hartford CT 06106

Call Sign: KB1UHZ
Manuel A Dearce
55 Roxbury St 1st Flr
Hartford CT 06114

Call Sign: KA1RSN
Modesta Lebron
163 S Whitney
Hartford CT 06105

Call Sign: N1WHJ
Wojciech W Sieczek
78 S Whitney St
Hartford CT 06106

Call Sign: KA1RSM
Federico Lebron
163 S Whitney St
Hartford CT 06105

Call Sign: KB1EVQ
Ann M Gruden
16 Sherbrooke Ave
Hartford CT 061063838

Call Sign: WP4NOS
Angelo L Gonzalez
22 South Whitney St
Hartford CT 06106

Call Sign: KM1S
Neville V King
11a Sterling St
Hartford CT 06112

Call Sign: KX1R
Armand A Korzenik
120 Terry Rd
Hartford CT 06105

Call Sign: KB1WFJ
Robert L Day Iii
100 Trumbull St Apt 210
Hartford CT 06103

Call Sign: AA1FQ
Bradley F Ware
221 Trumbull St Apt 2103
Harford CT 06106

Call Sign: KA1TKB
Ildelfonso Calderon
99b Van Block Ave
Hartford CT 06106

Call Sign: N1YIC
Luis A Nieves
34 Vernon St - Apt 404
Hartford CT 06106

Call Sign: KB1GJI
Tomas A Marquez
8 Vine St Apt 2a
Hartford CT 06112

Call Sign: W1HXU
John P Tyskiewicz
77 W Euclid St
Hartford CT 06112

Call Sign: KA1WMX
Ronald Thompson Sr
117 W Morningside St
Hartford CT 06112

Call Sign: KB1AKK
Edgardo Rodriguez
79 Ward St
Hartford CT 06106

Call Sign: KB1TAG
Cara C Spencer
978 West Blvd
Hartford CT 06105

Call Sign: KB1RMN
J P Zimmerman
80 Wethersfield Ave
Hartford CT 06114

Call Sign: WB1DJL
Mariana W Armstrong
88 Wethersfield Ave
Hartford CT 06114

Call Sign: KA1TFN
Hector Alcantara
50 Willar St Apt 304n
Harford CT 06105

Call Sign: KA1RYA
Michael A Velez Sr
7 Woodland St
Hartford CT 06105

Call Sign: K1PUO
William H Spedding
15 Woodland St
Hartford CT 06105

Call Sign: KB1GRM
Haines Brown
30 Woodland Street 8-D
Hartford CT 06105

Call Sign: KB6EIT
Edward J White
20 Woodside Cir
Hartford CT 06105

Call Sign: KA1TUO
Ramon Gonzalez
150 Word St
Hartford CT 06106

Call Sign: KA1RST
Margie E Hutton
Hartford CT 06103

Call Sign: N1LMR
Alton E Jones
Hartford CT 06143

Call Sign: N1NFD
James S Gibson
Hartford CT 06141

Call Sign: NP4H
Nomar Vizcarrondo Leon
Hartford CT 061260656

Call Sign: WA1UBQ
David M Berin
Hartford CT 061320001

FCC Amateur Radio Licenses in Harwington

Call Sign: KB1OJS
Matthew R Hall
174 Wildcat Hill Rd
Harwington CT 06791

Call Sign: W1GSS
Arthur W Jakubiak

46 Beechwood Dr
Harwinton CT 06791

320 Harmony Hill Road
Harwinton CT 06791

59 Mountain View Dr
Harwinton CT 06791

Call Sign: KB1SFL
Martin J Rinko
275 Burlington Rd
Harwinton CT 06791

Call Sign: N1WEY
Henry H Tessman Jr
18 Highview Dr
Harwinton CT 06791

Call Sign: KA1DDO
John M Shaggy
83 Orchard Hill Rd.
Harwinton CT 06781

Call Sign: W1FSC
John E Sedlack
323 Burlington Rd
Harwinton CT 06791

Call Sign: N1SRM
Nicholas D Molino
275 Hill Rd
Harwinton CT 06791

Call Sign: KA1UCQ
Frances E Rice
720 Plymouth Rd
Harwinton CT 06791

Call Sign: KB1UAA
Mark A Ferrecchia
11 Campville Hill Rd
Harwinton CT 06791

Call Sign: W1VLF
Paul A Cianciolo
57 Huntington Dr
Harwinton CT 06791

Call Sign: KB1JKN
Michael J Mastrobattisto
36 Rocky Rd W
Harwinton CT 06791

Call Sign: WA1HUE
Jay C Peterson
59 County Line Rd
Harwinton CT 06791

Call Sign: N1GVP
Mary W Fox
14 Lenor Dr
Harwinton CT 06791

Call Sign: W1HTH
Leon L Ruot
204 Scoville Hill
Harwinton CT 06791

Call Sign: KB1GL
William J Mc Baine
Davis Rd
Harwinton CT 06791

Call Sign: WO1A
Colin P Fox
14 Lenor Dr
Harwinton CT 06791

Call Sign: N1VSO
Wallace M Drake
284 Scoville Hill Rd
Harwinton CT 06791

Call Sign: WA1YAA
Pasquale D Amato
Green Acres Rd
Harwinton CT 06790

Call Sign: KA1JFW
Michael J Conroy
193 Locust Rd
Harwinton CT 067912410

Call Sign: KB1VVC
Nathan T Hedrick
45 Silano Dr
Harwinton CT 06791

Call Sign: KB1TER
James A Pabilonia
96 Harmony Hill Rd
Harwinton CT 06791

Call Sign: KB1YQ
Joan M Niewinski
179 Mansfield Rd
Harwinton CT 06791

Call Sign: K1PUG
Henry R Cattey
41 Silo Dr
Harwinton CT 06791

Call Sign: KB1TES
Joan E Kirchner
96 Harmony Hill Rd
Harwinton CT 06791

Call Sign: KB1PNQ
Joanne L Endersby
50 Mountain View Dr
Harwinton CT 06791

Call Sign: KA1ICI
Terrence M Milanese
60 Westleigh Dr
Harwinton CT 06791

Call Sign: KA1EUQ
Keith M Dablain

Call Sign: KB1SLN
Christopher J Mckenna Sr

Call Sign: K1LQV
William C Ferrarotti

103 Whetstone Rd
Harwinton CT 06791

Call Sign: KB1BID
Kevin M Ferrarotti
103 Whetstone Rd
Harwinton CT 06791

Call Sign: K1ITW
Andrew J Kasznay Jr
172 Whetstone Rd
Harwinton CT 06791

Call Sign: N1JPY
David E Ross
244 Whetstone Rd
Harwinton CT 06791

Call Sign: W1FAN
David E Ross
244 Whetstone Rd
Harwinton CT 06791

Call Sign: N1UWR
Steven T Pinkowish
40 Wildwood Passway
Harwinton CT 06791

Call Sign: WA1WIM
Richard G Agoston
81 Wilson Pond Rd
Harwinton CT 06791

Call Sign: WA1VXG
Robert N D Amato
34 Windmill Dr
Harwinton CT 06791

Call Sign: K1ZSG
Donald G Nelson
Harwinton CT 06791

**FCC Amateur Radio
Licenses in Hebron**

Call Sign: K1PTI
J Peter Carbone Jr
5 Burnt Hill Rd
Hebron CT 06248

Call Sign: KA1NYH
Elaine D Phillips
310 Burnt Hill Rd
Hebron CT 06248

Call Sign: N1CBD
Thomas A Phillips
310 Burnt Hill Rd
Hebron CT 062481332

Call Sign: WA1EWQ
Gary J Sarra
84 Charles Ln
Hebron CT 06248

Call Sign: KB1FNK
Thomas R Corris
18 Country Ln
Hebron CT 06248

Call Sign: KB1LYB
Matthew F Griswold
75 Country Ln
Hebron CT 06248

Call Sign: K1NE
William H Becker
64 East St
Hebron CT 06248

Call Sign: KA1NYQ
Richard M Corris
255 East St
Hebron CT 06248

Call Sign: KB1DMU
Lorraine E C Corris
255 East St
Hebron CT 06248

Call Sign: AA1XI
Richard M Corris
255 East St
Hebron CT 06248

Call Sign: N1HP
Richard M Corris
255 East St
Hebron CT 06248

Call Sign: N1FUL
Daniel J Phelps
224 East St.
Hebron CT 06248

Call Sign: KB1KWC
Barbara L Kelly
1097 Gilead Rd
Hebron CT 06248

Call Sign: KB1QIA
Igor Parsadanov
905 Gilead St
Hebron CT 06248

Call Sign: KB1HSZ
Thomas L Kelly
1097 Gilead St
Hebron CT 06248

Call Sign: KB1JNX
William E Kelly
1097 Gilead St
Hebron CT 06248

Call Sign: KB1HLE
Michael C Thornton
17 Hickory Dr
Hebron CT 06248

Call Sign: N1KPX
Thomas J Chlupsa
287 Jagger Ln
Hebron CT 06248

Call Sign: N1JQT
Robert S Rydziel
89 Joel Dr
Hebron CT 06248

Call Sign: N1OUG
Robert R Armstrong
136 London Rd
Hebron CT 06248

Call Sign: N1JYN
Gregory M Long
383 Old Colchester Rd
Hebron CT 062311623

Call Sign: N1GOF
Florence A Graham
2 River Road
Hebron CT 06248

Call Sign: KB1IGT
Christopher F O Neill
65 Slocum Road
Hebron CT 06248

Call Sign: KB1NXD
Kurt W Meyerhardt
9 Tannery Hill Lane
Hebron CT 06248

Call Sign: WB2UUM
Robert A Schenck
245 W Main St
Hebron CT 06248

Call Sign: K2CU
Robert A Schenck
245 W Main St
Hebron CT 06248

Call Sign: K1YWB
William H Hills
248 W Man St
Hebron CT 06248

FCC Amateur Radio Licenses in Higganum

Call Sign: KB1HDC
Bruce C Grotta
53 Arkay Drive
Higganum CT 06441

Call Sign: W1DEX
Ernest A Woods Jr
550 Beaver Meadow Rd
Higganum CT 06441

Call Sign: K1MJF
Gary L Moody
384 Brainard Hill Road
Higganum CT 06441

Call Sign: N1GBN
William M Turner
173 Burr Road
Higganum CT 06441

Call Sign: W1YLS
John W Rogerson
Box 112 Christian Hill Rd
Higganum CT 06441

Call Sign: N1WGK
Frederick M Johnson Jr
51 Dish Mill Rd
Higganum CT 06441

Call Sign: WB1HBQ
Raymond F Hubner
9 Earl Roberts Rd
Higganum CT 06441

Call Sign: KA1BOE
Edna K Ege
16 Earl Roberts Rd
Higganum CT 064414001

Call Sign: WB1DCC
Richard A Ege

---

16 Earl Roberts Rd
Higganum CT 06441

Call Sign: KB1HGD
Joseph E Sharer
329 Killingworth Rd
Higganum CT 06441

Call Sign: WA1ZEK
Mark J Mokoski
944 Killingworth Rd
Higganum CT 06441

Call Sign: KB1GGZ
Town Of Haddam Ct
O.E.M.
944 Killingworth Rd
Higganum CT 064414405

Call Sign: KB1ILK
John A Hartzell
972 Killingworth Rd
Higganum CT 06441

Call Sign: W1JAH
John A Hartzell
972 Killingworth Rd
Higganum CT 06441

Call Sign: KB1VPK
Jacob V Hartzell
972 Killingworth Rd
Higganum CT 06441

Call Sign: N1JBQ
Joseph J Corda Jr
18 Laurel Grove Drive
Higganum CT 06441

Call Sign: KB1RNF
Diane M Petrilli
19 Laurel Grove Rd
Higganum CT 06441

Call Sign: N1KZN

John M Armando
9 Little City Road
Higganum CT 06441

Call Sign: KA1AB
William E Valerius
110 Morris Hubbard Rd
Higganum CT 06441

Call Sign: WB1ARC
American Red Cross
Central Conn Middlesex
Chapter
127 Nason Rd
Higganum CT 06441

Call Sign: K1HAD
Town Of Haddam Ct
O.E.M.
127 Nason Rd
Higganum CT 064414223

Call Sign: K1PU
Mark J Mokoski
127 Nason Rd
Higganum CT 064414223

Call Sign: N1YOS
Anthony P Mirabelli
19 Olson Pl
Higganum CT 06441

Call Sign: K1OCQ
Joseph R Therrien Sr
196 Pokorny Rd
Higganum CT 06441

Call Sign: K1OTN
Paul A Lewis
415 Saybrook Rd
Higganum CT 06441

Call Sign: WA1DIV
Hartford Public Hs Amateur
Radio Clb

415 Saybrook Rd
Higganum CT 06441

Call Sign: AB1QP
Frank A Yaskin
9 Sima Rd.
Higganum CT 06441

Call Sign: W1FK
Charles S Gillmor
29 Spencer Rd
Higganum CT 06441

Call Sign: N1IVK
Howard A Mc Auliffe
20 Thayer Rd
Higganum CT 06441

Call Sign: KW1V
David L Rose
Higganum CT 06441

Call Sign: N1OFN
William J Carson
Higganum CT 06441

Call Sign: KB1FYF
Robert A Norton Jr
Higganum CT 06441

**FCC Amateur Radio
Licenses in Huntington**

Call Sign: N1FRQ
Stephen G Ambrisco Jr
22 Barry Rd
Huntington CT 06484

Call Sign: WA1MIS
Paul J Murray
11 Carriage Dr
Huntington CT 06484

Call Sign: W1LRF
Charles A Mudre

30 Chamberlain
Huntington CT 06484

Call Sign: WA1FLA
George F Buckner
15 Christine Dr
Huntington CT 06484

Call Sign: KA1TMT
John J Morales
62 Dogwood Dr
Huntington CT 06484

Call Sign: KB1RJR
Nello A Fede
11 English Lane
Huntington CT 06484

Call Sign: K1MAR
Nicholas J Georgis
215 Fox Run
Huntington CT 06484

Call Sign: K1UAT
Staples H S Arc
215 Fox Run
Huntington CT 06484

Call Sign: WA1OOT
John Babina Jr
9 Freedom Way
Huntington CT 064845373

Call Sign: KB1BZL
Joaquin G Pereira
2 Hunters Ridge Rd
Huntington CT 064843536

Call Sign: KA1TIP
David G Alfano
32 Hurd St
Huntington CT 06484

Call Sign: KA1RPM
Daniel J Shepard

103 Lane St
Huntington CT 06484

Call Sign: KA1YYY
Earl L Augusta
91 Mill St
Huntington CT 06484

Call Sign: KA2INV
Eric K Le Strange
382 Mohegan Rd
Huntington CT 06484

Call Sign: KE1A
Jerry C Melson
36 Patricia Dr
Huntington CT 06484

Call Sign: KN1C
Nancy T Melson
36 Patricia Dr
Huntington CT 06484

Call Sign: WB1FER
Edward F Montagnino
5 Plante Lane
Huntington CT 06484

Call Sign: W1EFM
Edward F Montagnino
5 Plante Lane
Huntington CT 06484

Call Sign: K1DPO
Leo A Le Bel
27 Rolling Brook Ln
Huntington CT 064845760

Call Sign: W1RPG
Robert P Giuliani
26 Thompson St
Huntington CT 06484

Call Sign: W1CRS
Connecticut Radio Society

26 Thompson St
Huntington CT 06484

FCC Amateur Radio Licenses in Ivoryton

Call Sign: KA1DZF
M Samantha Geiger
253 Bushy Hill Rd
Ivoryton CT 06442

Call Sign: KD1CU
Alexander Proudfit
C/O Ingram
Ivoryton CT 06442

Call Sign: N1KZL
Thomas E Deal
68 Mares Hill Rd
Ivoryton CT 06442

Call Sign: N1PLW
Joanne B Deal
68 Mares Hill Rd
Ivoryton CT 06442

Call Sign: N1ZHT
Sarah J Deal
68 Mares Hill Rd
Ivoryton CT 06442

Call Sign: KA1IFS
Sandra J Mc Curdy
5 N Winds Dr
Ivoryton CT 06442

Call Sign: WA1GTP
Richard S Mc Curdy
5 Northwinds Dr
Ivoryton CT 06442

Call Sign: N1LUV
Leon K Chalker
64 Pond Meadow Rd
Ivoryton CT 06442

Call Sign: AB2OA
Shirley A Budney
Ivoryton CT 06442

Call Sign: K1ZHG
Louis R Budney
Ivoryton CT 06442

FCC Amateur Radio Licenses in Jewett City

Call Sign: N1FEJ
Rodney P Derosier
14 Bow Ln
Jewett City CT 06351

Call Sign: WV1F
Glenn E Derrah
6 Browning Rd
Jewett City CT 063512616

Call Sign: KB1VMW
Mark A Wells
220 Bundy Hill Rd
Jewett City CT 06351

Call Sign: KA1MAF
David B La Fleur Sr
56 December Dr
Jewett City CT 06351

Call Sign: KU1S
James P Gagliardo Sr
634 Hopeville Rd 46
Jewett City CT 06351

Call Sign: K1NNP
Donald N Lefrancois
21 Ilewicz Dr
Jewett City CT 06351

Call Sign: KA1YTD
Timothy P Sharkey
11 Lenox Ave

Jewett City CT 06351

Call Sign: N1KPF
Mark R Goodenow
46b Main St
Jewett City CT 06351

Call Sign: KB1NHM
Arnold J Daley
35 Pleasant View St Apt
104
Jewett City CT 06351

Call Sign: KA1GUK
Norman R Bourassa Jr
23 South Main St Apt 1
Jewett City CT 063512260

Call Sign: AK1G
Gary S Kuzmenko
171 Stone Hill Rd
Jewett City CT 06351

Call Sign: WB1GVK
Christine L Kuzmenko
171 Stone Hill Rd
Jewett City CT 06351

Call Sign: KA1CII
Dene E King
Jewett City CT 06351

FCC Amateur Radio Licenses in Kensington

Call Sign: KA1KSG
Louis C Provini
39 Beechwood Ln
Kensington CT 06037

Call Sign: N1WIB
Larry J Criniti
291 Brooke Meadow Rd
Kensington CT 06037

Call Sign: KA0LPW
Cirillo Berardozzi
35 Burnham St
Kensington CT 06037

Call Sign: KB1QQL
Daniel J Menard
34 Camels Back
Kensington CT 06037

Call Sign: N1OQB
Thomas Plawski
149 Carriage Dr
Kensington CT 06037

Call Sign: KB1YB
Dean A Baruffi
173 Cole Lane
Kensington CT 06037

Call Sign: K1ACE
Dennis J Pisko
42 Cole Ln
Kensington CT 06037

Call Sign: KA1ILD
Sebastian F Scarfe
57 Crater Ln
Kensington CT 06037

Call Sign: K1KFD
Jeffrey F Pajor
153 Dayl Dr.
Kensington CT 06037

Call Sign: K1HFZ
Jeffrey F Pajor
153 Dayl Dr.
Kensington CT 06037

Call Sign: N1WKT
Edward A Linn
622 Edgewood Rd
Kensington CT 06037

Call Sign: N1TUR
Raymond D Bosso
105 Four Rod Rd
Kensington CT 06037

Call Sign: KA1RAV
Barbara D Pavano
1017 Four Rod Rd
Kensington CT 06037

Call Sign: KA1RAX
Lynn R Rustigian
145 Glen St
Kensington CT 06037

Call Sign: N1ZJP
Ronald E King
30 Harris St
Kensington CT 06037

Call Sign: KB1RPE
Karl G Lewis
56 Hartland Terrace
Kensington CT 06037

Call Sign: WA1ZGB
Amedeo D Zovich
79 Heather Ln
Kensington CT 06037

Call Sign: N1JBH
Ronald C Manchesi
107 Hickory Hill Road
Kensington CT 06037

Call Sign: KA1MWS
Sarah E Ferrero
639 High Rd
Kensington CT 06037

Call Sign: N1YID
Joseph S Guerrera
685 High Rd
Kensington CT 06037

Call Sign: KB1NKZ
Nicholas W Fucello
29 Kelly Ann Court
Kensington CT 06037

Call Sign: N1LLO
Nicholas W Fucello
29 Kelly Ann Court
Kensington CT 06037

Call Sign: NF1P
Nicholas W Fucello
29 Kelly Ann Court
Kensington CT 06037

Call Sign: WV3X
Nicholas W Fucello
29 Kelly Ann Court
Kensington CT 06037

Call Sign: WV1Q
Nicholas W Fucello
29 Kelly Ann Court
Kensington CT 06037

Call Sign: WV3X
Nicholas W Fucello
29 Kelly Ann Court
Kensington CT 06037

Call Sign: W1WI
Nicholas W Fucello
29 Kelly Ann Court
Kensington CT 06037

Call Sign: W1UE
Adam J Dickon
1161 Kensington Rd
Kensington CT 06037

Call Sign: KA1FCN
Stanley A Tomusiak
1670 Kensington Rd
Kensington CT 060373522

Call Sign: N1SQF
Ronald F Gombotz
21 Mallard Ln
Kensington CT 06037

Call Sign: KB1GJM
Brian C Baker
306 Mooreland Rd
Kensington CT 06037

Call Sign: W1HNF
Edward G Mazuronis
72 Mountain View Dr
Kensington CT 060372945

Call Sign: KA1SXZ
John M Stifel
232 Percival Ave
Kensington CT 06037

Call Sign: KB1LYC
Matthew C Odishoo
311 Percival Ave
Kensington CT 06037

Call Sign: KB1MCO
Matthew C Odishoo
311 Percival Ave
Kensington CT 06037

Call Sign: N1CXJ
David J Cavanaugh
5 Pheasant Run
Kensington CT 06037

Call Sign: KA1MOP
Anthony Dagata
81 Ridgewood Ln
Kensington CT 06037

Call Sign: KA1YVN
Thomas E O Brien
32 Schultz Rd
Kensington CT 06037

Call Sign: N1PYW
William M Moore
19 Tower Ave
Kensington CT 06037

Call Sign: WA1IDY
Joseph A Sak
150 Vineyard Dr
Kensington CT 06037

Call Sign: KA1UEJ
Joseph A Diorio
28 Warner Rd
Kensington CT 06037

Call Sign: KC1JV
Edward H Matthews
26 Winding Meadow Drive
Kensington CT 06037

Call Sign: KA1VS
John Godzyk
112 Woods Edge Ct
Kensington CT 06037

Call Sign: KA1WVW
Jeffrey F Pajor
Kensington CT 060370043

Call Sign: N1NAL
Gerald T Wroblewski
Kensington CT 06037

Call Sign: WA5VKC
F Paul Haney
Kensington CT 06037

FCC Amateur Radio Licenses in Kent

Call Sign: W1CAH
Melvin D Eckert
381 Kent Cornwall Rd
Kent CT 067571206

Call Sign: W4EV
George E De Vilbiss
92 Macedonia Rd
Kent CT 06757

Call Sign: WA1CYI
Angus R Mc Farland
59 Segar Mountain Rd Box
631
Kent CT 06757

Call Sign: WA2VGS
David Genovese
22 St.Johns Acres
Kent CT 06757

Call Sign: W6NOL
Robert T Eaton
Kent CT 06757

**FCC Amateur Radio
Licenses in Killingly**

Call Sign: N1VIT
Albert A Leonard
Killingly CT 062430302

**FCC Amateur Radio
Licenses in Killingworth**

Call Sign: KB1LGD
James E Feldhouse
68 Alders Bridge Rd
Killingworth CT 06419

Call Sign: N1ZEG
Cynthia E Baran
121 Bar Gate Tr
Killingworth CT 06419

Call Sign: N1XME
Joseph M Wicklow Iii
121 Bar Gate Trail
Killingworth CT 06419

Call Sign: N1ZRJ
Joseph M Wicklow Iv
121 Bar Gate Trail
Killingworth CT 06419

Call Sign: N1ZEH
Robert L Bousquet
125 Bar Gate Trail Rd
Killingworth CT 06419

Call Sign: N1MWU
Michael A Boccia
11 Beckwith Rd
Killingworth CT 06419

Call Sign: N1BQQ
H Grey Knuth
32 Boulder Trail
Killingworth CT 06419

Call Sign: KA1TZZ
Margaret H Butler
166 Chestnut Hill Rd
Killingworth CT 06419

Call Sign: N1DCS
Caesar J Rondina
69 Chittenden Rd
Killingworth CT 06419

Call Sign: K1MMM
Albert N Lafreniere Sr
78 Chittenden Rd
Killingworth CT 064192414

Call Sign: W1EGS
Milton F Johnson
18 Country Club Trail
Killingworth CT 06419

Call Sign: N1ZII
Billy W Bassett
45 Granite Hill Rd
Killingworth CT 06419

Call Sign: N1ZIJ
Shirley J Bassett
45 Granite Hill Rd
Killingworth CT 06419

Call Sign: KB1PRR
Benjamin L Townsend
162 Green Hill Rd
Killingworth CT 06419

Call Sign: KW1R
Benjamin L Townsend
162 Green Hill Rd
Killingworth CT 06419

Call Sign: KM1A
John B Hill
29 Kelseytown Rd
Killingworth CT 06419

Call Sign: WA1YVE
Stephen C Anderson
46 Kelseytown Rd
Killingworth CT 06419

Call Sign: W1UX
Yves A Feder
2 N Chestnut Hill Rd
Killingworth CT 06419

Call Sign: KB1OZH
Michael S Haaga
177 North Chestnut Hill Rd
Killingworth CT 06419

Call Sign: KA1RJS
Linda S Skernick
2 North Chestnut Hill Road
Killingworth CT 06419

Call Sign: KA1DJX
S Mark Guk
60 Pond Meadow Rd
Killingworth CT 06419

Call Sign: KB1OZF
Ewan C Mark
74 Pond Meadow Rd
Killingworth CT 06419

Call Sign: K1CJJ
Robert J Hurle
415 Roast Meat Hill Rd
Killingworth CT 06419

Call Sign: KB1RLG
Peter F Burdett
590 Route 148
Killingworth CT 06419

Call Sign: W1PFB
Peter F Burdett
590 Route 148
Killingworth CT 06419

Call Sign: N1WGM
Jeffrey Reilly
804 Route 148
Killingworth CT 06419

Call Sign: KA1YBR
James S Tourgee
313 Route 148W
Killingworth CT 06419

Call Sign: KC1FS
Stephen T Athanas
580 Rt 148
Killingworth CT 06417

Call Sign: N1YQN
Bernard W Gordon
559 Rt 81
Killingworth CT 06419

Call Sign: N1EEI
Jeffrey M Whynall
44 Running Brook Dr
Killingworth CT 06419

Call Sign: WA1KPD
Carl H Nord
16 Saddlebrook Dr
Killingworth CT 06419

Call Sign: KD1MA
Robert F Tobey
27 Saddlebrook Dr
Killingworth CT 06419

Call Sign: KB1UCX
James D Grady Jr
15 Sugar Hill Rd
Killingworth CT 06419

Call Sign: WA1DVS
Harold C King Sr
1 Whitewood Rd
Killingworth CT 06417

Call Sign: W1KAC
Stuart H Dudley
Killingworth CT 06419

Call Sign: KB1OZG
Donald B Mcdougall
67 Alders Bridge Rd
Killlingworth CT 06419

**FCC Amateur Radio
Licenses in Lakeside**

Call Sign: N1TKP
Caroline Maselli
47 John Weik Rd
Lakeside CT 06758

Call Sign: N1TKQ
Michael J Maselli
47 John Weik Rd
Lakeside CT 06758

**FCC Amateur Radio
Licenses in Lakeville**

Call Sign: KA1LSG
George W Wahlberg Jr
Belgo Rd
Lakeville CT 06039

Call Sign: WA1BAL
Bart A Perrotti
Rte 1 Hotchkiss Rd
Lakeville CT 06039

Call Sign: KB1AWU
Malcolm R Labatt Simon
417 Lime Rock Rd
Lakeville CT 06039

Call Sign: KA1HOG
John B Palmer
Porter St
Lakeville CT 06039

Call Sign: W0PRD
Peter R Douglas
85 Reservoir Rd.
Lakeville CT 06039

Call Sign: KB1CEO
Sarah M Parsons
46 Sharon Dr
Lakeville CT 06039

Call Sign: WA1OTZ
John R Parsons
46 Sharon Rd
Lakeville CT 06039

Call Sign: W1LUA
Mascony Amateur Radio
Society
177 Sharon Rd
Lakeville CT 06039

Call Sign: WA1NWJ
Robert K Weber
177 Sharon Rd
Lakeville CT 06039

Call Sign: K1LEE
K Lee Collins
5 White Hollow Rd
Lakeville CT 06039

**FCC Amateur Radio
Licenses in Lebanon**

Call Sign: KB1ETR
Lee A Schuett
269 Babcock Hill Rd
Lebanon CT 06249

Call Sign: N1NAU
Allen I Gittleman
177 Bascom Rd
Lebanon CT 06249

Call Sign: KB1IRJ
Allen I Gittleman
177 Bascom Rd
Lebanon CT 06249

Call Sign: N1NAU
Allen I Gittleman
177 Bascom Rd
Lebanon CT 06249

Call Sign: K1WHU
William N Bourey
714 Beaumont Hwy
Lebanon CT 06249

Call Sign: KB1QDA
Alice Biron
281 Beaumont Hwy Apt 5
Lebanon CT 062491139

Call Sign: N1VIG
Cindy Dansker
336 Clubhouse Rd
Lebanon CT 06249

Call Sign: WA1HML

Fred C Misbach Jr
217 Exeter Rd
Lebanon CT 06249

Call Sign: KE1EO
Shirow Kinoshita
625 Exeter Rd
Lebanon CT 06249

Call Sign: W3EP
Emil Pocock
625 Exeter Rd
Lebanon CT 06249

Call Sign: KB1NHO
Angelo J Pontillo
791 Exeter Rd
Lebanon CT 06249

Call Sign: KB1SHI
Christopher J Bibeau
42 Fowler Rd
Lebanon CT 06249

Call Sign: KB1GUJ
Jaison E Stein
185 Goshen Hill Rd
Lebanon CT 06249

Call Sign: KB1URH
Jason A Pressler
377 Goshen Hill Rd
Lebanon CT 06249

Call Sign: K1PLS
Peter L Solari
1040 Goshen Hill Rd
Lebanon CT 06249

Call Sign: K1ITT
Philip J Godeck Sr
63 Lake Shore Dr
Lebanon CT 06249

Call Sign: KO6RE

Tom E Wheeler
164 Leonard Bridge Road
Lebanon CT 06249

Call Sign: KB1TWK
Robert D Abbey
213 Mccall Rd
Lebanon CT 06249

Call Sign: W1RDA
Robert D Abbey
213 Mccall Rd
Lebanon CT 06249

Call Sign: KB1SMK
Jeffrey S Sorrell
224 Oliver Rd
Lebanon CT 06249

Call Sign: N1JMI
Jeffrey S Rickabaugh
29 Rita Drive
Lebanon CT 06249

Call Sign: WB1CCP
James H Toon
25 Second St
Lebanon CT 062492021

Call Sign: KB1UOJ
Steven W Hussey
748 Tobacco St
Lebanon CT 06249

Call Sign: KB1EVW
Dana Peterson
228 Trumbull Highway
Lebanon CT 06249

Call Sign: KB1EEM
Dixie Lee A Abell
1231 Trumbull Hwy
Lebanon CT 06249

Call Sign: KB1HLY

Jason A Fraser
Lebanon CT 06249

Call Sign: NA1RC
Natchaug Amateur Radio
Club
Lebanon CT 06249

Call Sign: AB1IX
Charles B Olsen
Lebanon CT 06249

FCC Amateur Radio Licenses in Ledyard

Call Sign: KA1YFI
Sean R Thorne
17 Adios Ln
Ledyard CT 06339

Call Sign: KB1LQH
Charles M Hollis
6 Autumn Way
Ledyard CT 06339

Call Sign: KB1SKG
Todd E Schultz
66 Avery Hill Rd
Ledyard CT 06339

Call Sign: N4WYH
Theodore H Czarnecki
126 Avery Hill Rd
Ledyard CT 063391011

Call Sign: KA1CMW
Edythe H Brown
17 Blacksmith Dr
Ledyard CT 06339

Call Sign: KA1IJA
Roberta A Brown
17 Blacksmith Dr
Ledyard CT 06339

Call Sign: WB1EUL
Stuart J Brown
17 Blacksmith Dr
Ledyard CT 06339

Call Sign: W1EUL
Stuart J Brown
17 Blacksmith Dr
Ledyard CT 06339

Call Sign: N1EWR
Kenneth J Chasteen
1939 Center Groton Rd
Ledyard CT 06339

Call Sign: N1YFU
Joann M Longton
1925 Center Groton Rd
Ledyard Ct
Ledyard CT 06339

Call Sign: W1JRY
Armas A Sini
4 Chestnut Ln
Ledyard CT 06339

Call Sign: KB1LXK
Thomas W Lawler
26 Chriswood Trace
Ledyard CT 06339

Call Sign: K1DER
Thomas W Lawler
26 Chriswood Trace
Ledyard CT 06339

Call Sign: KB1LZK
Kimberly M Lawler
26 Chriswood Trace
Ledyard CT 06339

Call Sign: K1MMY
Kimberly M Lawler
26 Chriswood Trace
Ledyard CT 06339

Call Sign: KL7IGD
James W John
55 Chriswood Trace
Ledyard CT 06339

Call Sign: W1SNG
H Huntingto Smith
75 Church Hill Rd
Ledyard CT 06339

Call Sign: N1NRZ
Larry D Allgood
59 Coachman Pike
Ledyard CT 06339

Call Sign: K1SFC
George C Ellsworth
483 Col Ledyard Hwy
Ledyard CT 06339

Call Sign: KA1YEC
Steven M Peabody
399 Colonel Ledyard Hwy
Ledyard CT 06339

Call Sign: N1XKF
Daniel Service
25 Country Club Dr
Ledyard CT 06339

Call Sign: N1OZA
Frederick W Davies Jr
33 Country Club Dr
Ledyard CT 06339

Call Sign: KB1DZA
Daniel P Service
25 Country Club Dr.
Ledyard CT 06339

Call Sign: KB1AQK
Allen C Fernald Jr
11 E Flintlock Rd
Ledyard CT 06339

Call Sign: N1ZEM
Gregg H Lindner
21 Iron St
Ledyard CT 06339

Call Sign: KB1GDL
James E Cornell
6 Johnnie Court
Ledyard CT 063391022

Call Sign: KB1WLC
Norman Breed
15 Lake St
Ledyard CT 06399

Call Sign: W3TMC
Thomas M Crawford
152 Lambtown Rd
Ledyard CT 06339

Call Sign: KA1YJG
William P Spigel
226 Lambtown Rd
Ledyard CT 06339

Call Sign: KB1BDZ
Gabrielle N Paradis
226 Lambtown Rd
Ledyard CT 06339

Call Sign: KB1BEA
Michael C Spigel
226 Lambtown Rd
Ledyard CT 06339

Call Sign: NE1A
John M Spigel
226 Lambtown Rd
Ledyard CT 06339

Call Sign: W1AAA
Amateur Wireless Assoc Of
South Eastern Ct
226 Lambtown Rd

Ledyard CT 06339

Call Sign: W1NAN
Nancy P Spigel
226 Lambtown Rd
Ledyard CT 06339

Call Sign: W1AKA
Michael C Spigel
226 Lambtown Rd
Ledyard CT 063391928

Call Sign: W1AN
John M Spigel
226 Lambtown Rd
Ledyard CT 06339

Call Sign: K1ATA
Michael C Spigel
226 Lambtown Rd
Ledyard CT 063391928

Call Sign: W1DX
Amateur Wireless Assoc Of
South Eastern Ct
226 Lambtown Rd
Ledyard CT 06339

Call Sign: WB1HKM
Larry T Purcell
791 Lantern Hill Rd
Ledyard CT 06339

Call Sign: KB1OXC
Larry T Purcell
791 Lantern Hill Rd
Ledyard CT 06339

Call Sign: N1SZZ
Larry T Purcell
791 Lantern Hill Rd
Ledyard CT 06339

Call Sign: KB1GPU
Mark E Titterington

13 Linden Ln
Ledyard CT 06339

Call Sign: WD6ABC
Ronald G Nordstrom
39 Meetinghouse Ln
Ledyard CT 06339

Call Sign: WA1YAP
Ellis C Tucker
328 Pumpkin Hill Rd
Ledyard CT 06384

Call Sign: N1LAC
Margaret M Simon
390 Pumpkin Hill Rd
Ledyard CT 06339

Call Sign: N1LAD
Russell J Simon
390 Pumpkin Hill Rd
Ledyard CT 06339

Call Sign: KB1WXD
Andrew P Wawrzynowicz
463 Pumpkin Hill Road
Ledyard CT 06339

Call Sign: KA1WYC
Joseph P Gates
24 Seabury Ave
Ledyard CT 06339

Call Sign: KA1WNN
John T B Campbell
417 Shewville Rd
Ledyard CT 06339

Call Sign: KA1HNZ
Gerald E Chadwick
55 Silas Deane Rd
Ledyard CT 06339

Call Sign: N1GRJ
David L Hemond

81 Silas Deane Road
Ledyard CT 06339

Call Sign: KA1IHR
Michael S Seaton
84 Spicer Hill Rd
Ledyard CT 06339

Call Sign: W1FWE
James H Seaton
84 Spicer Hill Rd
Ledyard CT 063390035

Call Sign: N1AKZ
Keith E Griffin
12 Sunset Ave
Ledyard CT 06339

Call Sign: W2LOR
Keith E Griffin
12 Sunset Ave
Ledyard CT 06339

Call Sign: KA1SHO
Howard M Auten
Ledyard CT 06339

Call Sign: KF6UX
Richard C Kopplin
Ledyard CT 06339

Call Sign: N1RSK
J Mark Venable
Ledyard CT 06339

Call Sign: KB1EQP
Reynaldo Texidor
77 Indiantown Rd
Leydard CT 06339

**FCC Amateur Radio
Licenses in Lisbon**

Call Sign: KB1GVY
Daniel M Wrobel

229 B Bundy Hill Rd
Lisbon CT 06351

Call Sign: KB1PAA
Richard F Bloom
35 Baron Dr
Lisbon CT 06351

Call Sign: WB2LNE
Gordon L Lang
26 Ethel Acres
Lisbon CT 06351

Call Sign: KB1RPJ
David E Fuller
5 John St
Lisbon CT 06351

Call Sign: KW1A
Clement R White
61 Kimball Rd
Lisbon CT 06351

Call Sign: KA1GHH
Peter Kovacs
Rfd 3 Kimball Rd
Lisbon CT 06351

Call Sign: KB1UMQ
Zach Rice
62 Kinsman Hill Rd
Lisbon CT 06351

Call Sign: N1SRA
Daniel A Novak
24 Lower Blissville Rd
Lisbon CT 063513211

Call Sign: KB1QQM
Lawrence F Garvin
103 North Burnham
Highway
Lisbon CT 06351

Call Sign: W1SBV

George R Simoneau
3 Pleasant View Cove
Lisbon CT 06351

Call Sign: W1IBS
Robert L Zoner
41 Rex Rd
Lisbon CT 063512822

Call Sign: N1WPJ
Robert P Chubka
37 River Rd
Lisbon CT 06351

Call Sign: KB1FHQ
Robert A Barrett
345 River Rd
Lisbon CT 06351

Call Sign: W1VWL
Robert A Barrett
345 River Rd
Lisbon CT 06351

Call Sign: KB1JNF
Victor S Moore
526 River Rd
Lisbon CT 063513226

Call Sign: W1SSN
Victor S Moore
526 River Rd
Lisbon CT 063513226

Call Sign: WA1ZFU
Benjamin A Vincent Sr
307 S Burnham Hwy Rfd 2
Lisbon CT 06351

Call Sign: KB1VGS
William M Rutz
312 S Burnham Way
Lisbon CT 06351

Call Sign: W1EDJ

Earl D Johnson
16 Tunnel Hill Court
Lisbon CT 06351

**FCC Amateur Radio
Licenses in Litchfield**

Call Sign: KD1TR
Kenneth L Ernhout
36 Old Farm Rd.
Litchfied CT 06759

Call Sign: WA1HZF
Brian J Morgan
Rr 1 Beach St
Litchfield CT 06759

Call Sign: KA1DCC
Bernard H Stairs
Box 246
Litchfield CT 06759

Call Sign: KA1EYZ
John S Bolus
E Chestnut Hill Rd R 2 Box
300
Litchfield CT 06759

Call Sign: KA1TJE
Van C Bockus
Box 314
Litchfield CT 06759

Call Sign: W1EZE
Joseph Di Blasi
5 Dickerson Ct
Litchfield CT 06759

Call Sign: AB1ZB
Al Suttles
845 Eli Bunker Rd
Litchfield CT 06759

Call Sign: N1LXZ
Joseph L Peschko Jr

Box 211 Great Hill Rd
Litchfield CT 06759

Call Sign: KB1BCI
Richard H Bialoglowy
37 Harris Rd
Litchfield CT 06759

Call Sign: N1BGK
Bruce R Little
Mike Rd
Litchfield CT 06759

Call Sign: KB1UFU
Ethan A Ide
325 Norfolk Rd
Litchfield CT 06759

Call Sign: KB1TOR
Paul F Gibb Jr
339 Norfolk Rd
Litchfield CT 06759

Call Sign: WA1WGG
John S Glenn
Norfolk Rd At Weed Rd
Litchfield CT 06759

Call Sign: WA1ODZ
Howard E Kerpelman
6 Osborn Ln
Litchfield CT 06759

Call Sign: W1WFL
Thomas W Ferguson Jr
Sheldon Ln
Litchfield CT 06759

Call Sign: WA1IVH
Steven B Sayles
612 South Plains Rd
Litchfield CT 06759

Call Sign: KA1CYI
Carol A Andrews

366 South St
Litchfield CT 06759

Call Sign: N1AQB
Leon F Andrews
366 South St
Litchfield CT 06759

Call Sign: KB1KGQ
James F Lynch Jr
416 South St
Litchfield CT 06759

Call Sign: N3JFL
James F Lynch Jr
416 South St
Litchfield CT 06759

Call Sign: W1MJF
Matthew J Fitzgibbons
161 South Street
Litchfield CT 06759

Call Sign: KB1WM
Avery L Jenkins
44 Torrington Rd
Litchfield CT 067591642

Call Sign: W1REL
John E Ducci
366 Torrington Rd
Litchfield CT 06759

Call Sign: KB1ETS
Wamogo Regional High
School Amateur Radio Club
98 Wamogo Road
Litchfield CT 06759

Call Sign: WA1MOG
Wamogo Regional High
School Amateur Radio Club
98 Wanogo Road
Litchfield CT 06759

Call Sign: KC2DXV
Herman Robert Ladenhauf
Wells Run Unit C2
Litchfield CT 06759

Call Sign: KB1CBT
International Police Assoc
Radio Club
154 West St
Litchfield CT 06759

Call Sign: WA1ECA
Frank J Dlugokinski
154 West St
Litchfield CT 06759

Call Sign: WA1QFQ
Raymond J Terlaga
Litchfield CT 067591111

Call Sign: K2LME
David B Collins
45 Bill Hill Rd
Lyme CT 06371

Call Sign: KB1JND
Fredrik T Holth
159 Blood St
Lyme CT 06371

Call Sign: K1FPP
Richard T Monahan
165 Blood St
Lyme CT 06371

Call Sign: WA1RAE
John W Ronski
28 Brush Hill Rd
Lyme CT 06371

Call Sign: KC1EG
Richard R Dailey

Cove Rd Box 1066
Lyme CT 06371

Call Sign: K1UQV
Ronald Tidmarsh
328 Grassy Hill Rd
Lyme CT 063713312

Call Sign: KB1DYX
Thomas S Davies
332 Joshuatown Rd
Lyme CT 06371

Call Sign: WM1M
David E Amacher
127-8 Joshuatown Rd
Lyme CT 06371

Call Sign: WA1FOK
John C Courtney
50 Macintosh Rd
Lyme CT 06371

Call Sign: N1QKV
Richard E Bireley
60 Mount Archer Rd
Lyme CT 06371

Call Sign: N1QKU
Linda E Bireley
60 Mt Archer Rd
Lyme CT 06371

Call Sign: N1QKX
Kenneth D Plimpton Jr
26 Sterling City Rd
Lyme CT 06371

Call Sign: KA6PDD
Robert B George
20 Amber Trail
Madison CT 06443

Call Sign: WA1IWU
Francis J Mahan
18 Aylesbury Cir
Madison CT 06443

Call Sign: KA1IFR
Thomas N Jennings
74 Beaver Pond Rd
Madison CT 06443

Call Sign: N1FJN
Bernd Gigas
59 Beechwood Dr
Madison CT 06443

Call Sign: WB1EYD
Julius P Biehler Jr
43 Bishop Ln
Madison CT 06443

Call Sign: N1JXT
Alfred A Trulli Jr
70 Blinnshed Rd
Madison CT 06443

Call Sign: KA1NQZ
Ross Sayers
1089 Boston Post Rd
Madison CT 06443

Call Sign: KB1JHY
David A Steines
290 Bradley Corners
Madison CT 06443

Call Sign: N4BLN
Kenneth E Gray Jr
47 Bradley Corners Road
Madison CT 06443

Call Sign: K1NWC
Nicholas W Cerjanec
26 Copperstone Ln
Madison CT 06443

Call Sign: N1QYA
Stephen F Fuest
201 Durham Rd
Madison CT 06443

Call Sign: NP3V
Henry J H Perry
688 Durham Rd
Madison CT 06443

Call Sign: KA1HYG
Dennison H Mac Donald
798 Durham Rd
Madison CT 06443

Call Sign: N1XUW
Jeffery B Higgins
2215 Durham Rd
Madison CT 06443

Call Sign: N1ZEI
Gretchen T Higgins
2215 Durham Rd
Madison CT 06443

Call Sign: N1MUP
Gregory T Norrie
2430 Durham Rd.
Madison CT 06443

Call Sign: N1RRN
Spider J Bulyk
31 Field Brook Rd
Madison CT 06443

Call Sign: N1RRM
Jamin Bulyk
31 Fieldbrook Dr
Madison CT 06443

Call Sign: W1CIM
Paul Mary
164 Five Field Rd
Madison CT 06443

Call Sign: K1PVT
William L De Benedetto
32 Flintlock Rd
Madison CT 06443

Call Sign: K1VW
John Thomas
44 Garnet Park Rd
Madison CT 06443

Call Sign: KA1UVY
Keith R D Alessio
13 Green Hill Rd
Madison CT 06443

Call Sign: N1QQV
Kenneth E Freedman
820 Green Hill Rd
Madison CT 06443

Call Sign: KA1CYR
Keith R Ainsworth Esq
31 Green Springs Drive
Madison CT 06443

Call Sign: N1GDQ
Pauline M Garber
101 Hammonasset
Meadows Rd
Madison CT 06443

Call Sign: W1XI
Brad T Garber
101 Hammonasset
Meadows Rd
Madison CT 06443

Call Sign: KB1GDZ
Burkard J Schlott
64 Harkness Dr
Madison CT 06443

Call Sign: K1BJS
Burkard J Schlott

64 Harkness Dr
Madison CT 06443

Call Sign: W1PBB
Austin Ross
49 Hartford Ave
Madison CT 06468

Call Sign: KA1MMG
Craig P Olinsky
16 Highview Rd
Madison CT 06443

Call Sign: WA1HJS
Mel Olinsky
16 Highview Rd
Madison CT 06443

Call Sign: WA1QZU
Ronnie G Olinsky
16 Highview Rd
Madison CT 06443

Call Sign: N1UTM
Ben P Dare
29 Highview Rd
Madison CT 06443

Call Sign: KB1EIE
Benjamin D Goldman
160 Horse Pond Rd
Madison CT 06443

Call Sign: KB1MFV
Benjamin D Goldman
160 Horse Pond Rd
Madison CT 06443

Call Sign: N1SWN
Quentin H Bailey
337 Horse Pond Rd
Madison CT 06443

Call Sign: KA1IYN
James H Emery

314 Horsepond Rd
Madison CT 064432403

82 Mungertown Rd
Madison CT 06443

404 Race Hill Rd
Madison CT 064431665

Call Sign: KD1FN
George M Smith Jr
10 Horseshoe Ln
Madison CT 06443

Call Sign: W2LBJ
Howard J Langerman
5 Nichols Hill Dr
Madison CT 064431803

Call Sign: KB1PFK
Jared M Wolff
197 Racehill Rd
Madison CT 06443

Call Sign: KA1QS
Terry F Sinclair
39 Jefferson Park Dr
Madison CT 06443

Call Sign: KA1QFG
John P Prete
46 Old Post Rd
Madison CT 06443

Call Sign: N1VXF
Ray B Burton Iii
80 River Edge Farm Rd
Madison CT 06443

Call Sign: KA1EEZ
John H Garwood
133 Laurel Crest Rd
Madison CT 06443

Call Sign: WA1OOC
Bernard L Knudsen
107 Old Toll Rd
Madison CT 06443

Call Sign: WA2TWB
Thomas J Padberg
17 Sandelwood Dr
Madison CT 06443

Call Sign: N1KEC
Robert O Rawson
273 Legend Hill
Madison CT 06443

Call Sign: KA1SMJ
Jon D Epperson
218 Opening Hill Rd
Madison CT 06443

Call Sign: N1NVA
James F Malone
23 Scotland Ave
Madison CT 06443

Call Sign: KB1DCT
James De B Domville
24 Legend Hill Rd
Madison CT 06443

Call Sign: N1BRF
Donald C Epperson Sr
218 Opening Hill Rd
Madison CT 06443

Call Sign: N1XUI
Jeffrey J Kamen
72 Scotland Rd
Madison CT 06443

Call Sign: KB1EHO
Steven D Bell
12 Maple Ave
Madison CT 064433253

Call Sign: WB2KHA
Brian A Stroehlein
276 Opening Hill Rd
Madison CT 06443

Call Sign: W1HTM
Craig A Peffer
130 Scotland Rd
Madison CT 06443

Call Sign: KE1GV
Charles C Walden
15 Matthew Court
Madison CT 06443

Call Sign: N1WKV
Douglas E Smart
P.O.Box 211
Madison CT 06443

Call Sign: N1YNG
Scott G Gammons
398 Summer Hill Rd
Madison CT 06443

Call Sign: K1UAX
Howard S Weiss
87 Middle Beach Rd
Madison CT 064433006

Call Sign: WB1BUC
Joseph D Urban
63 Princess Dr
Madison CT 06443

Call Sign: K1FO
Stephen J Powlishen
816 Summer Hill Rd
Madison CT 064431604

Call Sign: N1SKK
Joseph J Cernak

Call Sign: N1HDV
John L Hornby

Call Sign: N1TM
Thomas E Magera

23 Thames Way
Madison CT 06443

Call Sign: N1JIH
John F Penders Iv
424 Warpas Rd
Madison CT 06443

Call Sign: WA1ZTD
Frank A Brindisi Jr
116 Wildcat Rd
Madison CT 06443

Call Sign: W1WTU
Norman J Potter
206 Wildcat Rd
Madison CT 064432414

Call Sign: N1ILM
Robert C Gerard
Madison CT 06443

Call Sign: KB1EKF
Christopher J Forrest
Madison CT 06443

Call Sign: KB1JNW
Eric T Oppegaard
Madison CT 06443

**FCC Amateur Radio
Licenses in Manchester**

Call Sign: KB1TVE
Gerald A Bujaucius
88 Ambassador Dr Unit B
Manchester CT 06042

Call Sign: KF6LIC
Michael W Belmore
28c Ambassador Drive
Manchester CT 06042

Call Sign: KB1QJE
Kurt T Wagner

6 Amherst Dr
Manchester CT 06042

Call Sign: KB1QJR
Kurt T Wagner
6 Amherst Dr
Manchester CT 06040

Call Sign: K1MTB
Kurt Wagner
6 Amherst Dr
Manchester CT 06040

Call Sign: KB1TVB
John F Boardman
138 Amherst Dr
Manchester CT 06042

Call Sign: KD1OO
Leroy S Olsen
112 Arnott Rd
Manchester CT 06040

Call Sign: KA1MYD
Kenneth P Charles Jr
8 Autumn St
Manchester CT 06040

Call Sign: W1IWQ
Paul E Dutelle
92 Avondale Rd
Manchester CT 06040

Call Sign: WB1DTP
Donald C Ostberg
23 Barry Rd
Manchester CT 06040

Call Sign: KB1QJG
Robert E Dunphy
98 Barry Road
Manchester CT 06042

Call Sign: W1DDT
Robert E Dunphy

98 Barry Road
Manchester CT 06042

Call Sign: KB1HCE
Edward K Mc Kenney
61 Bette Dr
Manchester CT 06040

Call Sign: KB1QJC
Scott L Somes
41 Bigelow St
Manchester CT 06040

Call Sign: W1EZF
Robert E Werner Jr
8 Bishop Dr
Manchester CT 06040

Call Sign: WA1NXC
Theodore Ferreira
76 Bolton St
Manchester CT 06040

Call Sign: KB1EPL
Mary-Ellen E Ferreira
76 Bolton St
Manchester CT 06040

Call Sign: KB1ULV
Anthony J St Marie
23 Bonner Rd
Manchester CT 06042

Call Sign: KB1LUB
William S Stanek
277 Braod St
Manchester CT 06040

Call Sign: KB1VE
Barry A Cyr
40 Bretton Rd
Manchester CT 06040

Call Sign: KB1IXQ
Kurt J Krukas

110 Bretton Rd
Manchester CT 060403330

Call Sign: KA1ABM
Arthur A Fettig
129 Bretton Rd
Manchester CT 06040

Call Sign: KB1NAF
Donald J Vinci
133 Briarwood Dr
Manchester CT 06040

Call Sign: W1BYN
William S Stanek
277 Broad St
Manchester CT 06040

Call Sign: N1WFC
Robert E Otten
34 Brookview Cir
Manchester CT 06040

Call Sign: KB1UFW
Kevin A Holian Borgnis
465 Buckland Hills Dr Apt
30223
Manchester CT 06042

Call Sign: KD1ZV
Anthony P Colonna
39 Buckland St Apt 2212
Manchester CT 06042

Call Sign: KB1ENF
Cliff E Carlson
242 Bush Hill Rd
Manchester CT 06040

Call Sign: KB1AYW
Stephen J Brady
291 Bush Hill Rd
Manchester CT 06040

Call Sign: N1RIG

Stephen J Brady
291 Bush Hill Rd
Manchester CT 06040

Call Sign: N1TPZ
William H Podolny
140 Butternut Rd
Manchester CT 06040

Call Sign: KB1JKA
Cathy E Phelps
82 Cambridge St
Manchester CT 06040

Call Sign: KB1QNY
William E Rettig
82 Carman Rd
Manchester CT 06042

Call Sign: N1VSP
Brian J Kellogg
106 Carpenter Rd
Manchester CT 06040

Call Sign: WA1JQX
John J Kellogg
106 Carpenter Rd
Manchester CT 06040

Call Sign: KA1JIY
Richard G Hubbard Jr
17 Castle Rd
Manchester CT 06040

Call Sign: KB1SQC
Manchester C.E.R.T.
75 Center St
Manchester CT 06040

Call Sign: K9OEM
Manchester C.E.R.T.
75 Center St
Manchester CT 06040

Call Sign: KB1LWO

Mark A Baldwin
86 Charis Rd
Manchester CT 060408263

Call Sign: N1WKO
Christopher J Kelling
261 Charter Oak St
Manchester CT 06040

Call Sign: KB1TCT
Ed D Halley Jr
86 Church St
Manchester CT 06040

Call Sign: KC8HSX
Regina M Halley
86 Church St.
Manchester CT 06040

Call Sign: KA1ZER
Dan G Breen
20 Coburn Rd
Manchester CT 06040

Call Sign: W1NMP
Stanley G Best
53 Coburn Rd
Manchester CT 06040

Call Sign: KB1TVT
Marc A Thurston
16 Columbia Dr
Manchester CT 06042

Call Sign: K1MSJ
Marc A Thurston
16 Columbia Dr
Manchester CT 06042

Call Sign: KB1TXO
David B Anderson
120 Coop Sawmill Rd
Manchester CT 06040

Call Sign: KB1LUC

Patrick R Sklenar
75 Cougar Dr
Manchester CT 06040

Call Sign: N1PRS
Patrick R Sklenar
75 Cougar Dr
Manchester CT 06040

Call Sign: KB1JJY
Francis A Maffe Jr
116 Croft Dr
Manchester CT 06040

Call Sign: KB1KVZ
Robert T Barker
86 Dartmouth Rd
Manchester CT 06040

Call Sign: KB1TVA
Raymond E Baker Jr
48 Deepwood Dr
Manchester CT 06040

Call Sign: KB1RMP
Judith Rose
191 Deer Run Trail
Manchester CT 06042

Call Sign: KB1TMV
Robert P Cleary
68 Delmont St
Manchester CT 06042

Call Sign: K1QPJ
Leonard J Witkowski
230 Deming St Apt 125
Manchester CT 06042

Call Sign: WA1EDR
M Lorraine Witkowski
230 Deming St Apt 125
Manchester CT 06042

Call Sign: KB1JJZ

George D Lillenstein
39a Downey Dr
Manchester CT 06040

Call Sign: AB1GL
George D Lillenstein
39a Downey Dr
Manchester CT 06040

Call Sign: W1MTR
Malvin G Darling
54 Downey Dr Apt D
Manchester CT 06040

Call Sign: KC8SFG
Poorna Chand Jyotula
113 Downey Drive Apt C
Manchester CT 06040

Call Sign: KB1WYO
Kathleen A Hauser
396 East Center St
Manchester CT 06040

Call Sign: KB1WQR
Patricia F Albers
171 East Center St 20
Manchester CT 06040

Call Sign: KB1QJB
Ronald C Tasse
171 East Center St Apt 2-D
Manchester CT 06040

Call Sign: W1RCT
Ronald C Tasse Mr
171 East Center St Apt 2-D
Manchester CT 06040

Call Sign: KB1JJX
Raymond F Gagnon
39 Eastland Dr
Manchester CT 06040

Call Sign: KB1QJD

Jill D Lavoie-Gagnon
39 Eastland Dr
Manchester CT 06042

Call Sign: KA1WVX
Eric A Davidove
63 Elm St 114
Manchester CT 06040

Call Sign: KB1MZQ
Aaron A Bieber
91 Elm St Apt 229e
Manchester CT 06041

Call Sign: KA1NAI
Klim Pesesky
150 Elvree St
Manchester CT 06042

Call Sign: KA1TBU
Leigh H Cleveland
23 Essex St
Manchester CT 06040

Call Sign: N1MXD
John L Muschko
11 Fairfield St
Manchester CT 06040

Call Sign: KA1KWM
Samuel J Robb Jr
34 Finley St
Manchester CT 06040

Call Sign: K1FOV
Robert B Schettler
31 Flower St
Manchester CT 06040

Call Sign: KB1JJV
Dean R Gates
70 Foley St
Manchester CT 060404808

Call Sign: KB1VRS

John J Terase
2 French Rd
Manchester CT 06042

Call Sign: KB1KIZ
Larry R Butler
105 Garth Road
Manchester CT 06040

Call Sign: KB1QNV
Collins D Johnston Ii
4 Grandview St
Manchester CT 06040

Call Sign: KB1JJT
Eileen Wilson
23 Green Farms Ln
Manchester CT 06040

Call Sign: W1HOP
Leon L Kramer
31 Green Manor Rd
Manchester CT 06040

Call Sign: KB1WQS
Stephen L Belmore Jr
136 Green Manor Rd
Manchester CT 06042

Call Sign: KA1CTP
Neva L Slater
113 Greenwood Dr
Manchester CT 06040

Call Sign: KA1HVF
Robert J Dusza Jr
242 Grissom Rd
Manchester CT 06040

Call Sign: KB1FQU
Lori A Dusza
242 Grissom Road
Manchester CT 06040

Call Sign: KB1UUL

Scott C Schumacher
48 Grove St Apt 1
Manchester CT 06042

Call Sign: KB1HCI
Todd G Henkel
45 Hamilton Dr
Manchester CT 06040

Call Sign: WU1Z
Joseph G Dubiel Jr
5 Hendee Rd
Manchester CT 06040

Call Sign: KB1LUE
John P Ledonne
44 Henry St
Manchester CT 060403523

Call Sign: N1JYH
James J Misiek
81 High St
Manchester CT 06040

Call Sign: N1VHA
Charles W Stone
167 High St
Manchester CT 06040

Call Sign: KB1LUF
James P Gregory Jr
204 High St
Manchester CT 06040

Call Sign: K1PJQ
Warren Thurnauer
24 Hillcrest Rd
Manchester CT 06040

Call Sign: N1ZNA
David B Bidwell
17 Hillcrest Road
Manchester CT 06040

Call Sign: KB1QNU

Bruce W Kramer
88 Hilliard Street
Manchester CT 06042

Call Sign: N1BRU
Bruce W Kramer
88 Hilliard Street
Manchester CT 06042

Call Sign: N1KNT
Donald A Dubiel
492 Hillstown Rd
Manchester CT 06040

Call Sign: KB1QNW
Matthew R Costa
557 Hillstown Road
Manchester CT 06040

Call Sign: KA1AEZ
Joseph P Carcia Jr
59 Holl St
Manchester CT 06040

Call Sign: KB1TUZ
Christopher H Andersen
97 Hollister St
Manchester CT 06042

Call Sign: KB1AGD
John A Nelson
205 Hollister St
Manchester CT 06040

Call Sign: WB1GIB
Stuart M Bass
254 Hollister St
Manchester CT 06040

Call Sign: KB1TVQ
Susan L Nagy
172 Homestead St Apt M
Manchester CT 06042

Call Sign: KB1OSW

Carlos H Jusem
25 Jeffrey Alan Dr
Manchester CT 06042

Call Sign: KB1JIR
Ronald L Potter
38 Jeffrey Alan Dr
Manchester CT 06040

Call Sign: W1RGC
Richard Claing
20 Joan Circle
Manchester CT 060406321

Call Sign: KB1TVI
Karen S Claing
20 Joan Circle
Manchester CT 06040

Call Sign: W1KSC
Karen S Claing
20 Joan Circle
Manchester CT 06040

Call Sign: KB1JJU
Richard Claing
20 John Circle
Manchester CT 060406321

Call Sign: KG6BF
James F Williams
111 John Olds Dr Apt 110
Manchester CT 06040

Call Sign: KB1QJK
Charles D Yaeger
66 Joyce Lane
Manchester CT 06040

Call Sign: KB1TVN
Anita M Gillespie
49 Karen Dr
Manchester CT 06042

Call Sign: W1AMG

Anita M Gillespie
49 Karen Dr
Manchester CT 06042

Call Sign: KB1MHJ
Mark G Meredith
550 Keeney St
Manchester CT 060407128

Call Sign: K1MGM
Mark G Meredith
550 Keeney St
Manchester CT 060407128

Call Sign: WA1CAN
Robert T Barker
52 Kingswood Drive
Manchester CT 06040

Call Sign: KA1ANM
James T Dodd Jr
131 Lake St
Manchester CT 06040

Call Sign: KM1U
Alfred D Kornfeld
88 Lamplighter Dr
Manchester CT 06040

Call Sign: KB1KWA
Madeline E Benyeda
37 Ledgecrest Ter
Manchester CT 06040

Call Sign: KB1KDE
Paul J Benyeda
37 Ledgecrest Terrace
Manchester CT 06040

Call Sign: KB1JFS
Joseph K Mccusker Jr
148 Lenox St
Manchester CT 06040

Call Sign: N1GBI

Raymond J Ponticelli
18 Lenti Dr
Manchester CT 06040

Call Sign: KB1DU
Robert J Voronovitch
38 Liberty St
Manchester CT 06040

Call Sign: KB1VRN
Jeffrey A Plasky
51 Litchfield St
Manchester CT 06040

Call Sign: N1TJK
Linda E German
46 Litchfield Street
Manchester CT 06040

Call Sign: N1TJM
Roy M German
46 Litchfield Street
Manchester CT 06040

Call Sign: KB1JKC
Madeline E Cainsilverstar
86 Lockwood St
Manchester CT 06040

Call Sign: KC0TGW
Joann A Post
91 Lookout Mountain Drive
Manchester CT 060406720

Call Sign: KC0UFY
James R Nieman
91 Lookout Mountain Drive
Manchester CT 06040

Call Sign: KB1MPM
Joann A Post
91 Lookout Mountain Drive
Manchester CT 060406720

Call Sign: KB1MPN

James R Nieman
91 Lookout Mountain Drive
Manchester CT 06040

Call Sign: KB1CAU
Kearsarge Amateur Radio
Society
7 Lorraine Rd
Manchester CT 06040

Call Sign: N7YZX
Terry L Christiansen
7 Lorraine Road
Manchester CT 060406322

Call Sign: N1BFI
C Daniel Thayer Jr
145e Love Lane
Manchester CT 060402680

Call Sign: K1AAF
Richard R Groff
14 Lucian St
Manchester CT 06040

Call Sign: N1JQX
Vincent J Lantieri
631 Lydall St.
Manchester CT 06040

Call Sign: N1SPD
Steven R Starski
71 Lyness St
Manchester CT 06040

Call Sign: KB1WQY
Cassandra J Parkman
411 Main St
Manchester CT 06040

Call Sign: KB1JJS
Neal E Wilson
399 Main St Unit 10
Manchester CT 060404152

Call Sign: WA1OSG
Bruce A Samborski
18 Markwood Ln
Manchester CT 06040

Call Sign: KB1RMR
Susan E Patten
33 Mather St
Manchester CT 06042

Call Sign: KB1TIP
Paul R Girard
104 Mather St
Manchester CT 06042

Call Sign: W1PT
Peter N Turbide
109 Mather St
Manchester CT 060422374

Call Sign: KB1IXR
Wendy Skeen
109 Mather St
Manchester CT 06040

Call Sign: W1CWR
Arthur J Plouff Memorial
Amateur Rad Station
109 Mather Street
Manchester CT 060422374

Call Sign: N1TUG
Myron Senczikowska
61 Meadow Lane
Manchester CT 06040

Call Sign: KD1NN
Wayne K Lowery
425 Meadowbrook Dr
Manchester CT 06040

Call Sign: KB1VRK
Michael J Murdock
239 Middle Tpke East
Manchester CT 06040

Call Sign: KB1RMT
Donald E Modean
78 Milford Rd
Manchester CT 06042

Call Sign: N1DUQ
Raymond J Murphy
150 N Elm St
Manchester CT 06040

Call Sign: WI7H
Jerome Anderson
24 N Fairfield St
Manchester CT 060405761

Call Sign: KB1BFG
Richard E Guilmette
80 N School St
Manchester CT 06040

Call Sign: KA1VLU
James T Ferranti Jr
158 North Elm St
Manchester CT 06040

Call Sign: KB1WQZ
Sarah J Pine
411 North Mainst 2
Manchester CT 06042

Call Sign: KB1TVJ
Nancy B Dolce
145 Oak Forset Dr
Manchester CT 06042

Call Sign: KB1QIZ
Ezequiel Alejandro
254 Oak St
Manchester CT 06040

Call Sign: W1YMS
Richard A Carocari
347 Oak St
Manchester CT 06040

Call Sign: KD1ZE
Peter O Baldwin
174a Oakland St
Manchester CT 06040

Call Sign: KF4ZFA
Anibal Velez
40 Olcott Apt 109
Manchester CT 06040

Call Sign: KB1CGI
Kathleen M Grover
29 Otis St
Manchester CT 06040

Call Sign: N1UYK
Kevin P Steffano
65 Oxford St
Manchester CT 06040

Call Sign: KB1TVH
David M Cannell
25 Park St
Manchester CT 06040

Call Sign: WA1ZUS
Joseph A Coscia
850 Parker Street Apt 123
Manchester CT 06042

Call Sign: KB1VRT
Laurinda Tuthill
137 Pine St
Manchester CT 06040

Call Sign: KB1GVN
Gordon M Lockwood
150 Pine St 131
Manchester CT 06040

Call Sign: W1GML
Gordon M Lockwood
150 Pine St 131
Manchester CT 06040

Call Sign: KB1NAE
Cheryl W Pringle
61 Plymouth Lane
Manchester CT 06040

Call Sign: N1WBO
William G Pringle Jr
61 Plymouth Ln
Manchester CT 06040

Call Sign: KB1VRW
Allen D Williams
149 Porter St
Manchester CT 06040

Call Sign: N1ALW
Allen D Williams
149 Porter St
Manchester CT 06040

Call Sign: KB1JJW
Thomas D Doody
215 Porter St
Manchester CT 06040

Call Sign: KB1QJF
Francene L Diana
26 Primer Rd
Manchester CT 06040

Call Sign: K1ELI
Francene L Diana
26 Primer Rd
Manchester CT 06040

Call Sign: N1GBH
Carol E Ponticelli
33 Primer Rd
Manchester CT 06040

Call Sign: KB1JKB
Jean K Devalve
118 Prospect St
Manchester CT 06040

Call Sign: KB1QNP
Ken Herold
8 Rachel Road Apt F
Manchester CT 06042

Call Sign: KB1QJL
Ralph C Gray
171 Ralph Road
Manchester CT 06040

Call Sign: KB1NQN
Lisa F Reiss
25 Raymond Rd
Manchester CT 06040

Call Sign: KB1NQO
Jacqueline M Reiss
25 Raymond Rd
Manchester CT 06040

Call Sign: KA1HVR
Kenneth A Reiss
25 Raymond Road
Manchester CT 06040

Call Sign: KA1DA
Everett E Newton
275 Redwood Rd
Manchester CT 06040

Call Sign: KB1VRV
James Q Wallin
30 Ridoe St
Manchester CT 06040

Call Sign: KB1VRD
Justin A Duran
65 Robert Rd
Manchester CT 06040

Call Sign: KA1WSG
Ellen L Rylander
36 Rossetto Dr
Manchester CT 06040

Call Sign: KA1WSH
Richard C Rylander
36 Rossetto Dr
Manchester CT 06040

Call Sign: KA1TMY
Joseph F Leva
34 Round Hill Rd
Manchester CT 06040

Call Sign: N1VEL
Sylvester S Pawlak
64d Ruby Dr
Manchester CT 06040

Call Sign: KB1GJC
Richard P Leible Jr
42 Russell St
Manchester CT 06040

Call Sign: KA1ANP
John G Carmichael
4 S Hawthorne St
Manchester CT 06040

Call Sign: KB1VRP
Danielle M Saffioti
157 Saint John St
Manchester CT 06040

Call Sign: N1TUP
Paul J Gibson
31 Santina Dr
Manchester CT 06040

Call Sign: W1KKS
Manchester Radio Club -
Est 1912
31 Santina Dr
Manchester CT 06040

Call Sign: W1OKY
Newington Amateur Radio
League Inc

31 Santina Dr
Manchester CT 06040

Call Sign: K8GGX
Rachel J Kaiser
33 Scarborough Rd
Manchester CT 06040

Call Sign: N1RSL
James W Fox
34 Server St
Manchester CT 06040

Call Sign: N1GVR
Alexander H Rydlewicz
46 Server St
Manchester CT 06040

Call Sign: W1UGY
Norman F Schaffer
23 Shallow Brook Ln
Manchester CT 06040

Call Sign: KB1QJN
Robert T Brown
74 South Farms Drive
Manchester CT 06040

Call Sign: WA1VKU
Peter E Beckwith
125 South Farms Drive
Manchester CT 06040

Call Sign: K1RTJ
Frederick P Richard
441 South Main St Apt 3
Manchester CT 06042

Call Sign: WB1CZO
Judith A Richard
441 South Main St Apt 3
Manchester CT 06043

Call Sign: KB1TVP
Mary L Gracyalny

429 Spring St
Manchester CT 06040

Call Sign: KB1LHQ
Robert Levesque
70 Spring Street
Manchester CT 06040

Call Sign: KB1VRJ
Elizabeth A Martinez
29 St John St
Manchester CT 06040

Call Sign: KB1MZA
Donald A Janelle
70 Steeplechase Dr
Manchester CT 06040

Call Sign: N1DAJ
Donald A Janelle
70 Steeplechase Dr
Manchester CT 06040

Call Sign: KB1RMZ
Tracy L Chartier
22 Strant St
Manchester CT 06040

Call Sign: KB1FBT
Robert R Kovach Ii
132 Strawberry Lane
Manchester CT 06040

Call Sign: KB1QJM
Christopher L Marvin
54 Strickland St
Manchester CT 06042

Call Sign: KB1KGV
Frank J Axiak
181 Summit St
Manchester CT 06040

Call Sign: KB1QIY
Teresa L Carter

221 Summit St
Manchester CT 06042

Call Sign: WA1IHE
Doris W Fraher
441 Summit St
Manchester CT 06040

Call Sign: N1CJG
Orest A Zajac
120 Sunrise Drive
Manchester CT 06040

Call Sign: N1ORK
Orest A Zajac
120 Sunrise Drive
Manchester CT 06040

Call Sign: W1FSH
Llewellyn H Melbert
93 Tanner St
Manchester CT 06040

Call Sign: W1CHT
George W Beauregard
35 Timber Trail
Manchester CT 06040

Call Sign: KA2YNE
Matthew D Gates
35 Timrod Rd
Manchester CT 06040

Call Sign: KB1TVR
William M Overton
103 Timrod Rd
Manchester CT 060406731

Call Sign: WB1EDU
Norman P Ward
293 Timrod Rd
Manchester CT 06040

Call Sign: N1VFZ
James D Burke Sr

815 Tolland Tpke
Manchester CT 06040

Call Sign: KB1NFI
Hugh W Brower
1131-0 Tolland Turnpike
157
Manchester CT 060421698

Call Sign: N1FZN
Carl E Petersen
30 Tower Rd
Manchester CT 060402831

Call Sign: N1MOT
James J Donovan
75 Union St
Manchester CT 06040

Call Sign: WA1YVF
John E Purcell
15 Valley View Rd
Manchester CT 060406917

Call Sign: KA1VGP
James T Philopena
16 Virginia Rd
Manchester CT 06040

Call Sign: N1RGJ
Charles P Avery
370 W Center St
Manchester CT 06040

Call Sign: W1DDL
William F Keehner
82 Walker St
Manchester CT 06040

Call Sign: KB1ONU
John E Gianopoulos
121 Walker St
Manchester CT 06040

Call Sign: W1JEG

John E Gianopoulos
121 Walker St
Manchester CT 06040

Call Sign: KB1LUD
Christopher P Mullinar
26 Walnut St
Manchester CT 06040

Call Sign: N1IEO
Seth G Mancini
77 Washington St
Manchester CT 06040

Call Sign: KB1IXP
Martha S Dupre Frances
87 West St
Manchester CT 06040

Call Sign: KB1QJA
Linda A Bycholski
448 Wetherell St
Manchester CT 06040

Call Sign: W1VIP
Linda A Bycholski
448 Wetherell St
Manchester CT 06040

Call Sign: KB1TIV
Brian C Clark
102 Wetherell St Unit 26
Manchester CT 06040

Call Sign: N1HMS
Arthur B Hurst
30 Winthrop Rd
Manchester CT 06040

Call Sign: KB1OSU
Kathryn L Wilson
263 Woodland St
Manchester CT 06042

Call Sign: W1SBK

Richard E Reichenbach
406 Woodland St
Manchester CT 06040

Call Sign: WA1UQH
Stephen B Uber
49t Woodland Street
Manchester CT 06042

Call Sign: KB1QJH
Jake C Nearine
31 Yale Drive
Manchester CT 06042

Call Sign: KB1QJP
Sheryl L Nearine
31 Yale Drive
Manchester CT 06042

Call Sign: WA1NBR
George D Bryan Jr
Manchester CT 06045

Call Sign: N1ZYX
Kim Neff
Manchester CT 06040

Call Sign: K1TSB
Timothy S Belmonte
Manchester CT 060450026

Call Sign: KB1KOH
P.V.R.A. Inc.
Manchester CT 06045

Call Sign: W1HDN
Pioneer Valley Radio Assn
Inc
Manchester CT 06045

Call Sign: AA1HD
P.V.R.A. Inc.
Manchester CT 06045

Call Sign: KB1RFA

P V R A
Manchester CT 06045

Call Sign: KB1WQX
Stanley H Ostrinsky
Manchester CT 06045

FCC Amateur Radio Licenses in Mansfield

Call Sign: N1UQN
James L Key
146 Atwoodville Rd
Mansfield CT 06250

Call Sign: N1TKI
Jarek Pizunski
17a Briar Cliff Rd.
Mansfield CT 06250

Call Sign: N1HUZ
Koon Hung Wong
40 East Brook Hts Apt E
Mansfield CT 062501653

Call Sign: WA1VFO
John D Jolls
456 Gurleyville Road
Mansfield CT 06268

FCC Amateur Radio Licenses in Mansfield Center

Call Sign: KB1MZT
Olivia K Schlosser
9 Atwoodville Lane
Mansfield Center CT
062501140

Call Sign: KB1JDZ
Armand G Biron
9 Atwoodville Ln
Mansfield Center CT
062501140

Call Sign: W1NRX
Armand G Biron
9 Atwoodville Ln
Mansfield Center CT
062501140

Call Sign: KA1GDR
Roy A Garrison
131d Bedlam Rd
Mansfield Center CT 06250

Call Sign: WB3DGB
David A Kloss
72 Beech Mountain Rd
Mansfield Center CT 06250

Call Sign: K1VRT
Donald N Lizee
48d Eastbrook Hgts Rd
Mansfield Center CT 06250

Call Sign: KD9MB
Russell A Grisamer
3 Heritage Square
Mansfield Center CT 06250

Call Sign: WA1VKS
William D Dittrich
26 Higgins Hwy
Mansfield Center CT 06250

Call Sign: W1IGC
Richard A Cheney
87 Highland Rd
Mansfield Center CT 06250

Call Sign: K1CBJ
John L Zatowski
24 Kaya Lane
Mansfield Center CT 06250

Call Sign: W1JLZ
John L Zatowski
24 Kaya Lane

Mansfield Center CT 06250

Call Sign: K1NLY
Harry I Barney Jr
37 Michele Ln
Mansfield Center CT 06250

Call Sign: W1SAQ
Kenneth W Fitts
96 Mulberry Rd
Mansfield Center CT 06250

Call Sign: K1RDL
Richard D Lafferty
6 Overlook Drive
Mansfield Center CT 06250

Call Sign: KB1SBE
Ethan C Drew
24 Pleasant Valley Rd
Mansfield Center CT 06250

Call Sign: KB1QHA
Michael J Darre
56 Riverview Road
Mansfield Center CT 06250

Call Sign: K3GAD
Thomas S Redmerski
83 Sawmill Brook Lane
Mansfield Center CT 06250

Call Sign: W1CWF
Bernard L Felton
83 Sawmill Brook Ln
Mansfield Center CT 06250

Call Sign: KB1SHS
Corinne M Rueb
297 Stafford Rd Apt 1
Mansfield Center CT 06250

Call Sign: KB1SHP
Kevin J Horan
527 Warrenville Rd

Mansfield Center CT 06250

Call Sign: KB1UQI
Eric J Reynolds
127 Wormwood Hill Rd
Mansfield Center CT 06250

Call Sign: N1FIT
Alice M Miner
464 Wormwood Hill Rd
Mansfield Center CT 06250

Call Sign: W1ODY
Edward E Miner
464 Wormwood Hill Rd
Mansfield Center CT 06250

Call Sign: N1EI
Charles N Fitts
Mansfield Center CT
062500097

Call Sign: N1KD
Rickie D George
Mansfield Center CT 06250

Call Sign: N1OKS
Mary L George
Mansfield Center CT 06250

Call Sign: N1PWH
Margaret Y Mc Carron
Mansfield Center CT 06250

**FCC Amateur Radio
Licenses in Mansfield
Depot**

Call Sign: KA1YCI
John G Le Conche
Mansfield Depot CT 06251

**FCC Amateur Radio
Licenses in Mansfield
Storrs**

Call Sign: N1QBR
Edward B Soltesz Sr
106 Fern Rd
Mansfield Storrs CT 06268

**FCC Amateur Radio
Licenses in Marion**

Call Sign: KA1KJZ
Ronald C Barnes
Marion CT 064440564

Call Sign: KA1SMP
Robert Pappas
Marion CT 06444

Call Sign: N1CUC
Terry T Perry
Marion CT 06444

Call Sign: N1FNM
Robert C Smith
Marion CT 06444

Call Sign: N1LGG
Owen Ames
Marion CT 06444

**FCC Amateur Radio
Licenses in Marlborough**

Call Sign: KB1VLY
Richard F Fontana Jr
4 Blackledge Dr
Marlborough CT 06447

Call Sign: N1XLX
Gordon H Thorner Jr
29 Dickinson Rd
Marlborough CT 06447

Call Sign: KB1PBO
Albert M Harmon
64 Dickinson Road

Marlborough CT
064471412

Call Sign: KB1PEO
Albert M Harmon
64 Dickinson Road
Marlborough CT
064471412

Call Sign: W1AMH
Albert M Harmon
64 Dickinson Road
Marlborough CT
064471412

Call Sign: KB1QGL
Rodney Madore
181 East Hampton Rd
Marlborough CT 06447

Call Sign: KA1NSQ
Robert R Watts
46d Edstrom Rd
Marlborough CT 06447

Call Sign: N1ZEJ
Robert D Mckinnon
174 Flood Rd
Marlborough CT 06447

Call Sign: KB1TAH
Michael A Ulloa
147 Flood Road
Marlborough CT 06447

Call Sign: KA1TAF
James A Carney
6 Hemlock Dr
Marlborough CT
064471017

Call Sign: W1CDD
Roger A Laine
6 Hickory Rd
Marlborough CT 06447

Call Sign: KB1IJX
Gregory J Lowrey
3 Hidden Woods Dr
Marlborough CT
064471270

Call Sign: KB1IYA
Anna L Hoberman
3 Hidden Woods Dr
Marlborough CT 06447

Call Sign: N1IH
Gregory J Lowrey
3 Hidden Woods Dr
Marlborough CT
064471270

Call Sign: KB1DWS
Timothy B Mather
347 Jones Hollow Rd
Marlborough CT 06447

Call Sign: WD0EXL
Daniel K Young
49 Kellogg Road
Marlborough CT 06447

Call Sign: W1PIO
Alvin W Winter
Marlborough Health Care
Marlborough CT 06447

Call Sign: KB1HWD
Holly J Wells
6 Millstone Dr
Marlborough CT 06447

Call Sign: N1XTJ
Donald L Bohman
5 Mystic Ln
Marlborough CT 06447

Call Sign: KY1F
Daniel G Brochu

8 Oak Drive
Marlborough CT 06447

Call Sign: KC1TY
Leroy H Brink
25 Phelps Rd
Marlborough CT 06447

Call Sign: WA1RZI
William V De Pietro Jr
11 Roberts Rd
Marlborough CT 06447

Call Sign: WA1SAY
Sandra L De Pietro
11 Roberts Rd
Marlborough CT 06447

Call Sign: W1LVT
Henry A Blais
22 S Main St
Marlborough CT 06447

Call Sign: KA1HJM
Donald Lack
355 S Main St
Marlborough CT 06447

Call Sign: KA1QQW
Robert J Rustigian
66 South Road
Marlborough CT 06447

Call Sign: N1FAZ
John L Benedetto
32 Virginia Rail Dr
Marlborough CT 06447

Call Sign: KA1XZ
James Kelly
9 Walnut Dr
Marlborough CT 06447

Call Sign: KA1XG
Douglas A Knowlton

10 Walnut Dr
Marlborough CT 06447

Call Sign: K1IHE
Anthony J Maiorano
43 Washington Rd
Marlborough CT 06447

Call Sign: KF6JAW
Welles F Hale Jr
174 West Road
Marlborough CT 06447

Call Sign: K1JJ
Thomas T Cathey
90 Windham Rd
Marlborough CT 06447

Call Sign: W1MZM
Vincent A Suprynowicz
Marlborough CT
064470235

Call Sign: K1RLV
Randall L Vardanian
Marlborough CT 06447

Call Sign: KA1TBW
Rudolph J Myjak
37 South Rd
Marlbourgh CT 06447

Call Sign: N1JGQ
Dmitri J Scranton
3 Paper Mill Rd
Marlobough CT 06447

FCC Amateur Radio Licenses in Melrose

Call Sign: KB1CHF
Beth A Grant
133 Melrose Rd
Melrose CT 06016

Call Sign: KA1NYG
Donald P Grant
189 Melrose Rd
Melrose CT 06016

FCC Amateur Radio Licenses in Meriden

Call Sign: KB3DEE
Candy L Couture
18 Ann Pl
Meriden CT 06450

Call Sign: N3ZWZ
Daniel V Couture
18 Ann Pl
Meriden CT 06450

Call Sign: KA1ZRD
Michael J Curtiss
36 Apple Wood Dr
Meriden CT 06450

Call Sign: KD0EMU
Sarah M Kubler Burress
104 Avery Ave
Meriden CT 06450

Call Sign: KD0EMQ
Thomas W Burress
104 Avery Ave.
Meridcn CT 06450

Call Sign: KB1DWY
Richard P Pasela
36 B Kiki Dr
Meriden CT 064512855

Call Sign: W1ATV
Walter S Yatzook Jr
77 Baker Ave
Meriden CT 06450

Call Sign: KB1TJC
Leonard A Butkiewicz

282 Baldwin Ave
Meriden CT 06450

Call Sign: W1WEE
Floyd W Steiner
92 Baldwin St
Meriden CT 06450

Call Sign: KQ1Q
Florentino Gonzalez
620 Bee St
Meriden CT 06450

Call Sign: WB1AOE
Kenneth S Post
37 Birdsey Ave
Meriden CT 06450

Call Sign: N2CGS
Peter Reimanis
50 Birdsey Ave
Meriden CT 064504821

Call Sign: AA1DQ
Donna M Schinitis
703 Blackstone Village
Meriden CT 06450

Call Sign: NA1I
Alphonse M Jaras
52 Boylston St N
Meriden CT 06450

Call Sign: KD1OY
Linwood G Brown
52 Boylston St. North
Meriden CT 06450

Call Sign: W1LB
Linwood G Brown
52 Boylston St. North
Meriden CT 06450

Call Sign: N1HCA
Susan G South

34 Brecken Ridge Ave 3
Meriden CT 06450

Call Sign: KB2PNB
Jose A Perez
75 Britannia St
Meridan CT 06451

Call Sign: KA1DRZ
Michael A Gura Jr
253 Britannia St
Meriden CT 06450

Call Sign: N1PXN
Grzegorz Kordalski
300 Britannia St Ap 43
Meriden CT 06450

Call Sign: KB1PNN
Robert B Gemma
447 Broad St Apt 2-6
Meriden CT 06450

Call Sign: KB1RBG
Robert B Gemma
447 Broad St Apt 2-6
Meriden CT 06450

Call Sign: N1LEU
David M Carrasquillo
663 Broad St. #16
Meriden CT 06450

Call Sign: KB1GZJ
William S Clark
60 Broadview Terrace
Meriden CT 06450

Call Sign: W1DWV
Henry Cunningham
89 Bronson Ave
Meriden CT 06451

Call Sign: KB1JTL
Steven J Carter

464 Brownstone Ridge
Meriden CT 06451

Call Sign: KT1Y
Alfred E Baron
672 Brownstone Ridge
Meriden CT 06451

Call Sign: N1LEX
Peter W Lowe
171 Bunker Ave
Meriden CT 06450

Call Sign: WA1MVJ
Edward T Stanton
66 Byron Rd
Meriden CT 064514900

Call Sign: WA1VXH
Christian D Sievert
79 Carriage Dr E
Meriden CT 06450

Call Sign: KB1GLN
Jonathan D Bennett
256 Chamberlain Hwy
Meriden CT 06451

Call Sign: N1UTH
Joseph W Chappo
310 Chamberlain Hwy
Meriden CT 06451

Call Sign: N1MOS
Bruce J Terrio
52 Clinton St
Meriden CT 06450

Call Sign: KA1TMB
Barry E Keeler
108 Collins Ave
Meriden CT 06450

Call Sign: KB1QAA
Matthew B Murdy

21 Colorado Ct
Meriden CT 06450

Call Sign: KA1JSA
James G Nemeth
71 Columbus Ave
Meriden CT 06451

Call Sign: N1BKE
Joel P Kleinman
55 Corrigan Ave
Meriden CT 064512874

Call Sign: WB1CBF
Charles L Vigue
6 Country Club Dr
Meriden CT 06450

Call Sign: KA1VNV
George B Dietrichsen
18 Country Ln
Meriden CT 06450

Call Sign: KA1VVX
Matthew B Dietrichsen
18 Country Ln
Meriden CT 06450

Call Sign: N1RMA
Joyce H Wruck
67 Country Ln
Meriden CT 06451

Call Sign: N1IOO
Patricia A Testa
399 Crown St
Meriden CT 06450

Call Sign: N1IXL
Philip A Testa Sr
399 Crown St
Meriden CT 06450

Call Sign: KR1K
Paul A Lidtke

160 Dana Ln
Meriden CT 06450

Call Sign: N1VMM
Tony R Pontello
46 Dexter Ave
Meriden CT 06450

Call Sign: N1NWW
Wilfred Guerin
72 Dogleg Dr
Meriden CT 06450

Call Sign: W1RIE
John F Zolnik
140 Dogwood Ln
Meriden CT 06450

Call Sign: KA1FGI
Charles R Mock
108 Draper Ave
Meriden CT 06450

Call Sign: KA1MRE
Cheryl L Mock
108 Draper Ave
Meriden CT 06450

Call Sign: KB1DNF
Timothy J Kirk
115 Dryden Dr
Meriden CT 06450

Call Sign: NU1Q
Nicholas Semon
1274 E Main St Unit C11
Meriden CT 06450

Call Sign: KB1PAK
James B Mcbride Jr
210 Eaton Ave
Meriden CT 06451

Call Sign: W1JBM
James B Mcbride Jr

210 Eaton Ave
Meriden CT 06451

Call Sign: KA1OMM
Lisa A Verdolini
60 Edgemark Acres Rd
Meriden CT 06450

Call Sign: N1VFI
Pablo Torres
347 Elm Street
Meriden CT 06450

Call Sign: WA1JKS
Joseph R Riccitelli
20 Fair St
Meriden CT 06450

Call Sign: KA1JFJ
John J Mule
547 Finch Ave
Meriden CT 06451

Call Sign: WA1SXS
Ronald F Brown
39 Forest Ave
Meriden CT 06451

Call Sign: N1URC
Jorge L Rivera
19 Foster St
Meriden CT 06451

Call Sign: KA1SQR
Stanley M Klemczak
70 Fowler Ave
Meriden CT 06450

Call Sign: W1OOC
Vincent J Sadlowski
179 Gale Ave
Meriden CT 06450

Call Sign: N1API
Al Kaiser

194 Glen Hills Rd
Meriden CT 064513832

Call Sign: W1JAX
Meriden & Wallingford
Packet Assn.
194 Glen Hills Rd
Meriden CT 064513832

Call Sign: N1LEZ
John M Schinitis
308 Glen Hills Rd
Meriden CT 06450

Call Sign: KA1WO
Larry M Gross
317 Glen Hills Rd
Meriden CT 06451

Call Sign: N1OKQ
Sarah D Sanford
107 Godek Hill Rd
Meriden CT 06450

Call Sign: KC7SAF
Shirley I Whiteside
65 Green Rd
Meriden CT 06450

Call Sign: KI7CV
William I Whiteside
65 Green Rd
Meriden CT 06450

Call Sign: KB1NCF
Charles R Schappert
76 Griswold St
Meridan CT 06450

Call Sign: KA1BRZ
Douglas N Gianino
80 Hanover Apt 512
Meriden CT 06451

Call Sign: KA1TMN

Stephen K Hull
1389 Hanover Ave
Meriden CT 064516251

David J Laliberte
34 Jeffrey Lane
Meriden CT 06451

JAIME A Mcgrath
78 Madison Ave Ext
Meriden CT 06451

Call Sign: N1IHY
Marianne K Albo
18 Harkins Ln
Meriden CT 06450

Call Sign: N1ORL
Irene M Kunsa
204 Johnson Ave
Meriden CT 06450

Call Sign: KB1MEK
Michael G Vereneau
18 Maple Ave.
Meriden CT 06450

Call Sign: N1TUK
David P Mich Sr
81 Hicks Ave
Meriden CT 06450

Call Sign: N2VII
Patrick S Murphy
55 Kennedy Dr
Meriden CT 06450

Call Sign: W1EYF
Richard C Ward
4 Marlson Rd
Meriden CT 06450

Call Sign: N1CZG
John J Panetta
129 Highland Ave
Meriden CT 064515356

Call Sign: KB1SFC
Bryan T Ragaini
38 Knob Hill Rd
Meriden CT 06451

Call Sign: KB1HCC
Jonathan K Winslow
57 Mattabasset Dr
Meriden CT 06450

Call Sign: W1YHO
Fernando S Polvani
55 Hilldise Ave
Meriden CT 06451

Call Sign: N1NTH
Roy G Aduskevicz
220 Knob Hill Rd
Meriden CT 06451

Call Sign: KA1TUR
Paul B Hastey
10 Mayflower Ln
Meriden CT 06450

Call Sign: WA1RXF
Terry M Smock
9 Hitchcock Dr
Meriden CT 06450

Call Sign: KE1AU
Robert E Kaczor
330 Knob Hill Rd
Meriden CT 06451

Call Sign: KB1AWI
Gary K Jones
41 Mayflower Ln
Meriden CT 06450

Call Sign: WA1YKU
Charles T Murphy Jr
24 Holly Lane
Meriden CT 064504749

Call Sign: N1VTE
Sarah K Kaczor
330 Knob Hill Rd
Meriden CT 06451

Call Sign: KB1KEA
Steven C Sola
34 Mckenzie Ave
Meriden CT 06451

Call Sign: W1FEF
Carl T Wirth
58 Horton Ave
Meriden CT 06450

Call Sign: N1LGF
Philip A Lozano
68 Laurel Hgts
Meriden CT 06450

Call Sign: KB1MNC
Barbara M Sola
34 Mckenzie Ave
Meriden CT 06451

Call Sign: W1ZCF
Edward F Bilger
161 Hourigan Dr
Meriden CT 06451

Call Sign: KA1PPD
Andrew M Curtis
368 Liberty St
Meriden CT 064504529

Call Sign: WA1LEV
Arthur D Noel
72-101 Meetinghouse Ridge
Meriden CT 06450

Call Sign: KB1TBL

Call Sign: KB1PFV

Call Sign: KA1QNZ

Victoria A Jaras
144 Metrocomet Drive
Meriden CT 06450

Call Sign: KB1FOF
John D Lugli
52 Mildred Rd
Meriden CT 06450

Call Sign: KA1ZDU
Adam S Podgorski Iii
58 Morton Rd
Meriden CT 06450

Call Sign: KA1ZSX
Jason J Frase
102 Murray St
Meriden CT 06450

Call Sign: KA1WAT
Michael E Woronick
1516 N Broad St
Meriden CT 06450

Call Sign: KA3LNF
Joseph A Gillner
882 N Colony Rd 36
Meriden CT 06450

Call Sign: N1SBC
Corina J De Felice
35 N Pearl St
Meriden CT 06450

Call Sign: N1HMX
Stephen P Milas
92 N Pearl St
Meriden CT 06450

Call Sign: WS1Y
Richard J Besitka
273 New Hanover Ave
Meriden CT 06451

Call Sign: WA1VHR

Sherman A Stiles
47 North Meadow Lane
Meriden CT 06450

Call Sign: K1WJL
David T Swedock
77 Oak St
Meriden CT 06450

Call Sign: KA1BRO
Kenneth J Tully
1051 Old Colony Rd 24
Meriden CT 06450

Call Sign: N1LFA
Paul A Turner
1001 Old Colony Rd Unit 4-
6
Meriden CT 064517924

Call Sign: WB1AUA
Gary Krancher
1502 Old N Colony Rd
Meriden CT 06450

Call Sign: W1BTZ
George P Raiselis
265 Paddock Ave
Meriden CT 06450

Call Sign: N1LFB
David A Turner
624 Paddock Ave
Meriden CT 06450

Call Sign: N4BXA
John R Adams
337 Parker Ave S
Meriden CT 064505954

Call Sign: KA1DMM
Lorraine D Biernacki
21 Parkview St
Meriden CT 064515232

Call Sign: WX1D
Daniel I Biernacki
21 Parkview St
Meriden CT 064515232

Call Sign: KA1IXG
Ruben Ramos
16 Peacock Dr
Meriden CT 06451

Call Sign: KC8PE
William P Hamley
211 Pomeroy Ave Apt 3102
Meriden CT 06450

Call Sign: KA1TCG
Jeffrey W Frazier
211 Pomeroy Avenue Apt
1103
Meriden CT 06450

Call Sign: N1LER
Robert S Taylor
27 Queen St
Meriden CT 06450

Call Sign: WB1GRF
Stanley A Lipka
330 Reservoir Ave
Meriden CT 06451

Call Sign: KB1FYH
Carol H Guay
39 Ridge View Rd
Meriden CT 06451

Call Sign: KA1TDF
Andrew A Cieburri
80 Ridgefield St
Meriden CT 06450

Call Sign: K1MKF
Mark K Flanagan
40 Ridgewood Rd
Meriden CT 06450

Call Sign: KB1AGT
Thomas A Olmsted
33 Rose Cir
Meriden CT 06450

Call Sign: KA1TXI
Michael D Wheeler
34 S Broad Ter
Meriden CT 06450

Call Sign: KB1PWB
Jackie Cornell
139 Sagamore Rd
Meriden CT 06450

Call Sign: KA1UQE
Gennaro Schiand Di Cola
10 Sage Hill Rd
Meriden CT 06450

Call Sign: N1NFH
David Nguyen
153 Sandy Ln
Meriden CT 06450

Call Sign: KA1FGK
Philip L Viger
41 Sherman Ave
Meriden CT 06450

Call Sign: KC1CK
Allan L Macdonald
29 South Avenue
Meriden CT 06451

Call Sign: WA1KLD
Joseph R Fratzel
119 Stevenson Rd
Meriden CT 06451

Call Sign: N1HOC
James A Cole
162 Suffolk Ct
Meriden CT 06450

Call Sign: WA1ZDZ
Victor W Cznarty
90 Sunbright Dr N
Meriden CT 06450

Call Sign: KC1PU
Robert W Woodtke Jr
73 Sunbright Dr S
Meriden CT 06450

Call Sign: N1ZTT
Paul J Zaler Jr
117 Sunset Ave
Meriden CT 06450

Call Sign: W1OKW
Paul J Zaler Jr
117 Sunset Ave
Meriden CT 06450

Call Sign: N1GWQ
Gerald S Hanson
139 Sunset Ave
Meriden CT 06450

Call Sign: KA1BEY
Leonard A Dudek
152 Sunset Ave
Meriden CT 06450

Call Sign: KA1TUP
Ralph P Parks Jr
34 Terrace Gardens
Meriden CT 06450

Call Sign: N1GNV
John A Bartscherer
30 Tremont St
Meriden CT 064502234

Call Sign: KA1YZC
Paul E Patnoad
120 Tumble Brook Rd
Meriden CT 06450

Call Sign: WA1PFV
Joseph A Gibson
95 Twiss Street
Meriden CT 06450

Call Sign: WA1GLJ
Edward J Trella
100 Valley View Dr
Meriden CT 06450

Call Sign: KA1ZGH
William D Trumpold
775 W Main St
Meriden CT 06450

Call Sign: N1SZM
Misael Medina
40 Warren St 1fl
Meriden CT 06450

Call Sign: KB1SKR
Andrey Kuznetsov
61 Washington St 1st Floor
Meriden CT 06451

Call Sign: KB1SIV
Jose E Gonzalez
20 Williams St
Meriden CT 06450

Call Sign: KB1IZO
Edward C Kroll
52 Wilson Ave
Meriden CT 064506916

Call Sign: N1RDS
Barbara J Crown
44 Winthrop Ter
Meriden CT 06450

Call Sign: N1GWU
Mark J Marion
68 Woodland Ridge
Meriden CT 06450

Call Sign: K1LHO
Michael G Ash
4 Woodmere Knoll
Meriden CT 06450

Call Sign: N1JEO
Joel T Curneal
Meriden CT 06450

Call Sign: N1URF
Raul Vega
Meriden CT 06450

Call Sign: N1XXU
Andrew M Purchia
Meriden CT 06450

Call Sign: W1NRG
Meriden Amateur Radio
Club
Meriden CT 06450

Call Sign: WA1LYT
Thomas A Coss
Meriden CT 06450

Call Sign: W1XPW
Nutmeg Hamfest Inc.
Meriden CT 06450

Call Sign: KB1MKU
Anthony Marino
Meriden CT 06450

Call Sign: AB1GD
Anthony Marino
Meriden CT 06450

Call Sign: W1TE
Anthony Marino
Meriden CT 06450

Call Sign: KB1UPR

Frank Darmofalski W1fd
Scholarship Fund
Meriden CT 06450

Call Sign: W1FD
Frank Darmofalski W1fd
Scholarship Fund
Meriden CT 06450

FCC Amateur Radio Licenses in Middlebury

Call Sign: K1BWI
Franklin A Boyd
155 Algin Dr
Middlebury CT 06762

Call Sign: WY1C
Joel A Giuditta
205 Carriage Dr.
Middlebury CT 06762

Call Sign: K1JAG
Joel A Giuditta
205 Carriage Dr.
Middlebury CT 06762

Call Sign: KB2BLV
Mark S Fromowitz
10 Chatham Court
Middlebury CT 06762

Call Sign: KA1VVE
Robert J Marzinotto
1254 Christian Rd
Middlebury CT 06762

Call Sign: KB1PBM
Robert J Marzinotto
1254 Christian Rd
Middlebury CT 06762

Call Sign: KB1PDN
Robert J Marzinotto
1254 Christian Rd

Middlebury CT 06762

Call Sign: KD1JJ
Donald W Maclean
4 Devon Court
Middlebury CT 06762

Call Sign: KB1HSX
Patricia L Supp
79 Foster St
Middlebury CT 06762

Call Sign: KA1AKL
Edmond C Loyot Jr
168 Green Hill Rd
Middlebury CT 06762

Call Sign: WA1YKR
Edmond C Loyot
168 Green Hill Rd
Middlebury CT 06762

Call Sign: KA1TLI
Cyril W Mellette
17 Jensen Dr
Middlebury CT 06762

Call Sign: KA1OQB
Peter C Partenio Jr
4 Nantucket Way
Middlebury CT 06762

Call Sign: WA1EJK
Andrew E Grace
107 Periwinkle Drive
Middlebury CT 06762

Call Sign: K1DMA
Thomas R Carroll
101 Porter Ave
Middlebury CT 06762

Call Sign: N1PWE
Scott C Crabtree
157 Southford Rd

Middlebury CT 06762

Call Sign: W1HXQ
Steven J Whitman
61 Stony Brook Road
Middlebury CT 06762

Call Sign: K1OVF
William E Williams
188 Three Mile Hill Rd
Middlebury CT 06762

Call Sign: KA1ZDO
Stanley E Dibble Jr
218 White Ave
Middlebury CT 06762

Call Sign: K1RDO
James M Barrett
863 Whittemore Rd
Middlebury CT 067623037

Call Sign: N1NUH
Joseph B Knowles
Middlebury CT 06762

Call Sign: AB1CN
David F Rabens
Middlebury CT 06762

FCC Amateur Radio Licenses in Middlefield

Call Sign: NO1F
Guy Puglisi
183 Jackson Hill Rd
Middlefield CT 06455

Call Sign: KB3IXO
Michael Goldweber
63 Lake Shore Drive
Middlefield CT 06455

Call Sign: KA1TDD
Michael T Hinchliff

14 Mattabeseck Rd
Middlefield CT 06455

Call Sign: N1IMT
Francis J Gilbert
34 Sylvan Ridge Dr
Middlefield CT 06455

Call Sign: KA1BSL
John W Yusza Iii
70 Whisper Wind Rd
Middlefield CT 06455

Call Sign: KA1LCA
Louise M Perkins
Middlefield CT 06455

Call Sign: N1JPK
Gary A D Amico
Middlefield CT 06455

FCC Amateur Radio Licenses in Middletown

Call Sign: KA1TFA
Raymond Acosta
80 Acacea Ct
Middletown CT 06457

Call Sign: KB1UTN
Karta S Khalsa
478 Arbutus St
Middletown CT 06457

Call Sign: KA1ROR
David L Todeschini
153 Ballfall Rd
Middletown CT 06457

Call Sign: WA1ZEA
Richard E Bengtson
727 Bear Hill Rd
Middletown CT 06457

Call Sign: KB1PBN

Wayne S Bartolotta
3 Blue Meadow Rd
Middletown CT 06457

Call Sign: K1WSB
Wayne S Bartolotta
3 Blue Meadow Rd
Middletown CT 06457

Call Sign: KA1INR
Ralph N Rogers
237 Boston Rd
Middletown CT 06457

Call Sign: N1LMK
Burton C Hirsch Sr
343 Bow Ln
Middletown CT 06457

Call Sign: W1BCH
Burton C Hirsch Sr
343 Bow Ln
Middletown CT 06457

Call Sign: KB1ENN
Jacob D Kirk
31 Broadview Pkwy
Middletown CT 06457

Call Sign: N1AWE
Patrick I Mc Laughlin
16 Burgundy Hill Ln
Middletown CT 06457

Call Sign: N1GUK
John E Ertle
102 Burgundy Hill Ln
Middletown CT 06457

Call Sign: KB1TJF
Jarrett Dorough
275 Burgundy Hill Ln
Middletown CT 06457

Call Sign: KB1LID

Jarrett Dorough
275 Burgundy Hill Ln
Middletown CT 06457

Call Sign: KB1TTV
Jonathan L Martin
601 Cambridge Commons
Middletown CT 06457

Call Sign: KC4BEC
Leo Libera
64 Carriage Crossing
Middletown CT 06457

Call Sign: KB1FCP
Matthew H Graves
48 Chauncey Rd
Middletown CT 06457

Call Sign: KG2IS
Miroslaw Barcikowski
38 Chelsea Ct
Middletown CT 06457

Call Sign: KB1AGB
John A Battista Jr
151 Cimarron Rd
Middletown CT 06457

Call Sign: N1ZTR
Karen L Hoover
188 Cimarron Rd
Middletown CT 06457

Call Sign: N3YER
Kenneth J Hoover
188 Cimarron Rd
Middletown CT 064572358

Call Sign: KE1LR
Kenneth J Hoover
188 Cimarron Rd
Middletown CT 064572358

Call Sign: KA1PPN

Howard I Gustafson
44 Clover St
Middletown CT 064575219

Call Sign: K1RNT
B Robert Mc Cormick
624 Congdon St W
Middletown CT 06457

Call Sign: KA1GLY
Roger R Berry
31 Cooley Ave
Middletown CT 06422

Call Sign: KB1KHE
Brian M Fudge
169 Country Club Rd
Middletown CT 06457

Call Sign: W1SP
Csp Amateur Radio Club
1111 Countryclub Rd
Middletown CT 064579294

Call Sign: KC2FFZ
Vincent S Gogluicci
63 Countryside Ln
Middletown CT 06457

Call Sign: K1JX
Clarke V Greene
92b2 Cynthia Ln
Middletown CT 06457

Call Sign: WB1AVA
Virginia A Greene
92b-2 Cynthia Ln
Middletown CT 06457

Call Sign: KB1HBV
Maxime P. Toussaint
Contest Club
102 Dora Drive
Middletown CT 06457

Call Sign: WB1DWZ
Maxime P Toussaint
Contest Club
102 Dora Drive
Middletown CT 06457

Call Sign: KB2VDC
Paul N Klein
180 Dove Lane
Middletown CT 06457

Call Sign: WA1FMX
Peter R Jacobson
192 Dove Lane
Middletown CT 06457

Call Sign: WA1VJZ
Joseph A Leal
635 E Main St
Middletown CT 06457

Call Sign: N1OFB
John R Moore
92 Eagle Hollow Dr
Middletown CT 06457

Call Sign: AB1CT
John R Moore
92 Eagle Hollow Dr
Middletown CT 06457

Call Sign: WA1ORT
Raymond E Chaffee
704 East St
Middletown CT 06457

Call Sign: W3RG
Robert T Gallagher
84 Eastbury Hill Drive
Middletown CT 06457

Call Sign: KD1JG
Robert E Cartier
112 Fieldbrook Rd
Middletown CT 06457

Call Sign: KB1LNL
Royal Charter Composite
Squadron
112 Fieldbrrok Road
Middletown CT 06457

Middletown CT 06457

Call Sign: N2XN
Robert W Stielau
20 Hillcrest Ave
Middletown CT 06457

Middletown CT 06457

Call Sign: K1OI
John R Pike
743a Long Hill Road
Middletown CT 06456

Call Sign: N8LSQ
Byron F Blake
4-Aug Forest Glen Circle
Middletown CT 06457

Call Sign: N1HCB
Stanley E Walker
49 Inverness Ln
Middletown CT 06457

Call Sign: N1HYY
Lorelei H Goldstein
49 Lorelei Cir
Middletown CT 06457

Call Sign: N1LEO
Sebastian Marino Jr
22 Frazier Ave
Middletown CT 06457

Call Sign: WB1AAB
Henry J Kmietek
56 Jefferson Ave
Middletown CT 06457

Call Sign: WA1VVD
Neal B Goldstein
49 Lorelei Circle
Middletown CT 06457

Call Sign: N1YFN
J. Martin Acevedo
105 George Street
Middletown CT 06457

Call Sign: KA1RIQ
Joseph S Garofald Jr
36 Lake St
Middletown CT 06457

Call Sign: KB1IRO
Derek J Hunt
106 Lorraine Terrace
Middletown CT 06457

Call Sign: W1XRK
J. Martin Acevedo
105 George Street
Middletown CT 06457

Call Sign: WA1JNO
N Gordon Johnson
89 Laurel Grove Rd
Middletown CT 064574011

Call Sign: KB1HDR
Gregory P Krukonis
62 Loveland St Apt 7
Middletown CT 06457

Call Sign: KB1FFE
Glenn W Feldhouse
49 Greenview Terrace
Middletown CT 06457

Call Sign: KB1FCR
Timothy E Shettleworth
713 Laurel Grove Rd
Middletown CT 06457

Call Sign: W1LFK
Charles D Parmelee
1 Mac Donough Place
Middletown CT 06457

Call Sign: KA1AAU
George H Anderson
216 Hendley St
Middletown CT 06457

Call Sign: KB1GHL
Dennis P Hurd
7 Lindsey Rd
Middletown CT 06457

Call Sign: KB1SYV
Jeffrey W Zercie
698 Main St Apt 2d
Middletown CT 06457

Call Sign: KA1AAV
Stacia J Anderson
216 Hendley St
Middletown CT 06457

Call Sign: KB1KUN
Francis J Ifkovic Iii
30 Lindsey Rd
Middletown CT 06457

Call Sign: KA1WDF
Theodore R Werner
300 Margarite Rd
Middletown CT 06457

Call Sign: W1FUW
Edmund J Mierz
138 Higby Rd

Call Sign: N1YZQ
Scott D Mc Naughton
481 Long Hill Rd

Call Sign: KA1ADX
George H Kupfer Sr
158 Markham St

Middletown CT 06457

Call Sign: KA1PSD
Michael J Curnow
65 Meech Road
Middletown CT 06457

Call Sign: N1DWN
Carl L Trumpold
77 Meriden Rd
Middletown CT 06457

Call Sign: KA1MES
Joseph Failla
366 Millbrook Rd
Middletown CT 06457

Call Sign: WA1ZUV
Thomas J Domkowski
585 Miner Street
Middletown CT 06457

Call Sign: W1YTZ
Daniel T Dombrowik
91 Mountain Laurel Drive
Middletown CT 064572407

Call Sign: KB1UVJ
Douglas A Brown
91 Murray St
Middletown CT 06457

Call Sign: KB1IYC
Gerald C Foster
106 New Field St Unit 2
Middletown CT 06457

Call Sign: N1FDN
Thomas J Kemp
134 Newfield St
Middletown CT 06457

Call Sign: N1OYE
Vance J Stroneski
328 Newfield St

Middletown CT 06457

Call Sign: WA1REX
Robert W Pettersen
352 Newfield St - Apt 812
Middletown CT 06457

Call Sign: KB1FAO
Hannah M Deal
865 Newfield St 1st Floor
Middletown CT 06457

Call Sign: WA1TMA
John G Leverton Jr
220 Newfield St Apt 613
Middletown CT 06457

Call Sign: K1FZL
Paul E Roberts
597 Newfield Street
Middletown CT 06457

Call Sign: KN1J
Charles J Czajka
81 Newtown St
Middletown CT 06457

Call Sign: KA1RJO
Joan P Dickinson
36 Norfolk St
Middletown CT 064574206

Call Sign: N1BBJ
Raymond I Dickinson
36 Norfolk St
Middletown CT 064574206

Call Sign: KB1QJY
Brent C Samulenas
34 Northwoods Lane
Middletown CT 06457

Call Sign: N1UJQ
Daniel C Falk
40 Nutmeg Court

Middletown CT 06457

Call Sign: KB1DCK
Daniel T Dombrowik
57 Old Mill Rd
Middletown CT 064572407

Call Sign: N1ODJ
Kenneth G Schmitz
24 Orange Rd
Middletown CT 06457

Call Sign: KB1PMV
Emergency Management
Westfield
79 Orchard Hill Lane
Middletown CT 06457

Call Sign: KA1FDW
Emergency Management
Westfield
79 Orchard Hill Lane
Middletown CT 06457

Call Sign: WB1ENI
Leopold J Zieller Jr
79 Orchard Hill Ln
Middletown CT 06457

Call Sign: KB1HDF
Anna M Stevens
227 Pearl St
Middletown CT 06457

Call Sign: WA1NBS
James S Piccirillo
13 Pinehurst Place
Middletown CT 06457

Call Sign: KF4IAM
William K De Kine
3 Primrose Ln
Middletown CT 06457

Call Sign: WB1FQB

David A Hobson
91 Prospect St
Middletown CT 06457

Call Sign: WA1ZKX
James L Carlson
192 Prout Hill Rd
Middletown CT 06457

Call Sign: KB1LYY
Emergency Management
Middletown
675 Randolph Rd
Middletown CT 06457

Call Sign: K1MTN
Emergency Management
Middletown
675 Randolph Rd
Middletown CT 06457

Call Sign: N1YBA
Lawrence W Lovell
875 Randolph Rd
Middletown CT 06457

Call Sign: KA1SZG
Paul L Fuller
1408 Randolph Rd
Middletown CT 064575114

Call Sign: N1GIN
Peter W Gillies
429 Ridge Rd
Middletown CT 06457

Call Sign: KB1ONL
Richard Lenoce
680 Ridge Rd
Middletown CT 06457

Call Sign: W1SJY
Peter W Gillies
429 Ridge Road
Middletown CT 06457

Call Sign: KC2MLH
Adam M Castracane
215 Ridgefield Drive
Middletown CT 06457

Call Sign: N4YA
Robert C Duncan
235 Ridgefield Drive
Middletown CT 06457

Call Sign: N1MWV
Joseph Formica
10 Rising Trl Dr
Middletown CT 06457

Call Sign: N1RFJ
Parlane W Reid
36 Roberta Dr
Middletown CT 064575510

Call Sign: N1QIA
Charles B Malloch
16 Roberts St
Middletown CT 06457

Call Sign: N1GNZ
Charles S Rollins Jr
168 Rose Cir
Middletown CT 06457

Call Sign: KB1KLV
Paul Erickson
158 Russell Street
Middletown CT 06457

Call Sign: N1PXL
Carl J Dombrowik
25 Russet Lane
Middletown CT 06457

Call Sign: KT1Z
Delice S Ferrara
1 Ryan St
Middletown CT 06457

Call Sign: WA1ZPG
Thomas J Wilmarth
1150 S Main St - Apt 409
Middletown CT 06457

Call Sign: N1RLB
Bernard W Pudvah
11 Sand Hill Rd
Middletown CT 06457

Call Sign: N1TPE
Carol C Pudvah
11 Sand Hill Rd
Middletown CT 06457

Call Sign: N1STH
John L Lewis Sr
38 Santangelo Cir
Middletown CT 06457

Call Sign: KA1IYO
Raymond J Laverty
2099 Saybrook Rd
Middletown CT 06457

Call Sign: KA1YDJ
Selena Timbro
121 Saybrook Rd.
Middletown CT 06457

Call Sign: N1IFJ
Stephen P Graham
71 Smith St
Middletown CT 06457

Call Sign: WA1UMD
Kenneth E Stiles
1150 South Main St. Apt.
221
Middletown CT 06457

Call Sign: N1VIH
Michael J Huard
200 Spencer Dr

Middletown CT 06457

Call Sign: N1KVN
Salvatore N Marino
80 Summer Hill Rd
Middletown CT 06457

Call Sign: N1LDF
Gene Marino
80 Summer Hill Rd
Middletown CT 06457

Call Sign: N1ZHW
Joanna A Slysz
82 Summer Hill Rd
Middletown CT 06457

Call Sign: KA1GPI
Andrew J Kasznay Iii
164 Talcott Ridge Drive
Middletown CT 06457

Call Sign: KA1BYX
Lamont E Charlebois
Toll Gate Rd
Middletown CT 06457

Call Sign: KB1RHW
Andrew R Zeller
4323 Town Brooke
Middletown CT 06457

Call Sign: KA1MXY
Martin K Nevius
621 Town Colony Dr
Middletown CT 06457

Call Sign: N1ZTJ
Edward J Krasniewski
142 Trolley Crossing
Middletown CT 06457

Call Sign: WA1YVG
Ginette A Purcell
171 Trolley Crossing Ln

Middletown CT 06457

Call Sign: KA1JTG
James W Hartzell Jr
24 Wall St
Middletown CT 06457

Call Sign: N1UQP
Edward M Judway
400 Washington St C3
Middletown CT 06457

Call Sign: KB1KIX
E Jonathan Hardy
500 Washington St Unit 5
Middletown CT 06457

Call Sign: N1YYI
Robert L Vincent
86 Westfield St
Middletown CT 06457

Call Sign: KJ4WU
Edward C Peterson
45 Westmont Drive
Middletown CT 06457

Call Sign: KB1UYD
Brett O Braccidiferro
173 Woodbury Circle
Middletown CT 06457

Call Sign: KB1WEJ
David W Sykes
9 Yellow Birch Rd
Middletown CT 06457

Call Sign: KR4GS
Anthony A La Penta Jr
9 Yellow Green Street
Middletown CT 06457

Call Sign: KB1DZC
Douglas G Schumann
Middletown CT 06457

Call Sign: WA1LUJ
Csp Amateur Radio Club
Middletown CT 064579294

Call Sign: KB1JEX
David T Hines
Middletown CT 06457

FCC Amateur Radio Licenses in Milford

Call Sign: N1QYC
Matthew T Smith
30 Alden Pl
Milford CT 06460

Call Sign: N1PLP
Chester J Malinowski
35 Anchorage Dr
Milford CT 06460

Call Sign: W1LCG
Robert W Harriman Sr
47 Andrews Ave
Milford CT 06460

Call Sign: KA1FZE
Mark J Makower
29 Argyle Rd
Milford CT 06460

Call Sign: KA1PZC
Arthur T Pelham
68 Atwater St
Milford CT 06460

Call Sign: KB1THC
Daniel L Johnson
21 Autumn Ridge Rd
Milford CT 06461

Call Sign: W4RGP
Robert G Paddock
29 Avery Ave.

Milford CT 06460   Milford CT 064612304   Milford CT 06460

Call Sign: KA1OHS
Edward M Owers
160 Berner Ter
Milford CT 06460

Call Sign: N1GGC
Bertha M Betso
75 Berwin St
Milford CT 06460

Call Sign: KB1FCN
Gus A Betso
75 Berwyn St
Milford CT 06460

Call Sign: KB1APB
Paul R De Cava
89 Berwyn St
Milford CT 06460

Call Sign: KB1APD
Patricia A De Cava
89 Berwyn St
Milford CT 06460

Call Sign: N1RLS
Craig A Chambers
22 Bonsilene St
Milford CT 06460

Call Sign: KB1AHL
Lisa A Fournier
1698 Boston Post Rd
Milford CT 06460

Call Sign: N1QAF
Danette C Kennedy
670 Boston Post Rd Unit 8
Milford CT 06460

Call Sign: KB1PLS
Joseph M Filakovsky
62 Boylston St

Call Sign: N1DNP
Joseph M Filakovsky
62 Boylston St
Milford CT 064612304

Call Sign: KB1MJS
Frank J Kudlicki
82 Boylston St
Milford CT 06460

Call Sign: NR1K
Roger N Borgersen
7 Brett Cliff Rd
Milford CT 06460

Call Sign: KA1PHB
Anne M Heath
61 Brewster Rd
Milford CT 06460

Call Sign: KB1GGJ
David A Blaise
16 Bridgeport Ave
Milford CT 06460

Call Sign: KB1ZN
Irving H Shiffrin
307 Bridgeport Ave
Milford CT 06460

Call Sign: KB1WHY
Christopher J Moorman
240 Broad St
Milford CT 06460

Call Sign: AA1ET
Marino V Wilson
51 Broadway
Milford CT 06460

Call Sign: KC1TW
James B Mc Keand
46 Brookdale Ave

Call Sign: KB1DRW
Conrad D Henning
103 Castle Ln
Milford CT 06516

Call Sign: KB1VSQ
Riley T Kinsella
41 Charles St
Milford CT 06460

Call Sign: KA1UKT
William J Hammer
150 Chatham Ave
Milford CT 06460

Call Sign: N1QYF
John A Kowalsky
161 Chatham Ave
Milford CT 06460

Call Sign: N1TIL
Belinda J Kowalsky
161 Chatham Ave
Milford CT 06460

Call Sign: N1CLF
John H Chutjian
58 Cherry St
Milford CT 06460

Call Sign: N1EHQ
Louis H Jackson
33 Christopher Dr
Milford CT 06460

Call Sign: KB1ACK
Vito Masi
65 Claremont Cir
Milford CT 06460

Call Sign: K1LKB
Clifford E Nitchke
63 Clark Hill Rd

Milford CT 06460   Milford CT 06460   Milford CT 06460

Call Sign: WA1AM   Call Sign: WA1LXF   Call Sign: KA1YVO
Darren P Zapotocky Jr   Richard J Wynkoop   John A Gordon
31 Cooper Ave   27 Dock Rd   71 Elgin Rd
Milford CT 06460   Milford CT 06460   Milford CT 06460

Call Sign: KB1AHM   Call Sign: KB1UAW   Call Sign: N1CJA
Robert E Smith   William J Sahlmann   Francis J Gormley
36 Coran Ct   43 Driftwood Lane   31 Essex Dr
Milford CT 06460   Milford CT 06460   Milford CT 06460

Call Sign: KA1RIJ   Call Sign: N8KDP   Call Sign: W1DXV
Connie Trapani   Steven G Cross   Richard D Stott
99 Cornfield Rd   752 E Broadway 2nd Fl   36 Ettadore Pk
Milford CT 06460   Milford CT 06460   Milford CT 06460

Call Sign: KG2J   Call Sign: AB1GM   Call Sign: W2LWB
Peter W Trapani   Nicholas J Colombo   John A Chiuchiolo
99 Cornfield Rd   75 East Rutland Rd   73 Fairview St
Milford CT 06460   Milford CT 06461   Milford CT 064604127

Call Sign: KB1ABO   Call Sign: KA1ZAR   Call Sign: N1EZG
Timothy E Olenski   Philip J Griffin Jr   George A Ambriscoe Jr
5 Crestwood Road   315 Edgefield Ave   4 Flax Mill Terr
Milford CT 06460   Milford CT 06460   Milford CT 06460

Call Sign: KA1TFH   Call Sign: N1MUR   Call Sign: N1JWX
John Premak   Jennifer A Raymond   Kenneth L Wilkens
92 Dale Dr   315 Edgefield Ave   5 Franklin Rd
Milford CT 064601980   Milford CT 06460   Milford CT 06460

Call Sign: WB1GTW   Call Sign: KA1RDM   Call Sign: WB1FSR
Robert A Foster   Paul Matar   Michael Rowe
41 Dalton Rd   259 Edgemont Rd   53 Grant St
Milford CT 064606909   Milford CT 06460   Milford CT 06460

Call Sign: N1ZSI   Call Sign: N3FCO   Call Sign: WA1YCX
Fred W Zander   Charles E Ray   Kenneth A Burton
49 Depot Rd   102 Elaine Rd   60 Grant St
Milford CT 064607032   Milford CT 06460   Milford CT 06460

Call Sign: KB1SWG   Call Sign: KB1WJY   Call Sign: KB1JHU
Sharon M Voris   Douglas N Grant   Scott Burton
140 Depot Rd   38 Elder St   60 Grant St

Milford CT 06460

Milford CT 06460

Milford CT 06460

Call Sign: KB1KBL
Lee Burton
60 Grant St
Milford CT 064605310

Call Sign: W1VW
William M Kosturko
97 Hill St
Milford CT 06460

Call Sign: AA1XE
Glenn J Green
39 Judson Pl
Milford CT 06461

Call Sign: KB1OIE
Edward K Cholakian
43 Greenfield Rd
Milford CT 06460

Call Sign: KA1WA
Benjamin J Zigun
22 Hillside Avenue
Milford CT 06460

Call Sign: KB1ILJ
Merritt F Brainard
55 Judson Place
Milford CT 06461

Call Sign: K1ZFQ
James E Hoffman
42 Gresham St
Milford CT 06460

Call Sign: KB1PGJ
Bruce R Rutkowski
23 Honeycomb Lane
Milford CT 06461

Call Sign: KB1FTZ
Allan L Johnson
84 Kent St
Milford CT 06460

Call Sign: N1DUL
James P Richards
147 Gulf St
Milford CT 06460

Call Sign: K1SLQ
Bruce R Rutkowski
23 Honeycomb Lane
Milford CT 064611622

Call Sign: KA1SPC
Louis Travis Jr
48 Kerema Ave
Milford CT 06460

Call Sign: KA1DCQ
Rachel S Van Etten
64 Gunn St
Milford CT 06460

Call Sign: WA1SFH
Douglas E Sharafanowich
168 Housatonic Dr
Milford CT 06460

Call Sign: KA1FAI
William J Mc Vinua
14 Liberty St
Milford CT 06460

Call Sign: KA1DCL
Earl W Dugan
147 Harrison Ave
Milford CT 06460

Call Sign: KB1VSP
Victor J Rice
41 Jenniffer Ln
Milford CT 06461

Call Sign: KB1RJP
Cheryl A Fernandes
9 Lincoln Ave
Milford CT 06460

Call Sign: KB1GFE
Sean W Quigley
57 Hawley Ave
Milford CT 06460

Call Sign: KA1WUW
Glenn J Green
39 Judson Pl
Milford CT 06460

Call Sign: W1RDQ
Edwin F Collins
31 Long Island View Rd
Milford CT 06460

Call Sign: W1LLM
Peter C Brockett Sr
51 High St
Milford CT 06460

Call Sign: N1MLX
Robin L Green
39 Judson Pl
Milford CT 06460

Call Sign: WA2YXC
Salvatore J Di Salvo
6 Manor House Lane
Milford CT 06460

Call Sign: W1HMZ
Emery E Schmittgall
78 Hill St

Call Sign: N1VJY
Craig P Green
39 Judson Pl

Call Sign: N1SY
Salvatore J Di Salvo
6 Manor House Lane

Milford CT 06460

Call Sign: K1NCO
Joseph G Sefcik
159 Marino Dr
Milford CT 06460

Call Sign: N1XYE
William Muir Jr
74 Marion Ave
Milford CT 06460

Call Sign: KE1BX
Ward C Willis
30 Marshall St
Milford CT 06460

Call Sign: W1VLS
Leroy A Milewski Sr
30 Marshall St
Milford CT 06460

Call Sign: KA1UIL
Jill A Johnson
76 Marshall St
Milford CT 06460

Call Sign: N1HAW
Glenn J Krieger
132 Mcquillan Dr.
Milford CT 06460

Call Sign: WS1F
Robert H Frey
136 Meadow Park Dr
Milford CT 06460

Call Sign: KA1TBM
Arthur M Ford Jr
103 Meadow St
Milford CT 06460

Call Sign: WR1H
Nicholas D Kefalas
156 Meadow St

Milford CT 06460

Call Sign: KB1CFU
Juan Reyes
66 Meeting House Ln
Milford CT 06460

Call Sign: KA1REN
Ann M Bouteiller
163 Melba St
Milford CT 06460

Call Sign: KB1APA
Robert W Couture
163 Melba St
Milford CT 06460

Call Sign: KA1OQF
Anthony S Jackson
10 Mercury Dr
Milford CT 06460

Call Sign: N1UNG
Carlene R Hurlock
144 Merwin Ave
Milford CT 06460

Call Sign: KB1HKT
Leslie M Abbott
467 Merwin Ave
Milford CT 06460

Call Sign: N1INH
David R Clark
516 Merwin Ave
Milford CT 06460

Call Sign: N1LUJ
Karen L Clark
516 Merwin Ave
Milford CT 06460

Call Sign: KA1OFE
Denise J Gontarz
551 Merwin Ave

Milford CT 064607136

Call Sign: WB1GTY
Richard J Gontarz
551 Merwin Ave
Milford CT 06460

Call Sign: W1FWB
Kevin M Gunther
2 Milford Point Rd
Milford CT 06460

Call Sign: N1QCG
Anthony N Duro
84 Milford Point Rd
Milford CT 06460

Call Sign: K1PXE
Peter S Motyl
495 Milford Point Rd
Milford CT 064605427

Call Sign: KB1CBD
Milford Amateur Radio
Repeater Association
495 Milford Point Rd
Milford CT 06460

Call Sign: WA1QMC
Joseph C Hobson
921 Milford Point Rd
Milford CT 06460

Call Sign: W1GWV
John Darak
34 Minuteman Dr
Milford CT 06460

Call Sign: KB1DUU
Kenneth J Jalbert
42 Monroe St
Milford CT 06460

Call Sign: N1DUG
Roger L Janesky

750 Naugatuck Ave
Milford CT 06460

Call Sign: KB1JIT
Donald R Vincelette
12 Noble Ave
Milford CT 06460

Call Sign: W1OPY
Stanley Newman
65 Noble Ave
Milford CT 06460

Call Sign: KB1WJT
Richard L Sieron
52 Nutmeg Ln
Milford CT 06461

Call Sign: N1UTJ
David E Gray
48 Olive St
Milford CT 06460

Call Sign: ND1E
Melville J Fenn Jr
505 Orange Ave
Milford CT 06460

Call Sign: NP2LN
Lawrence Hunter
39 Orlando St.
Milford CT 06460

Call Sign: NP2LS
Angela L Hunter
39 Orlando St.
Milford CT 06460

Call Sign: W1KUN
Alfred J Post
92 Overhill Rd
Milford CT 06460

Call Sign: W1ZTY
Harold J Carter Jr

39 Overlook Dr
Milford CT 06460

Call Sign: W1HHY
John C Matthews Sr
15 Page St
Milford CT 06460

Call Sign: W1AMS
Harris J Heyman
1 Parkland Pl
Milford CT 064607723

Call Sign: KA1QOW
Mildred I Blotney
11 Pearl Hill St
Milford CT 06460

Call Sign: KA1QQT
Bernard H Blotney
11 Pearl Hill St
Milford CT 06460

Call Sign: KA1DLE
Eileen T Smith
12 Pearl Hill St
Milford CT 06460

Call Sign: NC1G
Robert J Smith
12 Pearl Hill St
Milford CT 06460

Call Sign: N1PQP
Shirley G Barton
24 Pearson Ave
Milford CT 06460

Call Sign: K1TEY
Harold R Roy
39 Peck St
Milford CT 06460

Call Sign: KA1RZW
Theresa M Gormley

150 Penn Common
Milford CT 06460

Call Sign: K1SLQ
Richard G Rutkowski
364 Plains Rd
Milford CT 06460

Call Sign: KB1APP
David L Packa
164 Point Beach Dr
Milford CT 06460

Call Sign: KB1WY
Gary L Packa
164 Point Beach Dr
Milford CT 06460

Call Sign: KE1DB
Frances M Packa
164 Point Beach Dr
Milford CT 06460

Call Sign: N1MLW
William H Kates
97 Pomona Ave
Milford CT 06460

Call Sign: KB1AME
Anne E Corwin
359 Pond Point Ave
Milford CT 06460

Call Sign: N1RRL
Douglas A Lyon
521 Popes Island Rd
Milford CT 06460

Call Sign: N1NBG
Albert Y Fournier
1698 Post Rd
Milford CT 06460

Call Sign: K1LGM
Joseph S Bedlovies Jr

30 Ridge Street
Milford CT 06460

160 Shorefront
Milford CT 06460

44 Stevens St
Milford CT 0460

Call Sign: N1TCN
Dennis A Hoben
31d Robert Treat Dr
Milford CT 06460

Call Sign: K1MAL
Christopher F Altieri
160 Shorefront
Milford CT 06460

Call Sign: N1DWW
Kimberly A Michaud
85 Sunnyside Crt
Milford CT 06460

Call Sign: N1LQO
Mark Halbrook
160 Rock Ln
Milford CT 06460

Call Sign: N1TGE
Shawn M Benoit
32 Shweky Beach Way
Milford CT 064606076

Call Sign: N1EAL
Bruce J Michaud
85 Sunnyside Ct
Milford CT 06460

Call Sign: KA1UQI
Julie L Williamson
30 Rogers Ave
Milford CT 06460

Call Sign: N1PJL
Tracy R Boyer
1 Smiths Point
Milford CT 06460

Call Sign: N1QOE
Glenn J Williamson
141 Sunnyside Ct
Milford CT 06460

Call Sign: N2PLY
Matthew A Cohan
587 Roses Mill Road
Milford CT 06460

Call Sign: KB1VRC
Mark T Byers
64 Snowapple Ln
Milford CT 06460

Call Sign: N1WMU
Julie A Miller
141 Sunnyside Ct
Milford CT 06460

Call Sign: N1NGV
Kevin K Gallagher
36 S Kerema Ave
Milford CT 06460

Call Sign: WA2WIZ
Robert G Marrone
36 Soundview Avenue
Milford CT 064607877

Call Sign: WA1RGN
Franklin H Lindsay
502 Swanson Crescent
Milford CT 06460

Call Sign: N1SQA
Phillip S Hammel
70 Seabreeze Ave
Milford CT 06460

Call Sign: KB1OQM
Michael F Prete
97 Southwoodland Dr
Milford CT 06460

Call Sign: N1BSV
Thomas D Duggan
66 Timber Trail
Milford CT 06460

Call Sign: K2OT
Henry I Steckler
8d Seabreeze Ave
Milford CT 06460

Call Sign: N1DEC
Fred H Van Pala
11 Sperry St
Milford CT 06460

Call Sign: K1HUH
John Hubetsel
45 Tomahawk Ln
Milford CT 06460

Call Sign: KB1ABT
Robert E Chidsey Jr
41 Shea Ave
Milford CT 06460

Call Sign: KA1LZY
Hubert C Cossett
113 Springdale St
Milford CT 064607467

Call Sign: WA1VJN
Ralph Pascale
68 Tumblebrook Dr
Milford CT 06460

Call Sign: KB1JNG
Christopher F Altieri

Call Sign: N1LFD
Ronald M De Biaso

Call Sign: N1VJX
Shawn P Norris

28 Utica St
Milford CT 06461

Call Sign: KB1LDG
Stanley M Marczak
84 Utica St
Milford CT 06460

Call Sign: N1HBE
George W Mc Gann Jr
15 Valley View Rd
Milford CT 06460

Call Sign: KB1RRL
Mauro L Abrantes
50 Valley View Rd
Milford CT 06461

Call Sign: WA1MLA
Mauro L Abrantes
50 Valley View Rd
Milford CT 06461

Call Sign: K1MUF
Martin J Buchinger
142 W Town St
Milford CT 064603259

Call Sign: KA1QCP
David W Hurlburt
36 Wall Street
Milford CT 06460

Call Sign: KB1HLJ
Jonathan P Sandoval
141 Welch Point Rd
Milford CT 06460

Call Sign: KB1HLI
Joseph P Sandoval
141 Welch Point Road
Milford CT 06460

Call Sign: KA1BQC
Stewart E Damon

268 Welchs Point Rd
Milford CT 06460

Call Sign: KA1DLF
Stewart J Damon
268 Welchs Point Rd
Milford CT 06460

Call Sign: KA1ZDQ
Harold R Nowlin
460 Welchs Point Rd
Milford CT 06460

Call Sign: KA1GBD
Anne W Damon
268 Welchs Pt Rd
Milford CT 06460

Call Sign: N1TBA
Benjamin M Lucas
454 Welchs Pt Rd
Milford CT 06460

Call Sign: K1OEQ
Lester L Schoonmaker
28 Wcst Ave
Milford CT 06460

Call Sign: W1WKP
Frank R Soloman
128 West Ave
Milford CT 06460

Call Sign: KB1MKS
John R Soloman
128 West Ave
Milford CT 06460

Call Sign: W1WKP
John R Soloman
128 West Ave
Milford CT 06460

Call Sign: AB1IW
John R Soloman

128 West Ave
Milford CT 06460

Call Sign: W1WKP
John R Soloman
128 West Ave
Milford CT 06460

Call Sign: W1DME
Stephen G Ambrisco Sr
207 West Main St
Milford CT 06460

Call Sign: KB1ROO
Terrance S Fazekas Jr
370 West Rutland Rd
Milford CT 06461

Call Sign: N1MLZ
Robert A Fusaris
22 Whalley Ave
Milford CT 06460

Call Sign: KB1PJB
Philip V Marinaccio
881 Wheelers Farm Road
Milford CT 06461

Call Sign: K1PJR
Philip V Marinaccio
881 Wheelers Farm Road
Milford CT 06461

Call Sign: N1XUP
Timothy P Danehy
305 Wheelers Farms Rd
Milford CT 064601870

Call Sign: AB1DC
Timothy P Danehy
305 Wheelers Farms Rd
Milford CT 064601870

Call Sign: W1FUN
Richard M Haskell

5 Whitwell Street
Milford CT 06460

Call Sign: KA1RBD
William I Foster
75 Wilcox Rd
Milford CT 06460

Call Sign: KA1RBE
Judith L Foster
75 Wilcox Rd
Milford CT 06460

Call Sign: WA1YQE
Richard S Williamson
30 Wildflower Drive
Milford CT 06460

Call Sign: N1FEW
Daniel G Voldstad
65 Willow St
Milford CT 06460

Call Sign: KA1GBE
Raisa I Williamson
28 Wilson St
Milford CT 06460

Call Sign: KA1LIP
Tammy L Harvey
28 Wilson St
Milford CT 06460

Call Sign: WA1ZIG
Charles J Calandriello
39 Windsong Ln
Milford CT 06460

Call Sign: N1DRQ
Richard B Botsford
144 Wolf Harbor Rd
Milford CT 06460

Call Sign: W1CUX
Winkler C Gosch

Milford CT 06460

Call Sign: WA1LWD
Howard E Hecht
Milford CT 064600943

Call Sign: KB1GXO
Coastline Amateur Radio
Club
Milford CT 06460

Call Sign: N1EG
Coastline Amateur Radio
Club
Milford CT 06460

FCC Amateur Radio Licenses in Milldale

Call Sign: KA1KJY
Paul H Hemberger
Milldale CT 06467

Call Sign: N1JTB
Richard F Christian
Milldale CT 06467

FCC Amateur Radio Licenses in Monroe

Call Sign: WA1EAJ
Thomas C Bristovish
202 Barn Hill Road
Monroe CT 064682088

Call Sign: N1ISJ
Domenico D Zito Jr
381 Barn Hill Road
Monroe CT 064682000

Call Sign: KA1KT
William B Spencer
30 Beech Tree Lane
Monroe CT 06468

Call Sign: KB1CW
John R Doherty
23 Behrens Ter
Monroe CT 06468

Call Sign: KN1X
Thomas J Scanzillo
31 Bellevale St
Monroe CT 06468

Call Sign: N1YND
Clay A Huckins
75 Blake Rd
Monroe CT 06468

Call Sign: WA1PQN
Edward L Davidson
42 Blue Hills Rd
Monroe CT 06468

Call Sign: N1APO
David M Silverstone
32 Blueberry Hill Rd
Monroe CT 06468

Call Sign: KB1FBW
Louis R Kuti
9 Boulder Ridge Rd
Monroe CT 06468

Call Sign: KB1ODB
Erik Albrecht
15 Canterbury Lane
Monroe CT 06468

Call Sign: N1YNE
Jason W Malia
135 Church St
Monroe CT 06468

Call Sign: KB1GXQ
Michele L Pearson
171 Cross Hill Rd
Monroe CT 06468

Call Sign: KB1GWY
Scott R Pearson
171 Cross Hill Road
Monroe CT 064682316

Call Sign: KW1S
Scott R Pearson
171 Cross Hill Road
Monroe CT 064682316

Call Sign: KB1CIU
Kathryn Whitman
442 Cutlers Farm Rd
Monroe CT 064682116

Call Sign: KA1ATI
David Quong
20 East Dale Drive
Monroe CT 06468

Call Sign: KB1RLK
Cathy S Kohut
20 Easton Rd
Monroe CT 06468

Call Sign: KB1RLL
Christine A Clark
20 Easton Rd
Monroe CT 06468

Call Sign: KB1VFC
Kevin M Schnaitmann
130 Far Horizon Dr
Monroe CT 06468

Call Sign: KB2TXG
Mark R Cohen
10 Founders Way
Monroe CT 06468

Call Sign: KA1SUT
Donna M Mc Gough
22 Georges Ln
Monroe CT 06468

Call Sign: KU1G
John D Niski
109 Greenwood Ln
Monroe CT 06468

Call Sign: K1UQQ
David H Ambrose
265 Hammertown Rd
Monroe CT 064681308

Call Sign: WA1KRX
Douglas D Griffin
51 Hannah Ln
Monroe CT 06468

Call Sign: WB0GQS
William F Farren Iii
15 Hillside Ln
Monroe CT 06468

Call Sign: W1JFN
John F Nintzel
21 Hollow Tree Lane
Monroe CT 06468

Call Sign: KB1UHQ
Mark J Hughes
96 Hurd Ave
Monroe CT 06468

Call Sign: W1BDR
Mark J Hughes
96 Hurd Ave
Monroe CT 06468

Call Sign: W1NQY
Wilson J Moshier
51 Karen Dr
Monroe CT 06468

Call Sign: N1YNW
James C Boulton
20 Knorr Rd
Monroe CT 06468

Call Sign: N1YNF
Rich A Crawford
97 Lantern
Monroe CT 06468

Call Sign: KD1AH
Michael S Doery
36 Laurel Dr
Monroe CT 06468

Call Sign: K1BHY
Roger P Tavella
444 Moose Hill Rd
Monroe CT 06468

Call Sign: K1ZBD
Samuel C Lapidge
19 Moss Rd
Monroe CT 06468

Call Sign: K1BQ
Robert L Griffith
35 Mountainside Dr
Monroe CT 06468

Call Sign: WA1AAL
Joseph Oltra
140 Old Zoar Rd
Monroe CT 06468

Call Sign: KA1FVL
Colin G Andrews
243 Old Zoar Rd
Monroe CT 06468

Call Sign: WA1APP
David L Sporre
124 Old Zoar Rd A
Monroe CT 064681433

Call Sign: KB1STJ
Leon A Smith
131 Old Zoar Road
Monroe CT 06468

Call Sign: KA1UJV
Rachel A Fuchs
35 Pastors Walk
Monroe CT 06468

Call Sign: N1GIF
Robert W Fuchs
35 Pastors Walk
Monroe CT 06468

Call Sign: N1GKN
Russell R Booth Jr
331 Purdy Hill Rd
Monroe CT 06468

Call Sign: KB1OQE
Paul J Fernandes
46 Richmond Dr
Monroe CT 06468

Call Sign: W1QB
David T Richards
9 Round Hill Dr
Monroe CT 06468

Call Sign: WR3I
David T Richards
9 Round Hill Dr
Monroe CT 06468

Call Sign: K1JNH
Edward P Woodford
10 Saxony Dr
Monroe CT 06468

Call Sign: KA1GXM
Kevin S Barney
176 Stanley Rd
Monroe CT 06468

Call Sign: N1YNV
Robin F Wallace
62 Swendsen Dr
Monroe CT 06468

Call Sign: N1YNU
Eric E Haggstrom
42 Turkey Roost Rd
Monroe CT 06468

Call Sign: KB1IWX
Richard R Duckworth
52 Valley View Rd
Monroe CT 06468

Call Sign: KB1IWY
Brian R Duckworth
52 Valley View Rd.
Monroe CT 06468

Call Sign: N1JPE
John N Tuccio Sr
19 Weather Vane Hill
Monroe CT 06468

Call Sign: W1BHZ
Thomas R Carter
19 Webb Cir
Monroe CT 06468

Call Sign: WA1ZOA
Mary Ellen Pardee
24 Webb Cir
Monroe CT 06468

Call Sign: WA1YQH
William D Todd
358 Wheeler Rd
Monroe CT 064681900

Call Sign: N1MRD
James E Fogle
20 Williams Rd
Monroe CT 06468

Call Sign: KB1PLQ
Mark Morton
Monroe CT 06468

Call Sign: W1MEM

Mark Morton
Monroe CT 06468

Call Sign: AB1KH
David N Zembroski
Monroe CT 06468

**FCC Amateur Radio
Licenses in Moodus**

Call Sign: KB1SX
Thomas O Hagerth
9 Barberry Lane
Moodus CT 06469

Call Sign: KB4EM
Michael D Cornell
128 Cherry Swamp Road
Moodus CT 06469

Call Sign: K1PI
Michael D Cornell
128 Cherry Swamp Road
Moodus CT 06469

Call Sign: KA1FZG
Lora A Castronova
420 East Haddam-Moodus
Rd
Moodus CT 06469

Call Sign: W1GJK
Gregory J Kwasowski
74 Mott Ln
Moodus CT 06469

Call Sign: N1AFK
George H Perham
Po Box 646
Moodus CT 064690646

Call Sign: KD1F
Emil J Tillona
5 Scoville Landing
Moodus CT 06469

Call Sign: N1PXK
Stuart M Coleman Jr
140 Sillimanville Rd
Moodus CT 064691151

Call Sign: WA1CUZ
Neal Olderman
6 Southwinds Rd
Moodus CT 06469

Call Sign: KB1DGL
George H Perham
Moodus CT 064690646

Call Sign: N1QKW
Robert J Neudecker
Moodus CT 06469

Call Sign: N1QNF
Richard A Collis
Moodus CT 06469

Call Sign: W4RPR
Raymond P Richard
Moodus CT 06469

FCC Amateur Radio Licenses in Moosup

Call Sign: KB1JDY
George E Marczak
152 Lake St
Moosup CT 06354

Call Sign: KB1MDF
Joseph E Marczak
152 Lake St
Moosup CT 06354

Call Sign: KB1QCZ
Cindy M Marczak
152 Lake St
Moosup CT 06354

Call Sign: N1TGD
James A Bradbury
17 Linnell St
Moosup CT 06354

Call Sign: KB1IQY
Nimet Kulla
25 Linnell St
Moosup CT 06354

Call Sign: K1UOP
Robert A Niles
18 Mary Ave
Moosup CT 06354

Call Sign: N1NNV
Mert J Tenczar Jr
235 New Rd
Moosup CT 06354

Call Sign: K1BZK
Omer M Potvin
10 S Potvin Ave
Moosup CT 06354

Call Sign: N2TWB
James A Wyatt
39 Salisbury Ave
Moosup CT 06354

Call Sign: KB1FMM
Terry A Pipitone
9 Snake Meadow Rd
Moosup CT 06354

Call Sign: N1FEG
Henry B Murdoch Jr
37 Squaw Rock Rd
Moosup CT 06354

Call Sign: N1FEI
Ethel M Murdoch
37 Squaw Rock Rd
Moosup CT 06354

Call Sign: WA1GWM
Mark J Doyle
141 Sterling Hill Rd
Moosup CT 06354

FCC Amateur Radio Licenses in Morris

Call Sign: KB1UQC
Michael P Lefebure
25 Curtiss Hill Rd
Morris CT 06763

Call Sign: KB1HGW
Allen R Dwyer Iii
44 E Morris Ln
Morris CT 06763

Call Sign: N1FZX
Nathaniel Stein
102 Kenyon Rd
Morris CT 067631698

Call Sign: N1KAP
Richard Skilton
4 South St
Morris CT 06763

Call Sign: KA1VFI
Walter A Okoski
178 South St
Morris CT 06763

Call Sign: KA1VGB
Jennifer A Okoski
178 South St
Morris CT 06763

Call Sign: KA1DC
David A Silver
Morris CT 06763

Call Sign: KB1HCY
Tyler J Conlon
Morris CT 06763

Call Sign: W1WHL
Gordon W Shove
40 Amos St
Mount Carmel CT 06518

Call Sign: N1WXD
Richard D Grelle
25 Sunnyside Ave
Mount Carmel CT
065182526

FCC Amateur Radio
Licenses in Mystic

Call Sign: W1RFK
Milton R Eccleston
20 Academy Lane Apt 232
Mystic CT 06355

Call Sign: W1AXD
Clarence B Donath Jr
12 Alden St
Mystic CT 063552704

Call Sign: N2FYA
John J Valente
69 Algonquin Dr
Mystic CT 06355

Call Sign: WB3LID
Ronald W Minarik
375 Allyn St Unit 26
Mystic CT 06355

Call Sign: AE1I
Kurt F Hafner Jr
181 Ann Ave
Mystic CT 06355

Call Sign: KA1END
Donald J Pettini

14 Avery St
Mystic CT 06378

Call Sign: KA1ATP
Raymond E Mandry
182 Bel Aire Dr
Mystic CT 06355

Call Sign: KB1RQQ
Marcus W Aylor
35 Bern Ct
Mystic CT 06355

Call Sign: N1RJC
Thomas E Mc Carthy
Box 649
Mystic CT 06355

Call Sign: WF1C
John J Drew
51 Canterbury Rd
Mystic CT 06355

Call Sign: WA1VKK
Harold R Stevens
46 Church St
Mystic CT 06355

Call Sign: KA1KOJ
Kevin J Gilot
56 Cindy Ln
Mystic CT 063551404

Call Sign: NZ1I
Kevin J Gilot
56 Cindy Ln
Mystic CT 063551404

Call Sign: W1NZI
Sylvester J Haefner
175 Clift St
Mystic CT 06355

Call Sign: WA1YWM
Frank H Murphy

24 Clipper Dr
Mystic CT 063551921

Call Sign: KA1BLC
Raymond W Rancourt
173 Col Ledyard Hwy
Mystic CT 06355

Call Sign: KB1DOW
Archie J Cochrane
256 Colonel Ledyard Hwy
Mystic CT 06355

Call Sign: KC1YL
Susanne B Munyan
45 Crest Dr
Mystic CT 06355

Call Sign: N1MHV
Robert B Trester
83 Deerfield Ridge Dr
Mystic CT 06355

Call Sign: NR1Y
Robert P Rowe
15 E Forest Rd
Mystic CT 063553220

Call Sign: N1FEO
Gordon D Wallace
118 Edgecomb St
Mystic CT 06355

Call Sign: WA1WWG
Thomas R Tyler
6 Elm St
Mystic CT 06355

Call Sign: W1HDZ
James F Falcone
70 Fair Acres Cir
Mystic CT 06355

Call Sign: N9CBP
Kenny S Floering

72 Fair Acres Park Route 27
Mystic CT 06355

Call Sign: N3KMM
David B Lee
88 Farmstead Avenue
Mystic CT 06355

Call Sign: KA1WMS
Hugh F Holmes
1265 Flanders Rd
Mystic CT 06355

Call Sign: KB1MAJ
Robert L Brasher
326 Flanders Road
Mystic CT 06355

Call Sign: N1TSX
William W Green
98 Godfrey Rd
Mystic CT 06355

Call Sign: KB1QFS
James A Crawford
191 Godfrey Rd
Mystic CT 06355

Call Sign: KB1QID
James I Crawford
191 Godfrey Road
Mystic CT 06355

Call Sign: KL7HMD
Rufus M Clark
19 Godfrey St
Mystic CT 06355

Call Sign: KA1UKU
Dominick Amedio Jr
60 Harvard Ln
Mystic CT 06355

Call Sign: KB1KGN

Southeastern Connecticut
Contest Club
46 Hatch St
Mystic CT 06355

Call Sign: NW1E
Southeastern Connecticut
Contest Club
46 Hatch St
Mystic CT 06355

Call Sign: N1ETW
Thomas H Dexter
11 Hewitt Rd
Mystic CT 06355

Call Sign: N1JBM
Richard K Mahar
457 Hewitt Rd C1
Mystic CT 06355

Call Sign: KB1RQK
Alexander P Kelleher
169 High Meadow Ln
Mystic CT 06355

Call Sign: KB1IRP
Virginia D Bitting
261 High St
Mystic CT 06355

Call Sign: N1TVI
David C Cerreto
66 Hillside Dr
Mystic CT 06355

Call Sign: KB1TLO
Walter B Lincoln Jr
14 Holmes St
Mystic CT 06355

Call Sign: N1WBL
Walter B Lincoln Jr
14 Holmes St
Mystic CT 06355

Call Sign: N1OSP
Michael A Dennis
185 Indigo St
Mystic CT 06355

Call Sign: KB1RYL
Larry C Moxon
338 Indigo St
Mystic CT 06355

Call Sign: K1KRC
Larry C Moxon
338 Indigo St
Mystic CT 06355

Call Sign: KB1TBG
Saram
338 Indigo St
Mystic CT 06355

Call Sign: KB1TNP
Ross M Moxon
338 Indigo St
Mystic CT 06355

Call Sign: N1MGY
Saram
338 Indigo St
Mystic CT 06355

Call Sign: KB1TMO
Two Meter Operators
338 Indigo Street
Mystic CT 063551326

Call Sign: N1EKM
Arthur W Voldstad
186 Jerry Browne Road
Apt 3405
Mystic CT 063554011

Call Sign: W4KM
Dexter Anderson

186 Jerry Browne Road
Unit 3311
Mystic CT 063554011

Call Sign: KB3FAL
William G Repsher
30 Judson Ave
Mystic CT 06355

Call Sign: W1SOD
George H Hervey
492 Judson Ave
Mystic CT 063552112

Call Sign: N1MRP
Joseph S Marko
119 Lambtown Rd
Mystic CT 06355

Call Sign: KB2MNK
Howard C Dunn Iii
270 Lambtown Rd
Mystic CT 06355

Call Sign: KB1QWA
Daniel P Nelson
41 Lamphere Rd
Mystic CT 06355

Call Sign: KA1ANX
Paul M Mileski
339 Lantern Hill Rd
Mystic CT 063559801

Call Sign: KB1CEN
William B Watson
22 Mistuxet Ave
Mystic CT 06355

Call Sign: N1UQQ
Daniel G O Connor
18 Mystic Hill Rd
Mystic CT 06355

Call Sign: WA1SEA

Theodore T Tylaska
138 N Stonington Rd
Mystic CT 06355

Call Sign: N1XTA
Joseph W St Martin
50 New London Rd
Mystic CT 06355

Call Sign: W1NEC
Frank H Roberts
63 New London Rd
Mystic CT 06355

Call Sign: WA1GTX
Luther Palmer
473 New London Rd
Mystic CT 06355

Call Sign: N1IDX
Hugh J Holmes
18 Noank Ledyard Rd
Mystic CT 06355

Call Sign: KB1MAH
Michele A Kelly
78 Noank Ledyard Rd
Mystic CT 06355

Call Sign: AH6GZ
Timothy J Sprowls
402 Noank Rd
Mystic CT 06355

Call Sign: N1VWY
Mark J Wainston
102 Old North Rd
Mystic CT 063553288

Call Sign: KB1MVA
Stephen B Chisholm
47 Olso St
Mystic CT 06355

Call Sign: KB1MVB

Jean M Petryshyn
47 Oslo St
Mystic CT 06355

Call Sign: K1EV
William A Birtcher
66 Oxford Ct
Mystic CT 06355

Call Sign: N1LAP
David E Baumgarte
51 Patricks Court
Mystic CT 06355

Call Sign: KB1JAU
Thomas M Crawford
123 Payer Ln
Mystic CT 06355

Call Sign: WA1YDK
Donovan J Dyer
63 Quakertown Rd
Mystic CT 06355

Call Sign: WA1YVJ
Ruth F Dyer
63 Quakertown Rd
Mystic CT 06355

Call Sign: KA1WDT
John M Lee
14 Quarry Rd
Mystic CT 06355

Call Sign: KB1IYH
Frederick R Haberlandt
10 Rathbun Place
Mystic CT 06355

Call Sign: N1FH
Frederick R Haberlandt
10 Rathbun Place
Mystic CT 06355

Call Sign: AB1GZ

Kennon H Jones
12 Rhonda Dr
Mystic CT 06355

Call Sign: KD1GF
Cesare R Bellandese
107 Ridgewood Dr
Mystic CT 06355

Call Sign: WA8TT
David H Watt
1291 River Rd
Mystic CT 06355

Call Sign: W1TSJ
Richard E Metayer
30 Route 27
Mystic CT 06355

Call Sign: KC2BUA
Gary S Schmid
55 Rte 27
Mystic CT 06355

Call Sign: WA8GCR
Gary Schmid
55 Rte 27
Mystic CT 06355

Call Sign: N1CZU
Ward M Smith
7 Schooner Dr
Mystic CT 06355

Call Sign: W1JDL
Richard O Cheney
14 Skiff Ln Masons Is
Mystic CT 06355

Call Sign: W1CKR
West View Hills Arc
14 Steamboat Wharf Apt 10
Mystic CT 06355

Call Sign: KB1MTN

James J Loughlin Jr
35 West Mystic Ave
Mystic CT 06355

Call Sign: KE1IU
Mark C Noe
7 Whitehall Lane
Mystic CT 063551640

Call Sign: W1DQI
Ernest T Howell Jr
44 Wilcox Rd
Mystic CT 06355

Call Sign: NG1Y
Franklin L Lord Jr
59b Williams Ave
Mystic CT 06355

Call Sign: KA1PAX
Howard Katz
Mystic CT 06355

Call Sign: N1RJD
Daniel D Hatheway
Mystic CT 06355

FCC Amateur Radio Licenses in Naugattuck

Call Sign: KB1KRA
Lisa J Young
41 Morning Mist Rd
Naugattuck CT 06770

Call Sign: KB1THK
Caitlin D May
471 A Spring St
Naugatuck CT 06770

Call Sign: W1BBC
Frederick A Pritchard
75 Allerton Rd
Naugattuck CT 06770

Call Sign: K1JCS
William J Mancini
78 Allerton Rd
Naugatuck CT 06770

Call Sign: WB1CMH
Benedict J Danielczuk
151 Andrew Ave Apt 101a
Naugatuck CT 06770

Call Sign: KB1OHK
Joseph J Mclaine
17 B Walnut St
Naugatuck CT 06770

Call Sign: KB1MCP
Rudy D Fusco
701 Beacon Valley Rd Unit 3
Naugatuck CT 06770

Call Sign: N1JIX
Joseph M Verrilli
20 Bluebird Dr
Naugatuck CT 06607

Call Sign: KB1CRM
Margaret L Marra
59 Bluebird Dr
Naugatuck CT 06770

Call Sign: N0XRV
John M Burdis
7 Bradbury Street
Naugatuck CT 06770

Call Sign: KA1VIV
Geoffrey M Drawbridge
21 Briarwood Cir
Naugatuck CT 06770

Call Sign: WA1SSB
Joseph J Kotomski Jr
39 Cadbury Pl
Naugatuck CT 067703459

Call Sign: N1WCL
David P Blasko
5 Celentano Dr
Naugatuck CT 06770

Call Sign: N1OWT
Christian V Weatherford
21 Celentano Dr
Naugatuck CT 06770

Call Sign: KB1GBL
Colin S Radke
147 City Hill
Naugatuck CT 06770

Call Sign: WB1ALB
John L Hassenfeldt Sr
479 City Hill St
Naugatuck CT 06770

Call Sign: N1GUP
Floyd Doody
108 Clark Rd Box 99
Naugatuck CT 06770

Call Sign: KB1NUA
Stanley X Fofano
50-5 Coach Circle
Naugatuck CT 06770

Call Sign: KB1NWE
Stanley X Fofano
50-5 Coach Circle
Naugatuck CT 06770

Call Sign: N1RHL
James C Bradshaw
103 Craig Cir
Naugatuck CT 06770

Call Sign: N1ISL
Michael A Weber
258 Crestwood Dr
Naugatuck CT 06770

Call Sign: KB1HLK
Albert E Raymond
100a Donna Lane
Naugatuck CT 06770

Call Sign: WB1FZG
John R Lane
48 Donovan Rd
Naugatuck CT 06770

Call Sign: N1XTN
William E White Sr
157 E Waterbury Rd
Naugatuck CT 06770

Call Sign: KA1SUH
Joan T Chipokas
89 Field St
Naugatuck CT 06770

Call Sign: N1EZC
Jeffrey P Chipokas
89 Field St
Naugatuck CT 06770

Call Sign: NI1J
Jeffrey P Chipokas
89 Field St
Naugatuck CT 06770

Call Sign: K1ZJ
Jeffrey P Chipokas
89 Field St
Naugatuck CT 06770

Call Sign: KA1ZFF
William M Mc Kinney
835 Field St
Naugatuck CT 06770

Call Sign: KB1RGP
John V Talbot
28 Good Year Ave
Naugatuck CT 06770

Call Sign: N2IKI
Jonathan C Goodell
124b Greenwood St
Naugatuck CT 06770

Call Sign: KB1ASB
Harold R Doody
94 Hackett St
Naugatuck CT 06770

Call Sign: N2XZK
Anthony R Looby
155 High Ridge Road
Naugatuck CT 06720

Call Sign: KB1SFK
Joseph A Devine
92 Highland Ave Apt 2
Naugatuck CT 06770

Call Sign: K1XS
Kenneth A Hanks
19 Hillcrest Avenue
Naugatuck CT 06770

Call Sign: KA1WLT
David J Tomlinson
39 Horton Hill Rd 10i
Naugatuck CT 06770

Call Sign: KA1KSS
Fred T Desantis
34 Idleview Rd
Naugatuck CT 06770

Call Sign: N1ED
Edward J Gamache
242 Jones Rd
Naugatuck CT 06770

Call Sign: AA1GL
Robert J Mitchinson
33 Joseph Rd
Naugatuck CT 06770

Call Sign: KA1BSA
William J Silkowski
6 Kent St
Naugatuck CT 067703515

Call Sign: KA1ZGG
Judith R Silkowski
6 Kent St
Naugatuck CT 06770

Call Sign: KA1UFO
Reed Patterson
13 Lewis Cir
Naugatuck CT 06770

Call Sign: KB1JZN
Henry K Bacon
45 Lincoln Street
Naugatuck CT 06770

Call Sign: K1ROJ
Francis W Cassidy
36 Longview Ter
Naugatuck CT 067703445

Call Sign: KB1JDH
Jorge A Reyes Ii
111 Mallane Ln 4a
Naugatuck CT 06770

Call Sign: N1YXX
Vincent R Sosnowski
40 Manners Ave
Naugatuck CT 06770

Call Sign: KA1TTA
Glenn L Poirier
143 Manners Ave
Naugatuck CT 06770

Call Sign: KA1RWI
Donnell W Peil
18 May St
Naugatuck CT 06770

Call Sign: W1BGT
Murton W Lyon Sr
76 Mill St
Naugatuck CT 06770

Call Sign: KB1GBK
Lee R Radke
149 Millville Ave
Naugatuck CT 06770

Call Sign: N1OCJ
Patrick T Franzis
235 Millville Ave
Naugatuck CT 06770

Call Sign: WA1CGB
Daniel C Walsh Jr
204 Morning Dove Rd
Naugatuck CT 06770

Call Sign: KA1OPD
Michael J Young Sr
41 Morning Mist Rd
Naugatuck CT 06770

Call Sign: KB1VTJ
Richard S Gawronski
49 Mulberry St
Naugatuck CT 06770

Call Sign: NO1N
Paul P Zynosky
68 Mulberry St
Naugatuck CT 06770

Call Sign: W4PPZ
Paul P Zynosky
68 Mulberry St
Naugatuck CT 06770

Call Sign: W1IAN
David L Crawford
102 Mulberry St
Naugatuck CT 06770

Call Sign: N1WKW
Theresa M Fielder
193 Mulberry Street
Naugatuck CT 06770

Call Sign: WF0E
Robert A Fielder Jr
193 Mulberry Street
Naugatuck CT 06770

Call Sign: KB1WJX
Rocco W Magnanimo
1 New St
Naugatuck CT 06770

Call Sign: WA1ZSP
Kevin M Delgobbo
69 North Hoadley St.
Naugatuck CT 06770

Call Sign: KB1ITA
American Red Cross
Naugatuck Chapter
22 Park Pl
Naugatuck CT 067704102

Call Sign: KB1QCM
Samuel E Manickaraj
32 Pembrook Road
Naugatuck CT 067703354

Call Sign: KB1UCV
Michael R Abdullah
67 Quinn St
Naugatuck CT 06770

Call Sign: KB1QXE
Robert J Fritz
438 Quinn St
Naugatuck CT 06770

Call Sign: AB1KZ
Robert J Fritz
438 Quinn St

Naugatuck CT 06770

Call Sign: KN2DC
Robert J Fritz
438 Quinn St
Naugatuck CT 06770

Call Sign: W3LK
Lonnie J Kinley
438 Quinn Street
Naugatuck CT 06770

Call Sign: KB1TGS
David C Robinson Jr
10 Ridge Rd
Naugatuck CT 06770

Call Sign: KB1FRN
Brian P Simons
14 Rockwell Ave
Naugatuck CT 067702708

Call Sign: KB1AMD
Ryan F Morrissey
100 Round Hill Rd
Naugatuck CT 06770

Call Sign: WA1NQP
Richard F Morrissey
100 Round Hill Rd
Naugatuck CT 06770

Call Sign: N1IVL
Joseph M Sabia
1144 Rubber Ave
Naugatuck CT 06770

Call Sign: N1LQR
Joseph S Treczker Jr
27 Simisberry Rd
Naugatuck CT 06770

Call Sign: N1XCC
Karen A Bragg
39 Spencer St

Naugatuck CT 06770

Call Sign: N1XCD
Kurt L Bragg
39 Spencer St
Naugatuck CT 06770

Call Sign: N1JSW
Jason W Strano
415 Spring St
Naugatuck CT 06770

Call Sign: KB1DTD
Daniel J May
471a Spring St
Naugatuck CT 06770

Call Sign: NQ1X
Daniel J May
471a Spring St
Naugatuck CT 06770

Call Sign: N3YOK
JESSICA A Fricke
501d Spring Street
Naugatuck CT 06770

Call Sign: K1TG
Roger W Kuchera
270 Tawny Thrush Rd
Naugatuck CT 067704814

Call Sign: KA1IRO
Jean F Braley
119 Thunderbird Dr
Naugatuck CT 06770

Call Sign: WA1AES
Ernest J Malafronte Jr
526 Union City Rd
Naugatuck CT 06770

Call Sign: N1SZQ
Robert J Platzer
39 W Hill Ter

Naugatuck CT 067702310

Call Sign: WA2JYC
Mike D Mingle
119 Walnut St
Naugatuck CT 06770

Call Sign: KB1R
Harry L Alsdorf Jr
280 Wedgewood Dr
Naugatuck CT 06770

Call Sign: KB1FJX
Douglas Cummings
60 Whitney Place
Naugatuck CT 06770

Call Sign: KA1SYG
Peter J Fegley
Naugatuck CT 06770

Call Sign: W1JN
Joseph R Nehm
Naugatuck CT 06770

Call Sign: KB1EPU
Kenneth H Farrington
Naugatuck CT 06770

Call Sign: KB1TJE
Mark J Onofrio Sr
Naugatuck CT 06770

Call Sign: KB1WLW
Northrop Grumman
Amateur Radio Club
Naugatuck CT 06770

**FCC Amateur Radio
Licenses in New Britain**

Call Sign: KA1FOJ
John F De Angelis
89 Abbe St
New Britain CT 06051

Call Sign: WA1STO
Rosalie A White
34 Adele Rd
New Britain CT 06053

Call Sign: KB1JJL
David I Joslyn
110 Alexander Rd
New Britain CT 06053

Call Sign: N1DIJ
David I Joslyn
110 Alexander Rd
New Britain CT 06053

Call Sign: N1NTQ
Steven M Ege
341 Alexander Rd
New Britain CT 06053

Call Sign: KB1FTT
Nelson B Moncion
342 Arch St Apt 2n
New Britain CT 06051

Call Sign: W1NBM
Nelson B Moncion
342 Arch St Apt 2n
New Britain CT 06051

Call Sign: KD1CV
Robert B Forbes
10 Ash St
New Britain CT 06051

Call Sign: N1PFD
Augustine Z Santana
116 Austin St
New Britain CT 06051

Call Sign: WA2INB
William I Dunkerley Jr
275 Batterson Dr
New Britain CT 06053

Call Sign: KB1MNB
Reginald D Cone
48 Beechwood Dr
New Britain CT 06053

Call Sign: KA1QVL
Ann B Knope
96 Beechwood Dr
New Britain CT 06053

Call Sign: KC1IW
William J Knope
96 Beechwood Dr
New Britain CT 06053

Call Sign: N1MSR
Scott L Reed
174 Belmont St
New Britain CT 06053

Call Sign: KB1DCN
Robert E Dombrowik
179 Belridge Rd
New Britain CT 060531983

Call Sign: W1QJL
Eugene S Dombrowik
179 Belridge Rd
New Britain CT 06053

Call Sign: KB1UUC
Edward D Glaser
52 Benson St
New Britain CT 06051

Call Sign: KB1QQI
Paul J Labieniec
56 Biruta St Apt 1
New Britian CT 06053

Call Sign: W1DBS
John P Savonis
410 Blake Rd
New Britain CT 06053

Call Sign: KA1ZGJ
Orrin W Riggott Jr
42 Blodgett Roy Dr
New Britain CT 06053

Call Sign: AB1EL
Orrin W Riggott Jr
42 Blodgett Roy Dr
New Britain CT 06053

Call Sign: W1LDA
Andrew W Madrak
113 Blodgett Roy Dr
New Britain CT 06053

Call Sign: KB1DCQ
Lorraine R Muzzulin
232 Bond St
New Britain CT 06053

Call Sign: KA1KAD
Gennard Cistulli
250 Booth St
New Britain CT 06053

Call Sign: N1YYN
John M Villeux
230c Brittany Farms Rd
New Britain CT 06053

Call Sign: N1CRA
Christopher D O Hara
395 Brittany Farms Rd 132
New Britain CT 06053

Call Sign: K1LVZ
George F Clinton Jr
82 Brittany Farms Rd Apt
125
New Britain CT 060531243

Call Sign: KB1WYE
David M Victor

44 Brittany Farms Rd Apt
213
New Britain CT 06053

Call Sign: N1GEA
Franklin A Darius Jr
82 Brittany Farms Rd J343
New Britain CT 06053

Call Sign: KA1LHJ
John H Orkney
23 Buena Vista Ave
New Britain CT 06051

Call Sign: K1UDW
Gary J Robinson
503 Burritt St
New Britain CT 06053

Call Sign: N1TJZ
Michael T Cummiskey
92 Carlton St
New Britain CT 06053

Call Sign: KB1JTH
Marcial R Torres
25 Chapman St
New Britain CT 06051

Call Sign: N1GTV
Gray R Capo
135 Chestnut St
New Britain CT 06050

Call Sign: N1HEI
David J Czlapinski
222 Cianci Rd
New Britain CT 06053

Call Sign: KB1MFT
Scott A Calkins
241 Clark St
New Britain CT 06051

Call Sign: KB1ONN

Scott A Calkins
241 Clark St
New Britain CT 06051

Call Sign: N1DOX
Scott A Calkins
241 Clark St
New Britain CT 06051

Call Sign: N1SCR
Scott A Calkins
241 Clark St
New Britain CT 06051

Call Sign: N1GTT
Donald J Piascik Jr
23 Colt St
New Britain CT 06052

Call Sign: KB1LQG
Christopher W Butler
60 Commonwealth Ave
New Britain CT 060532914

Call Sign: W1VKW
Aime H Simoneau
35 Connecticut Ave
New Britain CT 06051

Call Sign: KB1NSR
Devon L Neal
123 Connecticut Ave
New Britain CT 06051

Call Sign: KA1ISP
Robert E Schnabel
30 Convoy Dr
New Britain CT 06051

Call Sign: KB1PIU
Richard D Ciervo
272 Corbin Ave
New Britain CT 06052

Call Sign: K1PFD

Lawrence M Campagnano
543 Corbin Ave
New Britain CT 06052

Call Sign: AA1NU
Rudolf W Bee
800 Corbin Ave
New Britain CT 06052

Call Sign: N1SBK
Robert J Wallace
1318 Corbin Ave
New Britain CT 06053

Call Sign: AA1HH
Carl R Walczewski
2161 Corbin Ave
New Britain CT 06053

Call Sign: KA1EPF
Geoffrey L Gidman
155 Country Club Rd
New Britain CT 06053

Call Sign: N1URV
Robert C Paonessa
15 Derby St
New Britain CT 06053

Call Sign: N1YPA
Rene L Reed
89 Dix Ave
New Britain CT 06051

Call Sign: N1GHI
Joseph S Manke
27 Dwight St
New Britain CT 06051

Call Sign: N2FDD
Wayne A Rappaport
744 East St
New Britain CT 06051

Call Sign: N1RYE

Christopher M Abucewicz
115 Eastwick Rd
New Britain CT 06053

Call Sign: WA1QQS
Philip T O Rilley
110 Elam
New Britain CT 06053

Call Sign: KB1HUW
Cristobal Maldonado
27 Elam Street Apt 2
New Britain CT 06053

Call Sign: N1QJC
Daniel Santiago
524 Ellis St
New Britain CT 06051

Call Sign: N1VKM
James L Hall
540 Ellis St
New Britain CT 06051

Call Sign: KB1CXL
Sixto Perez Jr
33 Euston St
New Britain CT 06053

Call Sign: KB1ECW
Geralou C Jamandre
111 F Brittany Farms Rd
New Britain CT 06053

Call Sign: KE1DZ
Tomasz Wisniewski
838 Farmington Ave
New Britain CT 06053

Call Sign: KA1KPI
Brandyce O Kenney
418 Farmington Ave Apt
C10
New Britain CT 06053

Call Sign: N1NAK
Jeffrey A Dutton
950 Farmington Avenue
Apt B22
New Britain CT 06053

Call Sign: N1JSA
Harry Vazquez
15 Fourth St
New Britain CT 06051

Call Sign: KB1EWM
Quentin D Hinton Iii
128 Fulton St
New Britain CT 06051

Call Sign: KA1ZIN
Alejandro Vargas
46 Gilbert St
New Britain CT 06052

Call Sign: N1LMN
Edward G Mazuronis Iii
505 Glen St
New Britain CT 06051

Call Sign: KB1GJJ
Edward N Landry Sr
35 Glen St Apt 4
New Britain CT 06051

Call Sign: KB1NYW
David T Axelby
24 Governor St
New Britain CT 06053

Call Sign: KA1KNZ
Linda A Ahlstrand
202 Hart
New Britain CT 06052

Call Sign: KB1GJF
Gregory J Kwasowski
137 Heather Ln
New Britain CT 060531960

Call Sign: KB1RUO
Barbara D Carlson
142 Henry St
New Britain CT 06051

Call Sign: N1UBA
Andy P Lundell
370 High St Apt G01
New Britain CT 06053

Call Sign: KB1PKN
Leona G Adams
323 Hillhurst Ave
New Britain CT 06053

Call Sign: W1LGA
Leona G Adams
323 Hillhurst Ave
New Britain CT 06053

Call Sign: N1CSM
Henry L Schuetze
86 Horseplain Rd
New Britain CT 06053

Call Sign: N1OIW
Gilman J Thereault
41 Jackson St
New Britain CT 06053

Call Sign: K1SZZ
Kristen L Anderson
57 Jefferson St #2
New Britian CT 06051

Call Sign: KC2CNA
Shawn M Anderson
57 Jefferson St 2
New Britian CT 06051

Call Sign: KB1RJM
Kristen L Anderson
57 Jefferson St 2
New Britian CT 06051

Call Sign: N1YOT
Erik R Bee
107 Joy Lane
New Britain CT 060531708

Call Sign: KA1KLE
Vincent Saraceno
137 Joy Ln
New Britain CT 06053

Call Sign: N1PJQ
Harry D Robertson
117 Jubilee St
New Britain CT 06051

Call Sign: KA1JCN
Julian A Mugarza
22 Judd Ave
New Britain CT 06051

Call Sign: N1YAO
Eric B Doody
200 Kelsey St
New Britain CT 06051

Call Sign: KB1QQQ
Lucy J Snow
50 Kensington Ave
New Britian CT 06050

Call Sign: KB1MYH
Arnold P Schwartz
27 Kenwood Dr
New Britain CT 06052

Call Sign: W1LDQ
Robert M Downes
225 Kenwood Dr
New Britain CT 06052

Call Sign: W1WZE
Stanley E Chapman
44 Kilbourne Ave
New Britain CT 06053

Call Sign: N1YLO
Andrzej Fiertek
95 Kim Dr
New Britain CT 06053

Call Sign: W1RRS
Herbert Anderson
38 Kimball Dr
New Britain CT 06051

Call Sign: N1XJY
Jesse J Stanley Jr.
8 Kimball Dr.
New Britain CT 06051

Call Sign: KA1SIR
Joseph L Guerette
62 Lawlor St 3rd Fl
New Britain CT 06051

Call Sign: KA1WIQ
Stefan H Potrawiak
124 Lewis Rd
New Britain CT 06053

Call Sign: N1XTI
Peter F Colapinto
384 Lewis Rd
New Britain CT 060531460

Call Sign: N1YBB
Eric M Colapinto
384 Lewis Rd
New Britain CT 06053

Call Sign: KE6SEH
Andrew S Miller
428 Lewis Rd
New Britain CT 06053

Call Sign: N1JXW
Mark E Anderson
58 Lincoln St
New Britain CT 06052

Call Sign: KB1RTM
Anthony P Philpin
617 Lincoln St
New Britain CT 06052

Call Sign: KB1CQM
Mark Fraello
270 Linwood St
New Britain CT 06052

Call Sign: WA1GCV
Eugene S Palmucci
90 Lorraine St
New Britain CT 06051

Call Sign: KB1QQN
Peter A Cistulli
65 Lucyan St
New Britian CT 06053

Call Sign: WA1WLE
John R David
10 Madison St
New Britain CT 06052

Call Sign: WA1VRP
Richard J David
12 Madison St
New Britain CT 06052

Call Sign: KA1WWS
John J Edmiston
6 Mansfield Ave
New Britain CT 06051

Call Sign: N1JQS
Joseph B Witkin
95 Marlin Rd
New Britain CT 06053

Call Sign: N1JQV
Miriam E Witkin
95 Marlin Rd
New Britain CT 060532138

Call Sign: WB1USN
Joseph B Witkin
95 Marlin Rd
New Britain CT 060532138

Call Sign: W1AGP
Allen G Pitts
43 Mill St
New Britain CT 06051

Call Sign: KB1GUA
James M Ellett Jr
14 Peace Court
New Britain CT 06051

Call Sign: KA1UTJ
Grazyna Kozodziejczak
19 Marwood Dr
New Britain CT 06053

Call Sign: KA1ZCW
Stanislaw Zabaglo
87 Millard St
New Britain CT 06051

Call Sign: KB1OQ
Daniel W Keifer
138 Pennsylvania Ave
New Britain CT 06052

Call Sign: KB1KUE
Lenny Kimball
22 May St
New Britain CT 06052

Call Sign: KB1BDH
Joseph Liudzius
101 Millard St
New Britain CT 06051

Call Sign: KA1DYZ
Maureen A Thompson
84 Pentlow Ave
New Britain CT 06053

Call Sign: KB1KUF
Yvonne M Kimball
22 May St
New Britain CT 060521012

Call Sign: KA1TGX
Isidro Santana
64 N St Apt 9c
New Britain CT 06050

Call Sign: N1QLN
William A Sanders
37 Pierremount Ave
New Britain CT 06053

Call Sign: KB1VIA
Orlik M Forde
116 Mcclintock St
New Britain CT 06053

Call Sign: N1YOR
Anthony F Otulak
127 Neanda St
New Britain CT 060532224

Call Sign: KB1UEE
Michael F Sanders
37 Pierremount Ave
New Britain CT 06053

Call Sign: N1NKK
Daniel F Lewis
116 Mckinley Drive
New Britain CT 06053

Call Sign: KC2QEF
Lincy H Castillo Negron
250 Nort St Apt 3b
New Britain CT 06051

Call Sign: N1QLN
Michael F Sanders
37 Pierremount Ave
New Britain CT 06053

Call Sign: AB1QJ
Daniel F Lewis
116 Mckinley Drive
New Britain CT 06053

Call Sign: NP3KH
Jose A Castillo Gomez
250 North St Apt 3b
New Britain CT 06051

Call Sign: WA1VCA
Geremia Te
102 Queen St
New Britain CT 06053

Call Sign: WA1YJP
John P Serbin
153 Merigold Dr
New Britain CT 06053

Call Sign: KA1GFY
Roberto Cardarelli
182 Oakland Ave
New Britain CT 06053

Call Sign: KB1MQN
Robert E Heyl
124 Queen St
New Britain CT 06053

Call Sign: KB1EOA
Allen G Pitts
43 Mill St
New Britain CT 06051

Call Sign: KB1IGC
Andres Quintana
23 Patton Dr
New Britain CT 06053

Call Sign: KA1HQV
Anthony Cocola
30 Randolph Ct
New Britain CT 06053

Call Sign: KA1HSD
Vincenzo Di Mauro
30 Randolph Ct
New Britain CT 06053

Call Sign: WB1L
Vincenzo Di Mauro
30 Randolph Ct
New Britain CT 06053

Call Sign: N1XDU
Samuel Romero
155 Resevoir Rd
New Britain CT 06052

Call Sign: N0ETY
Dean J Maluski
25 Rocky Hill Ave
New Britain CT 060513203

Call Sign: N1ETY
Dean J Maluski
25 Rocky Hill Ave
New Britain CT 060513203

Call Sign: KA1WZZ
Edward J Lechowicz Jr
104 Rocky Hill Ave
New Britain CT 06051

Call Sign: KA1SER
Angela M Beebe
112 Rocky Hill Ave
New Britain CT 06051

Call Sign: KB1GEK
American Red Cross
Central Conn Chapter
45 Russell St
New Britain CT 060521312

Call Sign: KB1EPE
Randall L Vardanian
325 S Main St

New Britain CT 06051

Call Sign: KB1OMM
John T Masterson
56 S Mountain Drive
New Britain CT 06052

Call Sign: AA1ST
James W Williams
54 Sefton Dr
New Britain CT 060532549

Call Sign: W1GFE
Alvin C Diedricksen
40 Seneca St
New Britain CT 06053

Call Sign: N1KJA
Thomas B Condren
55 Seneca Street
New Britain CT 06053

Call Sign: AA1RZ
Anthony J Nesta
92 Sexton St
New Britain CT 06051

Call Sign: KB1EPA
Efrain Vazquez
853 Slater Rd
New Britain CT 06053

Call Sign: KB2GGX
Jose A Ramos Jr
1389 Slater Rd.
New Britain CT 06053

Call Sign: KB1FRC
Marietta A Marquez
853 Slater Road
New Britain CT 06053

Call Sign: KB1KUC
Phillip A Liggett
85 Spring St 305

New Britain CT 06051

Call Sign: KD1JT
Dennis H Collin
151 Stanley St
New Britain CT 06051

Call Sign: W1SEG
Arthur J Buttero
1904 Stanley St
New Britain CT 06053

Call Sign: KA1ZOY
Andrzej B Winnik
67 Stonegate Rd
New Britain CT 06053

Call Sign: N1QHP
John C Larkin
194 Stratford Rd
New Britain CT 06053

Call Sign: KB1ALN
Leonard W Dorsey
136 Texas Dr
New Britain CT 06052

Call Sign: KB1PKO
Ethan M Sadoian
144 Thorniley St
New Britain CT 06051

Call Sign: KB1PKP
Nathaniel P Sadoian
144 Thorniley St
New Britain CT 06051

Call Sign: KB1OUQ
Mark P Buckovitch
115 Torkom Dr
New Britain CT 06053

Call Sign: KB1KUD
Richard E Godek
24 Vance St

New Britain CT 06052

Call Sign: KB1IGB
David J Behnke
54 Victoria Road
New Britain CT 06052

Call Sign: KR1SIS
Jon A Aparo
42 Wallace St
New Britain CT 06051

Call Sign: N1NXB
Arkadiusz Tadla
313 Washington St
New Britain CT 06051

Call Sign: K1FM
Anthony A Dorbuck
67 West Main St Apt 506
New Britain CT 06051

Call Sign: KA1WTO
Deborah K Shepard
230 Whiting Street #26
New Britain CT 06051

Call Sign: KB1BXN
Luis G Orriola
111 Willow St
New Britain CT 06051

Call Sign: KA1SXQ
Anthony P Rugens
102 Winthrop St
New Britain CT 06052

Call Sign: K1HEJ
Lawrence H Buck
262 Winthrop St
New Britain CT 06052

**FCC Amateur Radio
Licenses in New Canaan**

Call Sign: WA1BRR
Romeo J Ventres
507 Brookside Rd
New Canaan CT 06840

Call Sign: KB1FTW
Bert Tanner
203 Brushy Ridge Rd
New Canaan CT 06840

Call Sign: KA1GGM
William W Shields
336 Cedar Ln
New Canaan CT 06840

Call Sign: KA1NVF
Dave A Neiss
200 Charter Oak Rd
New Canaan CT 06040

Call Sign: WA1PBE
John L Frothingham
32 Country Club Rd
New Canaan CT 06840

Call Sign: ΛE1H
Carleton W Todd
59 Fawn Ln
New Canaan CT 06840

Call Sign: W1FEJ
Hugh C Bell
163 Ferris Hill Road
New Canaan CT 06840

Call Sign: K1BN
Martin J St George
119 Field Crest Rd
New Canaan CT 06840

Call Sign: KB1TJP
David J Stoller
409 Frogtown Rd
New Canaan CT 06840

Call Sign: K1OAS
Edward B Olson
169 Gerdes Rd
New Canaan CT 068406731

Call Sign: KB1EOC
Erik B Olson
169 Gerdes Rd
New Canaan CT 06840

Call Sign: K1OAS
Erik B Olson
169 Gerdes Rd
New Canaan CT 06840

Call Sign: KB1TPT
Benjamin J Saunders
285 Hawks Hill Rd
New Canaan CT 06840

Call Sign: N8MJU
Robert A Meade
172 Heritage Hill Rd
New Canaan CT 06840

Call Sign: N1RRO
John F Donlon
15 Hidden Meadow Ln
New Canaan CT 06840

Call Sign: WA2UMU
John H Linnartz
286 Jelliff Mill Rd
New Canaan CT 06840

Call Sign: N1IVO
W Scott Cluett Jr
73 Jennifer Ln
New Canaan CT 06840

Call Sign: N1ZAL
Tucker L Cluett
73 Jennifer Ln
New Canaan CT 06840

Call Sign: N1WSC
W Scott Cluett Jr
73 Jennifer Ln
New Canaan CT 06840

Call Sign: K1MRN
Alan C Fuller
182 Long Lots Rd
New Canaan CT 06840

Call Sign: N1CAT
Geoffrey L Pickard
320 Oenoke Ridge Rd
New Canaan CT 06840

Call Sign: N1TWW
Richard H Saunders
32 Knapp Ln
New Canaan CT 06840

Call Sign: WA1QBQ
John F Williams
256 Marvin Ridge Rd
New Canaan CT 06840

Call Sign: KB1CKK
John A Amarilios
1222 Oenoke Ridge Rd
New Canaan CT 068400028

Call Sign: WA1VXM
John M Kyles
84 Knollwood Ln
New Canaan CT 06840

Call Sign: N1XKS
Gabriel Chirinian
120 Middle Ridge
New Canaan CT 06840

Call Sign: K1JAA
John A Amarilios
1222 Oenoke Ridge Rd
New Canaan CT 068400028

Call Sign: KB1PSL
Arthur R Greenspon
111 Lake Wind Rd
New Canaan CT 06840

Call Sign: KA1LXZ
Sidney S Smith Iii
127 Middle Ridge Rd
New Canaan CT 068405059

Call Sign: N1VFW
Scott W Hamilton
181 Parish Rd
New Canaan CT 06840

Call Sign: N1KOD
William F Ruddock Iii
54 Lakeview Ave 18
New Canaan CT 06840

Call Sign: KB1ST
Sidney S Smith
127 Middle Ridge Rd
New Canaan CT 068405059

Call Sign: N8IWX
Matthew L Hoyt
194 Park St Unit 7
New Canaan CT 06840

Call Sign: KG4YYU
Oran J Spaulding Sr
186 Lakeview Ave C3
New Canaan CT 06840

Call Sign: KB1QXU
Norman E Toy
75 Nubel Lane
New Canaan CT 068406913

Call Sign: KB1PQL
Melissa M Clay
86 Pequot Lane
New Canaan CT 06840

Call Sign: N1CPO
Oran J Spaulding Sr
186 Lakeview Ave C3
New Canaan CT 06840

Call Sign: W1REQ
John L Gray
101 Oenoke Ln
New Canaan CT 06840

Call Sign: KB1PQM
Darin G Clay
86 Pequot Lane
New Canaan CT 06840

Call Sign: N1IVP
Theodore Teis
72 Locust Ave
New Canaan CT 06840

Call Sign: KA1PEJ
Sheila S Mc Mann
963 Oenoke Ridge
New Canaan CT 06840

Call Sign: K1WQF
G Howard Robbins
286 Ponus Ridge
New Canaan CT 06840

Call Sign: N1KSB
Joanne Teis
72 Locust Ave
New Canaan CT 06840

Call Sign: W2PCD
Renville H Mc Mann Jr
963 Oenoke Ridge
New Canaan CT 06840

Call Sign: N3KDJ
Philip W Scott
231 Ponus Ridge Road
New Canaan CT 068406017

Call Sign: WC1AAS
New Canaan Civil
Preparedness
33 Raymond St
New Canaan CT 06840

Call Sign: KB1GGI
Howard W Kelting
123 Richmond Hill Rd Unit
20
New Canaan CT 06840

Call Sign: W2QQ
Joseph P Giasi Jr
25 Running Brook Lane
New Canaan CT 068406547

Call Sign: KC1FN
James H Beall Jr
34 Scofield Ln
New Canaan CT 06840

Call Sign: K1EEZ
Richard T Kertesz
38 Selleck Pl
New Canaan CT 06840

Call Sign: AB1OF
Bert Holtappels
96 Seminary St
New Canaan CT 06840

Call Sign: KB1PXN
Elizabeth L Lab
479 Silvermine Rd
New Canaan CT 06840

Call Sign: KB1SUN
Anthony M O'connor Jr
752 Silvermine Rd
New Canaan CT 06840

Call Sign: K1OC
Anthony M O'connor Jr
752 Silvermine Rd

New Canaan CT 06840

Call Sign: K1EQW
James A Whitlock
133 Smith Ridge
New Canaan CT 06840

Call Sign: K1MIZ
Lawrence L Lanier
183 Smith Ridge Rd
New Canaan CT 06840

Call Sign: N1EVS
Craig E Steese
229 Smithridge Rd
New Canaan CT 06840

Call Sign: KB1USY
William E Hilson
39 Snowberry Lane
New Canaan CT 06840

Call Sign: KB1UJR
Jennifer E Lord
48 South Ave
New Canaan CT 06840

Call Sign: KB1BWC
Saxe Middle School 468
Saxe Middle School
Amateur Radio Club
South Avenue
New Canaan CT 06840

Call Sign: KA1TZR
Donald G Hudson
97 Southwood Dr
New Canaan CT 06840

Call Sign: W1CY
W Warren Barker
74 Springwater Ln
New Canaan CT 068406520

Call Sign: KA1ETF

Frank J Di Muzio
218 Summer St
New Canaan CT 06840

Call Sign: KB1HTQ
E Raymond Goodell
85 Thayer Dr
New Canaan CT 06840

Call Sign: KB1COO
Rick S Passero
11 Turning Mill Ln
New Canaan CT 06840

Call Sign: KB1PDM
Michael J Franco Jr
684 Valley Rd
New Canaan CT 068403335

Call Sign: WA9JNI
Steven E Buller
879 Valley Road
New Canaan CT 06840

Call Sign: W1POO
John H Caldwell
6 West Rd
New Canaan CT 06840

Call Sign: K8BUX
Randall S Meadows
356 West Rd
New Canaan CT 06840

Call Sign: N1TWU
Byron E Boots
254 White Oak Shade Rd
New Canaan CT 06840

Call Sign: KB1GEZ
William Ewing Iii
296 White Oak Shade Rd
New Canaan CT 06840

Call Sign: N1TFA

Patrick J Conroy
397 White Oak Shade Rd
New Canaan CT 06840

FCC Amateur Radio Licenses in New Fairfield

Call Sign: KB1IFD
Gary S Adams Sr
18 Albion Rd
New Fairfield CT
068124335

Call Sign: N1GSA
Gary S Adams Sr
18 Albion Rd
New Fairfield CT
068124335

Call Sign: KB1RFI
Michael V Podany
57 Ball Panel Rd E
New Fairfield CT 06812

Call Sign: N1OGC
Thomas M Moore
129 Ball Pond Rd
New Fairfield CT 06812

Call Sign: KA1VXQ
Brian D Morrison
9 Bigelow Rd
New Fairfield CT 06812

Call Sign: WB2BSO
Ronald E Graiff
52 Bogus Hill Rd
New Fairfield CT 06812

Call Sign: KB1HGL
Joseph J Stephens
9 Brush Hill Rd
New Fairfield CT 06812

Call Sign: N1JWU

Mary Lou Scebelo
8 Columbia Dr
New Fairfield CT 06812

Call Sign: W1PJN
William F Johnston
15 Crestway Knollcrest
New Fairfield CT 06812

Call Sign: KE1MG
Marco A Spinali
5 Curtis Ave
New Fairfield CT 06812

Call Sign: N2MZB
Marco A Spinali
5 Curtis Ave.
New Fairfield CT 06812

Call Sign: KA1ODG
Albert A Orioli
10 E Lake Rd
New Fairfield CT 06812

Call Sign: KA1EUE
Lee D Scott
9 E View Rd Knollcrest
New Fairfield CT 06812

Call Sign: KA1GAK
Quentin D Scott
9 E View Rd Knollcrest
New Fairfield CT 06812

Call Sign: KA1QAM
Donald R Benson
7 Elmwood Rd
New Fairfield CT 06812

Call Sign: KB1JNA
Richard P Volant
16 Fulton Dr
New Fairfield CT 06812

Call Sign: WX1T

Thomas E Coury
6 Hickory Lane
New Fairfield CT 06812

Call Sign: KA1HYL
Martin K Gucker
4 High Winds Road
New Fairfield CT 06812

Call Sign: N1OCM
Robert C Bell Jr
8 Hilltop Dr
New Fairfield CT 06812

Call Sign: KB1IIG
Svetlana N Bell
8 Hilltop Dr
New Fairfield CT 06812

Call Sign: N1XQT
Chris W Boyd
34 Indian Hill Rd
New Fairfield CT 06812

Call Sign: N1JVL
Eugene W Willingham Ii
15 Knollcrest Rd
New Fairfield CT 06812

Call Sign: N1GGL
Peter M Grob
2 Meadowbrook Rd
New Fairfield CT 06812

Call Sign: KD1JX
Robert W Bialack
12 Middleton Dr
New Fairfield CT 06812

Call Sign: KA1MLT
Anthony J Szklany
33 Milltown Rd
New Fairfield CT 06812

Call Sign: K1MLT

Anthony J Szklany
33 Milltown Rd
New Fairfield CT 06812

Call Sign: KA1EQZ
Hellmut Voigts
97 Pine Hill Rd
New Fairfield CT 06812

Call Sign: KA1WAX
Matthew R Ferretti
180 Pine Hill Rd
New Fairfield CT 06812

Call Sign: KB1ADB
Thomas H Thayer
12 Possum Dr
New Fairfield CT 06812

Call Sign: K1JOS
Jerry O Stern
16 Sail Harbour Dr
New Fairfield CT 06812

Call Sign: WB5NSG
Richard H Ingraham
19 Satterlee Rd
New Fairfield CT 06812

Call Sign: KA1DYH
Michael S Majewski
20 Shortwoods Rd
New Fairfield CT
068123216

Call Sign: W1KBW
Jon E Radder
25 Southview Rd.
New Fairfield CT 06812

Call Sign: WA2ZOA
Gerald R Mitkowski
304 State Rt. 39
New Fairfield CT 06812

Call Sign: WB1FSC
John C Henze
12 Sunset Dr
New Fairfield CT 06812

Call Sign: KB1KXW
John C Henze
12 Sunset Dr
New Fairfield CT 06812

Call Sign: K2TPX
John A Rogers
18 Sunswept Drive
New Fairfield CT
068124608

Call Sign: W1AS
Alan H Clair
5 Windward Dr
New Fairfield CT 06812

Call Sign: KA1WAW
Aaron S Radder
New Fairfield CT 06812

**FCC Amateur Radio
Licenses in New Hartford**

Call Sign: KA1BQJ
Thomas A Kruczek
35 Arrowhead Dr
New Hartford CT 06057

Call Sign: KB1KGR
Michael I Kruczek
35 Arrowhead Dr
New Hartford CT 06057

Call Sign: W1TXT
Thomas A Kruczek
35 Arrowhead Dr
New Hartford CT 06057

Call Sign: KB2AKY
Stephen P Nolan

20 Bakerville Terr
New Hartford CT 06057

Call Sign: N7ZRK
Scott N Luker
20 Bakerville Terrace
New Hartford CT 06057

Call Sign: KB1HNM
Alex S Mccray
6 Barella Rd
New Hartford CT 06057

Call Sign: KA1TDH
Deborah J Oscarson
70 Behrens Rd
New Hartford CT 06057

Call Sign: WA1TWX
Edward M Oscarson
70 Behrens Rd
New Hartford CT 06057

Call Sign: KA1RPE
Sheila C Allen
Rr 2 Box 153e
New Hartford CT 06057

Call Sign: KD1EU
Donald V Casella
75 Burwell Rd
New Hartford CT 06057

Call Sign: WA1YWW
Ernest J Mc Dermott
139 Burwell Road
New Hartford CT 06057

Call Sign: KA1TEO
Lester C Archer Jr
48 Cotton Hill
New Hartford CT 06057

Call Sign: N1YDA
Zygmunt S Michna

125 Cotton Hill Rd
New Hartford CT 06057

Call Sign: W1RBF
Kenneth L Payne
Lot 88 Davis Dr
New Hartford CT 06057

Call Sign: N1SAG
David W Hamm
11 Den Rd
New Hartford CT 06057

Call Sign: AA1RL
Christopher J Perrault
33 Den Rd
New Hartford CT 06057

Call Sign: N1MMM
Garry O Mc Cabe
37 E Cotton Hill Rd
New Hartford CT 06057

Call Sign: W1COJ
Garry O Mc Cabe
37 E Cotton Hill Rd
New Hartford CT 06057

Call Sign: KA1MTG
Warren J Kimberley
419 E Cotton Hill Rd
New Hartford CT 06057

Call Sign: KA7QNF
Lawrence A Buckley
481 East Cotton Hill Rd
New Hartford CT 06057

Call Sign: WA1DXA
William A Marchand
390 Famington River
Turnpike
New Hartford CT 06057

Call Sign: W1WAM

William A Marchand
390 Farmington River
Turnpike
New Hartford CT 06057

Call Sign: KB1IRK
William S Marchand
390 Farmington River
Turnpike
New Hartford CT 06057

Call Sign: KB1GGP
James A Bullard
51 Holcomb Hill Rd
New Hartford CT 06057

Call Sign: KB1KWT
Miranda D Bullard
51 Holcomb Hill Rd
New Hartford CT 06057

Call Sign: WB1HFT
Robert G Koether
93 Hoppen Rd
New Hartford CT 06057

Call Sign: KB1KET
Robert J Britton
72 Indian Meadow Rd
New Hartford CT 06057

Call Sign: KA1UHO
Robert E Brzozowy
20 Johnny Cake Ln
New Hartford CT 06057

Call Sign: K1XO
Timothy W Ferrarotti
25 Knollwood Dr
New Hartford CT
060573232

Call Sign: N1XZN
David Maraia
17 Laurelwood Pond Lane

New Hartford CT 06057

Call Sign: KB1MNE
Robert P Upson
1074 Litchfield Tpke
New Hartford CT
060573312

Call Sign: N1LQM
David F Rosati
160 Litchfield Turnpike
New Hartford CT 06057

Call Sign: KB1GGS
David J Wilcox
1261 Litchfield Turnpike
New Hartford CT
060573322

Call Sign: K1DJW
David J Wilcox
1261 Litchfield Turnpike
New Hartford CT
060573322

Call Sign: KB1KWQ
Sandra L Wilcox
1261 Litchfield Turnpike
New Hartford CT
060573322

Call Sign: KB1KWR
Ashley L Wilcox
1261 Litchfield Turnpike
New Hartford CT
060573322

Call Sign: KC1RW
Matthew S Rugens
33 Livery Pool Rd
New Hartford CT 06057

Call Sign: WB1FVW
Frank P Bares
93 Maillet Ln

New Hartford CT 06057

Call Sign: AA7ZM
Joseph R Nerney
220 Main St. Unit 1-C
New Hartford CT 06070

Call Sign: W1FIL
Joseph R Nerney
220 Main St. Unit 1-C
New Hartford CT 06057

Call Sign: N1YDH
Paul Minihan
116 Maple Hollow Rd
New Hartford CT 06057

Call Sign: KB1KWS
Evan S Beavers
24 Meadow View Ln
New Hartford CT 06057

Call Sign: N1OT
David V Santis
43 Prospect St. Apt. A.
New Hartford CT 06057

Call Sign: KB1PCK
Peter J Kandefer
41 South Rd
New Hartford CT
060573522

Call Sign: W1ATT
Nelson A Nicholson
418 South Rd
New Hartford CT 06057

Call Sign: N1SQI
Charles F Gelzinis
52 Tanglewood Road
New Hartford CT 06057

Call Sign: KB1AJX
Eileen P Levine

38 Timberline Rd
New Hartford CT 06790

Call Sign: WB2EQE
Mark R Levine
38 Timberline Rd
New Hartford CT 06057

Call Sign: K1TBA
William L Yoreo
570 Townhill Rd Box 1051
New Hartford CT 06057

Call Sign: N1ECY
Carol A Slabinski
462 W Hill Rd
New Hartford CT 06057

Call Sign: N8RA
Chester J Slabinski
462 W Hill Rd
New Hartford CT 06057

Call Sign: WA1UNO
Sarkis M Douaihy
60 Winchester Rd
New Hartford CT 06057

Call Sign: N1LOQ
William G Llewellyn
New Hartford CT 06057

Call Sign: NL7MO
Leslie I Rogers Jr
New Hartford CT 06057

Call Sign: WB1DJU
Wireless Operators Of
Winsted
New Hartford CT
060570053

Call Sign: WY1O
Perry T Green

New Hartford CT
060570053

FCC Amateur Radio Licenses in New Haven

Call Sign: K1PLN
Donald W Andrus
Amity Station
New Haven CT 06525

Call Sign: KB1PIO
David Gortler
342 Audubon Court
New Haven CT 06510

Call Sign: N1XBZ
Taeko Maehara
601 B Prospect St
New Haven CT 06511

Call Sign: KA1NRF
Lisa A Johnson
45 Beecher Pl
New Haven CT 06512

Call Sign: N1HFB
Joshua P Spoerri
15 Birch Dr
New Haven CT 06515

Call Sign: KB1INR
Tyson B Records
101 Bishop St 3rd Floor
New Haven CT 06511

Call Sign: N1UAH
Josue D Encarnacion
196 Blatchley Ave
New Haven CT 06513

Call Sign: KA1NNC
Steve D Johnson
139 Bradley St
New Haven CT 06511

Call Sign: KB1RLU
Stephen C Watson
1 Brewery Square Unit
S131
New Haven CT 06513

Call Sign: KB1VXE
Stephen C Watson
1 Brewery Square Unit
S131
New Haven CT 06513

Call Sign: KB1SEB
Susan E Malter
19 Burton St
New Haven CT 06515

Call Sign: KA1WI
Jacinto Lirola
147 Canner St
New Haven CT 06511

Call Sign: KC0DZS
Garrett M Leahy
111 Canner St 1l
New Haven CT 06511

Call Sign: N1UED
Robert C Norris
2141 Chapel Street
New Haven CT 06515

Call Sign: N1KSD
Peter D Staffa
177 Chestnut St
New Haven CT 06511

Call Sign: KA1UZU
Daniel M Rittel
265 College Apt 9n
New Haven CT 06510

Call Sign: KC1IN
Frank X Oboyski

135 Concord St
New Haven CT 06512

Call Sign: N1DVT
Ralph K Maynard
620 Dixwell Ave
New Haven CT 06511

Call Sign: K1PLR
Harry A Arsenault
241 Dixwell Avenue - Unit
406
New Haven CT 06511

Call Sign: KB1CIW
Robert K Stephens
40 Donna Dr A6
New Haven CT 06513

Call Sign: KB1SIT
Teresa C Stephens
40 Donna Dr Unit A6
New Haven CT 06513

Call Sign: N1EFU
Carlos Reyes
199 Dover St
New Haven CT 06513

Call Sign: AA1IQ
Samuel J Barbiero Sr
22 Downing St
New Haven CT 06513

Call Sign: KB1BWG
Derek C Haspeslagh
175 Dwight St
New Haven CT 06511

Call Sign: K1CCU
Hubert B Bradburn
251 E Rock Rd
New Haven CT 06511

Call Sign: KE4DHE

Derrick L Wilson
11 Earl Street
New Haven CT 06515

Call Sign: KA1SPQ
Michael F Toth
315 Eastern St Apt D1702
New Haven CT 06513

Call Sign: N1HOR
William D Smith
315 Eastern St Bldg 1715
New Haven CT 06513

Call Sign: N1TJQ
Alan B Schultz
321 Eastern Street
New Haven CT 06513

Call Sign: KB1ITJ
Marjorie W Powers
311 Eastern Street E 804
New Haven CT 06513

Call Sign: KA1SOX
Thomas L Ransom
320 Edgewood Ave
New Haven CT 06511

Call Sign: KA1ZHD
David Low
511 Ellsworth Ave
New Haven CT 06511

Call Sign: KA1VQP
Chet Thompson
581 Elm St
New Haven CT 06511

Call Sign: KA1VJD
Norman C Keul
Saybrook College 242 Elm
St
New Haven CT 06511

Call Sign: KB1IP
Raymond W Henry
975 Elm St.
New Haven CT 06511

Call Sign: KB1TXU
Richard C Kollanda Ii
19 First Ave
New Haven CT 06513

Call Sign: KB1ERP
Henry W Farkas
37 Florence Ave
New Haven CT 065123944

Call Sign: KA1TLN
Richard J Galella
99 Fort Hale Rd
New Haven CT 06513

Call Sign: W1TFT
William P Blumenfeld
360 Fountain St
New Haven CT 06515

Call Sign: KB1UPD
David K Mcpike
149 Fountain St 4
New Haven CT 06515

Call Sign: KA1QNL
Allen B Blakely
17 Fountain Ter
New Haven CT 06515

Call Sign: KC1VP
Christopher H Genly
95 Fountain Ter
New Haven CT 06515

Call Sign: KB1UDX
Todd C Wormell
113 Frederick Ave 2l
New Haven CT 06515

Call Sign: N1RNT
Robert M Luby Jr
106 Front St
New Haven CT 065133927

Call Sign: N1NJJ
Joseph G Moffo
25 Gold St
New Haven CT 06519

Call Sign: KA1RZL
Raymond H Paige Jr
99 Good Year St
New Haven CT 06511

Call Sign: KB1CHZ
Jackie H Williams
26 Highview Ln
New Haven CT 06513

Call Sign: N1RWH
Yuewu Xu
24 Hillhouse Ave
New Haven CT 06520

Call Sign: KI6UKZ
Robert B Carleton
56 Hillside Place #4
New Haven CT 06511

Call Sign: KB1WRR
Robert B Carleton
56 Hillside Place #4
New Haven CT 06511

Call Sign: N1EAB
Robert P Castiglione
5 Hopkins Dr
New Haven CT 06512

Call Sign: WA1YGF
Roger S Hess
86 Howard Ave
New Haven CT 06519

Call Sign: KC2MED
Luis A Amar
79 Kimberly Ave. Apt#2
New Haven CT 06519

Call Sign: N1NQH
Daniel H Mc Nulty
104 Lawncrest Rd
New Haven CT 06515

Call Sign: KA1TIG
Biagio L Fronte
280 Lighthouse Rd
New Haven CT 06512

Call Sign: WI1T
Ladislav Brazina
308 Lighthouse Rd
New Haven CT 06512

Call Sign: KE1GN
Marc Antony R Foreman
50 Lilac St
New Haven CT 06511

Call Sign: W1GHU
Wade G Holcomb
185 Linden St
New Haven CT 06511

Call Sign: KB1KTB
Terry E Utterback
18 Mansion St
New Haven CT 06512

Call Sign: KB1GPC
Norbert N Gradowski
161 Maple St
New Haven CT 06511

Call Sign: KB1JTM
Alexander Scheirer
47 Maplewood Rd
New Haven CT 06515

Call Sign: KA1ODY
Gary Matican
107 Marlin Dr
New Haven CT 06515

Call Sign: KA1MJ
George F Mancini
143 Meadow View St
New Haven CT 06512

Call Sign: N3ZVG
Ryan M Rubin
40 Mechanic Street 1st Fl
New Haven CT 06511

Call Sign: KB1NTV
Karl B Geertz
242 Nicoll St
New Haven CT 06511

Call Sign: WC1ACL
Office Of C D New Haven
200 Orange St
New Haven CT 06510

Call Sign: KA1UBQ
Omur I Bozma
516 Orange St 57
New Haven CT 06520

Call Sign: KB1RXN
Christopher F Collins
53 Pearl St Apt 3
New Haven CT 06511

Call Sign: N1PQT
Alfred J Verrilli
322 Peck St
New Haven CT 06513

Call Sign: N1UNP
Christine M Marsee
66 Perkins St
New Haven CT 06513

Call Sign: KB1GPZ
Luis Rodriguez
151 Portsea Street
New Haven CT 06519

Call Sign: KA1UBP
Billur Barshan
15 Prospect St Dept Of Ee
New Haven CT 06520

Call Sign: N1RYG
Patricia A Brotschul
55 Raynham Road
New Haven CT 06512

Call Sign: KB1TXS
Mario A Fernandez Jr
203 Rosette St
New Haven CT 06519

Call Sign: KA2DAY
Thomas M Webster
428 Smith Ave
New Haven CT 06513

Call Sign: N1LFC
Dominic J Scoppetto
616 Smith Ave
New Haven CT 06513

Call Sign: KB1GLD
James D Olson
908 State St
New Haven CT 06511

Call Sign: K1YVU
A Walter Jacobson
195 Stimson Rd
New Haven CT 06511

Call Sign: W1EKZ
Raymond A Boffa
30 Stuyvesant Ave
New Haven CT 06512

Call Sign: KA1VMB
Colonious King
91 Taylor Ave
New Haven CT 06515

Call Sign: W1YU
Yale Univ Amateur Radio
Club
79 Warren Street
New Haven CT 065115765

Call Sign: KB1TXM
Linda M Shepardson
79 Warren Street Apt 3
New Haven CT 06511

Call Sign: KB1JNY
Robert A Wisniewski
168 West Rock Ave
New Haven CT 065152223

Call Sign: N1ATB
John D Weinland
879 Whalley Ave 2nd Floor
New Haven CT 06515

Call Sign: KI4HBI
Elvin Torres
1015 Whalley Ave Apt C14
New Haven CT 06512

Call Sign: KB1TBM
Stephen J Anderson
467 Whalley Ave Unit H
New Haven CT 06511

Call Sign: N1UNQ
Sherryl A Prelesnik
467 Whalley Ave Unit S
New Haven CT 06511

Call Sign: KB1TJD
Gaianne G Jenkins
608 Whitney Ave
New Haven CT 06511

Call Sign: KB1VJO
Norimasa Yoshimizu
815 Whitney Ave Apt 3
New Haven CT 06511

Call Sign: KB1TOF
Brian C Merry
400 Whitney Ave Apt 7
New Haven CT 06511

Call Sign: KB2ZUZ
Kurt R Heumiller
206 Willow St 1st Floor
New Haven CT 06511

Call Sign: N1YPB
Jason E Lee
63 Winchester Ave Apt 2
New Haven CT 06511

Call Sign: N1RAZ
Peilin Tia
Yale Station
New Haven CT 06520

Call Sign: KC0FMO
Paul A Vierthaler
New Haven CT 06520

Call Sign: N1RBJ
David P Reddy
New Haven CT 06536

Call Sign: N1UAG
Josue D Encarnacion
New Haven CT 06513

Call Sign: WA1DTE
Mary L Sharron
New Haven CT 06533

Call Sign: KC2GOI
Myron A Johnson
New Haven CT 06511

Call Sign: KB1LVS
Myron A Johnson
New Haven CT 06511

Call Sign: KB1VCL
Doris I Barrett
New Haven CT 06520

FCC Amateur Radio Licenses in New London

Call Sign: KA1BES
Richard L Thibeault
11 Admiral Dr
New London CT
063204201

Call Sign: KB1HDP
Zachary M Brusca
36 Aitchinson Dr
New London CT 06320

Call Sign: KB1HDQ
Mark J Brusca
36 Aitchinson Dr
New London CT 06320

Call Sign: WB2QIJ
Michael J Brusca
36 Aitchison Dr
New London CT 06320

Call Sign: K1OV
Michael J Brusca
36 Aitchison Dr
New London CT 06320

Call Sign: KB1GWA
Stacey E Brusca
36 Aitchison Dr
New London CT 06320

Call Sign: W1HGE
Jack Van Verdeghem

527 Alewife Parkway
New London CT 06320

Call Sign: N1NXG
Daniel L Harrison
19 Ashcraft Rd
New London CT
063205110

Call Sign: N0VOC
Mark P Zanghetti
107 B Niles Hill Road
New London CT 06320

Call Sign: KB1QOG
Juan A Concepcion
14 Bristol St Apt 11
New London CT 06320

Call Sign: KB1EQL
Luigi Visco
314 Broad St
New London CT 06320

Call Sign: W1ISW
Luigi Visco
314 Broad St
New London CT 06320

Call Sign: KB1HNT
Daniel Docker
17 Center St
New London CT
063205316

Call Sign: KB1PWP
Clara J Hoverman
7162 Chase Hall
New London CT 06320

Call Sign: KB1PNC
Nicholas M Monacelli
7529 Chase Hall
New London CT 06320

Call Sign: KB1MBB
Simon P Barr
8767 Chase Hall
New London CT 06320

Call Sign: KB1LWV
Grant C Wyman
Uscga 7041 Chase Hall
New London CT 06320

Call Sign: KB1LWU
Joseph M Nowicki
Uscga 7205 Chase Hall
New London CT 06320

Call Sign: KB1LWW
Jonathan D White
Uscga 7268 Chase Hall
New London CT 06320

Call Sign: KB1LWT
Joshua D Brandt
Uscga 8769 Chase Hall
New London CT 06320

Call Sign: KB1MTO
Eleanor L Dahl
7830 Chase Hall Us Coast
Guard Academy
New London CT 06320

Call Sign: KB1NZB
Nicholas D Herndon
7418 Chase Hall Uscga
New London CT 06320

Call Sign: KB1VGU
Tara R Fitzgerald
7546 Chase Hall Uscga
New London CT 06320

Call Sign: KB1OZD
Mark E Coddington
97 Chester St Apt H
New London CT 06320

Call Sign: WA1WRI
Ronald A Booth
14 Colman St 12
New London CT 06320

Call Sign: K1MSG
George Malcolm Brown
37 Cottage Street
New London CT 06320

Call Sign: WA1VOB
Cynthia B Suntup
2 Cove View Rd
New London CT 06320

Call Sign: N1RAX
Stephen D Gibbs
45 Crescent St
New London CT 06320

Call Sign: N1JCY
George E Peabody Sr
223 Crystal Ave
New London CT 06320

Call Sign: W1GEP
George E Peabody Sr
223 Crystal Ave
New London CT 06320

Call Sign: KC2GXU
Johnathan D Porco
330 Crystal Ave #18
New London CT 06320

Call Sign: WB1ADT
Eileen R Jacobs
43 Dart St
New London CT 06320

Call Sign: K1HYQ
Richard A Darling
26 Dell Ave
New London CT 06320

Call Sign: N1YPQ
Eric G Lofvenborg
23 Fitch Ave
New London CT 06320

Call Sign: N1JVX
Robert I Hayford Jr
148 Gardner Ave
New London CT 06320

Call Sign: W1ICT
James P Shores
344 Glenwwod AVE.
New London CT 06360

Call Sign: N1GHN
Michael C Parrott
33 Granite St Apt 106
New London CT 06320

Call Sign: KA1SJH
Donald E White
40 Hawthorne Dr
New London CT 06320

Call Sign: KA3OUU
John J Frank
108 Hawthorne Dr Apt 4e
New London CT 06320

Call Sign: KB1CEY
Barbara A Lewis
18 Hawthorne Dr N Apt 5
New London CT 06320

Call Sign: KI4FWI
Alex J Pecoraro
19 Hawthorne Dr Unit 120
New London CT 06321

Call Sign: K2ZQL
William J Soukey
62-3 Hawthorne Dr. N.
New London CT 06320

Call Sign: KB1SFA
Gregory W Maine
108 Hawthorne Drive North
Apt 5a
New London CT 06320

Call Sign: K6KCS
Kelly C Seals
4 Holly Terrace
New London CT 06320

Call Sign: KA1TDY
Chester H Colby
149 Huntington St Apt 408
New London CT 06320

Call Sign: N1RAW
Roger A Edwards
11 Lincoln Ct
New London CT 06320

Call Sign: KB1NZI
Joseph Benin
15 Mohegan Ave
New London CT 06320

Call Sign: WA2HLP
Christopher B Steiner
270 Mohegan Ave
New London CT 06320

Call Sign: KB1PSG
Perry D Susskind
270 Mohegan Ave
New London CT 06320

Call Sign: W1CGA
Uscg Academy Dee - 27
Uscga Cadet Amateur Radio
Club
Mohegan Ave
New London CT
063204195

Call Sign: KB1LWQ
Benjamin J Lee
15 Mohegan Ave 7214
New London CT 06322

Call Sign: KB1LWS
Bradley R Clemons
15 Mohegan Ave 7675
New London CT 06323

Call Sign: KB1MBE
Philip S Baxa
13 Mohegan Ave Chase
Hall 8829
New London CT 06320

Call Sign: KB1MBA
Nadia S Cazaubon
15 Mohegan Ave Chase
Hall 8834
New London CT 06320

Call Sign: KE1CF
Warren H Axtell
504 Montauk Ave
Ncw London CT 06320

Call Sign: WA1EJB
Dan Weissman
29 Mott Ave
New London CT 06320

Call Sign: K1HL
Harry Leiser
62 Mott Ave
New London CT 06320

Call Sign: KB1IPB
Robert W Krenicki
111a Niles Hill Rd
New London CT 06320

Call Sign: KA1LJB
George R Pritchett
47 Ocean Ave

New London CT 06320

Call Sign: KA1UYR
Richard C Lee
46 Parkway S
New London CT 06320

Call Sign: N1KIS
Steven P Caplowe
292 Pequot Ave
New London CT 06320

Call Sign: KA1CSH
Richard L Humphreville
824 Pequot Ave
New London CT 06320

Call Sign: KB1AWF
Albert D Ardao
292 Pequot Ave 4-0
New London CT 06320

Call Sign: KE1LC
William S Morse
292 Pequot Ave Apt 4c
New London CT 06320

Call Sign: WD3S
Paul D Berkman
605 Pequot Avenue
New London CT 06320

Call Sign: W1RPQ
Frederic T Nazro
36 Pkwy S
New London CT
063202034

Call Sign: K1YJG
Joseph A Konrad
33 Plant St
New London CT
063204419

Call Sign: WB1HBF

Richard J Ryan
25 Prospect St
New London CT 06320

Call Sign: N1HFO
Kevin M Keast
Uscga
New London CT 06320

Call Sign: KB1OAZ
Maca Ryan
Uscga
New London CT 06320

Call Sign: KB1VGR
Catherine Leknes
Uscga Chase Hall Box 8875
New London CT 06320

Call Sign: KA1KAU
Maria A Campbell
331 Vauxhall St
New London CT 06320

Call Sign: N1LAE
Kenneth S Campbell
331 Vauxhall St
New London CT
063203837

Call Sign: WA4QXT
George W Sebastian
89 Vietes St
New London CT 06320

Call Sign: KG4TDA
Carlos J Delvalle
10 W Pleasent St
New London CT 06320

Call Sign: KB1HNS
William E Magill
15 West St
New London CT 06320

Call Sign: N1MPW
Robert C Niedojadlo
91 West St
New London CT 06320

Call Sign: W1GGU
J Kenneth Fahey
166 Willetts Ave
New London CT
063204819

Call Sign: KA1UNR
Loren A Burnett
283 Willetts Ave
New London CT 06320

Call Sign: KB1LIM
Deborah D Skinner
247 Williams St
New London CT 06320

Call Sign: KA1TYH
Luanne Benshimol
4 Winchester Rd
New London CT 06320

Call Sign: KE5GUG
Keoni A Hutton
New London CT 06320

FCC Amateur Radio Licenses in New Milford

Call Sign: K1WNT
Roger G Hornecker
20 Aspetuck Pines
New Milford CT 06776

Call Sign: KA1SNQ
Daisy M Hornecker
20 Aspetuck Pines
New Milford CT 06776

Call Sign: N1NGS
Russell B Cook

340 Aspetuck Rd
New Milford CT 06776

Call Sign: KA1OLY
Charles W Horgen
36 Barker Rd
New Milford CT 06776

Call Sign: K1OLY
Charles W Horgen
36 Barker Rd
New Milford CT 06776

Call Sign: KB1IER
Paris J Thalassinos
8 Bonnie Vue Ln
New Milford CT 06776

Call Sign: K1OP
Leonard A Casacalenda
14 Bradbury Rd
New Milford CT 06776

Call Sign: KB1WTC
John F Wittmann
1 Brentwood Dr
New Milford CT 06776

Call Sign: KB1OYZ
Claudia Waldvogel
5 Brookview Ln
New Milford CT
067762544

Call Sign: KB1OZA
Ralf Waldvogel
5 Brookview Ln
New Milford CT
067762544

Call Sign: KI1RA
Ralf Waldvogel
5 Brookview Ln
New Milford CT
067762544

Call Sign: KI2RA
Claudia Waldvogel
5 Brookview Ln
New Milford CT
067762544

Call Sign: N1LDE
Peter G Pfeifer
130 Candlewood Lake Rd N
New Milford CT 06776

Call Sign: K1RCK
Robert T Bruce Jr
151 Candlewood Lake Rd N
New Milford CT 06776

Call Sign: KA1HAN
Nelson J Gaudenzi
94 Candlewood Lk Rd N
New Milford CT 06776

Call Sign: K2ZVA
Paul C Kroll Ii
179 Carmen Hill 2
New Milford CT 06776

Call Sign: KB1PVX
Joseph W Goodell
16 Carriage Dr
New Milford CT 06776

Call Sign: K1JWG
Joseph W Goodell
16 Carriage Dr
New Milford CT 06776

Call Sign: K1YJQ
Richard J Slivka
11 Cedar Vale Dr
New Milford CT
067764633

Call Sign: N8RIN
Letha D Walters

32 Chapin Road
New Milford CT 06776

Call Sign: W8ZY
Gary M Walters
32 Chapin Road
New Milford CT 06776

Call Sign: KB1PXX
Christopher P Lundgren
9 Charterhouse Rd
New Milford CT 06776

Call Sign: WA1WTH
Peter J Morrisroe
27 Cornwall Dr
New Milford CT 06776

Call Sign: N1MIC
Michael J Laudenslager
8 Deer Woods Drive
New Milford CT 06776

Call Sign: WA6SHQ
David R Carlson
28 Dodd Road
New Milford CT 06776

Call Sign: WA1WXC
David R Carlson
28 Dodd Road
New Milford CT 06776

Call Sign: N1RBD
David P Kirkwood
6 Eagle Dr
New Milford CT
067764576

Call Sign: KB1BKU
Laurence G Villar Jr
9 Fordyce Ct
New Milford CT 06776

Call Sign: KA1QWB

Stephen P Clark
78 Fort Hill Road
New Milford CT 06776

Call Sign: KB1LEV
Michael K Onorato
15 Gaffney Rd
New Milford CT 06776

Call Sign: N1ILW
Bonnie F Lieberman
46 Gaffney Road
New Milford CT 06776

Call Sign: WA1UZO
Michael T Lieberman
46 Gaffney Road
New Milford CT 06776

Call Sign: KE1AI
James P Delancy Jr
11 Geiger Rd
New Milford CT 06776

Call Sign: N1UIH
James P Delancy Sr
11 Geiger Rd
New Milford CT 06776

Call Sign: N1UII
Tammi R Delancy
11 Geiger Rd
New Milford CT 06776

Call Sign: KB1FVG
Northville Amateur Radio
Asociation
11 Geiger Rd
New Milford CT 06776

Call Sign: NA1RA
Inc. Northville Amateur
Radio Association
11 Geiger Rd
New Milford CT 06776

Call Sign: KB1VNO
William J Blizman
2 Goodhill Rd
New Milford CT 06776

Call Sign: ND1X
John W Profita Jr
13 Granite Rd
New Milford CT 06776

Call Sign: W3IHC
William J Thebert
2 Gretl Ln
New Milford CT 06776

Call Sign: KB1COE
KRISTINA R Swindell
6 Hayfield Road
New Milford CT 06776

Call Sign: KA1YGH
John B Brady
8 Hearthstone Ter
New Milford CT
067762126

Call Sign: WA1IRF
Richard V La Russo
23 Hine Rd
New Milford CT 06776

Call Sign: K0XP
Steven M Harrison
145 Housatonic Avenue
New Milford CT 06776

Call Sign: N1YGE
Thomas G Cooper
2 Laurel Dr
New Milford CT 06776

Call Sign: N1PXT
Scott J Campbell
428 Litchfield Rd

New Milford CT 06776

Call Sign: KB1HSQ
David L Hughes Jr
424 Long Mountain Road
New Milford CT 06776

Call Sign: KB1LVF
Geoffrey Stratman
25 Meetinghouse Ter
New Milford CT 06776

Call Sign: N8QMW
Robert O Scillitoe
18 Meredith Lane
New Milford CT 06776

Call Sign: KB1WBW
Charles F Pomeroy Iii
9 Mountain View Dr
New Milford CT 06776

Call Sign: N1WHP
Russell V Pribanic
120 Mt View Dr
New Milford CT 06776

Call Sign: KC1ZC
Glenn S Curtiss
4 Mtn View Dr
New Milford CT 06776

Call Sign: KC2HNM
Joseph A Santaniello
21 Norton Lane
New Milford CT 06776

Call Sign: N2LTK
Donald G Mc Callion Jr
60 Old Ridge Rd
New Milford CT 06776

Call Sign: KL7IOP
Clayton H Norman
18 Old Town Park Rd

New Milford CT
067764228

Call Sign: N1BXP
Michael F Bloch
One Sterling Ridge
New Milford CT 06776

Call Sign: W1TYS
John J Broadbrook Sr
20 Overlook Dr
New Milford CT
067764742

Call Sign: KD4JUH
Elmer M Sinclair
7 Park Ln W
New Milford CT
067762314

Call Sign: KB1BZW
Robert J Grant Jr
2 Pleasant St
New Milford CT 06776

Call Sign: KB1MWU
Elizabeth S Mullis
63 Prospect Pl
New Milford CT 06776

Call Sign: KB1MQB
James O Mullis Jr
63 Prospect Place
New Milford CT 06776

Call Sign: N1OUJ
Jack Fernandes
95 Pumpkin Hill Rd
New Milford CT 06776

Call Sign: KB1CAV
Peter T Richardson
52 Putnam Rd
New Milford CT 06776

Call Sign: N1ZYO
Thomas A Tucker
27 Revere Rd
New Milford CT 06776

Call Sign: N1ZYP
Linda A Tucker
27 Revere Rd
New Milford CT 06776

Call Sign: KB1CLL
David E Freeman
87 River Rd
New Milford CT 06776

Call Sign: N1TGK
Judy L Etzler
9 Serena Ln
New Milford CT 06776

Call Sign: N1XWP
Eleanore L Etzler
9 Serena Ln
New Milford CT 06776

Call Sign: N8WXQ
Frank M Etzler
9 Serena Ln
New Milford CT 06776

Call Sign: WB2NOV
Louis M Venezia
126 Sherman Rd
New Milford CT 06776

Call Sign: WB2NOW
Maria C Venezia
126 Sherman Rd
New Milford CT 06776

Call Sign: N1GUY
Jody S Cipot
28 Sherwood Dr
New Milford CT 06776

Call Sign: KA1TGB
Terry F Profita
44 Squire Hill Rd
New Milford CT 06776

Call Sign: W2DAB
John H Reynolds
60 Squires Hill Rd
New Milford CT 06776

Call Sign: K2JSQ
George F Neumann
17 Stephanie Dr
New Milford CT 06776

Call Sign: WA1BZI
Harriett G Edson
6 Sundance Rd
New Milford CT 06776

Call Sign: KB1NGO
John C Rinciari
10 Sundance Rd
New Milford CT 06776

Call Sign: WA1ZSQ
Laurence A Bourdillon
24 Twin Oaks
New Milford CT 06776

Call Sign: KB1CPO
Gregory S Sottosanti
8 Violet Hill Lane
New Milford CT 06776

Call Sign: WS1Q
Paul F Kleppin
12 Warwick Dr
New Milford CT 06776

Call Sign: KC1XU
Keith Y Mortensen
131 Washington Ridge Rd
New Milford CT 06776

Call Sign: N1IEN
Penny Kern
131 Washington Ridge Rd
New Milford CT 06776

Call Sign: W1EOY
Richard M Moreau
9 Wedgewood Dr
New Milford CT 06776

Call Sign: KB1MGE
John T Nixon
2 Wedgewood Drive
New Milford CT 06776

Call Sign: N1GMD
Howard P Lapidus
290 Wellsville Ave
New Milford CT 06776

Call Sign: KB1KIE
Calvin T Daniels
330 Wellsville Ave
New Milford CT 06776

Call Sign: AB1EC
Calvin T Daniels
330 Wellsville Ave
New Milford CT 06776

Call Sign: N1SIJ
Peter D Homberg
334 Wellsville Ave
New Milford CT 06776

Call Sign: KB1IJW
Darren Devall
23a Wellsville Ave
New Milford CT 06776

Call Sign: N1NYY
Darren Devall
23a Wellsville Ave
New Milford CT 06776

Call Sign: K2SBI
Leith A Mangels
21 Willow Road
New Milford CT
067763228

Call Sign: N1NY
Robert D Dugan
209 Willow Springs
New Milford CT 06776

Call Sign: N1VIR
Tom P Mullen Jr
120 Wynwood Dr
New Milford CT 06776

Call Sign: KM1M
Stephen D Kish
New Milford CT 06776

Call Sign: N1FFG
Herb Goldman
New Milford CT 06776

Call Sign: WA1JBN
Robert J Yourwith
New Milford CT 06776

Call Sign: KB1SOJ
James Lalli
New Milford CT 06776

FCC Amateur Radio Licenses in New Preston

Call Sign: W1LZE
Henry T Gibson
16 Hinckley Rd
New Preston CT 06777

Call Sign: KA1ZBU
Charles S Cook
80 Kielwasser Rd
New Preston CT 06777

Call Sign: N1RHI
Daniel R Delancy
7 New Milford Tpke
New Preston CT 06777

Call Sign: KA1YXT
Howard C Lockwood Iii
16 New Preston Hill Rd
New Preston CT 06777

Call Sign: K1RGW
Robert G Weber
5 Slaughterhouse Road
New Preston CT 06777

Call Sign: W1TGN
Laurance A Weber
229 W Shore Rd
New Preston CT 067771304

Call Sign: KA1MMM
Sean A Banks
New Preston CT 06777

Call Sign: NF1E
Arthur J Banks
New Preston CT 06777

FCC Amateur Radio Licenses in New Preston Marble

Call Sign: N1AQV
Jerrold D Hornak
34 Garland Rd
New Preston Marble D CT
067772112

Call Sign: KD1UK
Robin K Delancy
7 New Milford Tpke
New Preston Marble D CT
06777

FCC Amateur Radio Licenses in Newington

Call Sign: KC1J
Thomas R Hogerty
35 5c Woodsedge Dr
Newington CT 06111

Call Sign: W1QAH
Nicholas Soroka
41 Atwood St
Newington CT 06111

Call Sign: KB1JTG
Adam C Castro
111 Audubon Ave
Newington CT 06111

Call Sign: N1TUL
David J Kent
24 B Cambridge Dr
Newington CT 06111

Call Sign: KA1ZDK
Philip J Schmitt
189 Back Ln
Newington CT 06111

Call Sign: N1NBJ
Eric Rosow
42 Baldwin Ct
Newington CT 06111

Call Sign: N2PXS
Martin K Winterling
97 Barkledge Dr
Newington CT 06111

Call Sign: KB1VBP
Michal M Nowicki
100 Barn Hill Ln
Newington CT 06111

Call Sign: W1RSX
Michael E White

9 Beacon Court
Newington CT 06111

Call Sign: WB1DWR
Peter T Kohanski
16 Berkeley Cir
Newington CT 06111

Call Sign: KB1MYG
John Andrews
4 Berkeley Circle
Newington CT 06111

Call Sign: K3AHF
Lawrence B Crone
2210 Berlin Turnpike
Newington CT 061310600

Call Sign: KB1RHT
Robert A Regina
38 Birchlawn Terr
Newington CT 06111

Call Sign: WA1RJR
Newington High School
Amateur Radio Club
151 Boylston St
Newington CT 06111

Call Sign: WB1CRH
Thomas J Vesci
151 Boylston Street
Newington CT 06111

Call Sign: KA1NDD
Bertrand A Rankin
33 Brace Rd
Newington CT 06111

Call Sign: KA1RQV
Lee A Dawson
124 Brentwood Rd
Newington CT 06111

Call Sign: N1NMV

Michael A Reinbold
38 Briarwood Rd
Newington CT 06111

Call Sign: N1OLS
Mary Ann V Yukna
38 Briarwood Rd
Newington CT 06111

Call Sign: N1FCH
Allyson T Hurder
53 Broadview
Newington CT 06111

Call Sign: KA1SIQ
Ann D Hurder
53 Broadview St
Newington CT 06111

Call Sign: KB1ASG
John L Annino
82 Brockett St
Newington CT 06111

Call Sign: W1VJA
Vincent J Alianiello Jr
241 Brockett Street
Newington CT 06111

Call Sign: KB1TSB
Gregory K Rannou
56 Brook St
Newington CT 06111

Call Sign: N1QEK
Thakorbhai U Patel
191 Brookside Rd
Newington CT 06111

Call Sign: N1ZAW
Matt S D Amore
213 Brookside Rd
Newington CT 06111

Call Sign: KB1FTS

John M Hoyle
31 Buck St
Newington CT 06111

Call Sign: KA1YAV
Stacey K Fitch
206 Buena Vista Ave
Newington CT 06111

Call Sign: KB1LMS
Laura E Demaio
22 Burdon Ln
Newington CT 06111

Call Sign: KE1JN
William G Besenyei
30 Butternut Ln
Newington CT 061114289

Call Sign: KA1UWW
David C Bagioni
127 Cambridge Dr
Newington CT 06111

Call Sign: W1AAL
Anthony A La Penta Jr
27 Candlewyck Dr
Newington CT 06111

Call Sign: KB1NFU
Steve J Cultrera
38 Carriage Hill Dr
Newington CT 06111

Call Sign: N1GCS
Gary H Gatzen
192 Carriage Hill Dr
Newington CT 06111

Call Sign: KA1CQW
Paul S Bonazinca
314 Cedar St 4b
Newington CT 06111

Call Sign: WA1TPB

John J Arusiewicz
69 Centerwood Rd
Newington CT 06111

Call Sign: N1AWD
Joseph F Seiler Jr
135 Cherry Hill Dr
Newington CT 06111

Call Sign: K1QEN
Stuart A Mc Fadyen
207 Cherry Hill Dr
Newington CT 06111

Call Sign: N1SYA
Stanley Kaufman
265 Cherry Hill Dr
Newington CT 06111

Call Sign: KB1EZA
Richard Carlson
288 Cherry Hill Dr
Newington CT 06111

Call Sign: KB1BVV
Christine J Gwiazdowski
133 Church St
Newington CT 06111

Call Sign: N1QDP
James A Marks
438 Church St
Newington CT 06111

Call Sign: WA1OBV
Edward T Intravia
112 Churchill Dr
Newington CT 06111

Call Sign: N1CNV
William D Unghire
86 Clarendon Terrace
Newington CT 06111

Call Sign: KB1YE

Charles H Shooshan Iii
60 Clifford Street
Newington CT 061113807

Call Sign: N1HFI
Charles S Wilson
278 Connecticut Ave
Newington CT 061112115

Call Sign: AK1Y
Jerome J Bycul
34 Coolidge Ave
Newington CT 06111

Call Sign: KB1HVL
Stephen R Kelly
18 Coronado Dr
Newington CT 061115006

Call Sign: KB1NMO
Ethel M Kramer
37 Coronado Dr
Newington CT 061115007

Call Sign: KB1OJP
Justin M Baldini
100 Coronado Dr
Newington CT 06111

Call Sign: K1RLF
Justin M Baldini
100 Coronado Dr
Newington CT 06111

Call Sign: N1EBV
Ferdinand A Belcamino
26 Cortland Way
Newington CT 061115332

Call Sign: KA1ZXP
David N Woznica
48 Cortland Way
Newington CT 06111

Call Sign: KB1GEW

Dennis T Callanan
26 Crown Ridge
Newington CT 06111

Call Sign: KA1KQY
Lorraine S Evans
550 Cypress Rd
Newington CT 06111

Call Sign: N1JTL
Harry H Abery Jr
18 Dalewood Road
Newington CT 061112524

Call Sign: AB1ER
Harry H Abery Jr
18 Dalewood Road
Newington CT 061112524

Call Sign: K1SXF
Donald H Scagel
102 Day St
Newington CT 06111

Call Sign: W1VT
Zachary H J Lau
80 E Robbins Ave
Newington CT 061113913

Call Sign: N1VH
Mary E Lau
80 E Robbins Ave
Newington CT 061113913

Call Sign: WA1WNG
John M Maljanian
96 Eddy Ln
Newington CT 06111

Call Sign: KB1LUX
Holly H Harlow
11 Edmund St
Newington CT 06111

Call Sign: KB1LUY

Raymond C Harlow
11 Edmund St
Newington CT 06111

Call Sign: KB1LUZ
Sean J Harlow
11 Edmund St
Newington CT 06111

Call Sign: N1FNN
Raymond F Grogan Jr
52 Elton Dr
Newington CT 06111

Call Sign: KB1RJO
Ryan C Sheehan
45 Elton Drive
Newington CT 06111

Call Sign: N1TUH
Klaus D Schmidt
36 Fairfield Ave
Newington CT 06111

Call Sign: KB1KBK
Theresa Gogluicci
41 Fairfield Ave
Newington CT 06111

Call Sign: K1VIN
Vincent S Gogluicci
41 Fairfield Avenue
Newington CT 06111

Call Sign: KA1ZOJ
Mary E Kalinoski
25 Faith Rd Apt 4
Newington CT 06111

Call Sign: KA1SYB
Donald F Mc Kay
46 Flagler St
Newington CT 06111

Call Sign: N1MCI

H Carl Gold
20 Forest Dr
Newington CT 061113117

Call Sign: WA2ASQ
Paul J Hausleben
129 Fox Run Court
Newington CT 06111

Call Sign: KB1IIP
Daniel Sayad
11 Fox Run Ct
Newington CT 06111

Call Sign: WB2KXY
Randy P Sigman
245 Foxboro Dr
Newington CT 06111

Call Sign: N1HIO
Kathleen D Bagioni
52 Francis Dr
Newington CT 06111

Call Sign: KB1POV
Rocky Hill Amateur Radio
Club
21 Garfield Street
Newington CT 06111

Call Sign: KB1FMY
Mark J Dzamba
53 Garvan St
Newington CT 061112021

Call Sign: KB1FMZ
Pamela D Dzamba
53 Garvan St
Newington CT 061112021

Call Sign: KB1GXJ
Stephen E Walden
58 Glenview Dr
Newington CT 06111

Call Sign: KB1MOZ
Janet L Rocco
121 Glenview Drive
Newington CT 06111

Call Sign: W1JLR
Janet L Rocco
121 Glenview Drive
Newington CT 06111

Call Sign: N1PBC
Neil R Owens
49 Golf St
Newington CT 06111

Call Sign: KB1DMT
Mario L Sousa Jr
26 Hall St
Newington CT 06111

Call Sign: W1VVK
Jack E Mahar
37 Hampton Ct
Newington CT 06111

Call Sign: K1VQZ
Henry A Seagren
16 Harding Ave
Newington CT 06111

Call Sign: KA1YHR
Dorothy A Szczabrowski
89 Harding Ave
Newington CT 06111

Call Sign: KA1SLL
Bernadette G Capella
172 Harding Ave
Newington CT 06111

Call Sign: WA1CRO
David J Capella
172 Harding Ave
Newington CT 06111

Call Sign: KB1DDX
Michael J Phelps
124 Harris Drive
Newington CT 06111

Call Sign: KA1KBI
Kenneth J Albert
205 Hartford Ave
Newington CT 06111

Call Sign: N1QJI
Kee C Tang
31 Henry Ave
Newington CT 06111

Call Sign: KA1PCL
Patrick M Clow
187 Hickory Hill Ln
Newington CT 06111

Call Sign: KA1NCB
Robert Burger
55 High Gate Rd A3
Newington CT 06111

Call Sign: N1RFO
James A De Lorso
39 Highland St
Newington CT 06111

Call Sign: KB1HLF
Helen W Dalton
147 Hillcrest Ave
Newington CT 06111

Call Sign: K1GQO
Alfred J Dessert
224 Hillcrest Ave
Newington CT 061113519

Call Sign: KB1KUJ
Elmer Oder
30 Horizon Hill Rd
Newington CT 06111

Call Sign: WB1FAG
Hugo Hernandez
123 Howard St
Newington CT 06111

Call Sign: KB1KKB
Christopher L Ham
185 Hunters Ln
Newington CT 061114555

Call Sign: W1GJW
William A La Penta
34 Indian Hill Rd
Newington CT 061113407

Call Sign: KB1GSX
Cory Lachance
11 Indian Hill Road
Newington CT 061113408

Call Sign: KA2EMT
Cory Lachance
11 Indian Hill Road
Newington CT 061113408

Call Sign: W1FXQ
Alexander Cohen
42 Jeffrey Ln
Newington CT 061111616

Call Sign: N1VMQ
Fernand R Philippon
105 Kenlock St
Newington CT 06111

Call Sign: N1EIQ
Gary P Husmer
2-Jul King Arthurs Way
Newington CT 06111

Call Sign: K0BOG
Charles B Skolaut
4 King Arthurs Way - Apt 5
Newington CT 06111

Call Sign: N0TIK
Mary I Skolaut
4 King Arthurs Way - Apt 5
Newington CT 06111

Call Sign: KC1IHS
Mary I Skolaut
4 King Arthurs Way - Apt 5
Newington CT 06111

Call Sign: KC7HBB
Lyle E Davieau
29 Kinnear Avenue
Newington CT 06111

Call Sign: KA1BPU
Thomas G Perdion
43 Knollwood Rd
Newington CT 061112565

Call Sign: N1HVT
Mary Ann Perdion
43 Knollwood Rd
Newington CT 06111

Call Sign: AB1AL
Mary Ann Perdion
43 Knollwood Rd
Newington CT 06111

Call Sign: AB1AM
Thomas G Perdion
43 Knollwood Rd
Newington CT 061112565

Call Sign: KB1SPI
Raymond D Lee
15 Ledgecrest Dr
Newington CT 06111

Call Sign: N3BH
John E Spangler
66 Ledgecrest Dr
Newington CT 06111

Call Sign: KB1SST
Maynard C Freeman
81 Linwood Ave
Newington CT 06111

Call Sign: KB1DMW
Rose Anne S Lawrence
335 Lloyd St
Newington CT 061112325

Call Sign: KB1DMX
Richard E Lawrence
335 Lloyd St
Newington CT 061112325

Call Sign: KB1BHM
Peter A Ruchwa
27 Lucas Cir
Newington CT 06111

Call Sign: KB1BHB
Valerie P Wislo
30 Lucas Cir
Newington CT 06111

Call Sign: N1NIV
Steven D Wislo
30 Lucas Cir
Newington CT 06111

Call Sign: WA1SOP
Joseph Patriss Jr
110 Lydall Rd
Newington CT 06111

Call Sign: K5FUV
William E Kennamer
225 Main St
Newington CT 06111

Call Sign: KA1JPA
Joanne B Morin
225 Main St
Newington CT 06111

Call Sign: KA1UFZ
Lisa A Kustosik
225 Main St
Newington CT 06111

Call Sign: KB1BZS
Central Connecticut Qrp
Club
225 Main St
Newington CT 06111

Call Sign: W1AW
Arrl Hq Operators Club
225 Main St
Newington CT 06111

Call Sign: W1INF
Arrl Hq Operators Club
225 Main St
Newington CT 06111

Call Sign: KB1INJ
Laird Campbell Memorial
Hq Operators Club
225 Main St
Newington CT 06111

Call Sign: W1HQ
Laird Campbell Memorial
Hq Operators Club
225 Main St
Newington CT 06111

Call Sign: KB1KJC
Maria Somma
225 Main St
Newington CT 06111

Call Sign: AB1FM
Maria Somma
225 Main St
Newington CT 06111

Call Sign: KB1NED
Debra A Jahnke

225 Main St
Newington CT 06111

Call Sign: K1DAJ
Debra A Jahnke
225 Main St
Newington CT 06111

Call Sign: KB1NJU
Katie Breen
225 Main St
Newington CT 06111

Call Sign: KB1ODH
Janice Wytas
225 Main St
Newington CT 06111

Call Sign: KB1OKV
Diane H Szlachetka
225 Main St
Newington CT 06111

Call Sign: KB1OKW
Susan Fagan
225 Main St
Newington CT 06111

Call Sign: KB1QAW
Carol A Michaud
225 Main St
Newington CT 06111

Call Sign: W1ZOE
Zoe E Belliveau
225 Main St
Newington CT 06111

Call Sign: KB1RPF
Micah J Murray
225 Main St
Newington CT 06111

Call Sign: KB1ULQ
Kathleen M Glass

225 Main St
Newington CT 06111

Call Sign: KB1VUV
Amanda Grimaldi
225 Main St
Newington CT 06111

Call Sign: KB1TXQ
Guy P Paquette
83 Main St Apt 2d
Newington CT 06111

Call Sign: N7IAL
Mary E Lau
83 Main St Apt 9a
Newington CT 061111326

Call Sign: K1SFA
S Khrystyne Keane
225 Main Street
Newington CT 06111

Call Sign: K1TTY
The Fr James P. Mccaffrey
Memorial Radio Club
225 Main Street
Newington CT 06111

Call Sign: W1BQS
Stanley C Perkoski
336 Maple Hill Ave
Newington CT 06111

Call Sign: KB1DMV
Walter P Soucy
490 Maple Hill Ave
Newington CT 06111

Call Sign: N1KWJ
Frederick S Jarvis
34 Meadow St
Newington CT 06111

Call Sign: KA1WLG

Mark I Siegel
57 Meadowview Court
Newington CT 06111

Call Sign: KA1QVF
Robert D Williams
53 Miami Ave
Newington CT 06111

Call Sign: KA1SXS
Nicholas B Shinkaruk
195 Miami Ave
Newington CT 06111

Call Sign: N1HVO
David S Burgess
97 Moreland Ave
Newington CT 06111

Call Sign: N1KB
John C Hennessee
110 Moylan Ct
Newington CT 06111

Call Sign: W1KLY
Stephen R Kelly
162 Nicholson Street
Newington CT 06111

Call Sign: K4ANC
Adam C Castro
49 Noble St
Newington CT 06111

Call Sign: WA2ITD
Robert A Kulesa
105 Old Farm Dr
Newington CT 06111

Call Sign: N1FCL
Robert J Maciorowski
16 Paris Lane
Newington CT 06111

Call Sign: KA1MJN

Ernest R Glabau Sr
80 Patriot Ln
Newington CT 06111

Call Sign: KB1AYV
Matthew R Feshler
37 Pine St
Newington CT 06111

Call Sign: N1NYN
Mark H Pearl
2 Quail Court
Newington CT 06111

Call Sign: KA1OTL
John E Guyan Jr
40 Quincy Ln
Newington CT 061111021

Call Sign: NC1L
Wilfred G Moore
92 Reservoir Rd
Newington CT 06111

Call Sign: KB1WBV
Sandro Dibacco
90 Revere Drive
Newington CT 06111

Call Sign: W1VLA
Michael Lentini
78 Ridgeway St
Newington CT 061113727

Call Sign: KB1HVU
Monica L Golec
21 River Camp Dr
Newington CT 06111

Call Sign: KB1HVV
Christopher M Golec
21 River Camp Dr
Newington CT 06111

Call Sign: KA1QVG

John M Oman
54 Robbins Ave
Newington CT 06111

Call Sign: W1JMO
John M Oman
54 Robbins Ave
Newington CT 06111

Call Sign: N1VVD
Thomas Giantonio
190 Robbins Ave
Newington CT 06111

Call Sign: KB1MPK
Zoe E Belliveau
190 Roseleah Ave
Newington CT 06111

Call Sign: KA1JLH
Richard D Coan
19 Saddle Hill Cir
Newington CT 06111

Call Sign: KC1VX
Paul G Arvai Iii
30 Salem Dr
Newington CT 06111

Call Sign: N1IYA
Deborah C Arvai
30 Salem Dr
Newington CT 06111

Call Sign: KB1LKC
James C Failla Iii
63 School House Rd
Newington CT 061114033

Call Sign: KB1EHF
Andrew B Schiller
84 Settlers Knoll
Newington CT 06111

Call Sign: KB1FNF

Andrew B Schiller
84 Settlers Knoll
Newington CT 06111

Call Sign: AB1BA
Andrew B Schiller
84 Settlers Knoll
Newington CT 06111

Call Sign: KA1NTD
Walter Miller
19 Seventh St
Newington CT 06111

Call Sign: N1UFA
Veronica S Underwood
59 Sleepy Hollow Rd
Newington CT 06111

Call Sign: WB1FSB
Marian S Anderson
26 Spruce St
Newington CT 06111

Call Sign: KM1O
Thomas M Namnoum
55 Spruce St
Newington CT 06111

Call Sign: N1CMA
Eleanor L Namnoum
55 Spruce St
Newington CT 06111

Call Sign: KB1BDI
Sarah E Gantnier
131 Stoddard Ave
Newington CT 06111

Call Sign: KB1JRY
Richard B Lewis
189 Stoddard Ave
Newington CT 06111

Call Sign: KA1VGW

John P Ericson
34 Summit St
Newington CT 06111

Call Sign: KA1JJL
Michael G Carpentieri
44 Surrey Dr A2
Newington CT 06111

Call Sign: N1QOC
Anthony W Collins
23 Theodore St
Newington CT 06111

Call Sign: W1HRJ
Paul J Bedoian Sr
21 Tremont St
Newington CT 06111

Call Sign: K1YMA
Harold Kritzman
91 Tremont St
Newington CT 06111

Call Sign: KB1FQX
Robert S Bedoian
21 Tremont Street
Newington CT 06111

Call Sign: W1HRJ
Robert S Bedoian
21 Tremont Street
Newington CT 06111

Call Sign: KB1PCU
Ellen Leonard
30 Trotter Lane
Newington CT 061115333

Call Sign: KB1PRP
Armando Landrian
38 Tunxis Rd
Newington CT 06111

Call Sign: KB1TEX

Armando A Landrian
38 Tunxis Rd
Newington CT 06111

Call Sign: WB2BLV
Michael A Graziano
38 Valley View Dr
Newington CT 06111

Call Sign: N1AFU
Martin A Erlandson
120 Vincent Dr
Newington CT 06111

Call Sign: KA1NHN
Frederick W Heinrichs
237 Vineyard Ave
Newington CT 06111

Call Sign: N1YYE
Wayne G Haley
34 Wakeley Rd
Newington CT 061113159

Call Sign: N1FCN
Edward C Sullivan
78 Webster Ct
Newington CT 06111

Call Sign: N1QEI
Frank J Slogeris
83 Webster Ct
Newington CT 06111

Call Sign: N1RSJ
Greti V Fodor
101 Webster Ct
Newington CT 06111

Call Sign: N1RSM
Richard S Genovese
101 Webster Ct
Newington CT 06111

Call Sign: KB1AGH

Frederick C La Voie
134 Webster Ct
Newington CT 06111

Call Sign: N1QEO
Gerald Reardon
56 Welles Dr N
Newington CT 06111

Call Sign: WB1FIF
Maurice R Miles
372 Willard Ave
Newington CT 06111

Call Sign: N1LNP
Marc K Frantz
288 Williamstown Ct
Newington CT 06111

Call Sign: KB1NXO
Amy Hurtado
115 Windmill Lane
Newington CT 06111

Call Sign: N1WHY
David J Gasner
89 Winslow Dr
Newington CT 06111

Call Sign: KA1HQK
John Di Sarro
134 Winslow Dr
Newington CT 061114926

Call Sign: N1YPF
James J Chrzanowski
35 Woodbridge Rd
Newington CT 06111

Call Sign: WB9RRU
Scott H Gee
60 Woodbridge Road
Newington CT 06111

Call Sign: WS1K

Jerry Ellis
35-2b Woodsedge Dr
Newington CT 061114271

Call Sign: KG2LL
Jerry Ellis
35-2b Woodsedge Dr
Newington CT 061114271

Call Sign: KG2LL
Jerry Ellis
35 Woodsedge Dr Apt 2b
Newington CT 06111

Call Sign: WA1VMA
William V Yushkevich Jr
85 Woodsedge Dr Apt 4c
Newington CT 06111

Call Sign: K1MK
Michael J Keane
Newington CT 061310291

Call Sign: KB1DCJ
Edward Majewski
Newington CT 061310252

Call Sign: N1FOZ
Mark D Gamble
Newington CT 06111

Call Sign: N2YCQ
Ronald C Bogaert
Newington CT 061310713

Call Sign: N2YDS
Philippe Bogaert
Newington CT 061310713

Call Sign: NU1AW
International Amateur Radio
Union
Newington CT 061310905

Call Sign: NX1L

Naoki Akiyama
Newington CT 061310855

Call Sign: W1NB
New Britain Radio
Ramblers
Newington CT 061310713

Call Sign: WA1VLX
Robert V Andersen
Newington CT 06131

Call Sign: WV1X
Steven R Ewald
Newington CT 061310855

Call Sign: KB1NMA
Siesta Wireless Society
Newington CT 061310384

Call Sign: KB1OQO
Siesta Wireless Society
Newington CT 061310384

Call Sign: KB1RLY
The Fr James P. Mccaffrey
Memorial Radio Station
Newington CT 061310291

Call Sign: KB1RWL
Newington Amateur Radio
League
Newington CT 06111

Call Sign: KB1RWS
Boston College High School
Arc
Newington CT 06131

Call Sign: NA1RL
Newington Amateur Radio
League
Newington CT 06111

Call Sign: WA1NWS
George E Blantin
4 Aunt Park Ln
Newtown CT 06470

Call Sign: KA1EFQ
William D Cosgrove
9 Bari Dr
Newtown CT 06470

Call Sign: KB1TWD
Jeffrey J Zibluk
30 Birch Hill Rd
Newtown CT 06470

Call Sign: AB1HN
Daniel S Furphy
3 Black Walnut Dr
Newtown CT 06470

Call Sign: KB1PKR
Christal J Furphy
3 Black Walnut Dr
Newtown CT 06470

Call Sign: N1VPM
Jason E Luckenbaugh
40 Brookwood Dr
Newtown CT 06470

Call Sign: KC1TR
Robert J Schroeder
71 Castle Hill Rd
Newtown CT 06470

Call Sign: W1EJH
Ernest J Martin
27 Castle Meadow Rd
Newtown CT 06470

Call Sign: WA1FHD
Frank E Furze Jr

27 Castle Meadow Rd
Newtown CT 06470

Call Sign: N1PJF
Barbara A Butler
43 Castle Meadow Rd
Newtown CT 06470

Call Sign: KB1LVW
Leslie Murray
24 Cedar Hill Rd
Newtown CT 064702214

Call Sign: WA1HOZ
Gerard L Belanger
62 Cedar Hill Rd
Newtown CT 06470

Call Sign: KB1LYO
Louis Belanger
62 Cedar Hill Rd
Newtown CT 06470

Call Sign: N1ZMI
Barry G Smith
11 Crossbrook Rd
Newtown CT 064701733

Call Sign: KA1VVF
Alastair C Sellars
68 Currituck Rd
Newtown CT 06470

Call Sign: N1IGO
Eugene R Travis
97 Currituck Rd
Newtown CT 06470

Call Sign: WB2SHG
Howard M Winkler
149 Currituck Rd
Newtown CT 06470

Call Sign: N1ORQ
Douglas W Lindell

6 Daves Ln
Newtown CT 06470

Call Sign: N1UJS
Robert F Busino
5 Diamond Drive
Newtown CT 06470

Call Sign: KB1MPV
Leslie A Busino
5 Diamond Drive
Newtown CT 06470

Call Sign: KA1NXL
Tracy A Brown
7 Ferris Rd
Newtown CT 06470

Call Sign: KB1UQX
Clifford M Scharf
13 Flat Swamp Rd
Newtown CT 06470

Call Sign: KB1CIV
Philip J Barackman
42 Grand Pl
Newtown CT 06470

Call Sign: WA1DYI
Paul D Murphy
17 Greenleaf Farms Rd
Newtown CT 06470

Call Sign: KB1LJP
Benjamin P Cruson
174 Hanover Rd
Newtown CT 06470

Call Sign: N1GTN
Rosemarie D Moseley
191 Hanover Rd
Newtown CT 06470

Call Sign: N1GUU
William F Moseley Jr

191 Hanover Rd
Newtown CT 06470

Call Sign: KA1VJC
Laura M Morgan
40 Hattertown Rd
Newtown CT 06470

Call Sign: N1TGO
George E Martin
83 Hattertown Rd
Newtown CT 06470

Call Sign: AC8O
Robert H Keegan
106 Head Of Meadow Rd
Newtown CT 06470

Call Sign: KB1PDL
Michael P Chevalier
143 Headow Of Meadow
Rd
Newtown CT 06470

Call Sign: KA1TZM
Howard M Smith
7 Hyvue Dr
Newtown CT 06470

Call Sign: W1ER
John E Traub
19 Hyvue Dr
Newtown CT 06470

Call Sign: N1EVD
Albert W Clemence
12 John Beach Rd
Newtown CT 06470

Call Sign: KB2CER
Philip T Morgan
3 Juniper Rd
Newtown CT 06470

Call Sign: K2RE

James F Wolff Jr
29 Key Rock Road
Newtown CT 06470

Call Sign: N1CUO
Joseph J Girgasky Iii
7 Lake Rd
Newtown CT 06470

Call Sign: W1CM
Joseph J Girgasky Iii
7 Lake Rd
Newtown CT 06470

Call Sign: N1UJU
Alan T Fletcher
14 Lantern Dr
Newtown CT 064702735

Call Sign: KB1NRN
Erik Dawe
2 Madison Dr
Newtown CT 06470

Call Sign: K2EMR
Kenneth Lerman
55 Main St
Newtown CT 06470

Call Sign: KB1NNI
James M Pearson Sr
25 Maltbie Rd
Newtown CT 06470

Call Sign: KA1UBG
John J Hanna Ii
14 Mount Nebo Rd
Newtown CT 064702434

Call Sign: KC6GAC
John F Bingham
16 Mt Nebo Rd
Newtown CT 06470

Call Sign: K1OJP

Robert S Grossman
45 Mt Pleasant Rd
Newtown CT 06470

Call Sign: KB1LJQ
Alex M Snow
22 N Branch Rd
Newtown CT 06470

Call Sign: NF1K
Andrew D Cartoun
9 Newfield Ln
Newtown CT 06470

Call Sign: KB1LZT
George M Bennett
17 Oak Ridge Dr
Newtown CT 06470

Call Sign: K1GMB
George M Bennett
17 Oak Ridge Dr
Newtown CT 06470

Call Sign: KB1OFP
Andrew H Hsu
17 Old Castle Dr
Newtown CT 06470

Call Sign: N1TGN
Vincent J Cannavo
6 Old Gate Ln
Newtown CT 06470

Call Sign: AA1DV
Allen G Kellogg
13 Ox Hill Rd
Newtown CT 06470

Call Sign: WA1VSI
Richard M Margules
13 Palestine Rd
Newtown CT 06470

Call Sign: WB9RQG

Joseph G Aschauer
45 Parmalee Hill Rd
Newtown CT 06470

Call Sign: KB1KIF
Brenden R Walsh
7 Parmalee Park Pl
Newtown CT 06470

Call Sign: KB1PKQ
Gregory D Jurman
21 Pebble Rd
Newtown CT 06470

Call Sign: KB1OQQ
Anthony J Raiani
23 Plumtrees Road
Newtown CT 06470

Call Sign: AA8BO
Mike H Summerer
5 Pumpkin Lane
Newtown CT 06470

Call Sign: N1VFE
James R Hill
62 Queen St
Newtown CT 064702124

Call Sign: WB1EZA
J David Goldin
19 Russett Road
Newtown CT 06470

Call Sign: WA5SGW
Kenneth E Stephenson
13 Saw Mill Ridge Rd
Newtown CT 06470

Call Sign: KB1NFD
Patricia Stephenson
13 Sawmill Ridge Rd
Newtown CT 06470

Call Sign: KQ2M

Robert L Shohet
51 Scudder Rd
Newtown CT 06470

Call Sign: KB1LMR
James G Hilton
2 Sealand Dr
Newtown CT 06470

Call Sign: KA1TFM
Katie M Johnstone
11 Stone Fence Lane
Newtown CT 06470

Call Sign: N1JXJ
Jane M Johnstone
11 Stone Fence Lane
Newtown CT 06470

Call Sign: N1JXK
Erik M Johnstone
11 Stone Fence Lane
Newtown CT 06470

Call Sign: KB1NUI
William M Mcdonough
55 Sugar St
Newtown CT 06470

Call Sign: KB1MWW
Andrew B Lamarche
161 Taunton Hill Rd
Newtown CT 06470

Call Sign: KA1NXM
John W Warner
12 Taunton Ridge Rd
Newtown CT 06470

Call Sign: KB1OOF
Nicholas R Maccharoli
11 Towns End Rd
Newtown CT 06470

Call Sign: N1VNM

Donald W Stowe
32 Washbrook Rd
Newtown CT 06470

Call Sign: KB1LYM
David A Shugarts
19 Wendover Rd
Newtown CT 06470

Call Sign: KB1LYN
Andrew R Shugarts
19 Wendover Rd
Newtown CT 06470

Call Sign: N1HUV
Richard F Ruscoe
11 Wills Rd
Newtown CT 06470

Call Sign: N1PNT
Michelle M Thompson
Newtown CT 06470

Call Sign: KB1KQD
Robert G Taylor
Newtown CT 06470

Call Sign: KB1SOP
James G Zeranski
Newtown CT 06470

FCC Amateur Radio Licenses in Niantic

Call Sign: N1OKJ
Robert M Silva
30 Attawan Rd
Niantic CT 06357

Call Sign: N1IIP
Roger S La Flamme
102 Bayview Rd
Niantic CT 06357

Call Sign: K1WWU

Thomas N Cairns
54 Bellaire Rd
Niantic CT 063573346

Call Sign: KA1UWF
Hugo Zimmer
Bishop Bay Dr 10
Niantic CT 06357

Call Sign: KB1MAM
Kenneth F Lecara
29 Black Point Rd
Niantic CT 06357

Call Sign: N1CDV
James S Zoldy Sr
5 Blueberry Ln
Niantic CT 063571943

Call Sign: WA1JGL
Dennis M Perruccio
7 Burnap Rd
Niantic CT 06357

Call Sign: KA1STP
Robert C Preston
6 Churchwood
Niantic CT 06357

Call Sign: W1JJR
Jacob J Rosen
10 Compass Court
Niantic CT 06357

Call Sign: KB1KNA
Anne E Budding
34 Cubles Dr
Niantic CT 06357

Call Sign: W1VRP
John C Amaral
7 Cypress Way
Niantic CT 06357

Call Sign: KB1PGK

John S Kopchik
33 Damon Heights Rd
Niantic CT 06357

Call Sign: AE1N
Louis E Cote
38 Damon Heights Rd
Niantic CT 06357

Call Sign: KK1D
Peter J Rovero
42 Damon Heights Rd
Niantic CT 06357

Call Sign: WR1E
Roger B Thurlow
149 Flanders Rd
Niantic CT 06357

Call Sign: KE4YPJ
Grant M Miller
5 Forest Road
Niantic CT 06357

Call Sign: KB1FPB
April L Lowell
11 Gada Rd
Niantic CT 06357

Call Sign: K1LDR
George E Ryalls
72 Giants Neck Rd
Niantic CT 06357

Call Sign: N1CZW
Nicholas A Gianacoplos
40 Greencliff Dr.
Niantic CT 06357

Call Sign: WB1HLU
John R Robinson
80 Hillcrest Rd
Niantic CT 06357

Call Sign: N1URS

William A Kramm
70 Hope St
Niantic CT 06357

Call Sign: WW1CK
Clifford J Kramm
70 Hope St
Niantic CT 06357

Call Sign: W1WAK
William A Kramm
70 Hope St
Niantic CT 06357

Call Sign: KB1IXZ
Michael A Bekech
84 Hope St
Niantic CT 063570135

Call Sign: WA1ONA
James B Hall Jr
6 Hudson Lane
Niantic CT 063571968

Call Sign: KB1UVH
Robert C Turner
40 Lake Ave
Niantic CT 06357

Call Sign: K1JVJ
Jack A Plane
8 Lake Ave Ext
Niantic CT 06357

Call Sign: K1TUK
William L Konrad
54 Laurel Hill Dr
Niantic CT 06357

Call Sign: N1YFB
Bernard M Mc Guinness
29 Laurel St
Niantic CT 063572624

Call Sign: KA1IAX

Daniel F Lowell
91 Lee Farm Drive
Niantic CT 06357

Call Sign: WO1J
Nicholas P Yonclas
417 Main St
Niantic CT 06357

Call Sign: N1REE
Clifford J Kramm
423 Main St
Niantic CT 06357

Call Sign: K2HWU
Wallace R Lowe
417 Main St - Crescent
Point
Niantic CT 06357

Call Sign: KC1CP
Peter C Matson
417 Main St Apt 103
Niantic CT 063573150

Call Sign: W1ACM
Albert C Moutran
468 Main Street Apt 214
Niantic CT 06357

Call Sign: N1HAV
Charles E Bowers
22 Mc Elaney Dr
Niantic CT 06357

Call Sign: KA1JCJ
Peter F Wilhelmsen
5 Meadow St
Niantic CT 06357

Call Sign: W1TEZ
Edward S Dana
21 N Main St
Niantic CT 06357

Call Sign: N1VGW
Charles H Benson
6 North Drive
Niantic CT 06357

Call Sign: N1BOW
Philip J Zocco
7 Oakwood Rd
Niantic CT 06357

Call Sign: KB1VZK
Truxtun E Brodhead
58 Oswegatchie Hills Rd
Niantic CT 06357

Call Sign: KB1HCV
East Lyme Office Of
Emergency Management
P O Drawer 519
Niantic CT 06357

Call Sign: KA1IPH
Ernest W Jones
14 Park Ln
Niantic CT 06357

Call Sign: KA1LDB
Harvey S Rogers
29 Park Pl
Niantic CT 06357

Call Sign: KB1LYD
Herbert L Lindblom
150 Pennsylvania Ave
Niantic CT 06357

Call Sign: WQ1N
James E Themig
26 Pleasant Dr
Niantic CT 06357

Call Sign: N1LVK
Frank S Replogle Jr
1 Pontiac Dr
Niantic CT 06357

Call Sign: W1NSI
Richard C Storrs
River Bank
Niantic CT 06357

Call Sign: KB1PDH
Laura N Abel
61 River View Rd
Niantic CT 06357

Call Sign: KE2TL
John C Abel
61 Riverview Rd
Niantic CT 06357

Call Sign: AB1HK
John C Abel
61 Riverview Rd
Niantic CT 06357

Call Sign: K1AMS
A Michael Schindler
91 Riverview Road Unit 9a
Niantic CT 06357

Call Sign: WA1WUH
Charles A Rowbotham
123 Roxbury Rd
Niantic CT 06357

Call Sign: W1QAI
Charles M Tinker Jr
200 Roxbury Rd
Niantic CT 063571011

Call Sign: KB1DPP
John O Primo
19 Sleepy Hollow Rd
Niantic CT 06357

Call Sign: W1JOP
John J Primo
19 Sleepy Hollow Rd
Niantic CT 06357

Call Sign: KB1PRY
Dorothea P Stribling
41 So Cobblers Court
Niantic CT 06357

Call Sign: KB1GDK
Robert G Lavoie
68 Society Rd
Niantic CT 06357

Call Sign: KB1GJS
Chad B Lavoie
68 Society Rd
Niantic CT 06357

Call Sign: KA1CRZ
Robert G Lavoie
68 Society Road
Niantic CT 06357

Call Sign: N1OUP
James F Mc Gillivray
1 South Drive
Niantic CT 06357

Call Sign: K1BY
John H Templeton
7 Stone Cliff Dr
Niantic CT 06357

Call Sign: AA1QY
Frank E Geluso
5 Strawberry Ln
Niantic CT 063571936

Call Sign: W1RED
David E Reed
10 Surrey La
Niantic CT 06357

Call Sign: N1QKY
Nancy R Reed
10 Surrey Ln
Niantic CT 06357

Call Sign: WA1ZWG
David E Reed
10 Surrey Ln
Niantic CT 06357

Call Sign: KB1RPO
Christine H Wohlgemuth
85 Terrace Ave
Niantic CT 06357

Call Sign: KB1MCT
Forrest E Andrews
86 Terrace Ave
Niantic CT 06357

Call Sign: AA1CF
Fred V Gwyer
97 W Main St
Niantic CT 06357

Call Sign: KB1WFA
Ira Spector
21 Wells St.
Niantic CT 06357

Call Sign: N1YBC
Philip C Simmons
5 Windfall Lane
Niantic CT 063571247

Call Sign: W1OEM
East Lyme Office Of
Emergency Management
Niantic CT 06357

Call Sign: KA4TUM
Harry D Mc Cutcheon
4 Peach Tree La
Niantie CT 06357

**FCC Amateur Radio
Licenses in Noank**

Call Sign: N1DIX

Montague G Miller
201 Elm St Apt 1-7
Noank CT 06340

Call Sign: N1QFE
Susanne A Huber
92 Front St
Noank CT 06340

Call Sign: K1OEA
William G Gaynor
490 Groton Long Point Rd
Noank CT 06340

Call Sign: WD1E
Kenneth F Richard
681 Groton Long Pt Rd
Noank CT 06340

Call Sign: W1ENB
William W Walker
30 High
Noank CT 06340

Call Sign: K1EE
Edward H Eckelmeyer
75 High St
Noank CT 06340

Call Sign: KB1AVH
Thomas D Leary
20 Morgan Point
Noank CT 06340

Call Sign: KA1ZNY
Donald L Treworgy
91 Noble Ave
Noank CT 06340

Call Sign: W1PBN
Thomas A Saragosa
24 Osage Ln
Noank CT 06340

Call Sign: KB1JMM

Judith A Drake
68 Prospect Hill Rd
Noank CT 06340

Call Sign: KB1JMN
David M Drake
68 Prospect Hill Rd
Noank CT 06340

Call Sign: WB1BXK
Michael P Gozzo
225 Prospect Hill Road
Noank CT 06340

Call Sign: N1VGA
William B Andrews
107 Seneca Dr
Noank CT 06340

Call Sign: W1ENI
Edward B Amatrudo
45 Spicer Ave
Noank CT 06340

Call Sign: N1SXV
John K Andersen
37 Sylvan St
Noank CT 063405742

Call Sign: KB1CJP
Brian A Brousseau
25 West View Ave
Noank CT 06340

Call Sign: N1EIL
Claiborne C Van Zandt Jr
Noank CT 06340

Call Sign: N1VOK
Andrew G Attanasio
Norfolk CT 06058

FCC Amateur Radio Licenses in North Branford

Call Sign: KB1WH
John Sykes Jr
37 Altieri Rd
North Branford CT 06471

Call Sign: KC1NB
Michael K Loukides
229 Branford Rd 310
North Branford CT 06471

Call Sign: KA1QZH
Douglas A Wilmott
43 Brook Ln
North Branford CT 06471

Call Sign: KA1YIC
Lawrence L Bee Jr
20 Church Street
North Branford CT 06471

Call Sign: KA1UWD
Donald J Turecek
16 Clear Lake Manor Rd W
North Branford CT 06471

Call Sign: KB1STM
George A Colafati Jr
24 Edward Rd
North Branford CT 06471

Call Sign: N1KGD
Laureen B Mongillo
6 Frederick St
North Branford CT 06471

Call Sign: KJ1V
John A O Connor
4 Glen Cir
North Branford CT 06471

Call Sign: KB1VCK
Arne G Hansson
75 Great Hill Rd
North Branford CT 06471

Call Sign: W1ZEU
John J Britt
25 Highfield Ln
North Branford CT 06471

Call Sign: KB1UVI
James A Raymond Jr
4 Lake Rd
North Branford CT 06471

Call Sign: KA1QFM
Christine H Harrison
87 North St
North Branford CT 06471

Call Sign: W1LQZ
Victor A Stancliff
88 Notch Hill Rd
North Branford CT 06471

Call Sign: W1YVC
Ian Isdale
88 Notch Hill Road Unit
140
North Branford CT 06471

Call Sign: N1HAX
Donald L Izzo
24 Rivaldi Drive
North Branford CT 06471

Call Sign: KA1SXI
James E Mc Cue
5 Rose Ln
North Branford CT 06471

Call Sign: KB1URS
Nicholas M Brenckle
126 Sea Hill Road
North Branford CT 06471

Call Sign: W1ESV
Franklin D Swezey
15 Sunset Rd W

North Branford CT 06471

Call Sign: KA1RJQ
Eugene J Modzelewski
312 Twin Lakes Rd
North Branford CT
064711220

Call Sign: N1LXU
Lillian M Steeves
381 Twinlakes Rd
North Branford CT 06471

Call Sign: AA1VM
Daniel L Steeves
381 Twinlakes Rd
North Branford CT 06471

Call Sign: WB1GXO
Stephen P Syrotiak
86 Valley Rd
North Branford CT 06471

Call Sign: WB1HFF
Cecelia D Syrotiak
86 Valley Rd
North Branford CT 06471

Call Sign: N1KSY
Donald A Krahl
279 Valley Rd
North Branford CT 06471

**FCC Amateur Radio
Licenses in North Canaan**

Call Sign: N1SVL
John F Brown
16 Barlow St
North Canaan CT 06018

**FCC Amateur Radio
Licenses in North Canton**

Call Sign: N1IIR

Christopher C Stratton
2 Andrew Dr
North Canton CT 06059

Call Sign: WA1PIU
Barbara Cassada
35 Deer Run Rd
North Canton CT 06059

Call Sign: WA1JLC
Joseph M Hagel
7 Scoville Rd
North Canton CT 06059

**FCC Amateur Radio
Licenses in North
Franklin**

Call Sign: KB1HNP
Thomas H Seidel
14 Bullard Rd
North Franklin CT 06254

Call Sign: N1MWM
Nicholas J Sobestanovich
23 Hyde Park Rd
North Franklin CT 06254

Call Sign: WA1QDX
John W Chamberlain
46 Meeting House Hill
Road
North Franklin CT 06254

Call Sign: KB1CTD
Richard L Provost
19 Plains Rd
North Franklin CT 06254

Call Sign: KB1DED
Louis R Herman
North Franklin CT 06254

**FCC Amateur Radio
Licenses in North Granby**

Call Sign: KB1PYY
Brent D Robertson
22 Cider Mill Heights
North Granby CT 06060

Call Sign: WA1PJU
Hilding W Olin
170 East St
North Granby CT 06060

Call Sign: N1PDD
Thomas R Johnston
9 Gloucester Ln
North Granby CT 06060

Call Sign: KB1GW
Glenn P Swanson
25 Heather Lane
North Granby CT 06060

Call Sign: W1ALI
Giacinto J Reale Jr
139 Loomis St
North Granby CT 06060

Call Sign: KB1MNH
Howard R Baird
39 Northwoods Rd
North Granby CT 06060

Call Sign: KD1AF
Edward R Darcy
63 Silver St
North Granby CT 06060

Call Sign: N1KKN
Kenneth N Isenberg
148 Silver St
North Granby CT 06060

**FCC Amateur Radio
Licenses in North
Grosvenordale**

Call Sign: K1TBQ
David S Ostrowski
Rr 1 Box 851
North Grosvenordale CT
06255

Call Sign: K1EZB
Richard A Rocheleau
110 Main St
North Grosvenor Dale CT
06255

Call Sign: KB1DNN
Matthew G Clark
17 Mountain Hill Rd
North Grosvenordale CT
06255

Call Sign: AB1DX
Oliver L Richards
12 Rachel Dr
North Grosvenordale CT
06255

Call Sign: N1RFW
Antony G Judd
1201 Riverside Dr
North Grosvenordale CT
06255

Call Sign: KB1VBX
Alan C Pratt
31 Seastrand Rd
North Grosvenordale CT
06255

Call Sign: K1ZKR
Milton P Columbus
89 Stawicki Rd
North Grosvenordale CT
06255

Call Sign: N1TYO
Thomas P Popiak
56 Valley Rd

North Grosvenordale CT
06255

Call Sign: N1NNL
Marvin J Wilbur
12 Whittemore Ave
North Grosvenordale CT
06255

Call Sign: K1VSC
Ronald D Pariseau
North Grosvenordale CT
062550376

Call Sign: N1UBO
Scott D Robinson
North Grosvenordale CT
062550885

Call Sign: KB1VMX
The 807's Group
North Grosvenordale CT
06255

Call Sign: K1EOS
The 807's Group
North Grosvenordale CT
06255

**FCC Amateur Radio
Licenses in North Guilford**

Call Sign: W1WEB
Vincent Scalise
438 County Rd
North Guilford CT 06437

Call Sign: N1OFM
Scott Cameron
867 Hoop Pole Rd
North Guilford CT 06437

**FCC Amateur Radio
Licenses in North Haven**

Call Sign: K1YLV
Jeffrey N Wayne
61 Allendale Dr
North Haven CT 06473

Call Sign: K1NMZ
Arthur R Davis
38 Butler Rd
North Haven CT 06473

Call Sign: N1TTT
Frank S Jablonski
9 Drazen Dr
North Haven CT 06473

Call Sign: WA1ZLR
Carolyn A Wayne
61 Allendale Dr
North Haven CT 06473

Call Sign: W1AMF
Robert B Munro
29 Butler Road
North Haven CT 06473

Call Sign: KA1BHP
Lauren E Brown
39 Edison Dr
North Haven CT 06473

Call Sign: K1EJL
John H Goodrich Sr
113 Bailey Rd
North Haven CT 064732610

Call Sign: WI1G
Robert B Munro
29 Butler Road
North Haven CT 06473

Call Sign: WB1BYW
Phillip J Brown
39 Edison Dr
North Haven CT 06473

Call Sign: W1NRE
Lyn H Cyr
83 Bayayrd Ave
North Haven CT 06518

Call Sign: W1IG
Robert B Munro
29 Butler Road
North Haven CT 06473

Call Sign: WA1ZKR
Gordon V Olsen
160 Garfield Ave
North Haven CT 06473

Call Sign: KA1GTO
John P Golino
36 Blakeslee Ave
North Haven CT 06473

Call Sign: WB1DZI
Eunice J Falcigno
44 Carriage Dr
North Haven CT 06473

Call Sign: KB1BER
Mary Ann Viscio
104 Grove Rd
North Haven CT 06473

Call Sign: K1VZZ
Frank E Morse Jr
119 Blakeslee Ave
North Haven CT 064731919

Call Sign: WB1DZJ
Brett P Falcigno
44 Carriage Dr
North Haven CT 06473

Call Sign: WA1OIH
Louis Viscio
104 Grove Rd
North Haven CT 06473

Call Sign: KA1BIA
Donald M Maki
9 Bowling Grn Dr
North Haven CT 06473

Call Sign: KB1DMY
Anthony J Lengvinis
91 Chapel Hill Rd
North Haven CT 06473

Call Sign: KB1BGH
Lynda A Kalkowski
1034 Hartford Tpke
North Haven CT 06473

Call Sign: KB1RRY
Michael P Kelly
29 Butler Rd
North Haven CT 06473

Call Sign: K1SCM
Howard A Stebbins
6 Coach Dr
North Haven CT 064731511

Call Sign: N1GTL
James G Kalkowski
1034 Hartford Tpke
North Haven CT 06473

Call Sign: W1MPK
Michael P Kelly
29 Butler Rd
North Haven CT 06473

Call Sign: N1SBG
Robert A Anastasio
8 Donmar Ct
North Haven CT 06473

Call Sign: KE1AY
Donald G Mitchell
1682 Hartford Tpke
North Haven CT 06473

Call Sign: KB1DJF
Patrick E Logan
2065 Hartford Tpke
North Haven CT 06473

Call Sign: W1WCG
Frank C Van Cleef Iii
42 Larson Dr
North Haven CT 064731800

Call Sign: W1NDT
Robert Lombardo
45 Pool Rd
North Haven CT 06473

Call Sign: N1ZRI
Guy H Barnhart
1057 Hartford Turnpike
North Haven CT 064733039

Call Sign: KB1KZB
Gene Dinuzzo
51 Laydon Ave
North Haven CT 06473

Call Sign: N1NPZ
Stephen F Morley
28 Potter Rd
North Haven CT 06473

Call Sign: KB1VHX
Brian P Smith
1518 Hartford Turnpike
North Haven CT 06473

Call Sign: KA1BHX
James Dowers
26 Lincoln St
North Haven CT 06473

Call Sign: W1LV
Stephen F Morley
28 Potter Rd
North Haven CT 06473

Call Sign: W1UDQ
William T Davies Jr
79 Hartley St
North Haven CT 06473

Call Sign: N1VBS
Terry K Martin
13 Louis St
North Haven CT 06473

Call Sign: KB1PLR
Michael Schlereth
252 Quinnipiac Ave
North Haven CT 06473

Call Sign: W1OAS
Frederick M Burkle
97 Hartley St
North Haven CT 06473

Call Sign: N1EFD
Martin L Rudnick
123 Maple Ave
North Haven CT 06473

Call Sign: K1WMQ
Arthur J Fregeau
27 Renee Ln
North Haven CT 06473

Call Sign: N1FLY
Howard A Phillips
5 Hickory Hill Rd
North Haven CT 06473

Call Sign: N1EDY
Robert H Lynch
250 Maple Ave
North Haven CT 06473

Call Sign: KB1IZM
Jameson F Rivers
27 Renee Ln
North Haven CT 06473

Call Sign: KB1OFA
Vernon G Wulle
11 Hidden Pond Drive
North Haven CT 06473

Call Sign: N1VKN
Daniel M Sanford
585 Middletown Ave
North Haven CT 06473

Call Sign: AF1HS
Arthur J Fregeau
27 Renee Ln
North Haven CT 06473

Call Sign: KE1AV
David W Sanford
28 Hilltop Ter
North Haven CT 06473

Call Sign: W1JAK
August J Asor
20 Norway Road
North Haven CT 06473

Call Sign: W1GZX
Carleton H Burt
6 Samoset Ave
North Haven CT 064732622

Call Sign: N1XFL
Philip T Diperi
45 Juniper Drive
North Haven CT 06473

Call Sign: WA1WZU
Robert Lombardo
45 Pool Rd
North Haven CT 06473

Call Sign: WA1VML
Rico B Gattilia Jr
19 School Lane
North Haven CT 06473

Call Sign: WB1ENL
Robert A Tiroletto
35 Sentinel Hill Rd
North Haven CT 06473

Call Sign: KA1LRK
Paul A Amendola
126 Spring Rd
North Haven CT 06473

Call Sign: KA1POF
Edward E Varipapa
100 Spring Road
North Haven CT 06473

Call Sign: KB1FSG
Louis A Lettelleir
36 St John Street
North Haven CT 06473

Call Sign: W1WHF
South Central Conn Amat
Rad Assn Inc
84 State St
North Haven CT 06473

Call Sign: N1MMO
Mark J Petrone
1 Summer Ln
North Haven CT 06473

Call Sign: WB1CJP
Theodore R Ross
125 Tokeneke Dr
North Haven CT 06473

Call Sign: KD1RG
Clifford R Loos
6 Vincent Rd
North Haven CT 06473

Call Sign: KB1CIB
Joseph J Sciuto
8 William St
North Haven CT 06473

Call Sign: KA1VQE
Lorraine F Cavallaro
24 Wilson Ave
North Haven CT 06473

Call Sign: KA1VRX
Paul G Cavallaro Sr
24 Wilson Ave
North Haven CT 06473

Call Sign: N1WKU
Tawfiq E Al Ezz
North Haven CT 06473

Call Sign: KB1FYJ
Shari A O Mara
North Haven CT 06473

Call Sign: KB1KJN
George S Esposito
North Haven CT 064730765

Call Sign: N1ESP
George S Esposito
North Haven CT 06473

FCC Amateur Radio Licenses in North Stonington

Call Sign: KA1VMG
Andrew J Clark
93 Boombridge Rd
North Stonington CT 06359

Call Sign: KB1LFU
Richard J Marks Iv
15 Clarks Falls Rd
North Stonington CT 06359

Call Sign: K1RJM
Richard J Marks Iv
15 Clarks Falls Rd
North Stonington CT 06359

Call Sign: KA1TQM
Thomas J Cassidy
214 Clarks Falls Rd
North Stonington CT 06359

Call Sign: KA1TQI
James E Cowley Jr
226 Clarks Falls Rd
North Stonington CT 06359

Call Sign: KA1KAK
June C Stewart
452 Cossadack Hill Rd
North Stonington CT 06359

Call Sign: KA1KAL
L Lincoln Stewart
452 Cossaduck Hill Rd
North Stonington CT 06359

Call Sign: KA1KAM
G Russell Stewart Ii
452 Cossaduck Hill Rd
North Stonington CT 06359

Call Sign: N1TMU
Matthew T Beaudoin
9 Ella Wheeler Rd
North Stonington CT 06359

Call Sign: KE1LM
Peter B Davis
47 Jeremy Hill Rd
North Stonington CT
063591202

Call Sign: W1DVS
Peter B Davis
47 Jeremy Hill Rd
North Stonington CT
063591202

Call Sign: N1JSH
Gary E Smith

7 Kingswood Dr
North Stonington CT 06359

Call Sign: N1IBL
Calvin T Stafford
51 Mains Crossing
North Stonington CT 06359

Call Sign: KB1QBQ
David T Holliday
11 Mains Crossing Road
North Stonington CT 06359

Call Sign: WA1DOC
David T Holliday
11 Mains Crossing Road
North Stonington CT 06359

Call Sign: KB1CFC
Harry I Trice Jr
400 Providence New
London Tpke
North Stonington CT 06359

Call Sign: N1AEA
John E Ahern
20 Providence New London
Turnpike Lot 21
North Stonington CT 06359

Call Sign: K1PB
Robert H Reust
30 Ravenwood Rd
North Stonington CT 06359

Call Sign: KB1BGE
Herbert E Coon
135 Reutemann Rd
North Stonington CT 06359

Call Sign: N1LJB
Leonora B Gwyer
13 Rocky Hollow Rd
North Stonington CT 06359

Call Sign: N1ENN
Richard S Matthews
11 Tom Wheeler Rd
North Stonington CT 06359

Call Sign: KZ6S
Gregory R Allison
20 Tom Wheeler Rd
North Stonington CT 06359

Call Sign: KB1EQN
William A Grenier
North Stonington CT 06359

FCC Amateur Radio Licenses in North Windham

Call Sign: WA1NLA
George H Worrall Jr
229 Beaver Hill Rd
North Windham CT 06256

Call Sign: N1FEH
Lawrence C Laflamme
280 Beaver Hill Rd
North Windham CT 06256

Call Sign: KB1FPS
Rene E Roy
293 Beaver Hill Rd
North Windham CT 06256

Call Sign: W1OND
Arthur C Ayer Jr
33 Evelyn Dr
North Windham CT 06256

Call Sign: KB1BBJ
Douglas M Fornal
97 S Bear Hill Rd
North Windham CT 06256

Call Sign: WB1GLR
Chester G Rich

67 Virginia Dr
North Windham CT 06256

FCC Amateur Radio Licenses in Northfield

Call Sign: KA1UWX
Timothy E Scatena
Rfd 1 Campville Rd
Northfield CT 06778

Call Sign: N1URP
Judith E Hayward
14 Hilltop Ln
Northfield CT 06778

Call Sign: KB1TU
Gerard J Huber
22 Lazo Dr
Northfield CT 067782121

Call Sign: KA1LDG
Karen B Stronk
587 Northfield Rd
Northfield CT 06778

Call Sign: KK4DX
Lance K Stronk
587 Northfield Rd
Northfield CT 06778

FCC Amateur Radio Licenses in Northford

Call Sign: KC1NS
Nancy K Tipping
78 Alling Rd
Northford CT 06472

Call Sign: N1VSF
Karen E Tipping
78 Alling Road
Northford CT 06472

Call Sign: NZ1J

David L Tipping
78 Alling Road
Northford CT 06472

Call Sign: KA1SZQ
Daniel C Sohl
75 Berncliff Dr
Northford CT 06472

Call Sign: WA1TMQ
John J Ardine
16 David Ln
Northford CT 06472

Call Sign: KB1VTI
David H Roden
31 Evergreen Rd
Northford CT 06472

Call Sign: KB1JDL
Fred J Liedke Jr
38 Forest View Rd
Northford CT 06472

Call Sign: W1POP
Fred J Liedke Jr
38 Forest View Rd
Northford CT 06472

Call Sign: N1OKF
Robert A Parisi
5 Hickory Ln
Northford CT 06472

Call Sign: KA1IPN
Robert E Pietruszka
1963 Middletown Ave
Northford CT 06472

Call Sign: WA1PRJ
Arthur C Labaree
165 Mill Rd
Northford CT 064721518

Call Sign: KB1GWJ

Patrick W Six
66 Mountain View Terrace
Northford CT 06572

Call Sign: N1KJK
Rita Smith
58 Old Post Rd
Northford CT 06472

Call Sign: N1KGP
Martin P Staffa
112 Old Post Rd
Northford CT 06472

Call Sign: KB1MTE
Joseph Staffa
112 Old Post Rd
Northford CT 06472

Call Sign: KB1SIO
Michael A Staffa
112 Old Post Rd
Northford CT 06472

Call Sign: W1ERE
Irving T King
82 Old Tnpk
Northford CT 06472

Call Sign: N1LGH
Barbara K Stone
38 Old Turnpike
Northford CT 06472

Call Sign: W1RWS
Richard W Slayton
72 Oxbow Ln
Northford CT 06472

Call Sign: KB1NSY
Kenth B Astrom
41 Skylark Dr
Northford CT 06472

Call Sign: W1JKP

Kenth B Astrom
41 Skylark Dr
Northford CT 06472

Call Sign: KA1ASD
Malcolm W Wilcox
12 Snowbird Ln
Northford CT 06472

Call Sign: KB1KQU
Chris M Kohler
350 Totoket Rd
Northford CT 06472

Call Sign: KB1KTA
Pamela J Kohler
350 Totoket Rd
Northford CT 06472

Call Sign: N1PLT
Edward V Busch Ii
595 Totoket Rd
Northford CT 06472

Call Sign: KB1OQP
Steven J Farber
662 Totoket Rd
Northford CT 06472

Call Sign: K1IHZ
Calvin S Beck
794 Totoket Rd
Northford CT 06472

Call Sign: KB1CFY
Frank F Prochilo
810 Totoket Rd
Northford CT 064721467

Call Sign: KB9ZIS
Carl A Battista
808 Totoket Road
Northford CT 06472

Call Sign: KA1KYQ

Walter W Torfason
144 Village St
Northford CT 06472

Call Sign: N1ORK
Francis S Driscoll
144 Village St
Northford CT 06472

Call Sign: KA1SZN
Arthur C Anderson
58 Woodhouse Ave
Northford CT 06472

Call Sign: AK1O
Anthony J Vanacore
32 Woodland Dr
Northford CT 064721206

Call Sign: W1RFT
George J Marotto
12 Woodvale Dr
Northford CT 06472

**FCC Amateur Radio
Licenses in Norwalk**

Call Sign: N2QCA
Stephen M Holton
9 Alewives Rd
Norwalk CT 068502201

Call Sign: N1NB
Stephen M Holton
9 Alewives Rd
Norwalk CT 068502201

Call Sign: KB1VZX
Scott J Nette
5 Allen Court
Norwalk CT 06851

Call Sign: WA1RXA
Joseph A Beck Mr.
26 Ambler Dr

Norwalk CT 06851

Call Sign: N1YDL
John D Dropick
8 Anson Road
Norwalk CT 06850

Call Sign: KB1GPD
Priscilla Chung
28 Apple Tree Lane
Norwalk CT 06850

Call Sign: W2SSB
Priscilla Chung
28 Apple Tree Lane
Norwalk CT 06850

Call Sign: W2SSB
Neil R Ferri
28 Appletree Ln
Norwalk CT 06850

Call Sign: K2NF
Neil R Ferri
28 Appletree Ln
Norwalk CT 06850

Call Sign: W1YRT
Paul C Pokrop
44 Assisi Way
Norwalk CT 06851

Call Sign: K2BRY
Martin H Wincott
44 B Harbor Ave
Norwalk CT 06850

Call Sign: K1EHW
George J Peters
41 Barbara Dr
Norwalk CT 068515306

Call Sign: KA1WYU
George Swatland
65 Barbara Dr

Norwalk CT 06851

Call Sign: N1HGC
Anthony J Constantine
16 Beau St
Norwalk CT 06850

Call Sign: N1CAL
Alex E Novotnik Jr
4 Beverly Pl
Norwalk CT 06850

Call Sign: AA1DP
Willard E Bennett
36 Birchside Dr
Norwalk CT 06850

Call Sign: KA1ZEY
Ruth E Brown
13 Blue Mountain Ridge
Norwalk CT 06851

Call Sign: N1HFS
Theodore S Rosen
16 Bobwhite Dr
Norwalk CT 06851

Call Sign: K1PGA
Pablo C Aymerich
16 Bobwhite Drive
Norwalk CT 06851

Call Sign: N1GBO
Michael R Basso Jr
10 Boulder Rd
Norwalk CT 06854

Call Sign: N1RRF
John D Callahan
2 Bramble Lane
Norwalk CT 06850

Call Sign: N1JRV
Napoleon S Chenard
6 Broad St

Norwalk CT 06851

Call Sign: KC2HMP
Lauren M Henry
26 Bryan Road
Norwalk CT 06853

Call Sign: KB1SYF
Mary M Minnis
15 Burchard Lane
Norwalk CT 06853

Call Sign: WA2OQE
Hugh L Lupo
46 Calf Pasture Beach Road
Norwalk CT 06855

Call Sign: N1CYC
Ralph E Blechner
28 Catherine St
Norwalk CT 06851

Call Sign: KB1ABS
Venugopalan Muralidharan
33 Center Ave
Norwalk CT 06854

Call Sign: KA1WTX
Robert W Higbee
3 Channel Ave
Norwalk CT 06854

Call Sign: KE1IY
Jeffrey N Richter
12 Chelene Rd
Norwalk CT 06851

Call Sign: N1UNE
Mark A La Polt
24 Chelene Rd
Norwalk CT 06851

Call Sign: N1EXN
Gerald D Jarvis
54 Chestnut Hill Rd

Norwalk CT 06851

Call Sign: KB1PXR
Leigh Berkowitz
14 Cider Lane
Norwalk CT 06851

Call Sign: WX1LDB
Leigh Berkowitz
14 Cider Lane
Norwalk CT 06851

Call Sign: KA1YIQ
Philip I Berkowitz
14 Cider Ln
Norwalk CT 068513413

Call Sign: KA1ZBL
Solomon Berkowitz
14 Cider Ln
Norwalk CT 06851

Call Sign: WX1CT
Philip I Berkowitz
14 Cider Ln
Norwalk CT 068513413

Call Sign: KB1VWJ
Rachel L Ambrose
16 Cliff Street
Norwalk CT 06854

Call Sign: N1CML
Charles R Ball
49 Clinton Ave
Norwalk CT 06854

Call Sign: N1DWT
Vincent Clark
72 Comstock Hill Rd
Norwalk CT 06850

Call Sign: KA1ZTQ
Ray A Cooke
156 Connecticut Ave

Norwalk CT 06854

Call Sign: WA1TLA
Sam Tartaglia Jr
14 Country Club Rd
Norwalk CT 068515616

Call Sign: N1KZX
David R Mc Knight
42 Creeping Hemlock Dr
Norwalk CT 06851

Call Sign: K1REM
Herman D Parks
36 Creeping Hemlock Rd
Norwalk CT 06851

Call Sign: KB1KTV
Edward J Gombos
1 Daphne Dr
Norwalk CT 068513101

Call Sign: AB1ED
Edward J Gombos
1 Daphne Dr
Norwalk CT 068513101

Call Sign: N1II
Paul M Danzer
2 Dawn Rd
Norwalk CT 06851

Call Sign: WA1WTB
Steven J Danzer
2 Dawn Rd
Norwalk CT 06851

Call Sign: N1INM
Laurie D Gotch
21 Deerwood Ct
Norwalk CT 06851

Call Sign: W1TNM
Robert F Kane Jr
7 Deerwood Manor

Norwalk CT 06851

Call Sign: N1EV
Evelyn R Gross
32 Deerwood Manor
Norwalk CT 06851

Call Sign: KA1PJZ
Andrew J Kordas
3 Dorset Rd
Norwalk CT 06851

Call Sign: WA1RFH
Robert F Maslan Jr
28 Douglas Dr
Norwalk CT 06850

Call Sign: N1CDE
Bruno Zarkower
46 Douglas Dr
Norwalk CT 06850

Call Sign: KA1AJM
Herbert E Forger Sr
88 Dry Hill Rd
Norwalk CT 06851

Call Sign: KA1QBD
Jeannette Stewart
221 E Rocks Rd
Norwalk CT 06851

Call Sign: N6TRD
William F Waters
2 East Meadow Lane
Norwalk CT 06851

Call Sign: WB1ADS
Ignatius J Vetter
162 East Rocks Rd
Norwalk CT 06851

Call Sign: K1REC
Joseph C Strolin
21 Ellen St

Norwalk CT 06851

Call Sign: N2KMX
Brian N Vetter
18 Ells Street
Norwalk CT 06850

Call Sign: KA1YAM
Trevor L Viechweg
18 Elton Ct
Norwalk CT 06851

Call Sign: N8WTP
Laura A Shaw
34 Emerson St #2
Norwalk CT 06852

Call Sign: N1DWH
Anthony W Tripodi
16 Fairfield Ter
Norwalk CT 06851

Call Sign: KB1RJQ
Kathleen K Castleberry
50 Fairview Ave Apt 3K
Norwalk CT 06851

Call Sign: N1YV
Walner Cadet
49 Ferris Ave 2nd Floor
Norwalk CT 06854

Call Sign: WU1N
Walner Cadet
49 Ferris Ave 2nd Floor
Norwalk CT 06854

Call Sign: N1RRE
Thomas D Kirmayer
238 Fillow St
Norwalk CT 06850

Call Sign: KK2C
Thomas D Kirmayer
238 Fillow St

Norwalk CT 06850

Call Sign: KA1DWE
Albert P Mathieu
115 Fillow St 77
Norwalk CT 06850

Call Sign: W2LNK
Omachonu O Ogali
56 Fillow Street
Norwalk CT 06850

Call Sign: K2LNK
Omachonu O Ogali
56 Fillow Street
Norwalk CT 06850

Call Sign: KA1YVW
Ronald D Neilson
300 Flax Hill Rd 1
Norwalk CT 06854

Call Sign: N1UTK
Suzette M Vertrees
115 Flax Hill Rd 3
Norwalk CT 06854

Call Sign: N1UDK
Joseph R Pekar
13 Fordham Dr
Norwalk CT 06855

Call Sign: KB1UKE
Ed Fitzgerald
318 Foxboro Dr
Norwalk CT 06851

Call Sign: W1AGQ
Clarice P Giler
1226 Foxboro Drive
Norwalk CT 068511152

Call Sign: W1AGU
Roger R Giler
1226 Foxboro Drive

Norwalk CT 06851

Call Sign: KA1UBU
Jennie C Lombardi
1 Freedman Dr
Norwalk CT 06854

Call Sign: N1OLR
Jean B Richeme
3 Frost St
Norwalk CT 06850

Call Sign: AA1XV
Hugo W Catta
7 Fullin Ct
Norwalk CT 06851

Call Sign: KV1A
Kare Helberg
11 Geneva Rd
Norwalk CT 06850

Call Sign: W1TBW
David W Morse
18 Getner Trail
Norwalk CT 06854

Call Sign: N1PYJ
Eugene Suttenberg
45 Glen Ave
Norwalk CT 06850

Call Sign: K1OE
John F Stuart
1 Greenwood Place Main
House
Norwalk CT 06854

Call Sign: KB1LHP
Jason Farrow
6 Harbor View Ave
Norwalk CT 068544821

Call Sign: WC1ACV
Norwalk Civil Preparedness

23 Harriet St
Norwalk CT 06851

Call Sign: WT1Y
Edward H Bolton
23 Harriet St
Norwalk CT 06851

Call Sign: N1JRW
Richard G Bliss
6 Highland Ct
Norwalk CT 06854

Call Sign: K1RF
Steven B Dick
18 Holiday Dr
Norwalk CT 06851

Call Sign: KB1RSA
Samuel J Dick
18 Holiday Drive
Norwalk CT 068513403

Call Sign: NV1P
Samuel J Dick
18 Holiday Drive
Norwalk CT 068513403

Call Sign: KA1CKJ
Charles C Goodrich Iii
1 Horizon Dr 28
Norwalk CT 06854

Call Sign: N1PLH
Michael K Singewald
65 Howard Avenue
Norwalk CT 06855

Call Sign: KA1UTZ
John L Krause Jr
28 June Ave
Norwalk CT 06850

Call Sign: K1SFY
Albert E Marsden

2 Kellee Dr
Norwalk CT 06854

Call Sign: WB1AVG
Craig N Breny
7 Kingsbury Rd
Norwalk CT 068515606

Call Sign: KE4LYC
Pablo C Aymerich
2 Knoll St
Norwalk CT 06851

Call Sign: KB1VCQ
George F Flay Iii
16 Lakeview Dr
Norwalk CT 06850

Call Sign: AB1QK
George F Flay Iii
16 Lakeview Dr
Norwalk CT 06850

Call Sign: KE1IZ
Donald A Casavecchia
26 Laurel Street
Norwalk CT 06855

Call Sign: N1UQS
Raul Serrano
15 Leuvine St
Norwalk CT 06850

Call Sign: KB1O
Jean B Richeme
76 Lexington Ave
Norwalk CT 06854

Call Sign: AA1RJ
Jean B Richeme
76 Lexington Ave
Norwalk CT 06854

Call Sign: KD1CH
James S Rollinson Sr

42 Linden St
Norwalk CT 06851

Call Sign: KD5AHL
Scott K Smith
4 Lowe St #302
Norwalk CT 06854

Call Sign: KB1UP
Martin F Grace
306 Main Ave
Norwalk CT 06851

Call Sign: N1PPA
Frederick Klein
554 Main Ave
Norwalk CT 06851

Call Sign: N1PPC
Shirley Klein
554 Main Ave
Norwalk CT 06851

Call Sign: KB1WFW
Robert W Talley
304 Main Ave 239
Norwalk CT 06851

Call Sign: W1NLK
Greater Norwalk Amateur
Radio Club
304 Main Ave Box 115
Norwalk CT 06851

Call Sign: KB1FOY
Gnarc Contest Club
324 Main Ave Box 115
Norwalk CT 06851

Call Sign: N1EV
Gnarc Contest Club
324 Main Ave Box 115
Norwalk CT 06851

Call Sign: KD5IUU

David Smith
400 Main Avenue
Norwalk CT 06851

Call Sign: KB1HMG
Joseph P Orban Iii
100 Maywood Rd
Norwalk CT 06850

Call Sign: W1RME
John E Hughes
13 Midrocks Dr
Norwalk CT 06851

Call Sign: KB1WBI
Radu C Tarta
48 Midrocks Drive
Norwalk CT 06851

Call Sign: W1KWH
Paul Carothers
16 Mills St
Norwalk CT 06850

Call Sign: AA1JI
Howard Mehr
17 Mohawk St
Norwalk CT 06851

Call Sign: N1YP
Jean M Gaucheron
9 Morehouse Lane
Norwalk CT 06850

Call Sign: N1ZZ
Daniel W Gravereaux
9 Morehouse Lane
Norwalk CT 06850

Call Sign: N1OSR
Lawrence W Sheltmire
22 Morgan Ave
Norwalk CT 06851

Call Sign: KA1WCT

Joan T Hook
15 Muriel St
Norwalk CT 06851

Call Sign: WA1PFS
Irving H Hook
15 Muriel St
Norwalk CT 06851

Call Sign: KB1DZN
Morris K Hays
21 Myrtle St Ph
Norwalk CT 06855

Call Sign: K1CYW
Richard M Balas Sr
215 N Taylor Ave
Norwalk CT 06854

Call Sign: KA1UBZ
Kersten H K Schriel
21 Nelson Ave
Norwalk CT 06851

Call Sign: KA1UCA
Robert Gasiorowski
21 Nelson Ave
Norwalk CT 06851

Call Sign: W1ARS
Ronald W Kresge
375 Newtown Ave
Norwalk CT 068512538

Call Sign: WB1DEN
Charles R Pennington Iii
19 Noahs Ln
Norwalk CT 06851

Call Sign: W1NM
Nicholas A Amente
60 Noahs Ln Ext
Norwalk CT 06851

Call Sign: KB1SJD

Anthony J Cossuto
200 North Taylor Ave
Norwalk CT 06854

Call Sign: AA1NK
Lesly Saint Victor
11 Oak Street
Norwalk CT 06854

Call Sign: AB2FT
Keita Negishi
3 Oakwood Ave. Unit A19
Norwalk CT 06850

Call Sign: N1ECE
Donald J Steiner
9 Old Kings Hwy
Norwalk CT 06850

Call Sign: K1VMX
Donald A Radman
43 Old Rock Ln
Norwalk CT 06850

Call Sign: W1WNY
John F Ashton
13 Orchard Hill Rd
Norwalk CT 068513440

Call Sign: N1NHD
David G Richards
1 Ox Yoke Ln
Norwalk CT 06851

Call Sign: N1DBZ
Eugene G Karoscik
9 Park St Unit 106
Norwalk CT 06851

Call Sign: WK1Q
Todd Wright
11 Park St Unit 211
Norwalk CT 06851

Call Sign: N1KIT

Gregory C Bitondo Sr
38 Parkhill Ave
Norwalk CT 06851

Call Sign: W1GTQ
Nunzio R Bitondo
12 Phillips St
Norwalk CT 06850

Call Sign: KB1KIB
Gary S Jacobson
2 Pine Hill Ave
Norwalk CT 06855

Call Sign: N1DKB
Gary S Jacobson
2 Pine Hill Ave
Norwalk CT 06855

Call Sign: KB1KLS
Jean N Jacobson
2 Pine Hill Ave
Norwalk CT 06855

Call Sign: KB1LTX
Emma L Jacobson
2 Pine Hill Ave
Norwalk CT 06855

Call Sign: N1VHV
John-Erik Christensen
26 Prospect Ave Unit A10
Norwalk CT 06850

Call Sign: KG4WZQ
Richard L Davis
5 Quarry Lane
Norwalk CT 068511210

Call Sign: KG1W
Richard L Davis
5 Quarry Lane
Norwalk CT 068511210

Call Sign: KC1FB

James R Francoeur
8 Regency Dr
Norwalk CT 06851

Call Sign: N1PXO
Joseph L Labraga
23 Reservoir Ave
Norwalk CT 06850

Call Sign: KB1DKL
Kevin M Stovall
4 Robins Sq E
Norwalk CT 06854

Call Sign: KB1DKM
Marian E Stovall
4 Robins Sq E
Norwalk CT 06854

Call Sign: K1BR
Ralph R Lee
16c Rockmeadow Rd
Norwalk CT 06850

Call Sign: KB2JNW
Shaun C Gartenberg
16 Rockmeadow Rd Unit F
Norwalk CT 06852

Call Sign: KA1YAN
Ram H Sainani
281 Rolling Ridge Aiken St
Norwalk CT 06851

Call Sign: N1FSI
John S Herald Sr
11 Rome St
Norwalk CT 068515317

Call Sign: KB1WSA
Ian M Sidey
50 Roton Ave
Norwalk CT 06853

Call Sign: KB1QZK

Matthew Robinson
8 Rowayton Ct
Norwalk CT 06853

Toy T Alladin
52 Scribner Ave
Norwalk CT 06854

Suzanne C Hilson
6 Sherman Pl
Norwalk CT 06851

Call Sign: N1HWB
Robert P Daly
87 Rowayton Woods Dr
Norwalk CT 06854

Call Sign: K1WYQ
Toy T Alladin
52 Scribner Ave
Norwalk CT 06854

Call Sign: WB1U
Raymond D Hilson
6 Sherman Pl
Norwalk CT 06851

Call Sign: KB1QWC
Beth M Siegelbaum
57 Russell St
Norwalk CT 068551306

Call Sign: N1IVN
Jose L Artigas
136 Scribner Ave
Norwalk CT 06854

Call Sign: K1VMI
John E Kent Jr
8 Silent Grove Ct
Norwalk CT 06851

Call Sign: KA1WYO
Elizabeth A Bavor
4 Saddle Rd
Norwalk CT 06851

Call Sign: N1NQ
Jose L Artigas
136 Scribner Ave
Norwalk CT 06854

Call Sign: WB1EMZ
Barbara P Kent
8 Silent Grove Ct
Norwalk CT 06851

Call Sign: W1TOC
Gordon F Bavor
4 Saddle Rd
Norwalk CT 06851

Call Sign: N1GQJ
James P Mancusi Jr
184 Scribner Ave
Norwalk CT 06854

Call Sign: N1TWT
Russell Wright
10 Silent Grove Ct
Norwalk CT 06851

Call Sign: N1FZE
Duncan P Payne
17 Saddle Rd
Norwalk CT 06851

Call Sign: K1VKO
Arthur A Santella
45 Seaview Ave
Norwalk CT 06855

Call Sign: W1RGW
Russell Wright
10 Silent Grove Ct
Norwalk CT 06851

Call Sign: N1HKM
Lisbeth R Payne
17 Saddle Rd
Norwalk CT 06851

Call Sign: N1LRO
David R Marcus
3 Seir Hill Rd C5
Norwalk CT 06850

Call Sign: KB1UL
Glenn P York
34 Silvermine Ave
Norwalk CT 06850

Call Sign: N1ZD
Duncan P Payne
17 Saddle Rd
Norwalk CT 06851

Call Sign: KB1HMC
David L Gordon
3 Senga Rd
Norwalk CT 068542520

Call Sign: N1ASN
Richard Di Dia
5 Silwen Ln
Norwalk CT 06851

Call Sign: N1WYL
Edwin Huertas
63 Saddle Rd
Norwalk CT 06851

Call Sign: KB1IPM
Wmr Contest Club
18 Sheehan Ave
Norwalk CT 06854

Call Sign: KA2JDB
Mary A Frimmet
20 Splitrock Rd
Norwalk CT 06854

Call Sign: KA1WYQ

Call Sign: N1UDG

Call Sign: N2CBQ

Alfred Frimmet
20 Splitrock Rd
Norwalk CT 068544713

Call Sign: KA1WCS
Jose M Cruz
14 Spring Hill Ave 2nd
Floor
Norwalk CT 06851

Call Sign: N1IDB
Michael D Cloffi
21 Spring Hill Ave F
Norwalk CT 06850

Call Sign: WA1CTX
Lawrence F Colman
28 Spring St Apt 20
Norwalk CT 06854

Call Sign: N2VUF
Stephen D Apfelroth
5 Starlight Drive
Norwalk CT 068513424

Call Sign: K1NFF
Charles P Betts
17 Stephen Mather Rd
Norwalk CT 06850

Call Sign: KB1PXU
William R Bernstein
6 Studio Lane South
Norwalk CT 06850

Call Sign: KB1JGL
Mark E D'andrea
10 Sunlit Dr
Norwalk CT 06851

Call Sign: KA1NMW
Debra G Vargo
52 Toilsome Ave
Norwalk CT 06851

Call Sign: W1NDO
Ernest M Robinson
78 Toilsome Ave
Norwalk CT 06851

Call Sign: KC2BME
Mark S Halupa
18 Tracey Street
Norwalk CT 06850

Call Sign: KC2BUC
Cindy L Ng
18 Tracey Street
Norwalk CT 06850

Call Sign: N1HHH
Ellen M Banasik
4 Union Ave #11
Norwalk CT 06851

Call Sign: N1PAL
Walter N Broadhurst Jr
15 Victory Ct
Norwalk CT 06855

Call Sign: KE1DS
Walner Cadet
34 W Ave 2nd Fl
Norwalk CT 06854

Call Sign: KA1NGF
James M Bryson Jr
204 W Rocks Rd
Norwalk CT 06851

Call Sign: KB1JNO
Gaston Catta
83 Ward St
Norwalk CT 06851

Call Sign: K2QKA
Robert W Keene
40 William St
Norwalk CT 06851

Call Sign: KA1TKV
Henio Camacho
82 Wolfpit Ave
Norwalk CT 06851

Call Sign: WB1BPV
David H Hook
41 Wolfpit Ave Unit 1w
Norwalk CT 06851

Call Sign: KA1WBN
Martin G Diamond
41 Wolfpit Ave Unit 6b
Norwalk CT 06851

Call Sign: KA1IWN
Victor Di Meglio
10 Woodchuck Ln
Norwalk CT 06854

Call Sign: K2JAP
Frank C Derato
Norwalk CT 06852

Call Sign: W1KEN
Kenneth G Hildebrand
Norwalk CT 06856

FCC Amateur Radio Licenses in Norwich

Call Sign: W1UBM
Norma J Kornacki
66 11th St
Norwich CT 06360

Call Sign: KB1UEI
Kurt R Tetreault
24 Baltic Rd
Norwich CT 06360

Call Sign: K1KAM
Anthony L Jakubowski
99 Baltic Rd
Norwich CT 06360

Call Sign: KB1DYZ
Rodney J Reiter
105 Baltic St
Norwich CT 06360

Call Sign: KA1TXZ
Ernest W Gilman Jr
42 Beech St
Norwich CT 06360

Call Sign: KA1WUS
John J Fitzpatrick
19 Beechwood Blvd
Norwich CT 06360

Call Sign: W2NGE
Glenn F Taylor Jr
111 Briar Lane
Norwich CT 06360

Call Sign: KB1RFQ
The Norwich Free Academy
Ham Radio Club
305 Broadway
Norwich CT 06360

Call Sign: W1HLO
The Norwich Free Academy
Ham Radio Club
305 Broadway
Norwich CT 06360

Call Sign: N1XUH
Robert C Szarka
223 Browning Rd
Norwich CT 06360

Call Sign: KA1UWU
Thomas D Turner
593 Canterbury Tpke
Norwich CT 06360

Call Sign: N1KPW
Gregory A Peet Sr

528 Canterbury Turnpike
Apt 2
Norwich CT 06360

Call Sign: KB1EQO
Alan R Ruditzky
35 Caribou Drive
Norwich CT 06360

Call Sign: KA1WJV
Steven M Mercier
102 Central Ave
Norwich CT 06360

Call Sign: KA1QOA
Robert J Smith
6 Cherry Hill Rd
Norwich CT 063605202

Call Sign: KA1QPQ
Mark F Weber
19 Clay Ave
Norwich CT 06360

Call Sign: N1QHA
Albert J Fontaine Jr
51 Convent Ave
Norwich CT 06360

Call Sign: KB1DDQ
Kenneth M Noyes
26 Dalewood Dr
Norwich CT 06360

Call Sign: K1STS
Kenneth M Noyes
26 Dalewood Dr
Norwich CT 06360

Call Sign: N1SPU
Donald F Benac
9 Daniel St
Norwich CT 06360

Call Sign: W1ICN

Andre J Messier Jr
13 Debbie Ct
Norwich CT 06360

Call Sign: KB1RBH
Kevin M Walker
62 Division St
Norwich CT 06360

Call Sign: KB1CWY
Shannon S Carlos
112 Dunham
Norwich CT 06360

Call Sign: KB1CWZ
Mark S Carlos
112 Dunham St
Norwich CT 06360

Call Sign: KB1WDJ
Michael L Carlos
112 Dunham St
Norwich CT 06360

Call Sign: KB1BSK
Uconn Arc
247 Dunham St Apt 2
Norwich CT 06360

Call Sign: W1EBO
Woodrow W Guile
66 Eleventh St
Norwich CT 06360

Call Sign: W1YOC
Walter J Kornacki
66 Eleventh St
Norwich CT 06360

Call Sign: KA1RVG
John J Jakubielski
225 Elizabeth St
Norwich CT 06360

Call Sign: W1CT

John J Jakubielski
225 Elizabeth St
Norwich CT 06360

Call Sign: KA1WFK
JAMES W DUNION Phd
69 Elizabeth Street
Norwich CT 06360

Call Sign: W1IKY
Alexander A Grocki
16 Fountain St
Norwich CT 06360

Call Sign: WB1BRX
Dana L Burleson
24 Fowler Ave
Norwich CT 06360

Call Sign: KB1RAZ
John W Lake
204 Franklin Street Unit2
Norwich CT 06360

Call Sign: KB1AW
Tad A Church
32 G Church St.
Norwich CT 06360

Call Sign: W1CJN
Joseph J Schaffhauser
78 Geer Ave
Norwich CT 06360

Call Sign: KG6ENL
Gerald D Dugan
12 Gillette Rd.
Norwich CT 06360

Call Sign: KB1IFA
Jeremy R Minter
10 Grandview Ct
Norwich CT 06360

Call Sign: KB1DEE

Brian A La Salle
27 Hanes Ln Rfd 3
Norwich CT 06360

Call Sign: KA1KRD
Harold M Becker
209 Harland Rd
Norwich CT 06360

Call Sign: K1JN
Joseph A Natale
38 Hooper St Unit 20
Norwich CT 06361

Call Sign: KA1WXL
Wayne R Mc Curdy
11 Hunters Rd
Norwich CT 06360

Call Sign: WB1HJV
John P Jesmonth
136 Hunters Rd 141
Norwich CT 063601913

Call Sign: AB1FE
Wesley H Betler
23 Hunters Rd Lot 1
Norwich CT 06360

Call Sign: WQ1V
Frank J Trzesniowski
67 Lambert Dr
Norwich CT 06360

Call Sign: KA1FCM
Edward F Kane
382 Laurel Hill Rd
Norwich CT 06360

Call Sign: KA6PDG
Harry K Harkins
37 Lincoln Ave Apt 3
Norwich CT 06360

Call Sign: N1WPL

Larry R Ochs
106 Lucas Park Rd
Norwich CT 06360

Call Sign: K1TAY
Gordon E Simpson
31 Manwaring Rd
Norwich CT 06360

Call Sign: KA2JLB
William C Schramm
188 Mc Kinley Ave E
Norwich CT 06360

Call Sign: KB1FQR
Richard A Lasaracina
45 Michelle Drive
Norwich CT 06360

Call Sign: N1FHR
William J Pineault
4 Middle St
Norwich CT 06360

Call Sign: N1CFM
Henry J Schwab
303 Mohegan Park Rd Lot
14
Norwich CT 063602023

Call Sign: WA1ZRK
Francis R Lombardo
37 Mowry Ave
Norwich CT 06360

Call Sign: KA1ZMZ
Bruce R Adams
291 N Wawecus Hill Rd
Norwich CT 06360

Call Sign: KB1DYW
Elizabeth M Adams
291 N Wawecus Hill Rd
Norwich CT 06360

Call Sign: W1AYP
Ronald L Adams
305 N Wawecus Hill Rd
Norwich CT 06360

Call Sign: N3RPQ
Leonard A Schachter
323 New London Turnpike
Norwich CT 063602644

Call Sign: K1ZKY
Arthur P Heely
80 North St
Norwich CT 06360

Call Sign: KA1SGO
Philip W Cote Jr
90 North St Apt 5d
Norwich CT 06360

Call Sign: N1QGZ
Joseph S Hebert Jr
104 Norwich Ave. #H-2
Norwich CT 06360

Call Sign: KA1EL
Donald R Farrar
28 Oneco St
Norwich CT 06360

Call Sign: N1XCR
Andrew L Ault
19 Otrobando Ave
Norwich CT 06360

Call Sign: KB1DRJ
Raymond J Andrews Jr
13 Pleasant St
Norwich CT 06360

Call Sign: KB1PZO
William H Clarke
267 Prospect St
Norwich CT 063603234

Call Sign: W1ICH
William H Clarke
267 Prospect St
Norwich CT 063603234

Call Sign: KB1NAL
Leon P Kornilieff
20 Royal Oaks Dr
Norwich CT 06360

Call Sign: KC6LVQ
Scott O M Oney
30 Royal Oaks Dr
Norwich CT 06360

Call Sign: KA1OAE
Jeffrey P Seltzer
177 Scotland Rd
Norwich CT 06360

Call Sign: WA1ZEZ
Robert E Siemann
830 Scotland Rd
Norwich CT 06360

Call Sign: WB1DJF
Katherine P Siemann
830 Scotland Rd
Norwich CT 06360

Call Sign: WA1NYE
Daniel Deutsch
1 Sherwood Ln
Norwich CT 06360

Call Sign: N1VIU
Thomas S Veile
26 Slater Ave
Norwich CT 06360

Call Sign: N1CQV
Roland L Cote
78 Smith Ave
Norwich CT 06360

Call Sign: KA1JLL
G Scott Granados
52 Spring Garden
Norwich CT 06360

Call Sign: N1TSU
David G Keller
69 Spring Garden Ave
Norwich CT 06360

Call Sign: N1RAV
Robert L Booth
10 Stonecliff Ln
Norwich CT 06360

Call Sign: WB3LFG
Jason L Abbott
102 Stonington Rd   Apt
A-205
Norwich CT 06360

Call Sign: KA1WD
Wesley H Betler
104 Taftville Occum Rd
Norwich CT 06360

Call Sign: KB1RBI
Keith J Mutch Mr
1 Tanner Av
Norwich CT 06360

Call Sign: KB1IMD
Jason L Gurtz
7 Taylor Dr
Norwich CT 06360

Call Sign: KA1CQR
Charles A Newman
17 Thomas Ave
Norwich CT 06360

Call Sign: WA1ZFE
William L Daley
2 Tower Hill Rd
Norwich CT 06360

Call Sign: AK1B
Samuel D Boomer
8 Turnpike Pk
Norwich CT 06360

Call Sign: N1YSM
Joshua D Fegley
8 Twins Ct
Norwich CT 06360

Call Sign: N1WPK
David M Beatty Sr
665 W Thames St
Norwich CT 06360

Call Sign: KB1NKK
Wayne D Rosenfield Phd
D-Ground 326 Washington
St
Norwich CT 063602714

Call Sign: W5UMO
Wayne G Horn
66 Weber Farm Rd.
Norwich CT 06360

Call Sign: KA1VLS
Wayne M Simon
52 Westwood Park
Norwich CT 06360

Call Sign: K1QYC
Paul A Jette
45 Williams St
Norwich CT 06360

Call Sign: N1EFZ
Jan F Lindberg
86 Williams St
Norwich CT 06360

Call Sign: K1AFI
Paul W Taylor
175 Yantic Ln

Norwich CT 06360

Call Sign: N1NNS
Paul E Daley
Norwich CT 06360

Call Sign: KB1EUA
Edward J Gwozdz
Norwich CT 06360

Call Sign: K1WDR
Wayne D Rosenfield Phd
Norwich CT 063600329

FCC Amateur Radio Licenses in Nougatock

Call Sign: N1UNU
Joseph Torok
82 Rustling Reed Rd
Nougatock CT 06770

FCC Amateur Radio Licenses in Oakdale

Call Sign: KB1ISU
Donald L Pomroy
74 Beechwood Rd
Oakdale CT 06370

Call Sign: W1FKC
Donald L Pomroy
74 Beechwood Rd
Oakdale CT 06370

Call Sign: W1TYL
Tyl Middle School Amateur
Radio Club
166 Chesterfield Rd
Oakdale CT 06370

Call Sign: KA1OIJ
James R Mack
1071 E Lake Rd
Oakdale CT 06370

Call Sign: KA1NRC
John E Fast
1036 East Lake Road
Oakdale CT 06370

Call Sign: KA1WUP
Eldon L Laforge
85 Fellows Rd
Oakdale CT 06370

Call Sign: W1YH
Jewel D Brown
420 Fire St
Oakdale CT 063701806

Call Sign: W1TMX
Gary J Grimm Sr
131 Forsyth Rd
Oakdale CT 06370

Call Sign: KB1KMW
Emil F Soderberg
48 Georgia Rd
Oakdale CT 063700076

Call Sign: K1SZ
Roger R Chamberland
27 Leitao Dr
Oakdale CT 06370

Call Sign: KA1TBB
David W Menge
2 Michaels Way
Oakdale CT 06370

Call Sign: KA1UMC
Stephen P Koeberle
140 Noble Hill Rd
Oakdale CT 06370

Call Sign: WB1CFY
John F Dufrat
519 Norwich Salem Tpke
Oakdale CT 06370

Call Sign: KE4CEZ
Lester F Osborne Sr
29 Oak Hill Rd
Oakdale CT 06370

Call Sign: N1PUR
Keith A Macht
26 Oakhill Rd
Oakdale CT 06370

Call Sign: N1SQZ
Stephen M Rocketto
928 Old Colchester Rd
Oakdale CT 06370

Call Sign: WA1ZSW
Robert D Mac Gregor
1588 Old Colchester Rd
Oakdale CT 06370

Call Sign: KC2GRD
Edward K Beale
2 Partridge Holw
Oakdale CT 06370

Call Sign: KA1KLN
Christopher S Bekris
786 Route 163
Oakdale CT 06370

Call Sign: N1NKB
Jonathan M Genesky
1486 Route 163
Oakdale CT 06370

Call Sign: KD1XI
Gregory J Majewski
1176 Rt 163
Oakdale CT 06370

Call Sign: WA1YNC
Charles E Trotter
383 Rt 82
Oakdale CT 06370

Call Sign: KB1VMV
Alan G Middleton
776 Rte 163
Oakdale CT 06370

Call Sign: W1ICY
Michael J Sullivan
33 Simpson Ln
Oakdale CT 06370

Call Sign: N1OBR
Sean W Judge
134 Simpson Ln
Oakdale CT 06370

Call Sign: N1NNW
Michael F Gouthro Jr
29 Texas Dr
Oakdale CT 06370

Call Sign: K1GEP
Marlan K Fisher
20 Williams Rd
Oakdale CT 06370

Call Sign: N1LIU
William Rodriguez
Oakdale CT 063701524

Call Sign: N1NCW
William C Benson Jr
Oakdale CT 06370

Call Sign: KB1EJO
Paul D Campo
Oakdale CT 06370

**FCC Amateur Radio
Licenses in Oakville**

Call Sign: KB1INC
Robert W Bradshaw
43 Ann Ave
Oakville CT 06779

Call Sign: KA1MVN
Carlo Ciaburri
131 Bamford Ave
Oakville CT 06779

Call Sign: N1WUT
Nicola Ciaburri
131 Bamford Ave
Oakville CT 06779

Call Sign: N1TOK
Thomas L Calo
74 Cedar Ridge Drive
Oakville CT 06779

Call Sign: KB1KUU
James F Brooks
427 Davis St
Oakville CT 06779

Call Sign: N1UWX
Erna E Mueck
2 Emile Ave
Oakville CT 06779

Call Sign: N1UWY
Alois Mueck
2 Emile Ave
Oakville CT 06779

Call Sign: KA1RRG
Dorothy K Mc Grath
77 Jenks St
Oakville CT 06779

Call Sign: KB1HQC
Michael A Malanga
202 Main St
Oakville CT 06779

Call Sign: KB1VRO
Scott P Ruskay
189 Parkman St
Oakville CT 06779

Call Sign: K9TRL
Scott P Ruskay
189 Parkman St
Oakville CT 06779

Call Sign: KA1GKJ
Donald D Taylor
78 Shaw Farm Road
Oakville CT 067791466

Call Sign: N1VGD
Andrew D Cagno
25 Slade Ave
Oakville CT 06779

Call Sign: KA1EBW
William R Paige
100 Turner Ave
Oakville CT 06779

Call Sign: N1PNS
James M Perillo
430 Williamson Cir
Oakville CT 06779

Call Sign: W1ICI
Frank H Henjes
4 Cross Ridge Dr
Old Greenwich CT 06870

Call Sign: N1ZFQ
Heidi H Helmer
1465 E Putnam Ave 407
Old Greenwich CT 06870

Call Sign: KB1HMD
Marshall E Winokur
35 Edgewater Dr
Old Greenwich CT 06870

Call Sign: KB1VVX

George F Thalheim
2 Grace St
Old Greenwich CT 06870

Call Sign: KB1NPZ
Michael J Street
96 Havermeyer Lane
Old Greenwich CT 06476

Call Sign: K1IGP
Willis D Weirick
39 N Ridge Rd
Old Greenwich CT 06870

Call Sign: KA1RPV
Kenneth B Young
15 Old Wagon Rd
Old Greenwich CT 06870

Call Sign: KA1YVX
Alex C H Me Vay
7 Richmond Dr
Old Greenwich CT 06870

Call Sign: WZ1Y
Stephen Mecsery
21 Richmond Dr
Old Greenwich CT 06870

Call Sign: KA1SLH
Daniel W Slater
14 Stuart Dr
Old Greenwich CT 06870

Call Sign: W1PUV
Alexander Kulchuk
14 Tait Rd
Old Greenwich CT 06870

Call Sign: N1VUR
Oscar N Manero
22 Watch Tower Ln
Old Greenwich CT 06870

Call Sign: W1PMB
Russell V Lewis
20 Bill Hill Rd
Old Lyme CT 06371

Call Sign: K1WUD
Donald W Nelson
159 Blood St
Old Lyme CT 06371

Call Sign: K1QDS
Zacharias B Abbey Sr
17 Boston Post Rd
Old Lyme CT 06371

Call Sign: W1IJD
Robert H Mellen
117 Boston Post Rd
Old Lyme CT 06371

Call Sign: KA1YFP
Howard M Gordon
9 Coult Ln
Old Lyme CT 06371

Call Sign: N1MCC
Christian M Kocielo
9 Dutchess Drive
Old Lyme CT 06371

Call Sign: KB1NHJ
Matthew S Jewell
3 Fawn Trail
Old Lyme CT 06371

Call Sign: KB1ERC
Mark A Kramm
1 Fawn Trl
Old Lyme CT 06371

Call Sign: W1MAK
Mark A Kramm

1 Fawn Trl
Old Lyme CT 06371

4 Meetinghouse Ln
Old Lyme CT 06371

81 Rowland Rd
Old Lyme CT 06371

Call Sign: KB1FOZ
Benjamin R Williams
142 Four Mile River Road
Old Lyme CT 06371

Call Sign: KC1FT
Nicholas D Athanas
90 Mile Creek Rd
Old Lyme CT 06371

Call Sign: KA1HRP
Salvatore C D Aquila
7 Sandalwood Ln
Old Lyme CT 06371

Call Sign: KB1FPA
Brian Williams
142 Four Mile River Road
Old Lyme CT 06371

Call Sign: KB1MAN
Leon J Just
4 Millers Way
Old Lyme CT 06371

Call Sign: W1RFL
Thomas E Hooper
27 Shore Drive
Old Lyme CT 063711274

Call Sign: AA1XK
Brian Williams
142 Four Mile River Road
Old Lyme CT 06371

Call Sign: KB1TMD
Donald J Leroi
5 Myrica Way
Old Lyme CT 06371

Call Sign: W1ZZY
Robert C Recor
65 Shore Drive
Old Lyme CT 06371

Call Sign: KA1WNM
Marek Jastrzebski
61r Hartford Ave
Old Lyme CT 06371

Call Sign: W1NGI
Milton L Chatkin
24 Nottingham Dr
Old Lyme CT 06371

Call Sign: KA1IFV
Douglas S Tolderlund
61 Sill Ln
Old Lyme CT 06371

Call Sign: KB2MQ
Joseph V Migliaccio
34 Jericho Drive
Old Lyme CT 06371

Call Sign: N1TMX
Donald F Cundy
23 Oakridge Dr
Old Lyme CT 06371

Call Sign: N1PYY
Ronald D Purinton
114 Sill Ln
Old Lyme CT 06371

Call Sign: N1SPV
Paul Fiorentino
2 Lake Drive
Old Lyme CT 063711211

Call Sign: KD2BT
Julian B Lo
20 Old Stagecoach Rd
Old Lyme CT 06371

Call Sign: KB1JAX
Daniel D Mutchler
114 Sill Ln
Old Lyme CT 06371

Call Sign: N1DPB
Christopher H Robinson
23 Library Ln
Old Lyme CT 06371

Call Sign: N2EJK
Frances B Lo
20 Old Stagecoach Rd
Old Lyme CT 06371

Call Sign: W1FAR
Theodore J Gordon
1 Smilax Rd
Old Lyme CT 06371

Call Sign: KB1GPB
Thaddeus E Blake
9 Matson Ridge
Old Lyme CT 06371

Call Sign: N1EAY
Thomas J Mc Hale
7 Olivia Lane
Old Lyme CT 06371

Call Sign: N1SAU
Marguerite S Mangin
15 Tantummaheag Rd
Old Lyme CT 06371

Call Sign: KB1KQB
Evan J Flower

Call Sign: KB1BVF
Troy C Clark

Call Sign: W1FFS
Thomas V Mc Andrew

7 Whippoorwill Rd
Old Lyme CT 06371

Call Sign: K1KLO
Andrew Pfeiffer
132 Whippoorwill Rd
Old Lyme CT 06371

Call Sign: KC1FR
Dale P Athanas
67 Whippoorwill Road
Old Lyme CT 06371

Call Sign: KA1GKR
Donald M Sosnoski
6 Wychwood Rd
Old Lyme CT 06371

Call Sign: KA1URT
Elizabeth L Marsh
Old Lyme CT 063710159

Call Sign: N1WHE
Michael J Pascale
Old Lyme CT 06371

Call Sign: WA1PAV
George B Duncan
Old Lyme CT 06371

Call Sign: WA1ZFQ
Ernest R Messer Jr
Old Lyme CT 063714002

Call Sign: W1GAP
Gabriel A Panko
Old Lyme CT 063710712

FCC Amateur Radio Licenses in Old Mystic

Call Sign: W1IGU
George E Deneke
37 Rt 27
Old Mystic CT 06372

Call Sign: KA1TES
Bernard W Steadman
Old Mystic CT 063720466

Call Sign: KD1CI
Glenn R Giordano
Old Mystic CT 03672

FCC Amateur Radio Licenses in Old Saybrook

Call Sign: KA1SYP
George V Allen
55 Ayers Point Rd
Old Saybrook CT 06475

Call Sign: KB1QJU
Gordon L Hirshhorn
117 Ayers Point Road
Old Saybrook CT 06475

Call Sign: K1ZHR
Gordon L Hirshhorn
117 Ayers Point Road
Old Saybrook CT 06475

Call Sign: N1LXS
Robert F Barrila
4 Billow Rd
Old Saybrook CT 06475

Call Sign: KA1WJT
Scott C Mc Coid
57 Bokum Rd
Old Saybrook CT 06475

Call Sign: KB1NDY
Keith N Reynolds
1 Cinnamon Way
Old Saybrook CT 06475

Call Sign: W1EEM
Roger W Bryson Sr
13 Club House Lane

Old Saybrook CT 06475

Call Sign: K1VKF
Robert E Chatfield
26 Cottage Pl
Old Saybrook CT 06475

Call Sign: WA1BSX
Donald W Munger
11 Cricket Ct
Old Saybrook CT
064755096

Call Sign: N1QNW
Edward G Wolcott
18 Edwards Road
Old Saybrook CT 06475

Call Sign: KA1PFN
Herman H Gernhardt
8 Evans Ln
Old Saybrook CT 06475

Call Sign: WA1UNK
Richard S Patenaude
34 Fenwood Grove Rd
Old Saybrook CT 06475

Call Sign: KA1ELA
Albert L Canfield
6 Fenwood Pkwy
Old Saybrook CT 06475

Call Sign: K1WLG
George E Wall
175 Ferry Rd   #20
Old Saybrook CT 06475

Call Sign: N1JA
Joel R Anderson
13 George Dr
Old Saybrook CT 06475

Call Sign: WB1EJK
Judith M Anderson

13 George Dr
Old Saybrook CT 06475

Call Sign: KA1WUO
Jon B Collins
30 George Dr
Old Saybrook CT 06475

Call Sign: KB1ETZ
Michael A Palmieri
11 Indianola Dr
Old Saybrook CT 06475

Call Sign: N1JIG
Earl F Vincent
38 Ingham Hill Rd
Old Saybrook CT 06475

Call Sign: N1XHM
Robert R Harris
118 Ingham Hill Rd.
Old Saybrook CT 06475

Call Sign: KA1OX
Wayne K Baggott
7 Kenn Road
Old Saybrook CT 06475

Call Sign: KB1SV
Alfred D Meucci
12 Kitteridge Hill
Old Saybrook CT 06475

Call Sign: KC1JH
Kenneth G Burgess
92 Knollwood Dr
Old Saybrook CT
064752937

Call Sign: K1KKT
Kenneth G Burgess
92 Knollwood Dr
Old Saybrook CT
064752937

Call Sign: KB1KUT
William R Gesick
341 Main St
Old Saybrook CT 06475

Call Sign: N1EUJ
John J Schofield
22 Maplewood Rd
Old Saybrook CT 06475

Call Sign: W1OTO
Roger C Tryon
34 Meadowood Ln
Old Saybrook CT 06475

Call Sign: KC1A
Richard J Mc Sweegan
17 Middletown Ave
Old Saybrook CT 06475

Call Sign: W1MTY
Kenneth G Anderson
37 Mohican Rd
Old Saybrook CT 06475

Call Sign: W5VRW
Horton A Johnson
39 N Cove Rd
Old Saybrook CT 06475

Call Sign: KB1OPC
Jason D Blumenthal
10 Obed Trailne
Old Saybrook CT 06475

Call Sign: KA1RJV
James W Brinkerhoff Jr
54 Pennywise Ln
Old Saybrook CT 06475

Call Sign: KB1NE
Mark E Facey
2 Redbird Trail
Old Saybrook CT 06475

Call Sign: K1AZC
George B Nichols
2 Salt Meadow Ln
Old Saybrook CT 06475

Call Sign: KB1HCA
Werner R Werner
309 Schoolhouse Rd
Old Saybrook CT
064751009

Call Sign: W1WFJ
Frederick J Williams
65 Spring Brook Rd
Old Saybrook CT 06475

Call Sign: KA1WPE
Norman K Prevost
4 Summerfield Mews
Old Saybrook CT 06475

Call Sign: KB1TSJ
Peter L Dion
8 Windsor Oval
Old Saybrook CT 06475

Call Sign: KA1LOZ
Adam M Czepiel
Old Saybrook CT 06475

Call Sign: N1IWG
Charles E Sohl
Old Saybrook CT 06475

FCC Amateur Radio Licenses in Orange

Call Sign: N1WHU
Deborah A Cerilli
817 Acorn Rd
Orange CT 06477

Call Sign: N1WHV
Richard D Cerilli
817 Acorn Rd

Orange CT 06477

Orange CT 06477

Orange CT 064771042

Call Sign: W1CTC
Robert J Doolittle
473 Alling Farm Rd
Orange CT 06477

Call Sign: N1ESH
John D Gregory
778 Deer Run Lane
Orange CT 06477

Call Sign: N1LRK
Louis J Ferry
851 Glenbrook Rd
Orange CT 06477

Call Sign: KB1GBI
Sean M Oreilly
4203 Avalon Drive East
Orange CT 06477

Call Sign: WP4UF
Ramon I Suarez
190 Derby Ave
Orange CT 06477

Call Sign: WB1FHE
Richard A Mason
526 Gospel Ln
Orange CT 06477

Call Sign: AC1K
William S Bridges
547 Bishop Dr
Orange CT 06477

Call Sign: N1KWT
Jeremy M Hanken
208 Derby Ave
Orange CT 06477

Call Sign: N1CEC
Howard B Treat Jr
801 Grassy Hill Rd
Orange CT 06477

Call Sign: AD2X
Edward J Weinberg
554 Boston Post Rd # 203
Orange CT 06477

Call Sign: KB1FPH
Michael C Carlson
476 Derby Milford Road
Orange CT 06477

Call Sign: N1GIG
Trish Treat
801 Grassy Hill Rd
Orange CT 06477

Call Sign: WT1R
Bruce M Backer
272 Charles Ct
Orange CT 064771629

Call Sign: KB1JFY
Alain R Samson
618 Douglas Dr
Orange CT 06477

Call Sign: W1RJJ
George T Hine Jr
1034 Grassy Hill Rd
Orange CT 06477

Call Sign: KA1EBT
Marc J Metivier
950 Corn Cob Ln
Orange CT 064771004

Call Sign: AB1KQ
Joann M Raytar
362 Drummond Road
Orange CT 06477

Call Sign: KC1SL
Pasquale M Maturo
233 Harvester Rd
Orange CT 06477

Call Sign: K1AP
Edwin J Soltysiak
118 Cummings Dr
Orange CT 06477

Call Sign: AA1DZ
Stephen D Packard
689 Estelle Ct
Orange CT 06477

Call Sign: KB1FQO
Vincent L Vigliotti
270 Hawthorne
Orange CT 06477

Call Sign: KA1QFK
Mark A Soltysiak
118 Cummings Dr
Orange CT 06477

Call Sign: KB1SWH
Fred C Palmer
1003 Garden Rd
Orange CT 06477

Call Sign: KA1EIB
Edward F Hunihan
288 Hemlock Dr
Orange CT 06477

Call Sign: K1EDY
John M Carulli
272 Currier Dr

Call Sign: KA1LDN
Thomas P Hurley
1050 Garden Rd

Call Sign: WA1HZG
Lewis I Merritt
368 Hitchingpost Dr

Orange CT 06477

Call Sign: K1CVA
Robert S Reiss
324 Juniper Dr
Orange CT 06477

Call Sign: KA1OWX
Francis D Cavallaro
132 Kennedy Dr
Orange CT 06477

Call Sign: KB1SWF
Martha M George
424 Longmeadow Road
Orange CT 06477

Call Sign: WB1FHF
Seth W Mason
215 Midland Drive
Orange CT 06477

Call Sign: KB1QEX
Allen E Mushin
741 N Greenbrier Dr
Orange CT 06477

Call Sign: K1QEX
Allen Mushin
741 N Greenbrier Dr
Orange CT 06477

Call Sign: KB1SWI
Lynn M Knight
415 Narrow Lane
Orange CT 06477

Call Sign: KA1COF
Deane A Allen
376 Narrow Ln
Orange CT 06477

Call Sign: N1BUQ
Virginia F Allen
376 Narrow Ln

Orange CT 06477

Call Sign: K1LMK
Donald R Nielsen
528 New England Ln
Orange CT 06477

Call Sign: KB1KJX
Santo J Galatioto
170 Ohman Ave
Orange CT 06477

Call Sign: AB1DA
Santo J Galatioto
170 Ohman Ave
Orange CT 06477

Call Sign: WG1S
Santo J Galatioto
170 Ohman Ave
Orange CT 06477

Call Sign: AA1PT
John A Brown
126 Old Hickory Rd
Orange CT 06477

Call Sign: N1GMP
Hugh N Emerson
131 Old Tavern Rd
Orange CT 064773421

Call Sign: W1LZM
John F Lutters
227 Old Tavern Rd
Orange CT 06477

Call Sign: KB1SWL
Victoria Gagel
408 Old Tavern Rd
Orange CT 06477

Call Sign: KA1SPA
Robert D Strona
1082 Orange Center Rd

Orange CT 06477

Call Sign: N1ZUS
Stephen H Goldner
59 Putting Green Ln
Orange CT 064773158

Call Sign: W1AYS
Louis P Fiore
38 Red Cedar Cir
Orange CT 06477

Call Sign: N1VBJ
Stuart H Buchman
873 Robert Treat Ext
Orange CT 06477

Call Sign: K1QCG
Joseph Palmieri
141 Russell Ave
Orange CT 06477

Call Sign: KB1ASP
Glenn J Davis
282 Sarah Cir
Orange CT 06477

Call Sign: W1NHS
Frederick W Ring
456 Sportsman Rd
Orange CT 064772329

Call Sign: K1ACD
Thurland J Bristol Jr
84 Sunset Dr
Orange CT 06477

Call Sign: KB1SWM
Patricia Connolly
571 Treat Lane
Orange CT 06477

Call Sign: KA1WBS
Marisa E James
528 Treat Ln

Orange CT 06477

Call Sign: W1LFU
Daniel S Gaidosz
342 W River Rd
Orange CT 06477

Call Sign: KA1THU
Andrew E Bloch
499 Wagon Trail
Orange CT 06477

Call Sign: WA1MUI
Fred S Kantor
52 Wellington Dr
Orange CT 06477

Call Sign: N1NDX
Steven M Siegelaub
150 Wild Rose Drive
Orange CT 06477

Call Sign: NF1Y
Faustino J Russo
428 Windy Hill Rd
Orange CT 06477

FCC Amateur Radio Licenses in Oxford

Call Sign: N1DCR
George L Rommel
5 Butternut Lane
Oxford CT 06478

Call Sign: KB1GBJ
John M Joy
2 Cedar Ln
Oxford CT 064781225

Call Sign: NQ1B
Michael J Gurecki
32 Charter Oak Dr
Oxford CT 064781549

Call Sign: W1QB
David T Richards
268 Chestnut Tree Hill
Road
Oxford CT 06478

Call Sign: KA1IFQ
Michael S Martell
461 Chestnut Tree Rd
Oxford CT 06478

Call Sign: WB2SJA
Russell L Maiese
41 Cortland Place
Oxford CT 06478

Call Sign: K2EH
Russell L Maiese
41 Cortland Place
Oxford CT 06478

Call Sign: W1AWK
John J Fiore
7 Crest Rd
Oxford CT 06478

Call Sign: WA1WST
Philip P Rubino Jr
5 Davis Rd
Oxford CT 06483

Call Sign: K1PPR
Philip P Rubino Jr
5 Davis Rd
Oxford CT 06483

Call Sign: KB1VFD
Christopher D Rubino
5 Davis Rd
Oxford CT 06478

Call Sign: K1CDR
Christopher D Rubino
5 Davis Rd
Oxford CT 06478

Call Sign: KB1CPE
Douglass A Coy Mr
3 Deer Hollow Rd
Oxford CT 06478

Call Sign: K1KGP
Frank T Tonucci
5 Deer Hollow Rd
Oxford CT 06478

Call Sign: K1QKA
Norman E Turner
54 Dorman Rd
Oxford CT 06478

Call Sign: KB1WJZ
Joe Rasberry
16 Greenbriar Rd
Oxford CT 06478

Call Sign: N1YCH
Robert A Berg
48 Highland Rd
Oxford CT 06478

Call Sign: KA1CTT
Carl W Carlson
98 Hogsback Rd
Oxford CT 06478

Call Sign: AA1WM
Scott M Beisiegel
74 Jacks Hill Rd
Oxford CT 06478

Call Sign: KB1WNI
Henry E Konopka
8 Laura Lane
Oxford CT 06478

Call Sign: KA1IP
Richard I Bouchard
15 Laura Ln
Oxford CT 06478

Call Sign: N1NCV
Eugene W Du Paul
41 Little Punkup Rd
Oxford CT 06478

Call Sign: N1HQU
Richard A Hanrahan
6 Meadow Dr
Oxford CT 06478

Call Sign: K1ZZZ
Mark J Zavatsky
132 Meadowbrook Road
Oxford CT 06478

Call Sign: KB1FCS
Daniel S Kresina
113 Newgate Rd
Oxford CT 06478

Call Sign: K1SU
Frederick Maseizik
63 O Neill Rd
Oxford CT 064781532

Call Sign: WA1OPE
Peter Fryncko
7 Old State Rd 3
Oxford CT 06478

Call Sign: KB1RYJ
Joseph E Devine
34 Oxford Road
Oxford CT 06478

Call Sign: WA1VTB
Kenneth C Arifian
773 Oxford Road
Oxford CT 06478

Call Sign: NO1S
William H Emerson
10 Park Rd
Oxford CT 064781932

Call Sign: N1IBX
George A Sheehy Iii
415 Quaker Farms Rd
Oxford CT 06483

Call Sign: N1LZP
Jeffrey S Park
344 Riggs St
Oxford CT 06478

Call Sign: KB1WJU
Thomas J Gugliotti Jr
245 Riggs Street
Oxford CT 064781130

Call Sign: KB1QPU
Daniel J Carey
22 Rolling Hills Dr
Oxford CT 06478

Call Sign: KA1YTK
Thomas W Drew
586 Roosevelt Dr
Oxford CT 06483

Call Sign: KB1MZP
Gary W Kendall
5 Rose Dr
Oxford CT 06478

Call Sign: W1TS
Willard A Revaz
13 Scott Rd
Oxford CT 06478

Call Sign: K1PVD
Carl W Schmelzle
32 Silva Ter
Oxford CT 06478

Call Sign: KA1SHI
Richard B Sereque
28 Silva Tr
Oxford CT 06483

Call Sign: WA1ZGA
George Riccio
100 Stakum Cir A1
Oxford CT 06478

Call Sign: W1RIP
George Riccio
100 Stakum Circle Apt A-1
Oxford CT 06478

Call Sign: KA1FEI
Peter Mezger
3 Willow Street
Oxford CT 06478

Call Sign: KB1WLM
Michael D Konopka
74 Woodside Ave
Oxford CT 06478

Call Sign: KE1JD
William G Blackwood
75 Woodside Ave
Oxford CT 06478

**FCC Amateur Radio
Licenses in Pawcatuck**

Call Sign: N1VIV
Joseph J Carr
29 Aimee Dr
Pawcatuck CT 06379

Call Sign: N1NCY
James T Kenny
108 Brookside Ln
Pawcatuck CT 06379

Call Sign: WA4VWV
Stephen D Smith
107-15 Brookside Ln
Pawcatuck CT 06379

Call Sign: KA1HRJ

Willard J Deiger
108 Brookside Ln Apt 2
Pawcatuck CT 063791967

Call Sign: AJ1G
Christopher A Bowne
3 Carnot Ct
Pawcatuck CT 06379

Call Sign: KA1YKG
Benjamin C Bowne
3 Carnot Ct
Pawcatuck CT 06379

Call Sign: K1FLK
Robert A Harris
61 Castle Hill Rd
Pawcatuck CT 06379

Call Sign: WD6FDQ
Thomas H Hodgson
103 Castle Hill Rd
Pawcatuck CT 063791900

Call Sign: W3DNN
Thomas H Hodgson
103 Castle Hill Rd
Pawcatuck CT 063791900

Call Sign: N1HVZ
Albert F Hofer
343 Greenhaven Rd
Pawcatuck CT 06379

Call Sign: N1KHZ
Loreen S Hofer
343 Greenhaven Rd
Pawcatuck CT 06379

Call Sign: KA1ZOA
Allan V Johnson
478 Greenhaven Rd
Pawcatuck CT 06379

Call Sign: WB1DJD

John L Krupczak
30 Lathrop Ave
Pawcatuck CT 06379

Call Sign: KB1MHD
Doug D Brummund
30 Mary Hall Rd
Pawcatuck CT 06379

Call Sign: KB1FXB
Shaun T Welsh
61 Maryhall Road
Pawcatuck CT 06379

Call Sign: KB1LYE
Donald E Michel
139 North Anguilla Road
Pawcatuck CT 06379

Call Sign: WA1BQS
Richard W Canavan
6 Oakwood Ave
Pawcatuck CT 06379

Call Sign: W1CGI
Anthony Perrone Jr
12 Oakwood Ave
Pawcatuck CT 063792211

Call Sign: K1ZNQ
Harold E Rathbun
66 Palmer Neck Rd
Pawcatuck CT 06379

Call Sign: KA1TYL
Alice L Rathbun
66 Palmer Neck Rd
Pawcatuck CT 06379

Call Sign: N1OSQ
Paul M Menard
16 Palmer Street
Pawcatuck CT 06379

Call Sign: W1PAM

Robert M Stellmaker
123 Pequot Trl
Pawcatuck CT 06379

Call Sign: KA1ULQ
Kenneth L Lanphere
114 River Rd
Pawcatuck CT 06379

Call Sign: NU1M
Daniel C Keane
8 Robinson St
Pawcatuck CT 06379

Call Sign: W9ZNY
Gregory G Lindholm
51 Russell Ave.
Pawcatuck CT 06379

Call Sign: W1RLE
Robert T Cowley Sr
30 Schiller Ave
Pawcatuck CT 06379

Call Sign: N2BYW
Dean Schaffer Md
40 Stewart Rd
Pawcatuck CT 06379

Call Sign: KB1JNB
Nicholas J Seager
94 Stillman Ave
Pawcatuck CT 06379

Call Sign: NB3L
Diana M Paetzell
912 Stonington Rd
Pawcatuck CT 06379

Call Sign: KA1QMS
Antonio R Cassata
1 Woodland Ct
Pawcatuck CT 06379

Call Sign: AA1RA

Kenneth A Webb
Pawcatuck CT 06379

Call Sign: KA1FRH
Ernest G Young
Pawcatuck CT 06379

Call Sign: KB1UHA
Mark D Tetlow
Pawcatuck CT 06379

FCC Amateur Radio Licenses in Pequabuck

Call Sign: KB1KWW
Michael J Maffia
Pequabuck CT 067810176

FCC Amateur Radio Licenses in Pine Meadow

Call Sign: N1WVS
Joseph J Zakrzewski
33 Satans Kingdom Rd Box 53
Pine Meadow CT 06061

Call Sign: AA1QX
John P Zakrzewski
Pine Meadow CT 06061

FCC Amateur Radio Licenses in Plainfield

Call Sign: KB1AEH
Edward F Sullivan
36 Babcock Ave
Plainfield CT 06374

Call Sign: N1ZHD
Evan G Scarborough
18 Beechwood Blvd
Plainfield CT 063742101

Call Sign: N1HVQ

Miguel C Diaz
145 Cemetary Rd Apt N
Plainfield CT 06374

Call Sign: WA1ZNU
Daniel A Davis
18 Fernwood St
Plainfield CT 06374

Call Sign: KB1JAV
Myrna J Allen
85 Flat Rock Rd
Plainfield CT 06374

Call Sign: KA1WZA
Richard M Allen
85 Flat Rock Road
Plainfield CT 06374

Call Sign: KB1UZT
Derek S Crocker
22 Greene Ave
Plainfield CT 06374

Call Sign: K1ROL
Derek S Crocker
22 Greene Ave
Plainfield CT 06374

Call Sign: KB1OJR
Eric M Swanson
16 James St
Plainfield CT 06374

Call Sign: KA1JKD
Jack J Chesanek Jr
358 Kate Downing Rd
Plainfield CT 06374

Call Sign: K1DNW
Edward J Sochon
407 Kate Downing Rd
Plainfield CT 06374

Call Sign: WA1FCA

Joseph J Bell
110 Ledgewood Acres
Plainfield CT 06374

Call Sign: N1HFX
Michael J Martell
74 Lillibridge Rd
Plainfield CT 06374

Call Sign: N1RNU
Joan A Martell
74 Lillibridge Rd
Plainfield CT 06374

Call Sign: KB1IZN
Philip H Brown
30 Major Dr
Plainfield CT 06374

Call Sign: KB1JNC
Matthew Z Brown
30 Major Dr
Plainfield CT 06374

Call Sign: N1YKH
Michael J Grimaldi Sr
20 Major Drive
Plainfield CT 063741720

Call Sign: KB1HAR
Leeann J Grimaldi
20 Major Drive
Plainfield CT 063741720

Call Sign: W1PHB
Philip H Brown
30 Major Drive
Plainfield CT 06374

Call Sign: KB1BY
John G Landis
1035 Norwich Rd
Plainfield CT 06374

Call Sign: N1JAE

Arnold E Sharkey
1105 Norwich Rd
Plainfield CT 06374

Call Sign: N1LZX
David M Fehnel
21 Oak Wood Blvd
Plainfield CT 06374

Call Sign: WB3IRO
David M Fehnel
21 Oak Wood Blvd
Plainfield CT 06374

Call Sign: N1TNT
Jay J Palazzo
45 Oakwood Blvd.
Plainfield CT 06374

Call Sign: KG6DNU
James M Washington
66 Pickett Rd
Plainfield CT 063741634

Call Sign: KB1VHP
Frank M Mackey
10 Robin Rd
Plainfield CT 06374

Call Sign: KB1VHQ
Patricia E Mackey
10 Robin Rd
Plainfield CT 06374

Call Sign: K1BTD
Keith D Collins
22 Shepard Hill Rd
Plainfield CT 06374

Call Sign: KG5TA
Gregory B Bain
224 Spaulding Rd
Plainfield CT 06374

Call Sign: N5IKQ

Phyllis B Bain
224 Spaulding Rd
Plainfield CT 06374

Call Sign: WA1HAL
Rodney K Gardiner
Starkweather Rd
Plainfield CT 06374

**FCC Amateur Radio
Licenses in Plainville**

Call Sign: N1JME
James M Ellett Jr
33 Alderson Avenue
Plainville CT 06062

Call Sign: N1AHY
Francis W Maranda
27 Ashford Rd
Plainville CT 06062

Call Sign: K1RM
Vincent S Sgroi
6 Autumn Ln
Plainville CT 06062

Call Sign: KB1QOO
Blue Devil Contest Club
6 Autumn Ln
Plainville CT 06062

Call Sign: WX7T
Blue Devil Contest Club
6 Autumn Ln
Plainville CT 06062

Call Sign: N1HIN
Richard P Mc Ginley
19 Beechwood Rd
Plainville CT 06062

Call Sign: K1IDM
Donald L Rio
37 Bel Aire Dr

Plainville CT 06062

Call Sign: N1VGV
Michael D Banks
4 Bel-Aire Drive
Plainville CT 060621002

Call Sign: N1VVE
Sean W Hyjek
220 Broad St
Plainville CT 06062

Call Sign: KB1GAJ
Malachi W Ege
282 Camp St
Plainville CT 06062

Call Sign: KB1GCS
Micah H Ege
282 Camp St
Plainville CT 06062

Call Sign: KB1IWZ
Mitchell J Underwood Jr
22 Canterbury Ln
Plainville CT 06062

Call Sign: KB1IPE
Michael D Ersevim
69 Chester St
Plainville CT 06062

Call Sign: KA1QWI
Roger A Kratka
213 Cooke St
Plainville CT 060621402

Call Sign: KB1OWK
David A Chevrette
15 Cronk Rd - Unit 9
Plainville CT 06062

Call Sign: W1DAC
David A Chevrette
15 Cronk Rd - Unit 9

Plainville CT 06062   Plainville CT 06062   Plainville CT 06062

Call Sign: KB1UYE   Call Sign: N1JPI   Call Sign: N1JGR
Lawrence A Hamilton Jr   Robert R Albrecht   Ricardo W Castrogiovanni
39 Diamond Ave   57 Jefferson St   27 Madison St
Plainville CT 06062   Plainville CT 06062   Plainville CT 06062

Call Sign: K1FXD   Call Sign: KB1ULW   Call Sign: KB1SNL
Donald L Thatcher   Michael P Dalena   Nicholas R Castrogiovanni
75 Diamond Ave   20 Johnson Ave   27 Madison St
Plainville CT 06062   Plainville CT 06062   Plainville CT 06062

Call Sign: N1NYJ   Call Sign: KA1BJS   Call Sign: KB1HDZ
Mario Cajar   Dean A Goldsmith   Nickolas C Boodley
338 East Street Apt. B-2   2 Jude Rd   45 Maple St 39
Plainville CT 06062   Plainville CT 060621118   Plainville CT 06062

Call Sign: KA1GMS   Call Sign: KB1IEU   Call Sign: N1JC
Mark S Kurowski   John J Sarra   James P Calandriello
11 Exeter Avenue   3 Kari Rd   62 Maxine Road
Plainville CT 06062   Plainville CT 06062   Plainville CT 060621056

Call Sign: KB1SNM   Call Sign: N1NVC   Call Sign: KB1UIH
Tyler D Clemens   Joan J Vallee   Thomas J Mcconnell
87 Farmington Ave   139 Laurel Court   3 Mel Rd
Plainville CT 06062   Plainville CT 06062   Plainvillc CT 06062

Call Sign: KB1UIK   Call Sign: N1NVD   Call Sign: WB1FEP
Reade Clemens   Rosaire J Caron   Ronald R Russell
87 Farmington Ave   139 Laurel Court   46 Metacomet Rd
Plainville CT 06062   Plainville CT 06062   Plainville CT 06062

Call Sign: N1SPC   Call Sign: K1WEP   Call Sign: WA1HRK
Bruce W Vicinus   David A Hoyt   Vincent D Mercadante
246 Farmington Ave   23 Lincoln St   47 Metacomet Rd
Plainville CT 060621320   Plainville CT 06062   Plainville CT 06062

Call Sign: N1NAM   Call Sign: N1OJR   Call Sign: KB1SNK
Carole M Dimock   Richard E Greenleaf   Jane M Gerke
10 Hardwood Rd   17 Locust St   63 N Washington St
Plainville CT 060621210   Plainville CT 06062   Plainville CT 06062

Call Sign: N1GLA   Call Sign: KA1DRU   Call Sign: N1JWF
Neil F Fitzgerald   Raymond T Swanson   Albert P Gerke
100 Hilltop Rd Rr 1   64 Mac Arthur Rd   63 N Washington St - Apt 3

Plainville CT 06062

Call Sign: KB1FYD
Robert J Pelletier
100 Northampton Ln Unit
C24
Plainville CT 06062

Call Sign: KA1IHF
John B Gladysz Jr
97 Northwest Dr
Plainville CT 06062

Call Sign: W1YOL
Arthur S Lake
2 Paul St
Plainville CT 060623008

Call Sign: KA1HZG
Giuseppe Rizzo
16 Pequot Rd
Plainville CT 06062

Call Sign: KB1OLF
Albert Entralgo
80 Pershing Dr Ct
Plainville CT 06062

Call Sign: N1IEC
Glenn E Williams
50 Pierce St Unit 12
Plainville CT 06062

Call Sign: WB1ETL
Herbert W Tenney
41 Pinnacle Rd
Plainville CT 06062

Call Sign: WB1FSN
Marjorie C Tenney
41 Pinnacle Rd
Plainville CT 06062

Call Sign: N1YZP
James E Kilcoin Iii

25 Plum Tree Rd
Plainville CT 06062

Call Sign: KA1DZS
Raymond K Seymour
38 Provencher Dr
Plainville CT 06062

Call Sign: AA1WU
Ronald M Melanson
134 Red Stone Hill
Plainville CT 06062

Call Sign: K1MWF
Lee J Burns
175 Red Stone Hill
Plainville CT 060622629

Call Sign: WA1NEZ
Bertrand L Thompson Jr
31 Rockwell Ave
Plainville CT 06062

Call Sign: W1KYD
Peter F Zakrzewski Sr
22 Rosemont Dr
Plainville CT 06062

Call Sign: N1MFC
Jesse W Marson
44 Shuttle Meadow Rd
Plainville CT 06062

Call Sign: KB1BFK
Jacek Orzol
14 Testa Dr
Plainville CT 06062

Call Sign: N1YFO
Edward G Bruce Jr
21 Tomlinson Ave
Plainville CT 06062

Call Sign: KA1GBG
Robert H Mundy Jr

190 Tomlinson Ave 3a
Plainville CT 060627076

Call Sign: KB1LZJ
James D Simone
190 Tomlinson Ave Apt 3c
Plainville CT 06062

Call Sign: WA1NMF
Paul J Dzilenski
22 Tyler Farms Road
Plainville CT 06062

Call Sign: W1ORG
Maurice H Lindquist
35 Wayne Dr
Plainville CT 06062

Call Sign: KB1UII
Edward M Krampitz Jr
49 Webster St
Plainville CT 06062

Call Sign: KB1UIJ
Dolores F Krampitz
49 Webster St
Plainville CT 06062

Call Sign: K1TLK
Tammy L Krauss
129 West Main St Apt 1
Plainville CT 06063

Call Sign: KD1GB
Joseph D Terrien Sr
15 West Pine Way Unit 18
Plainville CT 06062

Call Sign: N1GOJ
Peter J Keyes
71 White Oak Ave A2
Plainville CT 06062

Call Sign: KB1JGK
John P Callaghan

71 White Oak Avenue Unit
A5
Plainville CT 06062

Call Sign: K1HAH
John P Callaghan
71 White Oak Avenue Unit
A5
Plainville CT 06062

Call Sign: KA1ZOM
David A Taft
371 Woodford Ave 32
Plainville CT 06062

Call Sign: KB1VWI
Insurance City Repeater
Club
22 Woodside Lane
Plainville CT 060621225

Call Sign: K1CRC
Insurance City Repeater
Club
22 Woodside Lane
Plainville CT 060621225

Call Sign: K1DFS
Charles I Motes Jr
22 Woodside Ln
Plainville CT 06062

Call Sign: N1KCJ
Rita M Motes
22 Woodside Ln
Plainville CT 06062

Call Sign: N1PBD
James I Motes
22 Woodside Ln
Plainville CT 06062

Call Sign: N1GCV
Steven B Moss
35 Benny Dr
Plantsville CT 06479

Call Sign: W1SBM
Steven B Moss
35 Benny Dr
Plantsville CT 06479

Call Sign: K1TDO
Todd D Olsen
6 Carter Lane Apt #18
Plantsville CT 064791529

Call Sign: KB1OLA
Shane Taurinski
10 Cummings St
Plantsville CT 06479

Call Sign: WB1BVS
Salvatore T Rafala
76 De Fashion St
Plantsville CT 06479

Call Sign: N1LGJ
Robert J Baranski
119 Fern Dr
Plantsville CT 06479

Call Sign: WA1YBB
James J Casey
105 Green Valley Dr
Plantsville CT 06479

Call Sign: WA1UTV
Gary W Arseneau
126 Greystone Dr
Plantsville CT 06479

Call Sign: N1TXL
James W O Connell
86 Jubilee Dr
Plantsville CT 06479

Call Sign: W1JRT
William L Cornell
19 Knox Dr
Plantsville CT 06479

Call Sign: N1FQF
Robert A Smicz
3 Lois Ave
Plantsville CT 06479

Call Sign: KB1LAF
Charles A Dudac
267 Manor Rd
Plantsville CT 06479

Call Sign: AB1HB
Charles A Dudac
267 Manor Rd
Plantsville CT 06479

Call Sign: N1QNI
Mark W Gardner
27 Marboy Drive
Plantsville CT 064791517

Call Sign: W1ARW
Mark W Gardner
27 Marboy Drive
Plantsville CT 064791517

Call Sign: KB1VLZ
Gregory P Morin
383 Marion Ave
Plantsville CT 06479

Call Sign: K1OTI
Raymond L Thomas Jr
836 Marion Ave
Plantsville CT 06479

Call Sign: KB1NKM
Stanley G Tomalesky
125 Mariondale Dr
Plantsville CT 06479

Call Sign: KB1NKN
Helene Tomalesky
125 Mariondale Dr
Plantsville CT 06479

Call Sign: N3TFT
Joseph Tomalesky
125 Mariondale Drive
Plantsville CT 06479

Call Sign: N1OQC
Michael D Johnson
60 Maxwell Dr
Plantsville CT 06479

Call Sign: N1FQG
Christopher L Riedel
78 Milldale Ave
Plantsville CT 06479

Call Sign: KB1DVC
Jon A Aparo
529 Mount Vernon Road
Plantsville CT 06479

Call Sign: KC1EN
Kevin J Bernard
262 Mt Vernon Rd
Plantsville CT 06479

Call Sign: N1PZI
Christine C Grant Mulvey
116 Norton St
Plantsville CT 06479

Call Sign: KA1TFO
Lisa Leonard
1165 Old Turnpike Rd
Plantsville CT 06479

Call Sign: WB1GIR
Richard V Rosengrant
87 Parkview Dr
Plantsville CT 064791933

Call Sign: K1KSQ
Carl C Plourde
603 Prospect St
Plantsville CT 06479

Call Sign: N1FPJ
Stephen A Cisowski
775 Prospect St
Plantsville CT 06479

Call Sign: KB1EEQ
Kevin J Legat
1045 S Main St
Plantsville CT 06479

Call Sign: KB1SFD
Kevin J Legat
1045 S Main St
Plantsville CT 06479

Call Sign: W1KKG
Sperry B Skilton
970 S Main St Apt 206
Plantsville CT 064791693

Call Sign: KD1RQ
Laurence G D Addario
24 Silo Dr
Plantsville CT 06479

Call Sign: KB1SIS
Gail C Mihalakos
1175 South Main St Unit 2
Plantsville CT 06479

Call Sign: NC1D
Raymond D Desrochers Jr
861 South Main Street Unit
29
Plantsville CT 06479

Call Sign: N1EVR
John G Schoenfeld
28 Summer St
Plantsville CT 06479

Call Sign: KA1ILC
Robin M Seitz
138 Summit St
Plantsville CT 06479

Call Sign: KA1ILH
Harold C Bacon
138 Summit St
Plantsville CT 06479

Call Sign: KA1KVT
Lydia G Peeters
138 Summit St
Plantsville CT 06479

Call Sign: W1ECV
Southington Amateur Radio
Assoc Inc
138 Summit St
Plantsville CT 064791125

Call Sign: KB1QFO
Mary A Bacon
1381/2 Summit Street
Plantsville CT 06479

Call Sign: W1MVN
Francis V Porter
50 Whitlock Ave
Plantsville CT 06479

Call Sign: KB1MZF
David L Ames
Plantsville CT 064790212

FCC Amateur Radio Licenses in Pleasant Valley

Call Sign: KB1NLF
Scott M Bruen
75 N Canton Rd
Pleasant Valley CT 06063

Call Sign: W1NLF
Scott M Bruen
75 N Canton Rd
Pleasant Valley CT 06063

Call Sign: N1BWS
Dale D Nebelsky
64 Pleasant Valley Rd
Pleasant Valley CT 06063

Call Sign: KB1IKS
Paul A Herzog
PO Box 99
Pleasant Valley CT 06063

Call Sign: KA1OAK
George M Murphy
Pleasant Valley CT 06063

Call Sign: KB1BXI
Raucus Caucus
Pleasant Valley CT 06063

Call Sign: WA1MMZ
Robert H Judd
Plcasant Vallcy CT 06063

Call Sign: WM1B
Susan E Fredrickson
Pleasant Valley CT 06063

Call Sign: KB1GGQ
Richard A Weinberg
Pleasant Valley CT 06063

Call Sign: N1NEH
Ronald L Mc Clain
18 Hillside Ave
Plymouth CT 06782

Call Sign: KA1MJX
Charles A Brewer Jr

16 Lake Plymouth Blvd
Plymouth CT 06782

Call Sign: KA1MPJ
Barbara M Brewer
16 Lake Plymouth Blvd
Plymouth CT 06782

Call Sign: KB1ADI
John H Curley Jr
217 Lake Plymouth Blvd
Plymouth CT 06782

Call Sign: N1WQJ
Harold W Day Jr
375 Lake Plymouth Blvd
Plymouth CT 06782

Call Sign: W1HJG
Daniel L Fellin
419a Mount Tobe Rd
Plymouth CT 06782

Call Sign: KB1BHH
Scott J Zurawel
Schrowback Rd
Plymouth CT 06782

Call Sign: N1SXR
Carol A Coon
31 South St
Plymouth CT 06782

Call Sign: NO1C
James G Pepides
419 South St
Plymouth CT 067822714

Call Sign: KB1CNU
Claude A West
11 Fox Hill Rd
Pomeret CT 062580252

Call Sign: W1BRF
Quinnebaug Valley Radio
Club
1 Quasset Rd
Pomfret CT 06258

Call Sign: KB1KBG
Keith R Eslinger
220-4 Babbit Hill Rd
Pomfret Center CT 06259

Call Sign: KA1HTX
James S Castle
422 Brooklyn Rd
Pomfret Center CT
062592406

Call Sign: N1PTI
George A Rukstela
4 Fire Tower Rd
Pomfret Center CT 06259

Call Sign: KA1UFH
Robin L Cipot
16 Firetower Rd
Pomfret Center CT 06259

Call Sign: KR1U
Robert S Eslinger
20 Gary School Rd
Pomfret Center CT
02599801

Call Sign: KA1UGP
Robert V Lavoie Jr
466 Hampton Rd
Pomfret Center CT 06259

Call Sign: N1SFJ
Robert A Griggs

535 Hampton Rd
Pomfret Center CT
062592012

Call Sign: KB1SBD
Kerry L Clark
278 Paine Rd
Pomfret Center CT 06259

Call Sign: KB1QDC
Kevin M Clark
278 Paine Road
Pomfret Center CT 06259

Call Sign: WB9CLJ
Glen R Dash
90 Quassett Rd.
Pomfret Center CT 06259

Call Sign: KB1NAK
Gregory D Konney
69 Ragged Hill Rd
Pomfret Center CT 06259

Call Sign: N1RCP
Clayton W Welch
127 Searles Rd
Pomfret Center CT 06259

Call Sign: W1DWX
Alfred C Dion Sr
Seely Brown Village Apt
202
Pomfret Center CT 06259

Call Sign: KB1JPZ
Jacqueline L Sembor
269 Taft Pond Rd
Pomfret Center CT 06259

Call Sign: KB1DNO
Frances M Rollinson
182 Wrights Crossing Rd
Pomfret Center CT 06259

Call Sign: KE1LI
Paul M Rollinson
182 Wrights Crossing Rd
Pomfret Center CT 06259

Call Sign: KB1EZU
Rebecca M Rollinson
182 Wrights Crossing Rd
Pomfret Center CT 06259

Call Sign: KB1JPY
Jennifer K Rollinson
182 Wrights Crossing Rd
Pomfret Center CT 06259

Call Sign: W1HST
Irvin S Rosen
458 Wrights Crossing Rd
Pomfret Center CT 06259

FCC Amateur Radio Licenses in Poquonock

Call Sign: N1YKB
Donald S Sheldon
Poquonock CT 060640284

FCC Amateur Radio Licenses in Portland

Call Sign: KB1WOI
Christian J Gould
5 Bell Ct
Portland CT 06480

Call Sign: N1YFP
George E Scheer Jr
24 Brooks Lane
Portland CT 064801531

Call Sign: N1YIY
Babette P Scheer
24 Brooks Lane
Portland CT 064801531

Call Sign: KB1GCR
Todd R Scheer
24 Brooks Lane
Portland CT 064801531

Call Sign: KB1QQO
Barbara W Felgate
1 Brush Pasture Lane Unit
201
Portland CT 06480

Call Sign: N1JGP
David J Blais
19 Coe Ave Ext
Portland CT 06480

Call Sign: N1PFD
David J Blais
19 Coe Ave Ext
Portland CT 06480

Call Sign: N1MT
Mark P Toussaint
36 Cote Lane
Portland CT 06480

Call Sign: WB1ADO
John R Larrabee
3 Dogwood Dr
Portland CT 06480

Call Sign: K1BIY
Franklin G Barker
9 Edgewood Rd
Portland CT 06480

Call Sign: WA1VNN
Milton L Bloomquist
4 Elizabeth Rd
Portland CT 06480

Call Sign: KA1VQC
Robert A Cone
14 Elizabeth Rd
Portland CT 06480

Call Sign: N1OOC
Roger L Jean
9 Freestone Ave
Portland CT 06480

Call Sign: K1MBI
Lambros Lambrinides
21 Freestone Ave
Portland CT 064801817

Call Sign: KA1VTX
Brian D Sargent
4 Greenview Dr
Portland CT 06480

Call Sign: WA1ELE
Edward P Zakowich
231 Main St
Portland CT 06480

Call Sign: KA1MWR
Matthew J Florentz
319 Main St
Portland CT 06480

Call Sign: K1GAW
Leon R Case
484 Main St
Portland CT 064801528

Call Sign: N1WGL
Bruce D Nelson
170 Marlborough St
Portland CT 06480

Call Sign: KB1WSE
Jason R Tetlow
30 Michele Dr
Portland CT 06480

Call Sign: WA1ZJT
Marra C Giuliano
280 Middle Haddam Rd
Portland CT 06480

Call Sign: N1JML
Bernie C Jarzabek Jr
16 Myrtle Road
Portland CT 06480

Call Sign: K1MGO
Douglas B Sargent
11 Pear Orchard Rd.
Portland CT 064804606

Call Sign: W1STT
Emanuel J Rame
322 Penfield Hill Rd
Portland CT 06480

Call Sign: AA1GX
Theodore Trudel
92 Pepperidge Road
Portland CT 064801343

Call Sign: N1OYF
TRACEY A Krasniewski
1330 Portland Cobalt Road
Portland CT 06480

Call Sign: KB1OUP
Peter Mcdougall
22 Prospect St
Portland CT 06480

Call Sign: KB1OUR
Dylan S Mcdougall
22 Prospect St
Portland CT 06480

Call Sign: KB1DWX
Charles Joe Kolenda
7 Riverview St Ext
Portland CT 064801971

Call Sign: WA1BAR
Erroll H Drinkwater
202 Rose Hill Rd
Portland CT 06480

Call Sign: W1RJ
Bruce E Thivierge
18 Rustic Terrace
Portland CT 06480

Call Sign: KB1ULP
James Z Martel
36 Sand Hill Rd
Portland CT 06480

Call Sign: K1CMM
Donald B Gouin
52 South Rd
Portland CT 06480

Call Sign: W1EDH
Middlesex Amateur Radio
Society
52 South Rd
Portland CT 06480

Call Sign: AA1OL
Bruce E Thivierge
3 Stoner Ter
Portland CT 06480

Call Sign: WA2YKG
Andrew P Jarosik
21 Taylor Dr
Portland CT 064801211

Call Sign: K1APJ
Andrew P Jarosik
21 Taylor Dr
Portland CT 064801211

Call Sign: KB1QBN
John Kalinowski
9 Wagon Wheel Ln
Portland CT 06480

Call Sign: K1DUQ
John Kalinowski
9 Wagon Wheel Ln

Portland CT 06480

Call Sign: N1GLJ
Frederick M Cohan
16 Woodland Rd
Portland CT 06480

Call Sign: N1FLV
Lon K Travis
Portland CT 06480

Call Sign: N1LMP
Michael A Stemmler
Portland CT 06480

Call Sign: WB1ARF
Brian D Gouin
Portland CT 06480

Call Sign: KB1OUS
Charles B Shaffer
Portland CT 06480

Call Sign: KB1OUT
Matthew C Shaffer
Portland CT 06480

Call Sign: KB1OXD
Ryan C Shafter
Portland CT 06480

Call Sign: KB1OXE
Alexander M Shaffer
Portland CT 06480

FCC Amateur Radio Licenses in Preston

Call Sign: N1APP
Helen H Lavallee
Rt 165 Box 669
Preston CT 06365

Call Sign: KD5JIA
Mertissa M Schmittroth

111 Branch Hill Rd
Preston CT 06365

Call Sign: W1SBH
Alvan E Lawrence
121 Brickyard Rd
Preston CT 06365

Call Sign: KA1EBO
Ignatz A Melgey
59 Bunny Road
Preston CT 06365

Call Sign: N4GCN
Harold A Davison
9 Doolittle Rd
Preston CT 06365

Call Sign: KA1YXF
Peter R Leibert
39 Krug Rd
Preston CT 06365

Call Sign: N1LJK
Damon M Leibert
39 Krug Rd
Preston CT 06365

Call Sign: KA1YCJ
Gary R Cardot
21 Lewis Rd
Preston CT 06360

Call Sign: KB1IRN
Robert G Byrnes
5 Lincoln Park Rd Ext Apt C
Preston CT 06365

Call Sign: KA1PFM
Mark P Hewitt
57 Long Society Rd
Preston CT 06365

Call Sign: WB1DIW

Patricia A Marino
61 Mc Climon Rd
Preston CT 06365

Call Sign: WB1DJA
John V Marino
61 Mc Climon Rd
Preston CT 06365

Call Sign: KA1CBL
Michael K Nylen
51 Miller Rd
Preston CT 06365

Call Sign: N1ITJ
Mark T Renouf
45 Preston Plains
Preston CT 06360

Call Sign: W1LBD
Joseph J Wall
153 R Rt 12
Preston CT 06365

Call Sign: KA1ZHP
Christopher C Oat
142 River Rd
Preston CT 06365

Call Sign: KA1ZPZ
David A Oat
142 River Rd
Preston CT 06365

Call Sign: K1DCT
David C Thackston
244 Route 2
Preston CT 06365

Call Sign: KD1YI
Donald N Renouf
45 Rt 164
Preston CT 06365

Call Sign: WA1YRD

Richard J Fields
255 Rt 2a
Preston CT 06360

Call Sign: WA1JCI
Ronald J Rheaume
15 Stanton Ln
Preston CT 063658029

Call Sign: KA1FFP
Fred C Wissell
35 Swantown Rd
Preston CT 06365

Call Sign: KA1HRE
Fred E Wissell
35 Swantown Rd
Preston CT 06365

FCC Amateur Radio Licenses in Prospect

Call Sign: KA1KJT
William M Berzinskas
44 Bronson Rd
Prospect CT 06712

Call Sign: KB1RRG
Joseph R Hawthorne
5 Cambridge Dr
Prospect CT 06712

Call Sign: KB1RRM
Brian J Hawthorne
5 Cambridge Dr
Prospect CT 06712

Call Sign: W7YY
William F Mc Casland
6 Candee Rd
Prospect CT 06712

Call Sign: KA1RVX
Robert E Carson
17 Candee Rd

Prospect CT 06710

Call Sign: W1AMJ
Peter K Miller
14 Chandler Dr
Prospect CT 06712

Call Sign: KB2SSM
Hrvoje Podnar
108 Cheshire Rd
Prospect CT 06712

Call Sign: KB1FSX
John M Foege
12 Clark Hill Road
Prospect CT 06712

Call Sign: N1ZNF
Anthony F Di Meco Sr
10 Coer Rd
Prospect CT 067121614

Call Sign: WA1PEI
Jonathan W Krofssik Sr
33 Coer Rd
Prospect CT 06712

Call Sign: KA1JGC
Barbara A Cable
11 Maple Dr
Prospect CT 067121020

Call Sign: W1DIG
Louis D Cable Jr
11 Maple Dr
Prospect CT 067121020

Call Sign: KB1MEL
Matthew T Comeau
16 Maria Hotchkiss Rd Unit
1
Prospect CT 06712

Call Sign: N1WSL
Leo G Grondine

57 Putting Green
Prospect CT 06712

Call Sign: N1YZO
Daryll J Christensen
28 Putting Green Lane
Prospect CT 06712

Call Sign: N1QDA
Conrad H Sheldon
12 Putting Green Ln
Prospect CT 06712

Call Sign: N1TAM
Michael J Sheldon
12 Putting Green Ln
Prospect CT 06712

Call Sign: N1ZFD
Thomas M Sheldon
12 Putting Green Ln
Prospect CT 06712

Call Sign: KA1YQK
Jerry S Burr
4 Radio Tower Rd
Prospect CT 06712

Call Sign: KA1NTB
Mark A Proul
10 Radio Tower Rd
Prospect CT 067121836

Call Sign: KB1SL
Leslie J Proul
10 Radio Tower Rd
Prospect CT 06712

Call Sign: N1DMC
Dolores A Proul
10 Radio Tower Rd
Prospect CT 06712

Call Sign: N1KFA
John R Moscariello Jr

6 Saunders Lane
Prospect CT 06712

Call Sign: N1QYE
John Vasil
50 Scott Rd
Prospect CT 06712

Call Sign: KB1KUV
Christopher K Bedard
72 Smokerise Circle
Prospect CT 06712

Call Sign: WV2LKM
Steven H Waldmann
135 Summit Rd
Prospect CT 06712

Call Sign: KA1QND
Barbara L Charland
154 Summit Rd
Prospect CT 06712

Call Sign: WA1IKJ
Raymond D Charland
154 Summit Rd
Prospect CT 06712

Call Sign: KB1WVS
William W Moroz Jr
18 Sunrise Drive
Prospect CT 06712

Call Sign: N1VGC
Peter A Cipriano
201 Sycamore Drive
Prospect CT 06712

Call Sign: KB1FGC
Richard J Guerrera
19 Terry Rd
Prospect CT 06712

Call Sign: KD1XQ
John J Durbin Jr

4 Vaillan Ct
Prospect CT 06712

Call Sign: W1JZA
William A Hulstrunk
81 Waterbury Rd
Prospect CT 06712

Call Sign: KB1KYT
Raymond E Lush
48 Waterbury Rd Rt 69
Prospect CT 06712

Call Sign: KA1PWC
Timothy P Meehan
21 Williams Dr
Prospect CT 06712

Call Sign: KA1DIL
Timothy P Meehan Jr
52 Williams Dr
Prospect CT 06712

Call Sign: N1EBE
Thomas E Woundy
22 Woodcrest Dr
Prospect CT 06712

Call Sign: KB1PDI
Kevin T Stelmaszek
Prospect CT 06712

FCC Amateur Radio Licenses in Putnam

Call Sign: W1EQ
Robert C Garceau
110 Breault St
Putnam CT 06260

Call Sign: N0FQY
William E Wilson
312 Church Street
Putnam CT 06260

Call Sign: N1OQN
Normand T Savary Jr
25 Cleveland St
Putnam CT 06260

Call Sign: KA1TGU
Floyd D Loomis
590 Five Mi River Rd
Putnam CT 06260

Call Sign: KB1MZS
Timothy S Auclair
63 Five Mile River Rd
Putnam CT 06260

Call Sign: KB1TIM
Timothy S Auclair
63 Five Mile River Rd
Putnam CT 06260

Call Sign: N1DSE
Sherwood B Bauer
59 Gary School Rd Rfd 2
Putnam CT 06260

Call Sign: KB1SBB
Scott A Chartier
40 Groveland Ave
Putnam CT 06260

Call Sign: KB1ORX
Thomas W Sansoucy
48 Heritage Road
Putnam CT 06260

Call Sign: KB1UWC
Angela S Henrichon
136 Killingly Ave
Putnam CT 06260

Call Sign: WB1GPG
Richard C Holbrook
86 Latici St
Putnam CT 06260

Call Sign: KA1LYO
Omer M Bruneau
56 Meehanies St
Putnam CT 06260

Call Sign: KA1MAD
Beatrice D Bruneau
56 Meehanies St
Putnam CT 06260

Call Sign: KA1LYS
Carol F Kennett
41 North
Putnam CT 06260

Call Sign: KA1LYQ
Paul H Kennett
41 North St
Putnam CT 06260

Call Sign: N1LSJ
Ronald A Kimball
16 Park Road
Putnam CT 06260

Call Sign: WB1DXW
Richard A Parker
32 Perry St
Putnam CT 06260

Call Sign: KB1STY
John P Tetreault Sr
73 Prospect St
Putnam CT 06260

Call Sign: KB1TJJ
John P Tetreault Sr
73 Prospect St
Putnam CT 06260

Call Sign: N1JTZ
John P Tetreault Sr
73 Prospect St
Putnam CT 06260

Call Sign: KB1SJT
William A Mullen
268 River Rd
Putnam CT 06260

Call Sign: N1MD
Michael L Therrien
476 River Rd
Putnam CT 06260

Call Sign: N1TLN
Lea M Therrien
476 River Rd
Putnam CT 06260

Call Sign: KB1BBI
Ruth L Rhodes
207 Sabin St Unit 60
Putnam CT 06260

Call Sign: N1RFK
Norman E Beausoleil
99 Smith St.
Putnam CT 06260

Call Sign: KA1MCX
Neal C Eslinger
23 Sunnyside Ave
Putnam CT 06260

Call Sign: KA1MPH
William E Owen
37 Thompson Ave
Putnam CT 06260

Call Sign: KB1ENX
Paul S Raymond
21 Vandale St
Putnam CT 06260

Call Sign: KB1FEP
Wendy M Jalette
21 Vandale St
Putnam CT 06260

Call Sign: NE1N
Donald J Hodges
66 Wilkinson St
Putnam CT 06260

Call Sign: KB1GLR
Edward S Beckman
50 Woodstock Ave
Putnam CT 06260

Call Sign: KA1KXX
Caleb A Warner
124 Woodstock Ave
Putnam CT 06260

Call Sign: KA1LMN
Roger E Lamothe Jr
341 Woodstock Ave
Putnam CT 06260

Call Sign: KB1TMT
Mark R Brodeur
379 Woodstock Ave
Putnam CT 06260

Call Sign: W5VDJ
Norma R Wheeler
218 Woodstock Ave Apt 13
Putnam CT 06260

Call Sign: KB1ODY
Steve Theriault
Putnam CT 06260

Call Sign: KB1QDU
William J Gradie
Putnam CT 06260

Call Sign: KB1TXR
Adam J Sansoucy
Putnam CT 06260

**FCC Amateur Radio
Licenses in Quaker Hill**

Call Sign: N1DCE
Theodore J Wirth
9 Best View Rd
Quaker Hill CT 06375

Call Sign: WA4LNG
Jack Morgan
3 Chapman Ave
Quaker Hill CT 06375

Call Sign: AA1SV
Austin J Wolfe
18 Chapman Ave
Quaker Hill CT 06375

Call Sign: WE1G
Walter N Kuhn Sr
9 Charles Ave
Quaker Hill CT 06375

Call Sign: W1EOZ
James A Archer
13 Faulkner Dr
Quaker Hill CT 06375

Call Sign: N1UKX
Lauri D Lundgren
12 Hempstead Drive
Quaker Hill CT 06375

Call Sign: KE1LW
Erick L Walters
2 John Ave
Quaker Hill CT 06375

Call Sign: KS1U
George Blahun Jr
7 Mamacoke Road
Quaker Hill CT 06375

Call Sign: N1WNW
Kevin M Callahan
99 Old Colchester Rd
Quaker Hill CT 06375

Call Sign: KD1QF
Raymond W Hasse
145 Old Colchester Rd
Quaker Hill CT 06375

Call Sign: WA9WMQ
John J Vopicka Iii
273 Old Colchester Rd
Quaker Hill CT 06375

Call Sign: N2UST
Sean F Lester
161 Old Norwich Rd
Quaker Hill CT 06375

Call Sign: WE1K
Harold E Nash
181 Old Norwich Rd
Quaker Hill CT 06375

Call Sign: KB1EXV
Robert D Collins
17 Porter St
Quaker Hill CT 06375

Call Sign: N1AMO
Donald P Ward
6 Rosemary Ln
Quaker Hill CT 06375

FCC Amateur Radio Licenses in Quinebaug

Call Sign: KB1VDM
Joseph Donovan Jr
5 Donovan Dr
Quinebaug CT 06262

Call Sign: N1OCA
Kevin R Freeland
111 Old Turnpike
Quinebaug CT 06262

Call Sign: KB1VCB
Albert G Lafleur

4 Paul Ave
Quinebaug CT 06262

Call Sign: K1AGL
Albert G Lafleur
4 Paul Ave
Quinebaug CT 06262

Call Sign: KB1VDL
Stephen F Benoit
11 Poulin Dr
Quinebaug CT 06262

Call Sign: N1TLO
David H Randall
Quinebaug CT 06262

FCC Amateur Radio Licenses in Redding

Call Sign: KA1KPS
James L Sugden Jr
186 Black Rock Tpke
Redding CT 06875

Call Sign: KB1TNL
George D Meschi
382 Black Rock Tpke
Redding CT 06896

Call Sign: WA1TXR
Gerhard J Frank
120 Blackrock Tnpk
Redding CT 06876

Call Sign: AB1CB
Gerhard J Frank
120 Blackrock Tnpk
Redding CT 068962515

Call Sign: N1DFR
Jerome E Nevins
41 Chalburn Road
Redding CT 06896

Call Sign: W1CEE
Davis M Bernhardt
10 Deacon Abbott Rd
Redding CT 06896

Call Sign: KA1AXI
Lawrence A Kulowiec
48 Gallows Hill Rd
Redding CT 06896

Call Sign: KA1DNL
William P Pardee
46 Goodridge Rd
Redding CT 068962614

Call Sign: KB1RLP
Adam T Kaufman
27 Great Meadow Rd
Redding CT 06896

Call Sign: W1GAE
John E Pfeifer
3 Great Pasture Rd
Redding CT 06896

Call Sign: N1LOV
Bennett H Pardee
60 Greenbush Rd
Redding CT 06875

Call Sign: KB1BZN
Eurico Costa
24 Hopewell Woods Rd
Redding CT 06896

Call Sign: KB1BSX
G Han Van Oostendorp
18 Huckleberry Rd
Redding CT 06896

Call Sign: K2GX
Joseph M Sand
9 Ledgewood Rd
Redding CT 06896

Call Sign: N2INX
Antonia M Sand
9 Ledgewood Rd
Redding CT 06896

Call Sign: W1DCC
Leonard E Dryer
16 Little Boston Ln
Redding CT 068962807

Call Sign: N2DHA
Nicholas S Kozloff Jr
6 Little River Lane
Redding CT 06896

Call Sign: W1NSK
Nicholas S Kozloff Jr
6 Little River Lane
Redding CT 06896

Call Sign: KB1FKH
Krista L Brown
96 Marchant Rd
Redding CT 06896

Call Sign: K1LSF
Walter G Rodiger Jr
3171 Meadow Ridge
Redding CT 068963227

Call Sign: KB1HDA
Andrew R Camp
55 Orchard Dr
Redding CT 06896

Call Sign: KB1HDB
Ann L Camp
55 Orchard Dr
Redding CT 06896

Call Sign: N1GKJ
Kent D Mac Farlane
67 Pocahontas Road
Redding CT 06896

Call Sign: N1CRW
Ira Stone
11 Sherman Tpke
Redding CT 06896

Call Sign: N1JXH
Thomas E Hoyt
14 Sunny View Dr
Redding CT 06896

Call Sign: KB1KXV
Josephus F G Degroot
30 Sunnyview Dr
Redding CT 06896

Call Sign: AB1DO
Josephus F G Degroot
30 Sunnyview Dr
Redding CT 06896

Call Sign: KB1UQE
Peter Q De Groot
30 Sunnyview Dr
Redding CT 06896

FCC Amateur Radio Licenses in Redding Center

Call Sign: WA1WTA
Hjalmar W Anderson Jr
Redding Center CT 06875

FCC Amateur Radio Licenses in Redding Ridge

Call Sign: W1AQT
Robert H Peck
91 Pine Tree Rd
Redding Ridge CT 06876

FCC Amateur Radio Licenses in Ridgefield

Call Sign: WB1AKH

John J Preli
23 Armand Pl
Ridgefield CT 068773001

Call Sign: KA1LUD
Stephen Szabolcsi
73 Ashbee Ln
Ridgefield CT 06877

Call Sign: K1HM
Harold D Maney Jr
510 Barrack Hill Rd
Ridgefield CT 06877

Call Sign: W1FTT
Edward M Peters
591 Barrack Hill Rd
Ridgefield CT 06877

Call Sign: N1AWJ
Marvin Fleischman
171 Bob Hill Rd
Ridgefield CT 06877

Call Sign: NA1C
Sebastian Van Engelen
171 Bob Hill Rd
Ridgefield CT 06877

Call Sign: K1IFJ
John F Sanders
Box 502
Ridgefield CT 06877

Call Sign: W1BKL
Charles F Rudolph
4 Brookside Rd
Ridgefield CT 06877

Call Sign: N1PE
Francis R Sileo
34 Bryon Ave
Ridgefield CT 068774426

Call Sign: KB1SOK

Jeffrey S Lundberg
45 Cooper Hill Rd
Ridgefield CT 06877

Call Sign: KB1TWC
Richard J Proctor Jr
31 Cooper Hill Road
Ridgefield CT 06877

Call Sign: KB1GSI
Anthony H Yonda
41 Craigmoor Rd S
Ridgefield CT 06877

Call Sign: W1AHY
Anthony H Yonda
41 Craigmoor Rd S
Ridgefield CT 06877

Call Sign: KB1CXP
Robert D Dobbin
499 Danbury Rd
Ridgefield CT 06877

Call Sign: KB1KCI
Arthur J Tolda
54 Danbury Rd 324
Ridgefield CT 06877

Call Sign: W1RNA
Richard N Aarons
638-15 Danbury Road
Ridgefield CT 06877

Call Sign: N1RNA
Richard N Aarons
638-15 Danbury Road
Ridgefield CT 06877

Call Sign: N1XMD
William I Allen
20 Fairview Ave
Ridgefield CT 06877

Call Sign: KB1ROK

Brenda L Finkbeiner
41 Farm Hill Rd
Ridgefield CT 06877

Call Sign: KA1WBL
Francis T Dolen
203 Farmingville Rd
Ridgefield CT 06877

Call Sign: N2DVX
John M Ahle
120 Fire Hill Rd
Ridgefield CT 06877

Call Sign: W1JMA
John M Ahle
120 Fire Hill Rd
Ridgefield CT 06877

Call Sign: KB1NQU
R-Com
120 Fire Hill Rd
Ridgefield CT 06877

Call Sign: KR1COM
R-Com
120 Fire Hill Rd
Ridgefield CT 06877

Call Sign: WB9YYG
Daniel J Pisano Jr
3 Glenbrook Ct
Ridgefield CT 06877

Call Sign: K3SOC
Paul J Bracken
22 Green Ln
Ridgefield CT 068773017

Call Sign: KF6IEJ
Fumio Ikeda
36 Grove Street
Ridgefield CT 06877

Call Sign: KB1FOD

Shiro Sakai
36 Grove Street
Ridgefield CT 06877

Jack L Spieth
118 Holmes Rd
Ridgefield CT 06877

Amy Breslin
10 Keeler Close
Ridgefield CT 06877

Call Sign: AA1WY
Shiro Sakai
36 Grove Street
Ridgefield CT 06877

Call Sign: KB1GXH
Robert L Wisnieff
200 Holmes Rd
Ridgefield CT 06877

Call Sign: KB1OFR
Philipp H Baumann
95 Keeler Dr
Ridgefield CT 06877

Call Sign: KC1XR
David W Harris
9 Hamilton Rd
Ridgefield CT 06877

Call Sign: W1SNF
Robert L Wisnieff
200 Holmes Rd
Ridgefield CT 06877

Call Sign: W1AOK
Denis Sharon
133 Knollwood Dr
Ridgefield CT 06877

Call Sign: KB1FKV
Wayne W Chou
25 Hauley Place
Ridgefield CT 06877

Call Sign: N5HYT
John B Hamilton
12 Huckleberry Ln
Ridgefield CT 06877

Call Sign: K1QPP
Peter A Annunziato
49 Lakeside Dr
Ridgefield CT 06877

Call Sign: N1PJE
James N Bodurtha
56 Hayes Ln
Ridgefield CT 06877

Call Sign: K2HMR
Michael W Richter
41 Hunter Ln
Ridgefield CT 06877

Call Sign: WK1D
Martin J Carr
63 Lawson Lane
Ridgefield CT 06877

Call Sign: WB1EGA
Oswald Inglese Jr
34 Hobby Dr
Ridgefield CT 068771930

Call Sign: KA2MBP
Nicholas J Gallo Jr
10 Island Hill Ave
Ridgefield CT 068774021

Call Sign: KB1OFS
Benjamin P Myers
42 Lawson Ln
Ridgefield CT 06877

Call Sign: KB1WCY
Sander O Pool
44 Holmes Rd
Ridgefield CT 06877

Call Sign: WA2JHV
David F Stroberg
10 Jefferson Dr
Ridgefield CT 06877

Call Sign: W4DXE
William J Hancock
126 Limestone Rd
Ridgefield CT 06877

Call Sign: W1SOP
Sander O Pool
44 Holmes Rd
Ridgefield CT 06877

Call Sign: KD1NV
Edward Kanowitz
51 Jefferson Dr
Ridgefield CT 06877

Call Sign: KD1SB
Jose F Helu Jr
356 Limestone Rd
Ridgefield CT 068772635

Call Sign: KB1WE
John W Spieth
118 Holmes Rd
Ridgefield CT 06877

Call Sign: N1KZZ
Joseph J Kanowitz
51 Jefferson Dr
Ridgefield CT 06877

Call Sign: K1DR
Richard J Rosevalt
64 Lincoln Ln
Ridgefield CT 06877

Call Sign: NG1M

Call Sign: KB1BGS

Call Sign: WB1CUJ

Francis M Waters Jr
32 Linden Rd
Ridgefield CT 06877

Call Sign: KB6YBS
Leslie W Thilow
11 Mamanasco Road
Ridgefield CT 06877

Call Sign: KB1HWW
Peter D Tannheimer
213 Mimosa Circle
Ridgefield CT 06877

Call Sign: KB1UQW
Curtis A Tilton
154 Minuteman Rd
Ridgefield CT 06877

Call Sign: KB1RJL
Paul J Roche
729 N Salem Rd
Ridgefield CT 06877

Call Sign: N1PJR
Paul J Roche
729 N Salem Rd
Ridgefield CT 06877

Call Sign: KB1OFO
Jeffery A Scott
285 No Salem Rd
Ridgefield CT 06877

Call Sign: KB1TWV
Amy Cohen
121 North St
Ridgefield CT 06877

Call Sign: KB1TWW
Robert Cohen
121 North St
Ridgefield CT 06877

Call Sign: N1CUI

Ward Carpenter
275 North St
Ridgefield CT 08772512

Call Sign: K1RFD
Jonathan P Taylor
118 Nursery Rd
Ridgefield CT 06877

Call Sign: KB1ROM
Mark Heminway
4 Old Denbury Rd
Ridgefield CT 06877

Call Sign: N1TBM
Luis H Rodriguez Jr
197 Old Stagecoach Rd
Ridgefield CT 06877

Call Sign: K1UHF
Del J Schier
126 Old West Mountain Rd
Ridgefield CT 06877

Call Sign: KB1ROZ
George Clark
33 Oscaleta Rd
Ridgefield CT 06877

Call Sign: KB1RPA
Susan Clark
33 Oscaleta Rd
Ridgefield CT 06877

Call Sign: N1WHQ
William A Loomis
23 Overlook Dr
Ridgefield CT 06877

Call Sign: KB1MWV
Richard N Aarons
33 Partridge Dr
Ridgefield CT 06877

Call Sign: KB1SOI

George G Siburn
105 Peaceable Ridge
Ridgefield CT 06877

Call Sign: N1SVU
Herbert R Schwamb
119 Poplar Rd
Ridgefield CT 06877

Call Sign: WB1DUZ
Joseph H Freer
9 Pound St
Ridgefield CT 06877

Call Sign: WB1EDO
John M Freer
9 Pound St
Ridgefield CT 06877

Call Sign: WA8UNS
Thomas Q Kimball
57 Prospect Street Apt 36
Ridgefield CT 06877

Call Sign: KB1WUS
Gary R Busch
546 Ridgebury Rd
Ridgefield CT 06877

Call Sign: KB1VLP
Adam A Lussier
94 Riverside Dr
Ridgefield CT 06877

Call Sign: KB1OFQ
Anthony G Markert
64 Rock Rd
Ridgefield CT 06877

Call Sign: N1XMC
Ralph E Libby
126 Round Lake Rd
Ridgefield CT 06877

Call Sign: AD4EC

Hirohito Sakai
68 Sarah Bishop Rd
Ridgefield CT 06877

Call Sign: N1MIT
Charles A Mittelstadt
6 Sherwood Rd
Ridgefield CT 068771916

Call Sign: KB1KHB
Kathleen H Barrett
9 Shields Ln
Ridgefield CT 06877

Call Sign: W1WJB
William J Barrett
9 Shields Ln
Ridgefield CT 06877

Call Sign: KB1DCM
Kenneth A Wright
104 Silver Spring Rd
Ridgefield CT 06877

Call Sign: WA2FBU
Timothy J Mc Gee
6 Skytop Rd
Ridgefield CT 06877

Call Sign: W1MQ
Stanley L Lawrynovicz
58 Soundview Rd
Ridgefield CT 06877

Call Sign: KB1OFT
James L Belote
25 Spireview Rd
Ridgefield CT 068771816

Call Sign: N1DKP
Rene E Franks
71 Stonecrest Rd
Ridgefield CT 068772521

Call Sign: AK8V

Jonathan P Taylor
93 Stonecrest Road
Ridgefield CT 06877

Call Sign: KB1RXA
Christopher H Day
38 Thunderhill Lane
Ridgefield CT 06877

Call Sign: KB1NCN
Walter K Wieland
6 Todds Rd
Ridgefield CT 068771821

Call Sign: WA1LCE
Ronald W Braun
43 Twin Ridge Rd
Ridgefield CT 06877

Call Sign: KB1RMJ
Gerald R Blank
22 Twixt Hills Rd
Ridgefield CT 06877

Call Sign: KA1RAB
Ronald J Raymond Jr
17 Walnut Grove Rd
Ridgefield CT 06877

Call Sign: KA1RAC
Ronald J Raymond Iii
17 Walnut Grove Rd
Ridgefield CT 06877

Call Sign: N1WHN
James Cutolo
23 Walnut Hill Rd
Ridgefield CT 06877

Call Sign: N2IVK
Robert M De Bartolo
254 West Lane
Ridgefield CT 06877

Call Sign: K1OUD

Charles D Williamson
253 Wilton Rd E
Ridgefield CT 06877

Call Sign: KB1ODR
Laura E Halloran
42 Wilton Rd W
Ridgefield CT 06877

Call Sign: KB1ODQ
Timothy M Halloran
42 Wilton Rd West
Ridgefield CT 06877

Call Sign: WA2EVH
Rodney M Gould
Ridgefield CT 06877

FCC Amateur Radio Licenses in Riverside

Call Sign: N1TS
Edward G Briggs
54 Crawford Terrace
Riverside CT 06878

Call Sign: KA1UBS
James V Coleman
5 Dialstone Ln
Riverside CT 06878

Call Sign: KA1RPW
Walter W Pendleton
1117 E Putnam Ave Suite 225
Riverside CT 068781333

Call Sign: N1RRG
Lee R Zoubek
2 Ernel Dr
Riverside CT 06878

Call Sign: KB1HYE
Keith J Callahan
104 Florence Rd

Riverside CT 06878

Call Sign: W1TPK
George E Hall
57 Gilliam Ln
Riverside CT 06878

Call Sign: KE1GB
Frank J Carr
25 Griffith Rd
Riverside CT 06878

Call Sign: W1BKR
William F Baker
2 Highgate Rd
Riverside CT 06878

Call Sign: N1GQF
Keith G W Smith
37 Jones Park Dr
Riverside CT 06878

Call Sign: N1JPX
David M Renton
15 Leeward Ln
Riverside CT 06878

Call Sign: N1JPZ
Philip B Renton
15 Leeward Ln
Riverside CT 06878

Call Sign: N1IBH
Martha D Johns
118 Lockwood Rd
Riverside CT 06878

Call Sign: W2JU
Alec S Berman
146 Lockwood Rd
Riverside CT 06878

Call Sign: KM1L
John E Mann
65 Long Meadow Rd

Riverside CT 06878

Call Sign: N1BTJ
Victor F Mann Jr
65 Long Meadow Rd
Riverside CT 068781125

Call Sign: W1ELO
Philip J Priore Jr
48 Longmeadow Rd
Riverside CT 06878

Call Sign: KB1NTN
Carl Lancaster
41 Old Orchard Rd
Riverside CT 06878

Call Sign: KB1EBS
John M Behne
8 Oval Ave
Riverside CT 068782128

Call Sign: KB1DSE
Seiichiro Nozaki
67 Summit Rd
Riverside CT 068782105

Call Sign: KA1ODN
George J Helmer Iii
12 Wesskum Wood Rd
Riverside CT 06878

Call Sign: K1GMC
John S Mcknight
Riverside CT 068780336

FCC Amateur Radio
Licenses in Riverton

Call Sign: KA1IWF
Kathleen M Palaski
229 Mill St
Riverton CT 06065

Call Sign: WA1TSJ

Daniel J Palaski
229 Mill St
Riverton CT 06065

Call Sign: KB1EHZ
Rebecca L Palaski
229 Mill St
Riverton CT 06065

Call Sign: WA1HRE
Matthew F Tyszka Jr
189 Old Forge Rd
Riverton CT 06065

Call Sign: N1GJK
Daniel F Lamont
446 Park Rd
Riverton CT 06065

Call Sign: KA1VFG
Mark Skaret
153 Riverton Rd
Riverton CT 06065

Call Sign: N1LXW
Robert J Miller
Riverton CT 06065

FCC Amateur Radio
Licenses in Rockfall

Call Sign: WA1TEU
William T Jagoda
43 Derby Rd
Rockfall CT 06481

Call Sign: KB1IYB
Stephen J Giarratana
69 Ross Rd
Rockfall CT 06481

Call Sign: N1SFE
Paul R Bourque
Rockfall CT 064810223

Call Sign: WA1VVG
Thomas H Lynch Jr
Rockfall CT 06481

FCC Amateur Radio Licenses in Rockville

Call Sign: KE1ET
George J Rakus
21 Court St Apt 2-B
Rockville CT 060663668

Call Sign: KC1QU
William T Marley
1 Emerald Dr
Rockville CT 06066

Call Sign: WA1HYF
Alan Hanusiak
37 Grand Ave
Rockville CT 06066

Call Sign: KB1ATA
Ernest R Golnik Jr
2 Grant St
Rockville CT 06066

Call Sign: N1UCW
Alan L Schulz
10 Harlow St Apt D
Rockville CT 06066

Call Sign: KB1LFE
George P Sedlik Jr
15 Janet Ln
Rockville CT 06066

Call Sign: N1NAV
Beverly M Fernandez
27 Lawrence St Apt 1
Rockville CT 06066

Call Sign: W1OPB
Harry W Bachiochi
22 Liberty St

Rockville CT 06066

Call Sign: N1KEH
Mike L Albert
26 Liberty St
Rockville CT 06066

Call Sign: KB1GWZ
Dennis G Strait
52 Mountain St
Rockville CT 06066

Call Sign: K1EXK
William H Zaleski
19 N Terrace
Rockville CT 06066

Call Sign: K1GWT
Edward G Crosby Jr
52 Park St
Rockville CT 06066

Call Sign: N1JSO
Steven K Manner
52 Prospect St
Rockville CT 06066

Call Sign: AE1CT
Gary F North
116 Prospect St   Apt 3
Rockville CT 06066

Call Sign: WW1T
Klaus J Kingstorf
74 Talcott Ave
Rockville CT 06066

Call Sign: KB1NWD
Robert S Poulios
Rockville CT 060660025

FCC Amateur Radio Licenses in Rocky Hill

Call Sign: KA1ZDN

Joseph R Graveline
124 Barnyard Rd
Rocky Hill CT 06067

Call Sign: KA1JY
Brian D Ellsworth
8 Barry Pl
Rocky Hill CT 06067

Call Sign: KB1TTM
James R Plourde
49c Brookwood Dr
Rocky Hill CT 06067

Call Sign: N1OGB
Robert A Lapointe Jr
62 Butternut Lane
Rocky Hill CT 06067

Call Sign: KB1SCS
Carey E Harmon
30 C Robbins Lane
Rocky Hill CT 06067

Call Sign: N1OTW
Patrick M Tangncy
9 Chapin Ave
Rocky Hill CT 06067

Call Sign: KA1QJR
Christopher L Dunn
35 Chapin Ave
Rocky Hill CT 06067

Call Sign: KB1IGD
William J Puro
57 Chapin Ave
Rocky Hill CT 060672323

Call Sign: KB1NKT
Mark S Harris
23 Clemens Court
Rocky Hill CT 06067

Call Sign: KB1NKU

Cody A Harris
23 Clemens Court
Rocky Hill CT 06067

Call Sign: K1MSH
Mark S Harris
23 Clemens Court
Rocky Hill CT 06067

Call Sign: KB1BKH
Paul R Harrington
50 Cold Springs Road Apt 317
Rocky Hill CT 06067

Call Sign: N1QDO
Tracy A Bedlack
87 Copper Beech Dr
Rocky Hill CT 06067

Call Sign: KA1UGJ
Beatrice L Clinton
16 Crestridge Rd
Rocky Hill CT 060671211

Call Sign: N1KVM
David A Soderstrom
70 Deerfield Run
Rocky Hill CT 06067

Call Sign: N1PYX
James J De Bacco
7 Dividend Rd
Rocky Hill CT 06067

Call Sign: KF6GOK
Wolfgang Leibauer
295 Farmstead Rd
Rocky Hill CT 06067

Call Sign: N1ZAV
Alan F Brannan
345 Farmstead Rd
Rockyhill CT 06067

Call Sign: N1PFG
Paul G Stryker
129 Forest St
Rocky Hill CT 06067

Call Sign: KD1MX
Richard B Green
39 Fox Hill Drive
Rocky Hill CT 06067

Call Sign: N1TVA
Mike J Scanlon
39 Fox Hill Drive
Rocky Hill CT 06067

Call Sign: N1ERR
Paul P Benedetto
594 France St
Rocky Hill CT 06067

Call Sign: K1AAS
Neil G Gordes
741 France St
Rocky Hill CT 06067

Call Sign: KB1TIE
Connecticut Wide Area
Digital Group
50 Goff Brook Lane
Rocky Hill CT 06067

Call Sign: KB1TIF
Rocky Hill Donkey Duster
Digital Club
50 Goff Brook Lane
Rocky Hill CT 06067

Call Sign: WD1STR
Connecticut Wide Area
Digital Group
50 Goff Brook Lane
Rocky Hill CT 06067

Call Sign: KB1USV

Connecticut Wide Area
Digital Group
50 Goff Brook Lane
Rocky Hill CT 06067

Call Sign: KB1USW
Connecticut Wide Area
Digital Group
50 Goff Brook Lane
Rocky Hill CT 06067

Call Sign: K1DIG
Connecticut Wide Area
Digital Group
50 Goff Brook Lane
Rocky Hill CT 06067

Call Sign: KA1KFR
Joyce E Navaroli
50 Goff Brook Ln
Rocky Hill CT 06067

Call Sign: KB1CDI
Rocky Hill Donkey Dusters
50 Goff Brook Ln
Rocky Hill CT 06067

Call Sign: KJ1Q
James N Navaroli
50 Goff Brook Ln
Rocky Hill CT 06067

Call Sign: WB1ADN
Catherine W Pillsbury
8 Grimes Rd
Rocky Hill CT 060672404

Call Sign: WB1AJS
Lewis A Pillsbury Jr
8 Grimes Rd
Rocky Hill CT 060672404

Call Sign: N1VFH
Stephen P Gross
1315 Harbor View Drive

Rocky Hill CT 06067

Call Sign: N1YYC
David R Munnett
2 Henry St
Rocky Hill CT 06067

Call Sign: KB1AE
Donald M Roog
46 Joiners Road
Rocky Hill CT 06067

Call Sign: K1JTH
John T Hart Jr
1e Lathrop Lane
Rocky Hill CT 06067

Call Sign: KB1LYA
Aaron W Griswold
65 Little Oak Ln
Rocky Hill CT 06067

Call Sign: N1YIF
Edward S Partridge
2589 Main St
Rocky Hill CT 06067

Call Sign: KB1TLN
Kim M Dotolo
2855 Main St
Rocky Hill CT 06067

Call Sign: KB1LFT
Rocky Hill Fire Amateur
Radio Club
3050 Main St
Rocky Hill CT 06067

Call Sign: K1RHF
Rocky Hill Fire Amateur
Radio Club
3050 Main St
Rocky Hill CT 06067

Call Sign: W1UHQ

Normand E Sicard
856 Maple St
Rocky Hill CT 06067

Call Sign: KA1ZTZ
Aleksandra Michalski
25 Marshall Rd
Rocky Hill CT 06067

Call Sign: NR1D
Kent A Thomas
29 Mountain View Drive
Rocky Hill CT 06067

Call Sign: WS1O
Brian J Battles
38 New Britain Ave
Rocky Hill CT 060671131

Call Sign: KB1NTX
Robert E Wakefield Iii
495 Orchard St
Rocky Hill CT 06067

Call Sign: N1PUC
Andrew S Marteka
2k Penn Pl
Rocky Hill CT 06067

Call Sign: N1TDK
Nicola A Corsi
215 Pheasant Dr
Rocky Hill CT 06067

Call Sign: N1EJN
John V Francis
76 Quail Dr
Rocky Hill CT 06067

Call Sign: KB1NZR
Alton H Gloer Iii
17 Rachel Dr
Rocky Hill CT 06067

Call Sign: WA1MXM

Florence L Legowski
135 Raymond Rd
Rocky Hill CT 06067

Call Sign: NQ1R
Robert J Inderbitzen
58 Riverview Road
Rocky Hill CT 06067

Call Sign: KA1NPP
Diane L Dunn
14 Rocamora Road
Rocky Hill CT 06067

Call Sign: WB1EXV
Philip R Dunn
14 Rocamora Road
Rocky Hill CT 06067

Call Sign: KJ5FF
Christopher Williamson
1800 Silas Deane Hwy Apt
310n
Rocky Hill CT 060671563

Call Sign: KB1EIU
Craig R Flanagan
270 Silo Drive
Rocky Hill CT 060671920

Call Sign: KA1HQ
George Bugai
72 Springbrook Dr
Rocky Hill CT 06067

Call Sign: N1QNQ
Michael V Natale Jr
153 Stonehill Dr
Rocky Hill CT 06067

Call Sign: W1LGB
Sirio S D Amato
11 Textbook Ave
Rocky Hill CT 06067

Call Sign: KA1PUF
Lester M Mc Gowan
1 Webber Rd
Rocky Hill CT 06067

Call Sign: N1DKU
Harvey S Peck
287 West St
Rocky Hill CT 06067

Call Sign: KA1DLM
John A Pelczar
20 Westmeadow Rd
Rocky Hill CT 060671041

Call Sign: KA1KNQ
Pauline M Pelczar
20 Westmeadow Rd
Rocky Hill CT 06067

Call Sign: KA1SLD
Elizabeth M Pelczar
20 Westmeadow Rd
Rocky Hill CT 060671041

Call Sign: KA1TPM
Patricia L P Rossi
20 Westmeadow Rd
Rocky Hill CT 060671041

Call Sign: WA1LFH
James D Oleksiw
143 Woodfield Crossing
Rocky Hill CT 060672908

Call Sign: KB1NMM
Eileen R Awsiukiewicz
261 Woodfield Crossing
Rocky Hill CT 06067

Call Sign: W1NYC
Eileen R Awsiukiewicz
261 Woodfield Crossing
Rocky Hill CT 06067

Call Sign: WA1DEM
Gary P Awsiukiewicz
261 Woodfield Crossing
Rocky Hill CT 06067

Call Sign: W1GPA
Gary P Awsiukiewicz
261 Woodfield Crossing
Rocky Hill CT 06067

Call Sign: WW1LP
Anthony A La Penta Jr
44 Woodland Road
Rocky Hill CT 06067

Call Sign: N1USP
Marla W Kennedy
93 Wynding Brook Dr
Rocky Hill CT 06067

Call Sign: N1HJH
Daniel J Klin
90 Wynding Brook Drive
Rocky Hill CT 06067

Call Sign: KA1KZA
Matthew R Yoo
83 Wyndingbrook Dr
Rocky Hill CT 06067

Call Sign: KB1PVZ
Scott Holl
Rocky Hill CT 06067

Call Sign: W1BBC
Scott Holl
Rocky Hill CT 06067

FCC Amateur Radio Licenses in Rogers

Call Sign: W1PMR
Theodore D Szafranski
Rogers CT 062630193

FCC Amateur Radio Licenses in Rowayton

Call Sign: WA1AKC
Joseph F De Lorenzo
41 Arnold Ln
Rowayton CT 06853

Call Sign: KB1GFC
Scott G Kuhner
10 Craw Ave
Rowayton CT 06853

Call Sign: KB1KFE
Leslie B York
3 Crooked Lane
Rowayton CT 06853

Call Sign: KA1VWP
Michael Harvey Smith
19 Indian Spring Rd
Rowayton CT 06853

Call Sign: K1DLT
Marvin H Kronenberg
23 Ledge Road
Rowayton CT 06902

Call Sign: KB1FBX
Thomas W Robinson
8 Rowayton Ct
Rowayton CT 06853

Call Sign: K2PRB
Louis P Pataki Jr
7 Steepletop Rd
Rowayton CT 06853

Call Sign: WA1VWU
John G Macari
19 Thomes St
Rowayton CT 06853

FCC Amateur Radio Licenses in Roxbury

Call Sign: N1DAV
John D Skewis
195 Apple Ln
Roxbury CT 06783

Call Sign: K1CO
Charles F O Rourke
197 Apple Ln
Roxbury CT 06783

Call Sign: WA2WCB
Michael D Arsenie
17 Garnet Rd
Roxbury CT 06783

Call Sign: KB1AFW
Edward A Bouley
49 Garnet Rd
Roxbury CT 06783

Call Sign: KA1SOM
Mark D Stracks
45 Gold Mine Rd
Roxbury CT 06783

Call Sign: N1GUC
David M Stracks
45 Gold Mine Rd
Roxbury CT 06783

Call Sign: N1OZK
Richard B Stracks
45 Goldmine Rd
Roxbury CT 06783

Call Sign: WA1JOY
Kurt A Anderson
18 Hickory Lane
Roxbury CT 06783

Call Sign: K1GDW
Fred C Spannaus
295 North St Rt 199
Roxbury CT 06783

Call Sign: W2PLL
Paul J Plishner
271 South Street
Roxbury CT 06783

Call Sign: KB1GHU
Harold O Roeske
Roxbury CT 06783

FCC Amateur Radio
Licenses in Salem

Call Sign: N1MCD
David L Bronson
3 Buckley Rd
Salem CT 06420

Call Sign: KA1TYN
John R Murphy Jr
59 Buckley Rd
Salem CT 06420

Call Sign: KA1PRN
Henry D Cordell
229 Buckley Rd
Salem CT 06415

Call Sign: N1MCG
Robert J Aiksnoras
10 Cherry Tree Rd
Salem CT 06420

Call Sign: W1JO
Richard J Rainville
126 Cockle Hill Rd
Salem CT 06420

Call Sign: WB5SAB
Carl L Zorn
346 Darling Rd
Salem CT 06415

Call Sign: K1DM
Michael E Mc Kaughan

23 Fairy Lake Rd
Salem CT 06420

Call Sign: WB1ACS
Shirley B Neddo
71 Forest Dr
Salem CT 064203725

Call Sign: N1ANY
Peter Sawitsky
24 Gardner Lake Heights
Salem CT 06420

Call Sign: KC1OA
William S Georgian
104 Hartford Rd
Salem CT 06420

Call Sign: NQ1G
Gary J Mc Manus
58 Hill Top Trl
Salem CT 06420

Call Sign: KA1WZW
Teresa D Drew
58 Hilltop Tr
Salem CT 06420

Call Sign: AA1JN
Anthony J Griggs
122 New London Rd
Salem CT 06420

Call Sign: N1OXP
Justin A Griggs
122 New London Rd
Salem CT 06420

Call Sign: K1VGA
John H Visneuski
315 Old New London Rd
Salem CT 064202099

Call Sign: W1ICB
Douglas K Bingham

Rfd 3
Salem CT 06415

Call Sign: N1MOU
Michael J Sabolesky
94 Round Hill Road
Salem CT 06420

Call Sign: KA1NEJ
Darryl E Balaski
379 Round Hill Road
Salem CT 06420

Call Sign: K1WA
David J Pietraszewski
139 Sullivan Rd
Salem CT 06420

Call Sign: KB1JAW
Ralph F Boles
125 Way Rd
Salem CT 06420

Call Sign: N1SVI
Bruce E Lloyd
72 Witch Meadow Rd
Salem CT 06420

FCC Amateur Radio Licenses in Salisbury

Call Sign: KA1SNB
James F Fox
Twin Lakes Rd Box 59a
Salisbury CT 06068

Call Sign: KA1RA
David A Chard
Salisbury CT 06068

FCC Amateur Radio Licenses in Sandy Hook

Call Sign: KB1OFU
Jason M Adams

73 Bennetts Bridge Rd
Sandy Hook CT 06482

Call Sign: KB1OGD
Jason M Adams
73 Bennetts Bridge Rd
Sandy Hook CT 06482

Call Sign: W1USF
Paul R Heetmann
4 Camelot Crest Rd
Sandy Hook CT 06482

Call Sign: N1CVL
Charles J Hegenauer
1 Chimney Swift Dr
Sandy Hook CT 06482

Call Sign: WA9EQL
Barry P Meyer
11 Cobblers Mill
Sandy Hook CT 06482

Call Sign: KB1OJM
John T Kukla
21 Cobblers Mill Rd
Sandy Hook CT 06482

Call Sign: KB1NFF
Austin G Baldour
17 Grays Plain Rd
Sandy Hook CT 06482

Call Sign: WA2DQI
Donald E Sullivan
109 Haley Lane
Sandy Hook CT 064821703

Call Sign: KB1NFH
Jason R Howell
48 High Rock Rd
Sandy Hook CT 06482

Call Sign: N1GRF
Mark E Pelletier

7 Homer Clark Ln
Sandy Hook CT 06482

Call Sign: KB1NFE
Brandon Adsitt-Weiner
24 Jo Mar Dr
Sandy Hook CT 06482

Call Sign: KA1VVD
Clark M Sellars
Lakeview Ter
Sandy Hook CT 06482

Call Sign: KB1MWX
Patrick D Schaedler
7 Longview Rd
Sandy Hook CT 06482

Call Sign: K1LAW
Ronald J Leddy
29 Lyrical Ln
Sandy Hook CT 06482

Call Sign: K1MYG
New Milford Vhf Society
29 Lyrical Ln
Sandy Hook CT 06482

Call Sign: N1GQG
Anne M O Connell
9 Maple Dr
Sandy Hook CT 06482

Call Sign: N1GVC
James J O Connell
9 Maple Dr
Sandy Hook CT 06482

Call Sign: N3LMC
Judi M Boyle
2 Marlin Rd
Sandy Hook CT 06482

Call Sign: WA3KBE
Glenn E Boyle

2 Marlin Rd.
Sandy Hook CT 06482

Call Sign: KB1IWN
Anthony W Kmetetz
46 Old Green Rd
Sandy Hook CT 06482

Call Sign: KA1SVL
Bernard S Cayne
8 Old Green Rd Rd 2
Sandy Hook CT 06482

Call Sign: K6VWM
Douglas W Sherman
34 Osborne Hill Rd
Sandy Hook CT 064821500

Call Sign: WA1SOV
Peter C Mc Nulty
8 Settlers Ln
Sandy Hook CT 06482

Call Sign: KA2JCY
Dennis J Brinkmann
32 Still Hill Rd
Sandy Hook CT 06482

Call Sign: K1DEN
Dennis J Brinkmann
32 Still Hill Rd
Sandy Hook CT 06482

Call Sign: KB1LG
William R Ames
5 Turkey Roost Rd
Sandy Hook CT 06482

Call Sign: KC2RAY
Raymond J Hoesten
46 Underhill Rd
Sandy Hook CT 06482

Call Sign: WA1MGO
Paul J Clapis

15 Valley Field Rd
Sandy Hook CT 06481

Call Sign: KB1IRL
Scott W Beals
11 Walker Hill Rd
Sandy Hook CT 06482

Call Sign: W1FRP
Scott W Beals
11 Walker Hill Rd
Sandy Hook CT 06482

Call Sign: W1LAR
Lawrence A Ross
36 Watkins Dr.
Sandy Hook CT 06482

Call Sign: KB1LYP
John H Will Iii
2 Zoar Road
Sandy Hook CT 06482

Call Sign: N1ILD
Gerald J Mullen
Sandy Hook CT 06482

Call Sign: KB1OVQ
Sandy Hook Vol Fire &
Rescue Inc.
Sandy Hook CT 06482

FCC Amateur Radio Licenses in Scotland

Call Sign: K1MZZ
Joseph E Gauvin
Palmer Rd
Scotland CT 06264

Call Sign: N7PRD
Jason L Bousquet
62 Pudding Hill Rd
Scotland CT 062640116

Call Sign: KB1SHM
James F Meikle
Scotland CT 06264

FCC Amateur Radio Licenses in Seymour

Call Sign: KB1WCO
Eric S Ingersoll
3 A Daisy Drive
Seymour CT 06483

Call Sign: W1WFN
George Jarvis
7 Argyle Cir
Seymour CT 06483

Call Sign: KA1RSE
Mark R Orner
49 Balance Rock Rd
Seymour CT 06483

Call Sign: KB1ISI
Peter A Stark
81 Balance Rock Rd Apt 19
Seymour CT 06483

Call Sign: KB1LJF
Garet D Holcomb
49 Balance Rock Road 17
Seymour CT 06483

Call Sign: WA1YHK
Thomas J Mc Alee
53 Birchwood Rd
Seymour CT 06483

Call Sign: W1XQ
Paul J Gregory
99 Botsford Rd
Seymour CT 06483

Call Sign: WB1CML
Charles S Betkoski
126 Botsford Rd

Seymour CT 06483

Call Sign: KB1LTZ
Roberta M Betkoski
126 Botsford Rd
Seymour CT 06483

Call Sign: KA1A
Charles S Betkoski
126 Botsford Rd
Seymour CT 06483

Call Sign: N1CT
Kevin J Nintzel
50 Briarwood Drive
Seymour CT 064833045

Call Sign: WB1GHV
Mary J Simonu
36 Brookdale Rd
Seymour CT 06483

Call Sign: KA1CNK
Steven R Marti
46 Buckingham Rd
Seymour CT 06483

Call Sign: N1NJT
Brett A Bechtel
39 Canfield Rd
Seymour CT 06483

Call Sign: KB1PZC
Stephanie M Hopwood
37 Chamberlain Rd
Seymour CT 06483

Call Sign: KB1UNZ
John N Raymond
35 Colony Rd
Seymour CT 06483

Call Sign: WN1RAY
John N Raymond
35 Colony Rd

Seymour CT 06483

Call Sign: KA1OMR
Brian M Solt
22 Culver St
Seymour CT 06483

Call Sign: KK1V
David B Conway
190 Eastwood Drive
Seymour CT 06483

Call Sign: KA1HEW
Roger A Dilliber
15 Elmwood Dr
Seymour CT 06483

Call Sign: KA1HAK
George T Monroe Jr
29 Greenwood Cir
Seymour CT 06483

Call Sign: KB1FOB
Ryan J Farrington
28 Greenwood Circle
Seymour CT 06483

Call Sign: KB1GEB
Richard I Farrington
28 Greenwood Circle
Seymour CT 06483

Call Sign: KB1HSY
Molly E Farrington
28 Greenwood Circle
Seymour CT 064832458

Call Sign: K1RLZ
William A Roberts
8 Hemlock Rd
Seymour CT 06483

Call Sign: K1LBH
Glen E Norton
48 Heritage Drive

Seymour CT 06483

Call Sign: W0JAY
Oran J Spaulding Jr
10 Housatonic Terr
Seymour CT 06483

Call Sign: N7DLG
Holly A Spaulding
10 Housatonic Terr
Seymour CT 06483

Call Sign: WA1PUX
Bruce E Felper
6 Jacko Dr
Seymour CT 06483

Call Sign: N1YAE
George S Andrews
7 Oak Hill Rd
Seymour CT 06483

Call Sign: W1DBY
Derby Emergency
Operations Club
7 Oak Hill Rd
Seymour CT 06483

Call Sign: N1DPF
William J Duggan
5 Oakwood Drive
Seymour CT 06483

Call Sign: K1YVZ
Edward S Olsen
6 Olsen Dr
Seymour CT 06483

Call Sign: N1VGI
William D Wheeler
14 Paramount Dr
Seymour CT 06483

Call Sign: WA1EHF
Dennis A Grindrod Sr

68 Pearl St
Seymour CT 064833708

Call Sign: WA1NBM
Sharon A Grindrod
68 Pearl St
Seymour CT 06483

Call Sign: N1OLM
Charles F Woodin
3 Poplar Dr
Seymour CT 06483

Call Sign: N1LUF
Mark J Goulet
9 Riviera Ter
Seymour CT 06483

Call Sign: WB1HIY
Robert P Yazluk
285 S Main St
Seymour CT 06483

Call Sign: W1EGL
William F Brown
872 S Main St
Seymour CT 064833235

Call Sign: N1OYR
Joseph F Mihalcik
7 Stanley Dr
Seymour CT 06483

Call Sign: N1WLS
Raoul J I Michaud
16 Stanley Dr
Seymour CT 06483

Call Sign: KA1QPH
John L Barto Jr
120 W Church St
Seymour CT 06483

Call Sign: W1LSQ
Stanley S Smalec

164 Walnut St
Seymour CT 064833629

Call Sign: N1ALA
Frank J Lang
27 Wood St
Seymour CT 06483

Call Sign: KB1TGX
Barron R Dubois Jr
Seymore CT 064830177

Call Sign: KB1QQA
John D Popik
Seymour CT 06483

FCC Amateur Radio Licenses in Shady Hook

Call Sign: N1VCR
Robert G Miller
Shady Hook CT 06482

FCC Amateur Radio Licenses in Sharon

Call Sign: WA1VIU
Wallace E Chase
195 A Amenia Union Rd
Sharon CT 06069

Call Sign: W1UMO
Frank M Campbell
129 Butter Rd
Sharon CT 06069

Call Sign: KA1IUW
Keith A Garovoy
Calkinstown Rd
Sharon CT 06069

Call Sign: N1BUF
Nicholas P Tosches
22 Clark Hill Road
Sharon CT 06069

Call Sign: K1SVI
Stig O Juhlin
173 East St
Sharon CT 06069

Call Sign: WA1COX
Edward M Vanicky Sr
197 East St
Sharon CT 06069

Call Sign: WA1HEY
Anne M Vanicky
East St 364
Sharon CT 06069

Call Sign: W1BAA
Rt 41 Southern Berkshire
Amateur Radio Club
Gay St
Sharon CT 06069

Call Sign: WB1CEI
Edward H Wilbur
92 Gay Street
Sharon CT 06069

Call Sign: K1LAR
Robert R Hotaling Jr
75 Jackson Hill Rd
Sharon CT 06069

Call Sign: K1ONH
Robert R Hotaling
1 Lovers Ln
Sharon CT 06069

Call Sign: N1BSA
Christopher F Plescia
17 Red Rock Rd
Sharon CT 06069

Call Sign: K1SS
Sidney X Shore
205 Sharon Valley Rd

Sharon CT 060690603

Call Sign: KB1DJE
David J Supino
83 Westwoods Road
Sharon CT 06069

Call Sign: WA1AGA
William F Kiernan
32 Windy Ridge Rd
Sharon CT 06069

Call Sign: KB1BJZ
Marion J Buehrle
Sharon CT 06069

Call Sign: N1GIS
William E Buehrle Jr
Sharon CT 06069

**FCC Amateur Radio
Licenses in Shelton**

Call Sign: KB1NCP
William J Smith
10 Angell Ave
Shelton CT 06484

Call Sign: KA1MQM
Brian E Krieger
35 Arthurs Court
Shelton CT 06484

Call Sign: WA1ILU
Stephen C Maude
267 Beardsley Rd
Shelton CT 06484

Call Sign: N1OSS
Robert H Sennett Jr
5 Big Horn Rd
Shelton CT 06484

Call Sign: KB1TD
Robert H Axtell

85 Birdseye Rd
Shelton CT 06484

Call Sign: KA1FWC
Brian R Eastman Sr
29 Brentley Drive
Shelton CT 06484

Call Sign: KA1SOZ
John R Vitka
10 Bruce Dr
Shelton CT 06484

Call Sign: W1JXR
William R Heil Sr
236 Buddington Rd
Shelton CT 06484

Call Sign: KA1VRW
Donald H Roth
26 Button Rd
Shelton CT 06484

Call Sign: K2YKX
Donald H Roth
26 Button Rd
Shelton CT 06484

Call Sign: N1UAI
Samuel J Conigliaro
46 Catlin Pl
Shelton CT 06484

Call Sign: N1PDE
Robert M Camara
21 Catlin Place
Shelton CT 06484

Call Sign: K1CWH
William J Gazsi
135 Center St
Shelton CT 06484

Call Sign: KD1WX
Thomas P Evans

6 Christine Dr
Shelton CT 06484

Call Sign: W1JC
Thomas P Evans
6 Christine Dr
Shelton CT 06484

Call Sign: N1PLM
Lisa A Mycko
108 Cliff St
Shelton CT 06484

Call Sign: N1GIV
Jeffrey W Haynes
29 Colonial Village
Shelton CT 06484

Call Sign: N1HAR
Yukio Masuda
97 Country Pl
Shelton CT 06484

Call Sign: WB1FKO
David J Preschel
20 Courtland Dr
Shelton CT 06484

Call Sign: WB1FNA
Marvin M Preschel
20 Courtland Dr
Shelton CT 06484

Call Sign: K1EIR
Barbara A Lombardi
85 Cranston Ave
Shelton CT 06484

Call Sign: WA1PTR
Walter M Spader Sr
15 Cribbins Ave
Shelton CT 06484

Call Sign: K1ODY
Robert M Tonucci

45 Cribbins Ave
Shelton CT 06484

Call Sign: KD7IUI
Ronald C Baktis
20 Cross Street
Shelton CT 064843341

Call Sign: N1BDF
Jon Krijgsman
3 Dartmouth Dr
Shelton CT 06484

Call Sign: KG4CPL
James R Boyles
89 Dickinson Drive
Shelton CT 06484

Call Sign: W1WWB
James R Boyles
89 Dickinson Drive
Shelton CT 06484

Call Sign: KB1VXM
Steven E Kruk
175 Division Ave
Shelton CT 06484

Call Sign: KB1JLM
Eric Fine
11 Doe Place
Shelton CT 06484

Call Sign: N2IYG
Ulrich Deuschle
10 Dogwood Ln
Shelton CT 06484

Call Sign: N1QOH
Louis J Havanich Jr
159 E Village Rd
Shelton CT 064841706

Call Sign: KB1QPX
Edward M Risko

319 East Village Rd
Shelton CT 06484

Call Sign: W1FQS
Gerard T Paul
498 Elk Run Drive
Shelton CT 06484

Call Sign: K1IGE
Henry Pessah
2 Fairlane Dr
Shelton CT 06484

Call Sign: KA2LFI
Jeanne M Kellogg
36 Fairlane Dr
Shelton CT 06484

Call Sign: KB1RNL
Nicholas A Pinto
14 Farmill Street
Shelton CT 06484

Call Sign: KA1TFI
Louis Carbone
20 Fifth Ave
Shelton CT 06484

Call Sign: KB1WFU
John E Todd
39 Florence Drive
Shelton CT 06484

Call Sign: N1SCQ
Lee H Van Iderstine
348 Green Rock
Shelton CT 06484

Call Sign: KB1LQR
James M Clark
193 Grove St
Shelton CT 06484

Call Sign: N1BXF
Richard G Tallberg Sr

117 Howe Ave
Shelton CT 06484

Call Sign: N1IKC
Charles R Perillo Jr
30 Hull St
Shelton CT 06484

Call Sign: K1UUR
John P Ellison
126 Hunters Cr
Shelton CT 06484

Call Sign: K1GFD
Charles W Teichert Iii
26 Huntington Heights
Shelton CT 064842968

Call Sign: KB1NSI
David C Ellis
308 Huntington St
Shelton CT 06484

Call Sign: KB1UQG
David C Ellis
308 Huntington St
Shelton CT 06484

Call Sign: W1DCE
David C Ellis
308 Huntington St
Shelton CT 06484

Call Sign: KB1NYB
Walter M Roog
16 Jefferson St
Shelton CT 06484

Call Sign: N1LUI
Lisa T Edmonds
27 Jenyfer Ct
Shelton CT 06484

Call Sign: WS1G
Keith A Edmonds

27 Jenyfer Ct
Shelton CT 06484

Call Sign: KA1W
David P Haller
24 Jodie Ln
Shelton CT 06484

Call Sign: N1IEM
John G Vargoshe
15 Kazo Dr
Shelton CT 06484

Call Sign: KA1LZL
David J Lombard
88 Kings Highway
Shelton CT 06484

Call Sign: N1WCN
Frank E Almeida
72 Kneen St
Shelton CT 06484

Call Sign: KA1YND
Lauren B Kovarczi
103 Lane St
Shelton CT 06484

Call Sign: KA1ZGE
Robyn N Shepard
103 Lane St
Shelton CT 06484

Call Sign: N1LPD
Scott N Shepard
103 Lane St
Shelton CT 06484

Call Sign: K1VRD
Earl L Sisson
16 Liberty St
Shelton CT 06484

Call Sign: N1KPR
Robert W Betts

8 Little Fawn Dr
Shelton CT 06484

Call Sign: KF1N
Linda H Barry
87 Long Hill Ave
Shelton CT 064843214

Call Sign: AB1MZ
David Power
214 Long Hill Ave
Shelton CT 06484

Call Sign: N1OLO
John G Kalotai
456 Long Hill Ave
Shelton CT 06485

Call Sign: KB1HVD
Alfred J Febbroriello
100 Longmeadow Rd
Shelton CT 06484

Call Sign: W1AZT
Mark A Paskus
3 Maler Ave
Shelton CT 06484

Call Sign: KB1RCV
Robert J Korolyshun
123 Maltby St
Shelton CT 06484

Call Sign: KA2EKA
Joseph A Ippolito Jr
57 Maple Ln
Shelton CT 06484

Call Sign: W1EKA
Joseph A Ippolito Jr
57 Maple Ln
Shelton CT 06484

Call Sign: KB1HCX
John W Kopchik

35 Martinka Dr
Shelton CT 06484

Call Sign: W1WG
Earle T Fairbanks
127 Meadow
Shelton CT 06484

Call Sign: K1EIC
Elizabeth L Doane
92 Mohegan Rd
Shelton CT 064842448

Call Sign: W1HAD
Mohegan Amateur Radio
Club
92 Mohegan Rd
Shelton CT 064842448

Call Sign: KA1FJV
Robert S Cline Jr
215 Mohegan St
Shelton CT 06484

Call Sign: K1FBI
John F Zvonek
8 N Meadow Ridge Dr
Shelton CT 06484

Call Sign: K1TSU
Elio J Di Camillo
17 N Meadow Ridge Dr
Shelton CT 06484

Call Sign: KB1SSK
William M Carter
55 New St
Shelton CT 06484

Call Sign: WB1AHA
James S Ramsey
75 Nicholdale Rd
Shelton CT 06484

Call Sign: WA1YYZ

Lorraine C Di Camillo
17 North Meadow Ridge Rd
Shelton CT 06484

Call Sign: N1IZQ
John V Nole
133 Oak Ave
Shelton CT 06484

Call Sign: W1JVM
John Masulli
19 Ojibwa Trail
Shelton CT 06484

Call Sign: N1RHM
Brian H Twohig
153 Okenuck Way
Shelton CT 06484

Call Sign: KB1WUQ
Joseph J Norton
19 Partridge Ln
Shelton CT 06484

Call Sign: N1VNL
Timothy M Bagley
45 Pawtucket Ave
Shelton CT 064845546

Call Sign: KA1OJX
Diana L Tyszka
9 Raymond Ln
Shelton CT 06484

Call Sign: K1RVM
Emil W Bleston
19 Revere Rd
Shelton CT 06484

Call Sign: KA1GSS
Vincent J Stanton
661 River Rd
Shelton CT 06484

Call Sign: AB1JC

Lawrence J Reed
5 Rodia Ridge Rd
Shelton CT 06484

Call Sign: N1JQD
James C Miller
36 Sagamore Rd
Shelton CT 06484

Call Sign: W1GNK
James T Sherwood
99 Shelton Ave
Shelton CT 06484

Call Sign: KA1WFY
Paul D Bienkowski
108 Shelton Ave
Shelton CT 06484

Call Sign: KB1TZT
Michael C Johnston
331 Shelton Ave
Shelton CT 06484

Call Sign: N1MCJ
Michael C Johnston
331 Shelton Ave
Shelton CT 06484

Call Sign: KB1SWK
Joseph W Han
19 Sherwood Ln
Shelton CT 06484

Call Sign: N1HNM
Dean A Del Franco Sr
9a Shinnacock Trail
Shelton CT 06484

Call Sign: W1BFS
Joseph M Krynitzky
279 Sound View Ave
Shelton CT 06484

Call Sign: KB1SIX

Mark S Holden
275 Soundview Ave
Shelton CT 06484

Call Sign: WB1FEN
John O Young Jr
54 Stendahl Dr
Shelton CT 06484

Call Sign: N1BEV
Paul F Reilly
62 Sunny Side Dr
Shelton CT 06484

Call Sign: N1AAL
Joseph M Swiatek Jr
28 Tamarac Ridge Cir
Shelton CT 06484

Call Sign: KB1LQS
Robert J Giuliani
26 Thompson St
Shelton CT 06484

Call Sign: K1RJG
Robert J Giuliani
26 Thompson St
Shelton CT 06484

Call Sign: KA1ICA
Ronald J Cerreta
20 Timberlane Dr
Shelton CT 06484

Call Sign: KA1CVY
Ronald J De Rosa
39 Timberlane Dr
Shelton CT 06484

Call Sign: W1ZQT
Theodore S Kaszuba
59 Timberlane Dr
Shelton CT 06484

Call Sign: W1COA

John P Van Duyne
515 Trading Post Lane
Shelton CT 06484

Call Sign: KB1WFV
Joan D Todd
15 Trolley Bridge Road
Shelton CT 06484

Call Sign: KB1FGL
Daniel E Pagliaro
43 Tuxedo Ave
Shelton CT 06484

Call Sign: K1RRR
Gilbert C Kellersman Jr
31 United Place
Shelton CT 06484

Call Sign: W1TAR
Andrew M Svatek
15 Waterford Lane
Shelton CT 064845449

Call Sign: KB1UIO
Manoj S Pillai
81 Wells Ave
Shelton CT 06484

Call Sign: KB1UIS
Manu M Pillai
81 Wells Ave
Shelton CT 06484

Call Sign: KB1UIM
Manish M Pillai
C/O Gene James 81 Wells
Avenue
Shelton CT 06484

Call Sign: KB1UIN
Alex Kuncheria
81 Wells Avenue
Shelton CT 06484

Call Sign: KB1UIQ
Nisha M Mohan
81 Wells Avenue
Shelton CT 06484

Call Sign: KB1UIR
Madhu S Mohan
81 Wells Avenue
Shelton CT 06484

Call Sign: WA1INL
Samuel E G Banks
243 Weslel Heights
Shelton CT 06484

Call Sign: WD1M
Robert W Gilmore
76 West St
Shelton CT 06484

Call Sign: WB1CSE
Frank B Waldhaus
35 Weybosset St
Shelton CT 064844042

Call Sign: KA1ONO
Mitchell Krzyzewski
89 William St
Shelton CT 06484

Call Sign: K1PFY
Charles R Karpowicz
2 Winchester Dr
Shelton CT 06484

Call Sign: N1SKG
Bradley R Sagendorf
2 Windsor Rd
Shelton CT 06484

Call Sign: KA1UNJ
Edward R Voccola
98 Woodland Pk
Shelton CT 06484

Call Sign: N1RHN
Paul H Zito
155 Wooster St
Shelton CT 06484

Call Sign: N1ZAN
Anthony R Molinaro
Shelton CT 06484

FCC Amateur Radio Licenses in Sherman

Call Sign: KB1JTO
Steven M Lurcott
17 Brookside Ln
Sherman CT 06784

Call Sign: N1RXQ
Jeffrey A Lagarto
6 Candleview Dr
Sherman CT 06784

Call Sign: KB1LFH
Matthew J Fitzgibbons
1 Cedar Ln
Sherman CT 06784

Call Sign: KA1HAM
Michael J Gaudenzi Sr.
37 Cozier Hill Rd
Sherman CT 06784

Call Sign: KB1GAU
David F Ritter
32 Cozier Hill Road
Sherman CT 06784

Call Sign: KB1GAV
Mark B Ritter
32 Cozier Hill Road
Sherman CT 06784

Call Sign: N1ORX
Melvin M Peoples
44 Green Pond Rd

Sherman CT 06784

Call Sign: K2YFQ
Gilbert E Vazquez
169 Green Pond Rd
Sherman CT 067842116

Call Sign: N2AZS
Lawrence S Schopfer
8 Holiday Point Road
Sherman CT 06784

Call Sign: N1RQN
William E Heinz
8 Old Greenwoods Rd
Sherman CT 06784

Call Sign: N1RQQ
Jo Ann Heinz
8 Old Greenwoods Rd
Sherman CT 06784

Call Sign: N1GLH
Shirley I Crocco
11 Orchard Beach Rd
Sherman CT 06784

Call Sign: KB1CHX
William M Chuisano
66 Route 55 W
Sherman CT 06784

Call Sign: KB1JGI
Frederick A Robinson
12 Upland Pastures Rd
Sherman CT 06784

Call Sign: N1XMB
Daniel P O Connell Sr
76 Wakeman Rd
Sherman CT 06784

Call Sign: KB1JJK
George T Zinn
Sherman CT 06784

FCC Amateur Radio Licenses in Simsbury

Call Sign: K1ZOX
Paul R Luksic
19 Walker Dr
Simsburg CT 06070

Call Sign: KB1NVC
Christopher M Catalano
18 Alder Rd
Simsbury CT 06070

Call Sign: KB1ABL
Adam B Libros
25 Alder Road
Simsbury CT 06070

Call Sign: WA1ZEV
Steven E Shore
8 Banks Rd
Simsbury CT 06070

Call Sign: N3TVX
Sanjay G Bajekal
67 Blue Ridge Drive
Simsbury CT 06070

Call Sign: N1EXH
Karl A Boehm
153 Bushy Hill Rd
Simsbury CT 06070

Call Sign: N1FPY
Ralph J E Boehm
153 Bushy Hill Rd
Simsbury CT 06070

Call Sign: WA1WWA
Norma W Mellen
290 Bushy Hill Rd
Simsbury CT 06070

Call Sign: N1SZD

Ronald L Ouellette
304 Bushy Hill Rd
Simsbury CT 06070

Call Sign: KB1KUA
Gregory W Esthus
358 Bushy Hill Rd
Simsbury CT 06070

Call Sign: KB1KWB
Colby A Esthus
358 Bushy Hill Rd
Simsbury CT 06070

Call Sign: KA1ZOQ
Ganiford C Graml
404 Bushy Hill Rd
Simsbury CT 06070

Call Sign: AA1ZE
Ganiford C Graml
404 Bushy Hill Rd
Simsbury CT 06070

Call Sign: N1JQQ
Christopher M Jackson
477 Bushy Hill Rd
Simsbury CT 060702910

Call Sign: W1TNS
Charles R Newton
9 Buttonwood Dr
Simsbury CT 06070

Call Sign: N1FDO
Robert L Branham
31 Canton Rd
Simsbury CT 06070

Call Sign: W1AMC
Bradley Busque Mr.
77 County Road
Simsbury CT 06070

Call Sign: KB1NUY

Robert W Proctor
1 Cricket Lane
Simsbury CT 06070

Call Sign: KB1NUZ
Derek W Proctor
1 Cricket Lane
Simsbury CT 06070

Call Sign: KB1NVM
Connor J Proctor
1 Cricket Lane
Simsbury CT 06070

Call Sign: AJ1N
Philip Accardi
7 Dominique Ln
Simsbury CT 06070

Call Sign: W1HSG
Walter C Bernkopf
2 E View Dr
Simsbury CT 060703010

Call Sign: KA1UVE
Charles J Scanlon
2 Eagle Ln
Simsbury CT 06070

Call Sign: N1FSJ
James K Clark
31 Fairview St
Simsbury CT 06070

Call Sign: KB1KUB
Ralph F Dietz
21 Fawn Brook Ln
Simsbury CT 06070

Call Sign: N1GUD
Olive J Lavnikevich
62 Fernwood Dr
Simsbury CT 06070

Call Sign: N1GWI

Nicholas J Lavnikevich
62 Fernwood Dr
Simsbury CT 06070

Call Sign: N1JQU
Edward C Shefler Jr
447 Firetown Rd
Simsbury CT 06070

Call Sign: KB1VRU
Laurel S Urda
471 Firetown Rd
Simsbury CT 06070

Call Sign: N2KNU
William S Middelaer
279 Firetown Road
Simsbury CT 06070

Call Sign: WA1UNV
Glenn A Swartzentruber
6 Fleetwood Dr
Simsbury CT 06070

Call Sign: N1TCS
Albert E Dorman
6 Forest Ln
Simsbury CT 06070

Call Sign: W1AH
William E Neff Jr
Mc Lean Home 75 Great
Pond Rd
Simsbury CT 06070

Call Sign: N1IXF
Richard E Cady
5 Gregory Lane
Simsbury CT 060701628

Call Sign: N1LMS
Eric H Miller
2 Gretel Ln.
Simsbury CT 06070

Call Sign: W1CNY
Robert J Rinaldi
23 Grimes Ln
Simsbury CT 06070

Call Sign: KB1PFZ
Jay Jedlicka
11 Hampden Circle
Simsbury CT 06070

Call Sign: KB1PGC
Jace Jedlicka
11 Hampden Circle
Simsbury CT 06070

Call Sign: N1IWK
Craig B Korsen
475 Hopmeadow St
Simsbury CT 06070

Call Sign: N1LEE
Charles R Whitman
125 Hoskins Rd
Simsbury CT 06070

Call Sign: N1IF
David G Fletcher
8 Hunting Ridge Dr
Simsbury CT 06070

Call Sign: KB1GAB
David G Fletcher
8 Hunting Ridge Drive
Simsbury CT 060701807

Call Sign: KB1NVD
Joseph M Bailey
25 Laurel Dr
Simsbury CT 06070

Call Sign: WA1UQM
Robert J Rossetti
14 Library Lane
Simsbury CT 06070

Call Sign: N1KBY
Jeffrey R Hugabone
21 Litchfield Drive
Simsbury CT 06070

Call Sign: K1AO
Robert A Thompson
4 Owens Brook Cir
Simsbury CT 06070

Call Sign: KB1EJ
Robert A Barney Sr
2 Russell Ln
Simsbury CT 06070

Call Sign: KB1FNZ
Michael D Bubnash
30 Longview Drive
Simsbury CT 06070

Call Sign: KJ2T
Kai J Thompson
4 Owens Brook Circle
Simsbury CT 06070

Call Sign: WA1WMO
James E Long
20 Sanctuary Dr
Simsbury CT 06070

Call Sign: KB1NWB
Christopher Loftus
7 Meadow Crossing
Simsbury CT 06070

Call Sign: K1ARO
Richard J Madrak
4 Paine Rd
Simsbury CT 06070

Call Sign: KB1DXL
Ralph M Cook Jr
22 Simsbury Landing
Simsbury CT 06070

Call Sign: KB1SIU
Alan J Tausch
16 Metacom Dr
Simsbury CT 06070

Call Sign: KB1VRH
Fumio E Kaneko
5 Park Rd
Simsbury CT 06070

Call Sign: W1JC
Thomas V Evans
113 Stratton Brook St
Simsbury CT 06070

Call Sign: KB1TKP
Peter J Draghi
15 Michael Rd
Simsbury CT 06070

Call Sign: N1VXY
Barry J Shelley
38 Pine Glen Rd
Simsbury CT 06070

Call Sign: KA3YXN
David J Pieri
7 Tallwood Ln
Simsbury CT 06089

Call Sign: KB1NYV
Andrew F Rich
25 Minister Brook Drive
Simsbury CT 06070

Call Sign: KA1VCN
Michael A Sperber
55 Pine Glen Road
Simsbury CT 06070

Call Sign: KA1FVC
Richard P Bonczek
150 Tariffville Rd
Simsbury CT 06081

Call Sign: KA7JZV
Marilyn L Tarantino
21 Neal Dr
Simsbury CT 06070

Call Sign: W1PUM
John F Raye
19 Ridge Rd
Simsbury CT 06070

Call Sign: W1SFC
Richard P Bonczek
150 Tariffville Rd
Simsbury CT 06081

Call Sign: N1TCP
Gregory M Bird
72 Old Meadow Plain Rd
Simsbury CT 06089

Call Sign: K1QJD
Richard E Johnston
29 Ridge Rd
Simsbury CT 06070

Call Sign: KB1FJC
Phillip A Viets
107 West St
Simsbury CT 06070

Call Sign: K1AOB
Robert A Thompson
4 Owens Brook Cir
Simsbury CT 06070

Call Sign: N1PCM
Charles V Chandler
10 Robin Rd
Simsbury CT 06070

Call Sign: KE1GS
Paul J Campagnola
34 Wheeler Rd
Simsbury CT 06070

Call Sign: KB1SQR
Albert C Kodet
19b Wiggins Farm Dr
Simsbury CT 06070

**FCC Amateur Radio
Licenses in Somers**

Call Sign: KB1SMA
Daniel J Marceau
9 Autumn Lane
Somers CT 06071

Call Sign: N1NIJ
Richard E Zacharkow
36 Bilton Rd
Somers CT 060711040

Call Sign: WB1AAP
Roland F Gladwin
Blue Ridge Dr
Somers CT 06071

Call Sign: W3SM
Stephen E Moynihan
80 Bridle Path Drive
Somers CT 060711021

Call Sign: W1MWP
John C Welch
56 Colonial Dr
Somers CT 06071

Call Sign: WA1RUV
Carl F Alsing
129 Colorado Dr
Somers CT 06071

Call Sign: KB1SLX
Joseph H Kelley
91 Colton Rd
Somers CT 06071

Call Sign: W1CDT
C Daniel Thayer Jr

10 Colton Road
Somers CT 06071

Call Sign: W1ILV
Mark W Grochowski
31 Colton Road
Somers CT 06071

Call Sign: WA1UXK
William J Olesik
15 Concord Terrace
Somers CT 06071

Call Sign: K1LXD
Rae S Bristol
17 County Rd
Somers CT 06071

Call Sign: N1DYX
William F Childs
184 County Rd
Somers CT 06071

Call Sign: KB1RMY
David A Dunn
100 Four Bridges Road
Somers CT 06071

Call Sign: KB1OER
Peter C Debrino
23 Goodwin Dr
Somers CT 06071

Call Sign: K1PMD
Peter C Debrino
23 Goodwin Dr
Somers CT 06071

Call Sign: KB1VQL
Nicholas A Flebotte
12 Gracie Dr
Somers CT 06071

Call Sign: AA0CA
Fred L Thompson

54 Green Tree Lane
Somers CT 06071

Call Sign: N0XAG
Helen M Thompson
54 Green Tree Lane
Somers CT 06071

Call Sign: K7UGQ
Donald C Johnson
19 Haystack Ln
Somers CT 06071

Call Sign: WB1ARX
Francis P Gowash
42 Hickory Hill Dr
Somers CT 06071

Call Sign: KB1TLW
Thomas F Manning
58 Highland View Dr
Somers CT 06071

Call Sign: KB1SLY
Robert E Kozaczka Jr
42 Kibbe Dr
Somers CT 06071

Call Sign: N1YYB
Deborah J Roy
125 Kibbe Grove Rd
Somers CT 060711111

Call Sign: KB1JAT
Yankee Wireless
Association
125 Kibbe Grove Rd
Somers CT 060711111

Call Sign: WB1AAK
Robert F Tremblay
139 Kibbe Grove Rd
Somers CT 060711111

Call Sign: W1MG

Michael E Gruber
125 Kibbe Grove Road
Somers CT 060711111

Call Sign: W1MY
Yankee Wireless
Association
125 Kibbe Grove Road
Somers CT 060711111

Call Sign: KB1VRG
Kathleen N Gilbert
336 Main St
Somers CT 06071

Call Sign: KB1ERH
Town Of Somers
Emergency Operations
Center
600 Main St
Somers CT 06071

Call Sign: W1SOM
Town Of Somers
Emergency Operations
Center
600 Main St
Somers CT 06071

Call Sign: KB1BEI
Peter Krzywicki
635 Main Street
Somers CT 06071

Call Sign: WA1RRS
Timothy J Simoes
141 Michele Dr
Somers CT 06071

Call Sign: KA1EDA
Frank M Falcone Jr
294 Mountain Rd
Somers CT 06071

Call Sign: KB1VQM

Richard W Gauvreau Jr
424 Mountain Rd
Somers CT 06071

Call Sign: K1RWG
Richard W Gauvreau Jr
424 Mountain Rd
Somers CT 06071

Call Sign: N1DLL
John Makar
23 Mountain Rd Box 128
Somers CT 060710128

Call Sign: KB1LEC
Grant E Genlot
23 Newsome Rd
Somers CT 06071

Call Sign: KC1V
George J Collins
105 Ninth District Rd
Somers CT 06071

Call Sign: KB1VQN
David P Mccaffrey
249 Ninth District Rd
Somers CT 06071

Call Sign: K1ZJH
Peter J Bertini
20 Patsun Rd
Somers CT 060711810

Call Sign: KA1GUH
Nancy A Bertini
20 Patsun Rd
Somers CT 06071

Call Sign: KB1VQJ
Peter C Bezzini Iii
41 Pleasant View Dr
Somers CT 06071

Call Sign: KB1QGM

Douglas G Maxwell
Po Box 887
Somers CT 06071

Call Sign: K1PQE
Susan G Oswell
13 Robert St
Somers CT 06071

Call Sign: N1ZOH
David T Brown
24 Rosehaven Rd
Somers CT 06071

Call Sign: AB1GR
Hiromichi Fukuda
94 Scully Rd
Somers CT 06071

Call Sign: KA1Z
Hiromichi Fukuda
94 Scully Rd
Somers CT 06071

Call Sign: W1YUN
Dudley N Lathrop
40 Shady Glen Ln
Somers CT 06071

Call Sign: KA1ZXM
Catherine M Bernier
187 Springfield Rd
Somers CT 06071

Call Sign: N1OLP
Thomas R Nelson
464 Springfield Road
Somers CT 06071

Call Sign: N1MRB
Emily C Mc Kenzie
698 Stafford Rd
Somers CT 06071

Call Sign: N1PLB

Peter P Pelkey
440 Turnpike Rd
Somers CT 06071

Call Sign: N1TTA
Kimberly C Quirk
298 Watchaug Rd
Somers CT 060711111

FCC Amateur Radio Licenses in Somersville

Call Sign: N1EUD
Whitney L Bradley Jr
24 Shaker Rd
Somersville CT 06072

Call Sign: KB1VQX
Marian L Beland
Somersville CT 06072

Call Sign: K9MLB
Marian L Beland
Somersville CT 06072

FCC Amateur Radio Licenses in South Britain

Call Sign: N1OLU
John G Lipsett Jr
South Britain CT 06487

FCC Amateur Radio Licenses in South Glastonbury

Call Sign: W1HNJ
Michael W Marinaro
250 Coldbrook Rd
South Glastonbury CT
06073

Call Sign: WN1M
Michael W Marinaro
250 Coldbrook Rd

South Glastonbury CT
06073

Call Sign: N1XHK
Kelly K Tofil
181 Great Pond Rd
South Glastonbury CT
06073

Call Sign: KB1TEV
Sean Jackson
166 Grindle Brook Rd
South Glastonbury CT
06073

Call Sign: K1VIJ
Wayne E Merrick
14 High Ridge Rd
South Glastonbury CT
060733214

Call Sign: KB1SUP
Brad Boris
88 Homestead Dr
South Glastonbury CT
06073

Call Sign: KB1SUS
Smith L Philip
88 Homestead Dr
South Glastonbury CT
06073

Call Sign: KA1HCV
Bruce A Fraser
22 Lakewood Cir
South Glastonbury CT
060732311

Call Sign: KA1LSY
Laura L Fraser
22 Lakewood Cir
South Glastonbury CT
060732311

Call Sign: N1FWL
Parvez A Bukhari
40 Redwood Lane
South Glastonbury CT
060732912

Call Sign: KN1GHT
Peter J Knight
14 Southgate Dr
South Glastonbury CT
06073

Call Sign: KB1GAA
David A Maddock Jr
184 Wassuc Road
South Glastonbury CT
06073

Call Sign: KB1PXY
Maynard L Marquis Jr
South Glastonbury CT
06073

Call Sign: AB1KE
Maynard L Marquis Jr
South Glastonbury CT
06073

FCC Amateur Radio Licenses in South Kent

Call Sign: N7PCG
Paul D Morton
183 Geer Mountain Rd
South Kent CT 06785

FCC Amateur Radio Licenses in South Lyme

Call Sign: KA1NIF
Kenneth L Green
South Lyme CT 063760477

FCC Amateur Radio Licenses in South Meriden

Call Sign: KB1IS
Arthur D Short
147 Charles St
South Meriden CT 06450

Call Sign: KA1FSO
Keith L Moore
145 Dana Ln
South Meriden CT 06450

Call Sign: KB1AUC
Richard L Meyer
162 Godek Hill Rd
South Meriden CT 06450

Call Sign: KB1EEP
David R Petruzielo
162 Godek Hill Rd
South Meriden CT 06451

Call Sign: N1QAD
Linda J Petruzielo
162 Godek Hill Rd
South Meriden CT 06451

Call Sign: WA1OMZ
Randy W Petruzielo
162 Godek Hill Rd
South Meriden CT 06451

Call Sign: N1URD
David J Solkoske
37 Hillside St
South Meriden CT 06451

Call Sign: N1LFY
Stephen M Polce
9 Keats Rd
South Meriden CT 06450

Call Sign: N1LFZ
Nicholas O Polce
9 Keats Rd
South Meriden CT 06450

Call Sign: KB1GWL
Jonathon E Polce
9 Kents Rd
South Meriden CT 06451

Call Sign: WA1TRY
Richard H Aubin
168 Knob Hill Rd
South Meriden CT
064514930

Call Sign: N1LGE
Robert B Munson Jr
16 Raymond Dr
South Meriden CT 06450

FCC Amateur Radio Licenses in South Norwalk

Call Sign: N4LCF
Peter H Willcox
36 Dock Rd
South Norwalk CT 06854

Call Sign: KA1YAT
Orlando W Martin
284 Ely Ave 2nd Floor
South Norwalk CT 06854

Call Sign: N1JDX
Gilberto V Nieves
228 Ely Avenue 1st Floor
South Norwalk CT 06854

Call Sign: WY1T
Jose A Serrano Sr
2 Hanford Place Apt 2c
South Norwalk CT
068543001

Call Sign: W1FHM
Gerald A Gorden
6 Iris Ct
South Norwalk CT 06854

Call Sign: KB1AHO
Eligio Crespo Jr
5 Laura St
South Norwalk CT 06854

Call Sign: WG1HM
William T Baldwin
4 Neptune Ave 3rd Fl
South Norwalk CT
068544718

Call Sign: KB1AMT
Carlos Nieves
4 Oak St
South Norwalk CT 06854

Call Sign: W1IGR
Kenneth B Benson
23 Park Ln
South Norwalk CT 06854

Call Sign: KB1LGS
Gabriel A Aufiero
50 Water St Apt 305
South Norwalk CT 06854

Call Sign: KB1ALP
Oscar Serrano
80 Woodward Ave
South Norwalk CT 06854

FCC Amateur Radio Licenses in South Windham

Call Sign: N1QNG
Craig J Robbins
14 Babcock Hill Rd
South Windham CT 06266

Call Sign: KB1SHK
Alan F Estell
45 Babcock Hill Rd
South Windham CT 06266

Call Sign: KB1LQF
Christian H Robison
127 Babcock Hill Rd
South Windham CT 06266

Call Sign: KA1ZEQ
Craig E Durand Mr
South Windham CT 06266

FCC Amateur Radio Licenses in South Windsor

Call Sign: N1UCJ
Daniel F Schroll
23f Amato Drive
South Windsor CT 06074

Call Sign: KB1RMQ
Michael B Pollack
54 Andreis Trail
South Windsor CT 06074

Call Sign: K1MBP
Michael B Pollack
54 Andreis Trail
South Windsor CT 06074

Call Sign: AA1WP
James F Williams
25-4 Arthur Drive
South Windsor CT 06074

Call Sign: N3AVN
Stephen E Alexander
80 Ash Road
South Windsor CT
060741520

Call Sign: KB1UIL
Rishi Narayana Nadimpally
7 Austin Circle
South Windsor CT 06074

Call Sign: KB1UIP

Vivek Bejugama
7 Austin Circle
South Windsor CT 06074

Call Sign: W1AMW
James R Hosking
90 Beelzebub Rd
South Windsor CT 06074

Call Sign: W1ECI
John W Tencza
141 Beelzebub Rd
South Windsor CT
060742278

Call Sign: K1IED
Larry F Skilton
72 Brook St
South Windsor CT 06074

Call Sign: K1IWM
Linda R Skilton
72 Brook St
South Windsor CT 06074

Call Sign: KB1DWW
Thomas J Morelli
320 Brookfield St
South Windsor CT
060741206

Call Sign: KC0APQ
Lori A Campbell
419 Buckland Rd
South Windsor CT 06074

Call Sign: WA9IFM
Joseph D Stengel
95 Carriage Dr
South Windsor CT 06074

Call Sign: WA1WKQ
Hipocrates J Restrepo
16 Carson Way
South Windsor CT 06074

Call Sign: KA1WNT
Charles F Catania Jr
503 Chapel Rd
South Windsor CT 06074

Call Sign: KB1HTC
Cesar E Rodriguez
762 Clark St
South Windsor CT 06074

Call Sign: W1IKL
Alfred F Yacovone
177 Clinton Dr
South Windsor CT 06074

Call Sign: N1GAG
Denise E Cologne
98 Country View Drive
South Windsor CT 06074

Call Sign: N1QHN
Edmund F Piela
7 Deerfield Ln
South Windsor CT 06074

Call Sign: KB1FLV
Christopher M Hack
91 Deerfield Ln
South Windsor CT 06074

Call Sign: KB1FGK
Christopher M Hack
45 Diane Dr
South Windsor CT 06074

Call Sign: KD1XJ
Richard E Fletcher
190 Diane Dr
South Windsor CT 06074

Call Sign: N1JNV
Matthew L Galin
75 Diane Drive
South Windsor CT 06074

Call Sign: W1EA
Matthew L Galin
75 Diane Drive
South Windsor CT 06074

Call Sign: K1AOY
Edward G Oppelt
682 Ellington Rd
South Windsor CT 06074

Call Sign: KA1YCB
Charles M Sellers
840 Ellington Rd
South Windsor CT 06074

Call Sign: KB1HLN
Adam R Pacheco
1374 Ellington Rd
South Windsor CT 06074

Call Sign: KB1HLO
Joshua C Pacheco
1374 Ellington Rd
South Windsor CT 06074

Call Sign: KA1DFJ
David J Barth
2534 Ellington Rd
South Windsor CT 06074

Call Sign: W1DKE
Fred L Babbitt
2560 Ellington Rd
South Windsor CT
060742203

Call Sign: KB1WFI
Mary G Beaulieu
2780 Ellington Rd
South Windsor CT 06074

Call Sign: KB1NKV
Emily P Shea
21 Elm St

South Windsor CT 06074

Call Sign: WB1FVS
Thomas A Delnicki
130 Felt Rd
South Windsor CT 06074

Call Sign: WA1VJH
Garnet Drakiotes
70 Fitch Meadow Lane
South Windsor CT 06074

Call Sign: KB1PRN
Paul F Dunia
78 Garnet Lane
South Windsor CT 06074

Call Sign: AA1MC
William A Eichner
16 Greenfield Dr
South Windsor CT 06074

Call Sign: N1WWZ
Marc E Nevue
229 Griffin Rd
South Windsor CT 06074

Call Sign: K1EHC
Joseph F Saczyk
515 Griffin Rd
South Windsor CT 06074

Call Sign: N1KVQ
Peter C Haggerty
713 Griffin Rd
South Windsor CT 06074

Call Sign: N1HWQ
Christopher A Gearhart
176 Kent Ln
South Windsor CT 06074

Call Sign: N1IAH
Harry G Saddock Jr
47 Le Foll Blvd

South Windsor CT 06074

Call Sign: WA1OWS
John R Huff
263 Le Foll Blvd
South Windsor CT 06074

Call Sign: KB1JLX
Nicholas D Saddock
47 Lefoll Blvd
South Windsor CT 06074

Call Sign: W1OBI
Leonard C Mc Farland Sr
213 Long Hill Rd
South Windsor CT 06074

Call Sign: WA1SLA
David A Goodwin
1512 Main St
South Windsor CT 06074

Call Sign: KB1KUG
Walter E Carlson
31 Maple St
South Windsor CT 06074

Call Sign: KB1FOC
Brian Heath
2008 Mill Pond Drive
South Windsor CT 06074

Call Sign: N1VIF
Emil Bruce Botti
428 Niederwerfer Rd
South Windsor CT 06074

Call Sign: KA1ETL
Robert D Lannan
460 Niederwerfer Rd
South Windsor CT 06074

Call Sign: KB1KJP
Richard I Chang
41 Norman Dr

South Windsor CT 06074

South Windsor CT 06074

South Windsor CT 06074

Call Sign: W1FVU
Robert H Pavey
100 Northview Dr
South Windsor CT 06074

Call Sign: N1ACM
David L Jordan
163 Robert Dr
South Windsor CT 06074

Call Sign: KB1KIY
Christine R Ostrowski
M5 St Marc Circle
South Windsor CT 06074

Call Sign: K1RDK
Syril D Bragg
442 Oakland Rd
South Windsor CT 06074

Call Sign: N1CRB
Edward P Assarabowski
12 Sally Dr
South Windsor CT 06074

Call Sign: W1WHO
Rodney W Midford
303 Strawberry Lane
South Windsor CT 06074

Call Sign: WA1YSF
Barry R Loos
6 Old Farm Rd
South Windsor CT 06074

Call Sign: KB1PON
Ulf J Jonsson
100 Sally Dr
South Windsor CT 06074

Call Sign: W1FKI
William J Mc Teague
43 Summerwood Lane
South Windsor CT 06074

Call Sign: N1RFN
Diane M Intino
65 Perrin Ln
South Windsor CT 06074

Call Sign: K1ULF
Ulf J Jonsson
100 Sally Dr
South Windsor CT 06074

Call Sign: KB1MLL
Stephen A Nettleton
65 Sycamore Rd
South Windsor CT
060743529

Call Sign: KB1LUU
Conrad J Lavoie
807 Pleasant Valley Rd
South Windsor CT 06074

Call Sign: KB1PLL
Wayne H Wilhelm
70 Scantic Meadow Rd
South Windsor CT 06074

Call Sign: N1GHR
Daniel L Aldrich
30 Willow St
South Windsor CT 06074

Call Sign: KB1FAS
Melissa A Stone
949 Pleasant Valley Rd 2-4
South Windsor CT 06074

Call Sign: N1USX
Thomas W Piantek
170 Scantic Meadow Rd
South Windsor CT 06074

Call Sign: N1WIE
Raymond J Tautic Jr
63 Willow St
South Windsor CT
060743125

Call Sign: K1AZF
Thomas J Oppelt Jr
72 Pond Ln
South Windsor CT 06074

Call Sign: W1BMY
Harvey I Weiner
67 Scott Dr
South Windsor CT 06074

Call Sign: KA1KNW
Gregory Jarvis
South Windsor CT 06074

Call Sign: K1EBJ
Lloyd E Jones Jr
20 Ridge Rd
South Windsor CT 06074

Call Sign: KC1NF
Arthur E Champagne Jr
262 Scott Dr
South Windsor CT 06074

Call Sign: N1ZOK
Thomas J Gromak
South Windsor CT 06074

Call Sign: N1KPI
Alvena T Jones
20 Ridge Rd

Call Sign: KA1UJO
Frank D Burns
45 Sele Dr

Call Sign: KB1KST
Diane Shippee
South Windsor CT 06074

Call Sign: KA1RNU
Donald F Henry
Box 297 Route 171
South Woodstock CT 06267

Call Sign: NM1Q
Thomas E Francis
South Woodstock CT 06267

Call Sign: W1TEF
Thomas E Francis
South Woodstock CT 06267

**FCC Amateur Radio
Licenses in Southbury**

Call Sign: WA2JIO
Lila J Howard
440 A Heritage Village
Southbury CT 06488

Call Sign: WA2KPA
Richard B Howard
440 A Heritage Village
Southbury CT 06488

Call Sign: KD1TQ
Richard B Locher
736 A Heritage Village
Southbury CT 064881312

Call Sign: KI4YMU
Diane C Gaughan
13 B Heritage Village
Southbury CT 06488

Call Sign: KB1BFY
Arthur W Hinkson
53 B Heritage Village
Southbury CT 06488

Call Sign: KB1CQS
Donald P Chabot
14 Bridle Path Rd
Southbury CT 06488

Call Sign: KA1PVW
James P Alfano
114 Burma Rd
Southbury CT 06488

Call Sign: KA1PWP
Deborah C Alfano
114 Burma Rd
Southbury CT 06488

Call Sign: KA1USW
David A Diamond
128 Burma Rd
Southbury CT 06488

Call Sign: KA1VQI
Gary Diamond
128 Burma Rd
Southbury CT 06488

Call Sign: W2ENF
Charles P Koehler
81 C Heritage Village
Southbury CT 064881660

Call Sign: WA1TKC
John E Andrews Jr
57 Charter Oak Rd
Southbury CT 06488

Call Sign: KB1GUD
Vincent Da Grosa
78 E Heritage Village
Southbury CT 06488

Call Sign: KA1NIZ
Shirley R Korte
231 E Heritage Village
Southbury CT 06488

Call Sign: KB1NYL
Volker W Fritz
Flag Swamp Rd
Southbury CT 06488

Call Sign: W1ICJ
Gary R Simons
9 Gate Post Ln
Southbury CT 06488

Call Sign: N1RYH
John J Long
114 Georges Hill Rd
Southbury CT 06488

Call Sign: W9MRM
John W Boeckel
1232 Georges Hill Rd
Southbury CT 06488

Call Sign: WA5YXW
Aubrey J Mays
125 Grassland Rd
Southbury CT 06488

Call Sign: WB5QGC
Harriet F Mays
125 Grassland Rd
Southbury CT 06488

Call Sign: WA1NLS
Harriet F Mays
125 Grassland Rd
Southbury CT 06488

Call Sign: KA1KP
Joseph Parker
93 Hampton Court
Southbury CT 064883907

Call Sign: N1DPP
Jennie Rose Parker
93 Hampton Court
Southbury CT 064883907

Call Sign: N1BVL
Donald D Mac Kenzie
11c Heritage Crest
Southbury CT 06488

Call Sign: KA1NMO
John Warren
647b Heritage Village
Southbury CT 06488

Call Sign: WA2ILY
William J Kerber
541b Heritage Vlg
Southbury CT 064886662

Call Sign: KB1JGJ
Joe A Glynn
108a Heritage Village
Southbury CT 06488

Call Sign: N1JVF
John G Winter
662b Heritage Village
Southbury CT 06488

Call Sign: W2MXX
Bernard D Plakun
566b Heritage Vlg
Southbury CT 06488

Call Sign: KA1ZUZ
Louise Austin
127b Heritage Village
Southbury CT 06488

Call Sign: W1RRU
William R Goetz
685b Heritage Village
Southbury CT 06488

Call Sign: N1RVR
Otto H Kortegast
739a Heritage Vlg
Southbury CT 06488

Call Sign: KB1SOL
Jack W Riling
270d Heritage Village
Southbury CT 06488

Call Sign: KB1AZO
Gerald V Schnutt
752a Heritage Village
Southbury CT 06488

Call Sign: N1UDJ
Herbert C Franson
751d Heritage Vlg
Southbury CT 064885316

Call Sign: N1XLY
Huntley H Holmes
364b Heritage Village
Southbury CT 064881716

Call Sign: KG4EZS
Richard D Lonergan
81a Heritage Village
Southbury CT 06488

Call Sign: N1JVN
Kenneth L Weiner
198 Hickory Ln
Southbury CT 06488

Call Sign: W2BUE
Carl M Backer
587c Heritage Village
Southbury CT 06488

Call Sign: N1AAS
A Keith Eaton Jr
830a Heritage Village
Southbury CT 06488

Call Sign: W1NG
Kenneth N Bolin
132 High Meadow Dr
Southbury CT 06488

Call Sign: KA1ZVA
Jerome R Ferber
602a Heritage Village
Southbury CT 06488

Call Sign: KA1TRG
Roy K Tonning
860a Heritage Village
Southbury CT 06488

Call Sign: WB1AIO
Lawrence W Zimmer
31 High Point Rd
Southbury CT 06488

Call Sign: W2NYN
Albert J Davidson
606b Heritage Village
Southbury CT 06488

Call Sign: KB1NPV
Robert A Rogowski
949b Heritage Village
Southbury CT 06488

Call Sign: WB1DRE
Anthony J Zarcone
27 Hillside Rd
Southbury CT 06488

Call Sign: KB1IWF
Robert N Greene
619a Heritage Village
Southbury CT 06488

Call Sign: W6RPA
Walter R Baranger Sr
202a Heritage Vlg
Southbury CT 06488

Call Sign: KB1CGV
Bernadette V Hamad
261 Hinman Ln
Southbury CT 06488

Call Sign: KB1LI
Albert E Urkawich
150 Holly Hill Ln
Southbury CT 06488

Call Sign: KB1AL
Albert E Urkawich
150 Holly Hill Ln
Southbury CT 06488

Call Sign: WI1W
Albert E Urkawich
150 Holly Hill Ln
Southbury CT 06488

Call Sign: KB1AL
Albert E Urkawich
150 Holly Hill Ln
Southbury CT 06488

Call Sign: WA1GBY
William J Kilbride
94 Ichabod Rd
Southbury CT 06488

Call Sign: N1ACI
Terry L Brenn
310 Jacob Rd
Southbury CT 064882780

Call Sign: N1AAJ
Ronald J Hluska
665 Jeremy Swamp Rd
Southbury CT 06488

Call Sign: KB1PJI
David A Polmon
957 Kettletown Rd
Southbury CT 06488

Call Sign: W1HRD
David A Polmon
957 Kettletown Rd
Southbury CT 06488

Call Sign: WB6SVP
William C Kleinhofer
150 Kettletown Road 166
Southbury CT 06488

Call Sign: NA1BK
William C Kleinhofer
150 Kettletown Road 166
Southbury CT 06488

Call Sign: KA1PFO
Brian P Lebert
129 Lake Mere Dr
Southbury CT 06488

Call Sign: KA1NBR
John L Trzaski
95 Low Bridge Rd
Southbury CT 06488

Call Sign: N1EGK
Jeanne M Soares
323 Luther Dr
Southbury CT 06488

Call Sign: NA1S
Vincent A Soares
323 Luther Dr
Southbury CT 06488

Call Sign: AB1OW
Evan Jones
920 Main Street North
Southbury CT 06488

Call Sign: K2RBY
Evan Jones
920 Main Street North
Southbury CT 06488

Call Sign: WA1ZIW
Jack O Stringer Jr
95 N Georges Hill Rd
Southbury CT 06488

Call Sign: K2RBY
Jack Jones
920 N Main St
Southbury CT 06488

Call Sign: KB1FW
Henry A Jensen Jr
104 Old Field Rd
Southbury CT 06488

Call Sign: K0UL
Thomas D Schreiner
365 Old Poverty Rd
Southbury CT 06488

Call Sign: KA9KOZ
Rochelle Metcoff
484 Old Woodbury Rd
Southbury CT 064881932

Call Sign: KA9KPA
William S Metcoff
484 Old Woodbury Rd
Southbury CT 064881932

Call Sign: N1NIQ
Chris T Thompson
59 Painter Road
Southbury CT 06488

Call Sign: K1ESF
Bruce A Palmer
34 Palmer Rd
Southbury CT 06488

Call Sign: KA1IRQ
Denise S Cohen
149 Palmer Rd
Southbury CT 06488

Call Sign: N1KYB
Richard A Miska
190 Palmer Rd
Southbury CT 06488

Call Sign: KA1PNL
Guy Puglisi
160 Patriot Road
Southbury CT 06488

Call Sign: N1EEY
Kenneth L Ratkevich
1304 Purchase Brook Rd
Southbury CT 06488

Call Sign: KA1ZCC
Gary A Tomlinson
1380 Route 67
Southbury CT 06488

Call Sign: KB1TZS
Kevin S Byler
61 Russian Village Road
Southbury CT 06488

Call Sign: WB1DEO
Robert A Grover
196 Scout Rd
Southbury CT 06488

Call Sign: KA2BDZ
Joseph R M Ruggiero
245 Skyview Dr
Southbury CT 06488

Call Sign: KB1VRM
Todd J Onze
493 South Britain Rd
Southbury CT 06488

Call Sign: K9OCT
Todd J Onze
493 South Britain Rd
Southbury CT 06488

Call Sign: AB1IL
Chad E Gatesman
343 Strongtown Road
Southbury CT 06488

Call Sign: W1CEG
Chad E Gatesman
343 Strongtown Road
Southbury CT 06488

Call Sign: N1RBX
Steve Marcello
65 Turrill Brook Dr
Southbury CT 06488

Call Sign: KA1MVV
Joseph Ratkevich
707 W Purchase Rd
Southbury CT 06488

Call Sign: WA1DUC
Frank J Makray
167 West Flat Hill Rd.
Southbury CT 06488

Call Sign: AB1EN
Steven V Reinhardt
160 Woods Way Dr
Southbury CT 06488

Call Sign: W1KF
Steven V Reinhardt
160 Woods Way Dr
Southbury CT 06488

Call Sign: N1BDN
Sigmund G Bookbinder
Southbury CT 06488

Call Sign: WA1UKD
Winship Barn - One
Winship Dr H V Radio
Electronics
Southbury CT 06488

**FCC Amateur Radio
Licenses in Southington**

Call Sign: K1STM

Anne M West
43 Academy Street Apt 102
Southington CT 064893259

Call Sign: N1IWT
John M West
43 Academy Street Apt 102
Southington CT 064893259

Call Sign: N1QYY
John P Bottiglieri
87 Acre Way
Southington CT 06489

Call Sign: KB1UWS
Alan S Morrison
101 Alder Ln
Southington CT 06489

Call Sign: WA1RED
Irving C Carlson Sr
644 Andrew St
Southington CT 06489

Call Sign: KB1BWL
Rolling Thunder Contest
Club
358 Andrews St
Southington CT 06489

Call Sign: N1QDQ
Peter C Brunelli
358 Andrews St
Southington CT 06489

Call Sign: N1ILV
Roger H Rousseau
106 Arlington Dr
Southington CT 06489

Call Sign: N1JFQ
Colleen W Rousseau
106 Arlington Dr
Southington CT 06489

Call Sign: K1KQV
Nelson J Campagnano
86 Beecher St
Southington CT 06489

Call Sign: KB1GUB
Frederick E Sokolowski
116 Belleview Ave
Southington CT 06489

Call Sign: KA1WIF
Allen E Horner
216 Belleview Ave
Southington CT 06489

Call Sign: N1QVD
David D Arre
330 Belleview Ave
Southington CT 06489

Call Sign: W1SBI
Raymond G Maccio
49 Berkley Ave
Southington CT 06489

Call Sign: KB1BTV
Ragged Mountain Radio
Collective
117 Berlin Ave
Southington CT 06489

Call Sign: W1GVT
John J Mc Nassor Jr
218 Berlin Ave
Southington CT 06489

Call Sign: N1FSO
William F Putney
223 Berlin Ave
Southington CT 06489

Call Sign: N1LRN
Brian Corbino
167 Berlin Street
Southington CT 06489

Call Sign: W2JFN
Mason F Cox
703 Berry Patch Way
Southington CT 06489

Call Sign: KB1UWT
Lisa Dorau
80 Brentwood Dr
Southington CT 06489

Call Sign: N1GCN
Robert S Nicoletti
32 Bridle Path Drive
Southington CT 06489

Call Sign: WK1S
John W Mc Laughlin
81 Bruce Ave
Southington CT 06489

Call Sign: N1AN
George R Lucian
183 Budding Ridge Rd
Southington CT 06489

Call Sign: KA1KTD
William G La Cells
178 Butternut Ln
Southington CT 06489

Call Sign: KB1EYU
Lance R Kilburn
197 Butternut Ln
Southington CT 06489

Call Sign: KA1TRY
Jeffrey A Garlick
138 Carey Street
Southington CT 06489

Call Sign: KA1YB
Thomas E Gaffney
80 Cedar Drive
Southington CT 06489

Call Sign: KA1VCB
Glenn A Powell
3 Chaffee Ln
Southington CT 06489

Call Sign: KB1QQ
Robert J Conner
3 Chaffee Ln
Southington CT 06489

Call Sign: WB1FQZ
Craig M Zoll
350 Churchill St
Southington CT 06489

Call Sign: KA1YLK
Albert J Ferreri
38 Ciccio Rd
Southington CT 06489

Call Sign: N1MP
Martin J Peshka Iii
22 Ciccio Road
Southington CT 064892163

Call Sign: W1PED
Mark H Schumacher
106 Ciccolella Ct
Southington CT 06489

Call Sign: WA1TJB
Gary L Smith
130 Ciccolella Ct
Southington CT 064891354

Call Sign: KB1KTZ
Carl Fosse
75 Claudia Dr
Southington CT 06489

Call Sign: KB1TEY
Edward C Janelle
83 Clearview Ct
Southington CT 06489

Call Sign: K1AKP
Helen M Zadrick
11 Coolidge St
Southington CT 06489

Call Sign: W1JHC
Russell E Magnuson
180 Debbie Dr
Southington CT 06489

Call Sign: K1HSN
Robert T Stathis
141 Foley Dr
Southington CT 064894413

Call Sign: N1NZ
Nickolas Zadrick
11 Coolidge St
Southington CT 064893616

Call Sign: KB1KTY
Joseph Spagna
88 Doe Meadow Ct
Southington CT 06489

Call Sign: N1EZM
Elizabeth J Stathis
141 Foley Dr
Southington CT 064894413

Call Sign: N1YXD
Mark D Noble
67 Darling St
Southington CT 06489

Call Sign: N1JBU
Albert C Bryant
217 Dunham Lot 16
Southington CT 06489

Call Sign: N1RQP
Natalie V Woodman
55 Ford St
Southington CT 06489

Call Sign: KB1ORB
Mark D Noble
67 Darling St
Southington CT 06489

Call Sign: KB1OFW
Brian A Schollin
61 East Mountain Dr
Southington CT 06489

Call Sign: WB1FYN
William A Lexton
36 Garden Gate Rd
Southington CT 06489

Call Sign: KD1ZO
Alberto Nieves
19a Darling St
Southington CT 06489

Call Sign: KA1DBS
CHARLES R Demarco Jr
1452 East St
Southington CT 06489

Call Sign: KB1LNE
Lionel A Thadieo
159 Harness Dr
Southington CT 064891864

Call Sign: KB1DMS
Deane Y Bartley
550 Darling St 6e
Southington CT 06489

Call Sign: KA1EGI
Oscar W Suess
55 Eastview Rd
Southington CT 06489

Call Sign: KA1ZDI
William A Cugno
434 Hart St
Southington CT 06489

Call Sign: KB1EGT
Christopher D Gatto
15 Darling St Apt C
Southington CT 06489

Call Sign: KB1TFC
Kurt S Ryder
342 Edgewood Circle
Southington CT 06489

Call Sign: WA1DUG
Guy A Buckland
75 High Ridge Rd
Southington CT 06489

Call Sign: WA1UCY
Steven D Edick
30 David Dr
Southington CT 06489

Call Sign: N1RYO
Paul P Brunelli
51 Faye Ln
Southington CT 06489

Call Sign: KB1VJM
Giuseppe Lombardo
322 Hightower Rd
Southington CT 06489

Call Sign: KB1TEZ
Charles E Hobson Jr
88 Dawn Lane
Southington CT 06489

Call Sign: WB1EOC
Pete C Noyes
1485 Flanders Rd
Southington CT 06489

Call Sign: WB1DXD
James M Hackett
102 Highwood Ave
Southington CT 06489

Call Sign: N1SIA
Thomas J O'hare
124 Hobart St
Southington CT 06489

Call Sign: KA1ZDR
Dominick C Mazza
14 Kiefer Rd
Southington CT 06489

Call Sign: W1GFL
Pasco A Maiorano
46 Lucy Ct
Southington CT 064892424

Call Sign: N1RCJ
Norbert H Beauchemin
316 Hobart St
Southington CT 06489

Call Sign: WB1FLW
Joanne M Duncan
55 Kingswood Dr
Southington CT 064894114

Call Sign: W1WC
David A Bauchiero
304 Main St
Southington CT 06489

Call Sign: W1DNJ
Frank H Mitchell
528 Hobart St
Southington CT 06489

Call Sign: KB1CKZ
Bashar G Betros
78 Laning St 7c Bldg 3
Southington CT 06489

Call Sign: KB1RBC
Mary Ann Bauchiero
304 Main St
Southington CT 06489

Call Sign: N1NWN
Jay J Mongillo
14 Howard Ave
Southington CT 06489

Call Sign: N1VZJ
Walter J Hyjek Jr
112 Lee Dr
Southington CT 06489

Call Sign: KA1LYF
Roger D Graffam
236 Malcein Dr
Southington CT 06489

Call Sign: KA1MJY
William S Chan
70 Jeremy Woods Dr
Southington CT 06489

Call Sign: KA1JKN
Paul N Dinnean
46 Lincoln Dr
Southington CT 06489

Call Sign: KB1TXN
Ronald E St Pierre
19 Maple Rock Rd
Southington CT 06489

Call Sign: N1FPO
Paula Lenge
328 Jude Ln
Southington CT 06489

Call Sign: N1FNE
Rodney J Lane
78 Loper St
Southington CT 064891812

Call Sign: N1IJH
Philip J Passero Jr
124 Maplewood Rd
Southington CT 06489

Call Sign: N1PXR
Dennis A Vitali
173 Juniper Rd
Southington CT 06489

Call Sign: KB1TFA
David L Brennan
118 Loper St
Southington CT 06489

Call Sign: KA2BIF
Roderick S Kalbfleisch
117 Mckenzie Dr
Southington CT 06489

Call Sign: WA1RD
David R Ward
246 Juniper Rd
Southington CT 06489

Call Sign: KA1WCO
Rhonda M Lane
78 Loper Street
Southington CT 064891812

Call Sign: N1CPD
Robert S Josefiak
72 Meander Ln
Southington CT 06489

Call Sign: W1QH
David R Ward
246 Juniper Rd
Southington CT 06489

Call Sign: N1FND
Vernon R Tompkins
91 Lowery Dr
Southington CT 06489

Call Sign: KB1TET
Peter M Kurtz
31 Melissa Ct
Southington CT 06489

Call Sign: N1MVT
Thomas E Gale
413 Meriden Ave
Southington CT 06489

Call Sign: KA1GMT
Frank A Lapico
1319 Meriden Ave
Southington CT 04689

Call Sign: KA1NXX
Jan C Rogus
250 Meriden Waterbury Rd
Southington CT 06489

Call Sign: WA1JKR
John P Rogus Jr
250 Meriden-Wtby Tnpk
Southington CT 06489

Call Sign: KB1TFD
Nancy S Voisine
216 Monarch Dr
Southington CT 06489

Call Sign: N1NAH
Taft E Armandroff
54 Mooreland Dr
Southington CT 06489

Call Sign: KB1TFB
Charles Miceli
24 Morningside Lane
Southington CT 06489

Call Sign: N1JJX
Michael P Nagorski
1662 Mount Vernon Road
Southington CT 06489

Call Sign: N1NGT
Denise L Nagorski
1662 Mount Vernon Road
Southington CT 06489

Call Sign: W2PAL
Harry J Woods
19 Mountain View Rd
Southington CT 06489

Call Sign: W1GXG
Charles F Drozd
1717 Mt Vernon Rd
Southington CT 06489

Call Sign: N1YAD
Mark A Moran
106 Oak
Southington CT 06489

Call Sign: K1LZZ
George G Buzel
47 Old Turnpike Rd
Southington CT 064893633

Call Sign: KB1OLV
Michael D Ullmeyer
99 Pheasant Rd
Southington CT 06489

Call Sign: K1PYT
Harold E Gerrish Jr
26 Pine Grove Rd
Southington CT 06489

Call Sign: WB1BVQ
Albert J Frascatore
38 Plaza Ave
Southington CT 06489

Call Sign: N1ECB
Joseph S Rogus
476 Pleasant St
Southington CT 06489

Call Sign: N1UIR
Steven G Raleigh
288 Pond View Dr
Southington CT 06489

Call Sign: N1OKG
Beverly L Ames
355 Pond View Dr
Southington CT 064893953

Call Sign: N1SA
Stephen J Ames
355 Pond View Dr
Southington CT 06489

Call Sign: N1SA
Beverly L Ames
355 Pond View Dr
Southington CT 064893953

Call Sign: KB1ERB
Samuel J Sweet
36 Pondview Dr
Southington CT 064893945

Call Sign: KB1PAJ
Richard T Lukas
123 Pondview Dr
Southington CT 06489

Call Sign: KK1F
Richard T Lukas
123 Pondview Dr
Southington CT 06489

Call Sign: N1FIH
Anthony J Telesha
24 Pratt St Apt 105
Southington CT 064894246

Call Sign: KB1CVX
Robert P Mc Comb
273 Queen St 9a
Southington CT 064891932

Call Sign: KB1VNT
Daniel J Coogan
191 Queen St Apt E 15
Southington CT 06489

Call Sign: KA1SZT
Cheryl L Shaia
285 Queen Ter Apt 1f
Southington CT 06489

Call Sign: N1GUE
Harold T Heath
12 Red Oak Dr
Southington CT 06489

Call Sign: KA1QVJ
Stephen A Logue
62 Round Hill Rd
Southington CT 06489

Call Sign: KB1SBR
Branden C Hughes
62 Round Hill Rd
Southington CT 06489

Call Sign: K1NQM
Thomas E Gomberg
65 Royal Oak Dr
Southington CT 06489

Call Sign: W1TK
Ronald J Wakefield
12 Royal Oak Drive
Southington CT 06489

Call Sign: K1TVF
Robert E Anderson
139 Rustic Oak Dr
Southington CT 06489

Call Sign: K1MQW
James D Dicklow
53 Rye Hill Dr
Southington CT 064891331

Call Sign: KA1GKA
Wilbert E Senna
68 S End Rd
Southington CT 064893958

Call Sign: KB1JYY
Alan J Lisitano
930 S End Rd
Southington CT 064894144

Call Sign: KB1MYK
Brenda J Lisitano
930 S End Rd
Southington CT 06489

Call Sign: W1LOZ
Alan J Lisitano
930 S End Rd
Southington CT 064894144

Call Sign: N1ITT
Alan Lisitano
930 S End Rd
Southington CT 064894144

Call Sign: KA1VNU
Jennifer Hinckley
475 Savage St
Southington CT 06489

Call Sign: N1GZO
Katherine A Capodicasa
15 Secondo Ct
Southington CT 06489

Call Sign: N8BZX
William J Vorih
53 Shagbark Dr.
Southington CT 06489

Call Sign: AI1G
Joseph Lombardo
978 Shuttle Mdw Rd
Southington CT 06489

Call Sign: KA1QCM
Elizabeth M Lombardo
978 Shuttle Meadow Rd
Southington CT 06489

Call Sign: WA1P
Joseph Lombardo
978 Shuttle Meadow Rd
Southington CT 06489

Call Sign: WB1CTN
Elizabeth M Lombardo
978 Shuttle Meadow Rd
Southington CT 06489

Call Sign: KA1WDK
Michael J Moriarty
68 Skyline Dr
Southington CT 06489

Call Sign: KA1ANJ
Michael H Baldwin
54 South Center Street
Southington CT 06489

Call Sign: KB1MYL
Lori E Lisitano
930 South End Rd
Southington CT 064894144

Call Sign: KB1MYM
Del-Lor R Lisitano
930 South End Rd
Southington CT 06489

Call Sign: W1BTU
Willard R Ballou
28 Stuart Dr
Southington CT 06489

Call Sign: W1GST
Edward P Surveski Sr
47 Sunnybrook Hill Rd
Southington CT 06489

Call Sign: KB1QQK
Steven C Briggs
5 Sunset Ridge Dr
Southington CT 06489

Call Sign: NG1J
Francis J Vesci
16 Taylor Lane
Southington CT 06489

Call Sign: W1NK
Francis J Vesci
16 Taylor Lane
Southington CT 06489

Call Sign: KB1TTO
John M Tassie
236 Thistle Lane
Southington CT 06489

Call Sign: KD1WN
Richard D Ryan
15 Vermont Court
Southington CT 06489

Call Sign: N1CV
Vincenzo Calandra
338 W Center St
Southington CT 064892338

Call Sign: KA1RBQ
Anthony F Cop
55 Washington Dr
Southington CT 064894329

Call Sign: N1GTU
Blaine Morin
77 Welch Rd
Southington CT 06489

Call Sign: K1VC
Vincenzo Calandra
338 West Center Street
Southington CT 064892338

Call Sign: KB1AXY
Craig J Begin
64 Wheeler Village
Southington CT 06489

Call Sign: KB1UAU
Wilton F Hawes Ii
11 Whippoorwill Rd
Southington CT 06489

Call Sign: N7EMW
Richard E Post
193 Winding Ridge Rd
Southington CT 06489

FCC Amateur Radio Licenses in Southport

Call Sign: W1WUZ
John Sabo
Acorn Ln
Southport CT 06490

Call Sign: N1WHS
Phyllis A Sternberg
66 Barberry Rd
Southport CT 06490

Call Sign: N1BGF
Leo J Heile
Cedar Brook Ln
Southport CT 06490

Call Sign: WA1DKK
Myron J Hinckley
600 Cedar Rd
Southport CT 06490

Call Sign: KD1SX
John H Bisack Ii
340 Half Mile Rd
Southport CT 06490

Call Sign: WB9FPW
Walter S Ciciora
45 Hulls Farm Rd
Southport CT 064901027

Call Sign: WJ1M

Joseph Meo
115 Hulls Hwy
Southport CT 06490

Call Sign: WA2NXR
Jerome L Schulman
770 Hulls Hwy
Southport CT 068901074

Call Sign: KA1JTV
Frank J Gallinelli
657 Mill Hill Rd
Southport CT 06490

Call Sign: KB1GFG
Walker S Vought
301 Sasco Hill Rd
Southport CT 06490

Call Sign: N1YKC
Gurdon Perry
95 Southport Woods Dr
Southport CT 06490

Call Sign: KA1UBV
Wallace E Stern
224 Southport Woods Dr
Southport CT 06490

Call Sign: N1GTS
Perry C Engel
40 Taylor Pl
Southport CT 06490

Call Sign: AA1W
Philip P Tomasky
73 Warner Hill Rd
Southport CT 068903041

Call Sign: N1PLO
Anthony S Carbone
411 Westford Dr
Southport CT 06490

Call Sign: WA9NIZ

Jeffrey L Walden
210 Woodrow Ave.
Southport CT 06890

Call Sign: N1HOT
Peter J Moeller
Southport CT 06490

**FCC Amateur Radio
Licenses in Stafford**

Call Sign: N1JGS
Peter J Kovaleski
93 Delphi Rd
Stafford CT 06076

Call Sign: KB1RNB
Brian J Beley
187 East St
Stafford CT 06076

Call Sign: KI4QDN
Timothy M Carpenter
15a Wales Rd
Stafford CT 06076

Call Sign: N1EBQ
Bruce D Wittig
Stafford CT 06075

Call Sign: KB1JVH
Anthony P Ostrowski
Stafford CT 060750279

Call Sign: KB1QJZ
Gale A Eberly
Stafford CT 06075

**FCC Amateur Radio
Licenses in Stafford
Springs**

Call Sign: W1CKI
William D Mottes
4 Blodgett Rd

Stafford Springs CT 06076

Call Sign: KB1GBX
Eric J Molitoris
93 Buckley Hwy
Stafford Springs CT 06076

Call Sign: KB1GVO
Edward Molitoris
93 Buckley Hwy
Stafford Springs CT 06076

Call Sign: KB1WQD
Scott Small
9 Charter Ave
Stafford Springs CT 06076

Call Sign: KB1TJA
Christopher M Grohs
39 Charter Rd
Stafford Springs CT 06076

Call Sign: W1FDJ
Donald E Swift
6 Clearview
Stafford Springs CT 06076

Call Sign: KB1PYN
Mark Morrison
23 Clearview Drive
Stafford Springs CT 06076

Call Sign: KB1HLB
Everett A Bradway Jr
2 Crystal Lake Rd
Stafford Springs CT 06076

Call Sign: K9CZY
Brian J Beley
187 East St
Stafford Springs CT 06076

Call Sign: KB1PYM
Albert J Beland
89 Furnace Ave Unit S - 2

Stafford Springs CT 06076

Call Sign: K9TIA
Albert J Beland
89 Furnace Ave Unit S - 2
Stafford Springs CT 06076

Call Sign: KA1PVZ
Kenneth W Paradis
25 Gulf Rd
Stafford Springs CT 06076

Call Sign: KA1PWA
Thomas W Paradis
25 Gulf Rd
Stafford Springs CT 06076

Call Sign: N1VEE
Ronald W Braun
9 John St
Stafford Springs CT 06076

Call Sign: WA1DMX
Michael J Pyrch
39 Mayflower Hill Road
Stafford Springs CT 06076

Call Sign: K1ALT
Edward A Roberts
272 Monson Rd
Stafford Springs CT 06076

Call Sign: WA1CCQ
Norman F Bliss
45 Monson Rd.
Stafford Springs CT 06076

Call Sign: KA1ZNM
Sandra N Miller
2 Oakridge Dr
Stafford Springs CT 06076

Call Sign: W1HWG
Charles H Stevens
18 Olympic Ave

Stafford Springs CT 06076

Call Sign: KB1PRZ
Alan L Jacewicz
7 Ridge Rd
Stafford Springs CT 06076

Call Sign: N1ADK
Alan L Jacewicz
7 Ridge Rd
Stafford Springs CT 06076

Call Sign: N1DR
Alan L Jacewicz
7 Ridge Rd
Stafford Springs CT 06076

Call Sign: N1XOJ
David K Michaud
25 Spencer Road
Stafford Springs CT 06076

Call Sign: N1IUF
Tracey J Collier
86 Tolland Ave
Stafford Springs CT 06076

Call Sign: KB1WQK
Laurie A Pray
123 Tolland Ave
Stafford Springs CT 06076

Call Sign: KA1JZX
Phillip S Lucas
44 Tolland Ave 58
Stafford Springs CT
060761386

Call Sign: KF4SMR
Thomas G Griffin
44 Tolland Ave.
Stafford Springs CT 06076

Call Sign: W1FPV
Arthur L Guerra

33 W Stafford Rd
Stafford Springs CT 06076

Call Sign: N1AIU
Earl S Dawson
110 W Stafford Rd
Stafford Springs CT 06076

Call Sign: W1DFT
David H Johnson
141 W Stafford Rd
Stafford Springs CT 06076

Call Sign: W1EY
David H Johnson
141 W Stafford Rd
Stafford Springs CT 06076

Call Sign: AA1J
David H Johnson
141 W Stafford Rd
Stafford Springs CT 06076

Call Sign: W1EY
David H Johnson
141 W Stafford Rd
Stafford Springs CT 06076

Call Sign: N1WYH
Thomas F Stachelsky
Stafford Springs CT 06076

FCC Amateur Radio Licenses in Staffordville

Call Sign: KA1GXB
Robert L Hatch
12 Dunay Rd
Staffordville CT 06077

Call Sign: KA1FZK
Barbara J Palmberg
8 Reservoir Drive
Staffordville CT 06077

Call Sign: N1UCK
Shane P Reichle
74 Wales Rd
Staffordville CT 06077

FCC Amateur Radio Licenses in Stamford

Call Sign: WA1WGZ
William B Cookson
155 Acreview Dr
Stamford CT 06903

Call Sign: KB2TPF
Richard E Seligson
67 Apple Tree Dr
Stamford CT 06906

Call Sign: KB1JMT
Robert M Louth
35 Applebee Rd
Stamford CT 06905

Call Sign: AA1C
Tuckerman S Jalet
52 Aquila Road
Stamford CT 06902

Call Sign: KA1LLL
Anthony S Kucis
30 Archer Ln
Stamford CT 06905

Call Sign: WB1BSI
Paul J Mc Kenna
784 Atlantic St
Stamford CT 06902

Call Sign: KB1EVS
Malcolm M Dickinson Iii
69 Auldwood Rd
Stamford CT 069027815

Call Sign: W1KLI
Edward A Faubel

8 Ayres Dr
Stamford CT 06905

444 Bedford Street 1n
Stamford CT 06901

75 Birchwood Rd
Stamford CT 06907

Call Sign: N8CNC
Stephen T Norman
170 Barclay Dr
Stamford CT 06903

Call Sign: KB1UOB
Christina E Kovacs
141 Belltown Rd
Stamford CT 06905

Call Sign: WA1FZK
Jonathan D Cline
48 Black Twig Pl
Stamford CT 06903

Call Sign: N1GSD
Willard H Kemp Iii
37 Beal St
Stamford CT 06902

Call Sign: N1JRU
Alan M Quell
236 Belltown Rd
Stamford CT 06905

Call Sign: KB1UKA
Franco Becchi
62 Blue Ridge Dr
Stamford CT 06903

Call Sign: N1GSF
Luisa Kemp
37 Beal St
Stamford CT 06902

Call Sign: KB1OKS
Matthew S Cirillo
236 Belltown Rd
Stamford CT 06905

Call Sign: KB1LPH
Yonatan T Schechter
89 Blue Ridge Dr
Stamford CT 06903

Call Sign: KA1UBO
Elissa L Bucciarelli
1435 Bedford St
Stamford CT 06902

Call Sign: W1AMQ
Alan M Quell
236 Belltown Rd
Stamford CT 06905

Call Sign: N1AWN
Lee D Brauer
71 Boulderol Road
Stamford CT 06903

Call Sign: KB1WKY
Georgi T Todorov
500 Bedford St 111
Stamford CT 06901

Call Sign: W1CE
Alan M Quell
236 Belltown Rd
Stamford CT 06905

Call Sign: KA1LLH
David L Stewart Jr
113 Bouton St West
Stamford CT 06907

Call Sign: K1GTT
Georgi T Todorov
500 Bedford St 111
Stamford CT 06901

Call Sign: KB1QBZ
Jon Perelstein
141 Belltown Road
Stamford CT 06905

Call Sign: K1GF
Frederick S Wardwell Sr
69 Briar Brae Rd
Stamford CT 06903

Call Sign: KA2ALT
Gennaro L Russo
1500 Bedford St 304
Stamford CT 069054725

Call Sign: WB2RYV
Jon Perelstein
141 Belltown Road
Stamford CT 06905

Call Sign: N1UCO
Joseph A Barone
121 Bridge Street
Stamford CT 06905

Call Sign: KB1ADV
Carmine G Bucciarelli
1435 Bedford St 5c
Stamford CT 06905

Call Sign: KB1OMK
Stephanie R Cirillo
236 Belltown Road
Stamford CT 06905

Call Sign: W1IOP
Alexander J Koda
129 Brook Run Ln
Stamford CT 06905

Call Sign: KB1UJZ
Laura J Augustyn

Call Sign: KA1ROA
David Gregory Jr

Call Sign: KB1IFX
Frank X Cassella

62 Buckingham Dr
Stamford CT 06902

Call Sign: N1MXU
Thomas S Kovacs
39 Burwood Ave
Stamford CT 06902

Call Sign: KB1VTQ
Sri Satya Parthiva
Hno 970 C Hope St Apt 4
Stamford CT 06907

Call Sign: N1SNU
Bruce W Spaulding
126 Cedarwood Rd
Stamford CT 06903

Call Sign: KB1GHE
Dennis W Muehring
20 Chatfield St
Stamford CT 06907

Call Sign: KA0VOM
Larry G Gettinger
87 Clover Hill Dr
Stamford CT 06902

Call Sign: KA2HWJ
Kevin W Multer
96 Clover Hill Drive
Stamford CT 06902

Call Sign: KA1LXX
Evelyn M Heath
227 Club Rd
Stamford CT 069052125

Call Sign: W1BWK
Spencer R Heath
227 Club Rd
Stamford CT 069052125

Call Sign: KB1LHN
Ryan P Smith

53 Cody Dr
Stamford CT 06905

Call Sign: N1ATS
Irving M Neitlich Mr
180 Colonial Rd. # B-1
Stamford CT 06906

Call Sign: N1WDP
Wilner St Jean
135 Courtland Ave Unit 26
Stamford CT 06902

Call Sign: KA1FOT
Dennis R Tidrick
65 Cousins Road
Stamford CT 06903

Call Sign: AB1K
Diran Varzhabedian
601 Cove Rd
Stamford CT 069026125

Call Sign: N1HIX
George R Payne Sr
33 Crestview Ave
Stamford CT 06907

Call Sign: N1YNO
Christopher Clark
90 Crestview Ave
Stamford CT 06907

Call Sign: KB1RMK
Louis P Perry
57 Cross Rd
Stamford CT 06905

Call Sign: N1JSU
Martin A Cooper
6 Dann Dr
Stamford CT 06905

Call Sign: N1LNL
Arthur Weber

96 Dannell Dr
Stamford CT 06905

Call Sign: N5JHT
John H Tull Jr
80 Davenport Dr
Stamford CT 06902

Call Sign: N1DSK
Gregory A Doorakian
98 Diamond Crest Ln
Stamford CT 06903

Call Sign: NM1E
Mary A Doorakian
Diamond Crest Ln
Stamford CT 06903

Call Sign: NS2F
Tore A Smedman
209 Dolphin Cove Quay
Stamford CT 06902

Call Sign: WB2WYZ
Edward Jacobson Md
293 East Hunting Ridge
Road
Stamford CT 06903

Call Sign: KA1IIW
Marc C Malloch
54 Edgewood Ave
Stamford CT 06907

Call Sign: W3EIC
Jonathan E Solomon
4 Edice Road
Stamford CT 06905

Call Sign: N1VSZ
Melissa J Gluck
43 Elm Tree Pl
Stamford CT 06906

Call Sign: KB1HPX

Kevin M Behilo
5 Elm Tree Pl 3
Stamford CT 06906

Call Sign: N1OOA
Anthony A Prizio I Iii
116 Farms Rd
Stamford CT 06903

Call Sign: KB1DUA
Steven A Bander
22 Fieldstone Cir
Stamford CT 06902

Call Sign: N1NDA
Brian S Lessin
8 Four Brooks Cir
Stamford CT 06903

Call Sign: K1JWX
A Albert Goldberg
323 Four Brooks Rd
Stamford CT 06903

Call Sign: AG1B
A Albert Goldberg
323 Four Brooks Road
Stamford CT 06903

Call Sign: KB1CDW
Frantz Joseph
201 Franklin St
Stamford CT 06901

Call Sign: N1WYE
Barry S Barkinsky
97 Franklin St 2a
Stamford CT 069011309

Call Sign: N2CN
Andrew B Siegel
113 Gary Rd
Stamford CT 06903

Call Sign: KB1PIY

Adam B Siegel
113 Gary Road
Stamford CT 06903

Call Sign: W1PBH
Jacob V Garrecht
1 Givens Ave
Stamford CT 06902

Call Sign: KA1VWO
Michael P Durbin
30 Glenbrook Rd 3f
Stamford CT 06902

Call Sign: KB1QNM
Sean M Sullivan
30 Glenbrook Rd Unit 8d
Stamford CT 06902

Call Sign: K1ONZ
Robert L Worsley Ii
668 Glenbrook Rd Unit 8d
Stamford CT 06906

Call Sign: N1CUS
Charles A Dianis
421 Glenbrook Road Unit 2
Stamford CT 06906

Call Sign: KA1QDC
Richard J Casey
30 Golf View Circle
Stamford CT 06905

Call Sign: WA1PDK
Lawrence F Stoler
140 Grove Street Apartment
3k
Stamford CT 06901

Call Sign: N1MFV
Andrew V Schanck
88 Haig Ave
Stamford CT 06905

Call Sign: KB1CQZ
Donald K Grossberndt
287 Hamilton Ave 2d
Stamford CT 06902

Call Sign: N1ZFS
James A Markus Jr
287 Hamilton Ave Unit 4i
Stamford CT 06902

Call Sign: KB1UKH
Adam Williams
15 Harbor St Floor 2
Stamford CT 06897

Call Sign: KA1YVV
David R Herz
18 Hemlock Dr
Stamford CT 06902

Call Sign: KB1UHP
James M Freire
200 Henry Street 2405
Stamford CT 06902

Call Sign: K1BIM
Francis L Hajdu
105 High Clear Dr
Stamford CT 06905

Call Sign: WA1UON
Henrietta G Hajdu
105 High Clear Dr
Stamford CT 06905

Call Sign: KB1NYK
Geoffrey K Parker
1525 High Ridge Rd
Stamford CT 06903

Call Sign: N1NNG
James W Murdock Iii
2440 High Ridge Rd
Stamford CT 06903

Call Sign: N1NOA
James W Murdock Iv
2440 High Ridge Rd
Stamford CT 06903

Call Sign: N1NOB
Hunter R Murdock
2440 High Ridge Rd
Stamford CT 06903

Call Sign: N1QNL
Charles C Murdock
2440 High Ridge Rd
Stamford CT 06903

Call Sign: N1SNW
Kathryn L Murdock
2440 High Ridge Rd
Stamford CT 06903

Call Sign: K1EAN
Thomas Lyman Jr
3045 High Ridge Rd
Stamford CT 06903

Call Sign: KC2HSS
Omachonu O Ogali
65 High Ridge Rd #361
Stamford CT 06905

Call Sign: KB1QXR
Chris W Demisch
65 High Ridge Rd 546
Stamford CT 06902

Call Sign: N1WQA
Maureen E Leffand
65 High Ridge Rd 653
Stamford CT 06905

Call Sign: WA2YAX
Leonard S Leffand
65 High Ridge Road Suite
531
Stamford CT 06905

Call Sign: N1GWO
Joseph M Pregio
35 Hilltop Ave
Stamford CT 06907

Call Sign: KB1QIK
Matt E Smith
77 Hirsch Rd
Stamford CT 06905

Call Sign: W1UDV
Edward R Guider
1336 Hope
Stamford CT 06907

Call Sign: KE1IE
Peter Spyropoulos
187 Hope St
Stamford CT 06906

Call Sign: KA2RKK
Margaret P Heffler
409a Hope St
Stamford CT 06906

Call Sign: KB1VTR
Ramana Venkata
970 Hope St Apt 4
Stamford CT 06907

Call Sign: WA1ZCX
James F Bongo Jr
63 Hope St Unit 23c
Stamford CT 06906

Call Sign: KB2AAN
Jennifer L Brand-Kobetitsch
455 Hope Street Apt 3h
Stamford CT 06906

Call Sign: N1IDC
Peter Calcano
143 Hoyt St Apt 1s
Stamford CT 06905

Call Sign: W2DZF
Benjamin F Newton
111 Hubbard Ave
Stamford CT 06905

Call Sign: N1RNH
Vinicio Cifre
34 Hundley Ct
Stamford CT 06902

Call Sign: KB1PIZ
Matthew W Canil
506 Hunting Ridge Road
Stamford CT 06903

Call Sign: AA1MP
Robert A Castrignano
157 Idlewood Dr
Stamford CT 06905

Call Sign: AB2KY
Frank B Boscamp
10 Indian Rock Rd
Stamford CT 06903

Call Sign: WA1VUU
John R Finn
27 Ivy St
Stamford CT 069022205

Call Sign: KA1UDU
Michael Fortunato
144 Joffre Ave
Stamford CT 06905

Call Sign: WR1AIE
Dick Rosevalt Memorial
Amateur Radio Club
147 Joffre Avenue - Apt 2
Stamford CT 069052933

Call Sign: K1TA
Thomas J Alessi
147 Joffre Avenue - Apt 2

Stamford CT 069052933

Call Sign: N2MZG
Robert S Murch
233 Jonathan Dr
Stamford CT 06903

Call Sign: N1ILR
Luke A Williams
5 Kenilworth Dr E
Stamford CT 06902

Call Sign: N2CLA
Michael G Considine
50 Kensington Rd
Stamford CT 06905

Call Sign: WD4JRF
Richard O Avery
45 Lancaster Pl
Stamford CT 06905

Call Sign: N1SL
Mark G Lowenstein
79 Larkspur Rd
Stamford CT 06903

Call Sign: KB1RJS
Adam S Borawski
60 Lawn Ave Apt 22
Stamford CT 06902

Call Sign: W1ASB
Adam S Borawski
60 Lawn Ave Apt 22
Stamford CT 06902

Call Sign: KB1TGW
Donna P Librandi
58 Ledge Lane
Stamford CT 06905

Call Sign: KA1KGY
Loren M Cubbison
26 Ledge Ln

Stamford CT 06905

Call Sign: KB1IFY
William R Librandi
58 Ledge Ln
Stamford CT 069053322

Call Sign: WB2SPU
Fryderyk Tyra
40 Limerick St
Stamford CT 06902

Call Sign: KB1SON
Robert P Valenti
27 Lindstrom Rd 8c
Stamford CT 06902

Call Sign: KE6ZQL
Frances M Ross
27 Lindstrom Rd Apt 3c
Stamford CT 06902

Call Sign: W1ASK
B Eric Cooper
55 Linwood Ln
Stamford CT 069034702

Call Sign: KA1RNX
Walter W Garrity
63 Little John Ln
Stamford CT 06907

Call Sign: N1UMI
John M Bell
1327 Long Rdg Rd
Stamford CT 06903

Call Sign: KA1RAD
Alan J Longveil
241 Loveland Rd
Stamford CT 06905

Call Sign: AA1WD
Alan J Longveil
241 Loveland Rd

Stamford CT 06905

Call Sign: N1ILX
Henry H Moore
251 Main St 308
Stamford CT 06901

Call Sign: N1MUQ
Charles D Woodside
66 Malvern Rd
Stamford CT 06905

Call Sign: KB1NCO
Nallasamy Ponnusamy
101 Maple Tree Ave Apt -
2a
Stamford CT 06906

Call Sign: KB3CZA
Andrew Rosca
9 Maple Tree Ave. A1
Stamford CT 06906

Call Sign: WA1VRQ
Joseph A Kardos Jr
46 Martin Street
Stamford CT 069026242

Call Sign: W1MQA
John H Stokes
26 Melrose Ave
Stamford CT 06902

Call Sign: N1CHD
Chester J Piorkowski
46 Mercedes La
Stamford CT 06905

Call Sign: KB1FBV
Alfonso C Sgritta
103 Midland Ave
Stamford CT 06906

Call Sign: K3LWO
Richard P Sabreen

121 Mill Spring Ln
Stanford CT 06903

Call Sign: WB6COI
Wilbert M Chun
328 Mill Road
Stamford CT 06903

Call Sign: KD1UL
Thomas W Young
47 Mitchell St
Stamford CT 06902

Call Sign: N1PAN
David J Connolly
39 Mitzi Rd
Stamford CT 06905

Call Sign: N1OGI
Burton L Piaser
26 Mohawk Trail
Stamford CT 06903

Call Sign: W1GUP
Hawley C Oefinger
1758 Newfield Ave
Stamford CT 069035130

Call Sign: KB1VKK
Joseph C Lacerenza
29 Newfield Ct
Stamford CT 06905

Call Sign: K8HSC
Paul B Kraus
Nine Old Long Ridge Rd
Stamford CT 069031620

Call Sign: KB1LUI
Michael T Calvert
27 Northill St - Apt 6a
Stamford CT 06907

Call Sign: N1RZA
Vinicio Cifre

29 Nurney St 2nd Fl
Stamford CT 06902

Call Sign: WA1SC
Vinicio Cifre
29 Nurney St 2nd Fl
Stamford CT 06902

Call Sign: KA1HFZ
Leo F De Rosa
18 Nutmeg Ln
Stamford CT 06905

Call Sign: N1EOF
John H Gagnon
233 Oaklawn Ave
Stamford CT 06905

Call Sign: KB1TWX
Terrence Papazidis
285 Oaklawn Ave
Stamford CT 06905

Call Sign: WA1JBO
Terrence Papazidis
285 Oaklawn Ave
Stamford CT 06905

Call Sign: KB1IFV
Joseph M Ballerini
223 Ocean Drive East
Stamford CT 06902

Call Sign: WA1ZST
Raymond L Loibl
66 Old Barn Rd
Stamford CT 06905

Call Sign: KB1QXQ
James Urrata
9 Orchard St
Stamford CT 06902

Call Sign: KB8NAA
Eileen M Conway

156 Overbrook Drive
Stamford CT 069061017

Call Sign: W1AWX
Lee E Atkins
122 Palmers Hill Rd Apt
1108a
Stamford CT 069022135

Call Sign: N1OZB
William G Simons
122 Palmers Hill Road
#1211
Stamford CT 06902

Call Sign: KB1BJE
Gautam Srikanth
47 Park St
Stamford CT 069026004

Call Sign: KA1BVE
Terrence S Martin
30 Pellom Pl
Stamford CT 06905

Call Sign: W1TSM
Terrence S Martin
30 Pellom Pl
Stamford CT 06905

Call Sign: KB1MUD
Anthony J Cortese
528 Pepper Ridge Rd
Stamford CT 06905

Call Sign: KB1OAS
Connecticut Amateur Radio
Association
528 Pepper Ridge Rd
Stamford CT 06905

Call Sign: KA1DKM
William K Birch
31 Pepperidge Rd
Stamford CT 06905

Call Sign: K1MII
Shirley K Kronenberg
7 Phaiban Ln
Stamford CT 06902

Call Sign: W1GOZ
James W Momberg
30 Phaiban Ln
Stamford CT 06902

Call Sign: N2NJC
Alan E Selkin
21 Princess Court
Stamford CT 06903

Call Sign: KB1RWE
Mustafa B Ozcay
91 Prospect St Apt 1
Stamford CT 06901

Call Sign: KR4ZX
Glenn Kinen
77 Prospect St Apt9g
Stamford CT 06901

Call Sign: N1ZFR
Thomas Neil Wynne Jr
31 Ralph St
Stamford CT 06902

Call Sign: N1REW
Randall D Stone
81 Ridge Brook Dr
Stamford CT 06903

Call Sign: W1HC
Charles C Allen
147 Ridgecrest Rd
Stamford CT 06903

Call Sign: N1HYH
Gerald W Shields Jr
46 Riding Stable Tr
Stamford CT 06903

Call Sign: WB2AKN
Richard L Feffer
1145 Riverbank Rd
Stamford CT 069032710

Call Sign: KB1DUB
Matthew Terenzio
1329 Riverbank Rd
Stamford CT 06903

Call Sign: AB1NT
John S Winterle
1260 Rock Rimmon Rd
Stamford CT 06903

Call Sign: WB1GRB
John C Sabini Jr
102 Rock Spring Rd Apt A
Stamford CT 06906

Call Sign: W2NUD
Harvie E Schwartz Jr
88 Rockrimmon Rd
Stamford CT 06903

Call Sign: KA1PSI
Roman Balzar
51 Rolling Ridge Rd
Stamford CT 06903

Call Sign: KA1PPV
Joseph Molon
121 Rolling Wood Drive
Stamford CT 06905

Call Sign: WA1LSF
Michael S Heath
64 Round Hill Dr
Stamford CT 06903

Call Sign: KB1EJA
Evgin Heath
64 Round Hill Dr
Stamford CT 06903

Call Sign: KB1GXL
Guven Derkunt
64 Round Hill Dr
Stamford CT 069031516

Call Sign: N1LNS
Ralph M Altomare Jr
10 Rushmore Cir
Stamford CT 06905

Call Sign: N1FNZ
James B Fullman
Scofieldtown Rd And
Woodley Ln
Stamford CT 06903

Call Sign: KB1QXP
William A Dudas
269 Seaside Ave
Stamford CT 06902

Call Sign: K1POK
Samuel W Daskam
38 Settlers Trl
Stamford CT 06903

Call Sign: KA1DDU
Jeffrey W Bankson
55 Severance Dr
Stamford CT 06905

Call Sign: KF6CBT
Sebastian Wolf
55 Severance Drive (App.
2)
Stamford CT 06905

Call Sign: N1NSM
Frank J Melo
30 Shelburn Rd Apt F2
Stamford CT 06902

Call Sign: W1KAV
Martin H Cash Jr

4 Sherwood Rd
Stamford CT 06905

Call Sign: KA1WCA
Vincent E Mobilio
38 Sherwood Rd
Stamford CT 06905

Call Sign: KA1YAK
Judith Ann Mobilio
38 Sherwood Rd
Stamford CT 06905

Call Sign: WB1ABS
Franklyn H Pinney
1361 Shippan Ave
Stamford CT 06902

Call Sign: N1SNV
Hai H Nguyen
1404 Shippan Ave
Stamford CT 06902

Call Sign: KA1UBM
Peter D Cushing
1559 Shippan Ave
Stamford CT 06902

Call Sign: KB1EBT
Peter A Covello
1860 Shippan Ave
Stamford CT 06902

Call Sign: N1FFT
Arthur S Rich
320 Shippan Ave 123
Stamford CT 06902

Call Sign: AA1LD
Leonid Soliterman
521 Shippen Ave #207
Stamford CT 06902

Call Sign: WA2IDF
Steven M Loeb

2241 Shippan Avenue
Stanford CT 06902

Call Sign: KB1QZH
Franklyn A Ballentine Jr
42 Silver St
Stamford CT 06902

Call Sign: KE1IF
Michael F Corrado
33 Sleepy Hollow Ln
Stamford CT 06907

Call Sign: WA2HAR
Wayne C Pride
290 Sound View Ave
Stamford CT 06902

Call Sign: N1VDE
Sidney D Zacharias
59 Soundview Ave
Stamford CT 06902

Call Sign: KC1XT
Robert G Marrone
290 Soundview Ave
Stamford CT 069027128

Call Sign: KB1IFW
Frank L Brantner Jr
185 Southfield Ave
Stamford CT 06902

Call Sign: WD5GEY
Paul J Block
94 Southfield Ave 1605
Stamford CT 06902

Call Sign: N1ZFP
Edward J Esposito
6 Stanwick Cir
Stamford CT 06905

Call Sign: KA1DKD
Pearl Leferson

85 Sterling Pl
Stamford CT 06907

Call Sign: W1LUH
Joseph Leferson
85 Sterling Pl
Stamford CT 06907

Call Sign: N1RQZ
James E Williams
542 Stillwater Rd
Stamford CT 06902

Call Sign: KB1QBY
Andrew P Pezzimenti
309 Straberry Hill Ave
Stamford CT 06902

Call Sign: WB1BSJ
Benjamin Goldschein
91 Strawberry Hill Ave
Stamford CT 06902

Call Sign: KB2NER
Jaime Gil Jr
44 Strawberry Hill Ave 2f
Stamford CT 06902

Call Sign: W1FLH
Wilson P Ralston
1 Strawberry Hill Ave Apt
12a
Stamford CT 06902

Call Sign: N1YLU
Bruce A Urban
91 Strawberry Hill Ave Apt
831
Stamford CT 06902

Call Sign: KA1VWT
Patrick J Leyden
91 Strawberry Hill Ave Unit
1126
Stamford CT 06902

Call Sign: K1UL
Jack Alexander
108 Studio Rd
Stamford CT 06903

Call Sign: N1ABT
Thomas Condon
14 Sun Dance Cir
Stamford CT 06905

Call Sign: N1MWQ
Michael J Capasse
189 Sundance Rd
Stamford CT 06905

Call Sign: KA1MJG
Anne S Peskin
127 Thornridge Dr
Stamford CT 069035123

Call Sign: KA1MJH
Bernard A Peskin
127 Thornridge Dr
Stamford CT 069035123

Call Sign: KC6VGT
Jack R Buchmiller
16 Timber Lane
Stamford CT 069051732

Call Sign: N1XCA
Maurice L Turoff
36 Timber Mill Rd
Stamford CT 06903

Call Sign: KA1ZLH
Miriam Villarini
133 Tresser Blvd 8b
Stamford CT 06901

Call Sign: KB1TJO
Vlad Ionescu
54 Van Buskirk Ave -3
Stamford CT 06902

Call Sign: WA1EJJ
John R Nolan
41 Very Merry Rd
Stamford CT 06903

Call Sign: KA1NGG
Ernest C Laug
33 Vincent Ave
Stamford CT 06905

Call Sign: KA1YVT
Kathie F Laug
33 Vincent Ave
Stamford CT 06905

Call Sign: W1EE
Stamford Amateur Radio
Assocation Inc
33 Vincent Ave
Stamford CT 06905

Call Sign: N1GZJ
Benjamin A Cariri
1 W Hill Rd
Stamford CT 06902

Call Sign: N4YAX
Amiel H Goldberg
159 W Hill Rd
Stamford CT 069021706

Call Sign: N1VUS
Robert A Mizelle
17 Wake Robin Ln
Stamford CT 06903

Call Sign: N1QNM
Mark Vignola
211 Wardwell St
Stamford CT 06902

Call Sign: WB2HTJ
Thomas C Agoston

1450 Washington Blvd
N902
Stamford CT 06902

Call Sign: K1FC
Frederick E Cunningham
118 Webbs Hill Rd
Stamford CT 06903

Call Sign: N1OVH
Michael E Cunningham
118 Webbs Hill Rd
Stamford CT 06903

Call Sign: KB1SQS
Malcolm C Kelley
20m Weed Hill Ave
Stamford CT 06907

Call Sign: KB1TJN
Ian Lachowski
29 Weedhill Ave
Stamford CT 06907

Call Sign: KB1MXT
William M Straus
187 West Ave Unit 8
Stamford CT 069025556

Call Sign: N1YSI
Alexander W Blocker
46 West Glen Dr
Stamford CT 06902

Call Sign: KY1Q
Jeanine Cariri
1 Westhill Rd
Stamford CT 06902

Call Sign: N1FOB
Helen Buskirk Cannella
909 Westover Rd
Stamford CT 06902

Call Sign: N1NVG

Mark Ressler
226 Westwood Rd
Stamford CT 06902

Call Sign: WA1ISL
William H Nevins
321 Westwood Rd
Stamford CT 06902

Call Sign: N1PZE
Michael S Pappalardo
341 Westwood Rd
Stamford CT 06902

Call Sign: WD1A
Siebe Schaaf
116 Wildwood Rd
Stamford CT 06903

Call Sign: N2MPL
Stephen M Hart
420 Wildwood Rd
Stamford CT 06903

Call Sign: N1UJR
Ricardo L Rodriguez
77 Willard Terrace
Stamford CT 06903

Call Sign: K1JXF
William H Scully
276 Wire Mill Rd
Stamford CT 06903

Call Sign: WA1DLF
Harold Martin
476 Wire Mill Rd
Stamford CT 06903

Call Sign: WA1FVZ
Bruce M Balog
22 Woodbury Ave
Stamford CT 06907

Call Sign: KB1TJM

Luis R Cardez
44 Wright St
Stamford CT 06902

Call Sign: WB1M
Vinicio Cifre
24 Wrigth Street
Stamford CT 06902

Call Sign: WA1SC
Vinicio Cifre
24 Wrigth Street
Stamford CT 06902

Call Sign: N1MXW
Thomas C Chang
22 Yale Ct
Stamford CT 06905

Call Sign: KA1KVC
Robert A Johnson
Stamford CT 06905

Call Sign: KB1AFT
James E Phelan
Stamford CT 069050481

Call Sign: N1KZW
Gregory D Mortensen
Stamford CT 06907

Call Sign: KB1HWY
Fairfield Amateur Radio
Technical Society
Stamford CT 06907

Call Sign: KB1IFP
New England Shriners
Radio Club
Stamford CT 069070825

Call Sign: KB1LQT
Susan I Goodman
Stamford CT 06904

Call Sign: KB1LQU
James W Goodman
Stamford CT 06904

FCC Amateur Radio Licenses in Stepney

Call Sign: W1RZB
August V Mackro
139 Pepper St
Stepney CT 06468

FCC Amateur Radio Licenses in Sterling

Call Sign: WA1GWP
Skeet L Gray
Rt 14 Box 201
Sterling CT 06377

Call Sign: KB1IRR
Dorothymae Gahner
34 Grove St
Sterling CT 06377

Call Sign: KB1HOV
Timothy J Gahner
34 Grove St.
Sterling CT 06377

Call Sign: N1NNQ
Leo A Kolek
77 River Rd
Sterling CT 06377

FCC Amateur Radio Licenses in Stevenson

Call Sign: KB1SJC
John N Carrano
Stevenson CT 06491

FCC Amateur Radio Licenses in Stoney Creek

Call Sign: N1VBY
Kenneth W Rocklin
14 West Point Rd
Stoney Creek CT 06405

Call Sign: KA1ZQQ
Dennis C Pollock
327 Al Harvey Rd
Stonington CT 06378

Call Sign: W1RT
Joseph R De Bragga
Rfd 1 Box 239
Stonington CT 06378

Call Sign: K1YEI
Alan P Bentz
52 Cove
Stonington CT 06378

Call Sign: KB1AUT
Frederic W Wilson
31 Cove Rd
Stonington CT 06378

Call Sign: N1LIV
Edgar E Tattersall
50 Cove Rd
Stonington CT 06378

Call Sign: W1KE
James N Crum
100 Cove Rd
Stonington CT 06378

Call Sign: N1FHX
Robert G Hauser
23 Front St
Stonington CT 06378

Call Sign: KC0ERL

Brennan P Downes
9 Grand St #6
Stonington CT 06378

Call Sign: N1VWX
Philip Lopresto Jr
10 Heritage Dr
Stonington CT 06378

Call Sign: KB1IUU
William L Walker
16 Hill Ave
Stonington CT 06378

Call Sign: N1SPW
Joseph A Miller
42 Island Rd
Stonington CT 06378

Call Sign: KB1VMT
Frank E Lionelli
80 Island Rd
Stonington CT 06378

Call Sign: KB1FNT
Robert K Sundman
9 Meadow Ave
Stonington CT 06378

Call Sign: KA1UUX
George A Cassidy
37 Noyes Ave
Stonington CT 06378

Call Sign: N1KEF
Mary Jane Cassidy
37 Noyes Ave
Stonington CT 06378

Call Sign: KC1WP
George K Harris
15 Shawondassee
Stonington CT 06378

Call Sign: WO2B

Robert J Bailey
13 Shawondassee Dr
Stonington CT 06378

Call Sign: KD1WS
Charles R Miller
22 Water St
Stonington CT 06378

Call Sign: KL1LY
Charles H Beck
123 Water St Unit 3
Stonington CT 06378

Call Sign: KA1KAJ
James O Malo
11 Wheeler Brook Park Lot
5
Stonington CT 063781629

Call Sign: KA1YNB
Joan Z Huettl
Stonington CT 06378

Call Sign: KE1CU
Joseph A Rocklin
14 West Point Rd
Stony Creek CT 06405

Call Sign: WB1DUK
John D Drury
52a Clovermill Rd
Storrs CT 06268

Call Sign: KB1NIX
Donald A Soucie Jr
8 Baxter Rd
Storrs CT 06268

Call Sign: N1LJQ
William J Cook Jr
Box 21
Storrs CT 06268

Call Sign: KA1RMS
Scott L Carey
123 Cedar Swamp Rd
Storrs CT 06268

Call Sign: KB1OHJ
Scott L Carey
123 Cedar Swamp Rd
Storrs CT 06268

Call Sign: KB1IQI
Joseph C Dowden
75 Cheney Dr
Storrs CT 06268

Call Sign: N1FWE
Peter A Rawitscher
343 Codfishfalls Rd
Storrs CT 06268

Call Sign: KA1UNZ
James J Martin
38a Crystal Ln
Storrs CT 06268

Call Sign: KB1TSW
Eric M Kurz
10 Eastwood Rd
Storrs CT 06268

Call Sign: KA1ASI
William J Riesen
42 Farmstead Rd
Storrs CT 06268

Call Sign: KA1ASJ
Grace F Riesen
42 Farmstead Rd
Storrs CT 06268

Call Sign: KA1ASK
John W Riesen
42 Farmstead Rd
Storrs CT 06268

Call Sign: N1QIO
William E Shakalis
32 Fellen Road
Storrs CT 06268

Call Sign: KA1BBH
Milton R Morgan
32 Fern Rd
Storrs CT 06268

Call Sign: WB1FPU
Arc Of Westfield State
College
220 Forest Dr
Storrs CT 06279

Call Sign: KC1M
Karen M Riggin
423 Gurleyville Rd
Storrs CT 06268

Call Sign: KB1LRV
Sheila J Thompson
57 Hillyndale Rd
Storrs CT 06268

Call Sign: WA1DHW
Rene A Lizee
15 Holly Dr
Storrs CT 06268

Call Sign: KA1RMR
Rami D Marcus
180 Hunting Lodge Rd
Storrs CT 06268

Call Sign: KA1ROZ
Lawrence H Marcus
180 Hunting Lodge Rd
Storrs CT 06268

Call Sign: N1WME
David W Butler
357 Hunting Lodge Rd
Storrs CT 06268

Call Sign: KB1OHL
Gregory A Fusco
661 Middle Tpk
Storrs CT 06268

Call Sign: KB1ORY
Edwin G Buttell
611 Middle Tpke Apt 8A
Storrs CT 06268

Call Sign: N1HWS
Edwin E Passmore
668 Middle Turnpike
Storrs CT 06268

Call Sign: KA1RMT
Eric Donkor
48 Northwood Rd Apt 48
Storrs CT 06268

Call Sign: N1WOQ
Albert C Ching
23 Rockridge Rd
Storrs CT 06268

Call Sign: KA1BR
Barry L Wollman
18 Russet Ln
Storrs CT 06268

Call Sign: W4ORU
Leon J Gobin
1 Silo Cir Apt A204
Storrs CT 06268

Call Sign: K1ZSD
Gerald E James
782 Storrs Rd
Storrs CT 06268

Call Sign: N1XLW
Theodore J Busky
72 Timber Dr
Storrs CT 06268

Call Sign: N1REF
Gary D Lavigne
10 Woodland Rd
Storrs CT 06268

Call Sign: KB1WRC
Michael H Sweeney
265 Woodland Rd
Storrs CT 06268

Call Sign: KD7LLB
Scott C Huff
5c Zygmunt Dr
Storrs CT 06268

FCC Amateur Radio Licenses in Storrs Mansfield

Call Sign: KB1TIS
Henry J Dube
28 Hillpond Dr
Storrs Mansfield CT 06268

Call Sign: K1EXN
Henry J Dube
28 Hillpond Dr
Storrs Mansfield CT 06268

Call Sign: N1SAX
George R Kerr
1 Silo Circle Apt A 101
Storrs Mansfield CT 06268

Call Sign: KC7EBR
Roger M Ricard
1096 Stafford Rd
Storrs Mansfield CT
062681812

Call Sign: W1HM
William Outerson
4d Sycamore Dr
Storrs Mansfield CT
062682000

Call Sign: N1LLT
Bruce A Kay
386 Browns Rd
Storrs-Mansfield CT 06268

Call Sign: KB1DYQ
Steven J Toce
504 Middle Tpk
Storrs-Mansfield CT 06268

FCC Amateur Radio Licenses in Stratford

Call Sign: K1HAM
Robert I Curtis
162 A Bison Ln
Stratford CT 06497

Call Sign: KA1QGF
Benjamin N Estra
526 A Chapokele Ln
Stratford CT 066148313

Call Sign: K3JZU
James L Deese
589 A North Trail
Stratford CT 06614

Call Sign: N1XYO
Charles E Kazian
513 A Opa Ln
Stratford CT 06614

Call Sign: KA1PXK
Ellen S Pecoroni
70 Alexandra Dr
Stratford CT 06497

Call Sign: WA1FKP
Richard W Pecoroni
70 Alexandra Dr
Stratford CT 06497

Call Sign: K1QVX
Robert J Ruskin
95 Alexandra Dr
Stratford CT 06497

Call Sign: WA1ZPL
Evelyn B Ruskin
95 Alexandra Dr
Stratford CT 06497

Call Sign: KB1WJV
Scott H Sharp
165 Alexandra Drive
Stratford CT 06614

Call Sign: N1PCK
Richard T Kobelis
51 Allencrest Dr
Stratford CT 06497

Call Sign: W1SYG
Joseph M Sebas Jr
146 Ann Ter
Stratford CT 06497

Call Sign: N1XYN
Christopher R Spodnick
130 Avon St
Stratford CT 06497

Call Sign: KA3TPG
Susanna E Harding
12 B Algonquin Lane
Stratford CT 06614

Call Sign: KA1EPS
Charles W Wilkerson
100 Beacon St
Stratford CT 06497

Call Sign: WA1UND
John J Becker
Beaver Dam Rd
Stratford CT 06497

Call Sign: AF1X
James R Elliott
89 Blakeman Pl. 2nd Floor
Stratford CT 06615

Call Sign: N1NXZ
Lawrence E Peck
108 Boswell St
Stratford CT 06497

Call Sign: KB1GXB
Andrew M Svatek
495 Brinsmayd Ave
Stratford CT 06614

Call Sign: WA1THI
John A Takacs
235 Bunnyview Dr
Stratford CT 066141906

Call Sign: N1AH
Adam E Hosa Jr
40 California St
Stratford CT 06615

Call Sign: W1KDY
Muriel S Moreau
255 California St
Stratford CT 06615

Call Sign: N1KOH
Gregory T Segla
41 Canaan Court Bldg-78
Stratford CT 06614

Call Sign: W1DML
John A Kekacs
205 Carol Rd
Stratford CT 06497

Call Sign: WD1X
Raymond E Campofiore
178 Castle Dr
Stratford CT 06497

Call Sign: K1AMO
Jacob J Katz
616a Cherokee Ln
Stratford CT 064978228

Call Sign: N1WLR
Greg M Traverse
105 Clinton St
Stratford CT 06497

Call Sign: N1XYP
Michael R Corona
30 Colony St
Stratford CT 06497

Call Sign: N1UNS
Arthur E Schulz
45 Cottage Pl
Stratford CT 06497

Call Sign: N2RWS
Paul R Koorse
119 Creston Road
Stratford CT 06614

Call Sign: W1WKW
Stephen G Skarupa
215 Cutspring Rd
Stratford CT 06497

Call Sign: KB1JCK
Christopher M Ruskin
200 Deerfield Dr
Stratford CT 06614

Call Sign: KB1EY
David J Wisniewski
121 Delaware Dr
Stratford CT 06614

Call Sign: N1CMW
John A Wisniewski
121 Delaware Dr
Stratford CT 06614

Call Sign: N1SDL
Louis J Petriel Jr
33 Disbrow St
Stratford CT 06497

Call Sign: K1NFK
Alan R Soloman
941 East Broadway
Stratford CT 06615

Call Sign: KA1KCC
Robert W Graves
2232 Elm St
Stratford CT 06497

Call Sign: K1LOM
Seth L Horen
2050 Elm Street
Stratford CT 06615

Call Sign: WA1BGG
Stephen J Pavluvcik
265 Emerald Pl
Stratford CT 06497

Call Sign: N1LNT
Dawn M Smeltzer
510 Emerald Pl
Stratford CT 06497

Call Sign: N1VGT
Arthur L Cartier Iii
107 Emerson Dr
Stratford CT 06614

Call Sign: N1XLJ
Laurie E Cartier
107 Emerson Dr
Strattford CT 06614

Call Sign: K1CTH
Erwin S Botsford
285 Fairfax Dr
Stratford CT 06497

Call Sign: K1ICD
Frank J Serra
46 Greenlawn Ave
Stratford CT 06497

Call Sign: K1RFN
Anthony C Serra Sr
290 Hollywood Ave
Stratford CT 06497

Call Sign: K1BUI
Anthony C Vena
197 Ferndale Ave
Stratford CT 06497

Call Sign: KA1USK
Donald K Deyo Sr
235 Henry Ave 12r
Stratford CT 06497

Call Sign: N1WFS
Kipp A Taylor
46 Holmes St
Stratford CT 06497

Call Sign: KB7HEO
Jeffrey M Arkenberg
91 Flagler Ave
Stratford CT 06614

Call Sign: KB2NMZ
Mark C Sekelsky Sr
1185 Hillside Ave
Stratford CT 06497

Call Sign: KB1AYO
Albert F Kovalik
64 Jackson Ave
Stratford CT 06497

Call Sign: N9CAT
John B Arkenberg
91 Flagler Ave
Stratford CT 06614

Call Sign: KB1SKC
Angus M Maciver
245 Hilltop Dr
Stratford CT 06614

Call Sign: KB1TWF
Gus P Csuka
1685 James Farm Rd
Stratford CT 06614

Call Sign: KB1FBU
Craig H Gilbert
146 Floral Way
Stratford CT 06615

Call Sign: W1AMM
Angus M Maciver
245 Hilltop Dr
Stratford CT 06614

Call Sign: WB1GDI
Michael F Morra
240 Judith Terrace
Stratford CT 066141051

Call Sign: N1BLT
Craig H Gilbert
146 Floral Way
Stratford CT 06615

Call Sign: AA1JQ
Gottfried Kloyer
266 Hilltop Dr
Stratford CT 066142809

Call Sign: N1DOS
Curtis L Dumas
134 Kenyon St
Stratford CT 06497

Call Sign: KB1YC
Mary E Damon
157 Floral Way
Stratford CT 06497

Call Sign: N1PDF
Brian L Mc Cann
331 Hilltop Dr
Stratford CT 06497

Call Sign: N1PLN
Mary Janice Ligouri
154 Kenyon St
Stratford CT 06497

Call Sign: KA1CQ
Joseph C De Caro
412 Freeman Ave
Stratford CT 06614

Call Sign: N1HUG
Roy T Thompson
35 Hitching Post La
Stratford CT 066142227

Call Sign: K1PLJ
Mary Janice Ligouri
154 Kenyon St
Stratford CT 066142556

Call Sign: WA2FFX
Gene S Glick
145 Gem St
Stratford CT 06614

Call Sign: KB1RJT
Brenda D Martin
576 Hollister St
Stratford CT 06615

Call Sign: KB1SUO
Vicki L Dumas
134 Kenyon Street
Stratford CT 06614

Call Sign: N2SYD
Michael D Galaty
221 King Street #3
Stratford CT 06615

Call Sign: WA1GBX
John E Howe
92 Lawlor Terrace
Stratford CT 06497

Call Sign: KD1SN
Mark E Malasics
444 Light St
Stratford CT 06497

Call Sign: WB1GDG
Calvin T Harris Sr
105 Lindsley Pl
Stratford CT 066157016

Call Sign: N1PLL
John K Hamilton
108 Linton St
Stratford CT 06497

Call Sign: N2GZG
Christopher S Lemos
650 Longbrook Ave
Stratford CT 06614

Call Sign: W1BEA
Joseph Vitko
925 Longbrook Ave Unit
107
Stratford CT 06497

Call Sign: KB1RJU
Jeffrey R Reichle
248 Lordship Road
Stratford CT 06615

Call Sign: N1JIY
David O Schoennagel
60 Luanne Rd
Stratford CT 06497

Call Sign: KA1BJR
John F Brennan
1305 Main St
Stratford CT 064977048

Call Sign: N1ZJB
Cindy A Jump
1630 Main St
Stratford CT 06497

Call Sign: N1PKQ
Leo D Crader
1800 Main St
Stratford CT 06497

Call Sign: KB1JIU
Arthur F Gumbus
5629 Main St
Stratford CT 06614

Call Sign: KB1HVE
Joseph J Belisari Jr
7365 Main St 138
Stratford CT 06614

Call Sign: N1KOG
Eric T Barton
1168 Main St A8
Stratford CT 06615

Call Sign: WA1WLA
Constantine Thomas
3620 Main Str
Stratford CT 06614

Call Sign: W1SWL
Arthur F Gumbus
5629 Main Street
Stratford CT 06614

Call Sign: KN1Y
Thomas H Ryan
260 Marcroft St
Stratford CT 06497

Call Sign: N1LXY
William M Charney
235 Mary Ave
Stratford CT 06497

Call Sign: KA1MWL
Roman F Garbacik
80 Matthew Dr
Stratford CT 06615

Call Sign: N1UUU
Andrew Kozel
70 Meadow Brook Rd
Stratford CT 06614

Call Sign: AA1HY
Adam E Hosa Jr
65 Morehouse Ave
Stratford CT 06497

Call Sign: WW1I
Adam E Hosa Jr
65 Morehouse Ave
Stratford CT 06614

Call Sign: KB1EWF
Stephen E Foisey
51 Morningside Ter
Stratford CT 06614

Call Sign: KA1SMV
Milton Milewski
225 Nassau Rd
Stratford CT 06497

Call Sign: KA1CR
James H Bonney
25 Newtown Ave
Stratford CT 06497

Call Sign: WA1CSJ
John Zarifian
150 Nichols Ave
Stratford CT 06497

Call Sign: KA1DCM
Kenneth M Franco
1047 Nichols Ave
Stratford CT 06497

Call Sign: KB1JLN
Jonathan M Gottfried
1621 North Peters Ln
Strafford CT 06614

Call Sign: N1YJE
Lynn Bloom
185 Old Coach Lane
Stratford CT 06614

Call Sign: KA1OYS
Leonard J Bloom Jr
185 Old Coach Ln
Stratford CT 06614

Call Sign: KA1MB
James H Moore Jr
621a Onondaga Ln
Stratford CT 06497

Call Sign: KB1DNY
Jason M Chormanski
180 Patricia Dr
Stratford CT 066141094

Call Sign: W1KPN
Florian J Fox Sr
219 Plymouth St
Stratford CT 06497

Call Sign: K1HVP
Robert J Koripsky
240 Post Oak Rd
Stratford CT 06497

Call Sign: N1XQQ
Peter E Gall
420 Prayer Spring Road
Stratford CT 06614

Call Sign: KB1HRK
Timothy J Ford
468 Prospect Dr
Stratford CT 06615

Call Sign: KB1PFO
Vincent A Vizzo
119 Quail St
Stratford CT 06614

Call Sign: KB1RML
Derby Emergency
Operations Club
119 Quail St
Stratford CT 06614

Call Sign: KB1PGD
Kevin D Lyman
109 Quail Street
Stratford CT 06614

Call Sign: KB1PTU
Debra L Lyman
109 Quail Street
Stratford CT 06614

Call Sign: W1KPC
Henry W Chorobik
40 Red Coach Dr
Stratford CT 064972238

Call Sign: N1KZS
James J Ligouri Iii
170 Reut Dr
Stratford CT 06497

Call Sign: N2XQL
Kathleen H Colish
39 Richard
Stratford CT 06614

Call Sign: N2XQK
John L Colish
39 Richard Circle

Call Sign: KA1UUT
Robert R Gaulin
621 Riverdale Dr
Stratford CT 06497

Call Sign: K1TMW
Alan G Thorpe
636 Robin Ln
Stratford CT 066142483

Call Sign: W1RHF
Joseph R Koundry
60 Rockaway Ave
Stratford CT 064975630

Call Sign: KA1SDN
Donald R Graham
45 Ross Dr
Stratford CT 06497

Call Sign: KA1CJZ
Edward A Harcarik
36 Rowland St
Stratford CT 06614

Call Sign: K1SPX
Edward A Harcarik
36 Rowland St
Stratford CT 06614

Call Sign: KA2WAP
David W Moy
170 San Gabriel Avenue
Stratford CT 06614

Call Sign: N1PCL
Darleen J Koetsch
25 Sanford Pl
Stratford CT 06497

Call Sign: KA1EOU
Michael Abramowitz
221 Second Ave

Stratford CT 066157725

Call Sign: KB1WBE
Stratford Emergency
Operations Club
221 Second Avenue
Stratford CT 06615

Call Sign: W1SFD
Stratford Emergency
Operations Club
221 Second Avenue
Stratford CT 06615

Call Sign: KA1DLO
Joseph J Karcsmar
578 Sedgewick Ave.
Stratford CT 06615

Call Sign: N1FRR
Harry R Davis
93a Seminole Ln
Stratford CT 064978148

Call Sign: N1SPZ
Michael J Mardis
164 Soundview Ave
Stratford CT 06615

Call Sign: KC1EC
Cary A Cieciuch
500 Soundview Ave
Stratford CT 06615

Call Sign: W1RAR
Richard Ruggiero
1362 South Avenue
Stratford CT 06615

Call Sign: N1NCU
Stephen A Grinvalsky Ii
65 St Michael Ave
Stratford CT 06614

Call Sign: KB1KDN

Samuel A Wellington
666 Stratford Ave
Stratford CT 06615

Call Sign: KA1YQH
Jean Tate
60 Sun Ridge Ln
Stratford CT 06497

Call Sign: KB1SS
Douglas P Waterhouse
187 Sunflower Ave
Stratford CT 06497

Call Sign: N1SFA
Steven P Lewkowicz
359 Swanson Ave
Stratford CT 066144513

Call Sign: KA1TXF
James S Cebik
144 Terrill Rd
Stratford CT 06497

Call Sign: W1JRV
George V Dlugos
244 Third Ave
Stratford CT 06497

Call Sign: KA1YQG
Joanne Kopko
245 Thompson St
Stratford CT 06615

Call Sign: KB1QPW
Sterrett S Pixley
220 Victory Street
Stratford CT 0615

Call Sign: N1IZE
Daryl W Guberman
1538 W Broad St
Stratford CT 06497

Call Sign: KB1BYZ

Walter P Turek
1205 Warner Hill Rd
Stratford CT 06497

Call Sign: W1NAJ
Edward A Gruler
Warner Hill Rd
Stratford CT 06497

Call Sign: W1HBU
A F Christopher
137 Warwick Ave
Stratford CT 06615

Call Sign: KB1WFY
Dawn M Sanders
157 Warwick Avenue
Stratford CT 06615

Call Sign: KB1MXS
Richard F Guglielmo
1584 West Broad St
Stratford CT 06615

Call Sign: KB1PYZ
Richard Ruggiero
681 Wigwam Lane
Stratford CT 06614

Call Sign: K1OAN
Elbridge W Watson
70 Wilbar Dr
Stratford CT 06497

Call Sign: W1FMU
Kenneth E Hallstrom
105 Wilbar Dr
Stratford CT 06497

Call Sign: N1LXV
Edward J Butler
295 Wilbar Dr
Stratford CT 06497

Call Sign: N1JTX

Edward G Johnson
552 Wilcoxson Ave
Stratford CT 066144237

Call Sign: N1WKK
Robert R Murray
118 Winter St
Stratford CT 06497

Call Sign: K1IPW
Joseph L Rich Sr
152 Woodcrest Ave
Stratford CT 06497

Call Sign: W1GMZ
Joseph P Molloy
437 Woodstock Ave
Stratford CT 06497

Call Sign: N1RRP
Richard A Watt
320 York St
Stratford CT 066157900

Call Sign: N1TGF
Jennifer M Watt
320 York St
Stratford CT 066157900

Call Sign: N1UNX
Elizabeth A Watt
320 York St
Stratford CT 066157900

Call Sign: N1UNZ
Mary E Watt
320 York St
Stratford CT 066157900

Call Sign: KB1S
Richard A Watt
320 York St
Stratford CT 066157900

Call Sign: KA1SHN

Barbara J Moyher
Stratford CT 066150331

Call Sign: N1KT
Housatonic Amateur Radio
Club
Stratford CT 066150331

Call Sign: N1UNT
Thomas W Moyher
Stratford CT 066150331

Call Sign: N1YCZ
Kathie A Powell
Stratford CT 06615

Call Sign: N1ZZY
Jennifer L Moyher
Stratford CT 066150331

Call Sign: WE1M
Gary T Moyher
Stratford CT 06615

Call Sign: W1KAP
Kathie A Powell
Stratford CT 06615

FCC Amateur Radio Licenses in Suffield

Call Sign: KA1CEC
James H Chain
865 Boston Neck Rd
Suffield CT 06078

Call Sign: KR1STI
Kristi L Bathgate
17 Braintree Court
Suffield CT 06078

Call Sign: KB1FLI
Charles E Housner
14 Brandywine Lane
Suffield CT 01077

Call Sign: K1CTV
Warren L Wright
48 Countryside Ln
Suffield CT 06078

Call Sign: KB1UQB
Ryan E Malley
20 Devine Rd
Suffield CT 06078

Call Sign: KA1JED
William H Myers
61 East St N
Suffield CT 06078

Call Sign: KA1ONZ
Thomas M Nowak
819 East St N
Suffield CT 06078

Call Sign: KA1MZE
Kenneth A Nebel
85 First St
Suffield CT 06078

Call Sign: K1WB
William A Borchers
460 Hale St
Suffield CT 06078

Call Sign: KB1CWS
Christopher E Basile
528 Hale St
Suffield CT 060782504

Call Sign: KA1OYO
Carlyle S Dewey
32c Harmon Dr
Suffield CT 06078

Call Sign: K1STP
Gerard J Surprenant
42b Harmon Dr
Suffield CT 06078

Call Sign: KC1AG
William S Shipp
1195 Hill St
Suffield CT 06078

Call Sign: AA1CG
Douglas A Wolfe Sr
209 Kent Ave
Suffield CT 06078

Call Sign: W1RFS
Robert F Siano
68 Kildeer Ln
Suffield CT 06078

Call Sign: KA1ERT
Marcus G Deane Sr
820 Mapleton Ave
Suffield CT 06078

Call Sign: N1AEH
Gregory D Stoddard
1500 Mapleton Ave
Suffield CT 06078

Call Sign: KB1RMU
Donald W Miner
1855 Mapleton Ave
Suffield CT 06078

Call Sign: KA1AJZ
Arthur L Fisher
6 Maybury Rd
Suffield CT 060782049

Call Sign: KA1PLL
Robert S Brooks
418 N Main St
Suffield CT 06078

Call Sign: AB1DB
Robert S Brooks
418 N Main St
Suffield CT 06078

Call Sign: AB1RB
Robert S Brooks
418 N Main St
Suffield CT 06078

Call Sign: KB1VDD
Suffield Emergency
Communications Team
418 North Main Street
Suffield CT 06078

Call Sign: N1QHE
Glenn O Pugh
1051 North St
Suffield CT 06078

Call Sign: KA1HTK
Ralph A Zavarella
1357 North St
Suffield CT 06078

Call Sign: K1WVX
William P Wing
59 Poole Rd
Suffield CT 06078

Call Sign: KB1VBO
Matthew R Willett
69 Poole Rd
Suffield CT 06078

Call Sign: WB1CKF
Marc J Rohrbacher
462 Remington St
Suffield CT 06078

Call Sign: KE1DM
Jorge A Messmer
7 Riverview Drive
Suffield CT 06078

Call Sign: K1BFG
Robert A Payne
32 Riverview Terrace

Suffield CT 06078

Call Sign: KA1ZCY
Howard L Pomeroy
183 Russell Ave
Suffield CT 06078

Call Sign: KA1FOP
William S Robotham Sr
6 Sandgate Ct
Suffield CT 06078

Call Sign: K1AZ
James S Grant
625 Taintor St
Suffield CT 06078

Call Sign: W1CTF
Bingham G Day
287 Thompsonville Rd
Suffield CT 06078

Call Sign: KB1AOO
Stuart L Brown
685 Thompsonville Rd
Suffield CT 06078

Call Sign: KB1KTC
John G Nicholas
584 Thrall Ave
Suffield CT 06078

Call Sign: W1JGN
John G Nicholas
584 Thrall Ave
Suffield CT 06078

Call Sign: KB1DNI
Glen R Garrity Sr
713a Thrall Avenue
Suffield CT 06078

Call Sign: KA1MJM
John Langh Jr
80 Valley View Dr

Suffield CT 060781424

Call Sign: K2SJY
Burton A Weinberg
90 Woodland Ter
Suffield CT 06078

Call Sign: K1CYD
George B Corcoran Jr
Suffield CT 06078

Call Sign: N1QKT
Ron F Tautic
Suffield CT 06078

Call Sign: KB1ONM
Richard Hodge
Suffield CT 06078

FCC Amateur Radio Licenses in Taconic

Call Sign: KA1VIB
Walter J Lang Sr
Preston Rd
Taconic CT 06079

FCC Amateur Radio Licenses in Tariffville

Call Sign: KA1ZDJ
John J Sarapina Jr
27 Church St
Tariffville CT 06081

Call Sign: KB1PRM
Adam B Libros
8b Elm Street
Tariffville CT 06081

Call Sign: W5AER
Arthur E Roberts
5 Hartland Road
Tariffville CT 060819612

Call Sign: KB1QJX
David O Blackford
42 Hayes Rd
Tariffville CT 06081

Call Sign: N1TCO
Patrick H Fuery
118 Hunters Ave
Taftville CT 06380

Call Sign: KB1DTE
Albert M Bolduc
25 Main St Apt 1a
Tariffville CT 060810375

Call Sign: KB1DHA
John P Aberg
12 N 3rd Ave
Taftville CT 06380

Call Sign: N1WGJ
Charles N Miclette
13 S B St
Taftville CT 06380

Call Sign: N1XOM
Brian C Donovan
14 Teal Circle
Tariffville CT 06081

Call Sign: N1EEH
Cory Reynolds
43 Tunxis Rd
Tariffville CT 06081

Call Sign: WB1ANE
Walter R Banzhaf
26 West Point Ter
Tariffville CT 06081

Call Sign: KA1FUW
Stephen P Pitaro
23 Wood Duck Ln
Tariffville CT 06081

Call Sign: N1HWR
Donald R Skinner
22 Wooster Rd
Tariffville CT 06081

Call Sign: KB1KIU
Christopher J Britting
Tariffville CT 06081

FCC Amateur Radio Licenses in Terryville

Call Sign: N1JVT
Pauline H Clukey
16 Abbott Avenue
Terryville CT 06786

Call Sign: WA1QHZ
Truman W Gustafson
6 Adams Dr
Terryville CT 06786

Call Sign: N1VCQ
Richard D Prior
62 Allentown Rd
Terryville CT 06786

Call Sign: K1EM
Clement P Paskus
4 Arrow Drive
Terryville CT 06786

Call Sign: N1HDJ
Cathleen M Paskus
4 Arrow Drive
Terryville CT 06786

Call Sign: KA2UCP
Thomas P Filecco Iii
163 Bemis St
Terryville CT 06786

Call Sign: KB1LKV
Thomas P Filecco Iii
163 Bemis St

Terryville CT 06786

Call Sign: KB1QFP
Carol A Filecco
163 Bemis St
Terryville CT 06786

Call Sign: W1WSO
Thomas P Filecco Iii
163 Bemis St
Terryville CT 06786

Call Sign: N1VC
Vincent L Coppola Jr
6 Bobbin Rd
Terryville CT 06786

Call Sign: KA1VIT
James E Coviello
11 Burnham St Apt 8
Terryville CT 06786

Call Sign: KB1GHV
Robert J Luther
80 Canal St
Terryville CT 06786

Call Sign: KB1GLM
Stephen J Luther
80 Canal St
Terryville CT 06786

Call Sign: WB1DAY
Robert A Klim
93 Dorothy Ln
Terryville CT 06786

Call Sign: N1VPN
Henry P Patnode
116 E Plymouth Rd
Terryville CT 06786

Call Sign: KB1CVK
Keith F Piwczynski
6 East Orchard St

Terryville CT 06786

Call Sign: KB1BQS
Students Of Plymouth Arc
21 Fall Mountain Lake Rd
Terryville CT 06786

Call Sign: KA1YBT
Michael T De Almeida
8 Fall Mountain Terrace
Terryville CT 06786

Call Sign: N1SPF
Howard E Miller
110 Fall Mt Lake Rd
Terryville CT 06786

Call Sign: K1TKP
John G White
16 Gosinski Park
Terryville CT 06786

Call Sign: KA1ZSR
Rosalie A Myers
9 Green Dr
Terryville CT 06786

Call Sign: KA1ZSS
Louis G Myers
9 Green Dr
Terryville CT 06786

Call Sign: N1YZR
John A Neveu
94 Harwington Ave
Terryville CT 06786

Call Sign: W1JAS
Joseph A Sanada Iii
27 Hillside Ave
Terryville CT 06786

Call Sign: N1DBK
Michael S Suchinski
33 Lake Forest Rd

Terryville CT 06786

Call Sign: N1OUR
Edwin J Gangloff Jr
14 Lovely St
Terryville CT 06786

Call Sign: WB1DAM
William E Broadwell
27 Lynn Ave
Terryville CT 06786

Call Sign: KB1UKM
Joseph T Cherneskie
27 Main St
Terryville CT 06786

Call Sign: N1BBH
Warren E Dion
412 Main St Apt 16
Terryville CT 067861340

Call Sign: KD1XH
Steven D Cahill
115 Main St Apt 4
Terryville CT 06786

Call Sign: N1CTH
William O Allread
16 Makara St
Terryville CT 06786

Call Sign: KB1DWT
Patricia A Daigle
27 Matthews St
Terryville CT 06786

Call Sign: N1WPB
Steven R Daigle
27 Matthews St
Terryville CT 06786

Call Sign: KB1VMY
Richard P Kreidel
12 Meadow St

Terryville CT 06786

Call Sign: K1RPK
Richard P Kreidel
12 Meadow St
Terryville CT 06786

Call Sign: KA1CIF
Richard T Lickwar
92 N Main St App 2
Terryville CT 06786

Call Sign: WB1DZU
Philip J Mazur
170 Old Waterbury Rd
Terryville CT 06786

Call Sign: KB1RRH
Michael S Hill
54 Pine View Ct
Terryville CT 06786

Call Sign: N1OUS
Kevin J Engle
205 Preston Road
Terryville CT 06786

Call Sign: W1ICV
Jane P Anderson
45 Ridge Rd
Terryville CT 06786

Call Sign: W1SP
C Vernon Anderson
45 Ridge Rd
Terryville CT 06786

Call Sign: WB1FUU
Richard A Grem
165 Summit View Rd
Terryville CT 06786

Call Sign: N1OGD
Robert D Engle
115 Town Hill Rd

Terryville CT 06786

Call Sign: K1KFX
Richard J Bellefleur
Box 148 Town Hill Rd
Terryville CT 06786

Call Sign: KA1AVV
Josephine S Malley
2 Virginia Rd
Terryville CT 06786

Call Sign: KI1D
Raymond T Malley Jr
2 Virginia Rd
Terryville CT 06786

FCC Amateur Radio Licenses in Thomaston

Call Sign: N1TTI
Gerald E Mosimann Jr
278 Atwood Rd
Thomaston CT 067871205

Call Sign: WA1MJT
Douglas W Benedict
45 Babbitt Rd
Thomaston CT 06787

Call Sign: WA1WPJ
Randal B Hathway
158 Babbitt Rd
Thomaston CT 06787

Call Sign: N1UHY
Timothy J Polowy
71 Babbitt Road
Thomaston CT 06787

Call Sign: KB1IKF
Franklin E Brody
Rr 2 Box 568
Thomaston CT 067870568

Call Sign: N1BBQ
Franklin E Brody
Rr 2 Box 568
Thomaston CT 067870568

Call Sign: WB3BEX
William M Mutter
150 Bristol St
Thomaston CT 067870285

Call Sign: KA1ICY
William J Arnauckas Jr
131 Cedar Mountain Rd
Thomaston CT 06878

Call Sign: KA1VGX
Lisa A Celone
348 Cedar Mtn Rd
Thomaston CT 06787

Call Sign: N1GBE
Ralph V Celone
348 Cedar Mtn Rd
Thomaston CT 06787

Call Sign: KB1WBA
Veronica A Celone
348 Cedar Mtn Rd
Thomaston CT 06787

Call Sign: KB1PJH
Scott D Stevenson
363 D Welton Way
Thomaston CT 06787

Call Sign: W1EQD
John Rahuba
120 Edwin Lane
Thomaston CT 06787

Call Sign: WB1HHF
Gregg J Rahuba Sr
120 Edwin Ln
Thomaston CT 06787

Call Sign: N1WUA
Ernest D Blanchard
578 Fenn Rd
Thomaston CT 06787

Call Sign: KA1TCI
Mathew Thier Jr
21 Future Rd
Thomaston CT 06787

Call Sign: KB1CGW
Gary D Kingsbury
175 Hickory Hill Rd
Thomaston CT 06787

Call Sign: AA1SR
Hugo L Vilkaitis
417 High St
Thomaston CT 06787

Call Sign: N1OLT
Michael T Daniels
881 High St Ext
Thomaston CT 06787

Call Sign: KA1IKZ
Joseph B Kelley
180 Jackson St
Thomaston CT 06787

Call Sign: N1ZMZ
Anthony Barbera
98 Judson St
Thomaston CT 06787

Call Sign: KU1M
John J Polowy
19 Marine St
Thomaston CT 06787

Call Sign: KU1L
Lawrence S Polowy
21 Marine St
Thomaston CT 06787

Call Sign: KU1K
William M Polowy
570 Moosehorn Rd
Thomaston CT 06787

Call Sign: KB1UOH
Charles J Russell
143 Pine Hill Rd 8a
Thomaston CT 06787

Call Sign: KA1JVM
Elisabeth K Bazin
64 Pleasant St
Thomaston CT 06787

Call Sign: KA1KBU
Robert J Bazin
64 Pleasant St
Thomaston CT 06787

Call Sign: KB1INE
Alan K Jayson
360 South Main
Thomaston CT 06787

Call Sign: WD5T
Thomas A Mannino
120 Valley View Road
Thomaston CT 06787

Call Sign: N1SIK
Stewart G Stanley Jr
Thomaston CT 06787

Call Sign: KB1GGT
Charles D Smith
Thomaston CT 067870221

Call Sign: K1CDS
Charles D Smith
Thomaston CT 067870221

Call Sign: K1HMR
Scott D Stevenson
Thomaston CT 06787

FCC Amateur Radio
Licenses in Thompson

Call Sign: KA1NDW
Elias Angelis
91 A Church St
Thompson CT 06277

Call Sign: W1KVM
Albin A Sheputa
Marianapolis School 26
Chase Rd
Thompson CT 062770368

Call Sign: K1ZXX
Gary A Hopkins
129 Church St
Thompson CT 06277

Call Sign: KB1NFZ
Eric R Fogg
38 County Home Rd Box B
Thompson CT 06277

Call Sign: WA1OEH
Vernon W Smith
42 E Thompson Rd
Thompson CT 06277

Call Sign: WA1OEI
Mildred L Smith
42 E Thompson Rd
Thompson CT 06277

Call Sign: N1RCW
Richard G Morrill
22 Green Ln
Thompson CT 06277

Call Sign: KB1VBZ
William R Poirier
7 Island View Terrace
Thompson CT 06277

Call Sign: K1WRP
William R Poirier
7 Island View Terrace
Thompson CT 06277

Call Sign: K1APE
Donald F Amirault
66 Labonte Rd Rr 1
Thompson CT 06277

Call Sign: N1PTA
James E Verge
181 Porter Plain Rd
Thompson CT 06277

Call Sign: KB1LHK
John A Szamocki
310 Quaddick Town Farm
Rd
Thompson CT 06277

Call Sign: K1CSP
John A Szamocki
310 Quaddick Town Farm
Rd
Thompson CT 06277

Call Sign: KB1PUM
Julie M Szamocki
310 Quaddick Town Farm
Rd
Thompson CT 06277

Call Sign: W1YQD
Wilfred J Arsenault
Box 129 Rich Rd
Thompson CT 06277

Call Sign: KB1LYR
Eric E Lariviere
102 Spicer Rd
Thompson CT 06277

Call Sign: KB1PRW
Timothy R Morin

128 Spicer Rd
Thompson CT 06277

Call Sign: K1GZE
Gerald B Stackpole
Sunset Hill Rd
Thompson CT 06277

Call Sign: KA1JKB
Ronald E O Grady
Thompson CT 06277

FCC Amateur Radio Licenses in Tobrington

Call Sign: W1WRI
George F Ruth
176 Westside Ln
Tobrington CT 06790

FCC Amateur Radio Licenses in Tolland

Call Sign: KA1TQC
Stephen C O Neal
32 Alfred Dr
Tolland CT 06084

Call Sign: W1GPO
John R Haserick Jr
25 Alta Vista Ave
Tolland CT 060842547

Call Sign: N1RNO
Joel Fontanella
14 Anthony Rd
Tolland CT 06084

Call Sign: N1NBL
David J Kirol
194 Anthony Rd
Tolland CT 06084

Call Sign: KB1GAQ
Edward J Levesque

248 Anthony Rd
Tolland CT 06084

Call Sign: N1ZLY
Linda M Rankin
67 Autumn Dr
Tolland CT 06084

Call Sign: KB1TIO
Steven D Morin
42 Avebury Ln
Tolland CT 06084

Call Sign: N1SKD
John D Lunderville
370 Babcock Rd
Tolland CT 06084

Call Sign: N1UAU
Janice G Lunderville
370 Babcock Rd
Tolland CT 06084

Call Sign: KA1KSD
Leonard A Bach
192 Bald Hill Rd
Tolland CT 06084

Call Sign: K1RIK
Richard C Osgood
12 Barbara Rd
Tolland CT 06084

Call Sign: KB1BTP
Richard C Osgood
12 Barbara Rd.
Tolland CT 06084

Call Sign: N1ZXL
Gregory J Vinci
239 Baxter St
Tolland CT 06084

Call Sign: KB1PYS
Irene M Vinci

239 Baxter St
Tolland CT 060843908

Call Sign: K1BXC
Daniel L Burbank
77 Carriage Dr
Tolland CT 06084

Call Sign: KB1EYS
Joan G Burbank
77 Carriage Dr
Tolland CT 06084

Call Sign: KB1MLG
Peder S Johnson
138 Cook Rd
Tolland CT 06084

Call Sign: WA1VOA
Paul R Umbdenstock
102 Crystal Lake Rd
Tolland CT 06084

Call Sign: KB1TKW
Nathan L Robinson
360 Crystal Lake Rd
Tolland CT 06084

Call Sign: K1GT
George L Titus
40 Elizabeth Lane
Tolland CT 06084

Call Sign: KB1QJT
Brian A Knight
92 Fox Ridge Kane
Tolland CT 06084

Call Sign: KB1BAK
Brian A Knight
92 Fox Ridge Kane
Tolland CT 06084

Call Sign: N1XTK
Keith A Randino

56 Garnet Ridge Dr
Tolland CT 06084

Call Sign: KB1KUQ
Kyle A Randino
56 Garnet Ridge Dr
Tolland CT 06084

Call Sign: KA1DTG
John W Gorsky Jr
188 Gehring Rd
Tolland CT 06084

Call Sign: WA1KQJ
Richard S Parker
459 Gehring Rd
Tolland CT 06084

Call Sign: KB1UVC
Fno1xt Contesters
38 Gerber Dr
Tolland CT 06084

Call Sign: W3XTT
Fno1xt Contesters
38 Gerber Dr
Tolland CT 06084

Call Sign: KD1JK
Philip G Dooley Jr
192 Goose Lane
Tolland CT 060843821

Call Sign: KB1VQQ
Todd M Rolland
265 Grahaber Rd
Tolland CT 06084

Call Sign: W1TMR
Todd M Rolland
265 Grahaber Rd
Tolland CT 06084

Call Sign: KA1YOV
Michelle A Amsden

23 Grant Hill Rd
Tolland CT 06084

Call Sign: KB1CEP
Tandy Employees Amateur
Radio Station Ct
23 Grant Hill Rd
Tolland CT 060843408

Call Sign: KB1LNV
International Single
Sidebanders
23 Grant Rd
Tolland CT 06084

Call Sign: N1JVS
Bonnie L Johnson
268 Hartford Tpke Unit B2
Tolland CT 06084

Call Sign: KB1TVL
Brian K Gay
9 Hillcrest Dr
Tolland CT 06084

Call Sign: WA1UYM
Francis J Pietlock Sr
432 Hunter Rd
Tolland CT 060842110

Call Sign: AC1V
Donald A Paolucci
139 Hurlbut Rd
Tolland CT 06084

Call Sign: K1BVY
Arthur D Gorshel
65 Kendall Mtn Rd
Tolland CT 06084

Call Sign: KA1QAR
Virginia B Cohen
238 Kozley Rd
Tolland CT 06084

Call Sign: W1CTX
Todd R Cohen
238 Kozley Rd
Tolland CT 06084

Call Sign: K1CPJ
Robert A Cohen
Kozley Rd
Tolland CT 06084

Call Sign: N1ASP
Jesse M Giammarino
23 Lemek Lane
Tolland CT 06084

Call Sign: KB1LKB
Frank J Fascione
63 Loehr Road
Tolland CT 06084

Call Sign: K1MAA
Frank J Fascione
63 Loehr Road
Tolland CT 06084

Call Sign: N1WYG
Dustin T Stachelsky
609 Merror Rd Apt 25
Tolland CT 06084

Call Sign: N1RIO
Herbert L Terban
483 Merrow Rd
Tolland CT 06084

Call Sign: N1UCA
Michael D Terban
483 Merrow Rd
Tolland CT 06084

Call Sign: W1JZC
Elwin B Gleason
150 New Rd
Tolland CT 06084

Call Sign: KB1PYQ
Eugene Curylo
17 Oakwood Lane
Tolland CT 06084

Call Sign: KB1RSQ
Eugene Curylo
17 Oakwood Lane
Tolland CT 06084

Call Sign: KB1JMV
James W Tuttle
195 Old Post Rd
Tolland CT 06084

Call Sign: KB1JMW
Seale W Tuttle
195 Old Post Rd
Tolland CT 06084

Call Sign: KB1TTT
Seale W Tuttle
195 Old Post Rd
Tolland CT 06084

Call Sign: WA1QFM
Daniel D Allen
520 Old Post Rd
Tolland CT 06084

Call Sign: N1FNV
Walter A Dimmock
614 Old Post Rd
Tolland CT 06084

Call Sign: KB1AGC
Robert G Bowser
177 Old Post Road
Tolland CT 06084

Call Sign: KA1RLA
Steven C Dube
202 Old Stafford Rd
Tolland CT 06084

Call Sign: KB1PYO
Thomas L Lebel
57 Pepperwood Dr
Tolland CT 06084

Call Sign: KA1ZE
Stanley W Hilinski Iii
17 Pilgrim Dr
Tolland CT 06084

Call Sign: KB1EYV
John F Commins Iii
67 Pine Hill Rd
Tolland CT 06084

Call Sign: KC4OXF
Riley H Cook
64 Plains Rd
Tolland CT 060842265

Call Sign: WB1CCF
Charles A Pitts
174 Plains Road
Tolland CT 06084

Call Sign: KB1QNQ
Adam N Conner
38 Reed Rd
Tolland CT 06084

Call Sign: AC1B
Roy H Auclair
123 Reed Rd
Tolland CT 060843239

Call Sign: W1QAP
Bernard W Smith Jr
112 Rhodes Rd
Tolland CT 06084

Call Sign: K1VI
Michael J Bragg
75 Robbie Rd
Tolland CT 06084

Call Sign: KA1YMG
Jeffrey M Bragg
75 Robbie Road
Tolland CT 06084

Call Sign: WO1C
Michael J Bragg
75 Robbie Road
Tolland CT 06084

Call Sign: N8HLE
Douglas D De Maw
320 S River Rd
Tolland CT 06084

Call Sign: W1CER
Douglas D Demaw
320 S River Rd
Tolland CT 06084

Call Sign: KB1VRL
Christopher Northrop
376 S River Rd
Tolland CT 06084

Call Sign: W1FB
Central Connecticut Qrp
Club
320 S River Road
Tolland CT 06084

Call Sign: KA1OCR
Bruce Feller
50 Shanda Lane
Tolland CT 06084

Call Sign: N1ZJM
Stephen A Fair
71 Shenipsit Lake Rd
Tolland CT 06084

Call Sign: KB1PYP
Bruce E Cropper
33 Sherry Circle
Tolland CT 06084

Call Sign: K1BEC
Bruce E Cropper
33 Sherry Circle
Tolland CT 06084

Call Sign: KA1UTK
Zbigniew J Kolodziejczak
13 Stacy Lane
Tolland CT 06084

Call Sign: KB4IMO
William N Eccles
106 Sugar Hill Rd.
Tolland CT 06084

Call Sign: KA1VWL
Richard D Sale
34 Summit Dr
Tolland CT 06084

Call Sign: KA1TSG
Sean T Donahue
46 Susan Dr
Tolland CT 06084

Call Sign: N1WLO
Monica A Rinaldi-Ellison
7 Tolland Farms Road
Tolland CT 06084

Call Sign: W3CNY
Monica A Rinaldi-Ellison
7 Tolland Farms Road
Tolland CT 06084

Call Sign: KB1PYT
Douglas A Racicot
21 Tolland Green
Tolland CT 06084

Call Sign: KB1DWZ
Donald S Grant
402 Tolland Stage Rd
Tolland CT 060842922

Call Sign: KA1TSB
Kevin C Clapp
476 Tolland Stage Rd
Tolland CT 06084

Call Sign: W1BTK
Robert L Kaylor Sr
1372 Tolland Stage Rd
Tolland CT 06084

Call Sign: N1NUG
Robert E Zielfelder Jr
64 Tolland Turnpike
Tolland CT 06084

Call Sign: N1UDX
Nicholas J Bourikas
72 Torry Rd
Tolland CT 06084

Call Sign: KC9BW
Brian G Clark
136 Torry Rd
Tolland CT 06084

Call Sign: K1PSY
Albert J Ruops
33 Vaalcom Rd
Tolland CT 06084

Call Sign: KB1FOA
Kevin M Romanick
183 Walbridge Hill Rd
Tolland CT 06084

Call Sign: KB1GKS
Odile R Romanick
183 Walbridge Hill Rd
Tolland CT 06084

Call Sign: K1KEV
Kevin M Romanick
183 Walbridge Hill Rd
Tolland CT 06084

Call Sign: KA1JIU
Richard P Mozzer
211 Wallbridge Hill Rd
Tolland CT 06084

Call Sign: KG4AVA
Joseph M Vesel
8 Winterbourne View
Tolland CT 06084

Call Sign: W1JMV
Joseph M Vesel
8 Winterbourne View
Tolland CT 06084

Call Sign: KB1WQV
Louis M Gugliotti
Tolland CT 06084

Call Sign: W1ZXP
Louis M Gugliotti
Tolland CT 06084

FCC Amateur Radio Licenses in Torrington

Call Sign: W1DND
Attilio L Avallone Jr
30 Aetna Ave
Torrington CT 06790

Call Sign: WB1CQI
Martin H Weingart
41 Aetna Ave
Torrington CT 06790

Call Sign: WB1CQH
Peter R Russo
127 Aetna Ave
Torrington CT 06790

Call Sign: KB1VVB
Thomas P Russo
127 Aetna Ave

Torrington CT 06790

Call Sign: N1HRH
Kenneth A Frizzo
217 Albrecht Rd
Torrington CT 06790

Call Sign: N1PSO
Mark C N Libby
334 Allison Dr
Torrington CT 06790

Call Sign: KB1GGN
Henry P Heim
20 Allison Drive
Torrington CT 06790

Call Sign: KB1ER
Joanna C Nettleton
122 Apter Dr
Torrington CT 06790

Call Sign: KB1OIF
Robert F Albreada Jr
25 Auburn Way
Torrington CT 06790

Call Sign: N1ZHK
Leon A Deloy Jr
105 B Camp Wahnee Rd
Torrington CT 06790

Call Sign: AA1CX
Alan C Pollinger
37 Ben Porte Ter
Torrington CT 06790

Call Sign: N1HBC
Alexander B Kilpatrick
32 Berry St
Torrington CT 06790

Call Sign: KB1UOK
David Goessinger
167 Berry St

Torrington CT 06790

Call Sign: N1PNR
Kevin C Gundlach
118 Bradford Rd
Torrington CT 06790

Call Sign: K1OLR
John D Tarter
156 Bradford Road
Torrington CT 06790

Call Sign: N1OUQ
Frederick C Hudak
33 Brightwood Ave
Torrington CT 06790

Call Sign: KB1KWV
Larry R Tashjian
398 Brightwood Ave
Torrington CT 06790

Call Sign: KB1NNL
James M Rourke
58 Carroll Dr
Torrington CT 06790

Call Sign: N1JMR
James M Rourke
58 Carroll Dr
Torrington CT 06790

Call Sign: KA1ZZE
Charles W Mitchell
78 Chelsea Ct
Torrington CT 06790

Call Sign: KB1CGC
Tabitha L Quinn
32 Christine St
Torrington CT 067905438

Call Sign: KA1OBJ
Jerry P Carillo Jr
47 Circle Dr

Torrington CT 06790

Call Sign: N1TVM
Michal S Rentschler
364 Circle Drive
Torrington CT 06790

Call Sign: N1HW
Howard W Baldwin Jr
97 Coolidge Ave
Torrington CT 06790

Call Sign: KB1JTN
Patrick T Baldwin
97 Coolidge Ave
Torrington CT 06790

Call Sign: K1HOW
Howard W Baldwin Jr
97 Coolidge Ave
Torrington CT 06790

Call Sign: KW1B
Howard W Baldwin Jr
97 Coolidge Ave
Torrington CT 06790

Call Sign: N1XQF
Jeffrey M Fitzgerald
27 Cooper St
Torrington CT 06790

Call Sign: W1LUP
Gordon F Benedict
158 Cypress Ct
Torrington CT 067903071

Call Sign: N1WUB
Terrence A Mahoney
8 Deercrest Dr
Torrington CT 06790

Call Sign: KA1IQ
Arthur B Palazzini Jr
49 Dibble St

Torrington CT 06790

Call Sign: KA1YSV
Edgar F Effs
41 Doman Dr
Torrington CT 06790

Call Sign: K1DXK
David Bock
2119 E Main St
Torrington CT 06790

Call Sign: KA1ZQV
John R Lukasavage Jr
106 E Pearl St
Torrington CT 06790

Call Sign: N1LOP
Anna B Lukasavage
106 E Pearl St
Torrington CT 06790

Call Sign: N1LOR
John R Lukasavage
106 E Pearl St
Torrington CT 06790

Call Sign: KB1LFI
Matthew M Dunn
85 Eastwood Rd
Torrington CT 06790

Call Sign: KA1TCJ
Lee W Carter
139 Edgewood Dr
Torrington CT 06790

Call Sign: KA1LTO
Jeanne E Senack
149 Edgewood Dr
Torrington CT 06790

Call Sign: KB1NML
John E Beauregard
188 Edgewood Dr

Torrington CT 06790

Call Sign: WA1RBL
Joseph R Eicher
73 Elmira Ave
Torrington CT 06790

Call Sign: KA1ZIK
Roland Berube Sr
61 Evans St
Torrington CT 06790

Call Sign: KB1DJM
James E Rebman
115 Fairlawn Dr
Torrington CT 06790

Call Sign: KA1GLP
Sidney S Axelrod
162 Fairlawn Dr
Torrington CT 06790

Call Sign: K1DXA
Philip W Bittel
329 Fairlawn Dr
Torrington CT 06790

Call Sign: KB1OJQ
John S Alexson
141 Farmstead Ln
Torrington CT 06790

Call Sign: WA1TNR
Christopher W Hafey
16 Field Street
Torrington CT 067904934

Call Sign: N1SAH
Peter J Narducci
53 Frederick Street
Torrington CT 06790

Call Sign: N1PJN
Peter J Narducci
53 Frederick Street

Torrington CT 06790

Torrington CT 06790

Torrington CT 06790

Call Sign: W1OQM
Anthony P Cisowski
217 Goshen Rd
Torrington CT 06790

Call Sign: KB1MYN
Joseph M Pathe
71 Holley Pl
Torrington CT 06790

Call Sign: K1DUV
Albert R Febbroriello
847 Litchfield St
Torrington CT 06790

Call Sign: W1TB
Gary J Della Ghelfa
112 Greenfield Drive
Torrington CT 06790

Call Sign: N1RDG
John J Rusckowski
170 Homestead Rd
Torrington CT 06790

Call Sign: KB1FTP
Robert S Magyar
115 Loretta Dr
Torrington CT 06790

Call Sign: KB1RAJ
Jeremy D French
428 Greenwood Rd
Torrington CT 06790

Call Sign: N1CDW
Dominic D Angelo
A 52 Hunter Crt
Torrington CT 06790

Call Sign: KB1VIQ
John J Papp
187 Lovers Lane Unit 29
Torrington CT 06790

Call Sign: NU1B
Stephen B Claar
315 Guerdat Rd
Torrington CT 06790

Call Sign: W1RWC
Richard W Carter
75 Lafayette St
Torrington CT 06790

Call Sign: KA1EXW
Richard W Kost
62 Lynn Hgts Rd
Torrington CT 06790

Call Sign: KB1RRI
Robert S Baldwin
453 Guerdat Rd
Torrington CT 06790

Call Sign: WB2TTA
Philip H Levy
173 Ledge Dr
Torrington CT 06790

Call Sign: WB1HHC
John J Kucera Jr
71 Margerie St
Torrington CT 067903649

Call Sign: KB1ETV
Theodore J Wanatowicz
270 High St Apt B-5
Torrington CT 06790

Call Sign: KB1DIQ
Suzanne M Mc Cray
121 Lindberg St
Torrington CT 067903434

Call Sign: N1MUL
Karen M Veronneau
330 Meyer Rd
Torrington CT 06790

Call Sign: KB1NSC
Leo A Martigneni
173 Highfield Dr
Torrington CT 067905826

Call Sign: N1ZVL
John T Mc Cray
121 Lindberg St
Torrington CT 067903434

Call Sign: N1ZXW
Jonathon O Veronneau
330 Meyer Rd
Torrington CT 06790

Call Sign: N1WLW
Robert M Dileo
134 Hillandale Blvd
Torrington CT 06790

Call Sign: N1ZVM
Shawn R Mc Cray
121 Lindberg St
Torrington CT 06790

Call Sign: WA1JBR
Douglas J Veronneau
330 Meyer Rd
Torrington CT 06790

Call Sign: KB1DHP
Gerrard A Amoroso
38 Hoffman St

Call Sign: N1ZVN
Wayne K Mc Cray
121 Lindberg St

Call Sign: KB1BBY
Scott W Frazer
185 Migeon Ave.

Torrington CT 06790

Call Sign: KB1OMZ
Cq Radio Club
1881 Mountain Ave
Torrington CT 06790

Call Sign: WA1EOC
Cq Radio Club
1881 Mountain Ave
Torrington CT 06790

Call Sign: K1DAV
David B Hyatt
1881 Mountain Rd
Torrington CT 06790

Call Sign: N1LOS
Gary A Rosa
231 New Litchfield St
Torrington CT 06790

Call Sign: N1UHX
Michael J Polowy
68 New Litchfield Street
Apt 1
Torrington CT 06790

Call Sign: K1FIX
Thomas A Fix
554 Norfolk Rd
Torrington CT 06790

Call Sign: KA1ZPT
Brian B Fix
554 Norfolk Rd
Torrington CT 06790

Call Sign: KB1MPR
Thomas J Preato Jr
1895 Norfolk Rd
Torrington CT 067902011

Call Sign: N1LKB
Robert F Stewart Iii

21-4 Oak Ave Ext
Torrington CT 06790

Call Sign: K1HOW
Howard W Baldwin Jr
140 Oak Ave.
Torrington CT 06790

Call Sign: KB1NNS
Russell E Masters
199 Oak Dr
Torrington CT 06790

Call Sign: N1PCP
Robert J Buchenholz
11 Oregon St
Torrington CT 06790

Call Sign: N1RFP
Ann A Buchenholz
11 Oregon St
Torrington CT 06790

Call Sign: N1RIC
Curt M Buchenholz
11 Oregon St
Torrington CT 06790

Call Sign: N1RIE,
Bruce R Buchenholz
11 Oregon St
Torrington CT 06790

Call Sign: KB1JDV
Paul J Winzler
77 Oxford Way
Torrington CT 06790

Call Sign: KA1JAZ
Thomas J English
21 Parson Ter
Torrington CT 06790

Call Sign: N1SBY
Lawrence T Kelson Jr

39 Prospect St
Torrington CT 06790

Call Sign: W1CH
Robert D Corbett
46 Prospect St
Torrington CT 06790

Call Sign: KA1NLU
Gail M Louchen
431 Prospect St
Torrington CT 06790

Call Sign: K1GML
Gail M Louchen
431 Prospect Street
Torrington CT 06790

Call Sign: KB1FJO
William P Schouten
112 Queens Rd
Torrington CT 06790

Call Sign: KB1IPL
Howard W Baldwin Jr
480 Riverside Ave
Torrington CT 06790

Call Sign: AB1BI
Howard W Baldwin Jr
480 Riverside Ave
Torrington CT 06790

Call Sign: N1HET
John F Piddock
251 Riverside Ave #1
Torrington CT 06790

Call Sign: KB1PVG
Miguel A De Jesus
342 Riverside Ave 1fl
Torrington CT 06790

Call Sign: KA6OEY
Debra L Chastain

357 Riverside Ave.
Torrington CT 067904529

Call Sign: KA1IO
Thomas F Eucalitto
20 Roulin St
Torrington CT 06790

Call Sign: KA1IFN
Beatrice E Colangelo
699 S Main St
Torrington CT 06790

Call Sign: W1TMU
Salvatore M Savoia
31 Scoville St
Torrington CT 06790

Call Sign: N1LGV
Brian E Kiernan
113 Settlers Ln
Torrington CT 06790

Call Sign: WA1ZOO
William A Shaffer
80 Shirley Rd
Torrington CT 067905916

Call Sign: KB1JAH
Margaret R Shaffer
80 Shirley Rd
Torrington CT 06790

Call Sign: K1KEA
Harry A Langenheim Jr
258 South Main St
Torrington CT 06790

Call Sign: WB1AKJ
Gregory J Peters Jr
67 Stoneridge Dr
Torrington CT 067903219

Call Sign: AA1HK
Diane M Johnstone

33 Sunset Ln
Torrington CT 067904235

Call Sign: K1BCI
C Q Radio Club
33 Sunset Ln
Torrington CT 067904235

Call Sign: WB1COB
David J Johnstone
33 Sunset Ln
Torrington CT 067904235

Call Sign: WV1M
Richard N Clukey Jr
261 Sycamore Drive
Torrington CT 06790

Call Sign: KB1MZR
Thomas A Latosek
31 Tognalli Drive
Torrington CT 06790

Call Sign: KA1LPL
Bernard F Yeski
249 Torcan Dr
Torrington CT 06790

Call Sign: KB1CVJ
Timothy N Quinn
3674 Torringford St.
Torrington CT 067905438

Call Sign: KA1FGR
Howard F Mitchell
116 Torringford W St
Torrington CT 06790

Call Sign: W1HQM
Donald F Thomas Jr
124 Torringford West St
Torrington CT 06790

Call Sign: KB1PRQ
Michael E Falls

171 Torringford West St
Torrington CT 06790

Call Sign: KA1LTP
Gerry R Levesque
193 Torringford West St
Torrington CT 06790

Call Sign: N1CXZ
Richard M Box
2251 Torringford West St
Torrington CT 067902520

Call Sign: N1BXB
Arnold W Staire
375 Torringford West Street
Torrington CT 067904049

Call Sign: KB1NZV
Angela J Capolupo
1410 Torringford West
Street
Torrington CT 06790

Call Sign: KJ1M
Arthur C Deming Jr
450 University Dr
Torrington CT 06790

Call Sign: N1ZVJ
Brett W Guralnick
218 W Pearl Rd
Torrington CT 06790

Call Sign: N1ZVK
Kenneth B Guralnick
218 W Pearl Rd
Torrington CT 06790

Call Sign: KA1GJS
Lee C Nietupski
254 W Side Ln
Torrington CT 06790

Call Sign: KA1GJT

Jean J Nietupski
254 W Side Ln
Torrington CT 06790

Call Sign: KB1MYO
Desiree D Delmastro
140 Washington Ave
Torrington CT 06790

Call Sign: KB1EUW
Robert A Cesca
146 Washington Ave
Torrington CT 067905168

Call Sign: AA1YK
Robert A Cesca
146 Washington Ave
Torrington CT 067905168

Call Sign: KB1LRT
Larry R Tashjian
140 Washington Ave.
Torrington CT 06790

Call Sign: N1KLA
George A Hegedty
122 Water St Apt 307
Torrington CT 06790

Call Sign: KB1NNK
Paul F Maxwell Jr
30 Wedgewood Dr
Torrington CT 06790

Call Sign: KA1FVN
Joseph A Benisch
190 Weed Rd
Torrington CT 06790

Call Sign: WA0OFB
Steven K Wilson
491 Weigold Rd
Torrington CT 067902036

Call Sign: WA1NGH

John T Zukowski Jr
270 West Hill Road
Torrington CT 06790

Call Sign: KA1TCH
Albert E Petrunti
77 White Pine Rd
Torrington CT 06790

Call Sign: KB1NWG
Network Operations Center
77 White Pine Rd
Torrington CT 06790

Call Sign: N1TCS
Network Operations Center
77 White Pine Rd
Torrington CT 06790

Call Sign: WB1GIK
Claus H Propfe
211 White Pine Rd
Torrington CT 06790

Call Sign: KA1HVW
Floyd J Hegedty Sr
52 Willow St Apt 38
Torrington CT 06790

Call Sign: N1IHM
William H Scheremeta
86 Wilmot St
Torrington CT 06790

Call Sign: KA1AWR
George A Miklos
68 Wilson Ave
Torrington CT 06790

Call Sign: K2DOC
Jon J Secor
81 Winesap Run
Torrington CT 06790

Call Sign: KA6FDW

Edward C Chastain
212 Winsted Rd
Torrington CT 067902929

Call Sign: KB1FQM
Debra L Chastain
212 Winsted Rd
Torrington CT 06790

Call Sign: N1IKQ
Robert J Nilsson
1229 Winsted Rd 41
Torrington CT 06790

Call Sign: K2BDD
Salvatore P De Muro
1229 Winsted Rd 91
Torrington CT 06790

Call Sign: N1SVJ
Donald R Aeschlimann
1229 Winsted Rd Unit 115
Torrington CT 06790

Call Sign: KA1TDS
David R Zolla
56 Winthrop St
Torrington CT 06790

Call Sign: K1EJS
Donald R Fantozzi Sr
107 Woodlawn Dr
Torrington CT 06790

Call Sign: KB1RUL
Joel S Hallenbeck
251 Wyoming Ave
Torrington CT 06790

Call Sign: K1KGQ
Joel A Weber
Torrington CT 067900064

Call Sign: K1SYN
Thomas W Grieco Jr

Torrington CT 06790

Call Sign: KA1GED
Charles E Devaux
Torrington CT 06790

Call Sign: N1VXB
Raymond T Kulinski
Torrington CT 067900185

Call Sign: W1ECR
Robert Bullock
Torrington CT 06790

**FCC Amateur Radio
Licenses in Trumbull**

Call Sign: K1EPT
George M Bekech
15 Arden Rd
Trumbull CT 06611

Call Sign: N1FWP
Herbert A Rosenberg
87 Arden Rd
Trumbull CT 066114441

Call Sign: KB8UYG
Clayton J Ramseyer
4131 Avalon Gates
Trumbull CT 06611

Call Sign: KJ4HTS
Stephen C Watson
11121 Avalon Gates
Trumbull CT 06611

Call Sign: N1MMA
Thomas A Morris
9233 Avelon Gates
Trumbull CT 06611

Call Sign: N1TTG
Louis B Weber
95 Beardsley

Trumbull CT 066115250

Call Sign: KB1RXB
Terrence A Flanagan
37 Beardsley Parkway
Trumbull CT 06611

Call Sign: KB1TAF
Terrence A Flanagan
37 Beardsley Parkway
Trumbull CT 06611

Call Sign: N1LUH
Stanley J Wuchek Jr
40 Beech St
Trumbull CT 066113512

Call Sign: N1SLK
Nicholas G Bohnsack
248 Blackhouse Rd
Trumbull CT 06611

Call Sign: KA1KXT
Mark F Mandello
11 Bonnie View Dr
Trumbull CT 06611

Call Sign: KB1AUF
Aaron J Keeler
385 Booth Hill Rd
Trumbull CT 06611

Call Sign: N1GXM
Jefre D Keeler
385 Booth Hill Rd
Trumbull CT 06611

Call Sign: KB1GUW
Michael J Brooks
75 Calhoun Ave
Trumbull CT 06611

Call Sign: N1VBK
Kenneth M Jezierny
21 Cardinal Cir

Trumbull CT 06611

Call Sign: N1RMK
John A Meyers
51 Cardinal Cir
Trumbull CT 06611

Call Sign: WA1CXE
Frank Gerratana
24 Chestnut Hill Rd
Trumbull CT 06611

Call Sign: N1BMZ
Henry J Lefcort
23 Chestnut Hill Road
Trumbull CT 06611

Call Sign: N1IIV
Charles C Rankin
477 Church Hill Rd
Trumbull CT 06611

Call Sign: WA1PKL
Louis S Evan
36 Clinton St
Trumbull CT 06611

Call Sign: N1MDP
Christopher R Huydic
24 Cobblers Hill Rd
Trumbull CT 06611

Call Sign: N1QBJ
Robert M Denman
64 Colony Ave
Trumbull CT 06611

Call Sign: WB2IOQ
Mark R Walter
177 Colony Ave
Trumbull CT 06611

Call Sign: WA1WRR
Bernard L Zebrowski
24 Columbine Dr

Trumbull CT 06611

Call Sign: N1FYO
Michael T Decerbo
28 Columbine Dr
Trumbull CT 06611

Call Sign: KA1ILN
David J Domogala
56 Coral Dr
Trumbull CT 06611

Call Sign: KB1GUX
George F Luft Iii
40 Cottage St
Trumbull CT 06611

Call Sign: KB1HVW
George F Luft Iii
40 Cottage St
Trumbull CT 06611

Call Sign: KB1MPI
Ronald A Zimmer
4 Crocus Lane
Trumbull CT 06611

Call Sign: KB1NTB
Alex D Zimmer
4 Crocus Lane
Trumbull CT 06611

Call Sign: KB1NTC
Shirlee E Glahn
4 Crocus Lane
Trumbull CT 06611

Call Sign: KB1DK
Robert F Kulacz
93 Crown St
Trumbull CT 06611

Call Sign: W1BPT
City Of Bridgeport
Emergency Operations Club

4 Daniels Farm Rd 128
Trumbull CT 06611

Call Sign: WA1TFA
Pasquale J Salvo
4 Daniels Farm Rd 196
Trumbull CT 06611

Call Sign: WA1PIX
George J Beloin Jr
4 Daniels Farm Rd Unit 275
Trumbull CT 06611

Call Sign: AB1OU
Michael T Grant
870 Daniels Farm Road
Trumbull CT 06611

Call Sign: W1AHS
Allen H Silberstein
4 Daniels Farms Rd 128
Trumbull CT 06611

Call Sign: KA1UTA
Michael K Levin
66 Deepdene Rd
Trumbull CT 06611

Call Sign: N1CIT
Wayne S Levin
66 Deepdene Rd
Trumbull CT 06611

Call Sign: KB1FTF
Roberto Zanchin
434 Edison Road
Trumbull CT 06611

Call Sign: N1PLJ
David J Chin
708 Fairchild Rd
Trumbull CT 06611

Call Sign: K1UOV
Salvatore N Feola Sr

39 Fairview Ave
Trumbull CT 06611

Call Sign: K1TEO
Jeffrey D Klein
11 Farmview Cir
Trumbull CT 06611

Call Sign: N1IOT
Bryan G Thirkield
24 Fawn Circle
Trumbull CT 06611

Call Sign: K1JAZ
Bryan G Thirkield
24 Fawn Circle
Trumbull CT 06611

Call Sign: KB1QPT
Sheldon Z Yessenow
48 Foxwood Rd
Trumbull CT 066114051

Call Sign: KA1KRM
Gloria R Bennett
8 Glenbrook Rd
Trumbull CT 06611

Call Sign: KD1PQ
Raymond M Schlesier
107 Governor Trumbull
Way
Trumbull CT 06611

Call Sign: W1FBO
Robert R Hair
14 Green Haven Rd
Trumbull CT 066112631

Call Sign: WA1ZKY
Kevin W Lindell
8 Greenfield Dr
Trumbull CT 06611

Call Sign: KB1HME

James W Vetromile
28 Greenwood Dr
Trumbull CT 06611

Call Sign: N1AYO
Steve Szabo
90 Haviland Dr
Trumbull CT 0611

Call Sign: KA1ENA
Ralph A Levesque
80 Hedgehog Cir
Trumbull CT 06611

Call Sign: KA1EFR
Deborah S Barlow
38 Highgate Road
Trumbull CT 06611

Call Sign: KB1KXY
Lawrence A Gross
50 Hills Point Rd
Trumbull CT 06611

Call Sign: W1LAG
Lawrence A Gross
50 Hills Point Rd
Trumbull CT 06611

Call Sign: KB1RHN
Mfcc American Red Cross
Radio Club
50 Hills Point Rd
Trumbull CT 06611

Call Sign: W1MFC
Mfcc American Red Cross
Radio Club
50 Hills Point Rd
Trumbull CT 06611

Call Sign: KA1FWL
Raymond J Brooks
2061 Huntington Tpke
Trumbull CT 06611

Call Sign: KA1ZFW
James G Savastano
142 Inwood Rd
Trumbull CT 06611

Call Sign: WB1X
Joe A Cassidy Jr
31 Jackson Dr
Trumbull CT 066111423

Call Sign: NM1O
Joe A Cassidy Sr
31 Jackson Drive
Trumbull CT 066111423

Call Sign: NM1P
Jean A Cassidy
31 Jackson Drive
Trumbull CT 066111423

Call Sign: K1OOZ
Karl H Paquee
53 Jerome Ave
Trumbull CT 066113742

Call Sign: KD1IS
Hiroya Nishida
31 Kenwood Ln
Trumbull CT 06611

Call Sign: N1RWI
Nan L Stern
44 Lafayette Dr
Trumbull CT 06611

Call Sign: N1RZH
Alan L Stern
44 Lafayette Dr
Trumbull CT 06611

Call Sign: WA1VAR
George J Lombardi
48 Larkspur Dr
Trumbull CT 066114652

Call Sign: N1QPJ
John C Overhiser
44 Laurel St
Trumbull CT 06611

Call Sign: KB1SJE
Albert Derouin
48 Leffert Rd
Trumbull CT 06611

Call Sign: KB1SJF
Vivian Derouin
48 Leffert Road
Trumbull CT 06611

Call Sign: KA1VFS
Janice P Wilson
8 Leighton Rd
Trumbull CT 06611

Call Sign: N1QFQ
Leopold J Felui Jr
42 Mac Arthur Rd
Trumbull CT 06611

Call Sign: K1ZXF
John G Wargo
4239 Madison Ave
Trumbull CT 06611

Call Sign: WB9FWK
Thomas J Foth
5099 Madison Ave
Trumbull CT 066111120

Call Sign: KB1LTW
David H Schadlich
26 Melrose Ave
Trumbull CT 06611

Call Sign: KA1PXW
Harry R Novak
21 Morris Ave
Trumbull CT 06611

Call Sign: W1VIY
Charles H Obert
47 Morris Ave
Trumbull CT 066113550

Call Sign: N1UA
John L Pratt
30 Nokomis Dr
Trumbull CT 06611

Call Sign: KB1QQG
Raymond D Luvara
14 Norwood Terrace
Trumbull CT 06611

Call Sign: KA1OQJ
Barbara R Hilinski
108 Old Dyke Rd
Trumbull CT 06611

Call Sign: N1AUF
Walter N Hilinski
108 Old Dyke Rd
Trumbull CT 06611

Call Sign: KB1UU
Randall S Kemp
18 Old Farm Rd
Trumbull CT 066114725

Call Sign: N1SKI
William B Chin
6 Old Hollow Rd
Trumbull CT 06611

Call Sign: K1WTB
Leonard Levi
10 Oldfield Rd
Trumbull CT 06611

Call Sign: KB1LGU
Jonathan P Mulla
35 Owl Hill Trail
Trumbull CT 06611

Call Sign: KA1NTG
Frank A Olsson
149 Palomino Pass
Trumbull CT 06611

Call Sign: N1RRJ
Steven R Alesevich
46 Park St
Trumbull CT 066113972

Call Sign: KB1LVV
John J Butkus
139 Pinewood Trail
Trumbull CT 06611

Call Sign: KA1CF
Chester Kadish
10 Pioneer Trail
Trumbull CT 06611

Call Sign: N1TKU
Cynthia Kadish
10 Pioneer Trail
Trumbull CT 06611

Call Sign: K1SWA
Lewis J Klunk Jr
22 Pleasant St
Trumbull CT 06611

Call Sign: WA1UDB
Jeffrey R Goldman
63 Plum Tree Ln
Trumbull CT 06611

Call Sign: KB2UHX
Scott A Vincent
186 Porters Hill Road
Trumbull CT 06611

Call Sign: W1MWT
Paul W Heiden Jr
7 Preston Rd
Trumbull CT 066111817

Call Sign: WA1UEP
Lois S Heiden
7 Preston Rd
Trumbull CT 06611

Call Sign: N1AEB
Frank C Sawicki
104 Roosevelt Dr
Trumbull CT 066112561

Call Sign: WA2TJR
Franklin T Merkler
19 Round Hill Rd
Trumbull CT 06611

Call Sign: W5TFM
Donald E Meyer
54 Salem Rd
Trumbull CT 06611

Call Sign: N1XGU
Claudio Borghesan
11 Scattergood Cir
Trumbull CT 06611

Call Sign: KB1VDJ
Michael J Miciukiewicz
78 Shawnee Rd
Trumbull CT 06611

Call Sign: K1MJM
Michael J Miciukiewicz
78 Shawnee Rd
Trumbull CT 06611

Call Sign: KA1HCX
Samuel A Green
43 Skating Pond Rd
Trumbull CT 06611

Call Sign: WA2CQH
George M Yahwak
25 Skytop Dr
Trumbull CT 06611

Call Sign: KA1TKK
Larry J Cohen
69 Stemway Rd
Trumbull CT 06611

Call Sign: KB1NYJ
Charles R Berezin
45 Stephanie Circle
Trumbull CT 06611

Call Sign: AG2K
Kenneth E Middleton
185 Sterling Rd.
Trumbull CT 06611

Call Sign: KB1ENB
Robert P Ostrover
30 Sunnycrest Rd
Trumbull CT 06611

Call Sign: N1KGM
Kevin W Cellini
49 Sunrise Ave
Trumbull CT 06611

Call Sign: N1KGN
Edmond L Cellini
49 Sunrise Ave
Trumbull CT 066111944

Call Sign: N1TIX
Edmond L Cellini Sr
49 Sunrise Ave
Trumbull CT 066111944

Call Sign: KB1NFT
Southern Connecticut Ares
49 Sunrise Ave
Trumbull CT 06611

Call Sign: KC1EOC
Greater Bridgeport
Emergency Operations Club
49 Sunrise Ave

Trumbull CT 06611

Call Sign: KB1LSV
Patrick J Keane
50 Sunrise Ave
Trumbull CT 06611

Call Sign: KA1NSG
Allan E Szabo Jr
33 Sunset Ave
Trumbull CT 06611

Call Sign: KA1FVY
Carole V Perregaux
37 Sunset Ave
Trumbull CT 06611

Call Sign: KA1SKX
Scott W Stiewing
63 Tanager Ln
Trumbull CT 06611

Call Sign: W1IOE
Donald E Allen
63 Tashua Rd
Trumbull CT 066111029

Call Sign: AB1AG
George F Luft Iii
27 Twin Circle Drive
Trumbull CT 06611

Call Sign: WA1ZCF
Peter J Ingrassia
18 Valley Rd
Trumbull CT 06611

Call Sign: KA1SQT
Jeffrey A Lamy
12 Valley View Rd
Trumbull CT 06611

Call Sign: N1SKJ
Victor L Martin
37 Valley View Rd

Trumbull CT 06611

Call Sign: KB2AMV
Debra C Graffeo Schmidt
20 Vazzano Pl
Trumbull CT 06611

Call Sign: KB2AMW
John R Schmidt
20 Vazzano Pl
Trumbull CT 06611

Call Sign: W1JBV
Norman S Howard
5 Westbrook Rd
Trumbull CT 06611

Call Sign: N1MUC
Paul A Litwinovich
205 White Plains Rd
Trumbull CT 06611

Call Sign: W2SAF
David T Larmon
130 Whitney Ave
Trumbull CT 06611

Call Sign: KB1HRY
Stephen P Baunach
27 Wisteria Dr
Trumbull CT 066114624

Call Sign: KA1CVX
Joseph T Casarin
4 Woodfield Dr
Trumbull CT 06611

FCC Amateur Radio Licenses in Uncasville

Call Sign: KA1RPL
Michael D Holmes
31 Allen Dr
Uncasville CT 06382

Call Sign: N1GBQ
Kenneth E Burrows
21 Baldwin Ct
Uncasville CT 06382

Call Sign: KA1BMV
Joseph P Stronski
56 Fowler Dr
Uncasville CT 06382

Call Sign: KB1DVH
Glenn D Andrews Jr
29 Joy Ln
Uncasville CT 06382

Call Sign: WB1GVJ
Carlisle M Fowler
16 Church Ln
Uncasville CT 06382

Call Sign: K1BMV
Joseph P Stronski
56 Fowler Dr
Uncasville CT 06382

Call Sign: KB1GVZ
Matthew R Morgan
185 Kitemaug Rd
Uncasville CT 06382

Call Sign: KB1NQQ
Richard J Martin
16 Cook Dr
Uncasville CT 06382

Call Sign: N1VXZ
Eric W Ehrenfels
84 Fowler Dr
Uncasville CT 06382

Call Sign: KB1EVP
Norman R Betty
34 Lisa Ln
Uncasville CT 06382

Call Sign: KB1PIT
Jodi L Martin
16 Cook Dr
Uncasville CT 06382

Call Sign: KA1IFG
Peter F Kerttula
23 Gair Ct
Uncasville CT 06382

Call Sign: W1NRB
Norman R Betty
34 Lisa Ln
Uncasville CT 06382

Call Sign: W1JOD
Jodi L Martin
16 Cook Dr
Uncasville CT 06382

Call Sign: N1DAT
Judith M Kerttula
23 Gair Ct
Uncasville CT 06382

Call Sign: KE6KCB
Lisa A Doyle
224 Maple Ave 3
Uncasville CT 06382

Call Sign: KB1RGJ
Chad E Rudolph
25 Cove Road
Uncasville CT 06382

Call Sign: N1LIZ
George R Markow
21 Heather Brook Rd
Uncasville CT 063822067

Call Sign: KA1PFL
Wayne E Hewitt
9 Mc Culley Pl
Uncasville CT 06382

Call Sign: KD4JJE
Joseph L Childress
19 Elton Court
Uncasville CT 06382

Call Sign: KA1HLA
Carole L Gosselin
46 Hillcrest Drive
Uncasville CT 06382

Call Sign: KA1MMH
William P Edwards
217 Moxley Rd
Uncasville CT 06382

Call Sign: KB1NHX
Jeffrey A Sutton
396 Fitch Hill Rd
Uncasville CT 06382

Call Sign: KA1KE
Alfred R Gosselin
46 Hillcrest Drive
Uncasville CT 06382

Call Sign: KA1OKW
Charles T Edwards
217 Moxley Rd
Uncasville CT 06382

Call Sign: N1ESA
Jeffrey A Sutton
396 Fitch Hill Rd
Uncasville CT 06382

Call Sign: K1JNR
Roy A Hilt
41 Jerome Rd
Uncasville CT 06382

Call Sign: KA1OKX
Ann M Edwards
217 Moxley Rd
Uncasville CT 06382

Call Sign: WB1BXJ
Roger P Arnold
1691 Norwich New London
Tpk
Uncasville CT 06382

Call Sign: KB1QFW
Christina A Martin
1851 Norwich New London
Trpk.
Uncasville CT 06382

Call Sign: KB1HHN
Michael A Tucker
31 Park Ave Ext
Uncasville CT 063821817

Call Sign: W1MCT
Michael A Tucker
31 Park Ave Ext
Uncasville CT 063821817

Call Sign: KA1DDZ
Joseph N Weymouth
154 Park Ave Ext
Uncasville CT 06382

Call Sign: WA1IWD
Ernest B Pollard Jr
180 Park Ave Ext
Uncasville CT 06382

Call Sign: W1LCJ
William H Page
136 Pollys Ln
Uncasville CT 06382

Call Sign: W1GRW
Joseph M Pollard Jr
51 Rainbow Dr
Uncasville CT 06382

Call Sign: K1GFL
Ernest L Yohe
16 Rankin Ct

Uncasville CT 06382

Call Sign: KA1UDI
Luciana N Cisotto
34 Rankin Ct
Uncasville CT 06382

Call Sign: N1ISX
Allison R Hilt
164 Raymond Hill Rd
Uncasville CT 06382

Call Sign: N1ZYB
Paul S Towne
26 Riched Ln
Uncasville CT 063821907

Call Sign: N1ZYC
Linda L Towne
26 Riched Ln
Uncasville CT 063821907

Call Sign: WB1GOX
Robert D Rainville
11 Ridge Dr
Uncasville CT 06382

Call Sign: NN1S
Thomas S Ziemski
19 Ridge Dr
Uncasville CT 06382

Call Sign: W1ELE
Edwin A Sylvia Jr
28 Vartellas Dr
Uncasville CT 06382

Call Sign: N1HFT
David E Whitehead
119d Woodland Dr
Uncasville CT 06382

Call Sign: WA1NUI
Sheldon A Gisser
Uncasville CT 06382

Call Sign: N1DWM
Richard J Martin
Uncasville CT 063820013

FCC Amateur Radio Licenses in Union

Call Sign: K1IM
Thomas E Nelson
24 Bradway Rd
Union CT 06076

Call Sign: K2LO
Northeastern Dx & Contest
Club
24 Bradway Rd
Union CT 06076

Call Sign: KE1HY
David H Herr
163 Cemetery Rd
Union CT 06076

Call Sign: N1ZPN
Allison R Herr
163 Cemetery Rd
Union CT 06076

Call Sign: K1HY
David H Herr
163 Cemetery Rd
Union CT 06076

FCC Amateur Radio Licenses in Union City

Call Sign: N1MMR
Thomas A Owens
118 Miller Dr Box 1133
Union City CT 06770

FCC Amateur Radio Licenses in Unionville

Call Sign: N1IAD
Steven F Sadlowski
68 Bidwell Square
Unionville CT 06085

Call Sign: N1SQX
Scott A Goetchius
12 Bliss Rd
Unionville CT 06085

Call Sign: K1CGU
Andrew R Smolen
72 Forest St
Unionville CT 060851202

Call Sign: N1MXC
Gregory J Noble
9 Hemlock Notch
Unionville CT 06085

Call Sign: KB1MCQ
Edward S Simonds
14 Hunters Ridge 8
Unionville CT 06085

Call Sign: KB1UTT
Andrew P Strupinski
20 Jefferson St
Unionville CT 06085

Call Sign: KA1SJO
Michael L Wolf
21 Jefferson St
Unionville CT 06085

Call Sign: KB1BFL
John L Wolk
70 Keene Pl
Unionville CT 06085

Call Sign: N1TJR
Eric M Solliday
77 Lido Rd
Unionville CT 06085

Call Sign: N1EXO
Truman E Alderman
230 Main St
Unionville CT 06085

Call Sign: N1JPG
Robert V Sagherian
29 Mohawk Dr
Unionville CT 06085

Call Sign: AA1MH
Marko Pavlic
126 Oak Ridge
Unionville CT 06085

Call Sign: KB1IFZ
Elsie M Mathews
P. O. Box 600
Unionville CT 06085

Call Sign: N1NEP
Andrew A Poitras
11 Pine Dr
Unionville CT 06085

Call Sign: N1ELV
John W Shepherd Jr
660 Plainville Ave
Unionville CT 06085

Call Sign: W1YXQ
Richmond A Brouker
8 River Rd
Unionville CT 06085

Call Sign: KB1GJH
Michael C Thayer
103 Webster St
Unionville CT 06085

Call Sign: N1URO
Richard B Rogers
110 Webster St
Unionville CT 060851056

Call Sign: K1NNC
John E Kruse
14 West Avon Rd
Unionville CT 06085

Call Sign: KB1CVO
Donald P Perrault Iii
114 West Avon Rd
Unionville CT 06085

Call Sign: W1UED
Perry F Williams
12 West District Rd
Unionville CT 06085

Call Sign: K1GZU
Gerald W Hemphill
85 West District Road
Unionville CT 06085

Call Sign: KA1BLZ
Walter S Urbowicz
63 Wooddale Dr
Unionville CT 06085

Call Sign: KA1FNI
Thomas H Hart
Unionville CT 06085

Call Sign: KB1EHE
Eric A Knight
Unionville CT 06085

Call Sign: N1RIG
Thomas J Brady
Unionville CT 06085

**FCC Amateur Radio
Licenses in Vernon**

Call Sign: W1DH
John L Giulietti
20 Beverly Road
Vernon CT 060666103

Call Sign: KA1VLV
Mark M Jackson
91 Blue Ridge Dr
Vernon CT 06066

Call Sign: W1SKA
Richard B Saich Jr
667 Bolton Rd
Vernon CT 06066

Call Sign: N1MM
Thomas F Wagner
301 Box Mountain Dr
Vernon CT 06066

Call Sign: N1UIP
Paul R Collin
97 Box Mountain Dr.
Vernon CT 060666304

Call Sign: KB1QNL
Cara E Sullivan
211 Brandy Hill Rd
Vernon CT 06066

Call Sign: KB1QNN
Claudia G Sullivan
211 Brandy Hill Rd
Vernon CT 06066

Call Sign: K1KYC
Roland C Jones
88 Brent Dr
Vernon CT 060666239

Call Sign: KB1RAT
Christopher M Fiore
27 Brighton Lane
Vernon CT 06066

Call Sign: WA1UVS
John J Fisher
6 Brighton Ln
Vernon CT 06066

Call Sign: KB1AML
Krishan M Agrawal
42 Brighton Ln
Vernon CT 06066

Call Sign: WA1GET
Delbert L Horn
16 Christopher Dr
Vernon CT 06066

Call Sign: KB1EYW
Alan R Jones
47 Crest Dr
Vernon CT 06066

Call Sign: KA1MVY
Theodore H Gunter
20 Dailey Cir
Vernon CT 06066

Call Sign: WB1CMV
Mark H Osbeck
38 Daryl Dr
Vernon CT 06066

Call Sign: W1COT
Robert E Leiper
47 Diane Dr
Vernon CT 06066

Call Sign: W1KZF
Bryan A Woods
11 Discovery Rd
Vernon CT 06066

Call Sign: KB1YF
Glenn S Kroll
7 Dobson Commons Circle
Vernon CT 06066

Call Sign: WA1ZWU
James Ferguson Jr
65 Dockerel Rd
Vernon CT 06066

Call Sign: N1VIK
Peter W Rado
19 Duncaster Ln
Vernon CT 06066

Call Sign: NQ1D
George R Holzman
166 Echo Dr
Vernon CT 06066

Call Sign: N1XGX
Richard S Liszewski
149 Evergreen Rd
Vernon CT 06066

Call Sign: N1BHF
Glen D Sykes
1 Fern St
Vernon CT 06066

Call Sign: KB1BVS
Norma F Baldwin
34 Foster Dr
Vernon CT 06066

Call Sign: WB1GIH
Kenneth D Milkie
6 Frederic Rd
Vernon CT 06066

Call Sign: KB1COD
Eric J Amsden
101 Grove St
Vernon CT 06066

Call Sign: N1WID
Joel C Kerr
144 Hany Ln
Vernon CT 06066

Call Sign: KB1MHM
Stanley C Barnes
239 Hany Ln
Vernon CT 06066

Call Sign: W1GHN
Stanley C Barnes
239 Hany Ln
Vernon CT 06066

Call Sign: WA1GFJ
Gabriel F Gargiulo
1134 Hartford Tpke - Unit
1a1
Vernon CT 06066

Call Sign: KB1WRA
Wesley D Newth Sr
859 Hartford Turnpike
Vernon CT 06066

Call Sign: KA1BYR
Harrison E S Koppe
1238 Hartford Turnpike Apt
80
Vernon CT 06066

Call Sign: K1BYS
Wilfred P Halliday
72 Hillside Manor Ave
Vernon CT 06066

Call Sign: KB1QNS
James L Hodges
3 Hilltop Ave
Vernon CT 06066

Call Sign: W1WDG
Wright D Gifford Jr
70 Hublard Dr
Vernon CT 06066

Call Sign: KB1NWA
James D Burr
76 Indian Trail
Vernon CT 06066

Call Sign: W1FEX
Leonel Syriac
1 Jan Drive

Vernon CT 06066

Call Sign: KB1WDH
Tam N Shane
36 Jeff Rd
Vernon CT 06066

Call Sign: KB1WDI
Christopher E Shane
36 Jeff Rd
Vernon CT 06066

Call Sign: KB1WDK
Rachael L Shane
36 Jeff Rd
Vernon CT 06066

Call Sign: AA4VW
Alexander W Smith
7 Jeff Road
Vernon CT 06066

Call Sign: KB1VQT
Deborah M Troesch
325 Kelly Rd M 39
Vernon CT 06066

Call Sign: KB1VQU
Joseph P Troesch
325 Kelly Rd M39
Vernon CT 06066

Call Sign: N1TUQ
John G Chvaral Jr
40 Kevin Dr
Vernon CT 06066

Call Sign: KB1JFH
Johan Van Achterberg
316 Lake St
Vernon CT 06066

Call Sign: WA1UUU
Dale A Whitney
48 Lakeview Dr Rfd 6

Vernon CT 06066

Call Sign: W1PCE
Robert J Meagher
293 Merline Rd
Vernon CT 06066

Call Sign: W1UTQ
Stephen V Taylor
172 Merline Road
Vernon CT 06066

Call Sign: N1WSM
Arthur T Grondine
26 Montauk Dr
Vernon CT 06066

Call Sign: KB1VQO
Peter J Orlowski Jr
34 Montauk Dr
Vernon CT 06066

Call Sign: N1ZXA
Gary P Marquis
60 Old Town Rd 88
Vernon CT 06066

Call Sign: N1PYV
Diane J Lux
60-158 Old Town Road
Vernon CT 06066

Call Sign: WA1OUH
David A Plis
94 Rambling Rd
Vernon CT 06066

Call Sign: N4ERB
David M Goldfarb
94 Richard Road
Vernon CT 060666315

Call Sign: N1TUJ
Eileen M Phelps
14 Ridgewood Dr

Vernon CT 06066

Call Sign: W1BRS
Bears Of Manchester
14 Ridgewood Dr
Vernon CT 06066

Call Sign: N1ANN
Ann M Gruden
88 Rolling View Dr
Vernon CT 06066

Call Sign: WA1QJF
Kenneth J Bernacky
34 Russell Dr
Vernon CT 06066

Call Sign: KA1QOJ
Rudolph A Gaydos Jr
65 Scott Dr
Vernon CT 06066

Call Sign: AA1IL
Ronald W Lesniak
10 Shady Brook Lane
Vernon CT 06066

Call Sign: KA1RZY
Jeffrey S Bell
12 Snipsic View Hgts
Vernon CT 06066

Call Sign: KB1JIS
Tabitha W Heavner-
Molitoris
101 South St 15
Vernon CT 06066

Call Sign: K1NSH
Tabitha W Heavner
Molitoris
101 South St 15
Vernon CT 06066

Call Sign: WA1QPV

William H Leland
655 Talcottville Rd Apt 168
Vernon CT 06066

Call Sign: KB1VQP
Zane C Pearson
655 Talcottville Rd Apt 92
Vernon CT 06066

Call Sign: KB1PGA
Matthew G Jussaume
35-31 Talcottville Rd. #171
Vernon CT 06074

Call Sign: N1NYL
Stephen B Marcus
83 Tracy Dr
Vernon CT 06066

Call Sign: WA1ZWZ
Hanna Marcus
83 Tracy Dr
Vernon CT 06066

Call Sign: N1COG
Alexander J Karr
31 Tracy Drive
Vernon CT 06066

Call Sign: KB1FLU
William F Campbell
214 Tracy Drive
Vernon CT 06066

Call Sign: W2GUN
William F Campbell
214 Tracy Drive
Vernon CT 06066

Call Sign: W1ULK
Paul L Wick
4 Tumblebrook Dr
Vernon CT 06066

Call Sign: KB1VQV

Linda P Woodrow
127 Union St
Vernon CT 06066

Call Sign: K1CC
Richard J Assarabowski
306 Vernon Ave
Vernon CT 06066

Call Sign: KK2Z
Zbigniew J Kossowski
306 Vernon Ave
Vernon CT 06066

Call Sign: KB1PNE
Leszek Fabjanski
306 Vernon Ave
Vernon CT 06066

Call Sign: N3QS
Leszek Fabjanski
306 Vernon Ave
Vernon CT 06066

Call Sign: KD1KD
Etienne G Olivier
324 Vernon Ave
Vernon CT 06066

Call Sign: KB1KLT
Rachel J Kaiser
205 Vernon Ave 152
Vernon CT 06066

Call Sign: KB1EPF
Stephen V Taylor
150 Vernon Ave Apt #414
Vernon CT 06066

Call Sign: N1WLQ
Joshua S Preston
142 Vernon Ave Unit 74
Vernon CT 06066

Call Sign: KF4EJK

Tommie Watkins Jr
205 Vernon Avenue
Vernon CT 06066

Call Sign: N1GTX
Steven P Kiely
64 Vernon Center Heights
Vernon CT 06066

Call Sign: N1LRP
David J Hansen Jr
22 West St
Vernon CT 060663008

Call Sign: KA1QVI
William T Burrows
Vernon CT 06066

Call Sign: N1SQT
Nancy S Mencel
Vernon CT 06066

Call Sign: W1AVK
Robert J West
Vernon CT 06066

FCC Amateur Radio Licenses in Vernon Rockville

Call Sign: KA1FFR
Robert E Mello
37 Barbara Rd
Vernon Rockville CT 06066

Call Sign: W1BYN
William F Stanek
269 Box Mountain Dr
Vernon Rockville CT 06066

Call Sign: KA1ERB
Eleanore D Rhodes
296 Box Mountain Dr
Vernon Rockville CT
060666309

Call Sign: K1SQN
Richard C Gaskill
165 Center Road
Vernon Rockville CT
060664104

Call Sign: KB1TII
Benjamin A Sheridan
36 Christopher Dr
Vernon Rockville CT 06066

Call Sign: KB1TIJ
Allen W Sheridan
36 Christopher Dr
Vernon Rockville CT 06066

Call Sign: KB1AWS
Allen W Sheridan
36 Christopher Dr
Vernon Rockville CT 06066

Call Sign: KB1TVU
William W Wardrop
37 Christopher Dr
Vernon Rockville CT
060662801

Call Sign: KA2DFN
Donald E Gibson
100 Dobson Rd Unit 20
Vernon Rockville CT 06066

Call Sign: KA1NH
Harry D Thomas
125 Dockerel Rd
Vernon Rockville CT
060665703

Call Sign: N1RZV
Alan T Baldwin
34 Foster Dr
Vernon Rockville CT 06066

Call Sign: K1GX

Paul Vitols
111 Grand Ave
Vernon Rockville CT
060663434

Call Sign: K1UAG
Harold A Wells
35 Heidi Dr
Vernon Rockville CT
060662807

Call Sign: N1TKL
Paul Sutkaitis
35 Kenwood Dr
Vernon Rockville CT 06066

Call Sign: W1SPI
Russell H Persson
333 Old Town Rd
Vernon Rockville CT 06066

Call Sign: N1NWK
Richard A Sander
86 Range Hill Dr
Vernon Rockville CT 06066

Call Sign: K1SW
Richard F Phelps
14 Ridgewood Dr
Vernon Rockville CT 06066

Call Sign: KB1TKQ
Lyle M Evans Sr
33 Rolling View Dr
Vernon Rockville CT 06066

Call Sign: N1EF
Eugene R Faltus
29 Scott Dr
Vernon Rockville CT 06066

Call Sign: N1RIN
Scott E Lent
99 Scott Dr
Vernon Rockville CT 06066

Call Sign: N1SSM
William J Mc Court
294 Talcottville Rd
Vernon Rockville CT 06066

Call Sign: KB1WOL
Charles R O'neill
655 Talcottville Rd 47
Vernon Rockville CT 06066

Call Sign: KB1TVK
James W Francoline
43 Tracy Dr
Vernon Rockville CT 06066

Call Sign: W1HJU
William G Dent
87 Tracy Dr
Vernon Rockville CT 06066

Call Sign: KB1TIQ
Stacey A Durante
86 Vernwood Dr
Vernon Rockville CT 06066

Call Sign: KB1TIR
Robert J Durante
86 Vernwood Dr
Vernon Rockville CT 06066

Call Sign: KB1TUW
Lawrence M Carter
94 West Street Unit 42
Vernon Rockville CT 06066

FCC Amateur Radio
Licenses in Voluntown

Call Sign: KA1WTT
Christopher M Schell
Box 531 A1
Voluntown CT 06384

Call Sign: W1OLO

Lester H Villeneuve
24 Bailey Rd
Voluntown CT 06384

Call Sign: N1OKV
James E Gervais
61 Beach Pd Rd
Voluntown CT 06384

Call Sign: N1OKK
Michael T Sullivan
471 Beach Pond Rd
Voluntown CT 06384

Call Sign: KD1LD
James E Mc Bride
662 Beach Pond Rd
Voluntown CT 06384

Call Sign: N1OKT
Laura A Charette
662 Beach Pond Rd
Voluntown CT 06384

Call Sign: N1UKW
Robert M Dillon
260 Beach Pond Road
Voluntown CT 063841908

Call Sign: N1VTD
Tina M Dillon
260 Beach Pond Road
Voluntown CT 06384

Call Sign: KB1KWM
Robert M Dillon
260 Beach Pond Road
Voluntown CT 063841908

Call Sign: N1UKW
Robert M Dillon
260 Beach Pond Road
Voluntown CT 063841908

Call Sign: N1XPE

Herbert J Margosian
165 Bennett Road
Voluntown CT 06384

Call Sign: KB1VDG
Paul B Hartman
257 Congdon Rd
Voluntown CT 06384

Call Sign: KB1VDH
Christopher E Hartman
257 Congdon Rd
Voluntown CT 06384

Call Sign: K1WQL
Timothy M Thomas
162 Cook Hill Rd
Voluntown CT 06384

Call Sign: KB1HYF
Paul A Ricard
759 Ekonk Hill Rd
Voluntown CT 06384

Call Sign: K1OQ
Woodrow A Wilson Jr
891 Ekonk Hill Rd
Voluntown CT 06384

Call Sign: KA1HWL
Paul W Kirsipuu
130 Gardner Rd
Voluntown CT 06384

Call Sign: N1IUV
Glenn K Phillips
80 Sheldon Rd
Voluntown CT 06384

Call Sign: KA1ZBG
George H Allard Jr
Voluntown CT 06384

FCC Amateur Radio
Licenses in Wallingford

Call Sign: KB1JL
Eric R Olsson
36 Algonquin Dr
Wallingford CT 06492

Call Sign: N1YGK
Leonard E Bienasz Jr
3 Beechwood Dr
Wallingford CT 06492

Call Sign: KA1YZH
Gary C Jacques
50 Brookvale Dr
Wallingford CT 06492

Call Sign: WA1GWZ
Leo A Perry
87 Algonquin Dr
Wallingford CT 06492

Call Sign: WB1GYZ
Robert A Biancur
24 Beechwood Dr
Wallingford CT 06492

Call Sign: N1ICZ
Carl B Morgan
18 Brookview Ave
Wallingford CT 06492

Call Sign: KA1NRX
Pierrette B Marshall
52 Alison Ave
Wallingford CT 06492

Call Sign: KA1UNW
Randall C Floberg
Box 441
Wallingford CT 06492

Call Sign: N1LET
Gary L Morgan
18 Brookview Ave
Wallingford CT 06492

Call Sign: KB1MZG
Guy Allard
23 Anna Dr
Wallingford CT 06492

Call Sign: N1RQO
Albert E Robinson
206 Brentwood Dr
Wallingford CT 06492

Call Sign: KB1SIN
William H Brooks
40 Brownstone Rd
Wallingford CT 06492

Call Sign: AC1C
Morton J Levy
122 Ashlar Village
Wallingford CT 064923093

Call Sign: N1SLH
Joanne D Robinson
206 Brentwood Dr
Wallingford CT 06473

Call Sign: KB1ETB
Jonathan W Matthews
34 Cardinal Dr
Wallingford CT 064924828

Call Sign: N1UF
Frederick T King
Ashlar Village 1102
Wallingford CT 06492

Call Sign: KB1IDK
James R Savage
19 Broadview Dr
Wallingford CT 064923349

Call Sign: KB1SYW
Shawn A Mcewen
8 Cheryl Ave
Wallingford CT 06492

Call Sign: KA1MJF
Mary Ann Stewart
Ashlar Village 3123
Wallingford CT 064923060

Call Sign: N1ZN
James R Savage
19 Broadview Dr
Wallingford CT 064923349

Call Sign: N0AHH
Shawn A Mcewen
8 Cheryl Ave
Wallingford CT 06492

Call Sign: W1KU
Robert K Dixon
4324 Ashlar Vlg
Wallingford CT 06492

Call Sign: KA1ISX
Mary E Corcoran
52 Broadview Dr
Wallingford CT 06492

Call Sign: W1MPO
Adwin J Rusczek Sr
96 Church St
Wallingford CT 06492

Call Sign: KB1UDK
Samantha Bergan
8 Ashley Ln
Wallingford CT 06492

Call Sign: KA1LLI
John G Corcoran
52 Broadview Dr
Wallingford CT 06492

Call Sign: W1PXA
Steve Hacku
10 Colonial Ln
Wallingford CT 06492

Call Sign: KB1DNE
Mark K Houde
16 Colonial Ln
Wallingford CT 06492

Call Sign: KA1GST
Rudolf J Schuster
30 Colonial Ln
Wallingford CT 06492

Call Sign: N1QWR
Gregory R Lindberg
233 Cook Hill Rd
Wallingford CT 06492

Call Sign: N1IHP
Stephen M Rittenhouse
49 Cooper Ave
Wallingford CT 06492

Call Sign: KB1GWM
Fredrik J Scimone
2 Country Way
Wallingford CT 06492

Call Sign: KB1GWN
John F Scimone
2 Country Way
Wallingford CT 06492

Call Sign: N9OZF
Peter A Nemenyi
27 Country Way
Wallingford CT 06492

Call Sign: K1NQI
James F Lincoln
12 Crestview Ter
Wallingford CT 064922006

Call Sign: KB1SUL
Robert J Friedland
16 Crestview Terrace
Wallingford CT 06492

Call Sign: KB1BRP
Arthur R Fenner Jr
4 Croydon Court
Wallingford CT 06492

Call Sign: KA1MWX
Paul J Stasieluk
22 Dana Blvd
Wallingford CT 064922076

Call Sign: N1OKR
Frank Ciccone
6 Davenport Pl
Wallingford CT 064922083

Call Sign: N1OKI
Chester R Betta
22 Donat Dr
Wallingford CT 06492

Call Sign: N1ZXS
Thomas W Wilson
1303 Durham Rd
Wallingford CT 064922611

Call Sign: N1GDU
Joseph M Delaney
1094 E Center St
Wallingford CT 06492

Call Sign: KD1QD
Gary D Nilson
865 E Center St Apt D
Wallingford CT 06492

Call Sign: KB1GWP
Joseph J Rish Sr
45 East St
Wallingford CT 06492

Call Sign: KA1BYW
Corinne M Jones
126 Eastside Dr
Wallingford CT 06492

Call Sign: N1XFR
James D Carmody Sr
66 Evergreene Condos
Wallingford CT 06492

Call Sign: N1KS
Kazuo Suzuki
10 Fairfield
Wallingford CT 06492

Call Sign: KA1UVR
Helen K Werns
20 Farm Hill Rd
Wallingford CT 06492

Call Sign: WA1UHH
George C Werns
20 Farm Hill Rd
Wallingford CT 06492

Call Sign: KA1QEF
John P Hamelin
17 Fawn Dr
Wallingford CT 06492

Call Sign: KB1DAR
Maureen P Hamelin
17 Fawn Dr
Wallingford CT 06492

Call Sign: AA1PH
Ronald L Crossley
25 Fox Run Dr
Wallingford CT 06492

Call Sign: KA1PEK
Frank J Bakanas
99 Grandview Ave
Wallingford CT 06492

Call Sign: KA1NBX
Kathleen A Pike
4 Grieb Ct
Wallingford CT 06492

Call Sign: KB1DWR
John R Pike Ii
4 Grieb Ct
Wallingford CT 06492

Call Sign: KB1OI
John R Pike
4 Grieb Ct
Wallingford CT 06492

Call Sign: WB8IMY
Steven R Ford
9 Grieb Ct
Wallingford CT 06492

Call Sign: KA1WGJ
Richard L Butcher
128 Hall Ave Apt 1
Wallingford CT 06492

Call Sign: WB1GGP
Jerald L Sheppard
16 Hallmark Dr
Wallingford CT 06492

Call Sign: KB1KHJ
Cherie P Freeman
5 Hampton Trail
Wallingford CT 06492

Call Sign: K1SOX
Brian J Freeman
5 Hampton Trail
Wallingford CT 06492

Call Sign: KB1SER
Shore Point Amateur Radio
Club
5 Hampton Trail
Wallingford CT 06492

Call Sign: W1SPC
Shore Point Amateur Radio
Club

5 Hampton Trail
Wallingford CT 06492

Call Sign: KB1INU
Anthony R Russo
115 Harrison Rd
Wallingford CT 06492

Call Sign: WA1SJX
Warren R Warzocha
8 Harrison Rd.
Wallingford CT 06492

Call Sign: KB1WDY
Patrick E Tuxbury
5 Harrison Road
Wallingford CT 06492

Call Sign: W1UFO
Michael A Cei
72 Henry St
Wallingford CT 064924722

Call Sign: N1RDR
James E Salvato
8 High Hill Rd
Wallingford CT 06492

Call Sign: N1LGC
Carl S Rodenhizer
189 High St
Wallingford CT 06492

Call Sign: WB1DZA
John W H Poulton
35 Highland Ave
Wallingford CT 06492

Call Sign: KB1HI
Brian J Curtiss
94 Highland Ave
Wallingford CT 06492

Call Sign: AB1AI
Brian J Curtiss

94 Highland Ave
Wallingford CT 06492

Call Sign: KB1IGK
Jason S Lapointe
94 Highland Ave
Wallingford CT 06492

Call Sign: N1YGM
John W Kruczek
219 Highland Ave
Wallingford CT 06492

Call Sign: N1OKH
Gregory H Butko
3 Hope Hill Rd
Wallingford CT 06492

Call Sign: N1YGN
George F Wruck
24 Jamestown Circle
Wallingford CT 06492

Call Sign: KA1CEN
David B Maclary
36 Johnson Rd
Wallingford CT 06492

Call Sign: KA1SYO
Walter H Uhle
6 Kovacs Pl
Wallingford CT 06492

Call Sign: K1JPA
Aaro O Koski
130 Long Hill Rd
Wallingford CT 064924934

Call Sign: N1CTJ
Alfred W Paz
1 Malchiodi Dr
Wallingford CT 06492

Call Sign: WA1WOA
Ellen C Deutsch

1 Malchiodi Dr
Wallingford CT 06492

Call Sign: KA1DWF
Harold R Carta
45 Maltby Ln
Wallingford CT 06492

Call Sign: KA1SE
Luke V Lauretano
15 Mansion Rd
Wallingford CT 06492

Call Sign: KB1GWK
Joel M Rinebold
194 Mansion Road
Wallingford CT 06492

Call Sign: N1RBL
David P Meyer
81 Marshall St
Wallingford CT 06492

Call Sign: W1DDX
Richard H Dillman Sr
Masonic Home 22 Masonic
Ave
Wallingford CT 06492

Call Sign: K1CXZ
Milton B Christman
55 Masonic Ave Apt 201
Wallingford CT 064923063

Call Sign: W1INQ
Versey H Mc Bride
Masonic Home & Hospital
Box 70
Wallingford CT 06492

Call Sign: N1LSN
Robert J Brady
104 Meadow St
Wallingford CT 06492

Call Sign: KB1UDY
Ernest W Frattini Sr
23 Mettler Dr
Wallingford CT 06492

Call Sign: N1QJR
Dominic D Ioime
106 Montowese Trail
Wallingford CT 06492

Call Sign: N1PHB
Michael R Mallinson
31 Morgan Dr
Wallingford CT 06492

Call Sign: WA1L
John V D Addario
202 N Airline Rd
Wallingford CT 06492

Call Sign: K1MWP
Samuel R Mac Donald
175 N Branford Rd
Wallingford CT 06492

Call Sign: KB1HPY
John L Pagano
617 N Elm St
Wallingford CT 06492

Call Sign: NR1B
William J Huggins
736 N Farms Rd
Wallingford CT 06492

Call Sign: KS1L
Louis R Maglione
977 N Farms Rd
Wallingford CT 06492

Call Sign: KA1HWR
Adolf S Pzedpelski
981 N Farms Rd
Wallingford CT 06492

Call Sign: KB1LEB
Stephen M Corneau
1005 N Main St Ext Apt S-9
Wallingford CT 06492

Call Sign: KC1HA
William Zebb
22 New England Dr
Wallingford CT 06492

Call Sign: KB1LWJ
Robert A Babcock V
20 Nod Brook Rd
Wallingford CT 06492

Call Sign: W0RAB
Robert A Babcock V
20 Nod Brook Rd
Wallingford CT 06492

Call Sign: K1LYP
John W Yusza Jr
251 North Airline Rd
Wallingford CT 06492

Call Sign: K1FLH
James H Condon Sr
311 North Airline Rd
Walingford CT 06492

Call Sign: KB1WYR
David Candela
68 Northfield Rd
Wallingford CT 06492

Call Sign: KA1EUZ
Donna K Valleau
4 Nutmeg Ct
Wallingford CT 06492

Call Sign: KA9CRG
Matthew J Valleau
4 Nutmeg Ct
Wallingford CT 06492

Call Sign: N1PBN
Thomas J Readey Jr
49 Osage Dr
Wallingford CT 06492

Call Sign: N1ZJS
Theresa A Readey
49 Osage Dr
Wallingford CT 06492

Call Sign: W1MKT
Thomas J Readey Jr
49 Osage Dr
Wallingford CT 06492

Call Sign: N1ZJT
Terrence M Readey
52 Osage Drive
Wallingford CT 06492

Call Sign: N1SST
Terrence M Readey
52 Osage Drive
Wallingford CT 06492

Call Sign: N1GOT
David W Scagnelli
12 Oxford Trail
Wallingford CT 064922626

Call Sign: WY1U
Timothy J Mik
5 Park Pond Cir
Wallingford CT 064922140

Call Sign: K1VDF
John D Blevins
60 Park Pond Cir
Wallingford CT 06492

Call Sign: WB1EBQ
Walter J Smith
192 Parker Farms Rd
Wallingford CT 06492

Call Sign: WB1EKI
Mark W Grochowski
53 Parker St
Wallingford CT 06492

Call Sign: KB1MXR
Dmitri Brook
53 Parker St C110
Wallingford CT 06492

Call Sign: KB1SUR
Dominic Scasino
9 Pelloni Hollow
Wallingford CT 06492

Call Sign: W1DOM
Dominic Scasino
9 Pelloni Hollow
Wallingford CT 06492

Call Sign: KA1ENR
Harvey W Kaetz
549 Pilgrims Harbor
Wallingford CT 06492

Call Sign: N1XIU
Richard J Hook
285 Pond Hill Rd
Wallingford CT 06492

Call Sign: KA1PCG
Robert N Hauser Jr
105 Prince St
Wallingford CT 06492

Call Sign: KB1MMS
Ronald A Slack
231 Quinnipiac St
Wallingford CT 06492

Call Sign: N1LGA
Michael F Tierney
1435 Rhey Ave
Wallingford CT 06492

Call Sign: WB1ABR
Kevin D Jacobson
27 Ridge Rd
Wallingford CT 06492

Call Sign: W1KDJ
Kevin D Jacobson
27 Ridge Rd
Wallingford CT 06492

Call Sign: KD1J
Kevin D Jacobson
27 Ridge Rd
Wallingford CT 06492

Call Sign: KB1CFB
Ronald V Paul
17 Ridgecrest Rd
Wallingford CT 06492

Call Sign: KB1KPL
Robert S Ross
34 Robert Ln
Wallingford CT 06492

Call Sign: N1NWP
William S Lyman Jr
219 S Orchard St
Wallingford CT 06492

Call Sign: WA1EET
Richard T Lostritto Sr
12 Saint Andrews Cir Unit 2
Wallingford CT 064925390

Call Sign: N1LES
Joseph M Murray
51 Schoolhouse Rd
Wallingford CT 06492

Call Sign: WB1GFI
Stanley C Hiriak
64 Schoolhouse Rd
Wallingford CT 06492

Call Sign: KB1APO
James J Sintay
5 Self Court
Wallingford CT 06492

Call Sign: KA1AXV
Roger W Dansereau
23 South Side Dr
Wallingford CT 06492

Call Sign: N1PBF
William B Munger Jr
15 Valley View Dr
Wallingford CT 06492

Call Sign: W1KSC
Philip V D Agostino
16 Shady Dr
Wallingford CT 06492

Call Sign: N1YMS
Alin J Lavariere
156 Southwind Drive
Wallingford CT 06492

Call Sign: KA1EEY
James F Cognetta
111 W Dayton Hill Rd
Wallingford CT 06492

Call Sign: KB1APW
Michael A Hill
7 Sharon Dr
Wallingford CT 06492

Call Sign: K1KBW
Robert E Albo
18 Stetson St
Wallingford CT 06492

Call Sign: KA1EAJ
Elmer N Paquette
121 W Dayton Hill Rd
Wallingford CT 064925324

Call Sign: W1KKF
William W Wawrzeniak
5 Shire Dr
Wallingford CT 06492

Call Sign: N1YMU
Miloslav Jungmann
6 Sunrise Cir
Wallingford CT 06492

Call Sign: W1SKP
Elmer N Paquette
121 W Dayton Hill Rd
Wallingford CT 06492

Call Sign: N1HJO
James G Cooke
17 Shire Dr
Wallingford CT 06492

Call Sign: KB1ERD
Miloslav Jungmann
6 Sunrise Cir
Wallingford CT 06492

Call Sign: KB1WON
Veterans
950 W Dayton Hill Rd
Wallingford CT 06492

Call Sign: KB1FYG
Michael V Camarata
37 Silliman Rd
Wallingford CT 064922035

Call Sign: K1UFS
Harry Subkowsky
4 Surrey Dr
Wallingford CT 06492

Call Sign: N1ZJQ
Zygmund S Loin Jr
59 Wallace Row
Wallingford CT 06492

Call Sign: KB1JDJ
Carol A Zipke
37 Silliman Rd
Wallingford CT 06492

Call Sign: KB1LRX
Paul J Ciezniak
11 Surrey Dr
Wallingford CT 06492

Call Sign: K1IIG
Stephen B Tripp
23 Wayne Rd
Wallingford CT 06492

Call Sign: N1LPY
Shelley A Lasker
123 Simpson Avenue
Wallingford CT 06492

Call Sign: K1SEZ
Paul J Ciezniak
11 Surrey Dr
Wallingford CT 06492

Call Sign: WA1LCR
Ronald E Fitch
12 Weatherside Dr
Wallingford CT 06492

Call Sign: W1OCB
George J Layman Sr
700 So Elm St
Wallingford CT 06492

Call Sign: N1HQY
William A Jens
4 Swan Ave
Wallingford CT 06492

Call Sign: KA1YL
Thomas F Cullen
2 Westview Dr
Wallingford CT 06492

Call Sign: N1XCE
James E Case
87 Wharton Br Dr
Wallingford CT 06492

Call Sign: WA1TAS
Bradley K Oestreicher
4 Wheatfield Drive
Wallingford CT 06492

Call Sign: KB1MDH
Zachary P Ribera
102 Woodhouse Ave
Wallingford CT 06492

Call Sign: KA1RWO
William H Wittstein
8 Woodland Dr
Wallingford CT 06492

Call Sign: KA1AXT
Thomas H Norrie
1174 Yale Ave
Wallingford CT 06492

Call Sign: N1KGY
Charles W Ayers
Wallingford CT 06492

Call Sign: N1OKM
Philip S Cook Iii
Wallingford CT 06492

Call Sign: N1TXK
Francis P Tomasiello
Wallingford CT 06492

Call Sign: N1URX
Martha A Floberg
Wallingford CT 06492

Call Sign: W1BV
Albert Schweitzer Institute
For The Humanities
Wallingford CT 064920550

Call Sign: KB1HLA
Rachel C Bonito
Wallingford CT 06492

Call Sign: KB1WYP
Jeffrey D Joy
Wallingford CT 06492

Call Sign: KB1EJT
Mike P Richo
75 Thorpe Ave
Wallington CT 06492

FCC Amateur Radio Licenses in Warehouse Point

Call Sign: K1CBA
Richard E Gwozdz
50 Scantic Rd
Warehouse Point CT 06088

FCC Amateur Radio Licenses in Warren

Call Sign: KB1QOP
George E Bates Iii
24 Anita Way
Warren CT 06754

Call Sign: KB1HNE
Jay F Wilson
28 Brickschool Rd
Warren CT 067591421

Call Sign: K1PNR
Irving K Reynolds Jr
90 Cornwall Rd
Warren CT 06754

Call Sign: KB1NZU
James A Schultz
165 Town Hill Rd
Warren CT 06754

Call Sign: KB1OST
Marcia A Schultz
165 Town Hill Rd
Warren CT 06754

Call Sign: KB1ABC
James A Schultz
165 Town Hill Rd
Warren CT 06754

Call Sign: N1YQQ
Douglas R Butler
27 Windy Ridge Rd
Warren CT 06754

FCC Amateur Radio Licenses in Washington

Call Sign: WA1PJY
John M Wyshynski
74 Hinkle Rd
Washington CT 06793

Call Sign: N2BIE
Xavier March
12 Painted Ridge Rd
Washington CT 06793

FCC Amateur Radio Licenses in Washington Depot

Call Sign: WA1MTQ
Frederick R Dahl
Baldwin Hill
Washington Depot CT 06794

Call Sign: N3HWM
Frank H Tomczyk Mr.
39 River Rd
Washington Depot CT 06794

Call Sign: KE6HKJ
Brian R Fernandez
145 Sabbaday Lane
Washington Depot CT
06749

Call Sign: K1BRF
Brian R Fernandez
145 Sabbaday Ln
Washington Depot CT
06794

Call Sign: K1HMT
William E Petruno Jr
22 Sunnyridge Rd
Washington Depot CT
06793

FCC Amateur Radio Licenses in Waterbury

Call Sign: N1EZE
Clifford L Aspinall
242 Alexander Ave
Waterbury CT 06705

Call Sign: KB1CGQ
Adalberto Rodriguez
292 Austin Rd Apt 5
Waterbury CT 06705

Call Sign: KP4MR
Miguel A Rivera
296 Austin Rd. Apt. 6
Waterbury CT 06705

Call Sign: N1QCY
Anthony A Valerio
63 Barbara St
Waterbury CT 06704

Call Sign: K1IVF
Jacob J Hanecak
33 Barrington Ln
Waterbury CT 06708

Call Sign: N1XGV
Gaetano T Amatruda
55 Barsalon Ave
Waterbury CT 06705

Call Sign: NF1F
Russell M Spencer
54 Bateswood Rd
Waterbury CT 06706

Call Sign: WP4KIF
Heriberto Garcia
41 Benjamin St
Waterbury CT 06706

Call Sign: KB1GEA
Noel A Gutierrez
324 Berkeley Ave
Waterbury CT 06704

Call Sign: KB1FYN
Raul O Pizarro
121 Beth Ln
Waterbury CT 06705

Call Sign: KA1UAT
Osward A Kaffana
30 Birchwood St
Waterbury CT 06708

Call Sign: KB1NJT
William D Saturno
248 Boyden St
Waterbury CT 06470

Call Sign: KB1JDW
Eugene A Field
263 Boyden St
Waterbury CT 06704

Call Sign: KA1KBW
Peter A Pecukonis
80 Bradley Ave
Waterbury CT 06708

Call Sign: N1TJS
Albert J Symonovich
14 Brewster St
Waterbury CT 067043001

Call Sign: KB1FXH
Jermaine A Chandler
36 Brookdale Lane
Waterbury CT 06705

Call Sign: N1XQH
Mark H Harold
134 Bunker Hill Ave Fl 2
Waterbury CT 06708

Call Sign: KA1NTC
Lewis E Greenwood
40 Byam Rd Apt 3
Waterbury CT 067053911

Call Sign: KB1BXK
Franklin Santiago
9 Carmen St
Waterbury CT 06706

Call Sign: KD1EY
Pierre E Ortiz
34 Chestnut Ave
Waterbury CT 06710

Call Sign: W1GTE
Gene R Schmidt
391 Chestnut Hill Ave
Waterbury CT 06704

Call Sign: WA1IXV
Victor Valletta Sr
440 Chipman St
Waterbury CT 06708

Call Sign: KE1EW
Gilberto Gonzalez
233 Chipman St Ext 2nd
Floor

Waterbury CT 06708

Call Sign: N1YLN
Edward A Olena
54 Clairmont 1st Fl.
Waterbury CT 06708

Call Sign: KB1TMC
Clare M Haney
54 Clairmont Avenue 1st
Floor
Waterbury CT 06708

Call Sign: KB1FSY
David P Mckenzie
105 Clinton St
Waterbury CT 06710

Call Sign: K1FSY
David P Mckenzie
105 Clinton St
Waterbury CT 06710

Call Sign: N1WQK
John W Hahn
364 Colonial Ave
Waterbury CT 067041316

Call Sign: N1KZU
William F Pryor
447 Congress Ave
Waterbury CT 06708

Call Sign: KB1HZY
Lisa M Capobianco
443 Country Club Rd
Waterbury CT 06708

Call Sign: KB1FGB
Thomas Capobianco
443 Country Club Road
Waterbury CT 06708

Call Sign: AA1XA
Thomas Capobianco

443 Country Club Road
Waterbury CT 06708

Call Sign: AF1W
John F Gordon
24 Darren Ct
Waterbury CT 067083903

Call Sign: KA1YZG
Donald A Melanson Sr
26 Deer Run Ln Apt 9
Waterbury CT 06705

Call Sign: KB1KGH
Donald A Melanson Sr
26 Deer Run Ln Apt 9
Waterbury CT 06705

Call Sign: W1BAR
Robert L Silvestri
81 Deerfield Ave
Waterbury CT 06708

Call Sign: WV1J
Roland T Hamel Jr
65 Deering Ln
Waterbury CT 06706

Call Sign: WA1INC
Roland T Hamel Jr
65 Deering Ln
Waterbury CT 06706

Call Sign: KA1EGJ
Gary L Rosengrant
85 Delaware Ave
Waterbury CT 067082444

Call Sign: K1TFF
Gary J Mc Guire
112 Delaware Avenue
Waterbury CT 067082445

Call Sign: N1MTB
Manuel J Torres

55 Dellwood Dr
Waterbury CT 06708

Call Sign: KA1BW
Andrew P Papanek
77 Draher St
Watebury CT 06708

Call Sign: N1ZIM
Joseph P Barocsi
5 E Fulkerson Dr
Waterbury CT 06708

Call Sign: N1NWO
Frank F Felber
168 E Main St
Waterbury CT 06702

Call Sign: KB1CGS
Juan Martinez
1660 East Main St Apt 5b
Waterbury CT 06705

Call Sign: K1RTS
Walter J Belsito Sr
142 Elliott Ave
Waterbury CT 06705

Call Sign: N1WET
Luis M De Jesus
22 Ellsworth Ave
Waterbury CT 06704

Call Sign: KB1VNQ
Lawrence M Hauser Jr
10 Esperon St
Waterbury CT 06705

Call Sign: KB1GBM
Margaret E Stubbs
176 Faber Ave
Waterbury CT 06704

Call Sign: KB1GBN
Richard W Stubbs

176 Faber Ave
Waterbury CT 06704

Call Sign: N1HMY
Douglas J Santoli
74 Fairfield Ave
Waterbury CT 06708

Call Sign: KB1KRB
William E Facer
251 Fairfield Ave
Waterbury CT 06708

Call Sign: KB1LMJ
Catherine E Facer
251 Fairfield Ave
Waterbury CT 06708

Call Sign: KB1LTY
William E Facer Jr
251 Fairfield Ave
Waterbury CT 06708

Call Sign: W1OLL
Edward F Derry
253 Fairlawn Ave
Waterbury CT 06705

Call Sign: N1BPE
James R White Sr
21 Farmwood Rd
Waterbury CT 06704

Call Sign: K1RMH
Russell M Harlow
112 Fern Cir
Waterbury CT 067082758

Call Sign: KC1WJ
William M Knapp
331 Forest Ridge Rd
Waterbury CT 06708

Call Sign: KA1YFL
Felix Cortes

21 Fox St
Waterbury CT 06708

Call Sign: KB1CPR
Alexander Cortes
23 Fox St
Waterbury CT 06708

Call Sign: KB1NCT
James J Bowler
153 Frske St
Waterbury CT 06710

Call Sign: NW7R
Raymond W Sumner
393 Gaylord Dr
Waterbury CT 06708

Call Sign: WA2OKS
George C Cuartero
3 Gayridge Road
Waterbury CT 06705

Call Sign: N2OKS
George C Cuartero
3 Gayridge Road
Waterbury CT 06705

Call Sign: KA1PUR
Sebastian A Vecca
25 Girard Ave
Waterbury CT 06704

Call Sign: KA1YED
Susan C Troupe
60 Grace Ave
Waterbury CT 06710

Call Sign: KF2XK
Paul B Iltchenko
60 Grace Ave
Waterbury CT 06710

Call Sign: WF1G
Paul B Iltchenko

60 Grace Ave
Waterbury CT 06710

Call Sign: K1KRY
Stanley Z Kugler Jr
147 Grandview Ave
Waterbury CT 067082508

Call Sign: W1XK
Stanley L Kugler
147 Grandview Ave
Waterbury CT 067082508

Call Sign: KA1WAV
Ross G Utter
134 Grandview Ave Suite
101
Waterbury CT 06708

Call Sign: KB1UVA
William M Legge
39 Granger St
Waterbury CT 06705

Call Sign: N1BPC
William H Box
47 Greenfield Avenue
Waterbury CT 06708

Call Sign: KA1ICW
John C Matheson
144 Grove St Apt 407
Waterbury CT 06710

Call Sign: W1DEE
Joseph A Di Leo
226 Haddad Rd
Waterbury CT 06708

Call Sign: KB1QAV
Kevin M Capobianco
92 Hallock Street
Waterbury CT 06706

Call Sign: N1ELH

Floyd E Hillman
103a Hamden Ave
Waterbury CT 067042752

Call Sign: KA1BXS
Robert J Senesac Jr
58 Harvard St
Waterbury CT 06704

Call Sign: KA1QYD
Mario A Varrone Sr
131 Heritage Dr
Waterbury CT 06708

Call Sign: KA1MEH
James A Baltrush
164 Hickory Hill Dr
Waterbury CT 06708

Call Sign: KA1OVQ
Robert L Butler
67 Highland Ave
Waterbury CT 06708

Call Sign: KA1ROS
Dorothy A Butler
67 Highland Ave
Waterbury CT 06708

Call Sign: KB1TKV
Robert J Colella
908 Highland Ave
Waterbury CT 06708

Call Sign: W1ELD
Robert J Colella
908 Highland Ave
Waterbury CT 06708

Call Sign: N1OYS
Edward C Lange Sr
1312 Highland Ave
Waterbury CT 06708

Call Sign: N1LHM

Anthony L Viola Sr
310 Highland Dr
Waterbury CT 06708

Call Sign: W1ALV
Anthony L Viola Sr
310 Highland Dr
Waterbury CT 06708

Call Sign: N1YAF
Roger J May
133 Highwood Rd
Waterbury CT 06708

Call Sign: W1SAG
Sharon A Grindrod
96 Hillcrest Avenue
Waterbury CT 06705

Call Sign: W1PPJ
Dennis A Grindrod Sr
96 Hillcrest Avenue
Waterbury CT 06705

Call Sign: KA1JMR
Carl M Cipriano
17 Hillview Ave
Waterbury CT 06704

Call Sign: N1LBY
Shari L Tidrick
380 Hitchcock Rd 161
Waterbury CT 06705

Call Sign: KB1IGE
Howard S Robins
380 Hitchcock Rd Unit 149
Waterbury CT 06705

Call Sign: N1SAD
William A Walker
126 Horseshoe Dr
Waterbury CT 06706

Call Sign: WB1AIE

David A De Angelis
23 Hutchinson St
Waterbury CT 06708

Call Sign: KU1F
Donald F Carpenter
111 Jersey St
Waterbury CT 06706

Call Sign: KA1ZED
Keith A Anderson
156 Jersey Street Apartment
3
Waterbury CT 06706

Call Sign: N1JVP
John F Wiehn
10 Jodie Cir
Waterbury CT 06706

Call Sign: K1OQK
Alvernon W Feero
122 Kelsey St
Waterbury CT 06706

Call Sign: K1SCN
Salvatore P Spino
52 Kenmore Ave
Waterbury CT 06708

Call Sign: WA1TCA
Jerry L Lloyd
31 Knoll Street
Waterbury CT 06705

Call Sign: KB1VHR
Louis E Pagan
173 Lakeside Blvd East
Waterbury CT 06708

Call Sign: N1HIP
Robert A Rudaitis
100 Larchmont Ave
Waterbury CT 06708

Call Sign: N1YLL
Raul Rebollo
152 Lincoln St
Waterbury CT 06710

Call Sign: WB1AIU
Joseph M Stofko Iii
297 Lincoln St
Waterbury CT 06710

Call Sign: W1AIU
Joseph M Stofko Iii
297 Lincoln St
Waterbury CT 06710

Call Sign: W2NG
Richard K Strobel
101 Longmeadow Drive
Waterbury CT 06706

Call Sign: N1MMP
Philip R Le Blanc
98 Lounsbury St
Waterbury CT 06706

Call Sign: WA1TBP
David J Genova
138 Macarthur Dr
Waterbury CT 06704

Call Sign: N1PFH
John D Slater
49 Maplewood St
Waterbury CT 06708

Call Sign: KA1EHD
James Dodds
72 Melbourne Ter
Waterbury CT 06704

Call Sign: KA1SEU
George P Miley
32 Meriden Rd
Waterbury CT 06705

Call Sign: KA1YTJ
Todd D Neuman
1358 Meriden Rd Apt 12
Waterbury CT 06705

Call Sign: KB1LEU
Francis J Delfino
219 Meriden Rd Ste 3
Waterbury CT 067051941

Call Sign: W1ATR
Francis J Delfino
219 Meriden Rd Ste 3
Waterbury CT 067051941

Call Sign: N1XZM
Jason J Brade
48 Meriden Road
Waterbury CT 06705

Call Sign: N1OBO
Scott L Gentile
47 Mildred Ave
Waterbury CT 06708

Call Sign: WA1OPD
Pat Finelli
13 Miller St
Waterbury CT 06704

Call Sign: NF1H
Elizabeth M Stotz
108 Moreland Ave
Waterbury CT 06705

Call Sign: N1VMO
Jennifer E Marshall
120 Mount Carmel Ave
Waterbury CT 06708

Call Sign: KB1MFU
John A Ramadei
2308 N Main St
Waterbury CT 06704

Call Sign: KA1WTH
Dennis M Conroy
3277 N Main St
Waterbury CT 06704

Call Sign: N1JWS
Armando Torres
1813 N Main St Apt D
Waterbury CT 06704

Call Sign: KB1AQT
Noela M Bourgoin
120-1 N Ridge Dr
Waterbury CT 06708

Call Sign: N1UHZ
Robert D Johnson
201 Newridge Ave
Waterbury CT 06708

Call Sign: WB1AVE
Raymond A Faber
2969 No Main St
Waterbury CT 06704

Call Sign: WA1ZMJ
Donald G Faber
3010 North Main St
Waterbury CT 06704

Call Sign: WA1CRS
Mark F Di Corpo
38 Oak Hill
Waterbury CT 06708

Call Sign: N1CHP
Michael P De Vivo
231 Park Rd
Waterbury CT 067082344

Call Sign: N1UCF
Jeffrey J Samoska
45 Pear St
Waterbury CT 067084921

Call Sign: WB1CUS
Kim M Myers
377 Pearl Lake Road
Waterbury CT 06706

Call Sign: KB1UAT
Theodore J Corcanges
152 Pinehurst Ave Unit 2
Waterbury CT 06705

Call Sign: KA1QXY
Fredrick M De Leon Jr
55 Piping Rock Rd
Waterbury CT 06706

Call Sign: KP4NW
Ramon Cancel
99 Platt St
Waterbury CT 06704

Call Sign: WP4KQ
Maria A Betancourt
99 Platt St
Waterbury CT 06704

Call Sign: N1VCW
Luis J Medina
62 Poplar St>
Waterbury CT 06708

Call Sign: KB2UKA
Douglas J Cerrato
34 Red Maple Lane
Waterbury CT 06704

Call Sign: KB1HQF
Tonya M Fennelly
129 Ridge Street
Waterbury CT 06706

Call Sign: N1EBG
Brian J Mongelluzzo
32 Ridgeland Drive
Waterbury CT 06708

Call Sign: N1MN
Eugene N Paolucci
31 Rosemount Ave
Waterbury CT 06708

Call Sign: N1WAF
Carman T Cartagena
1075 S Main St 4 Fl
Waterbury CT 06706

Call Sign: KB1EEN
John T Hart Jr
329 Schraffts Dr Apt 101
Waterbury CT 06705

Call Sign: KB1FEX
Kenneth J Jalbert
32 Starview Ave 2nd Floor
Apt
Waterbury CT 06708

Call Sign: KA2MSS
Joseph A Migliore Mr.
141 Stoddard Rd.
Waterbury CT 06708

Call Sign: W1QAJ
John J Tomasiewicz Sr
15 Stonybrook Rd
Waterbury CT 067053710

Call Sign: KB1CGT
Carlos M Ilarraza
33 Sumac St
Waterbury CT 06704

Call Sign: N1XLA
Jose D Rivera
33 Sumac St
Waterbury CT 06704

Call Sign: KB1VFF
Kenneth W Akins
25 Terrace Ave
Waterbury CT 06704

Call Sign: K1QFM
Nicholas J Parillo
56 Tracy Ave
Waterbury CT 06706

Call Sign: KP4UF
Aristalco Laracuente
Martinez
117 Tutor St
Waterbury CT 06704

Call Sign: KB1USS
Harvey O Watts
60 Vine St
Waterbury CT 06704

Call Sign: KB1HNG
Marc A Barbera
1024 W Main St
Waterbury CT 06708

Call Sign: N1IBO
Anthony T Vinciguerra
1157 W Main St
Waterbury CT 06708

Call Sign: KB1ASE
Jose Adorno
70 Walnut Ave
Waterbury CT 06704

Call Sign: N1XNS
Robert B Lovejoy
136 Washington St
Waterbury CT 06706

Call Sign: KA1FCH
Anthony J Zappone
150 Westmont Dr
Waterbury CT 06708

Call Sign: N1XBO
Michael D Griffin
158 Westmont Dr

Waterbury CT 06708

Call Sign: KA1JNG
John L Barbieri
89 Whittier Ave
Waterbury CT 06708

Call Sign: KC2EIK
Adelaida Sobrado
150 Willow Street 1st Floor
Waterbury CT 06710

Call Sign: NT1I
Richard A Jacovino
101 Woodbine St
Waterbury CT 06705

Call Sign: KE4TLK
James P Kelly Jr
47 Woodruff St
Waterbury CT 06708

Call Sign: K1FYS
David J Hales
56 Woodside Ave
Waterbury CT 06708

Call Sign: N1ZKY
Maribeth Cetola
98 Woodside Ave
Waterbury CT 06708

Call Sign: KA1JXW
John G Russo
104 Woodside Ave
Waterbury CT 067082504

Call Sign: WA1RJI
Greater Bridgeport Amateur
Radio Club
104 Woodside Ave
Waterbury CT 06708

Call Sign: N1TKN
David A Cetola

98 Woodside Avenue
Waterbury CT 06708

Call Sign: N1ZBT
Mark L Marcil
30 Wyoming Ave
Waterbury CT 06706

Call Sign: KC2GAZ
Felix D Nieves
39 Yale Street
Waterbury CT 06704

Call Sign: N1WAG
Maximo Torres
Waterbury CT 06710

FCC Amateur Radio Licenses in Waterford

Call Sign: N1MCY
Martin Kline
9 Baldwin Dr
Waterford CT 06385

Call Sign: KB1MAL
Paul S Kanfer
16 Baldwin Dr
Waterford CT 06385

Call Sign: KA1DOC
Paul S Kanfer
16 Baldwin Dr
Waterford CT 06385

Call Sign: W3QAN
Wayne G Shaffer
1 Beechwood Dr Apt 333
Waterford CT 06385

Call Sign: KS1I
Joseph P Kononchik
1 Betty Street
Waterford CT 06385

Call Sign: N1SPY
Harry J Neilan
4 Bishop St
Waterford CT 06385

Call Sign: K1KQW
Harry Sussman
191 Boston Post Rd
Waterford CT 06385

Call Sign: K1ARC
American Red Cross
Southeastern Ct Chapter
200 Boston Post Rd
Waterford CT 06385

Call Sign: KB1EJN
James E O Brien
349 Boston Post Rd
Waterford CT 06385

Call Sign: N1NNO
Charles I Hill
310 Boston Post Rd #32
Waterford CT 06385

Call Sign: KA1MIA
Charles R Edmonson Jr
26 Boston Post Rd 2 Fl
Waterford CT 06385

Call Sign: W1OPS
Howard R Cox
39 Braman Rd
Waterford CT 06385

Call Sign: WA1ZZO
Edward M Goldberg
91 Braman Rd
Waterford CT 06385

Call Sign: KB1UZJ
Nicholas P Constantine
211 Butlertown Rd
Waterford CT 06385

Call Sign: W1NYC
Lloyd H Chapel
88 Clark Ln
Waterford CT 06385

Call Sign: N1RAY
Charles B Werthman
2 Colonial Dr
Waterford CT 06385

Call Sign: KF1B
Edward S Eby
20 Colonial Dr
Waterford CT 06385

Call Sign: WA1AMO
Joseph J Bednarz Jr
13 Connshire Dr
Waterford CT 06385

Call Sign: KA1FBG
Robert E Handfield Sr
73 Dayton Rd
Waterford CT 06385

Call Sign: W1RAN
Edward L Raub Jr
12 Deerfield Rd
Waterford CT 06385

Call Sign: WA1MWD
Mitchell S Margolis
16 Doyle Rd
Waterford CT 06385

Call Sign: KA1VMH
Marvin R Sherriff
6 E Brook Dr
Waterford CT 06385

Call Sign: KB1DHV
John D Harrington
9 E Wharf Rd
Waterford CT 063852515

Call Sign: K1RVU
Max J Munsch
12 East Brook Dr
Waterford CT 06385

Call Sign: WA1GJL
Leonard Weinberg
15 Edgewood Ave
Waterford CT 06385

Call Sign: KA1ZRV
Stephen L Vlaun Sr
16 Fifth Ave
Waterford CT 06385

Call Sign: N5UGF
Joseph J Romano Jr
38 First Ave
Waterford CT 06385

Call Sign: WA1UXM
Stephen C Maginess
4 Goundry Dr
Waterford CT 06385

Call Sign: KA1TXT
Richard H West
25 Grabner Dr
Waterford CT 06385

Call Sign: N1EBA
Robert K Walter Iii
35 Greentree Dr
Waterford CT 06385

Call Sign: KC1MD
Jonathan L Levine
30 Gurley Road
Waterford CT 06385

Call Sign: N1DVY
Dean M White
11 Highland Dr
Waterford CT 06385

Call Sign: W1DCM
Thomas R Guadliana
21 Jordan Ter
Waterford CT 06385

Call Sign: WV1Z
Donald W Johnston
36 Kenyon Rd
Waterford CT 06385

Call Sign: N1OWN
Steven B Shortt
8 Kenyon Rd.
Waterford CT 06385

Call Sign: WA1YQI
Harrison A Fortier Jr
38 Lamphere Rd
Waterford CT 06385

Call Sign: W1HAF
Harrison A Fortier Jr
38 Lamphere Rd
Waterford CT 06385

Call Sign: KA1YXG
Nathan J Pupillo
6 Lark St
Waterford CT 06385

Call Sign: KB1RPK
Lawrence P Magee
9 Lee Rd
Waterford CT 06385

Call Sign: KB1RPP
Donna Magee
9 Lee Rd
Waterford CT 06385

Call Sign: WA1DD
Darryl L Del Grosso
13 Linda Ave
Waterford CT 06385

Call Sign: W1ECD
Alexander M Kasem Beg
39 Lloyd Rd
Waterford CT 06385

Call Sign: N1TYU
Curtis F Carlough
6 Locust Court
Waterford CT 063851506

Call Sign: N1WLI
Frederic C Carlough
17 Locust Court
Waterford CT 06385

Call Sign: N1KEJ
Theodore R Jones Jr
22 Lois Ave
Waterford CT 06385

Call Sign: KB1KHC
Bruce W Shewbrooks
4 Longview Ave
Waterford CT 06385

Call Sign: WA1GKU
Harold Margolis
55 Mackenzie Rd
Waterford CT 06385

Call Sign: KB1MAK
Thomas A Telage
14 Maginnis Pkwy
Waterford CT 06385

Call Sign: KA1SLB
William C Burch
7 Mallard Ln
Waterford CT 06385

Call Sign: KA1DDX
Roswell G Edgecomb
20 Mary St
Waterford CT 06385

Call Sign: KA1DDY
Eric C Strickland
32 Miner Ave
Waterford CT 06385

Call Sign: KQ1O
Arthur J Perry Jr
99 Niantic River Rd
Waterford CT 063851852

Call Sign: N1QYD
Margie A Petrilli
166 Niantic River Rd
Waterford CT 06385

Call Sign: KB1QQJ
Catherine C Chatfield
260 Niantic River Rd
Waterford CT 06385

Call Sign: KB1SAF
Catherine C Chatfield
260 Niantic River Rd
Waterford CT 06385

Call Sign: KB1PBP
Steven H Schoenberger
103 Oswegatchie Road
Waterford CT 06385

Call Sign: KB1JNE
David L Lindblom
13 Pamela Way
Waterford CT 06385

Call Sign: W1DLL
David L Lindblom
13 Pamela Way
Waterford CT 06385

Call Sign: KB1KFO
David L Lindblom
13 Pamela Way
Waterford CT 06385

Call Sign: AB1CU
David L Lindblom
13 Pamela Way
Waterford CT 06385

Call Sign: KB1LZC
Justin L Lindblom
13 Pamela Way
Waterford CT 06385

Call Sign: KB1ETQ
Scott S Hopper
16 Ridgewood Ave
Waterford CT 06385

Call Sign: KI1Y
Vincent E Castronova
62 Ridgewood Ave
Waterford CT 06385

Call Sign: KA1CIH
Robert E Mara
104 Ridgewood Ave
Waterford CT 06385

Call Sign: WA2Q
Keith D Kanoun
22 Robin Hill Road
Waterford CT 06385

Call Sign: K1QPV
Allen R Carpenter
30 Rockwood Dr
Waterford CT 06385

Call Sign: K1QWK
Ruth M Carpenter
30 Rockwood Dr
Waterford CT 06385

Call Sign: WB1EFV
Richard E Hix
200 Rope Ferry Rd
Waterford CT 06385

Call Sign: KB1VGT
Jared D Sparks
25 Roseleah Dr
Waterford CT 06385

Call Sign: WA1UVB
Richard D Dionne
36 Savi Ave
Waterford CT 063852224

Call Sign: WB1DJG
Albert A Knupp
18 Shawandassee Rd
Waterford CT 06385

Call Sign: WE1D
Gary A Slater
106 Shore Rd
Waterford CT 06385

Call Sign: KA1VOG
Aldo J Moretti
219 Shore Rd
Waterford CT 063853430

Call Sign: AA1UD
James M Howard
14 Spithead Rd
Waterford CT 06385

Call Sign: W1MCU
Margaret M Rogers
96 Spithead Rd
Waterford CT 06385

Call Sign: W1ZYJ
John H Rogers
96 Spithead Rd
Waterford CT 06385

Call Sign: N1JPW
John A Mc Garry
112 Stoneheights Dr
Waterford CT 06385

Call Sign: KA1KHW
Clifton J Brailey
47 Summer St
Waterford CT 06385

Call Sign: KE1LV
Edward F Hogan
21 Valley Street
Waterford CT 063853639

Call Sign: AI1T
James M Reid
17 Whaling Dr
Waterford CT 06385

Call Sign: K1LFI
Joseph A Cavanaugh
5 Wiemes Ct
Waterford CT 06385

Call Sign: WA1KMP
Margaret C Doucette
10 William St
Waterford CT 06385

Call Sign: KB1NHN
Christopher B Wright
61 Windward Way
Waterford CT 06385

Call Sign: N1APC
John R Watterson
30 Woodlawn Ave
Waterford CT 06385

Call Sign: KB1BZP
Southeastern Connecticut
Radio Amateur Mobile
Service
Waterford CT 06385

Call Sign: N1PFF
Paul M Brayne
Waterford CT 06385

Call Sign: W1NLC
Southeastern Connecticut
Radio Amateur Mobile
Service
Waterford CT 06385

Call Sign: KB1HNR
Gabriel A Panko
Waterford CT 063850029

FCC Amateur Radio Licenses in Watertown

Call Sign: N1VGF
Christopher James H Caesar
123 Barnes Rd
Watertown CT 06795

Call Sign: N1QCZ
Katherine M George
44 Buckwheat Hill Rd
Watertown CT 06795

Call Sign: KB1RRJ
Andrew L Rubman
1 Cannon Ridge Dr
Watertown CT 06795

Call Sign: KA1KLO
John H Smith
18 Cherry Ave
Watertown CT 06795

Call Sign: KB1MHO
Cuzco Contest Club
360 Cherry Ave
Watertown CT 067952818

Call Sign: WK1Q
Cuzco Contest Club
360 Cherry Ave
Watertown CT 067952818

Call Sign: KB1NGZ

Suzanne Khrystyne Keane
360 Cherry Ave
Watertown CT 067952818

Call Sign: KA1OLG
Jason J Molitierno
245 Cherry Avenue Unit
G15
Watertown CT 06795

Call Sign: KB1QCL
Christopher J Saraceno
31 Farmdale Rd
Watertown CT 06795

Call Sign: N1LMZ
Scott M Ligi
281 Fern Hill Rd
Watertown CT 06795

Call Sign: K1JTK
Michael J Defazio Sr.
109 Fern Hill Rd.
Watertown CT 067951512

Call Sign: KB1HNF
Jeffery J Fennelly
64 French St
Watertown CT 06795

Call Sign: N1GTW
James F De Marest Sr
102 French St
Watertown CT 06795

Call Sign: WA1JBS
James F Zilvitis Sr
46 Hart St
Watertown CT 06795

Call Sign: WB2VPT
Michael Israel
20 Hidden Pond Rd
Watertown CT 06795

Call Sign: K1DDY
Edward F Ryan
50 High St
Watertown CT 06795

Call Sign: KA1RBB
Gregory S Wolfe
116 Honey Hill
Watertown CT 06795

Call Sign: KA1RBA
Christopher S Wolfe
116 Honey Hill Rd
Watertown CT 06795

Call Sign: N1TVP
Jay P Fishcer
210 Hopkins Rd
Watertown CT 06795

Call Sign: N1VGE
Roger R Drouin
71 Inverary Rd
Watertown CT 06795

Call Sign: N1XQG
David E Buck
28 Iroquois Rd
Watertown CT 06795

Call Sign: W1QBF
Robert W Baldwin
54 Linkfield Rd
Watertown CT 06795

Call Sign: WR1V
Tyson Garbrecht
151 Mount Fair Drive
Watertown CT 06795

Call Sign: KA1LHT
Raymond A Frigon
83 Mt Fair Dr
Watertown CT 06795

Call Sign: N1WAL
Robin M Micket
146 Neill Drive
Watertown CT 06795

Call Sign: N1TVK
Jan J Guidess
150 Northfield Rd
Watertown CT 06795

Call Sign: W1PFB
Glenn H Wayne Jr
40 Nova Scotia Hill Rd
Watertown CT 06795

Call Sign: KB1VFG
James F Bebarski
211 Nova Scotia Hill Rd
Watertown CT 06795

Call Sign: KA1NTA
Colangelo Forino
472 Nova Scotia Hill Rd
Watertown CT 06795

Call Sign: KA1YHB
David Cortes Sr
472 Nova Scotia Hill Rd
Watertown CT 06795

Call Sign: KB1SXV
Ronald F Carver
675 Park Rd
Watertown CT 06795

Call Sign: KA1WLV
Pedro T Fernandes
235 Parkman St
Watertown CT 06779

Call Sign: KB1GGK
Krystal Wills
132 Porter St
Watertown CT 06795

Call Sign: N1TSC
Timothy S Tignor
59 Princeton Ter
Watertown CT 06795

Call Sign: NR1C
Michael S Tignor
59 Princeton Ter
Watertown CT 06795

Call Sign: KB1HCW
Victoria S Tignor
59 Princeton Terr
Watertown CT 06795

Call Sign: K1TPZ
Earl R Hon
150 Straits Tpke
Watertown CT 06795

Call Sign: N1SUO
Herman D Marggraff Jr
386 Straits Tpke
Watertown CT 06795

Call Sign: N1TYV
Michael E White
162 Westbury Park Rd
Watertown CT 06795

Call Sign: KB1ALZ
Cynthia A Halliwell
41 Wheeler St
Watertown CT 06795

Call Sign: N1ONJ
John E Halliwell
41 Wheeler St
Watertown CT 06795

Call Sign: K1SBM
Conrad J Stokes
Watertown CT 06795

Call Sign: WB1DDT

Stephen H Cammack
Watertown CT 06795

FCC Amateur Radio Licenses in Weatogue

Call Sign: KB1WFF
G Daniel Thomas
30 Blue Ridge Dr
Weatogue CT 06089

Call Sign: WA1SVS
Carlos J Garrett Iii
16 Colonial Drive
Weatogue CT 06089

Call Sign: KB1IXW
Glenn R Mcintyre
303 Hopmeadow St
Weatogue CT 06089

Call Sign: AB1LZ
William T Storey Iii
52 Red Stone Dr
Weatogue CT 06089

Call Sign: KB1VBB
East Granby Emergency
Communications Team
52 Red Stone Dr
Weatogue CT 06089

Call Sign: KA1WRS
Gerald R Iwan
20 Sunrise Ter
Weatogue CT 06089

FCC Amateur Radio Licenses in West Cornwall

Call Sign: W2QN
Halbert R Cliff
96 Dibble Hill Rd
West Cornwall CT 06796

Call Sign: N1RXO
Timothy L Locke
22 Lower River Rd
West Cornwall CT 06796

Call Sign: K1IWY
Jerry S Richter
33 Lower River Rd Box 66
West Cornwall CT 06796

Call Sign: KB1PQO
Marc D Simont
78 Pierce Lane
West Cornwall CT 06796

Call Sign: K1CTT
Marc D Simont
78 Pierce Lane
West Cornwall CT 06796

Call Sign: N1CDP
William F Brecher
57 Scoville Rd
West Cornwall CT 06796

Call Sign: KB1JTZ
Thomas M Brown
24 Sharon Goshen Tpk
West Cornwall CT 06796

Call Sign: N2CPP
Nevton D Dunn
19 Todd Hill Ext
West Cornwall CT 06796

Call Sign: W1UWV
Erich Richter Jr
33 Warren Tpke
West Cornwall CT 06796

FCC Amateur Radio Licenses in West Goshen

Call Sign: KA1OBL
John W George

153 Ives Rd
West Goshen CT 06756

**FCC Amateur Radio
Licenses in West Granby**

Call Sign: KB1VHO
Timothy C Maver
115 Firetown Rd
West Granby CT 06090

Call Sign: WA1VDX
Henry G Reluga
102 Higley Rd
West Granby CT 06090

Call Sign: KB1PIR
Gary C English
136 Higley Rd
West Granby CT 06090

Call Sign: KB1IPK
Jonathan M Kinsky
10 Moosehorn Rd
West Granby CT 06090

Call Sign: KB1KES
John F Kinsky
10 Moosehorn Rd
West Granby CT 06090

Call Sign: KB1REZ
Thomas J Bazyk
78 Simsbury Rd
West Granby CT 06090

Call Sign: KB1EAT
Stephen A Jakubowski
West Granby CT 06090

**FCC Amateur Radio
Licenses in West Hartford**

Call Sign: KB1MHK
David Bailey-Gates

1012 A Trout Brook Dr
West Hartford CT 06119

Call Sign: W1CBG
David Bailey-Gates
1012 A Trout Brook Dr
West Hartford CT 06119

Call Sign: KB1LPM
Chad A Thompson
30 Ahern St
West Hartford CT 06110

Call Sign: W1CKB
Chad A Thompson
30 Ahern St
West Hartford CT 06110

Call Sign: K8LSB
Marc B Goldstein
2657 Albany Ave
West Hartford CT 06117

Call Sign: WA1RYZ
Arnold L Chase
3115 Albany Avenue
West Hartford CT
061171858

Call Sign: KB1NWC
Brian M O'connell
18 Arlington Rd
West Hartford CT 06107

Call Sign: W1ASH
Robert F Moore
26 Auburn Rd
West Hartford CT 06119

Call Sign: KB1MXO
Jonathan C Flanders
30 Auburn Rd
West Hartford CT 06119

Call Sign: K3WFX

Scott P Bernstein
19 Avondale Rd
West Hartford CT 06117

Call Sign: KA1NRZ
Paul F Adomeit
39 Avondale Road
West Hartford CT 06117

Call Sign: N1RFF
Tomas M Foral
15 Baldwin St
West Hartford CT 06110

Call Sign: N1SPE
Donald G Olson
19 Baldwin St
West Hartford CT 06110

Call Sign: WA1VDZ
Francis P Dilion
27 Baldwin St
West Hartford CT 06110

Call Sign: N1OJQ
William A Nixon Iii
151 Balfour Dr
West Hartford CT 06117

Call Sign: KA1UU
Daniel M Friedman
49 Ballard Dr
West Hartford CT 06119

Call Sign: N1NEN
Albert A Bosco Jr
203 Ballard Drive
West Hartford CT 06119

Call Sign: N1ZJN
Walter C Barnes
27 Belcrest
West Hartford CT 06107

Call Sign: KB1MHL

Michael A Diaz
19 Berkshire Rd
West Hartford CT 06110

Call Sign: WA1CTZ
James S Capella
94 Bevarly Rd
West Hartford CT 06119

Call Sign: KB1OQY
Newton A Clark
270 Bloomfield Ave
West Hartford CT 06117

Call Sign: KA6DLE
Gary T Lieb
1130 Boulevard
West Hartford CT 06119

Call Sign: KB1LUT
Kenneth A Angle
1410 Boulevard
West Hartford CT 06119

Call Sign: KA1AJW
Paul S Cianci
107 Brace Rd
West Hartford CT 06107

Call Sign: W1WPR
Charles R Bender
23 Briarwood Rd
West Hartford CT
061072902

Call Sign: WA1VMC
Arline P Bender
23 Briarwood Rd
West Hartford CT 06107

Call Sign: K1MRM
George A Whelpley
44 Briarwood Rd
West Hartford CT 06107

Call Sign: KA1NJK
Brandon F Kampe
39 Brookmoor Rd
West Hartford CT 06107

Call Sign: AJ1K
Howard L Reuben
33 Brookside Blvd
West Hartford CT 06107

Call Sign: KA1MOD
Daniel Y Reuben
33 Brookside Boulevard
West Hartford CT
061071108

Call Sign: KB1NVL
Kimberly A Orzech
88 Brookside Dr
West Hartford CT 06107

Call Sign: KB1CGE
Jonathan I Kaufman
5 Brownleigh Rd
West Hartford CT
061171438

Call Sign: N1GDW
Joyce K Dickey
23 Brownleigh Rd
West Hartford CT
061171438

Call Sign: WV1W
Donald K Dickey
23 Brownleigh Rd
West Hartford CT 06117

Call Sign: KA1RBP
Ronald E Kwas
58 Brownleigh Rd
West Hartford CT 06117

Call Sign: W1SIS
Louis F Leonard

16 Brunswick Ave
West Hartford CT
061071711

Call Sign: N1ABL
Michael E Drechsler
25 Candlewood Dr
West Hartford CT 06117

Call Sign: N1ATH
Stephen D Perl
41 Candlewood Dr
West Hartford CT 06117

Call Sign: W1SHL
Stephan J Kaufmann
63 Carlyle Rd
West Hartford CT 06117

Call Sign: W1HUI
Douglas C Talbott
22 Claybar Dr
West Hartford CT 06117

Call Sign: WU1M
Michael A Berlin
63 Clifford Dr
West Hartford CT 06107

Call Sign: KB1IWI
 Aeronautical Mobile
Operators Club
63 Clifford Dr
West Hartford CT 06107

Call Sign: WE1FLY
 Aeronautical Mobile
Operators Club
63 Clifford Dr
West Hartford CT 06107

Call Sign: N1MZA
Perry S Mansfield
102 Clifton Ave
West Hartford CT 06107

Call Sign: KB1KOS
Thomas M Cote
123 Colonial St
West Hartford CT
061101811

Call Sign: WB0BOR
Kent A Sinram
43 Conard Dr
West Hartford CT
061073621

Call Sign: W1DGM
David G Mello
29 Cornell Rd
West Hartford CT 06107

Call Sign: KB1MPF
Andrew T Bieszad
15 Court Park
West Hartford CT 06119

Call Sign: WA2JUV
Samuel P Langweil
7 Crestwood Rd
West Hartford CT 06107

Call Sign: KA1ZTM
Jean Michel F Sibille
36 Crosshill Rd
West Hartford CT 06107

Call Sign: K1XA
Robert J Halprin
41 Crossroads Plaza #278
West Hartford CT 06117

Call Sign: K1BLT
Henry K Elliott
73 Cumberland Rd
West Hartford CT 06119

Call Sign: K1MGN
Harry Cohn

311 Cumberland Rd
West Hartford CT 06119

Call Sign: W1KGF
Morris Feigenbaum
65 Danforth Ln
West Hartford CT 06110

Call Sign: KA1GLW
Adelbert T Morency
44 Davenport Rd
West Hartford CT 06110

Call Sign: K1FTY
Frank C Hubbard
49 Davenport Rd
West Hartford CT 06110

Call Sign: KB1KTF
Steven I Adler
24 Edmund Pl
West Hartford CT 06119

Call Sign: N1IZC
Robert L Carlton
35 Ellsworth Rd
West Hartford CT 06107

Call Sign: N1OEO
William D Okeson
16 Fairfield Rd
West Hartford CT 06117

Call Sign: N1QOL
Jonathan M Hill
34 Fairview St Apt B6
West Hartford CT 06119

Call Sign: KC1Z
James R Mac Hardy
64 Fairwood Farms Dr
West Hartford CT 06107

Call Sign: W1MUW
Norma W Moskey

49 Fairwood Farms Drive
West Hartford CT
061073502

Call Sign: KA1OXW
Kathleen Cairns
724 Farmington Ave
West Hartford CT 06119

Call Sign: N1OQE
George W Cooper
1161 Farmington Ave
West Hartford CT 06107

Call Sign: KJ4HZR
Phillip Y Roland
3 Fawn Brook
West Hartford CT 06117

Call Sign: N1DN
Phillip Y Roland
3 Fawn Brook
West Hartford CT 06117

Call Sign: WA1PLG
Bern Solyn
100 Federal St
West Hartford CT 06110

Call Sign: KB1RMS
Edward C Mooney
383 Fern St
West Hartford CT 06119

Call Sign: WA1POI
Bruce R Kampe
500 Fern St
West Hartford CT 06107

Call Sign: K1BRK
Bruce R Kampe
500 Fern St
West Hartford CT
061071408

Call Sign: W1EA
Julius L Galin
60 Ferncliff Dr
West Hartford CT 06117

Call Sign: WA1KGQ
 Pioneer Valley Radio Assn
Inc
60 Ferncliff Dr
West Hartford CT 06117

Call Sign: KB1GHJ
Ronald F Cady
110 Four Mile Road
West Hartford CT 06107

Call Sign: WA1ISD
Stuart R Liftig
75 Foxridge Rd
West Hartford CT 06107

Call Sign: W1FLA
Jack Bass
89 Fuller Dr
West Hartford CT 06117

Call Sign: KB1HOU
Thomas F Gaffey Jr
19 Greenhurst Rd
West Hartford CT 06107

Call Sign: KA1KRP
Leslie S Andrew Jr
23 Grove St
West Hartford CT 06110

Call Sign: KA1NDE
Christopher J Andrew
23 Grove St
West Hartford CT
061101840

Call Sign: N1HQX
Janet C Andrew
23 Grove St

West Hartford CT 06110

Call Sign: N1WEW
Alexander Nweeia
91 Hartwell Rd
West Hartford CT 06117

Call Sign: KA1LF
Judith R Jordan
40 Henley Way
West Hartford CT 06117

Call Sign: WB1GKO
Allan Jordan
40 Henley Way
West Hartford CT 06117

Call Sign: KQ6KC
Matteo A Lo Grande
3 Hickory Ln
West Hartford CT 06107

Call Sign: KB1RWY
Barbara Cherry
64 High Farms Rd
West Hartford CT 06107

Call Sign: KB1RWZ
Thomas R Cherry
64 High Farms Rd
West Hartford CT 06107

Call Sign: KA1ZL
Steven A Stier
76 High Ridge Rd
West Hartford CT 06117

Call Sign: KC2DCT
Zoran Maricevic
103 High Ridge Rd
West Hartford CT 06117

Call Sign: N1CLW
Jeffrey S Katz
7 High Wood Road

West Hartford CT
061171117

Call Sign: KB1NRR
Tristan R Overstreet
5 Highland St Apt C5
West Hartford CT 06119

Call Sign: W1VJY
Melvin Stricker
34 Hilldale Rd
West Hartford CT 06117

Call Sign: KB1CGF
Garrett M Conway
40 Hilldale Rd
West Hartford CT 06117

Call Sign: KB1RUH
Peter C Lavoie
69 Hilltop Dr
West Hartford CT 06107

Call Sign: K1PCL
Peter C Lavoie
69 Hilltop Dr
West Hartford CT 06107

Call Sign: KA1DFC
Roman Luftglas
5 Hosmer Dr
West Hartford CT 06117

Call Sign: KB1EHY
Hilda I Sullivan
61 Jackson Ave
West Hartford CT 06110

Call Sign: N1KVS
Joel A Stoltz
15 Kirkwood Rd
West Hartford CT 06117

Call Sign: KB1HCZ
Jeremy M Stoltz

15 Kirkwood Rd
West Hartford CT 06117

Call Sign: KA1MLQ
Erik R Jensen
19 Laurel Dr.
West Hartford CT 06110

Call Sign: KA1VGF
Steven C Chambers
126 Lawler Rd
West Hartford CT 06117

Call Sign: KA1MJL
Link W La Porte
55 Layton St
West Hartford CT 06110

Call Sign: N1HGI
Gordon K Shand
62 Lemay St
West Hartford CT 06107

Call Sign: N1PVK
Jeffrey L Schmitt
97 Lemay St.
West Hartford CT 06107

Call Sign: WB1FXZ
Theodor M Simon
51 Linbrook Rd
West Hartford CT 06107

Call Sign: W1TXI
Edward E Hunt Jr
29 Longlane Rd
West Hartford CT 06117

Call Sign: W1UYP
Sylvia C Hunt
29 Longlane Rd
West Hartford CT 06117

Call Sign: WA1BXA

West Hartford Amateur
Radio Club
29 Longlane Rd
West Hartford CT 06117

Call Sign: N1JJC
Scott R Galin
81 Longlane Rd
West Hartford CT 06117

Call Sign: W1LOP
Scott R Galin
81 Longlane Rd
West Hartford CT 06117

Call Sign: W1MJM
Micah J Murray
Loomis Drive
West Hartford CT 06107

Call Sign: KA1TIE
Robert L Hoffman
25 Lovelace Dr
West Hartford CT 06117

Call Sign: KA1MCT
Adam M Kaplan
30 Lovelace Dr
West Hartford CT 06117

Call Sign: N1SPH
Edward T Brown
20 Lowell Rd
West Hartford CT 06119

Call Sign: KA1PKS
Michael A Elansky
25 Maiden Ln
West Hartford CT 06117

Call Sign: N1HUX
George W Rooney
59 Manchester Cir
West Hartford CT 06110

Call Sign: KA1MOE
Christopher M Coleman
14 Mansfield Ave
West Hartford CT 06117

Call Sign: N1FSQ
Mark H Jenks
96 Maplewood Ave
West Hartford CT 06119

Call Sign: N1LFR
John A Montgomery Jr
17 Middlefield Dr
West Hartford CT 06107

Call Sign: KB1VWO
Whitney F Stewart
146 Milton St
West Hartford CT 06119

Call Sign: W1WFS
Whitney F Stewart
146 Milton St
West Hartford CT 06119

Call Sign: N1ETM
Howard G Kirsner
101 Mohegan Dr
West Hartford CT 06117

Call Sign: W1HGK
Howard G Kirsner
101 Mohegan Dr
West Hartford CT 06117

Call Sign: N1AUR
Bert Sirkin
200 Mohegan Dr
West Hartford CT 06117

Call Sign: N1OPO
Thomas A Beach
120 Montclair Dr
West Hartford CT 06107

Call Sign: KB1TEW
Karl L Kuhn
143 Montclair Dr
West Hartford CT 06107

Call Sign: KA1GHM
Sam Pasco
Mountain Rd
West Hartford CT 06117

Call Sign: K1QPM
Roger B Jeanfaivre
1281 New Britain Ave
West Hartford CT 06110

Call Sign: N1PSJ
Daniel P Mc Nally
46 Newport Ave
West Hartford CT 06107

Call Sign: N1UAT
Matthew W Kilbourn
207 North Main Street
West Hartford CT 06107

Call Sign: KB1IQG
David N Greenfield
126 Norwood Rd
West Hartford CT 06117

Call Sign: N1VRD
Gregory E Watts
106 Oakwood Ave Apt A7
West Hartford CT 06119

Call Sign: WA2FTZ
Mark S Cronemeyer
112 Overbrook Road
West Hartford CT 06107

Call Sign: KB1ERS
Patrick Macomber
6 Oxford Dr
West Hartford CT
061071621

Call Sign: K1ERS
Patrick Macomber
6 Oxford Dr
West Hartford CT
061071621

Call Sign: KA1YKK
Roy S Perkins
622 Park Rd
West Hartford CT 06107

Call Sign: KX9X
Sean E Kutzko
47 Prescott St Apt B3
West Hartford CT 06110

Call Sign: N1EOL
Barry F Collord
41 Randal Ave
West Hartford CT
061101744

Call Sign: N1FEN
Sean P Collord
41 Randal Ave
West Hartford CT 06110

Call Sign: N1KCK
Michael J Taylor
42 Randal Road
West Hartford CT 06110

Call Sign: KA1MOC
Jay A Steinmetz
38 Ranger Ln
West Hartford CT 06117

Call Sign: NO1T
James A Yaeger
48 Ravenwood Rd
West Hartford CT 06107

Call Sign: KB1IGU
Julia A Cohn

80 Richmond Ln
West Hartford CT 06117

Call Sign: N1HDI
Ernest A Lefebvre
109 Richmond Ln
West Hartford CT 06117

Call Sign: KB1RGQ
Robert H Gale
183 Ridgewood Rd
West Hartford CT 06107

Call Sign: K3FN
James E Mackey
187 Ridgewood Rd
West Hartford CT
061073508

Call Sign: KB1YM
Douglas R Pagett
66 Rockledge Dr
West Hartford CT 06107

Call Sign: W1EPC
John B French
24 Rockwell Pl
West Hartford CT 06107

Call Sign: WA1YNI
Rex Roth
37 Royal Oak Dr
West Hartford CT 06107

Call Sign: N1EC
Martin F Levere
17 Rumford St
West Hartford CT 06107

Call Sign: WA1BJI
James E Kane
35 Rumford St
West Hartford CT
061073760

Call Sign: W1YER
Leonard G Rich
7 Rye Ridge Pky
West Hartford CT 06117

Call Sign: KB1EVK
Per V Wennerstrom
241 S Main St
West Hartford CT 06107

Call Sign: WA1PW
Per V Wennerstrom
241 S Main St
West Hartford CT 06107

Call Sign: KA1KEB
Mary L Kinnane
548 S Main St
West Hartford CT 06110

Call Sign: KB1EOY
William G Ewan
20 Sandhurst Dr
West Hartford CT
061073644

Call Sign: W1RTR
William G Ewan
20 Sandhurst Dr
West Hartford CT
061073644

Call Sign: KB1FNY
Veeta A Ewan
20 Sandhurst Drive
West Hartford CT 06107

Call Sign: KB1QQR
Paul R Taschereau Jr
64 Sedgwick Rd
West Hartford CT 06107

Call Sign: KB1NTU
Bryan M Lieblick
44 Seminole Cir

West Hartford CT 06117

Call Sign: WA1DBU
David M Siegel
52 Seneca Road
West Hartford CT 06117

Call Sign: N7OKQ
Richard E Andersen
54 Shadow Ln
West Hartford CT 06110

Call Sign: KA1URN
Marcel J Grenier
100 Shadow Ln
West Hartford CT 06110

Call Sign: N1PMR
Robert J Daly Jr
83 Shadow Ln Unit B1
West Hartford CT 06110

Call Sign: KB1DWV
Sally Ann D Derench
26 Sherwood Rd
West Hartford CT
061172738

Call Sign: N1XLU
Raymond C Derench
26 Sherwood Rd
West Hartford CT 06117

Call Sign: AB1NH
James R Livermore
2 Short Rd
West Hartford CT 06107

Call Sign: KB1VWN
George M Murphy
25 Smallwood Rd
West Hartford CT 06107

Call Sign: KA1OAK
George M Murphy

25 Smallwood Rd
West Hartford CT 06107

Call Sign: KB1SPJ
Marat F Kulakhmetov
499 South Main St
West Hartford CT 06110

Call Sign: KB1SZD
Rufat F Kulakhmetov
499 South Main St
West Hartford CT 06110

Call Sign: WA1SBS
Bramo P Ratti
102 St Charles St
West Hartford CT 06119

Call Sign: KA1HTN
David E Labenski
145 Steele Rd
West Hartford CT 06119

Call Sign: KA1HWC
Carolyn D Labenski
145 Steele Rd
West Hartford CT 06119

Call Sign: KA1KRL
John R Labenski
145 Steele Rd
West Hartford CT 06119

Call Sign: W1GEH
Robert Labenski
145 Steele Rd
West Hartford CT 06119

Call Sign: W1GZC
Leonard A Doughty
70 Sylvan Ave
West Hartford CT 06107

Call Sign: KB1DEB
Clifton T Baird

114 Thomas St
West Hartford CT 06119

Call Sign: KB1TIK
Ann-Marie St Jean
130 Thomas St.
West Hartford CT 06119

Call Sign: N1GOA
Robert Lebovitz
82 Timberwood Rd
West Hartford CT 06117

Call Sign: KA1RVW
Carol A Krohn
330 Tunxis Rd
West Hartford CT 06107

Call Sign: KB1NTW
Robert H Wilson
75 Uplands Dr
West Hartford CT
061071038

Call Sign: KA1ZOO
Harriet J Alvord
69 Van Buren Ave
West Hartford CT
061073051

Call Sign: KA1WDZ
William P Lind
45 W Hill Dr
West Hartford CT 06119

Call Sign: KA1FCT
Edward L Friedman
49 W Ridge Dr
West Hartford CT 06117

Call Sign: KA1PKR
Jon M Goldblatt
185 W Ridge Dr
West Hartford CT 06117

Call Sign: KA1ODV
James A Taylor Jr
55 Walden St
West Hartford CT 06107

Call Sign: WA1VMB
Edward M Prager
55 Walton Dr
West Hartford CT 06107

Call Sign: KB1FZZ
Bradley Busque
62 Warwick Street
West Hartford CT 06119

Call Sign: KA1UCN
Adam M Funkhouser
34 Washington Cir
West Hartford CT 06119

Call Sign: N1AF
Alan K Galin
30 West Maxwell Drive
West Hartford CT 06107

Call Sign: K1WY
William A Yoreo
24 Westfield Rd
West Hartford CT
061191533

Call Sign: KW1JY
Judith Yoreo
24 Westfield Rd
West Hartford CT
061191533

Call Sign: N1JY
Judith Yoreo
24 Westfield Rd
West Hartford CT
061191533

Call Sign: W1JNR
John N Ramsey

34 Westfield Rd
West Hartford CT 06119

Call Sign: N1QWQ
Richard E Lindberg
273 Westpoint Terr
West Hartford CT 06107

Call Sign: N1NYO
Matthew S Rosenthal
63 Westpoint Terrace
West Hartford CT 06107

Call Sign: N1RDF
Edward Rankin
39 Whitman Ave
West Hartford CT 06107

Call Sign: KA1DZW
Susanne M Farrah
70 Whitman Ave
West Hartford CT 06107

Call Sign: KA1ULY
Supriyo B Chatterjee
159 Whitman Ave
West Hartford CT 06107

Call Sign: KB1IGJ
Adam Q Khan
11 Wiltshire Ln
West Hartford CT 06117

Call Sign: KA1WMF
Peter A Herrmann
35 Wiltshire Ln
West Hartford CT 06117

Call Sign: K1GHJ
Alec R Bobrow
29 Winchester Drive
West Hartford CT 06117

Call Sign: KA1KOV
Robert S Burke

52 Woodmere Rd
West Hartford CT 06119

Call Sign: KB1TIB
William C Bigler
46 Woodridge Cir
West Hartford CT 06107

Call Sign: K1EXE
William C Bigler
46 Woodridge Cir
West Hartford CT 06107

Call Sign: KA1QVC
Randall Pease Jr
12 Woodruff Rd
West Hartford CT 06107

Call Sign: AA1DO
Albert Alvareztorres Jr
West Hartford CT
061330013

Call Sign: N1VIJ
Cynthe Aeon
West Hartford CT
061271363

Call Sign: N1YPG
William J Batayte Sr
West Hartford CT
061330175

Call Sign: KB1EOZ
Patricia A Gilbert
West Hartford CT
061330846

Call Sign: KB1FMU
Ranko Boca
West Hartford CT 06133

Call Sign: KB1RRZ
Thomas D Policelli
West Hartford CT 06137

FCC Amateur Radio
Licenses in West Hartland

Call Sign: WO1Z
Frank E Guptill
281 Pinehurst Rd
West Hartland CT 06091

Call Sign: KA1WEA
Robert H Lemp
West St
West Hartland CT 06091

FCC Amateur Radio
Licenses in West Haven

Call Sign: KB1TPS
Armand C Serio
21 4th Avenue
West Haven CT 06516

Call Sign: KB1SSR
Michael Cave
66 Aircraft Road
West Haven CT 06516

Call Sign: KA1VPL
Hobart N Stiles
75 Albion Ave
West Haven CT 06516

Call Sign: KA1FAL
Leon A Tomlinson
54 Alling St
West Haven CT 06516

Call Sign: KA1SNT
Edward W Jolley
54 Antrim St
West Haven CT 06516

Call Sign: KB1CHH
Kenneth E Wilhelm
31 Arlington St

West Haven CT 06516

Call Sign: KB1GXR
Edwin W Rhodes Iii
5 Bassett St Apt C-1
West Haven CT 06516

Call Sign: KB1SWJ
Edwin W Rhodes Iii
5 Bassett St Apt C-1
West Haven CT 06516

Call Sign: WA1LEI
Edwin W Rhodes Iii
5 Bassett St Apt C-1
West Haven CT 06516

Call Sign: N1ORW
Carl E Passafiume
106 Beatrice Dr
West Haven CT 065166519

Call Sign: W1ORS
Stratford Amateur Radio
Club Inc
106 Beatrice Dr
West Haven CT 06516

Call Sign: N1FNP
Anita L Ferron
109 Benham Hill Rd
West Haven CT 06516

Call Sign: N4GAA
Jayson T Ferron
109 Benham Hill Rd
West Haven CT 06516

Call Sign: KB1HTH
Arc Of Falls Church
109 Benham Hill Rd
West Haven CT 06516

Call Sign: K6OG
Arc Of Falls Church

109 Benham Hill Rd
West Haven CT 06516

Call Sign: KA8VYG
Charles E Ruotolo
297 Boston Post Road
West Haven CT 06516

Call Sign: WB1CSC
Joseph L Serphillips
45 Brower St
West Haven CT 06516

Call Sign: N1FNQ
Paul Di Grassi
70 Bull Hill Ln
West Haven CT 06516

Call Sign: KB1LIN
Barrett L Sporre
214 Campbell Ave
West Haven CT 06516

Call Sign: N1LFE
Brian J Freeman
998 Campbell Ave Apt 5
West Haven CT 06516

Call Sign: WA1KDG
Fred W Janis
38 Candee Ave
West Haven CT 06516

Call Sign: N1BYZ
Edward G Alberino Sr
63 Carlson Rd
West Haven CT 06516

Call Sign: KA1WDV
John F Vermeiren
38 Cherry Ln
West Haven CT 06516

Call Sign: KA1WVG
Fred L Johnstone

26 Chestnut St
West Haven CT 06516

Call Sign: N1EDX
Frank S Foster
99 Clark St
West Haven CT 06516

Call Sign: KA1RCS
Joseph A Giordano Jr
35 Claudia Dr Apt 117
West Haven CT 06516

Call Sign: N1ERN
Saverio J Rascati
130 Contact Dr
West Haven CT 06516

Call Sign: N1VAI
Paul P Bujalski
143 Cooper Rd
West Haven CT 06516

Call Sign: N1NMJ
Paul S Novak
17 Cottage St
West Haven CT 06516

Call Sign: KB1DND
Paul A Ferro
40 Court St
West Haven CT 06516

Call Sign: N1FTA
William K Barr
219 Court St
West Haven CT 06516

Call Sign: N1YJF
Michael J Macgregor
15 Crest St 22
West Haven CT 06516

Call Sign: N1NKM
William B Barnett Iii

52 Cullen Ave
West Haven CT 06516

Call Sign: N1UNW
Robin A Zander
14 Curtiss Ave
West Haven CT 06516

Call Sign: N1OXK
Ronald E Fink
62 Dana Street
West Haven CT 06516

Call Sign: W1KUK
Harold Roberts
49 Daniel Rd
West Haven CT 06516

Call Sign: WA1ZFZ
Michael A Serphillips
121 David St
West Haven CT 06516

Call Sign: KB1IWB
Deborah E Serphillips
121 David St
West Haven CT 065161200

Call Sign: N1WRM
Mark M Warner Jr
57 Dawson Ave Apt 3
West Haven CT 06516

Call Sign: NU1W
Peter J Keyes
131 Dogwood Rd B6
West Haven CT 06516

Call Sign: N1LQQ
Kevin M Frissora
59 Down Draft Circle
West Haven CT 06516

Call Sign: K1RCM
Sidney Yaffe

14 Easy Rudder Ln
West Haven CT 06516

207 Fresh Meadow Rd
West Haven CT 06516

86 Honey Pot Road
West Haven CT 06516

Call Sign: W1UOL
Francis M Mc Kernon
40 Easy Rudder Ln
West Haven CT 06516

Call Sign: W1EKB
Madeline B Simone
207 Fresh Meadow Rd
West Haven CT 06516

Call Sign: N1FAA
Christopher E Burns
86 Honey Pot Road
West Haven CT 06516

Call Sign: KA1PAD
John K Mc Carthy
200 Elm St #214
West Haven CT 06516

Call Sign: W1YUX
Kenneth M Bradley
5 Graham Ave
West Haven CT 065165816

Call Sign: W1HVN
Christopher E Burns
86 Honey Pot Road
West Haven CT 06516

Call Sign: W1TNU
Melvin Kleinman
15 Fair Sailing Rd
West Haven CT 06516

Call Sign: KB1LZS
Richard M Anderson
6 Grand Street
West Haven CT 06516

Call Sign: W1GC
Frederick H Brill
11 Howard St
West Haven CT 06516

Call Sign: K1AIP
William J Smallman Jr
128 Fairview Ave
West Haven CT 06516

Call Sign: KA1TPT
Michael J Jacobsen
82 Hemlock Street
West Haven CT 065161507

Call Sign: N1KFB
Gary W Serfass
Ivy Circle
West Haven CT 06516

Call Sign: N1FPK
John R Raccio Sr
24 Fern St
West Haven CT 06516

Call Sign: KA1YOX
Amanda L Murillo
27 Hickory St
West Haven CT 06516

Call Sign: N1OXR
Kathleen M Serfass
Ivy Circle
West Haven CT 06516

Call Sign: WB0ZTS
Kirby C Stafford Iii
484 First Ave 4
West Haven CT 06516

Call Sign: KA1YOY
Camilo E Murillo
27 Hickory St
West Haven CT 06516

Call Sign: WA3NOD
Henry A Schinnagel
46 Ivy St
West Haven CT 06516

Call Sign: KB1AOY
Nancee A Taylor
91 Fourth Ave
West Haven CT 06516

Call Sign: W1LOF
Stanley J Ciaburri
72 Hillside Ave
West Haven CT 06516

Call Sign: N1XLS
Stephen M Shine
475 Jones Hill Rd
West Haven CT 06516

Call Sign: KB1AOZ
Ronald G Taylor
941 Fourth Ave
West Haven CT 06516

Call Sign: W1ODB
Charles N Davidson
82 Hillside Ave
West Haven CT 06516

Call Sign: WA1GGN
Daniel R Shine Jr
475 Jones Hill Rd
West Haven CT 06516

Call Sign: W1EKA
S Solly Simone

Call Sign: KB1OLS
Christopher E Burns

Call Sign: KB1WJ
Peter P Zakalske

690 Jones Hill Rd Unit 21
West Haven CT 06516

Call Sign: N1KSE
Charles C Hill Iii
360 Jones Hill Road
West Haven CT 06516

Call Sign: W1JON
John Colavito
130 Jones Street
West Haven CT 06516

Call Sign: KB1OML
Paul D Mantegna
690 Joneshill Rd 30
West Haven CT 06516

Call Sign: N1CMI
Craig R Coleman
170 Kelsey Ave
West Haven CT 06516

Call Sign: WA1KCA
Anthony Chernick
30 Lamson St
West Haven CT 06516

Call Sign: K1NPG
Clifford S Beebe
173 Lamson St
West Haven CT 06516

Call Sign: WA1VRD
James F Collins
20 Laurel Place
West Haven CT 065166838

Call Sign: KB1QPZ
Rachel M Solveira
15 Laurel St
West Haven CT 06516

Call Sign: N1XOK
William J D Andrea Jr

165 Leete St
West Haven CT 06516

Call Sign: WB1EYU
William J Kane
618 Main St
West Haven CT 06516

Call Sign: W1WJK
William J Kane
618 Main St
West Haven CT 06516

Call Sign: N1SWQ
James F Pagliuca
511 Main St Apt 12
West Haven CT 06516

Call Sign: N1PVM
Michael A Radford
480 Main St Apt C3
West Haven CT 06516

Call Sign: KB1IJU
Rita Fagundo
278 Main St Apt F305
West Haven CT 06516

Call Sign: N1XQU
Diana P Cartier
40 Maitby Ave
West Haven CT 06516

Call Sign: N1VGS
Arthur L Cartier Jr
40 Maltby Ave
West Haven CT 06516

Call Sign: N1DLU
Nancy A Mc Gurrin
10 Marks Dr
West Haven CT 06516

Call Sign: NB1L
Michael E Mc Gurrin

10 Marks Dr
West Haven CT 06516

Call Sign: N2QHB
Gerald J Tancredi
26 Meadowbrook Rd
West Haven CT 06516

Call Sign: KA1BQD
Marianne M Damon
216 Milton Street
West Haven CT 06516

Call Sign: N1IAC
Dawson Blackmore Jr
39 Mohawk Drive
West Haven CT 065166722

Call Sign: KB1GEC
Donald V Iannuzzi
28 Morgan Lane
West Haven CT 06516

Call Sign: WS1I
Donald V Iannuzzi
28 Morgan Lane
West Haven CT 06516

Call Sign: N1KSF
James J Aportria
74 Morrissey Ln
West Haven CT 06516

Call Sign: N1ZLO
Jason A Cirillo
6 Mullen Rd
West Haven CT 06516

Call Sign: N1LFF
Gary R Felsted
63 Nashawena Ave
West Haven CT 06516

Call Sign: N1JIV
Jason J Zigmont

92 Ocean Ave
West Haven CT 06516

170 Richmond
West Haven CT 06516

686 Savin Ave
West Haven CT 06516

Call Sign: N1JYO
Lawrence B Mahoney
381 Ocean Ave
West Haven CT 06516

Call Sign: N1HNT
John R Carlo
81 Richmond Ave
West Haven CT 06516

Call Sign: WA1WDN
Robert J Marinoff Sr
275 Second Ave
West Haven CT 06516

Call Sign: N1GXO
Jeff M Johns
530 Orange Ave
West Haven CT 06516

Call Sign: KB1TJG
Harold Pollock
229 Richmond Ave
West Haven CT 06516

Call Sign: KA1YDC
Janet L Crosetti
Simon Pl
West Haven CT 06516

Call Sign: N1SUF
Diana E Tremonte
176 Park St
West Haven CT 06516

Call Sign: N1QGV
Paul E Mc Manus
3 Roberts St
West Haven CT 06516

Call Sign: KB1YO
Allan J Brown
20 Simos Ln
West Haven CT 06516

Call Sign: KC8BOA
Nathan G Rawling
84 Park Terrace Ave
West Haven CT 06516

Call Sign: KB1HKU
Karen E Asard-Moreland
87 Rockefellor Avenue
West Haven CT 06516

Call Sign: KB1NOJ
Dennis M Andrews
139 South St
West Haven CT 06516

Call Sign: KA1DMQ
William H Watts
1 Peck Ave 7
West Haven CT 06516

Call Sign: KA1ZMF
Robert E Moreland Jr
87 Rockfeller Ave
West Haven CT 06516

Call Sign: KB1EXE
Kenneth J Novicki
7 Spruce Peak Ln
West Haven CT 06516

Call Sign: KA1BPO
Angelo Rossi
41 Pheasant Rd
West Haven CT 06516

Call Sign: N1DLT
Mary B Burlock
43 Rodney St
West Haven CT 06516

Call Sign: N1KN
Kenneth J Novicki
7 Spruce Peak Ln
West Haven CT 065167703

Call Sign: KA1QGH
Charles T Reiss
101 Prospect Ave
West Haven CT 06516

Call Sign: N1DYH
Gary E Burlock Jr
43 Rodney St
West Haven CT 06516

Call Sign: KB1EXD
Christopher J Mcmillian
34 Strathmore Rd
West Haven CT 06516

Call Sign: N2UOV
Eric D Millard
93 Prospect Avenue
West Haven CT 06516

Call Sign: NB1M
Gary E Burlock Sr
43 Rodney St
West Haven CT 06516

Call Sign: KB1MPO
Gretchen Zukunft
34 Strathmore Rd
West Haven CT 06516

Call Sign: N1SUG
Margaret J Waltman

Call Sign: W1MJC
Jeanne A Poli

Call Sign: K1SPZ
Gretchen Zukunft

34 Strathmore Rd
West Haven CT 06516

Call Sign: N1DYG
Eligio Soto
62 Strathmore Rd
West Haven CT 06516

Call Sign: WA1BER
William M Welch Sr
34 Sunset Rd
West Haven CT 06516

Call Sign: WC1AAD
 West Haven Civil Defense
34 Sunset Rd
West Haven CT 06516

Call Sign: K1MF
Elliott E Eckert Jr
20 Terrace Ave
West Haven CT 065162627

Call Sign: WA1JYO
Vera M Klecowsky
370 Terrace Ave
West Haven CT 06516

Call Sign: N1ZQU
Sean A Pratt
309 Terrace Ave #44
West Haven CT 06516

Call Sign: W1NCL
Frank B Mercugliano
108 Thomas St
West Haven CT 06516

Call Sign: KA1VEJ
Anthony R Streeto
41 Thompson St
West Haven CT 06516

Call Sign: KA1ZAS
Cary A Green

17 Twin Circle Rd
West Haven CT 06516

Call Sign: KB1MOD
Jay S Kendall
77 Tyler Ave
West Haven CT 06516

Call Sign: AB1MV
Jay S Kendall
77 Tyler Ave
West Haven CT 06516

Call Sign: N2JK
Jay S Kendall
77 Tyler Ave
West Haven CT 06516

Call Sign: WA1TJT
Robert F Brill
85 Tyler Ave
West Haven CT 06516

Call Sign: W1GC
Robert F Brill
85 Tyler Ave
West Haven CT 06516

Call Sign: N1GSS
Mario J Fusaro
30 View St
West Haven CT 06516

Call Sign: K1MJL
Robert W Daly
22 Voss Road
West Haven CT 06516

Call Sign: N1KLD
Robert W Stanton
20 W Prospect St
West Haven CT 06516

Call Sign: N1GVA
Fred C Floberg

136 W Spring St
West Haven CT 06516

Call Sign: KA1WNS
Raymond J Collins
8 Washington Manor
West Haven CT 06516

Call Sign: KB1KQC
Robert C Morey
63 Westfield St
West Haven CT 06516

Call Sign: N1OXL
Kenneth S Bourque
239 Westwalk
West Haven CT 06516

Call Sign: N1OXM
Joan F Bourque
239 Westwalk
West Haven CT 06516

Call Sign: N1JKA
Kenneth A Frissora
West Haven CT 06516

**FCC Amateur Radio
Licenses in West Mystic**

Call Sign: N1JOB
Matthew J Snyder
West Mystic CT 06388

Call Sign: WA1ZVE
Stephen J Kondratowicz
West Mystic CT 06388

Call Sign: KB1NCD
Paul D Manoli
West Mystic CT 063880001

**FCC Amateur Radio
Licenses in West Norwalk**

Call Sign: N1QGW
Borivoj Boehm
6 Chipmunk Ln
West Norwalk CT 06850

**FCC Amateur Radio
Licenses in West Redding**

Call Sign: N1XWO
Dale D Wyatt
38 Deacon Abbott Rd
West Redding CT 06896

Call Sign: N3GJM
John C Kulp Jr
59 Farview Farm Rd
West Redding CT 06896

Call Sign: WA1TGE
Samuel A Mayer
9 Great Pond Ln
West Redding CT 06896

Call Sign: N1OJZ
Daniel L Brown
96 Marchant Rd
West Redding CT 06896

Call Sign: KA1LLG
Mark E Strauss
15 Orchard Drive
West Redding CT 06896

Call Sign: W1FTP
Barry Robinson
14 Peaceable St
West Redding CT 06896

Call Sign: KC1IS
Michael L Nelson
15 Peaceable St
West Redding CT 06896

Call Sign: N1PJM
Ryan S Alcott

30 Peaceable St
West Redding CT 06896

Call Sign: N1WVK
Peter A Kimball
21 Picketts Ridge Rd
West Redding CT 06896

Call Sign: WB4WZR
Christopher V Kimball
21 Picketts Ridge Rd Rd 2
West Redding CT 06896

Call Sign: NQ8Z
Christopher V Kimball
21 Picketts Ridge Rd Rd 2
West Redding CT 06896

Call Sign: K1ZKV
Jerome S Augustine
144 Seventy Acres Rd
West Redding CT
068962706

Call Sign: K1EB
John G Firtick
10 Silversmith Ln
West Redding CT 06896

**FCC Amateur Radio
Licenses in West Simsbury**

Call Sign: WA1VUH
Dieter Zinsmeister
13 Bridlepath Rd
West Simsbury CT 06092

Call Sign: WA1TZX
Judith K Townsend
49 Canton Rd
West Simsbury CT 06092

Call Sign: WA1TZY
Arthur G Townsend Jr
49 Canton Rd

West Simsbury CT
060922806

Call Sign: N1JGO
Herman R Schulz
10 Chestnut Hill Rd
West Simsbury CT 06092

Call Sign: KI4UMQ
Stephen M Hess
10 Clearfield Road
West Simsbury CT 06092

Call Sign: KB1HCJ
Joshua D Gilbert
19 Drumlin Rd
West Simsbury CT 06092

Call Sign: N1AFV
Robert J Petitjean
28 Drumlin Rd
West Simsbury CT 06092

Call Sign: N1DJQ
Helen B Kaplan
36 Drumlin Rd
West Simsbury CT
060922906

Call Sign: WA1OUI
David H Kaplan
36 Drumlin Rd
West Simsbury CT
060922906

Call Sign: KB1NUN
Keiko F Kaplan
36 Drumlin Rd
West Simsbury CT 06092

Call Sign: KB1PFF
Keiko F Kaplan
36 Drumlin Rd
West Simsbury CT 06092

Call Sign: WA1ZAC
Christopher R Johnson
42 Drumlin Road
West Simsbury CT 06092

Call Sign: KA1UKO
Janna S Gross
19 Madison Ln
West Simsbury CT 06092

Call Sign: N1PFN
Benjamin H Gross
19 Madison Ln
West Simsbury CT 06092

Call Sign: NY1P
Jeffrey B Gross
19 Madison Ln
West Simsbury CT 06092

Call Sign: WA1ICN
Ashley Lane Ii
135 Old Farms Rd
West Simsbury CT 06092

Call Sign: N1OKB
David A Klau
15 Pond Side Ln
West Simsbury CT 06092

Call Sign: KB1NVA
Gary Pandolfi
8 Quorn Hunt Rd
West Simsbury CT 06092

Call Sign: KB1NVB
Ethan J Pandolfi
8 Quorn Hunt Rd
West Simsbury CT 06092

Call Sign: KA1URZ
Mark I Jurras
27 Saddle Ridge Dr
West Simsbury CT 06092

Call Sign: N1YFM
David A Newitter
233 Stratton Brook Rd
West Simsbury CT 06092

Call Sign: KB1BJL
Cythia A Kern
57 Westledge Rd
West Simsbury CT 06092

Call Sign: N1SQK
Jack P Kern
57 Westledge Rd
West Simsbury CT 06092

FCC Amateur Radio Licenses in West Stafford

Call Sign: KA1KCQ
Bernard J Gaffney
11 Chestnut Hill
West Stafford CT 06076

FCC Amateur Radio Licenses in West Suffield

Call Sign: W1OQA
Norman A Gagne
47 Babbs Rd
West Suffield CT 06093

Call Sign: N1UCX
Stephen F Di Tommaso
214 Birch Rd
West Suffield CT 06093

Call Sign: N1GLM
Charles G Sutton Jr
255 Birch Rd
West Suffield CT 06093

Call Sign: W1EES
Harold C Chase
75 Chestnut Cir

West Suffield CT
060932100

Call Sign: W1VPF
Gladys V Chase
75 Chestnut Cir
West Suffield CT
060932100

Call Sign: WA1YMJ
George A Rossetti Jr
326 Lakeview Dr
West Suffield CT 06093

Call Sign: KB1VDA
David T Ryan
275 Lakeview Dr Sxt
West Suffield CT 06093

Call Sign: W1CPW
John A Gloria
556 N Grand St
West Suffield CT 06093

Call Sign: KB1LRO
Thomas J Sheridan Iii
1515 N Grand St
West Suffield CT 06093

Call Sign: KA1YU
Michael A Book
635 N Stone St
West Suffield CT 06093

Call Sign: N1DLQ
William H Chaney
1111 N Stone St
West Suffield CT 06093

Call Sign: KA1AZD
Richard A Gorski
1320 N Stone St
West Suffield CT 06093

Call Sign: KA1WVY

Miriam D Blackaby
1074 Newgate Rd
West Suffield CT 06093

Call Sign: KA1WWT
Mark E Blackaby
1074 Newgate Rd
West Suffield CT 06093

Call Sign: N1AYS
Bruce Millick
1170 Newgate Rd
West Suffield CT 06093

Call Sign: KB1PCJ
Robert C Howe
1321 North Grand St
West Suffield CT 06093

Call Sign: N1FKW
Robert J Bussolari
3852 Old Mountain Rd
West Suffield CT 06093

Call Sign: N1MAT
Dennis W Lombard
 Phelps Rd
West Suffield CT 06093

Call Sign: N1FGN
Leroy Musser Jr
148 S Grand St
West Suffield CT 06093

Call Sign: KE4IKP
Todd S Leahey
27 South Stone St.
West Suffield CT 06093

Call Sign: K1KI
Thomas W Frenaye
489 Warnertown Road
West Suffield CT 06093

Call Sign: W1SSB

Huckleberry Mountain
Contest Club
West Suffield CT 06093

Call Sign: KB1RNU
Bruce R Goulding
West Suffield CT 06093

FCC Amateur Radio Licenses in West Willington

Call Sign: KA1LYM
Leon Kouyoumjian
2 Adamec Rd
West Willington CT 06279

Call Sign: WB1CCJ
George W Saba
80 Krivanec Rd
West Willington CT 06279

Call Sign: N1SKF
James D Humphrey
21 Luchon Rd
West Willington CT 06279

Call Sign: N1MYG
Kathy A Majalian
70 Pinney Hill Rd Apt 1
West Willington CT 06279

Call Sign: KA1LWC
Terence A Sullivan
15 Ridgewood Rd
West Willington CT 06279

FCC Amateur Radio Licenses in Westbrook

Call Sign: KA1WXD
Marcy E Fuller
1732 Boston Post Rd
Westbrook CT 06498

Call Sign: WJ1T
Steven Dziadik
1732 Boston Post Rd.
Westbrook CT 06498

Call Sign: KB1VGE
Wayne R Norton
12 Cross Rd
Westbrook CT 06498

Call Sign: KA1RJP
Georgiana Porton
Drawer Z
Westbrook CT 06498

Call Sign: N1QVC
Leroy G Carter
416 E Pond Meadow Rd
Westbrook CT 06498

Call Sign: KB1WOR
Morgan D Barrett
990 East Pond Meadow Rd
Westbrook CT 06498

Call Sign: W1VVA
Donald P Relyea
655 East Pond Meadow
Road
Westbrook CT 06498

Call Sign: KA1VKE
Robert J Tombari
30 Economy Drive
Westbrook CT 06498

Call Sign: KA1WXG
Elizabeth A Nicholls
98 Edgewood Dr
Westbrook CT 06498

Call Sign: N1QVB
Richard H Tson
277 Essex Rd
Westbrook CT 06498

Call Sign: KB1KUO
James S Macgregor Iii
451 Essex Rd
Westbrook CT 06498

Call Sign: NY1M
Jeffrey J Kamen
821 Essex Rd
Westbrook CT 06498

Call Sign: N1TUB
Richard E Herman
959 Essex Rd
Westbrook CT 06498

Call Sign: KB1UVK
Philip M Einsmann Jr
1010 Essex Rd
Westbrook CT 06498

Call Sign: N1KZG
Robert R Smelings
1015 Essex Rd
Westbrook CT 06498

Call Sign: KA1SXJ
Matthew J Asensio
110 Fishing Brook Rd
Westbrook CT 06498

Call Sign: N1CWD
Jose M Asensio
110 Fishing Brook Rd
Westbrook CT 06498

Call Sign: KB1LTF
William D Spangler
210 Fishing Brook Rd
Westbrook CT 06498

Call Sign: KA1SXF
Jeffrey O Collins
130 Fishingbrook Rd
Westbrook CT 06498

Call Sign: KB1CXV
John A Staugaard
86 Grove Beach Rd N
Westbrook CT 06498

Call Sign: W1ZDX
Richard H Saunders
163 Hammock Rd N
Westbrook CT 064981744

Call Sign: K1LXP
Edward A Longo Md
44 Hammock Rd South
Westbrook CT 06498

Call Sign: KA1RRU
Linda B Longo
44 Hammock Rd South
Westbrook CT 06498

Call Sign: WD6GVR
Charles G Verba Jr
41 Linden Ave N
Westbrook CT 06498

Call Sign: KA1CEH
Lowndes A Smith
62 Little Stannard Beach
Road
Westbrook CT 06498

Call Sign: K1VYU
Ronald W Sizer
179 Malabar Dr
Westbrook CT 06498

Call Sign: KA1IFU
Sally A Sizer
179 Malabar Dr
Westbrook CT 06498

Call Sign: KA2OJX
Mary Ann Blank
38 Mink Rock Cir

Westbrook CT 064981561

Call Sign: N6IMT
Scott A Blank
38 Mink Rock Cir
Westbrook CT 064981561

Call Sign: KK1NBC
Scott A Blank
38 Mink Rock Cir
Westbrook CT 064981561

Call Sign: N1DIW
Gerald P Iovene
65 Mink Rock Cir
Westbrook CT 06498

Call Sign: W1FYG
Donald L Izzo
36 Muller Drive
Westbrook CT 06498

Call Sign: W1RLU
James H Williams
79 Norris Ave
Westbrook CT 06498

Call Sign: KB1MCG
Dalton S Marks
66 Ortner Dr
Westbrook CT 06498

Call Sign: W1APF
Dalton S Marks
66 Ortner Dr
Westbrook CT 06498

Call Sign: KB1UZM
Emmanuel C Louis
195 Pettipaug Rd
Westbrook CT 06498

Call Sign: KB1VNR
Steven R Nuhn
45 Plymouth Rd

Westbrook CT 06498

Call Sign: WA2IED
Peter E Barron
687 Pondmeadow Road
Westbrook CT 06498

Call Sign: KB1IUW
Daniel J Kinsman
5 South Lane
Westbrook CT 06498

Call Sign: K1LBG
Julius E Heck
430 Spencer Plain Rd
Westbrook CT 06498

Call Sign: N1OFL
Joel R Demers
430 Spencer Plains Road
Westbrook CT 06498

Call Sign: KB1OGH
William J Martyszczyk
2 Stone Hedge Rd
Westbrook CT 06498

Call Sign: AB1MS
William J Martyszczyk
2 Stone Hedge Rd
Westbrook CT 06498

Call Sign: KB1CQN
Kregg W Luca
64 Toby Hill Rd
Westbrook CT 06498

Call Sign: KB1DCY
Jane A Luca
64 Toby Hill Rd
Westbrook CT 06498

Call Sign: KB1EBB
Robert A Luca
64 Toby Hill Rd

Westbrook CT 06498

Call Sign: WA2CST
Paul E Dolengewicz
118 W Pond Meadow Rd 49
Westbrook CT 06498

Call Sign: W1EY
Edward F Kingsley
65 Wickham Ct
Westbrook CT 064982069

Call Sign: KB1BRD
Real Amateur Radio Club
Westbrook CT 06498

Call Sign: N1QLF
Marjorie G Mc Carthy
Westbrook CT 06498

Call Sign: W1BCG
Shoreline Amateur Radio
Club
Westbrook CT 06498

Call Sign: WW1L
Robert J Mc Carthy
Westbrook CT 06498

Call Sign: KB1NXZ
Gerard Ouellette
Westbrook CT 06498

Call Sign: W1JRD
Joel R Demers
Westbrook CT 06498

Call Sign: KB1QXF
Valley Shore Amateur
Radio Club
Westbrook CT 06498

Call Sign: W1EMD
Valley Shore Amateur
Radio Club

Westbrook CT 06498

Call Sign: KA1PQX
John R Fritz
60 Lancaster Rd Apt 31
Westhersfield CT 06109

Call Sign: W1OR
Gordon F Orelli
4 Blue Spruce Cir
Weston CT 06883

Call Sign: KB1LQX
THOMAS M Mc CUSKER
JR
34 Blueberry Hill
Weston CT 06883

Call Sign: WB2MRN
James A Conner
18 Briar Oak Dr
Weston CT 06883

Call Sign: N1SRN
Walter R Paul
135 Davis Hill Rd
Weston CT 06883

Call Sign: N1DHL
George E Beltz
10 Fresh Meadow Rd
Weston CT 06883

Call Sign: AB1KV
Michael A Smith
47 Greenlea Ln
Weston CT 06883

Call Sign: KD1CK

Mark Greeno
42 High Acre Rd
Weston CT 06883

Call Sign: W1LRR
Eugene F O Hare
68 Lyons Plain Rd
Weston CT 06883

Call Sign: KF2NC
G K Tsui
4 Nimrod Farm Rd
Weston CT 06883

Call Sign: KB1LTE
K1dr Repeater Club
96 Old Easton Turnpike
Weston CT 068832526

Call Sign: KA1UCY
Frederick W Feuerhake
14 Old Redding Rd
Weston CT 06883

Call Sign: WB2TPO
Mark S Lachs Md
33 Ridge Road
Weston CT 06883

Call Sign: KB1FDL
Stephen M Delay
17 Silver Ridge Common
Weston CT 06883

Call Sign: KB1UQH
Stephen M Delay Jr
17 Silver Ridge Common
Weston CT 06883

Call Sign: WA1OPG
David M Mangini
26 Soundview Farm
Weston CT 06883

Call Sign: K1YBY

Robert L Weinstein
46 Tannery Ln
Weston CT 06883

Call Sign: K1YHP
Joan A Weinstein
46 Tannery Ln
Weston CT 06883

Call Sign: WA2LRO
Richard A Cowan
27 Walker Ln
Weston CT 06883

Call Sign: KB1AJF
Ward M French Jr
36 Wildwood Ln
Weston CT 06883

Call Sign: WA1NND
Alfred I Wirtenberg
15 Wilson Rd
Weston CT 06883

Call Sign: KB1AB
John R Glover
Weston CT 06883

FCC Amateur Radio Licenses in Westport

Call Sign: KA1VVP
John W Shepherd Sr
7 Ambler Rd
Westport CT 06880

Call Sign: WA2DFJ
Dennis R Corsalini
4 Ambler Road
Westport CT 06880

Call Sign: KB1SIQ
Robinson A Batteau
6 Arlen Rd
Westport CT 06880

Call Sign: KB1CPY
Joseph M Carpenter
115 B Old Rd
Westport CT 06880

Call Sign: N1HSH
Edward M Bowers
14 Bauer Place
Westport CT 06880

Call Sign: K1YLK
Allen S Bomes
9 Bayberry Ln
Westport CT 06880

Call Sign: KB1UKF
Pamela L Joseph
24 Bermuda Road
Westport CT 06880

Call Sign: WB2PUA
Anthony H Handal
3 Blue Chip Ln
Westport CT 06880

Call Sign: N1RVZ
Frank D Dobyns
2 Bluewater Hill S
Westport CT 06880

Call Sign: KB1UKL
Barbra A Utting
20 Bobwhite Dr
Westport CT 06880

Call Sign: K1TTZ
Robert M Berler
3 Bruce Ln
Westport CT 06880

Call Sign: K1ISM
Richard E Brodie
37 Burr Farms Rd
Westport CT 06880

Call Sign: W1ZR
Joel R Hallas
54 Colony Rd
Westport CT 06880

Call Sign: KC2KJV
Joseph R Mule
17 Drumlin Rd
Westport CT 06880

Call Sign: N1MCB
Jon M Muro
18 Fairfield Ave
Westport CT 06880

Call Sign: KB1FBY
Nancy Hallas
54 Colony Rd
Westport CT 06880

Call Sign: NB1D
Leonard F Whitham
1655 E State St 47
Westport CT 06880

Call Sign: KB1WNZ
Bradley M Crescenzo
4 Fieldcrest Rd
Westport CT 06880

Call Sign: W1NCY
Nancy G Hallas
54 Colony Rd
Westport CT 068803704

Call Sign: K1NIY
Robert A Liftig
94 Easton Rd
Westport CT 06880

Call Sign: N1UDL
Vera Shanon
6 Fieldcrest Rd
Westport CT 06880

Call Sign: KB1WUU
Osvaldo L Alvarez
223 Compo Road South
Westport CT 06880

Call Sign: WA1DIH
Edward D Hyde Jr
27 Ellery Ln
Westport CT 06880

Call Sign: N2WQ
Rudy M Bakalov
18 Fillow Street
Westport CT 06880

Call Sign: KA1WYR
John J Kamon
25 Crescent Rd
Westport CT 06880

Call Sign: W1FYI
S Richard Kalt
8 Eno Ln
Westport CT 06880

Call Sign: KC2PYJ
Stiliyana Bankova
18 Fillow Street
Westport CT 06880

Call Sign: K1YMD
Vincent N Mac Ilvain
53 Cross Hwy
Westport CT 068802144

Call Sign: KB1IFC
Hiroshi Asada
21 Evergreen Pkwy
Westport CT 06880

Call Sign: K8ZB
Dimitar K Krastev
18 Fillow Street
Westport CT 06880

Call Sign: KB1SKD
ANNE Macilvain
53 Cross Hwy
Westport CT 068802144

Call Sign: W1GGG
Hiroshi Asada
21 Evergreen Pkwy
Westport CT 06880

Call Sign: KB1SIR
Justin M Sherman
2 Gordon Lane
Westport CT 06880

Call Sign: K1YMD
ANNE Macilvain
53 Cross Hwy
Westport CT 068802144

Call Sign: W1CFA
Hiroshi Asada
21 Evergreen Pkwy
Westport CT 06880

Call Sign: WA1VGT
Kenneth M Froehly
3 Great Marsh Rd
Westport CT 06880

Call Sign: W1YHW
Joseph W Hermenzie
189 Cross Hwy
Westport CT 06880

Call Sign: K9VFI
Stephen A Schwartz
10 Fairfield Ave
Westport CT 06880

Call Sign: KB1NVH
Jay R Franzese
22 Hales Road
Westport CT 06880

Call Sign: W1JRF
Jay R Franzese
22 Hales Road
Westport CT 06880

Call Sign: K1MLK
Paul A Bray Jr
16 Harbor Road
Westport CT 06880

Call Sign: WB2ZBV
John L Owens
20 Hills Lane
Westport CT 06880

Call Sign: N1YC
James A Brooks
15 Hitchcock Rd
Westport CT 06880

Call Sign: N2TIA
Kenneth L Stamm
17a Indian Hill Rd
Westport CT 06880

Call Sign: KA1NVH
Arete Seaton
2 Inwood Ln
Westport CT 06880

Call Sign: W1FSM
John C Seaton
2 Inwood Ln
Westport CT 06880

Call Sign: N1EEF
Moshe Shyevitch
7 Jansen Ct
Westport CT 06880

Call Sign: KB1QMD
Sumio Miyamoto
5 Janson Court
Westport CT 06880

Call Sign: W1JAL
Sumio Miyamoto
5 Janson Court
Westport CT 06880

Call Sign: N3HJ
Sumio Miyamoto
5 Janson Court
Westport CT 06880

Call Sign: W1PC
John H Minehan
10 Jennings Ct
Westport CT 06880

Call Sign: K1OF
Richard L Roznoy
5 Keyser Rd
Westport CT 06880

Call Sign: N1EKD
Cynthia Roznoy
5 Keyser Rd
Westport CT 06880

Call Sign: N1VBZ
Hans Peter Dohmen
5 Keyser Rd
Westport CT 06880

Call Sign: N1VCA
Joerg Bauerfeld
5 Keyser Rd
Westport CT 06880

Call Sign: N1VCB
Andreas Laumer
5 Keyser Rd
Westport CT 06880

Call Sign: W1CU
Jonathan A Cunitz
7 Lamplight Ln
Westport CT 06880

Call Sign: KB1OVL
Chalermpol Muangamphun
7 Lamplight Ln
Westport CT 06880

Call Sign: KY1A
Chalermpol Muangamphun
7 Lamplight Ln
Westport CT 06880

Call Sign: AB1PB
Neeranuch Muangamphun
7 Lamplight Ln
Westport CT 06880

Call Sign: WB2LUW
Harold J Levy
6 Lazy Brook Ln
Westport CT 06880

Call Sign: KD1KQ
Giovanni F Mioli
20 Long Lots Rd
Westport CT 06880

Call Sign: KB1UKK
Michael J Boyle
58 Long Lots Road
Westport CT 068803831

Call Sign: KC1TX
William D Hart
280 Main St
Westport CT 06880

Call Sign: KB1WFB
Charles G Lelievre
136 Main St Ste 202
Westport CT 06880

Call Sign: N1LLL
Charles G Lelievre
136 Main St Ste 202
Westport CT 06880

Call Sign: KB1EIQ
Scott T Bullard
18 Maple Ave N
Westport CT 06880

Call Sign: KG4MFP
David J Van Deventer
73 Old Hill Rd
Westport CT 06880

Call Sign: W2MUT
Edward H Rand
52 Regents Park
Westport CT 06880

Call Sign: KB1GQA
David P Land
21 Marine Ave
Westport CT 06880

Call Sign: KB1SBM
Augustus T Crocker Jr
85 Old Hill Road
Westport CT 06880

Call Sign: K1DCX
Martin A Yolles
24 Richmondville Ave
Westport CT 06880

Call Sign: N1YSH
David E Mrotek
21 Marion Rd
Westport CT 06880

Call Sign: KK1R
Augustus T Crocker Jr
85 Old Hill Road
Westport CT 06880

Call Sign: KA1NLF
Arlene Yolles
24 Richmondville Ave
Westport CT 06880

Call Sign: W9GMS
Edgar L Conant Jr
8 Meadow Brook Ln
Westport CT 06880

Call Sign: KA1LLK
Carl D Fleming
107 Old Rd
Westport CT 06880

Call Sign: KC8ULG
Kurt A Ringquist
23 Richmondville Ave.
Westport CT 06880

Call Sign: KA1OTK
John L Lowney
Mitchell Radio Assoc
Westport CT 06880

Call Sign: WB2OEM
Albert Goltzer
70 Patrick Rd
Westport CT 068801834

Call Sign: ND1L
Jesse Girard
2 River Oaks Rd
Westport CT 06880

Call Sign: KI4GBW
John W Bowman
72 Morningside Dr S
Westport CT 06880

Call Sign: WA1FVH
David P Levin
24 Punch Bowl Dr
Westport CT 06880

Call Sign: W1GSV
Alwin K Fraund
1 Rocky Ridge Rd
Westport CT 06880

Call Sign: KB1UKJ
Bettina G Stroll-Pass
11 N Sasco Common
Westport CT 06880

Call Sign: KB1AYJ
Duane E Minard Iii
17 Quentin Rd
Westport CT 06880

Call Sign: AB2T
Jordan M Zarembo
93 Roseville Rd
Westport CT 06880

Call Sign: W1WP
Holton E Harris
5 Newtown Tpke
Westport CT 06880

Call Sign: N1SRQ
Mary S Minard
17 Quentin Rd
Westport CT 06880

Call Sign: KA2RDD
Charles S Lowenstein
35 S Morningside Dr
Westport CT 06880

Call Sign: KB1SWO
Nicholas D Morgan
134 North Ave
Westport CT 06880

Call Sign: N1ATJ
Trevor J Marshall Jr
11 Redcoat Rd
Westport CT 068801410

Call Sign: K1JOP
Richard L Wysocki
14 Scofield Place
Westport CT 06880

Call Sign: N1ICR
Donna A Sussen
5 Sunset Strip
Westport CT 06880

Call Sign: N1YNC
Robert J Genader
24 Surf Rd
Westport CT 06880

Call Sign: K1DPL
David P Levin
69 Terra Nova Circle
Westport CT 06880

Call Sign: KB1KRE
D Douglas Hopkins
7 Thomas Rd
Westport CT 06880

Call Sign: WD4NXE
Keith J Ruskin
6 Tomahawk Ln
Westport CT 06880

Call Sign: N1RJZ
Kevin P Connell
36 Treadwell Ave
Westport CT 06880

Call Sign: N1RII
Mark M Yantachka
7 Vani Ct
Westport CT 06880

Call Sign: KB1IRW
Robert M Feinberg
3 Viking Green
Westport CT 06880

Call Sign: N1NQG
David H Page Jr
36 Westfair Dr
Westport CT 06880

Call Sign: N1QES
Richard D Shelton
11 White Woods Ln
Westport CT 06880

Call Sign: KA1YPS
Charles C Bevis
64 Whitney Glen
Westport CT 06880

Call Sign: KB1QPS
Mark J Modzelewski
6 Woodland Dr
Westport CT 06880

Call Sign: W1GIG
Timothy Walker
19 Woodside Ave
Westport CT 068803027

Call Sign: KB1EVU
Betty A Walker
19 Woodside Ave
Westport CT 06880

Call Sign: KC1PUP
Betty A Walker
19 Woodside Ave
Westport CT 06880

Call Sign: KB1CCV
Diana D Mrotek
Westport CT 06880

Call Sign: WB1GWI
Seth H Goltzer
Westport CT 06881

Call Sign: W1SHG
Seth H Goltzer
Westport CT 06881

**FCC Amateur Radio
Licenses in Wethersfield**

Call Sign: W1NYY
Thomas P Anselmo Sr
14b Fairway Dr
Wethersfield CT 06109

Call Sign: N1XHL
Sylvia M Moryl
39 Alison Ln
Wethersfield CT 06109

Call Sign: AA1BJ
Sebastian Urso
8 Back Ln
Wethersfield CT 06109

Call Sign: NJ1S
Robert J Garvey
10 Beech Tree Dr
Wethersfield CT 06109

Call Sign: W1LOP
Jeffrey N Galin
1807 Berlin Tnpk
Wethersfield CT 06109

Call Sign: W1JG
Jeffrey N Galin
1807 Berlin Tnpk
Wethersfield CT 06109

Call Sign: N1NMC
Drue A Hontz Jr
68 Beverly Rd
Wethersfield CT 06109

Call Sign: W1WZN
Arthur L Sperling
115 Black Birch
Wethersfield CT 061093516

Call Sign: K1NEP
Harriet L Sperling
115 Black Birch Rd
Wethersfield CT 06109

Call Sign: K1KRO
John R La Bella
17 Brookside Cir
Wethersfield CT 061091102

Call Sign: KB1BVU
Frederick A Arjune
22 Buckland Rd
Wethersfield CT 06109

Call Sign: KB1UFV
Robert J Bonin
35 Buckland Rd
Wethersfield CT 06109

Call Sign: N1YJX
John V Cusano
96 Cedar St
Wethersfield CT 06109

Call Sign: KA1AN
Richard H Davis
108 Cedar St
Wethersfield CT 061091406

Call Sign: KA1JCM
Winifred A Davis
108 Cedar St
Wethersfield CT 061091406

Call Sign: WA1JZT
Harold R Pfeiffer
180 Cedar St
Wethersfield CT 06109

Call Sign: AA1EZ
Larry G Hall
109 Center St
Wethersfield CT 06109

Call Sign: W1SX
Larry G Hall
109 Center St
Wethersfield CT 06109

Call Sign: N1NAS
David F Pingree
115 Charter Rd
Wethersfield CT 06109

Call Sign: WA1EEU
Walter P Piescik
157 Charter Rd
Wethersfield CT 06109

Call Sign: WA1QWH
John G Eppler
90 Church St
Wethersfield CT 06109

Call Sign: WA1PDF
Stephen D Mc Gee Sr
163 Church St
Wethersfield CT 06109

Call Sign: N1TJP
Frank P Berman
388 Church St
Wethersfield CT 06109

Call Sign: N1VGG
Derek Bylina
143 Clearfield Rd
Wethersfield CT 06109

Call Sign: K1PAI
Roger K Jeanfaivre
238 Clearfield Road
Wethersfield CT 06109

Call Sign: W1QBH
Richard J Hill
94 Clovercrest Rd
Wethersfield CT 06109

Call Sign: KA1GDX
Paul V Lombardo
67 Collier Rd
Wethersfield CT 06109

Call Sign: W1VMY
Paul P Lombardo
67 Collier Rd
Wethersfield CT 061093526

Call Sign: KA1ZUX
Jonathan M Arruda
433 Coppermill Rd
Wethersfield CT 06109

Call Sign: KD1LO
Arnold C Dunphy
47 Cross Hill Rd
Wethersfield CT 06109

Call Sign: K2BK
Paul J Coburn
9 Crystal Street
Wethersfield CT 06109

Call Sign: KB1WOJ
Robert J Kelley
201 Dale Rd
Wethersfield CT 06109

Call Sign: W1KEL
Robert J Kelley
201 Dale Rd
Wethersfield CT 06109

Call Sign: N1JJE
Thomas E Dunham Iii
34 Deming Place
Wethersfield CT 061091205

Call Sign: N1JPH
Kevin J Gurskis
47 Desmond Drive
Wethersfield CT 06109

Call Sign: WB1CPB
John P Babel
157 Dudley Rd
Wethersfield CT 06109

Call Sign: KE6GRP
Edward Figueroa
100 Executive Sq.
Wethersfield CT 061093818

Call Sign: KA1BU
Robert T Leonard
187 Fairlane Dr
Wethersfield CT 06109

Call Sign: KA1JTE
Antonio Coelho
64 Fairview Drive
Wethersfield CT 06109

Call Sign: KX1A
William J Webb
7 Fernwood St
Wethersfield CT 06109

Call Sign: KB1SCT
Philip J Lombardo
26 Forest Dr
Wethersfield CT 06109

Call Sign: KB1WOG
Peter J Avery
133 Fox Hill Rd
Wethersfield CT 06109

Call Sign: W1PJA
Peter J Avery
133 Fox Hill Rd
Wethersfield CT 06109

Call Sign: N1XAW
Krystyna Gorowski
301 Fox Hill Rd
Wethersfield CT 06109

Call Sign: KA1KQV
Ross W De May
108 Garden St
Wethersfield CT 06109

Call Sign: AA2SL
Christopher P Rozum
227 Garden Street
Wethersfield CT 061092326

Call Sign: KA1CA
Dominic L Fusco Jr
99 Glenwood Dr
Wethersfield CT 06109

Call Sign: W1WKG
Burton Booker
100 Goff Rd
Wethersfield CT 06109

Call Sign: KA1DFH
Walter M Styslo
35 Greenfield St
Wethersfield CT 06109

Call Sign: KB1BSJ
Central Connecticut Arc
35 Greenfield St
Wethersfield CT 06109

Call Sign: K1WMS
Walter M Styslo
35 Greenfield St
Wethersfield CT 06109

Call Sign: N1SFC
Robert D Welk Jr
109 Greenfield St
Wethersfield CT 061091611

Call Sign: WA1RMM
Fernando D Tavares
72 Ivy Ln
Wethersfield CT 06109

Call Sign: KA1ZXY
Zygmunt Michalski
135 Jameswell Rd
Wethersfield CT 06109

Call Sign: N1QVO
Selbourne G Brown
134 Jordan Ln
Wethersfield CT 06109

Call Sign: KB1BGY
Paul E Frankowski
210 Jordan Ln
Wethersfield CT 06109

Call Sign: N1QBQ
Sebastian J Cultrera
341 Jordan Ln
Wethersfield CT 06109

Call Sign: WB1ENT
Michelle A Bloom
24 La Cava Ln
Wethersfield CT 06109

Call Sign: KE3Z
Jonathan R Bloom
24 Lacava Ln
Wethersfield CT 06109

Call Sign: K1EPG
Eugene V Falcone
42 Lantern Ln
Wethersfield CT 06109

Call Sign: KA1HBW
Dominick A Armstrong
28 Lexington St
Wethersfield CT 06109

Call Sign: KA1SEW
Kathleen A Canty
8 Lindbergh Dr
Wethersfield CT 06109

Call Sign: KA1BQO
Joseph Zacchio
30 Livingston St
Wethersfield CT 06109

Call Sign: K1KPC
Edward S Milewski
38 Livingston St
Wethersfield CT 06109

Call Sign: KA1ZBJ
Martha A Partridge
117 Long Vue Dr
Wethersfield CT 06109

Call Sign: KA1ZBK
Russell W Partridge
117 Long Vue Dr
Wethersfield CT 06109

Call Sign: N1PNU
Dariusz Dziubinski
234 Longvue Dr
Wethersfield CT 06109

Call Sign: N1HSC
William C Herms Sr
255 Longvue Dr
Wethersfield CT 06109

Call Sign: N1HSD
Pamela S Herms
255 Longvue Dr
Wethersfield CT 06109

Call Sign: KA1ZEF
Linda W Nielson
418 Maple St
Wethersfield CT 06109

Call Sign: KB1VRF
Thomas F Gibson
28 Mapleside Dr
Wethersfield CT 06109

Call Sign: KB1LGR
Thomas V Chalkley
750 Nott St
Wethersfield CT 06109

Call Sign: KB1HSI
Neil J Gordon
712 Nott Street
Wethersfield CT 06109

Call Sign: KA1NIO
Frank N Giannini
49 Old Mill Rd
Wethersfield CT 06109

Call Sign: N1LCD
Bruce F Rothwell
19 Old Pewter Ln
Wethersfield CT 06109

Call Sign: KB1KGX
Richard J Gianetti Jr
20 Oxford St
Wethersfield CT 061091723

Call Sign: WA1UFC
Robert F Cottler
14 Palomina Way
Wethersfield CT 06109

Call Sign: KB1DCP
Blaise Riccio
24 Pheasant Run
Wethersfield CT 06109

Call Sign: KA1DFN
Charles Hanko
22 Prospect St
Wethersfield CT 061093755

Call Sign: KB1HYD
Mary M Hobart
259 Prospect St
Wethersfield CT 06109

Call Sign: K1MMH
Mary M Hobart
259 Prospect St
Wethersfield CT 06109

Call Sign: KB1MOI
Lisa R Tardette
10 Providence St
Wethersfield CT 06109

Call Sign: K1AH
Emile W Clede Jr
272 Ridge Rd
Wethersfield CT 061091019

Call Sign: WA1RFU
Walter G Cyrulik
599 Ridge Rd
Wethersfield CT 061092633

Call Sign: W1WRQ
Ward W Scott
65 Robbins Dr
Wethersfield CT 06109

Call Sign: KB1FRB
Diane L Strzemieczny
62 Schoolhouse Crossing
Wethersfield CT 06109

Call Sign: KB1VTG
Jayson D Fox
1077 Silas Deane Highway
282
Wethersfield CT 06109

Call Sign: N1QHT
C. Michael Millrod
1077 Silas Deane Hwy.
Wethersfield CT 06109

Call Sign: WA1HFQ
Joseph A Di Maggio
50 Southwell Rd
Wethersfield CT 06109

Call Sign: KB1CXK
Joseph A Clarizio
58 Stillwold Dr.

Wethersfield CT 06109

Call Sign: W1YNV
Alexander Janczyk
53 Sunset Blvd
Wethersfield CT 061094158

Call Sign: KB1KIS
James E Payette
208 Thornbush Road
Wethersfield CT 06109

Call Sign: W1RQN
Clifford A Maynard
164 Timber Trl
Wethersfield CT 06109

Call Sign: KB1THL
Anatoliy Oshur
13 Tinsmith Xing
Wethersfield CT 06109

Call Sign: K3PJA
Paul J Amodio
41 Town House Ln
Wethersfield CT 06109

Call Sign: KB1EPD
Paul J Amodio
41 Towne House Ln
Wethersfield CT 06109

Call Sign: W1UQK
Paul B Kuzmak
125 Two Brook Rd
Wethersfield CT 06109

Call Sign: KA1MYC
Leonard H Hanson
93 Two Stone Dr
Wethersfield CT 06109

Call Sign: AB1PF
Robert Palochko
52 Village Dr Apt 216

Wethersfield CT 06109

Call Sign: KB1HLL
Angela Steele
84 Village Drive - Apt 423
Wethersfield CT 06109

Call Sign: KB1HLM
Robert P Steele
84 Village Drive - Apt 423
Wethersfield CT 06109

Call Sign: KA2WKL
Steven Shoopak
44 Village Drive #126
Wethersfield CT 06109

Call Sign: N1APK
Richard J Fresher
29 Village Ln Apt 903
Wethersfield CT 06109

Call Sign: WA1ZQU
Martin C De Filippo
97 Waters View Dr
Wethersfield CT 06109

Call Sign: KB1TVZ
Jason C Parlante
741 Wells Rd
Wethersfield CT 06109

Call Sign: N1VOO
Luiz Fragoso
35 Wildwood Rd
Wethersfield CT 06109

Call Sign: KB1JDK
Spencer C Mahar
26 Willard St
Wethersfield CT 06109

Call Sign: W1VVK
Spencer C Mahar
26 Willard St

Wethersfield CT 06109

Call Sign: KB1VVD
Christian W Johnson
120 Willow St
Wethersfield CT 06109

Call Sign: KC1H
Felix G Sassano
476 Wolcott Hill Rd
Wethersfield CT 06109

Call Sign: KB1BFI
Maria T Santini
15 Wood Pond Dr
Wethersfield CT 06109

Call Sign: N1NAJ
Mary L Pergiovanni
60 Woodside Dr
Wethersfield CT 06109

Call Sign: W1DCP
John V Junokas Sr
43 Wright Rd
Wethersfield CT 06109

Call Sign: N1AFR
Richard T Paquette
Wethersfield CT 06109

FCC Amateur Radio Licenses in Willimantic

Call Sign: KB1FPR
Alicia L Varga
206 - G Foster Drive
Willimantic CT 06226

Call Sign: KA1ASG
Sidney Vernon
185 Birch St
Willimantic CT 06226

Call Sign: KA1VVG

Leo J Pageau
149 Bridge St
Willimantic CT 06226

Earl R White
240 High St
Willimantic CT 06226

Raymond P Maynard
93 Orchard Hill Lane
Willimantic CT 06226

Call Sign: K1ICQ
Michael J Rogers
75 Chapman St
Willimantic CT 06226

Call Sign: KB1SHL
Anne L Strate
191 High St Apt C
Willimantic CT 06226

Call Sign: KB1AKO
Susan R Blay
134 Orchard Hill Ln
Willimantic CT 06226

Call Sign: KB1PHG
Cheol-Min Kim
238 Foster Dr
Willimantic CT 062261559

Call Sign: N1WDN
Michael B Bergeron
27 Lauter Ave
Willimantic CT 06226

Call Sign: N1WMD
Greg R Gustavson
223 Oxbow Dr
Willimantic CT 06226

Call Sign: KB1PHH
Hyun-Soo Kim
238 Foster Dr
Willimantic CT 06226

Call Sign: KB1UWD
Sripati Sah
82 Lewiston Ave
Willimantic CT 06226

Call Sign: N9YES
John P Morahn
64 Park St 1st Floor
Willimantic CT 06226

Call Sign: KB1PIM
Chan-Soo Kim
238 Foster Dr
Willimatic CT 062261559

Call Sign: N1YTD
Jonathan A Duprey
258 Lewiston Ave
Willimantic CT 06226

Call Sign: N1YXK
Michael A Piercy
115 Pennywood Ln
Willimantic CT 06226

Call Sign: KD1IN
Dale L Smith
258 Foster Dr Apt A
Willimantic CT 06226

Call Sign: KA1BSS
Roddy J Mc Comber
1501 Main St
Willimantic CT 062261914

Call Sign: W1MUC
Thomas Pollitt Jr
141 Pleasant St
Willimantic CT 06226

Call Sign: KB1PIN
Soon Nam Choi
238 Foster Drive
Willimantic CT 06226

Call Sign: K1ILJ
Lloyd H Taylor Jr
45 Mountain St
Willimantic CT 06226

Call Sign: N2MPV
Peter A Morenus Jr
161 Pleasant St
Willimantic CT 06226

Call Sign: KB1SBG
Scott R Duplisea
27 Gem Dr
Willimantic CT 06226

Call Sign: KE1BT
George C Freeman
9 Mystic Ave
Willimantic CT 062263756

Call Sign: W1FMY
Harry Blumenthal
454 Pleasant St
Willimantic CT 06226

Call Sign: N4ZAR
Stephen C Miner
60 Greenwood St
Willimantic CT 06226

Call Sign: AA1PA
Richard Udal
150 N St
Willimantic CT 06226

Call Sign: KA1LPA
Maynard A Philbrook Jr
520 Pleasant St
Willimantic CT 06226

Call Sign: W1VNI

Call Sign: KB1WXB

Call Sign: KA1OBN

Richard C Du Vall
227 Prospect St
Willimantic CT 06226

Call Sign: WE1Y
Richard S Grillo
393 Prospect St
Willimantic CT 06226

Call Sign: W1WRN
George R Bombria
74 Quercus Ave
Willimantic CT 06226

Call Sign: KA1ZQT
Roland M Caldwell
33 Roanoak Ave.
Willimantic CT 06226

Call Sign: N1UIQ
Wayne R Heidelmark
400 S St
Willimantic CT 06226

Call Sign: KA1VDU
Brian A Gobin
18 Spring View Ln
Willimantic CT 06226

Call Sign: K1LEV
Sollie Brettschneider
440 Windham Rd
Willimantic CT 06226

Call Sign: W1HNA
Leonard E Insalaco
469 Windham Rd
Willimantic CT 06226

Call Sign: KB1KPD
Christopher D Reddy
Willimantic CT 06226

Call Sign: W1HNA
Douglas C Bertone Sr

Willimantic CT 06226

FCC Amateur Radio Licenses in Willington

Call Sign: WA1FJT
Lee F Goodell
16 Baxter Rd
Willington CT 06279

Call Sign: WB1FMP
Bruce L Moorash
33 Baxter Rd Unit 4a
Willington CT 06279

Call Sign: K1ACD
Bruce L Moorash
33 Baxter Rd Unit 4a
Willington CT 06279

Call Sign: N1GUS
Wayne A Rychling
59 Clint Eldredge Rd
Willington CT 06279

Call Sign: KB1VQK
Stephen T Bowen
132 Daleville Rd
Willington CT 06279

Call Sign: KB1KTG
Paul S Pribula
256 Jared Sparks Rd
Willington CT 06279

Call Sign: N1ZF
Paul S Pribula
256 Jared Sparks Rd
Willington CT 06279

Call Sign: K1ZE
Edward L Shekleton
51 Jared Sparks Road
Willington CT 06279

Call Sign: KA1NCR
William H Hodge Jr
33 Kollar Rd
Willington CT 06279

Call Sign: KB1LGC
Michael S Walker
90 Krivanec Rd
Willington CT 062791510

Call Sign: N1TPC
David A Nafis
48 Mirtl Rd
Willington CT 06279

Call Sign: KD7BLZ
Frank R Shoemaker
60 Old Farms Rd #109
Willington CT 06279

Call Sign: KA1SBP
Richard P Sarachek Jr
40 Old River Rd
Willington CT 062792226

Call Sign: KB1HKS
Daniel J Monti
42 Pinney Hill Rd
Willington CT 06279

Call Sign: KA1EBB
Shawn R Aldrich
352 River Rd
Willington CT 06279

Call Sign: KB1OQR
Stuart I Cobb
4 Tolland Tpk
Willington CT 06279

Call Sign: KC1ID
James H Kaminski Sr
41 Y Rd
Willington CT 06279

Call Sign: KG4BID
Michael J Vesel
Willington CT 06279

Call Sign: W1MJV
Michael J Vesel
Willington CT 06279

FCC Amateur Radio Licenses in Wilson

Call Sign: W1HXG
John Andruszko
25 Bristol St
Wilson CT 06095

FCC Amateur Radio Licenses in Wilton

Call Sign: W1IAF
Richard H Liebermann
27 Antler Ln
Wilton CT 06897

Call Sign: K1QHV
Dennis Jackson
19 Boas Ln
Wilton CT 068971301

Call Sign: WA1RPA
Alan B Wissinger
48 Collinswood Rd
Wilton CT 068971810

Call Sign: KA1UTY
Walter Sidas
28 Dorado Ct
Wilton CT 06897

Call Sign: N1ZTU
Daniel G Monroe
44 Forest Ln
Wilton CT 06897

Call Sign: KB1RQR

Richard S Ziegler
20 Fullin Ln
Wilton CT 068971001

Call Sign: KB1ZIG
Richard S Ziegler
20 Fullin Ln
Wilton CT 068971001

Call Sign: N1UNC
Richard H Hidgins Iii
45 Heather Ln
Wilton CT 06897

Call Sign: N1TKR
Richard Deutsch
64 Heather Ln
Wilton CT 06897

Call Sign: K1WMR
Wmr Contest Club
88 Hillbrook Rd
Wilton CT 06897

Call Sign: WB2FOX
Paul P Lauricella
21 Laurel Ln
Wilton CT 06897

Call Sign: KB1PUQ
Max O Spitzer
50 Musket Ridge Road
Wilton CT 06897

Call Sign: KB1PUR
Vlad G Spitzer
50 Musket Ridge Road
Wilton CT 06897

Call Sign: W1ZP
Vlad G Spitzer
50 Musket Ridge Road
Wilton CT 06897

Call Sign: W1MOS

Max O Spitzer
50 Musket Ridge Road
Wilton CT 06897

Call Sign: KA1WYT
Matthew E Robinson
52 Old Boston Rd
Wilton CT 06897

Call Sign: WB2JVB
Paul J Lourd
173 Old Boston Rd
Wilton CT 06897

Call Sign: N1MTE
Charles J Richards
59 Old Hwy
Wilton CT 06897

Call Sign: N1YCI
Eric V Nordlund
140 Old Mill Rd
Wilton CT 06897

Call Sign: N1TJG
David A Heiden
28 Pelham Lane
Wilton CT 06897

Call Sign: N1LQT
George W Kunzle
92 Pine Ridge Rd
Wilton CT 06897

Call Sign: KA1QYW
Walter S Hennig
177 Pipers Hill Rd
Wilton CT 06897

Call Sign: KA1AZJ
Hubert J Sebastian
93 Pond Rd
Wilton CT 06897

Call Sign: KA1ZTV

Brecknell M Dierolf
16 Powder Horn Hill
Wilton CT 06897

Call Sign: AE6RA
John G Horan
14 Range Road
Wilton CT 06897

Call Sign: WA1SIF
Peter Van Raalte
874 Ridgefield Rd
Wilton CT 06897

Call Sign: WB2EDD
Al S Koenig
42 Scribner Hill Rd
Wilton CT 06897

Call Sign: WA1GBJ
Donald H Stillman Jr
17 Spectacle Ln
Wilton CT 06897

Call Sign: W7EIZ
Carl J Tolonen
139 Spectacle Ln
Wilton CT 06897

Call Sign: W1TPL
Herman Yellin
152 Spoonwood Rd
Wilton CT 06897

Call Sign: K1WZB
Maurice D Bennett Jr
10 St Johns Rd
Wilton CT 06897

Call Sign: WA1ARO
Neil D Kleinfeld
68 St. Johns Road
Wilton CT 06897

Call Sign: KB1GTH

Randolph Ramirez
26 Stonecrop Lane
Wilton CT 06897

Call Sign: K1ROR
Randolph O Ramirez
26 Stonecrop Lane
Wilton CT 06897

Call Sign: KB1WYS
Daniel J Desimone
14 Tanners Dr
Wilton CT 068971117

Call Sign: N1XTH
Brian E Robinson
5 Village Walk
Wilton CT 068974035

Call Sign: KB1HVC
Jeffrey A Figurelli
116 Vista Road
Wilton CT 068971319

Call Sign: KB1KXZ
Anna Belle Reid
116 Vista Road
Wilton CT 06897

Call Sign: KB1MFC
Price A Figurelli-Reid
116 Vista Road
Wilton CT 06847

Call Sign: W1KHL
Calvin G Bennett
239 Westport Rd
Wilton CT 06897

Call Sign: KB1MSF
Clifford C Kaechele
8 Wolfpit Lane
Wilton CT 06897

Call Sign: K1DIH

Brian H Toubman
194 Wolfpit Rd
Wilton CT 068973418

Call Sign: KB1QPA
Richard Deutsch
Wilton CT 06897

FCC Amateur Radio Licenses in Winchester

Call Sign: N1CLZ
Allan W Buttrick Jr
124 Huntington Rd
Winchester CT 06098

Call Sign: KB1GDU
John M Hebert
101 Laurel Way
Winchester CT 06098

Call Sign: KB1GDY
Isaac B Hebert
101 Laurel Way
Winchester CT 06094

Call Sign: KB1RRK
Daniel T Butler
110 West Rd
Winchester CT 06098

FCC Amateur Radio Licenses in Winchester Center

Call Sign: W1YYY
Edward F Gebelein Jr
Winchester Center CT 06094

FCC Amateur Radio Licenses in Windham

Call Sign: K1KPW
Robert L Walsh

195 Ballamahack Rd
Windham CT 06280

Call Sign: N1YGZ
Charles E Brenker Ii
128 Bass Rd
Windham CT 06280

Call Sign: K1MGR
Walter F Wicks
Rt 14 Box 370
Windham CT 06280

Call Sign: KB1QFR
Laury A Lavoie
15 Cracow Ave
Windham CT 06280

Call Sign: N1NNN
John P Decker
20 George St
Windham CT 06280

Call Sign: N1VDC
Randal E Roy
19 Kodiak Dr
Windham CT 06280

Call Sign: N1YZC
Jan E Roy
19 Kodiak Dr
Windham CT 06280

Call Sign: WA1OHR
Everett L Paluska Sr
153 North Rd
Windham CT 062801311

Call Sign: KB1FKO
Devon A Conover
153 North Rd
Windham CT 06280

Call Sign: N1GCB
Wilmot F Dyer

89 Plains Rd
Windham CT 06280

Call Sign: KA1GEO
Oliver R Hayes
79 Scotland Rd
Windham CT 06280

FCC Amateur Radio Licenses in Windham Center

Call Sign: W5DHO
John N Harding
Box1
Windham Center CT
062800001

Call Sign: WB1FZB
Burton R Brown Iii
115 Oakwood Drive
Windham Center CT 06280

Call Sign: KA1DDC
Peter D Jones
43 Windham Center Rd
Windham Center CT 06280

FCC Amateur Radio Licenses in Windsor

Call Sign: N2GKL
Tokio Oishi
550 Marshall Phelps Rd
Windor CT 06095

Call Sign: KA1EBI
Robert H Pansky
168 Alcott Dr
Windsor CT 060952606

Call Sign: KA1EPI
Albert H Grimaldi
27 Alden Rd
Windsor CT 06095

Call Sign: KB1RSL
Charles V Powell
40 Alden Rd
Windsor CT 06095

Call Sign: KA1VAG
Renrick A Tulloch
60 Alden Rd
Windsor CT 06095

Call Sign: K1YKF
Gerard P Cavanaugh
65 Alden Rd
Windsor CT 06095

Call Sign: KB1CZR
Chris W Foote
23 Apple Tree Lane
Windsor CT 060951802

Call Sign: N1YJW
Matthew R Anderson
27 Arrowbrook Rd
Windsor CT 06095

Call Sign: KB1BLA
Marcus A Rice
66 Arrowbrook Rd
Windsor CT 06095

Call Sign: KB1IFQ
Repeater Group 533
82 Basswood Dr
Windsor CT 06095

Call Sign: WA1VOA
Repeater Group 533
82 Basswood Dr
Windsor CT 06095

Call Sign: N1SPI
Diane A Morelli
82 Basswood Rd
Windsor CT 06095

Call Sign: WB1GIC
Albert B Morelli
82 Basswood Rd
Windsor CT 06095

Call Sign: N1VXQ
Ronald A Ingraham Jr
16 Bellflower Rd
Windsor CT 06095

Call Sign: KB1KUH
Lois M Boling
4 Bent Rd
Windsor CT 06095

Call Sign: KB1KUI
Kenneth S Boling
4 Bent Rd
Windsor CT 06095

Call Sign: W2WTV
Gordon J Horn
20 Bent Road
Windsor CT 06095

Call Sign: KA1EPJ
Walter I Weymouth
629 Bloomfield Ave
Windsor CT 06095

Call Sign: WB2GQX
Seward E Ford
251 Bounty Way
Windsor CT 06095

Call Sign: KA1VAK
Ketan Kumar A Padalia
600 Bricklayer Rd
Windsor CT 06095

Call Sign: W1NEM
Windsor Emergency
Management
275 Broad St

Windsor CT 06095

Call Sign: N1WOS
Nuha Elmaghrabi
20 Broadleaf Cir
Windsor CT 06095

Call Sign: N1YKR
Ralph A Bragg
12 Brown Ave
Windsor CT 06095

Call Sign: N1WEX
Edwin C Barlow Jr
76 Capen St
Windsor CT 06095

Call Sign: KB1TMG
Kendall D Witham
18 Chelsea Lane
Windsor CT 06095

Call Sign: KB1RSM
Tyron A Mckinnis
115 Clover St
Windsor CT 06095

Call Sign: KB1TMI
Patrick J Dionne
102 Cobblestone Way
Windsor CT 06095

Call Sign: KA1GJB
Vincent W Wojtusik
45 Colton Street
Windsor CT 060953428

Call Sign: KB1BNL
Ronald A Seruille
77 Columbia Rd
Windsor CT 06095

Call Sign: WA1CRG
Joseph Joseph
28 Craigs Rd

Windsor CT 06095

Call Sign: KB1RSJ
Nathan G Varghese
35 Dewey Ave
Windsor CT 06095

Call Sign: KA1OAN
Mark Platti
51 Dewey Ave
Windsor CT 06095

Call Sign: KB1GJB
Mark D Butterfield
40 Dewey Avenue
Windsor CT 06095

Call Sign: N1TUI
Frank J Reynolds
19 Donna Lane
Windsor CT 06095

Call Sign: N1MTI
Paul Felgate
249 Dudley Town Rd
Windsor CT 06095

Call Sign: KA1OAS
William J Storey
49 E View Dr
Windsor CT 06095

Call Sign: W1UIY
Edward W Huntington
62 Eastview Dr
Windsor CT 06095

Call Sign: KB1BWR
Sean N Kallipolites
31 Elaine Mary Dr
Windsor CT 06095

Call Sign: N1NBC
Mark A Larsen
34 Elaine Mary Dr

Windsor CT 06095

Call Sign: KB1JSK
Marcellus D Davis
2849 Ellington Rd S
Windsor CT 06074

Call Sign: KB1BQW
Young Amateur Radio
League
50 Elm St
Windsor CT 060952915

Call Sign: N1OFO
Christoffel H Meijer
50 Elm St
Windsor CT 06095

Call Sign: KB3MRY
John C Ramos
111 Ethan Dr
Windsor CT 060951668

Call Sign: N1UEA
Jeremy V Pfeifer
77 Farmstead Ln
Windsor CT 06095

Call Sign: W1MLY
Russell C Mitchell
100 Farmstead Ln
Windsor CT 06095

Call Sign: WB1FTQ
Harry A Syring Jr
63 Filley Street
Windsor CT 060952919

Call Sign: WB5UVN
Jean A Conner
107 Gary Lynn Ln
Windsor CT 060951772

Call Sign: KB1GZT
Ryan M Conner

107 Gary Lynn Ln
Windsor CT 06095

Call Sign: KB1HCB
Evan P Conner
107 Gary Lynn Ln
Windsor CT 06095

Call Sign: N1WPG
Daniel K Wiford
184 Giddings Ave
Windsor CT 060953744

Call Sign: KB1BWQ
Jarod R D Shaw
125 Green Manor Ave
Windsor CT 06095

Call Sign: KA1DRQ
George W Christoph Iii
41 Hale Dr
Windsor CT 06095

Call Sign: KB1OLG
Michael M Dorval
28 Hampden Place
Windsor CT 06095

Call Sign: W1KZG
Carlton G Brown
73 Hayden Ave
Windsor CT 06095

Call Sign: AA1NT
Glen W Drake
160 Hayden Station Rd
Windsor CT 06095

Call Sign: KA1UDY
Robert A James
2d Heritage Dr
Windsor CT 06095

Call Sign: KB1NZH
Matthew J Karas

12 Heritage Dr Apt A
Windsor CT 06095

Call Sign: K1IN
William D Wilson
21 Heritage Drive - Apt D
Windsor CT 06095

Call Sign: KB1EEE
David R Oettle
272 High Path Rd
Windsor CT 060954132

Call Sign: WA8RUC
Michael M Whittlesey
120 Hilltop Rd.
Windsor CT 06095

Call Sign: KB1HDW
David F Blough
15 Hobson Ave
Windsor CT 06095

Call Sign: KB1HDX
Noah D Blough
15 Hobson Ave
Windsor CT 06095

Call Sign: KB1SRU
Luke A Blough
15 Hobson Ave
Windsor CT 06095

Call Sign: N1RNS
Michael T Green
54 Hollow Brook Rd
Windsor CT 06095

Call Sign: KB1EDY
Garret T De Jong
117 Hollowbrook Rd
Windsor CT 06095

Call Sign: K1LCS
Letia C Spain

3 Huntington Way
Windsor CT 06095

Call Sign: N1JYG
Louis B Simpson
61 Indian Hill Rd
Windsor CT 06095

Call Sign: N1WOT
Lindel J Cummings
22 Joshua Hill
Windsor CT 06095

Call Sign: KB1AGF
James A Fazio Jr
16 Juniper Rd
Windsor CT 06095

Call Sign: N2VTF
Michael J De May
7 Karen Circle
Windsor CT 06095

Call Sign: KB1BNN
Leah G Wallace
72 Kendrick Ln
Windsor CT 06095

Call Sign: KB1BWS
Kathleen A Lafferty
468 Kennedy Rd
Windsor CT 06095

Call Sign: KB1FQY
John P Szczepanik
475 Kennedy Rd
Windsor CT 060952239

Call Sign: K1ELU
Frank A Bill
532 Kennedy Rd
Windsor CT 06095

Call Sign: KB1BNM
Christopher S Smith

4 Kenneth Cir
Windsor CT 06095

Call Sign: KB1BNJ
Mark T Bielawiec
86 Lancaster Dr
Windsor CT 06095

Call Sign: WA1ZIP
Leon M Alford
426 Lantern Way
Windsor CT 060951650

Call Sign: KB2SFE
David J Morfit
42 Last Leaf Circle
Windsor CT 060954733

Call Sign: AC1W
J Donald Steisel
102 Lighthouse Rd
Windsor CT 060951212

Call Sign: K1SVH
Edward N Franco Sr
105 Longview Dr
Windsor CT 06095

Call Sign: N1YJY
Robert D Mayo
27 Loren Cir
Windsor CT 06095

Call Sign: KB1QHY
Oliver M Nigrosh
100 Ludlow Rd
Windsor CT 06095

Call Sign: K1WFK
William F Karlon Iii
57 Maple Ave
Windsor CT 06095

Call Sign: KI4UTC
Sophia M Beswick

40 Marble Faun Lane
Windsor CT 06095

Call Sign: WA1FSR
J Robert U Parent
889 Matianuck Ave
Windsor CT 06095

Call Sign: KB1EFV
David J Stanley
12 Matthew Ln
Windsor CT 06095

Call Sign: KB1EFW
Mark E Stanley
12 Matthew Ln
Windsor CT 06095

Call Sign: KB1LFC
William P Maragnano
334 Merriman Rd
Windsor CT 06095

Call Sign: KA1VAH
Bryan P Halay
10 Michael Ln
Windsor CT 06095

Call Sign: KA1EQA
Clayton C Van Gasbeck
67 Midian Ave
Windsor CT 06095

Call Sign: KB1HLG
Phillip R Van Gasbeck
67 Midian Ave
Windsor CT 06095

Call Sign: KB1DRG
Alan T Relyea
107 Milo Peck Ln
Windsor CT 06095

Call Sign: K1EBY
Frank D Collins

93 Mountain Rd
Windsor CT 06095

Call Sign: N1RNP
Jason G Kulas
97 Mountain Rd
Windsor CT 06095

Call Sign: KB1GVM
Dorothy C Wojcicki
159 Mountain Rd
Windsor CT 06095

Call Sign: KB1UUM
Desmond Ould
28 Olin St
Windsor CT 06095

Call Sign: N1ZLD
Pat C Gargiulo
20 Oxford Ln
Windsor CT 06095

Call Sign: KB1BNI
Eric S Avery
667 Palisado Ave
Windsor CT 06095

Call Sign: WB1GIL
Norbert J Hluchnik
1412 Palisado Ave
Windsor CT 06095

Call Sign: W1YDS
Walter F Lange
94 Park Ave
Windsor CT 06095

Call Sign: N1VCI
John W Avedisian
11 Parkwood Dr
Windsor CT 06095

Call Sign: N1VGH
Christopher W Le Vasseur

414 Pike Pl
Windsor CT 06095

Call Sign: WB9LXH
Jeffry K Kamenetz
422 Pike Place
Windsor CT 060951784

Call Sign: KB1RSI
Timothy J Coffey
58 Pilgrim Dr
Windsor CT 06095

Call Sign: N1YKS
James T Nelson
101 Pilgrim Dr
Windsor CT 06095

Call Sign: KB1RSO
Agustin R Vazquez
8 Pine Dr
Windsor CT 06095

Call Sign: KB1UND
James J Jaronczyk
20 Pine Dr
Windsor CT 06095

Call Sign: KA1VAL
Allyn R J Nelson Ii
130 Pine Ln
Windsor CT 06095

Call Sign: KA1SKG
Charles L Dube
1071 Plymouth St
Windsor CT 06095

Call Sign: N1TDW
George A Fuller
38 Poquonock Ave
Windsor CT 06095

Call Sign: KB1RSK
Joshua M Ritchie

43 Poquonock Ave Apt F
Windsor CT 06095

Call Sign: KB1FSI
Robert B Foster
96 Preston St
Windsor CT 06095

Call Sign: KB1RSH
Dylan M Hammerman
36 Quail Hollow Dr
Windsor CT 06095

Call Sign: N1YKA
Joseph E Provost
34 Rainbow Rd
Windsor CT 06095

Call Sign: AB1OD
Michael D Adams
488 Rainbow Rd
Windsor CT 06095

Call Sign: KA1EPU
Laverne E Anderson
23 Remington Rd
Windsor CT 06095

Call Sign: KB1WMN
Douglas E Peters
31 Ridge St
Windsor CT 06095

Call Sign: W1IRW
Richard T Blaisdell
31 Ridgewood Rd
Windsor CT 06095

Call Sign: KA1KZB
Philip J Calciano
48 Rood Ave
Windsor CT 06095

Call Sign: WB1CKM
Francis J Grottole

232 Rood Ave
Windsor CT 06095

Call Sign: W1SRE
Robert W Gray Iii
10 Sachem Hill Road
Windsor CT 06095

Call Sign: N1MDN
Joseph E Alfieri
22 Settler Cir
Windsor CT 06095

Call Sign: N1OF
Joseph E Alfieri
22 Settler Cir
Windsor CT 06095

Call Sign: N1WOR
Amanda L Reimer
109 Spring St
Windsor CT 06095

Call Sign: KB1TMH
Joe C Kiley
32 Spring St Apt 2
Windsor CT 06095

Call Sign: N1YMT
Douglas S Coates
12 Squire Rd
Windsor CT 06095

Call Sign: N1FQJ
Robert L Zweygartt
10 Sunnyside Cir
Windsor CT 06095

Call Sign: KB1HSV
Linda A Mullally
25 Taylor St
Windsor CT 06095

Call Sign: N1YMV
Nelson C Vieira

12 Tiffany Dr
Windsor CT 06095

Call Sign: W1VON
Ronald W Hahn
30 Timber Lane
Windsor CT 060953330

Call Sign: K1BNO
William R Eckert
24 Timber Ln
Windsor CT 06095

Call Sign: KB1RSN
Brendan J Allen
10 Valley View Dr
Windsor CT 06095

Call Sign: KB1MLH
Donald A Deming
67 Walnut Dr
Windsor CT 06095

Call Sign: K1ZFE
William J Sheedy
970 Windsor Ave
Windsor CT 060953424

Call Sign: N1UEB
Floris Vander Zwaard
1006 Windsor Ave
Windsor CT 06095

Call Sign: KA1VAJ
Manjula Annadurai
16 Winthrop Rd
Windsor CT 06095

Call Sign: KB1ZW
Richard A Wolos
Windsor CT 06095

Call Sign: KB1IVJ

Amateur Radio Club Of The
Vintage Communications
Museum Ct
Windsor CT 06095

Call Sign: W1VCM
Amateur Radio Club Of The
Vintage Communications
Museum Of Ct
Windsor CT 06095

Call Sign: KB1REY
So Sage Park Rd Windsor
High Radio Club
Windsor CT 06095

FCC Amateur Radio Licenses in Windsor Locks

Call Sign: KO1R
Joseph Krakol
38 Arlington Rd
Windsor Locks CT 06096

Call Sign: K1JJK
Joseph Krakol
38 Arlington Rd
Windsor Locks CT 06096

Call Sign: KA1PXS
Joseph F Bilodeau
59 Belaire Cir Box 178
Windsor Locks CT 06096

Call Sign: KB1MCH
Mark A Cote
59 Belaire Circle
Windsor Locks CT 06096

Call Sign: KA1DDM
James P Capoldo
73b Center St
Windsor Locks CT 06096

Call Sign: KB1BBT

Warren Goldthwait
66 Circle Dr
Windsor Locks CT 06096

Call Sign: AH6BV
Florentino V Encarnacion Jr
87 Circle Dr
Windsor Locks CT 06096

Call Sign: KB1AFX
Hanan S Al-Rayyashi
50 Dickerman Ave
Windsor Locks CT 06096

Call Sign: N1OUC
Robert G Toce
287 Elm St
Windsor Locks CT 06096

Call Sign: KA1MZD
Janice L Sturgis
287 Elm St Apt A6
Windsor Locks CT 06096

Call Sign: KB1KPC
Stephen C Ruffy
2 Fern St
Windsor Locks CT
060961406

Call Sign: N1XSJ
David P Joseph
15 First St
Windsor Locks CT 06096

Call Sign: N1KIQ
Alan W Roberts Jr
32 Grove St
Windsor Locks CT
060961806

Call Sign: KB1HET
Alan W Roberts Jr
32 Grove St

Windsor Locks CT
060961806

Call Sign: K1AWR
Alan W Roberts Jr
32 Grove St
Windsor Locks CT
060961806

Call Sign: NI1M
Harold V Tyrrell
486 Halfway House Rd
Windsor Locks CT 06096

Call Sign: W1UNW
Thomas K Unnold
7 Harrison St
Windsor Locks CT 06096

Call Sign: N0AZR
Kim D Yates
53 Leslie St
Windsor Locks CT 06096

Call Sign: W0PGZ
Harold E Yates
57 Leslie St
Windsor Locks CT 06096

Call Sign: N1YJV
Michael K Gaines
131 Oak Ridge Dr
Windsor Locks CT 06096

Call Sign: K1LAV
John F Lewis Sr
109 Orchard Hill Dr
Windsor Locks CT 06096

Call Sign: KE6TRI
Richard M Mortensen
130 Orchard Hill Drive
Windsor Locks CT
060962440

Call Sign: KC2FHO
Ian T Marchaj
9 Pleasant St
Windsor Locks CT 06096

Call Sign: N1ZXK
Theodore B Farver
11 Regina Drive
Windsor Locks CT 06096

Call Sign: KA1MM
Walter S Midura Jr
280 S Center St
Windsor Locks CT 06096

Call Sign: KB1QNR
Edna M Midura
280 S Center St
Windsor Locks CT 06096

Call Sign: KA1DRH
Joseph V Portuese
338 S Elm St
Windsor Locks CT 06096

Call Sign: N1WO
Michael F Navaroli
36 Sherwin Lane
Windsor Locks CT 06096

Call Sign: N1SSJ
Bret Mazur
97 Smalley Rd
Windsor Locks CT 06096

Call Sign: K1IEK
Richard W Ledgard
124 Southwest Ave
Windsor Locks CT 06096

Call Sign: KB1NFG
Glen A Goforth
205 Southwest Ave
Windsor Locks CT 06096

Call Sign: N1CCD
Robert A Topor
192 Spring St
Windsor Locks CT 06096

Call Sign: N1EGE
Steven M Ege
21 Spring St Apt A8
Windsor Locks CT 06096

Call Sign: N2EGE
Malachi W Ege
21 Spring St Apt A8
Windsor Locks CT 06096

Call Sign: K1EGE
Micah H Ege
21 Spring St Apt A8
Windsor Locks CT 06096

Call Sign: WB8RXB
James L Park Jr
13 Stevens St
Windsor Locks CT 06096

Call Sign: KB1CGX
Robert A Luksic
76 Suffield St
Windsor Locks CT 06096

Call Sign: AA1ER
Edward J Donohue
85b West St
Windsor Locks CT 06096

Call Sign: N1KIA
Thomas A Knapp
Windsor Locks CT 06096

Call Sign: N1YKD
Michael F Navaroli
Windsor Locks CT 06096

Call Sign: W3CFZ
Alfred W Bennett

Windsor Locks CT 06096

Call Sign: K1ICT
Walter S Millowicz
369 Lowell Davis Rd
Winsonville CT 06255

Call Sign: KB1NEM
Lauren A Buika
115 Southwest Avenue
Winsor Locks CT 06096

Call Sign: K1ALA
Lauren A Buika
115 Southwest Avenue
Winsor Locks CT 06096

| **FCC Amateur Radio Licenses in Winstead** |

Call Sign: KB1LQN
Milton S Pixley
5 Strong Terrace
Winstead CT 06098

Call Sign: KA1TDR
John W Bean
35 Arrowhead Dr Rfd 2
Winsted CT 06098

Call Sign: KA1HIE
Shirley A Volpe
63 Bank St
Winsted CT 06098

Call Sign: N1HFD
Mark G Anderson
9 Berg Street
Winsted CT 06098

Call Sign: W1UZ
Eugene J Sweeney
103 Bridge St
Winsted CT 06098

Call Sign: N1CRL
Alfred L Basso
Rfd 1 Bunnell St
Winsted CT 06098

Call Sign: KB1YS
E Morgan Durant
Rfd 3 Camron Pt
Winsted CT 06098

Call Sign: WB1AMW
Jerold E Silverio
26 Colony Dr
Winsted CT 060981809

Call Sign: KB1HZZ
Rachel L Bourquin
6 Cook St
Winsted CT 060981408

Call Sign: N1ZCW
Frank R Bourquin
6 Cook Street
Winsted CT 060981408

Call Sign: N1OVI
Anne Q Coloma
144 E Mountain Ave
Winsted CT 06098

Call Sign: KB1DTS
Robert E Nicol
219 E Wakefield Blvd
Winsted CT 06098

Call Sign: N1COL
Robert E Nicol
219 E Wakefield Blvd
Winsted CT 06098

Call Sign: WB1COE
Joseph A Torneo Jr
108 East Lake St
Winsted CT 06098

Call Sign: N1GFM
Gary F Monsam
307 East Wakefield Blvd
Winsted CT 06098

Call Sign: N1ENV
Mark Buslewicz
52 Holmes Dr
Winsted CT 06098

Call Sign: KB1GAN
Sarah E Hebert
101 Laurel Way
Winsted CT 06098

Call Sign: KB1LXD
Stephen M Oshana
39 Finn St
Winsted CT 06098

Call Sign: AA1XP
Mark Buslewicz
52 Holmes Dr
Winsted CT 06098

Call Sign: KB1GGO
Paul Parent
105 Laurel Way
Winsted CT 06098

Call Sign: KB1LZE
Vera D Richardson
39 Finn St
Winsted CT 06098

Call Sign: KB1LHT
Bruce D Stobbe
107 Indian Meadow Dr
Winsted CT 06098

Call Sign: KB1DYP
Allen D Hubbard Sr
11 Lewis St
Winsted CT 060982017

Call Sign: N1GWF
Brett N Flaherty
15 Front Street 2fl
Winsted CT 06098

Call Sign: KB1LHU
Debra L Stobbe
107 Indian Meadow Dr
Winsted CT 06098

Call Sign: N1EFP
Paul M Wooden
151 Main St
Winsted CT 06098

Call Sign: KA1TEL
Paul J Asselin
105 Gaylord Rd
Winsted CT 06098

Call Sign: KB1GGR
Robert I Platt
19 John St
Winsted CT 06098

Call Sign: KE1HP
Jeffrey W Bauer
480 Main St #15
Winsted CT 06098

Call Sign: KA1TDC
Brett A Marchand
146 Glendale Ave
Winsted CT 06098

Call Sign: KA1ITD
Jack De Pace
55 Lakeview Rd
Winsted CT 06098

Call Sign: KB1IUZ
Steven J Williams
187 Marshall St
Winsted CT 06098

Call Sign: K1VFF
William Hiller
175 Glendale Ave
Winsted CT 06098

Call Sign: KB1GAK
Arielle L Hebert
101 Laurel Way
Winsted CT 06098

Call Sign: K1SJW
Steven J Williams
187 Marshall St
Winsted CT 06098

Call Sign: WA1UME
Bernard C Levesque
194 Glendale Ave
Winsted CT 06098

Call Sign: KB1GAL
Cheryl A Hebert
101 Laurel Way
Winsted CT 06098

Call Sign: KA1AHS
Glenice L Mc Cormick
18 Morgan Brook Dr
Winsted CT 06098

Call Sign: WA1ZXL
Alice C Levesque
194 Glendale Ave
Winsted CT 06098

Call Sign: KB1GAM
Nathan J Hebert
101 Laurel Way
Winsted CT 06098

Call Sign: KA1AHX
Frank R Mc Cormick
18 Morgan Brook Dr
Winsted CT 06098

Call Sign: N1BJC
David V Santis
116 N Main St
Winsted CT 06098

Call Sign: WB1DQN
Vincent A Santis
116 N Main St
Winsted CT 06098

Call Sign: N1VS
Vincent A Santis
116 N Main St
Winsted CT 06098

Call Sign: KA1YTI
Daniel W Matthews
197 Oak St
Winsted CT 06098

Call Sign: KA1CWS
Donald F Fletcher
203 Old New Hartford Rd
Winsted CT 06098

Call Sign: KA1QVE
Pamela R Bauer
49 Palmer Ave
Winsted CT 06098

Call Sign: KA1TET
Cynthia A English
46 Park Pl
Winsted CT 06098

Call Sign: K2QAI
John J Phillips
472 Platt Hill Rd
Winsted CT 06098

Call Sign: KZ1N
Frank P Silvester
55 Pratt St
Winsted CT 06098

Call Sign: N1UQL
Stephen W Root
176 Pratt Street
Winsted CT 06098

Call Sign: N1LMJ
Willis I Leslie
121 Prospect St
Winsted CT 06098

Call Sign: N1MUJ
Joshua A Leslie
121 Prospect St
Winsted CT 06098

Call Sign: N1OQJ
Phyllis E Leslie
121 Prospect St
Winsted CT 06098

Call Sign: N1OVM
Rebecca E Kirk
121 Prospect St
Winsted CT 06098

Call Sign: KB1IZP
Wireless Operators Of
Winsted Arc
121 Prospect Street
Winsted CT 06098

Call Sign: W1EOO
Wireless Operators Of
Winsted
121 Prospect Street
Winsted CT 06098

Call Sign: WA1SYM
Vincent G Hunt
Rfd 2
Winsted CT 06098

Call Sign: KA1LTM
Suzanne L Dwyer
140 Ridge St

Winsted CT 06098

Call Sign: KA1LTN
William H Dwyer
140 Ridge St
Winsted CT 06098

Call Sign: KA1LTL
Brian T Lamont
111-9 Riverton Road
Winsted CT 06098

Call Sign: N1SHZ
Thomas L Sullivan Jr
94 Rockwell St
Winsted CT 06098

Call Sign: W1EOO
Anthony F Sorrentino
267 Rockwell St
Winsted CT 06098

Call Sign: WA1KXH
Robert G Nicosia
147 S Main St
Winsted CT 06098

Call Sign: N1DIR
Peter L Barnes
103 Shore Dr
Winsted CT 06098

Call Sign: N1RZU
Stephen W Owens
139 Smith Hill Road
Winsted CT 06098

Call Sign: KA1AMK
Kevin C Cooper
111 Torringford St Unit 6
Winsted CT 06098

Call Sign: KB1KWU
Karen R Klebe
130 Torrington Rd

Winsted CT 06098

Call Sign: N1SIL
Diane L Blaney
28 Union St
Winsted CT 06098

Call Sign: KA1VFM
Russel B Cassese
80 Upson Ave
Winsted CT 06098

Call Sign: KA1TCK
Edwin C Mitchell
349 W Lake St
Winsted CT 06098

Call Sign: N1ZNG
Earle W Corban
227 W Wakefield Blvd
Winsted CT 06098

Call Sign: KB1NSB
David W Jones
99 Waldron St
Winsted CT 06098

Call Sign: K1KUZ
David W Jones
99 Waldron St
Winsted CT 06098

Call Sign: NK1V
David W Jones
99 Waldron St
Winsted CT 06098

Call Sign: KA1VFH
Steven A Roberts
12 Wallens Hill Jct 3
Winsted CT 06098

Call Sign: KB1LTG
Jerry M Honeycutt Jr
37 Walnut St

Winsted CT 06098

Call Sign: N1UQZ
John P Bongiorno
275 Walnut St
Winsted CT 06098

Call Sign: KA1WPM
Dana A Borgman
72 Wetmore Ave
Winsted CT 060981244

Call Sign: N1DXE
John T Speziale
78 Wheeler St
Winsted CT 06098

Call Sign: KA1VFN
Harold F Carter
Winsted CT 06098

Call Sign: KA1WEV
Rita I Carter
Winsted CT 06098

Call Sign: N1SCB
Laurence J Lausier
Winsted CT 060980531

Call Sign: N1UNY
Andrew L Fleischmann
Winsted CT 06098

Call Sign: KB1JJM
Tristine A Sampson
Winsted CT 06098

FCC Amateur Radio Licenses in Winthrop

Call Sign: N1ABO
Jerry F Clark
25 Melody Ridge
Winthrop CT 06417

FCC Amateur Radio Licenses in Wolcott

Call Sign: KB1NKO
David W Hollis Iii
14 Allentown Rd
Wolcott CT 06716

Call Sign: WA1IXU
James J Ahrens
78 Bayview Cir
Wolcott CT 06716

Call Sign: W1JJA
James J Ahrens
78 Bayview Cir
Wolcott CT 06716

Call Sign: KB1OMV
Connecticut Digital
Repeater Association
78 Bayview Circle
Wolcott CT 06716

Call Sign: W1IXU
Connecticut Digital
Repeater Association
78 Bayview Circle
Wolcott CT 06716

Call Sign: KB1TW
Clement V Valerio Sr
217 Beach Rd
Wolcott CT 06716

Call Sign: KB1GBO
Frances M Flynn
309 Beach Rd
Wolcott CT 06716

Call Sign: KB1RHR
Jason Chin
37 Beacon Hill Blvd
Wolcott CT 06716

Call Sign: KB1DCL
Tammy A Sampson
276 Bound Line Rd
Wolcott CT 06716

Call Sign: KB1GZX
Anthony J Spagnoletti
43 Colonial Ct
Wolcott CT 06716

Call Sign: K1EFD
Charles J Brennan
40 Hampshire Dr
Wolcott CT 06716

Call Sign: WA1CYM
John R Wilson
Box 6202
Wolcott CT 06716

Call Sign: KO1A
Gary L Gibson
19 Copper Beech Rd
Wolcott CT 06716

Call Sign: WF1N
Anthony Spino
39 Hampshire Dr.
Wolcott CT 06716

Call Sign: WB1COU
Richard S Ziminsky
36 Brentwood Dr
Wolcott CT 06716

Call Sign: KA1WDJ
John J Kowchak
127 Farview Ave
Wolcott CT 06716

Call Sign: N1EBF
Philip A Mongelluzzo Jr
93 Hempel Drive
Wolcott CT 06716

Call Sign: N1EVC
Beatrix L Clark
126 Cancellaro Dr
Wolcott CT 06716

Call Sign: N1XNQ
Alan S Giroux
53 Finch Rd
Wolcott CT 06786

Call Sign: KB1RHS
Dennis Cleary Jr
57 Hemple Dr
Wolcott CT 06716

Call Sign: NX1E
Donald R Clark
126 Cancellaro Dr
Wolcott CT 06716

Call Sign: N1VII
Frank F Bruce Iv
6 Frisbie Cir
Wolcott CT 06716

Call Sign: KA1RRS
Thomas M Mc Donald
34 Hill Side Dr
Wolcott CT 06716

Call Sign: KA1UCP
Frederick J Weik
17 Catherine Dr
Wolcott CT 06716

Call Sign: N1WQM
Robert M Seretnhy
149 Garrigus Ct
Wolcott CT 06716

Call Sign: K1TMM
Thomas M Mc Donald
34 Hill Side Dr
Wolcott CT 06716

Call Sign: N1QCD
Thomas E Waltman
22 Catherine Drive
Wolcott CT 06716

Call Sign: WA1LOU
Stanley J Horzepa Jr
1 Glen Ave
Wolcott CT 06716

Call Sign: KB1TCR
Matthew A Bellemare
22 Hillside Dr
Wolcott CT 06716

Call Sign: N1UIL
Richard W Lachnicki
33 Cedar Point Rd
Wolcott CT 06716

Call Sign: KB1HLH
Michael A Zello
23 Hampshire Dr
Wolcott CT 06716

Call Sign: KB1GUC
Jeffrey N Mcadam
7 Ivy Lane
Wolcott CT 06716

Call Sign: KA1UMS
Raymond D Fasano Sr
129 Clinton Hill Rd
Wolcott CT 06716

Call Sign: W1VRU
Michael A Zello
23 Hampshire Dr
Wolcott CT 06716

Call Sign: KB1MNA
Michael J Mcadam
7 Ivy Lane
Wolcott CT 06716

Call Sign: K3KID
Connecticut Amateur Radio
League Of Youth Carly
7 Ivy Ln
Wolcott CT 06716

Call Sign: WA1SAG
Edward J Joseph Jr
34 Juniper Dr
Wolcott CT 06716

Call Sign: KA1JSL
Charles A Mitchell
3 Lancewood Ln
Wolcott CT 06716

Call Sign: WB1EDK
William E Hallock Jr
29 Long Swamp Rd
Wolcott CT 06716

Call Sign: N1RLV
William R Clair
79 Long Swamp Rd
Wolcott CT 06716

Call Sign: KB1KYP
Allen T Voghel
209 Long Swamp Rd
Wolcott CT 06716

Call Sign: WA1BXI
John V Karezna
196 Lyman Rd
Wolcott CT 06716

Call Sign: KA1PUV
Jean O Syssa
45 Lynwood Dr
Wolcott CT 06716

Call Sign: W1VNJ
Alfred A Syssa
45 Lynwood Dr
Wolcott CT 06716

Call Sign: KB1AXP
Robert C Heller
16 Mapleview Dr
Wolcott CT 06716

Call Sign: W1HLB
Louis R Monnerat Sr
33 Mapleview Dr
Wolcott CT 067161613

Call Sign: NQ1P
Deborah M Hillman
71 Mapleview Dr
Wolcott CT 06716

Call Sign: KD1YO
Barbara V Heller
16 Mapleview Drive
Wolcott CT 06716

Call Sign: KB1IXS
Vincent J Tarullo
29 Mountain View Dr
Wolcott CT 06716

Call Sign: N1LFO
Martin L Wiegner Iii
35 Munson Rd
Wolcott CT 06716

Call Sign: KB1GHF
Waterbury Area Chapter
American Red Cross
53 Orchard Lane
Wolcott CT 067162011

Call Sign: N1EMK
Scott S Slater Jr
53 Orchard Ln
Wolcott CT 06716

Call Sign: N1HAE
Scott S Slater Sr
53 Orchard Ln

Wolcott CT 06716

Call Sign: N1RIF
Scott S Slater Iii
53 Orchard Ln
Wolcott CT 06716

Call Sign: N1UFK
Emily J Slater
53 Orchard Ln
Wolcott CT 06716

Call Sign: AA1WT
Scott S Slater Jr
53 Orchard Ln
Wolcott CT 06716

Call Sign: KR1N
Michael W Baldino
165 Potuccos Ring Rd
Wolcott CT 06716

Call Sign: K1RZV
Frank J Rogers Jr
22 Rosemary Ln
Wolcott CT 06716

Call Sign: KB1JJN
Barry Dudelson
178 S Colman Rd
Wolcott CT 06716

Call Sign: AB1CF
Barry Dudelson
178 S Colman Rd
Wolcott CT 06716

Call Sign: AB1D
Barry Dudelson
178 S Colman Rd
Wolcott CT 06716

Call Sign: N1PVO
Gregory F Lafferty
2 Scovill Rd

Wolcott CT 06716

Call Sign: KB1OII
Michael V Macri
8 Seery Rd
Wolcott CT 06716

Call Sign: K1MVM
Michael V Macri
8 Seery Rd
Wolcott CT 06716

Call Sign: N1ADE
Philip A Mongelluzzo
891 Spindle Hill Rd
Wolcott CT 06716

Call Sign: N1RLA
Paul J Yeno
1182 Spindle Hill Rd
Wolcott CT 06716

Call Sign: KB1KQJ
Mark W Smith
12 Spindle Hill Rd Apt 3b
Wolcott CT 06716

Call Sign: KB1KQZ
David Evon
4 Split Rock Dr
Wolcott CT 06716

Call Sign: KB1KDD
Loren J Hisert
20 Spring Rd
Wolcott CT 06716

Call Sign: WA1QFN
Roy E Howe
96 Teresa Dr
Wolcott CT 06716

Call Sign: KA1GPE
David P Nadeau
8 Todd Hollow Road

Wolcott CT 067161107

Call Sign: N1TGI
Robert F Forgione
269 Todd Rd
Wolcott CT 06716

Call Sign: KA1RHU
Paul J Lambert
129 Tolsun Rd
Wolcott CT 06716

Call Sign: N1RID
Joseph R Stramondo
4 Val Ct
Wolcott CT 06716

Call Sign: N1TVO
Joseph A Stramondo
4 Val Ct
Wolcott CT 06716

Call Sign: KA1TZE
Robert M Ryan
63 Wihbey Dr
Wolcott CT 06716

Call Sign: KB1OIG
Robert J Weaver
43 Williams Court
Wolcott CT 06716

Call Sign: W1GTH
Robert J Weaver Sr
43 Williams Court
Wolcott CT 06716

Call Sign: KB1WXF
Walter J Belsito Sr
12 Wolf Hill Road 17d
Wolcott CT 06716

Call Sign: KA1MKP
Aimee L Rosengrant
1446 Woodtick Rd

Wolcott CT 06716

Call Sign: K1VHU
Anthony V Rinaldi Sr
19 Valley Rd
Wolcutt CT 06716

FCC Amateur Radio Licenses in Woodbridge

Call Sign: K1BEM
Robert H Schulz
504 Amity Rd
Woodbridge CT 065251605

Call Sign: N1ULL
Guy L Semon
545 Amity Rd
Woodbridge CT 06525

Call Sign: KA1ELY
Robert M Glassman
270 Amity Rd Ste 219
Woodbridge CT 06525

Call Sign: N1TAJ
Paul Z Hine
3 Apple Tree Ln
Woodbridge CT 06525

Call Sign: KB1GAO
Christopher K Lepensky
14 Beecher Rd
Woodbridge CT 06525

Call Sign: KB1GAP
Kelli J Lepensky
14 Beecher Rd
Woodbridge CT 06525

Call Sign: KB1SYC
Robert S Klatzkin
21 Bond Rd
Woodbridge CT 06525

Call Sign: KA1UYY
Michael S Sheehy
7 Bunker Hill Rd
Woodbridge CT 06525

Call Sign: KB1CIA
Sid Govindan
25 Dales Dr
Woodbridge CT 06525

Call Sign: KA1UYX
Zaneta Y Chung
10 Deepwood Rd
Woodbridge CT 06525

Call Sign: KC2CLE
Michael H Bloch
5 Diana Drive
Woodbridge CT 06525

Call Sign: KB1EWE
Nick T Santucci
10 Edgehill Dr
Woodbridge CT 06525

Call Sign: K1FHR
Martin J Kleinfeld
26 Evergreen Drive
Woodbridge CT 06525

Call Sign: KB1QEW
Lenn B Zonder
14 Fairview Rd
Woodbridge CT 06525

Call Sign: WB1CBS
Bradford Lott
8 Fieldstone Dr
Woodbridge CT 06525

Call Sign: N1ELW
Ronald M Dworkin
39 Hallsey Ln
Woodbridge CT 06525

Call Sign: KA1ZCZ
Allen H Heller
6 Hunters Ridge
Woodbridge CT 06525

Call Sign: KA1ZDA
David J Heller
6 Hunters Ridge
Woodbridge CT 06525

Call Sign: K1OOL
Chester F Bass
1188 Johnson Rd
Woodbridge CT 06525

Call Sign: KA1UZA
Jennifer M Marzullo
1681 Litchfield Tpke
Woodbridge CT 06515

Call Sign: W1ZJY
Daniel M Koenigsberg
6 Lois Dr.
Woodbridge CT 06525

Call Sign: W1WPD
Woodbridge Amateur Radio
Club
4 Meetinghouse Lane
Woodbridge CT 06525

Call Sign: KA1UYV
Thomas F Moore
16 Milhaven Rd
Woodbridge CT 06525

Call Sign: KB1IUG
Jonathan D Hubbard
33 Morris Rd
Woodbridge CT 06525

Call Sign: N2BYV
Yoram H Lirtzman
14 Nettleton Dr
Woodbridge CT 06525

Call Sign: W1YHL
Yoram H Lirtzman
14 Nettleton Dr
Woodbridge CT 06525

Call Sign: K1RH
Ralph M Hirsch
172 Newton Rd
Woodbridge CT 06525

Call Sign: K8KQO
Gary E Friedlaender
15 Old Still Rd
Woodbridge CT 06525

Call Sign: W1RPJ
Eric T Pierson
54 Orchard Rd
Woodbridge CT 065251123

Call Sign: KA1RLW
Lucille Morowitz
56 Ox Bow Ln
Woodbridge CT 06525

Call Sign: KB1GGV
Cinque Nove Nove Amateur
Radio Society
14 Oxbow Lane
Woodbridge CT 06525

Call Sign: K1PVT
Cinque Nove Nove Amateur
Radio Society
14 Oxbow Lane
Woodbridge CT 06525

Call Sign: K2RPM
Bruce E Torello
14 Oxbow Ln
Woodbridge CT 06525

Call Sign: W1GGT
Manson Van B Jennings

30 Prospect Ct
Woodbridge CT 06525

Call Sign: WA1UAF
Robert G Mc Carron
1224 Racebrook Rd
Woodbridge CT 06525

Call Sign: KA8ZFB
Erich C Altvater
18 Ranch Rd
Woodbridge CT 06525

Call Sign: W1CLJ
Charles L Jump
6 Raymond Street
Woodbridge CT 06525

Call Sign: KA1WEY
Marc D Lesser
205 Rimmon Rd
Woodbridge CT 06525

Call Sign: K1RU
Gene H Frohman
326 Rimmon Rd
Woodbridge CT 06525

Call Sign: AB1LO
Michael Apkon
20 Rock Hill Rd
Woodbridge CT 06525

Call Sign: KA1GYM
Michael B Bobrow
33 Rock Hill Rd
Woodbridge CT 06525

Call Sign: KA1GYN
Samuel N Bobrow
33 Rock Hill Rd
Woodbridge CT 06525

Call Sign: KB1NPG

Woodbridge Amateur Radio
Club
4 Meetinghouse Lane C/O
Brian Freeman
Woodbrige CT 06525

**FCC Amateur Radio
Licenses in Woodbury**

Call Sign: KB1OIH
Xuesi Mang
11 Bear Hill Rd
Woodbury CT 06798

Call Sign: KB1CFS
Dawn L Brownell
175 Bethlehem Rd
Woodbury CT 06798

Call Sign: KB1KQY
Garrett L Mitchell
212 Brushy Hill Rd
Woodbury CT 06798

Call Sign: K1ZTE
Russell J Domareck
23 Carriage Lane
Woodbury CT 06798

Call Sign: K1JJG
George K Fairbanks
152 Church Hill Rd
Woodbury CT 06798

Call Sign: NQ1H
Matthew C Fairbanks
152 Churchill Rd
Woodbury CT 06798

Call Sign: KB1WOH
Dominick F Spina
140 Curtis Rd Ext
Woodbury CT 06798

Call Sign: WA2NBG

Rayman G Mustafa
88 Curtiss Meadows
Woodbury CT 06798

Call Sign: KA1CU
Michael A Aurio
20 Farview Lane
Woodbury CT 06798

Call Sign: N1AOB
Stephen K Stone
418 Good Hill Road
Woodbury CT 06798

Call Sign: N1JVH
Colin J Petty
320 Grassy Hill Rd
Woodbury CT 06798

Call Sign: N1RML
Brian R Rhodes
15 Heritage Dr
Woodbury CT 06798

Call Sign: KD1AO
James J Werth
8 Hesseky Meadows Rd
Woodbury CT 06798

Call Sign: N1XNP
David L Lasiter Sr
29 Indian Ln
Woodbury CT 06798

Call Sign: W1DDJ
E Thomas O Hara
101 Judson Ave
Woodbury CT 06798

Call Sign: KB1AJK
Nicholas Caputo Jr
12 Lower Commons
Woodbury CT 06798

Call Sign: KB1BDY

Robert E Killing
529 Main St S
Woodbury CT 06798

Call Sign: N1SVT
Thomas J Davis
401 Middle Rd Tpke
Woodbury CT 06798

Call Sign: KB1KMD
Donald S Gamsjager
385 Middle Road Tnpk
Woodbury CT 06798

Call Sign: K1RMB
Barry W Maxwell
39 Minortown Rd
Woodbury CT 06798

Call Sign: K1MN
Lexington E Smith
153 Old Sherman Hill Rd
Woodbury CT 06798

Call Sign: WA1GJO
Robert C Peterson
592 Old Sherman Hill Rd
Woodbury CT 067984007

Call Sign: W1ZGZ
Carl G Braun
64 Orchard Ave
Woodbury CT 06798

Call Sign: AJ1U
Jonathan R Bernon
33 Owl Ridge Road
Woodbury CT 06798

Call Sign: WA2WIW
Christopher J Bottino
77 Plumb Brook Rd
Woodbury CT 06798

Call Sign: KA1EXO

Richard G Burr
148 Quassapaug Rd
Woodbury CT 06798

Call Sign: K1TXI
E Joel Mc Corkle
29 Stiles Rd
Woodbury CT 06798

Call Sign: KB1WCG
Christopher M Keane
519 Upper Grassy Hill Rd
Woodbury CT 06798

Call Sign: K1RMA
Donald W Richards Jr
660 Upper Grassy Hill Rd
Woodbury CT 06798

Call Sign: KB1HXG
Christina A Richards
660 Upper Grassy Hill Rd
Woodbury CT 06798

Call Sign: K1CWR
Donald E Sharpe
667 Upper Grassy Hill Rd
Woodbury CT 06798

Call Sign: KB1IWW
David J Szentmiklosy
669 Upper Grassy Hill Rd
Woodbury CT 06798

Call Sign: AB1CQ
David J Szentmiklosy
669 Upper Grassy Hill Rd
Woodbury CT 06798

Call Sign: N1ZS
David J Szentmiklosy
669 Upper Grassy Hill Rd
Woodbury CT 06798

Call Sign: WA1YKS

Charles G Loyot
36 Washington Ave
Woodbury CT 06798

Call Sign: WV1N
William R Schmidt
183 Washington Rd
Woodbury CT 06798

Call Sign: KB1HNH
Koen O Loeven
193 Washington Rd
Woodbury CT 06798

Call Sign: KB1TOS
Ralph A Panagrosso Jr
308 Washington Rd
Woodbury CT 06798

Call Sign: KB1HEA
Loreen M Heavens
74 Washington Rd W
Woodbury CT 06798

Call Sign: N1FNT
Ronald D Grossman
133 Westwood Road
Woodbury CT 06798

Call Sign: K1JBE
William C Noble
59 Woodbury Hill
Woodbury CT 06798

Call Sign: AA1FK
Thomas D Brownell
Woodbury CT 06798

Call Sign: N1VIQ
Andrew D Heavens
Woodbury CT 06798

Call Sign: N1YDO
Theodore G Crawford
Woodbury CT 06798

Call Sign: N1ZXV
Kristine Letsch
Woodbury CT 06798

Call Sign: WB2GYK
Stephen J Sant Andrea
Woodbury CT 06798

Call Sign: AG1YK
Stephen J Sant Andrea
Woodbury CT 06798

FCC Amateur Radio Licenses in Woodmont

Call Sign: N1DMZ
Charles A Pemberton Jr
207 Merwin Ave
Woodmont CT 06460

FCC Amateur Radio Licenses in Woodstock

Call Sign: N1VJA
Paul L Paradise
438 Barlow Cemetary Rd
Woodstock CT 06281

Call Sign: WB1DXX
John D Relahan
Rr 1 Box 215
Woodstock CT 06281

Call Sign: KA1NYC
Kenneth B Uguccioni
314 Child Rd
Woodstock CT 06281

Call Sign: KB1KLN
Jon J Normandin
31 Ellen Ln
Woodstock CT 062813006

Call Sign: KB1OXI

Edwin B Escoto
53 Herindeen Landing
Woodstock CT 06281

Call Sign: WA1QDA
Henry O Denno
73 Joy Rd
Woodstock CT 06281

Call Sign: KB1JQB
Timothy E Butler
86 Lebanon Hill Rd
Woodstock CT 06281

Call Sign: N1NTF
Gary A Hopkins
200 Old Hall Rd
Woodstock CT 06281

Call Sign: WA1LT
William A Lott
98 Peake Brook Rd
Woodstock CT 06281

Call Sign: K1EHG
Gurdon R Abell
172 Perrin Rd
Woodstock CT 06281

Call Sign: N1PTJ
Nathan M Adams
60 Rawson Rd
Woodstock CT 06281

Call Sign: KB1NAM
Paul H Chabot
11 Ridgewood Dr
Woodstock CT 06281

Call Sign: W1CIO
Paul H Chabot
11 Ridgewood Dr
Woodstock CT 06281

Call Sign: W1VPI

Earl H Brazeal Jr
518 Route 169
Woodstock CT 06281

Call Sign: W1NNZ
William A Kosche
Star Route
Woodstock CT 06281

Call Sign: KB1PUL
Clifford C French
177 Stone Bridge Rd
Woodstock CT 06281

Call Sign: KB1DNM
Colin R Cummings
174 W Quasset Rd
Woodstock CT 06281

Call Sign: W1BAN
Charles T Parham
Box 64 Wainwright Dr
Woodstock CT 06281

Call Sign: W1JGY
Warren O Rosenlund
46 Woodland Dr
Woodstock CT 062813033

Call Sign: K2VUI
Joseph E Green
Woodstock CT 06281

Call Sign: N1EDG
Edward C Ahern
Woodstock CT 06281

FCC Amateur Radio Licenses in Woodstock Valley

Call Sign: N1PTG
Leonard R Mathieu Sr
90 Barlow Cemetary Rd

Woodstock Valley CT
06282

Call Sign: KD1NC
Jo Lyn Jordan
21 Hemlock Drive
Woodstock Valley CT
06282

Call Sign: K1YN
George L Davis
1814 Rt 171
Woodstock Valley CT
06282

Call Sign: KB1QHC
Bradley H Sparks
15 Valley View Rd
Woodstock Valley CT
06282

Call Sign: W1AK
Bradley H Sparks
15 Valley View Rd
Woodstock Valley CT
06282

| FCC Amateur Radio Licenses in Xford |

Call Sign: N1HBL
Brian T Bassett
30 Old Farm Road
Xford CT 06478

| FCC Amateur Radio Licenses in Yatesville |

Call Sign: WA3APC
James S Cook
5 Kirtland Ct
Yalesville CT 06492

Call Sign: WA3ZZM
Karen Cook

5 Kirtland Ct
Yalesville CT 06492

Call Sign: W1ULL
Lawrence F Willard
17 Mountain View Rd
Yalesville CT 06492

Call Sign: W1SY
Robert L Warzocha
12 Wooding Rd
Yalesville CT 06492

Call Sign: KB1IXT
Albert L Steigler Jr
Yalesville CT 064927566

Call Sign: N1RIU
Jeffrey W Krystofolski
28 Grove St
Yaleville CT 06492

www.ingramcontent.com/pod-product-compliance
Lightning Source LLC
Chambersburg PA
CBHW081345280326

41927CB00042B/3071